THE LIFE AND WRITINGS OF

FREDERICK DOUGLASS

PHILIP S. FONER

The Life and Writings
of Frederick Douglass

Early Years, 1817-1849

INTERNATIONAL PUBLISHERS

NEW YORK

COPYRIGHT, 1950, BY

INTERNATIONAL PUBLISHERS CO. INC.

ISBN 13: 978-0-7178-0434-4
ISBN 10: 0-7178-0434-8

PRINTED IN THE U.S.A.

*To the Negro people of the United States
in gratitude for the great heritage
they have bestowed upon America,
and in the knowledge
that the principles and leadership
of Frederick Douglass
which served them
in their struggles for liberation
in the nineteenth century
will inspire them
and all progressive Americans
in the struggle
for full freedom and equality
for the Negro people.*

Contents

PREFACE 11

FREDERICK DOUGLASS *by Philip S. Foner* 15
    From Slavery to Freedom 15
    The Garrisonians and Abolition 28
    Anti-Slavery Agent 45
    A Chattel Becomes a Man 62
    Founding *The North Star* 75
    Editor and Publisher 84

WRITINGS AND SPEECHES OF FREDERICK DOUGLASS

Part One: From 1841 to the Founding
of *The North Star*

The Church and Prejudice, speech delivered at the
    Plymouth Church Anti-Slavery Society, December, 1841 103
To William Lloyd Garrison, November 8, 1842 105
To Maria (Weston) Chapman, September 10, 1843 110
The Folly of Our Opponents, *The Liberty Bell*, 1845 113
To William Lloyd Garrison, September 1, 1845 115
To William Lloyd Garrison, September 16, 1845 118
To William Lloyd Garrison, September 29, 1845 120
To R. D. Webb, November 10, 1845 122
To Thurlow Weed, December 1, 1845 123
To William Lloyd Garrison, January 1, 1846 125

To William Lloyd Garrison, January 27, 1846	129
To Francis Jackson, January 29, 1846	135
To Richard D. Webb, February 10, 1846	137
To William Lloyd Garrison, February 26, 1846	138
To Maria (Weston) Chapman, March 29, 1846	142
To Horace Greeley, April 15, 1846	144
To William Lloyd Garrison, April 16, 1846	149
To Anonymous, April 23, 1846	151
An Appeal to the British People, reception speech at Finsbury Chapel, Moorfields, England, May 12, 1846	154
To William Lloyd Garrison, May 23, 1846	165
The Free Church and Slavery, speech at Glasgow, Scotland, May 29, 1846	173
To the Editor of the *Protestant Journal,* July 23, 1846	179
To William A. White, July 30, 1846	181
To Maria (Weston) Chapman, August 18, 1846	184
To the Lynn Anti-Slavery Sewing Circle, August 18, 1846	186
To Samuel Hanson Cox, D.D., October 30, 1846	189
To Henry C. Wright, December 22, 1846	199
Farewell Speech to the British People, at London Tavern, London, England, March 30, 1847	206
To the Editor of the London *Times,* April 3, 1847	233
The Right to Criticize American Institutions, speech before the American Anti-Slavery Society, May 11, 1847	234
To Thomas Van Rensselaer, May 18, 1847	243
To William Lloyd Garrison, June 7, 1847	246
To the *Boston Daily Whig,* June 27, 1847	252
Bibles for the Slaves, *The Liberty Bell,* June, 1847	253
To William Lloyd Garrison, July 18, 1847	256
To Sidney Howard Gay (August, 1847)	256
To Sidney Howard Gay, August 20, 1847	259
To Sidney Howard Gay, September, 1847	262

CONTENTS

To Sidney Howard Gay, September 17, 1847	265
American Slavery, speech delivered at Market Hall, New York City, October 22, 1847	269
To J. D. Carr, November 1, 1847	278

Part Two: From the Founding of *The North Star* to the Compromise of 1850

Our Paper and Its Prospects, *The North Star*, December 3, 1847	280
To Our Oppressed Countrymen, *The North Star*, December 3, 1847	282
To Henry Clay, *The North Star*, December 3, 1847	284
Colored Newspapers, *The North Star*, January 8, 1848	291
The War with Mexico, *The North Star*, January 21, 1848	291
The North and the Presidency, *The North Star*, March 17, 1848	296
Peace! Peace! Peace! *The North Star*, March 17, 1848	300
Editorial Correspondence, *The North Star*, April 7, 1848	300
France, *The North Star*, April 28, 1848	303
To Julia Griffiths, April 28, 1848	306
What of the Night? *The North Star*, May 5, 1848	307
Northern Whigs and Democrats, *The North Star*, July 7, 1848	309
What Are the Colored People Doing for Themselves? *The North Star*, July 14, 1848	314
The Rights of Women, *The North Star*, July 28, 1848	320
The Revolution of 1848, speech at West India Emancipation celebration, Rochester, New York, August 1, 1848	321
An Address to the Colored People of the United States, *The North Star*, September 29, 1848	331
To Thomas Auld, September 3, 1848	336
The Blood of the Slave on the Skirts of the Northern People, *The North Star*, November 17, 1848	343
A Few Words to Our Own People, *The North Star*, January 19, 1849	347
Colonization, *The North Star*, January 26, 1849	350

CONTENTS

The Constitution and Slavery, *The North Star*, February 9, 1849	352
The Address of Southern Delegates in Congress to Their Constituents, *The North Star*, February 9, 1849	353
The Constitution and Slavery, *The North Star*, March 16, 1849	361
What Good Has the Free Soil Movement Done? *The North Star*, March 25, 1849	367
To Gerrit Smith, March 30, 1849	369
To H. G. Warner, Esq., *The North Star*, March 30, 1849	371
Comments on Gerrit Smith's Address, *The North Star*, March 30, 1849	374
"A Tribute for the Negro," *The North Star*, April 7, 1849	379
Colorphobia in New York! *The North Star*, May 25, 1849	384
The American Colonization Society, speech in Faneuil Hall, June 8, 1849	387
The Union of the Oppressed for the Sake of Freedom, *The North Star*, August 10, 1849	399
To W. M. Ratten, August 27, 1849	401
To Capt. Thomas Auld, formerly my master, September 3, 1849	403
Philadelphia, *The North Star*, October 19, 1849	406
Pumpkins, *The North Star*, October 19, 1849	407
The National League, *The North Star*, October 26, 1849	408
To Elizabeth Pease, November 8, 1849	411
Government and Its Subjects, *The North Star*, November 9, 1849	413
Zion Church School, *The North Star*, November 9, 1849	415
The Destiny of Colored Americans, *The North Star*, November 16, 1849	416
Mr. Whipper's Objections to the Proposed National League Considered, *The North Star*, December 14, 1849	419
REFERENCE NOTES	423
INDEX	445

PREFACE

In February, 1817, a Negro child was born in Maryland who was destined to become one of the nation's most distinguished citizens. Born a slave, he lifted himself up from bondage by his own efforts, taught himself to read and write, developed a great talent as lecturer, editor, and organizer, became a noted figure in American life, and gained world-wide recognition as the foremost spokesman for his oppressed people and courageous champion of many other progressive causes of his time.

The name of this man is Frederick Douglass. It should be a famous name in American history—placed beside the names of Jefferson and Lincoln. Yet only recently has it been rescued from the oblivion to which it was assigned by our historiography.

James Ford Rhodes' *History of the United States* devotes seven volumes to the period 1850-1870. Yet Rhodes leaves even the careful student with the impression that Douglass was just another of the many minor figures with which this exhaustive work is filled. John B. McMaster treats Douglass even more casually in the ten volumes of his *History of the People of the United States,* referring to him only once briefly and then not even taking the trouble to spell his name correctly. Edward Channing's six volumes had little room for mention and none for interpretation of Douglass' role. Professor Dwight L. Dumond of the University of Michigan, in his book, *The Anti-Slavery Origins of the Civil War,* finds space to present obscure white Abolitionists like Augustus Wattles and Calvin Waterbury, but Douglass is not so much as mentioned.

There have been several editions of Douglass' famous autobiography. But for over fifty years the bulk of his writings and speeches have remained buried in the yellowing pages of the press of that day, and scattered in the manuscript collections of various libraries and historical societies. Certain of Douglass' speeches and letters have been reprinted in Carter G. Woodson's *Negro Orators and Their Orations* and *The Mind of the Negro as Reflected by Letters Written During the Crisis,* 1800-1860. But no collected edition of Douglass' numerous speeches, which ranked him with the greatest of the nineteenth-century orators, was ever published. The great bulk of his letters remain in manuscript form. Few of the brilliant and eloquent editorials which appeared in *The North Star, Frederick Douglass' Paper, Douglass' Monthly,* and the *New National Era* have ever been reprinted. For a long time it was widely believed that ten volumes of Douglass' paper covering the period 1848 to 1860, the only copies available, had been lost when his house in Rochester had burnt to the ground in 1872.

"I have never been able to replace them," Douglass lamented late in his life, "and the loss is immeasurable. . . . If I have at any time said or written that which is worth remembering or repeating, I must have said such things between the years 1848 to 1860, and my paper was a chronicle of most of what I said during that time."

Six years ago I undertook to collect and prepare for publication the writings and speeches of Frederick Douglass. Through the kindness and help of a large number of historical societies and libraries as well as private individuals, I was not only able to obtain copies of all of Douglass' speeches and letters now available, but I was also able to assemble most of the issues of the paper which Douglass believed had disappeared forever.

The Life and Writings of Frederick Douglass will appear in four volumes entitled, *Early Years, The Pre-Civil War Decade, The Civil War,* and *Reconstruction and After.* Each volume includes the most important of Douglass' writings and speeches, letters, and editorials covering the period indicated, preceded by a study of the man and his times covering the same period.

There is good reason for this arrangement. No biography by itself can do the man full justice. For this we still have to read Douglass himself. Fortunately, this is no chore. These writings of a man whom slavery deprived of formal education constitute an important and distinctive contribution to our literature. Here is the clearest articulation of discontent, protest, militant action, and hope of the American Negro. Here one of the most brilliant minds of his time, constantly responsive to the great forces of his day, analyzes every important issue confronting the Negro and the American people generally during fifty crucial years in our history. Here are the eloquent words and penetrating thoughts that exerted a decisive influence on the course of national affairs for half a century and moved countless men and women to action in behalf of freedom. Most important of all, here are the militant principles of the outstanding leader of the Negro people whose ideas have remained vital and valid down to the present day.

Emphasis has been placed throughout these volumes on presenting Douglass' writings and speeches as they appeared in their original form. Passages have been omitted from several of the selections to avoid repetition arising inevitably from the nature of his journalistic work and his lecturing. These omissions have been properly indicated. There have also been a few editorial alterations in the selections to correct obvious misprints. Moreover, the writer has deemed it advisable to change the lower-case spelling of the word Negro to the upper-case spelling. The latter has become fairly general during the past generation as the result of continued pressure from the Negro people and their supporters, who justifiably pointed out that while other nationalities were honored with a capital letter, Negro continued to be spelled with a small n. Towards the end of his career Douglass began to use the upper-case spelling in his writings. It was the judgment of the writer that the upper case spelling of the word Negro should be used throughout these volumes.

Occasionally, too, the reader will come upon words in Douglass' speeches and writings which are correctly considered scurrilous and part of the parlance of the adherents of "white supremacy." In using them Douglass made it clear that he was doing so only to indicate the contempt expressed by the pro-slavery apologists for the Negro people. These words have not been fully spelled out in the present edition. By presenting these words in this form the writer believes that he best expresses the deepest indignation of all decent people at the slanderous attacks on the Negro people revealed in these epithets.

In all of Douglass' editorials and in most of his speeches, the original titles have been retained. The writer has supplied titles where they were missing or where more descriptive titles were considered advisable. The source of the originals of Douglass' writings and speeches has been placed at the end of each speech or article. The reference notes for Douglass' biography and for his writings and speeches have been placed at the end of each volume.

In the preparation of these volumes I have had the generous assistance and co-operation of the following: the libraries and personnel of the American Antiquarian Society, American Philosophical Library, the Frederick Douglass Memorial Association, Henry E. Huntington Library, the Historical Society of Pennsylvania, the Library Company of Philadelphia, the Library of Congress, New York Historical Society, Ohio State Archeological and Historical Society, Rutherford B. Hayes Memorial Association, the Schomburg Collection, New York, and the Wisconsin State Historical Society; the libraries of Fisk University, Harvard University, Moorland Foundation of Howard University, New York University, Oberlin College, Syracuse University, University of Rochester, and Yale University; the public libraries of Boston, New York City, and Rochester.

I also wish to thank Mr. Arthur B. Spingarn, Dr. Carter G. Woodson, and Mr. Henry P. Slaughter for making available to me writings and speeches of Frederick Douglass in their personal collections.

Mr. Doxey A. Wilkerson, Dr. Herbert Aptheker, and Elizabeth Lawson have kindly read this manuscript and offered valuable suggestions.

I wish to thank Mrs. Sophia O. Tevan for valuable assistance in preparing the manuscript for the printers.

PHILIP S. FONER

Croton-on-Hudson
January, 1950

FREDERICK DOUGLASS

From Slavery to Freedom

Once when Frederick Douglass was asked exactly when and where he was born, he replied: "I cannot answer; don't know my age. Slaves have no family records."[1] All any biographer of Douglass can say is that the man who was christened Frederick Augustus Washington Bailey and later became world famous as Frederick Douglass was born in February, 1817, somewhere in Tuckahoe, Talbot County, on the eastern shore of Maryland, the son of an unknown white father and Harriet Bailey, a slave.

Douglass never knew his father[2] and his knowledge of a mother who worked on a plantation twelve miles distant was "very scanty."[3] He had seen her four or five times, perhaps, up to the age of seven when the shadowy relationship was terminated by death. In his later life he recalled one of her rare, unexpected visits. She had walked the twelve miles after a long day's work and had brought him a large ginger cake. "I dropped off to sleep and waked in the morning to find my mother gone," he recollected. "I do not remember ever seeing her again. Death soon ended the little communication that had existed between us, and with it, I believe, a life—judging from her weary, sad, downcast countenance and mute demeanor—full of heartfelt sorrow."[4]

Douglass spent much of his early childhood in and around the slave cabin of his grandparents, Isaac (a free Negro) and Betsey Bailey. "Grandmamma Betty" was a warm-hearted person who spent her time making nets for catching shad and herring, planting seedling potatoes for nearby farmers, and nursing the children of her five daughters.[5]

When Douglass was seven years old, he was taken from his birthplace to the home of his master, Captain Aaron Anthony, on the banks of the river Wye. Captain Anthony owned three farms in Tuckahoe and about thirty slaves, but most of his time was spent in managing the twenty or thirty farms and the thousand slaves of Colonel Edward Lloyd. On the plantation Douglass lived like other slave children: brought in the cows in the evening, kept the chickens out of the garden, swept the front yard, ran errands, and did other simple chores.

It was here that Douglass first discovered the true face of slavery and the humiliations that went with it. Soon after his arrival at the plantation his Aunt Esther was given a brutal flogging. The seven-year-old Negro child was not to forget the tormented screams of the woman as each of the forty lashes with a heavy cowskin drew fresh blood. Later, he saw a cousin of his stagger wearily into the plantation, bare-footed, her neck and shoulders mutilated, open gashes on her head and her face streaming with blood. This was the work of a drunken overseer; the girl had dragged herself twelve miles to beg protection from her master. The young boy learned fast when he heard the master order the girl to go back to her torturer. She deserved "every bit of it," he shouted. And if she wasn't quick about leaving he would "take off the rest of the skin himself."

Life at the big house opened young Douglass' eyes. He compared the food-laden tables with the meager diet of the slave, and the fine clothes of the master and mistress with the slave's tattered wardrobe. The yearly wardrobe of a male slave consisted of two shirts and two pairs of trousers to be worn whatever the weather. These great contrasts remained with Douglass; they helped to create in him a burning hatred of the slave system.

His own experiences at the Lloyd plantation fed fuel to this hatred. He was yet to learn what it meant to be whipped with a cowhide, but he grew familiar with hunger and cold. Whatever the season he walked about almost naked, wearing only a coarse tow linen shirt which barely reached his knees. On cold nights he slept with his head and shoulders in a sack, but the frost bit into his feet breaking the skin open and forming deep gashes. He ate coarse boiled corn-meal—when he could edge his way to the trough on the kitchen floor where the mush was placed, and push aside the children scrambling for their portion. To add to his troubles, Aunt Katy, the cook, did not like him, and delighted in making him go without food. Several times a day he would follow the waiting girl to get the crumbs from the table cloth and the small bones flung out for the dogs and cats. He often fought with old Nep the dog for the crumbs which fell from the kitchen table.

It was only the kindness of Lucretia Auld, his master's daughter and wife of Captain Thomas Auld, which saved him from starvation. He would sing under her window, and it pleased her to reward him with a slice of bread and butter. It was also from Miss Lucretia that Douglass "received the first kindness that I ever experienced from one of a complexion different from my own."[6] He had been in a fight with another slave boy, receiving a heavy blow which left a scar on his face. He had come home screaming with pain. Lucretia Auld called him into the parlor, bound up his head, gave him a biscuit, and told him to go out to play with the other children. This simple act remained a bright memory in the bleak life of a slave child.

But such acts of kindness could not stop the constant pangs of hunger, nor make his coarse linen shirt seem any warmer on frosty days. Fortunately for young Douglass, another factor was at work. Slave labor in Maryland agriculture had ceased to be profitable. Consequently after 1820 it was common to farm slaves out to townspeople where they could be employed as house-servants and mechanics. This happened to Frederick Bailey.

In the spring of 1825 the eight-year-old slave was overjoyed to learn that he was being sent to Baltimore to live with Hugh Auld, a relative of the Anthony's. "Going to live at Baltimore laid the foundation, and opened the gateway, to all my subsequent prosperity," was the way Douglass put it.[7] This was to be the first of the many turning points in his eventful life.

For seven years Douglass worked for Hugh Auld, first as a household servant and later as an unskilled laborer in his shipyard. During the period he experienced comforts such as he had never known before. Yet he was seldom allowed to forget that he was a slave. Hearing his new mistress, Sophia Auld, read the Bible, a burning desire to learn to read consumed him. In response to his plea, his mistress taught him the alphabet and how to spell words of three or four letters. But the lessons ended the moment her husband learned of the boy's progress. In Douglass' presence, Hugh Auld forbade further instruction, shouting that "learning would *spoil* the best n———r in the world." Once a slave knew how to read there would be no keeping him![8]

These words only inspired the boy with a greater determination to learn. His former teacher was now the chief obstacle; as if to atone for her error, she kept constant vigilance over him, snatching any book or newspaper she saw in his hand, and making sure he could obtain no reading matter. But by various ingenious devices Douglass continued his education. He turned to school boys in the streets in out-of-the-way places where he could not be seen, and converted them into teachers. Out of his pocket would come the leaves of books he had raked "from the mud and filth of the gutter," a copy of his Webster's spelling book, and a slice of bread to pay for the lessons. While his tutors munched the bread, he talked to them about slavery. "Have not I as good a right to be free as you have?" he would ask the urchins. He was comforted by their sympathy and by their confidence that something would yet happen to make him free.[9]

With the first fifty cents he earned by blacking boots he bought the popular school book, *The Columbian Orator*.[10] This book deepened his hatred of slavery, and as he read and memorized the speeches of Chatham, Sheridan, and Fox in behalf of human rights, he began to understand his position. He was a victim of oppression, and if these great men were right, it was wrong that he or any man should be doomed to slavery. As he walked about the streets repeating to himself the words of Sheridan and Chatham, he kept asking himself: "Why am I a slave? Why are some people slaves, and others masters? Was there ever a time when this was not so? How did the relation commence?" He found no satisfactory answer to these questions, but when he heard his master and his friends denounce the Abolitionists, he resolved to discover who and what they were. Finally, in the columns of the *Baltimore American* he found a report that a vast number of petitions had been submitted to Congress, praying for the abolition of the internal slave trade. From that day, probably some time in February, 1833, "there was hope."

The thought of escaping from slavery frequently occurred to him. Two Irishmen whom he had met on the wharf advised him to run away to the North where he would be free. But he hesitated. He was still too young, and he wished to learn to write so that he himself could fill out the necessary pass.

While working in the shipyards he mastered the essentials of writing. During the slack periods he would copy the letters that made up the names of the ships; then using the streets as his school, his playmates as teachers, and the fences as his copybooks and blackboards, he learned to write. In later life in responding to a request for his autograph, he said: "Though my penmanship is not too fine it will do pretty well for one who learned to write on a board fence."[11]

In Baltimore Douglass enjoyed a life he never dreamed was possible when he was a slave on the plantation. He was much better fed and clothed, freely moved about the city, and was never whipped. Yet he could not escape the sufferings of slave life. He made the acquaintance of two slave girls who lived directly opposite the Aulds on Philpot Street. They were constantly being whipped by their sadistic mistress, and the head, neck and shoulders of the fourteen-year-old Mary were "literally cut to pieces." He watched with a heavy heart as the girl fought with the pigs for the garbage thrown into the street.

As he sat on Kennard's wharf, at the foot of Philpot Street, he saw men and women chained together being placed on board ships bound for New Orleans. He was profoundly moved by their piteous cries and their heavy footsteps as they moved from the slave pens to the vessels. Forty years later in a speech in Baltimore, he recalled this tragic sight and declared: "I then resolved that whatever power I had should be devoted to the freeing of my race."[12]

The comparative freedom of life in Baltimore was brought to an abrupt end as a result of Captain Anthony's death. The change of ownership placed Douglass in the possession of Thomas Auld, Anthony's son-in-law, a cruel, tight-fisted master who lived at St. Michaels, some thirty miles from Baltimore. The slave who returned to plantation life after seven years spent in the city was bound to get into difficulty with his new master. From books Douglass had learned of all the evils of slavery, and his hatred of the institution was deepened by the rigors of the plantation system after the comparative freedom of life in the city. He made no effort to hide his dissatisfaction with the meager diet provided by the kitchen at St. Michaels, and he infuriated Mr. and Mrs. Auld by his refusal to call his owner "Master" instead of "Captain."

When Douglass began to teach a Sunday School class for colored children, Master Auld decided that he had better take steps to provide his young slave with proper conditioning. Consequently, on the following Sunday, men armed with sticks and stones invaded the school, disrupted the class, and warned the teacher "to watch out." Douglass seemed determined to be another Nat Turner, said Master Auld, and if he did not mend his ways he would most certainly "get as many balls into him" as had the Negro slave rebel of 1831. Actually, Turner was hanged, but despite the inaccuracy, the warning indicated that trouble lay ahead.

Auld was not satisfied with merely a warning. Determined to crush young Douglass' spirit, he hired him out to Edward Covey, a professional slavebreaker. From January to August, 1834, the young slave was overworked, flogged daily, and was almost starved to death. After six months of such treatment, he was indeed "broken in body, soul and spirit." There seemed nothing left but either to kill Covey and then commit suicide or to fight back. Steeled by desperation and a combination of hope and fear, the youth found the courage to turn on his tormentor one day and soundly thrashed the Negro-breaker. The result was that Covey abandoned the whip and ignored Douglass for the four remaining months of hire. The slave never forgot the episode:

"This battle with Mr. Covey was the turning-point in my career. I was a changed being after that fight. I was nothing before, I was a man now . . . with a renewed determination to be a free man. . . . The gratification afforded by the triumph was a full compensation for whatever else might follow, even death itself. . . . I now resolved that, however long I might remain a slave in form, the day had passed forever when I could be a slave in fact. . . ."

Following his release, Douglass worked for two years on the plantation of a neighboring slaveowner, William Friedland. Conditions were a good deal better here; he had a kind master, enough food, was not overworked, and was even able to conduct a secret Sunday School for forty slaves. But kindness, food, and a few leisure hours were not enough. When he was at Covey's, beaten every day, he was concerned only with self-preservation. Now he began to think of freedom; the very privileges he enjoyed made him desire it the more. "If a slave has a bad master," he once explained, "his ambition is to get a better; when he gets a better, he aspires to have the best; and when he gets the best, he aspires to be his own master."[13]

Early in 1836 Douglass decided to escape. Together with other slaves, he planned to seize a canoe, paddle down the Chesapeake, and follow the North Star to freedom. But one of the men disclosed the plan before the fugitives could get away. As the leader of the group and originator of the conspiracy, Douglass was put in chains in the Talbot county jail. He expected to be sold to the slave traders and shipped to New Orleans, but his master balked when the idea was proposed by the planters in the neighborhood. Instead, Auld, hoping to subdue Douglass' insubordination by kindness, sent him back to Baltimore with a promise of freedom when he reached twenty-five—provided, of course, that he behaved himself.

For the next two years, from the summer of 1836 to the summer of 1838, Douglass worked in the Baltimore shipyards, first as an apprentice, then as a skilled caulker. During the first eight months of apprenticeship he came to know, through bitter experience, "the conflict of slavery with the interests of the white mechanics and laborers of the South." Forced to compete with slaves, the white workers found it impossible to get decent wages. Consequently they sought to keep slaves out of the trades, and demanded the ousting of all Negro artisans, free as well as slave.

When such a drive got under way at the shipyards of William Gardner on Fell's Point where Douglass was apprenticed, he became the victim of the campaign. Douglass was attacked many times. At one time, he fought his attackers so violently that it required four white apprentices, armed with bricks and heavy hand spikes, to finally lay him low. He was long to remember with bitterness how fifty white mechanics stood about during this brutal attack, some crying, "kill him—kill him—kill the d—d n———r, knock his brains out—he struck a white person." Much later in his life he came to understand that the southern white worker was almost as much the victim of the slave system as was the Negro.[14]

From Gardner's shipyards Douglass was transferred to a yard of which Hugh Auld was foreman. Here he rapidly became an expert caulker. Within a year, he was earning a dollar and a half a day, the highest wages paid caulkers in Baltimore. At first every penny of his earnings went to his master, but in May, 1838, he was able to persuade Auld to let him work for himself and in return would turn over a weekly payment of three dollars. Douglass bought his own tools and clothes, went about bargaining for his own employment, and every Saturday night handed over three dollars to his master.

In the evenings, after a day's work in the shipyard, Douglass extended his education. He met free Negroes who were well versed in literature, geography, and arithmetic, and he sought to learn from them. As a slave he was not able to join any of the forty benevolent institutions established by the free Negroes of Baltimore, but he was permitted to become a member of the East Baltimore Improvement Society as a special concession.[15] Here he took a prominent part in debates and here, too, he met Anna Murray, who afterward became his wife. Anna was one of twelve children of Bambarra and Mary Murray, slaves, and the first of their five children born in freedom, escaping by one month the fate of her older brothers and sisters born in slavery. At the age of eighteen she had left her parents' home in Denton, Maryland, and had gone to work as housekeeper for a well-to-do family in Baltimore. In the little circle of the East Baltimore Improvement Society she associated with free Negroes, but she was drawn to the slave, Frederick Bailey. They fell in love and planned to marry.

The meeting with Anna Murray intensified Douglass' desire for freedom. It was no longer a desire for himself alone. Freedom, now, would enable him to marry the woman he loved, not as a chattel but as a man.

Anna shared his feelings, encouraged him to escape and gave him her nine years' savings.

A dispute with Auld in the summer of 1838 hastened the day of escape. One Saturday evening, Douglass failed to turn over the three dollars to Hugh Auld and went instead with some friends to a camp meeting about twelve miles from Baltimore. Returning the next evening he was met with a furious outburst: "Now you scoundrel! You have done for yourself," Auld said. "You shall hire your time no longer. The next thing I shall hear of, will be your running away. Bring home your tools and your clothes, at once. I'll teach you how to go off in this way."[16]

In retaliation Douglass did not work the next week and on Saturday night there was no money to turn over. A violent quarrel followed which almost ended in blows. Douglass decided that the time had come for him to escape to the North. To allay Auld's suspicions he worked for a few weeks. On Saturday nights, he turned over his earnings to Auld who became so amiable that he returned twenty-five cents of it to Douglass, advising him to make good use of the money.

On Monday, September 3, 1838, Douglass bade farewell to Baltimore and slavery.

To effect his escape Douglass used a method familiar in southern seaport communities. He had had frequent contacts with free Negro sailors in the shipyards and had found them sympathetic to the plight of the slaves. From a sea-faring friend named Stanley who was his height, he borrowed a sailor's suit and a sailor's "protection," a paper listing the physical features of its owner who, as a free American sailor, could move about the country. (The suit was later returned to its owner by mail.) Douglass hopped the last car while a friend, Isaac Rhodes, threw his bundle into the moving train as it left the Baltimore station for Philadelphia. In this way he avoided buying a ticket which would have subjected him to the close scrutiny of the ticket agent who was bound to check the description on the "protection."

Fortunately, the conductor on the train was satisfied with the "protection." Nor did he pursue the matter further when Douglass replied, on being asked for the "free papers" which all free Negroes were required by Maryland law to produce on demand, that his "only pass was an American Eagle." Having passed the conductor's inspection, Douglass' chief worries seemed over, but at Wilmington his heart almost stopped beating. He ran into Frederick Stein, for whom he had once worked, and on a train bound south from Philadelphia, he caught sight of Captain

McGowan of Baltimore whom he knew intimately. But he was so perfectly disguised that neither of the men recognized him.

In the late afternoon of September 3, Douglass arrived in Philadelphia, where he "lived more in one day than in a year of ... slave life." The next day he was in New York City.[17]

Douglass' joy vanished rapidly as he walked the streets of the metropolis which the Abolitionists referred to as "the prolongation of the South," where "ten thousand cords of interests are linked with the Southern Slaveholder."[18] He was lonely and afraid. In New York City a fugitive slave was no safer than in Baltimore. And in the midst of the crisis of 1837, there were few opportunities for a free Negro to earn a livelihood. In desperation, Douglass finally revealed his plight to a passing sailor who introduced him to David Ruggles, the Negro secretary of the New York Vigilance Committee.[19]

For several days Douglass remained hidden in Ruggles' home and it was at this time that Anna Murray came North and joined him. On September 15, twelve days after his escape, they were married by the Rev. James W. C. Pennington, who had fled from a Maryland master ten years previously. Two days later they were on their way to New Bedford, Massachusetts, where Ruggles believed Douglass' skill as a caulker would secure him a livelihood. In his pocket the fugitive had his marriage certificate, a five-dollar bill which Ruggles had pressed upon him as the couple departed, and a letter of introduction to a Mr. Shaw in Newport whom they were to approach for funds if they did not have enough to carry them to New Bedford.

They arrived in Newport without funds to continue their trip by coach to New Bedford, but pushed ahead none the less, anxious to get to a place of safety. Their baggage, seized as security by the driver, was redeemed by Mr. and Mrs. Nathan Johnson, the family to whom they had been sent. The newlyweds felt at home immediately with this prosperous Negro family, who took great pains to make them forget their first experiences in the North. It was Johnson, moreover, who gave the name "Douglass" to his guest. In New York Frederick had dropped his two middle names, and changed Bailey to Johnson. As there were a great number of New Bedford Negroes with that name, his benefactor, who had just finished reading Sir Walter Scott's *Lady of the Lake,* suggested the name by which he was soon to be known on both sides of the Atlantic.

With Johnson's encouragement Douglass began his search for work as a free man. His first day's job was loading oil on a sloop bound for

New York, and dirty and back-breaking as it was, he went at it with a pleasure he had never experienced before. No master waited at the end of the day to rob him of his wages. Whatever he earned would be his own. The next day he sought work as a caulker—and made an important discovery. No one would hire him because white caulkers refused to work with Negroes. Forced to accept the fact that prejudice against Negroes was not confined to the South, he put aside his caulking clothes, borrowed a wood-horse and saw from Mr. Johnson and went in search of whatever work would come his way. There was no question of how hard, how dirty, and how menial it might be. For the next three years he sawed wood, shoveled coal, swept chimneys, rolled oil casks, drove a coach, carried the hod, waited on tables. His hands became hard. His earnings averaged only a dollar a day, but the family's scanty income was supplemented by Anna's earnings as a domestic servant. Her cheerful spirit, her thrift and economy helped immeasurably during those early days in New Bedford. The pillows, bed linen, dishes, knives, forks, and spoons, a trunk of clothing and furnishings which Anna had brought from Baltimore made their two rooms on Elm Street overlooking Buzzards Bay a comfortable home. While he worked with saw, buck, and axe, Anna was at the washboard adding her share to the daily earnings. Even after her children came (Rosetta was born in June, 1839, and Lewis sixteen months later), she worked as a domestic whenever she could spare time from her household duties.

The day-to-day task of eking out an existence for a growing family did not afford Douglass many opportunities to satisfy his longing for education. But he applied the same ingenuity that had stood him in good stead as a slave. "Hard work, night and day, over a furnace hot enough to keep metal running like water was more favorable to action than thought," he wrote later, "yet here I often nailed a newspaper to the post near my bellows and read while I was performing the up and down motion of the heavy beam by which the bellows were inflated and discharged."[20]

Soon after they had settled down in their new home, Douglass began to make himself a part of the Negro community of New Bedford. Having been class leader and choir member of the Sharp Street Methodist Church in Baltimore, he sought to renew his religious contacts. He joined a local Methodist church, but remained there only a short time. He discovered that Negroes were second-class communicants, sitting in a special section of the church. In disgust he walked out of the church, never to return. He tried other churches in New Bedford with the same result, and finally joined a small sect of his own people, the Zion Methodists, where he soon became a leading member of the congregation and a local preacher.[21]

Before he had left Baltimore Douglass had already heard of the Abolitionists and of their work to end slavery. He had received help from them en route to New Bedford, but actually he knew very little of their activities. Four months after he had come to New England there came into his hands a copy of William Lloyd Garrison's *Liberator*. So deeply was he moved by the paper that despite his poverty he became a regular subscriber. Every week he read the journal avidly, studying its principles and philosophy. "The paper became my meat and my drink," he wrote six years later. "My soul was set all on fire. Its sympathy for my brethren in bonds—its scathing denunciations of slaveholders—its faithful exposures of slavery—and its powerful attacks upon the upholders of the institution—sent a thrill of joy through my soul, such as I had never felt before!"[22]

Douglass was not satisfied to sit at home and thrill to the paper. He began to attend the Abolitionist meetings held by the Negro people of New Bedford. The first printed reference to Frederick Douglass appeared in the *Liberator* of March 29, 1839. It reported an anti-colonization meeting of the Negro citizens of New Bedford at the Christian Church on March 12, at which Douglass was one of the speakers in favor of resolutions condemning slavery, commending Garrison "as deserving of our support and confidence," and denouncing the African colonization movement in the following terms:

"That we are *American citizens,* born with natural, inherent and just rights; and that the inordinate and intolerable scheme of the American Colonization Society shall never entice or drive *us* from our native soil."

Douglass became more and more involved in the Abolitionist activities of the New Bedford Negroes. Every fortnight he attended a social meeting at the home of John Baily to discuss anti-slavery principles and events. A white Abolitionist who attended these sessions observed that in the discussions "the colored people acquire the habit of thinking and speaking; a circumstance which may, in a great measure, account for the self-possession of their manners, and the propriety and fluency of their language." Among these New Bedford Abolitionists Douglass was gradually assuming a position of leadership. On June 30, 1841, he was chairman at a meeting called to censure the Maryland Colonization Society for "threatening to remove the free colored people out of that state by coercion." The Negroes urged their brethren in Maryland to resist intimidation and condemned an attack on David Ruggles who had been roughly handled for combating segregation on the steamboat operating between New Bedford and Nantucket.[23]

On August 9, 1841, Douglass attended the annual meeting of the Bristol Anti-Slavery Society, held in New Bedford. Here in old Liberty Hall, a large, dilapidated building, with doors off their hinges, windows broken by stones thrown to break up Abolition proceedings, Douglass first heard William Lloyd Garrison. It was a red-letter day in the life of the young Negro, barely twenty-four years of age and but three years removed from slavery, because on that day, he saw in the editor of the *Liberator* the mission for his own life. "It may have been due to my having been a slave," he wrote toward the end of his life, "and my intense hatred of slavery, but no face and form ever impressed me with such sentiments as did those of William Lloyd Garrison." Douglass himself entered into the discussion and made a distinct impression upon the Abolitionist leader who reported to his paper that at the meeting were "several talented young men from New Bedford, one of them formerly a slave whose addresses were listened to by large and attentive audiences with deep interest."[24]

The following day, Douglass took his first vacation. With Garrison and forty other Abolitionists, white and Negro, he attended a convention at Nantucket. The trip was not without incident. Captain Phinney of the steamboat *Telegraph* refused to leave the dock until the Negro passengers aboard agreed to occupy separate quarters. Some of the delegates left, but, after a long delay, a compromise was worked out. All of the delegates went to the upper deck which was set aside for their use. During the sixty-mile voyage, the delegates, with Francis Jackson presiding, held an anti-slavery meeting on deck to protest the segregation practices of the steamship company.[25]

The next morning, August 12, at the convention in Athenaeum Hall, Douglass was called upon to speak by William C. Coffin, a New Bedford Abolitionist. Douglass, trembling and ill at ease, came forward to the platform and spoke with deep sincerity of his own life as a slave. Greatly stirred, Garrison followed with an exciting address using Douglass' remarks as his text. He asked the audience, "Have we been listening to a thing, a piece of property, or to a man?" "A man! A man!" came from five hundred voices. Then he asked if they would ever allow Douglass to be carried back to slavery and received a thunderous "No!" in reply. "Will you succor and protect him as a brother man—a resident of the old Bay State?" was the next question. "Yes!" shouted the audience with such vehemence that "the walls and roof of the Athenaeum seemed to shudder."

That evening Douglass spoke again, and, as in the morning, the group was moved by his eloquence. In his report of the convention, the *Anti-Slavery Standard* correspondent devoted special attention to the Negro delegate from New Bedford:

"One, recently from the house of bondage, spoke with great power. Flinty hearts were pierced, and cold ones melted by his eloquence. Our best pleaders for the slave held their breath for fear of interrupting him. Mr. Garrison said his speech would have done honor to Patrick Henry. It seemed almost miraculous how he had been prepared to tell his story with so much power. In the evening, which was to be the last meeting, he was again called forward, and listened to by a multitude with mingled emotions of admiration, pity and honor. . . .

"Then Garrison arose, and burst forth into a more eloquent strain than I had ever heard before. He eulogized, as he deserved, the fugitive who had just spoken and anathematized the system that could crush to the earth such men."[26]

Before the convention adjourned, John A. Collins, general agent of the Massachusetts Anti-Slavery Society, urged Douglass to become an active lecturer for the organization.[27] Douglass was reluctant to accept, doubting his own ability, but finally agreed to work for the society for three months. He was to travel with Stephen S. Foster, and, in addition to lecturing, was to get subscriptions for the *Liberator* and the *Anti-Slavery Standard*. His salary was to be four hundred and fifty dollars a year.

Douglass returned to New Bedford convinced that his usefulness as an Abolitionist agent would not last beyond the three month period. Events were rapidly to show how seriously he had underrated himself, and to prove that this was but the launching of a great career.

The Garrisonians and Abolition

For ten years after his Nantucket speech Douglass was part of a small but steadily growing army of men and women who constituted the Garrisonian wing of the anti-slavery movement. Around William Lloyd Garrison, the leader of this army, the fires of controversy still rage. A new school of historians has arisen who contend that the Garrisonian influence in the Abolitionist movement was relatively negligible and argue that by his intemperate and violent language Garrison actually did more to retard than advance the anti-slavery cause. Many historians, northern as well as southern, have long contended that the Garrisonians really brought on the Civil War by vilifying the slaveholders.

Although the recent studies revealing that the anti-slavery impulse came as much out of the West as out of New England have thrown valuable light on a hitherto neglected phase of the Abolitionist crusade,[1] the fact remains that the work of Garrison and his associates must still loom large in any analysis of the forces responsible for emancipation. Whatever his shortcomings, Garrison was the most indomitable figure among Abolition forces. He possessed to a marvelous degree an undivided devotion to the struggle, the supremacy of a single purpose, the stern stuff out of which a fighter for unpopular causes must be made. His uncompromising stand against slavery struck home with such force that it riveted the attention of all men on this cause.

Many Americans had written and spoken against slavery long before Garrison's day. Anti-slavery sentiment in America had its origins coincident with the introduction of slavery in the colonial period, and was greatly advanced by the literature produced just before and during the Revolutionary War. In his famous pamphlet published in Boston in 1764, *The Rights of the British Colonies Asserted and Proved,* James Otis denounced the institution of slavery and affirmed the Negro's inalienable right to freedom. Nathaniel Appleton of Cambridge, Massachusetts, writing in 1767, placed himself squarely for abolition at any cost because of man's "natural right to be free." Eight years later Thomas Paine published an essay, "African Slavery in America," in which he denounced slavery as no less immoral than "murder, robbery, lewdness and barbarity," and called upon Americans to "discontinue and renounce it, with grief and abhorrence." Thomas Jefferson, who had urged the Assembly in Virginia to emancipate the slaves in the colony as early as 1769, in the first draft of the Declaration of Independence, labeled the slave trade "a cruel war against human nature itself, violating its most sacred rights of life and liberty."

In his *Autobiography,* Jefferson relates what happened to this passage from the original draft of the Declaration of Independence:

"The Clause ... reprobating the enslaving of the inhabitants of Africa was struck out in complaisance to South Carolina and Georgia, who had never attempted to restrain the importation of slaves, and who on the contrary still wished to continue it. Our Northern brethren also I believe felt a little tender under these censures; for tho their people have very few slaves themselves yet they had been pretty considerable carriers of them to others."

Anti-slavery literature emphasized the inconsistency between slavery and the Declaration of Independence. Thus a correspondent who signed himself "Free Negro" asked: "Do the rights of nature cease to be such, when a Negro is to enjoy them? Or does patriotism in the heart of an African, rankle with treason?"

Under the impact of this revolutionary spirit, Negroes themselves, led by Absalom Jones, Prince Hall, and William Cuffee, became involved in the struggle; they protested the payment of taxes to a government denying them the rights of citizens; and they demanded freedom as a reward for fighting in defense of their country. Negroes also organized resistance to the slave trade and, in New England, even petitioned state legislatures for emancipation.[2]

These early protests against American slavery yielded rich rewards. By 1808 the African slave trade was abolished, slaves were freed in Vermont, New Hampshire, Massachusetts, and Ohio, and gradual emancipation was provided for in Rhode Island, Pennsylvania, New Jersey, New York, and Connecticut. Although slave labor in these states had already decreased in importance as an economic factor and was being replaced by free labor, these early anti-slavery activities hastened the day of freedom.

Beginning with the Pennsylvania Abolition Society in 1775, anti-slavery organizations spread throughout the North and the South. Until 1829, members of state and local bodies met in national meetings of the American Convention of Delegates from Abolition Societies.[3] But these meetings accomplished little of significance. Emancipation was still the ultimate goal, but the American Convention made no hard and fast rule as to how or when it could be secured. "The best method is still a question," it reported in 1821. "We cannot expect a speedy accomplishment of that event."[4]

There was always a small group of forthright and militant Abolitionists scattered through the Convention, but they were seldom heard and never countenanced by the conservatives who talked of gradual emancipation but did nothing to advance any program which might antagonize the vested interests. The reasons are fairly obvious. With the growth of the textile industry in England and New England, the invention of the cotton gin, and the expansion of the plantation system into the fertile land of the southwest, anti-slavery sentiment in the South gradually receded. By the late 1820's slavery represented a property interest amounting to billions of dollars, covering the whole plantation system and numerous northern industrial and commercial activities that rested upon servile labor. Small wonder so many anti-slavery men hesitated to antagonize this powerful economic and political alliance and could only give pious expressions in favor of gradual emancipation.

Whatever potential power there was in the American Convention of Delegates from Abolition Societies was dissipated by the rise of a new organization, the American Society for Colonizing the Free People of Colour of the United States. This organization disguised the issues and split the forces of the anti-slavery groups both in the North and South.

Formally organized on December 28, 1816, in the Hall of the House of Representatives in Washington, it was the culmination of colonizing efforts dating from the Revolutionary era. Prior to 1815, almost all colonization plans had called for the removal of Negroes, free or slave, all eventually to be emancipated. But the new society, dominated by southerners—the president and eight of the thirteen vice-presidents were from the South—was not only anti-Negro but pro-slavery. Such leaders as Andrew Jackson, Henry Clay, and Bushrod Washington gave the society great prestige but unfortunately many anti-slavery men, including even some who later became militant Abolitionists, threw their support to the new organization, believing they would find in the society the best answer to their problems.

Although by 1833, there were 97 local colonization societies in the North and 136 in the South, from 1820, the national society had been able to colonize only 2,885 Negro people. After the first enthusiasm, the society began to lose strength mainly because free Negroes opposed the plan; they refused to be uprooted, opposed being moved out of the country en masse, leaving hundreds of thousands of their people in slavery. The Negroes understood that the leaders of the Colonization Society were not interested in freeing slaves but in shipping troublesome Negroes out of the country, thereby strengthening their control over those who remained in bondage.[5]

In 1817, less than a month after the founding of the American Colonization Society, the free Negro people of Richmond and Philadelphia declared their opposition to any plan of deportation in the guise of repatriation. Other meetings followed in northern and border state centers. The delegates to the National Convention of the People of Color in Philadelphia in 1831 incorporated in their *Conventional Address* the declaration:

"The Convention . . . would respectfully suggest to that august body [the American Colonization Society] . . . that, in our humble opinion, . . . they are pursuing the direct road to perpetuate slavery, with all its unchristianlike concomitants, in this boasted land of freedom; and, as citizens and men whose best blood is sapped to gain popularity for that institution, we would, in the most feeling manner, beg of them to desist; or if we must be sacrificed to their philanthropy, we would rather die at home. . . ."[6]

Therefore, during the years when many white anti-slavery men were growing more cautious, the cause did not lack for militant fighters. The Negro people battled both slavery and the colonization movement and spoke out sharply on these issues. While the National Convention of the Delegates from Abolition Societies was offering a program which breathed gently upon the southern slaveholders and their northern allies, the Negro conventions came out boldly for human freedom. In 1827, *Freedom's Journal*, the first periodical published by Negroes in the United States, raised the demand for immediate emancipation of the slaves and conducted a brilliant campaign against the Colonizationists. Two years later, David Walker, the Boston agent for *Freedom's Journal,* issued his revolutionary *Appeal . . . to the Coloured Citizens of the world, but in particular, and very expressly to those of the United States* which was as advanced a call for the overthrow of slavery as anything to come from the Abolitionists in the next few decades.

Beginning with 1830 the anti-slavery crusade burst forth with a new intensity and within a few years was to establish itself as one of the most profound revolutionary movements in the world's history. The Negro slave rebellion in Virginia led by Nat Turner in September, 1831, was a portent of the sharply accelerating conflict between pro- and anti-slavery forces. On October 21, 1831, James Forten, the militant Philadelphia Negro reformer, wrote jubilantly that the Turner rebellion would strengthen the anti-slavery cause by "bringing the evils of slavery more prominently before the public. . . . Indeed we live in stiring [*sic*] times, and every day brings news of some fresh effort for liberty, either at home or abroad—onward, onward, is indeed the watchword."[7]

These were indeed stirring times. A new society was developing west of the Alleghenies, putting its mark on the social and political life of the entire country. A young labor movement was rising in the East, protesting the hardships of a rapidly expanding industrial system. Ecclesiastical revolts and religious revivals were asserting man's innate goodness and capacity for self-improvement, expressing this conviction in an interest in the weak and helpless—temperance reform, prison reform, and, logically, in the condition of the slave. It was an "age of great movements" which showed a "power to exalt a people," said William Ellery Channing, the New England liberal. "It was an era of sympathy with the suffering, and of devotion to the progress of the whole human race." This new anti-slavery movement was part of this great stirring, this upheaval, this effort to re-establish American democracy upon the principles of the Declaration of Independence. It was part of a great democratic and humanitarian impulse, for Abolitionism sprang up in a rich soil that gave us at the same time public education, woman's rights, peace, temperance, and utopian socialist movements.[8]

The leaders of the new anti-slavery movement had a great many differences of opinion on numerous matters—political action, "the woman question," non-resistance, disunion, the nature of the Constitution—but there was one idea which the majority held in common, and that was the inefficacy of "gradualism." They took their stand on immediate emancipation to save the nation from the sin of slave-holding. There was no time to waste. The eyes of the entire world were on them. It was their duty not only to themselves but to the slaveholder and to mankind the world over to save their brothers and sisters in bondage.

As we have shown, William Lloyd Garrison can scarcely be called a pioneer in the anti-slavery movement. Nor was he the first to raise the demand for the "immediate and complete emancipation" of the slaves. But it is to his credit that he was the first to build an organized movement capable of conducting a struggle to achieve this goal.

On Saturday, January 1, 1831, in Boston, Garrison issued the first number of the *Liberator,* through which for the next thirty-odd years he was to preach the gospel of the abolition of slavery. The first number contained an address to the public which sounded the keynote of Garrison's career. He announced his determination to attack the system of slavery until "every chain be broken, and every bondman set free." He repudiated every plan for gradual emancipation and proclaimed the duty of immediate and unconditional liberation of the slaves. Then announcing his program for the future, he boldly wrote:

"I will be as harsh as truth and as uncompromising as justice. . . . I will not equivocate—I will not excuse—I will not retreat a single inch—and I will be heard."[9]

To put into operation machinery with which to fight for his principles, Garrison organized the New England Anti-Slavery Society in 1832, and, in the following year, in Philadelphia, rallied the remnants of the local and national societies under a new organization known as the American Anti-Slavery Society. Soon after Garrison joined hands with George Thompson, Daniel O'Connell, Thomas Clarkson, and other Abolitionists in the British Isles, arousing international attention to the new movement.

The American Anti-Slavery Society rapidly attracted as active participants such men and women as Wendell Phillips, Arthur and Lewis Tappan, John Greenleaf Whittier, Maria Weston Chapman, Stephen S. Foster, Theodore D. Weld, Elijah P. Lovejoy, Gerrit Smith, Theodore Parker, Lucretia Mott, the Grimke sisters, and other well known people. Negroes shared in the leadership of the organization from its very inception. Several Negroes were delegates at the founding convention; three Negroes were among the sixty-two signers of the Declaration of Sentiments, and the Board of Managers included James G. Barbadoes of Massachusetts, Peter Williams of New York, Robert Purvis, James McCrummell, John B. Vashon and Abraham D. Shadd of Pennsylvania.[10]

The American Anti-Slavery Society was launched at a most critical period in the struggle over slavery. Cotton was king, and every southern institution, the schools, churches, and economic agencies which had criticized slavery before the invention of the cotton gin now paid homage to the new monarch whose throne rested on the labor of four million enslaved human beings. Economics books were rewritten to sing the great advantages of slave labor over free labor. The inferiority of the Negro was "proved" *a priori*. The Southerners devised the "Positive Good" theory which declared that slave labor was essential to the development and progress of the nation; that the Negro was destined, by all evidence, to be kept in a subordinate position; that slavery lifted a whole race of heathens to a Christian status; and that the institution improved the white people because it afforded leisure time for the development of culture and the arts. The ruling class was determined to permit no compromise between its economic interests and the pleas of humanitarians. The southern states prohibited manumission unless provision was made for the removal of the Negroes from the state. The status of slavery and the slave was summarized by the Supreme Court of North Carolina in 1829:

"The end [of slavery] is the profit of the master, his security, and the public safety. The subject is one doomed in his own person and his posterity to live without knowledge and without the capacity to make any thing his own, and to toil that another may reap the fruits. . . . The power of the master must be absolute to render the submission of the slave perfect. In the actual condition of things it must be so. There is no remedy. This discipline belongs to the state of slavery. . . ."[11]

Not without cause did the British Abolitionist, Charles Stuart, say: "Truly, your country, in all its leading outward features, is making itself a spectacle equally disgusting and ridiculous to all independent and manly intelligence. Applauding liberty, yet keeping slaves! Calling the slave trade piracy if practiced in Africa, but ready to wade through blood to honor and sustain it in America! Boasting of freedom, yet grasping tenaciously its gross idolatry of a white and its atrocious abhorrence of a colored skin."[12]

It was at this point, in the 'thirties, that the Abolitionists launched their campaign to capture the minds of the people and turn them against the system of oppression that was fastening the shackles of slavery even more securely upon the Negro people.

In the forceful Declaration of Sentiments adopted by the American Society at its founding convention, the delegates pledged:

"We shall organize anti-slavery societies, if possible, in every city, town, and village in our land.

"We shall send forth agents to lift up the voice of remonstrance, of warning, of entreaty and rebuke.

"We shall circulate unsparingly and extensively anti-slavery tracts and periodicals."[13]

The struggle to carry out this pledge was waged with a fervor, persistence and skill rarely matched in our history. The handful of Abolitionists worked out a thoroughgoing propaganda; circulated petitions by the thousands which they showered on Congress and state legislatures; appeared before legislative committees; sent out traveling agents; slipped printed handkerchiefs bearing anti-slavery slogans into bales designed for Southern markets, and mailed pictures depicting the cruelties of slavery. At the same time they did not neglect the free Negro people. Above all, they held anti-slavery meetings in every conceivable place, from a stable loft to a church. There was a round of annual meetings—meetings of the New York, the Massachusetts, the New England, the Western (Ohio), and the American Anti-Slavery Societies. Then there was the annual anti-slavery celebration of West India Emancipation on August 1st. There were anti-slavery bazaars, anti-slavery soirees, and anti-slavery festivals. Resolutions were passed, ardent speeches made and hymns were sung. Typical was the following stirring song written by Garrison:

> *I am an Abolitionist,*
> *I glory in the name*
> *Though now by Slavery's minions hissed*
> *And covered o'er with shame;*
> *It is a spell of light and power*
> *The watchword of the free:*
> *Who spurns it in the trial-hour,*
> *A craven soul is he!*[14]

The central features of Abolitionist agitation were the lecturers or "traveling agents"; the printing of newspapers and periodicals; the publication of books, leaflets (broadsides), and cartoons.

The system of "agents," who traveled from town to town explaining the principles of Abolitionism and forming local societies, was developed to a very high point by Theodore Weld, a master at all forms of agitation, and Elizur Wright, organizational genius of the American Society. Agents had to be of good moral character, sincere, fully steeped in the subject, financially trustworthy, and, as Wright wrote to Weld about one candidate: "Has he the *'vis Vividu,'* the galvanism that can reanimate the dead as well as the steadfastness that can withstand the onset of the living?" Meeting these qualifications, which might be investigated for a month or more, an agent would then begin his travels, "mobbed out of the big cities and pelted out of the little ones," jolting over primitive roads in hard coaches from day to day, speaking in barns, churches, taverns, schools, and private parlors—on the town common or in the nearest forest when nothing else could be had.

Since services rendered the slaves were freewill offerings, it followed that all able to do so should work without compensation. Others—those "who had no extrinsic means of livelihood"—were allowed "what they consider absolutely indispensable to a bare subsistence." The salaries were $8 a week if unmarried and those who had a wife and family at home received $600 a year and traveling expenses. The "Instructions to Agents" further adjured them to remember that "silver and gold are the Lord's" and to be frugal in their expenses. By way of implementing this advice, Elizur Wright scanned each agent's monthly expense and work reports with a stern, economical eye.[15]

These work reports convey in the simplest, most dramatic way the sincerity, courage, and self-sacrificing devotion of the anti-slavery agents. These traveling lecturers made every possible sacrifice and frequently went hungry. A mobbing was an every-day occurrence. James Russell Lowell's poem described Stephen S. Foster thus:

> *Hard by, as calm as summer even,*
> *Smiles the reviled and pelted Stephen;*
> *Who studied mineralogy*
> *Not with soft book upon the knee,*
> *But learned the properties of stones,*
> *By contact sharp of flesh and bones.*

The peak of achievement of the work of traveling agents came in 1836-37. Some seventy were selected, then summoned to a convention in New York City, to which about forty came. There Theodore Weld, as "the central luminary," held forth for a fortnight at the three daily sessions. Garrison wrote:

"The questions discussed were manifold—such as, what is slavery? What is immediate emancipation? Why don't you go to the South? The slaves, if emancipated, would overrun the North. The consequences of emancipation to the South. Hebrew servitude. Compensation. Colonization. Prejudice. Treatment and condition of our free colored population. Gradualism, etc., etc. All the prominent objections to our cause were ingeniously presented, and as conclusively shown to be futile."

Weld's prodigious efforts, added to a program of speaking from five to fifteen times in a single town, night after night, finished his speaking days forever. He lost his voice; and only long afterwards was he able to speak even in conversation without pain. He turned his talents, however, to writing at which he was equally a master.[16]

From its beginning, the American Society stressed the importance of publishing and distributing newspapers. Without reaching very large circulations, the Abolitionist papers multiplied in number and influence. In 1834 the *Liberator* had a weekly circulation of 2,300, and 75 per cent of its readers were Negro people. The weekly *Emancipator,* published by the New York Anti-Slavery Society, reached a circulation of 3,800 copies. There were 14 Abolitionist periodicals published in 1839, and 26 weeklies in 1843. By then the columns of many other newspapers had been opened to Abolitionist ideas and writers.

It required unremitting attention and sacrifice on the part of Abolitionist leaders and supporters to maintain their press. Selling at an average of two dollars a year, the anti-slavery weeklies operated at a loss. Financial campaigns were constantly undertaken, special appeals were made through the paper's columns, and agents had to remind audiences that a chief cause of the financial difficulties stemmed from the failure of subscribers to pay up their subscriptions. Most often the appeals would be heeded. Money would come in, sometimes generous contributions from wealthy donors like Gerrit Smith, a Peterboro, New York, landowner with varied reform interests, sometimes handsome legacies or a young lady's bracelet. Large contributions, however, were not too frequent, and most often the anti-slavery movement had to depend upon the receipt of letters such as the following from the West Boxford Female Anti-Slavery Society containing $2 and the statement:

> "We are a feeble band of small means but what we have we wish to appropriate to the best advantage.... 'The Cause' is one dear to our hearts, and it will be a source of the highest gratification to do anything for its advancement."[17]

One of the great contributions made by women to the Abolition movement was the accumulation of funds necessary to carry on the anti-slavery work. The Annual Anti-Slavery Fair, sponsored by the Female Anti-Slavery Societies, became a vital source of funds for the cause. The Fair was usually held the week before Christmas so that people could buy Christmas gifts and at the same time contribute to a cause dear to their conscience. All through the year female societies and sewing circles sewed and knitted. European friends made annual contributions of money and articles. In 1841 Mrs. Maria Weston Chapman who organized the Boston Fair for a period of twenty years, wrote to Lydia M. Child: "Petersburg, Paris, Geneva, Rome, London, Glasgow, all

Ireland, the lovely city of the Cape, and the Haitian city of Santiago are all contributors." Friendly merchants made donations or sold articles at wholesale prices to the ladies. In 1840 among the articles offered at the Boston Fair was "jewelry of friends who had renounced it for their own wearing for the sake of the cause" with the hope that the new wearers would learn to renounce it in the future!

Most of the Anti-Slavery Societies were poor; the largest income received for a single year by the American Society was $47,111.74; the Massachusetts Society collected approximately $6,000 annually and most state societies received only $3,000. Yet, despite their lack of funds, the Abolitionists carried "the word" into every nook and cranny of American life. They kept the community astir; they made people think and talk. The philosophy and the method of this unprecedented campaign for educating the American people were perfectly summed up by Wendell Phillips in the statement:

"Our aim is to alter public opinion. Did we live in a market, our talk should be of dollars and cents, and we would seek to prove only that slavery was an unprofitable investment. Were the nation one great, pure church, we would sit down and reason of 'righteousness, temperance, and judgment to come.' Had slavery fortified itself in a college, we would load our cannons with cold facts, and wing our arrows with arguments. But we happen to live in the world,—the world made up of thought and impulse, or self-conceit and self-interest, of weak men and wicked. To conquer, we must reach all."

As the campaign to "reach all" got under way, the ranks of the Abolitionists steadily increased. In 1834, there were 60 auxiliary societies; in May, 1835, there were 200; in May, 1836, there were 527. The number climbed to 1,000 in July, 1837; by 1838 it had jumped to 1,350 and in 1840 there were over 2,000 societies with a membership of 200,000.[18]

The rapid growth of Abolitionist sentiment during the 1830's was not merely the result of effective propaganda. Many Americans were seeing clearly that there was an identity of struggle for Negro freedom and for freedom for all people, and that the democratic rights of all people were threatened by the same power which kept millions of slaves in chains. There was a growing conviction among many people that to preserve their own civil and political liberties they had to support the struggle for the democratic rights of the Abolitionists to fight slavery.

This issue was crystallized by the struggle over the right of petition. For some years anti-slavery petitions were few in number. On December 12, 1831, John Quincy Adams, who was to lead the petition fight, presented fifteen petitions, which were referred to committees who reported against granting their plea. It was not until 1835 that petitions again reached Congress in sufficient volume to provoke discussion. With the beginning of 1836, however, they became headlines in the news. In the Senate, Calhoun introduced a motion against their reception which, after many weeks of debate, was defeated. A similar measure in the House provoked a debate lasting several weeks. Finally, the whole question of reception was referred to a special committee, at the head of which was Pinckney of South Carolina, which recommended that "all petitions relating to the subject of slavery or the abolition of slavery, shall, without being either printed or referred, be laid upon the table, and no further action whatever shall be had thereon." When the vote was taken, John Quincy Adams rose, and, instead of voting, pronounced the measure "a direct violation of the Constitution of the United States, the rules of this House, and the rights of my constituents."[19]

This was the famous "Pinckney gag," which, in various forms, was repeated each session until 1840, when it was made a standing rule of the House. Many Americans, however, who objected to Abolitionism, leaped to the defense of any group to petition Congress for whatever cause.

Step by step Abolitionism became identified with civil liberty. During the campaign in Congress to deprive the Abolitionists of the right of petition, the Philadelphia Trades' Union observed that the petitions of the Abolitionists and those of the trade unions in behalf of the ten-hour day received the same treatment. William Leggett, acting editor of the *New York Evening Post* and a spokesman for the labor movement during the Jacksonian era, attacked the government's interference with the mail privileges of the anti-slavery journals, and warned the workers that their journals would be next. When the Mayor of Philadelphia prevented Frances Wright, the courageous woman reformer, from lecturing in that city on the subject of slavery, the *National Laborer,* organ of the Philadelphia Trades' Union, the city central labor body, stated:

"The people need not be surprised at this, when they remember that it is the same Mayor who demanded the enormous bail of $2,500 for the appearance of the Schuylkill laborers to answer the charge of riot, who were afterwards discharged because there was no crime found against them."[20]

The increase in Abolitionist sentiment continued after 1840 as the aggressions of the slavocracy mounted. But the American Anti-Slavery Society did not reflect this increase. In 1840 the Society had reached its peak. The split in the organization between the Garrisonians and other Abolitionists stopped further growth.

The opponents of slavery were by no means solidly united in creed or strategy. One school insisted that the only proper and effectual instrument for the extermination of slavery was moral suasion; another maintained that moral suasion had to be buttressed by political action; and still another believed in direct, militant action and called for resistance in a physical sense.

Garrison and his followers were adherents of the first school of thought. They pledged major emphasis on the thesis that the way to get rid of slavery was to establish "in the hearts of men a deep and widespreading conviction of *the brotherhood of the human race;* that God hath indeed made of one blood all nations of men for to dwell on all the face of the earth"; that fighting evil with evil was to be condemned; that the slave should be urged not to resist his torturer with carnal weapons, for that was sin; that spiritual, not material means were the only moral way to achieve good. The warfare was to be no wild crusade, but a holy war, a sacred strife, waged not with earthly fire, "but with weapons fresh from the armory of God ... Prayer ... Faith ... and the word of God!" Said Wendell Phillips: "Those who cling to moral effort are the true champions in the fight ... We are working *with God,* and the times and the seasons are in His hands."[21]

Yet the Garrisonians never fell asleep at their moral weapons. The movement was always kept in vigorous operation. In spite of this, it became clear to many Abolitionists that moral suasion would not by itself free the slaves. The controversy over the right of petition encouraged many of them to seek abolition by political action and if necessary, even to form an independent political movement.

At first Garrison was favorable toward using the ballot-box against slavery. In an *Address to the Abolitionists of Massachusetts,* he wrote:

"Do not stay away from the polls. Go and scatter your votes. This is the true way to make yourselves felt. Every scattering vote you cast counts against the candidate of the parties; and you will serve as an effectual admonition to them, to nominate the next time, men whom you can conscientiously support."

But he opposed the formation of a political party by the Abolitionists on the grounds that it would be dangerous, if not fatal to the cause. He argued in this way:

"If we were a political party, the struggle for places of power and emolument would render our motives suspect, even if it did not prove too strong a temptation to our integrity. If we were a distinct party, every member of it must vote for its candidates, however he might disagree with them on other points of public policy. Experience seems to show that under a free government, there cannot be at one time, more than two powerful political parties."[22]

And very soon Garrison even retreated from his early endorsement of political action. He studied the Constitution and concluded that in giving "solemn guarantees" to slavery, it was "a covenant with death, and an agreement with hell." He cited the clause which legalized the slave trade for a period of twenty years; that which allowed the slave masters to swell their representation in Congress, and the clause which pledged the military power of the United States to put down servile rebellion and to enforce the fugitive slave law. These constituted a trinity of evil, and branded the Constitution a compact of fatal compromise. These provisions, moreover, expressed the exact purpose of its authors. Consistent Abolitionism was impossible under the Constitution. Slavery was intrenched in the fundamental law of the nation; consequently, anyone who would defend and uphold the Constitution, as was implicit in the act of voting and holding office, partook of the guilt of the slaveholders. As one of the Garrisonians put it: "The Abolitionists cannot conscientiously support or swear to support the Constitution. They cannot thus support God and mammon."

From denouncing the Constitution, Garrison moved next to denouncing the "blood-soaked" American Union, and, as early as 1832, led the Come-Outers (those who advocated leaving the Union). "There is much declamation about the sacredness of the compact which was formed between the free and slave States in the adoption of the Constitution," he write in the *Liberator* of December 29, 1832. "A sacred compact, forsooth! We pronounce it the most bloody and heaven-daring arrangement ever made by men for the continuance and protection of a system of the most atrocious villainy ever exhibited upon the earth . . ." Adopting as his watchword, "No Union with slaveholders," Garrison openly advocated the dissolution of the Union as the only means of freeing the slaves.

The Garrisonians fulminated against the churches as vigorously as they did against the state. They called "the church and clergy of the United States as a whole . . . a great *Brotherhood of Thieves,* inasmuch as they countenance the highest kind of theft, *i.e.,* man-stealing." Phillips remarked: "If I die before emancipation, write this for my epitaph. 'Here lies Wendell Phillips, infidel to a church that defended human slavery—traitor to a government that was only an organized conspiracy against the rights of men.'" Garrison not only denounced the churches as forming "the bulwark of American Slavery," but he repudiated the divine inspiration of the Scriptures. It was harmful, he argued, to refer to the Bible as the Holy Book, inasmuch as nobody knew who had written it or when it had been written. A staunch Anti-Sabbatarian, he held as superstition the setting aside of the first day of the week for religious purposes, attributing the practice to the machinations of the "priestcraft" for selfish ends.[23]

When to such beliefs was added Garrison's insistence that women should participate equally with men in the leadership of the anti-slavery societies, not a few Abolitionists were shocked. The "woman question" became a pivotal factor in the anti-slavery movement and a major issue in the conflict between Garrison and his opponents in the American Anti-Slavery Society. On May 7, 1839, the American Society at its annual convention voted, 180 to 140, to allow all *persons* present to be seated as members. One hundred and twenty members went on record as protesting the decision, stating that the right of women to speak, vote, and hold office was against the recognized rules of propriety, was a breach of faith against those who joined the society believing it to be an organization of men, that at the organizing convention the women did not sign the Declaration of Sentiments nor enroll as members, and that this was a step to enlist the anti-slavery movement in a cause foreign to its purpose.

Those in favor of women's participation, led by Garrison, stated that the constitution of the American Anti-Slavery Society made no distinction between men and women, but said, "All persons who consent to the principles" were to be admitted. The Executive Committee published a statement declaring that the action of the convention was not to be construed as committing the society to the principles of women's equality with men in public affairs; it became evident that there was a serious cleavage in the organization.[24]

The conflict reached its climax at the meeting of the American Society in 1840. Garrison's opponents, led by the Tappan brothers, attempted to capture the national society, to reverse the action allowing women to serve on committees with men, and to oust Garrison from a position of power. As every Abolitionist present was to have a vote, Garrison chartered a steamer at Providence to take a boatload of his followers to New York to save the society from falling into the hands of his opponents. A rallying cry went out through the *Liberator*. The response was prompt: over four hundred delegates were prepared to "preserve the integrity of the anti-slavery movement." Persons of all ages, color, and conditions, from veterans to new recruits, poured into the steamer. They filled the berths and floors in the cabins, and overflowed on the deck.

When the group arrived at the convention, they made "clean work of everything with crushing unanimity," to use Garrison's words. On a test vote Abby Kelley was nominated to the Business Committee by a vote of 557 to 451. Lucretia Mott, Lydia Maria Child, and Maria Weston Chapman were put on the executive committee. Some of the opposition delegates were so exasperated by the result that they left the meeting.

Garrison's opponents insisted that Abolition must be divorced from no-government, non-resistance, theological heterodoxy, and equality of the sexes. Garrison's doctrines, they claimed, weakened "the staff of accomplishment." Accordingly, Lewis Tappan, after the adoption of the resolution admitting women to membership, urged its opponents to meet in the lecture room under the church to organize a new society. All the ministers present accepted the invitation as did many others, and the American and Foreign Anti-Slavery Society was speedily organized.[25]

The new society recognized the "rightfulness of government," urged political action as a duty and declared that the admission of women to take part in its proceedings was an innovation "repugnant to the constitution of the society," "a firebrand in anti-slavery meetings, and contrary to the usages of the civilized world." Its program naturally drew within the organization the more conservative and prudent members of the old society, those who "could not swallow Garrison." But it also attracted those who disagreed with Garrison's presentation of the Constitution as a pro-slavery document and who believed firmly in the value of anti-slavery political action.

The American and Foreign Anti-Slavery Society never became a powerful organization, and expired after a feeble existence of thirteen years. Most of its members identified themselves with the Liberty Party.

They claimed that the Constitution had been misinterpreted, the text blameless, that it was, to the contrary, an Abolitionist document. Basing themselves on an anti-slavery constitutional interpretation the "New Orgs," as they were called, contributed to the growth of political Abolitionism.

Disgusted by the split in the movement and unwilling to join either organization, groups of anti-slavery men floundered about after 1840. Gerrit Smith expressed the viewpoint of the no-organization Abolitionists in a letter to Theodore D. Weld on July 11, 1840:

> "Like yourself, I can go neither with the Old nor New Anti-slavery Organization *at the present*. I am sick, heart sick, of the quarrels of abolitionists between themselves, and I apprehend that for *the present* at least, these organizations will be the occasion of keeping up and aggravating these quarrels. Could we all be in one Organization, and meet in it with fraternal harmony, then anti-slavery organization would be as dear to my heart as it ever was, and then it would be greatly and gloriously effective, as it once was."[26]

The schism affected the American Anti-Slavery Society to a considerable extent, the annual income dropping immediately from $47,000 to $7,000 and not rising above $12,000 until 1856. The number of local societies and the total membership immediately decreased and was never fully recovered. As a result the Garrisonians banded themselves more tightly together and, in defiance of their opponents, reaffirmed their purpose to maintain their program without modification. Once again they announced their intention to conduct a moral war against slavery, and avowed their confidence in conscience, reason, and discussion as the surest means with which to pull down the strongholds of oppression. Once more they denounced the "sectarian organizations called churches" to be "combinations of thieves, robbers, adulterers, pirates and murderers."[27] They branded the Constitution a pro-slavery document, and proclaimed as their slogan: "A Repeal of the Union between Northern Liberty and Southern Slavery is essential to the abolition of the one and the preservation of the other." On October 1, 1844, Garrison summed up his creed in a letter to Henry C. Wright:

> "Politically, the American Anti-Slavery Society has 'passed the Rubicon,' in regard to this blood-cemented Union; and on its banner is inscribed the motto, 'No Union with Slaveholders.' No step has yet been taken in our cause, so trying to those who profess to be abolitionists, or that is destined

to make such a commotion in Church and State. It will alienate many from our ranks, but their defection will be our gain. 'The battle is the Lord's,' not man's, and victory will be achieved not by numerical superiority—not by physical might or power—but by the Spirit of Truth, and the omnipotence of Love."[28]

Whatever the Garrisonians were guilty of, however impractical Garrison may have been concerning political and social processes, he and his followers, Negro and white, must be credited with rousing America's conscience to the extent that Abolition, a relatively unimportant issue in 1830, became by the 'fifties the all-important question which had to be faced by every man and woman.

Anti-Slavery Agent

Douglass joined the ranks of the Abolitionists at a time when his services were sorely needed. The slaveowners had succeeded in formulating a defense of slavery which was extremely disconcerting to the Abolitionists. They emphasized its divine origin and sanction, and argued that slavery was especially beneficial to the Negro, that the condition of the slave in the South was far better than that of the northern and the English factory worker. They argued that the vast majority of the northern anti-slavery agitators had never seen slavery as it really existed and consequently did not know what they were talking about.[1]

In support of their "peculiar institution" the slaveholders and their sympathizers let loose a flood of propaganda. They painted a most beautiful picture of slavery as "it really existed." There was so little work for the slaves to do, went these lyrical outbursts, that there were "few who cannot perform them by midday or within an hour or two afterwards"; they were "always provided with clothing and all necessary, though plain food"; their clothing consisted of "winter and summer suits, the former, a jacket, waist coat, and overalls of Welsh plains and the latter, osnaburg homespun or other substitutes. They have shoes, hats, and handkerchiefs and other little articles, such as tobacco, pipes, rum, etc." Furthermore, the slaves even possessed "most of the civil freedom of the white man," and enjoyed a measure of security entirely foreign to the workers in northern factories who could be dismissed at a moment's notice and who, during periods of unemployment, were left to starve in their miserable hovels.[2] Maryland was held up as the symbol of justice to the slave. One pamphleteer argued:

"Maryland enjoys what I deem the proud eminence of being of all the states, the first in friendliness toward the African. This state may be adduced as an example of the mixture of the two races without amalgmation and with least oppression."[3]

A number of Abolitionists had already exposed the lies of the pro-slavery propagandists. By citing evidence from southern newspapers in his masterly tract, *Slavery As It Is, the Testimony of a Thousand Witnesses,* Theodore Weld had demonstrated that slaves were "overworked, under-fed, have insufficient sleep, live in miserable huts, generally without floors, and with a single apartment in which both sexes are herded promiscuously; that their clothing serves neither the purposes of comfort nor common decency; that barbarous cruelty is inflicted upon them. . . ."[4]

Still the Abolitionists needed something concrete and irrefutable to offer to the very persuasive arguments coming from the South. Obviously the need could best be filled by the Negro himself. Who else could refute so effectively the testimony of those who upheld slavery and argued that the slaves actually benefited from their bondage? Small wonder that after 1840 the number of Negroes employed as Abolitionist agents "grew in leaps and bounds." As John A. Collins pointed out in a letter to Garrison early in 1842:

". . . The public have itching ears to hear a colored man speak, and particularly *a slave*. Multitudes will flock to hear one of this class speak. . . . It would be a good policy to employ a number of colored agents, if suitable ones can be found."[5]

When Garrison and his associates heard Douglass in Nantucket they recognized that here was a man who embodied all the qualities their cause needed. Here was a man, a slave for twenty-one years, who could bring to the lecture platform first-hand knowledge of the institution. What a contrast to the rosy picture painted by the pro-slavery propagandists was the ugly story of slavery as Douglass had seen and experienced it! Masters were not kind; slaves were not cared for morally and spiritually; hours of labor were not reasonable; slaves were not happy and contented; slavery was not beneficial to the Negro. Moreover, the terrible experiences Douglass cited had occurred in a state in which slavery practices were said to be comparatively mild! His story revealed how rotten was the moral fiber from which slavery was spun. What hypocrisy to speak of the religious beliefs of the slaveholder when a master could "come through" with his religion and immediately afterward gather a mob from his own white congregation to disperse a Sunday school conducted by a slave! How could the slaveholder claim God's sanction to a system which permitted Covey, the "slavebreaker," to lock up a young woman with a hired male slave for breeding purposes! Douglass recounted the wild joy of the Negro-breaker and his wife when the young woman gave birth to twins. There was no legal marriage for the slave; slave-breeding was the chief source of wealth in some of the southern states; the "best blood" of the Virginia whites could be found in the slave-markets of New Orleans; mulattoes were, for the most part, sold as mistresses for planters. The entire account was told with an absence of personal animus, for Douglass aimed his darts at no man. His target was always the *slave system* which robbed master and slave alike of the dignity of human beings. He insistently pointed out that the abuses of slavery were necessary to the maintenance of the system.

When Douglass told his story to the public, he spoke with unquestionable authority, a late "graduate from the 'peculiar institution' with his diploma written on his back," as John A. Collins used to say in introducing him. That his words carried conviction is evidenced by the amazing response to his lectures from the outset of his work as an agent for the Massachusetts Anti-Slavery Society.

During his first three months as a lecturer, Douglass traveled usually with John A. Collins, but at county-wide meetings they would be joined by Garrison, Pillsbury, Foster, Abby Kelley, and other leaders of the movement. Yet the presence of these veterans did not detract from the attention received by the new recruit. At Abington, Douglass' appearance "gave a fresh impulse to anti-slavery." A crowded audience at Georgetown listened enraptured, and, at a convention of the Worcester North Division Society, during the first week in October, 1841, a resolution was adopted welcoming him and extending to him "the right hand of fellowship." On hearing him at a convention of the Plymouth Society on November 4, the editor of the *Hingham Patriot* was reminded of Spartacus, the Gladiator.

"He is very fluent in the use of language," he wrote, " choice and appropriate language, too; and talks as well, for all we could see, as men who have spent all their lives over books. He is forcible, keen and very sarcastic; and considering the poor advantages he must have had as a slave, he is certainly a remarkable man." A similar report was sent from Rhode Island the following month by N. P. Rogers, editor of the Concord *Herald of Freedom*. Describing a meeting in Franklin Hall, Providence, Rogers wrote:

"The fugitive Douglass was up when we entered. This is an extraordinary man. He was cut out for a hero. In a rising for Liberty he would have been a Toussaint or a Hamilton. He has the 'heart to conceive, the head to contrive, and the hand to execute.' A commanding person over six feet, we should say, in height, and of most manly proportions. His head would strike a phrenologist amid a sea of them in Exeter Hall, and his voice would ring like a trumpet in the field. Let the South congratulate herself that he is a fugitive. It would not have been safe for her if he had remained about the plantation a year or two longer. . . . As a speaker he has few equals. It is not declamation—but oratory, power of debate. He has wit, arguments, sarcasm, pathos—all that first rate men show in their master efforts. His voice is highly melodious and rich, and his enunciation quite elegant, and yet he has been but two or three years out of the house of bondage."[6]

Douglass had journeyed to Rhode Island together with Rogers, Garrison, Pillsbury, Collins, Foster, and Abby Kelley in an effort to defeat the adoption of a state constitution restricting the suffrage to white persons. At first the Abolitionists had participated actively in the struggle led by Thomas Wilson Dorr for a wider extension of the limited franchise. (By 1841 Rhode Island was the only northern state which had not adopted white manhood suffrage.) But when the "People's Party" denied the suffrage to free Negroes in the new constitution which they submitted to the vote of the people, the anti-slavery men felt betrayed, and the Rhode Island Anti-Slavery Executive Committee issued a circular calling on all Abolitionists "to make a combined and vigorous effort against the proposed constitution." The Abolitionists held a series of enthusiastic meetings at which nearly a thousand dollars was raised to fight the proposed constitution. Several of these gatherings, addressed by Douglass, Foster, and Miss Kelley, were broken up by mobs opposed to "n——r voting," but the Abolitionists persisted and continued to denounce the "white" clause. Douglass made such a deep impression at the annual convention of the Rhode Island State Anti-Slavery Society that he was appointed on a committee "to go before the Suffrage convention to meet in this city next week, and protest in the name of the Abolitionists of this State, against the insertion of the word 'white' in the new constitution."[7]

From the beginning of his career as a lecturer, Douglass moved beyond the narrow limits prescribed for him by the Garrisonians. He had been hired to tell the story of his slave experiences, and in his first public addresses he discussed nothing else. But within two months, he was discussing the "progress of the cause." At the Hingham Anti-Slavery Convention, early in November, he launched into a discussion of the superiority of moral suasion over political action in the battle against slavery, and called for the dissolution of the American Union. He denounced the pledge of the North to return fugitives as "the bulwark of slavery" since it discouraged slaves "from making any attempts to gain their freedom," and he concluded that "he is no true Abolitionist who does not go against this Union."

There was nothing original in these remarks. Douglass was simply saying what Garrison and his colleagues had said many times. Yet they reveal that he was already widening his range on the platform. As early as mid-December, 1841, in a speech before the Plymouth County Anti-Slavery Society, Douglass struck the central theme of his career as an Abolitionist—the twin battle against slavery in the South and prejudice in the North. He denounced slavery, but reminded his audience that in Massachusetts he had been dragged out of railroad cars after paying his full fare; that in New Bedford he could not find work as a caulker, and in the same city he had seen Negroes discriminated against even in church.

"You degrade us [he cried bitterly] and then ask why we are degraded—you shut our mouths, and then ask why we don't speak—you close your colleges and seminaries against us, and then ask why we don't know more."[8]

Here was no mere copy of other Abolitionist lecturers. Here was a spokesman for his people who experienced their degradation every day of his life, and who could express in vivid, burning language the pent-up indignation of the American Negro.

Douglass may have contributed little that was original in his early anti-slavery speeches, but he did give the movement a newness of life that could not have been obtained otherwise. The speeches of most of the Garrisonians were by now pretty well set into a pattern, and everyone knew more or less what they would say. Each speech contained a fervent appeal for the slave, a denunciation of the slave system and of the church and politicians supporting it, a condemnation of the Constitution as a pro-slavery document, and a cry for separation from the South. Douglass utilized this formula in his speeches, but he also brought variety and freshness. He could denounce slavery and the slaveholders as bitterly as the other Garrisonians could, and his invectives were no less piercing. But he also injected into his speeches a sense of humor. He could thrill his listeners with an account of his battle with Covey, at the same time getting them to burst into laughter as he described the expression on the Negro-breaker's face as he went down in the filth of the cowpen. He could bring shouts of glee from the audience as he portrayed his master,

Mr. Auld, first being converted, the tears rolling down his cheeks as he worshipped God, then the same Mr. Auld, on the same day, dispersing a group of slaves who were assembled to worship the same God.

His fine sense of humor and mimicry was a keen weapon, and he used it devastatingly. At Faneuil Hall, the Cradle of Liberty, he enlivened a meeting one evening with "a very funny imitation of the way in which slaveholding clergymen would exhort their servants to obey their masters." He delivered this remarkable piece of mimicry time and again to the delight of his audiences and to the embarrassment of the southern clergy. In a canting tone of voice he would begin:

"They the ministers would take a text—say this:—'Do unto others as you would have others do unto you.' And this is how they would apply it. They would explain it to mean, 'slaveholders, do unto *slaveholders* what you would have them do unto you:' and then looking impudently up the slave's gallery . . . looking high up to the poor colored drivers and the rest, and spreading his hands gracefully abroad, he says (mimicking), 'And you too, my friends, have souls of infinite value—souls that will *labor diligently* to make your calling and election sure. Oh, receive into your souls these words of the holy apostle—Servants, be obedient to your masters.' (Shouts of laughter and applause.)

" 'Oh! if you wish to be happy in time, happy in eternity, you must be obedient to your masters; their interest is yours. God made one portion of men to do the working, and another to do the thinking; how good God is! Now you have no trouble or anxiety; but ah! you can't imagine how perplexing it is to your masters and mistresses to have so much thinking to do in your behalf! You cannot appreciate your blessings; you know not how happy a thing it is for you, that you were born of that portion of the human family which has the working, instead of the thinking to do! Oh! how grateful and obedient you ought to be to your masters! How beautiful are the arrangements of Providence! Look at your hard, horny hands—see how nicely they are adapted to the labor you have to perform! Look at our delicate fingers, so exactly fitted for our station, and see how manifest it is that God deigned us to be his thinkers, and you the workers—oh! the wisdom of God.' "

This sermon was usually followed by a parody on the "Heavenly Union," a hymn sung weekly in the churches of the South. The hymn itself ran as follows:

> *Come, saints and sinners, hear me tell*
> *The wonders of Emanuel.*
> *Who saved me from a burning hell*

> *And taught my soul with Him to dwell*
> *And gave me heavenly union.*
>
> *When Jesus from His throne on high*
> *Beheld my soul in ruin lie.*
> *He looked on me with pitying eye*
> *And said to me as he passed by,*
> *"With God you have no union."*

To Douglass it seemed that the very use of this hymn in worship, while the church sanctioned slavery, constituted extreme irony. Hence, he composed a travesty on the hymn, parts of which went:

> *Come, saints and sinners, hear me tell*
> *How pious priests whip Jack and Nell,*
> *And women buy, and children sell,*
> *And preach all sinners down to hell,*
>   *And sing of heavenly union.*
>
> *They'll bleat and bray and do like goats*
> *Gorge down black sheep, and strain at motes,*
> *Array their backs in fine black coats,*
> *Then seize their n——rs by their throats*
>   *And choke for heavenly union.*
>
> *They'll raise tobacco, corn and rye,*
> *And drive and thieve and steal and lie,*
> *And lay up treasure in the sky,*
> *By making switch and cowskin fly*
>   *In hope of heavenly union.*[9]

As reports from people who had heard Douglass poured into the *Liberator* and the *Anti-Slavery Standard*, the Massachusetts Abolitionists realized that they had gained an invaluable asset to the cause. In his annual report to the Society, John A. Collins bestowed lavish praise upon the young orator who had traveled with him to "upwards of sixty towns and villages" on a tour covering 3,500 miles.

"His descriptions of slavery," he wrote, "are most graphic, and his arguments so lucid, and occasionally so spiced with pleasantry, and sometimes with a little satire, that his addresses, though long, are seldom tedious, but are listened to with the most profound respect. He is capable of performing a vast amount of good for his oppressed race."[10]

Douglass responded eagerly to the invitation to continue as a lecturing agent for the Massachusetts Society.[11] The winter and spring of 1842 found him again stumping through eastern and central Massachusetts in company with Garrison, Samuel J. May, Charles Lenox Remond, and the Hutchinsons, "the minessingers of American freedom," a musically self-trained family who sang anti-slavery songs. Everywhere his speeches aroused enthusiasm. By his talks, said the *Herald of Freedom*, Douglass had "already made color not only honorable, but enviable." On May 25, 1842, a newspaperman, not especially friendly to Abolition, heard Douglass speak at the Gordon Street Chapel in Boston and came away with "a sentiment of respect for his talent, his good sense, and his zeal in a cause. . . ."

"We have seldom heard a better speech before a popular assembly," he wrote in the *Boston Courier* of May 26, 1842, "better, we mean, as to the language and the manner. Many of the speakers who followed him, and of a lighter complexion, men, who boasted that they were ministers, and who had, doubtless the advantage of education, which the man of color could never have enjoyed, might well be desirous of emulating the appropriateness of his elocution and gesticulation, and the grammatical accuracy of his sentences."

Writing to Garrison from Northbridge, a veteran Abolitionist observed:

"It has been my fortune to hear a great many anti-slavery lecturers, and many distinguished speakers on other subjects; but it has rarely been my lot to listen to one whose power over me was greater than Douglass, and not over *me* only, but over all who heard him."[12]

But the life of a Negro anti-slavery agent was not all applause and praise. Douglass was forced to face the most humiliating discrimination in hotels, steamboats and railway cars. He resolved soon after he began his work as a lecturer to protest politely but firmly against segregation in public places and on common carriers. Consequently he was frequently handled roughly. Usually when a conductor asked him to leave and sit in the Jim-Crow car, he would ask: "If you will give me any good reason why I should leave this car, I'll go willingly; but without such reason, I do not feel at liberty to leave." The conductor invariably replied by calling in assistants and together they would drag the resisting Negro into the car set aside for the Negro people along with several seats he managed to hold onto. Invariably, too, Douglass was left bruised and with his clothes torn.

In many communities hoodlums attacked anti-slavery speakers and disrupted their meetings. Douglass was always the first to be singled out. In the middle of his speech he was often forced to leave the building followed by a mob howling, "get the n——r!" "kill the damn n——r!" Frequently, the meeting was held out-of-doors as it was impossible in many communities to find a hall or church that would permit a Negro to use its facilities. In Concord, New Hampshire, one Sunday afternoon, Douglass stood on a street-corner and collected an audience by appealing to the sympathies of the church-goers. In Grafton, Massachusetts, he wrote and distributed a leaflet announcing: "Frederick Douglass, a fugitive slave, will lecture on Grafton Common this evening at 8 o'clock. All who wish to hear the workings of Slavery from one of its own recipients are invited to attend." Because the leaflets were distributed late in the afternoon, Douglass feared that the citizens would think the meeting was planned for the following night. So he got a bell and made the rounds announcing his own meeting.

"The shoemaker left his bench," wrote a citizen of Grafton, "the mother her domestic avocations, to listen to the sound of the bell and the voice of the fugitive bondman, who announced himself as the speaker of the evening. At the hour appointed a multitude assembled, and Frederic[k] drove into their midst, and in his anti-slavery chaise he addressed an attentive audience for more than an hour."[18]

Douglass drew courage to brave all sorts of difficulties for the cause by the sympathy of a number of his white Abolitionist friends who would never allow him to suffer discrimination alone. Once on hearing that Douglass was compelled to ride in a filthy Jim-Crow box-car, Wendell Phillips stepped to his friend's side in the presence of a group of cultivated spectators and walked with him straight into the miserable car, saying: "Douglass, if you cannot ride with me, I can ride with you." Men like Phillips would go hungry rather than eat in a dining-room from which Douglass was excluded.

From the middle of August until the end of October, 1842, Douglass was employed by the American Anti-Slavery Society. He spent these months with Collins and Abby Kelley touring western New York. On August 30, he spoke for the first time in Rochester where he was to spend twenty years of his life. He was deeply impressed by the cordial and progressive community and the warm reception he received at the home of Isaac and Amy Post, two locally prominent Abolitionists. The pleasant memory of his first visit to Rochester greatly influenced Douglass in the choice of the city for the publication of his weekly paper, *The North Star*, in the fall of 1847.[14]

On his return from western New York Douglass was hurled into the struggle around the Latimer case. George Latimer, a fugitive slave, had fled to Boston from Norfolk, Virginia, in October, 1842. He was arrested without a warrant and thrown into a Boston jail solely on a warrant order to the jailer of Suffolk County from James B. Gray who claimed to be his owner. Friends rallied to the slave's side and demanded a trial by jury. When Chief Justice Shaw denied the demand and refused to grant a writ of habeas corpus, the movement to save Latimer gained tremendous momentum.

Boston was wild with excitement. Placards were distributed and handbills posted throughout the city denouncing the outrage, and summoning the citizens to a meeting in Faneuil Hall "For the Rescue of Liberty!" "Agitate! Agitate!" cried the *Liberator* of November 11, 1842. "Latimer *shall go free!* . . . Be vigilant, firm, uncompromising, friends of freedom! friends of God!" Whittier sent a clarion call from Massachusetts to Virginia:

> *No slave hunt in our borders,*
> *no pirate on our strand!*
> *No fetters in the Bay State,*
> *no slave upon our land!*

In the first public letter he ever wrote, dated Lynn, November 8, 1842, Douglass informed Garrison that in New Bedford Remond and he had spoken day and night during the first week of November in behalf of "our outraged brother" who had been "hunted down like a wild beast and ferociously dragged through the streets of Boston." All the meetings had been characterized "by that deep and solemn feeling which the importance of the cause, when properly set forth, is always calculated to awaken."[15]

In mid-November Latimer was purchased from Gray for four hundred dollars, and then set free. Around this event, the Abolitionists organized a series of celebrations with Latimer as the central figure. Douglass, a prominent speaker at the celebrations, was moved by Latimer's freedom to unusual brilliance.[16] The reporter for the *Salem Register* could not forget Douglass' address at the festivities in his city:

"The most wonderful performance of the evening was the address of Frederick Douglass himself a slave only four years ago! His remarks and his manner created the most indescribable sensations in the minds of those unaccustomed to hear *freemen* of color speak in public, much more to regard *a slave* as capable of such an effort. He was a living, speaking, *startling* proof of the folly, absurdity and inconsistency (to say nothing worse) of slavery. Fluent, graceful, eloquent, shrewd, sarcastic, he was without making any allowance, a fine specimen of an orator. He seemed to move the audience at his will, and they at times would hang upon his lips with staring eyes and open mouths, as eager to catch every word, as any 'sea of upturned faces' that ever rolled at the feet of Everett or Webster, to revel in their classic eloquence. Douglass possesses great powers of humor, which he indulged freely on Monday evening in giving some of the neatest and severest home thrusts at the 'peculiar institution' of which he professed to be a *graduate,* which it was ever our fortune to hear."[17]

In 1843, Douglass was occupied with the Hundred Conventions through which the Garrisonians hoped to build a strong movement in the western states. At the tenth annual meeting of the American Anti-Slavery Society, a proposal to hold a series of conventions in the West had been discussed, but the meeting adjourned before action could be taken. When the New England Society met in May, 1842, the matter received prominent attention, and, Douglass, a member of the Executive Committee, had urged the adoption of the proposal. The motion was promptly carried.[18]

Douglass, Remond, George Bradburn, John A. Collins, Jacob Ferris, William A. White of Watertown and Sidney B. Gay, editor of the *Anti-Slavery Standard,* were selected as speakers to tour the West. The agents, divided into two groups, were to move singly or in pairs to various towns in a county, and occasionally unite and exchange services. When a county had been thoroughly canvassed, the agents were to assemble for a gigantic meeting before going on to the next county. The tour was scheduled to last six months.

Douglass and Remond left in July and held their first meetings in Vermont where they met with unreceptive audiences. At Middlebury, students of the Congregationalist College placarded the town with posters describing Douglass as an escaped convict from the state prison. From Vermont they went to Syracuse where, owing to the opposition of the leaders of the Liberty Party, they were unable to secure a church or hall for their meeting. Undaunted, Douglass held his first meeting in a park and was gratified to see his audience grow from five persons to five hundred. During the following two days they addressed their audience in an abandoned church.[19]

But the question of a meeting place was the least of the difficulties Douglass faced in Syracuse. John A. Collins had become an enthusiastic disciple of Fourierism, the program of utopian socialism expounded in the United States by Albert Brisbane, Horace Greeley and George Ripley. In 1843, it was gaining numerous adherents. When Collins arrived in Syracuse, he set out to make converts for his new cause. At the anti-slavery meetings, he argued that the Abolitionist movement was "a mere dabbling with effects," that if slavery were abolished and private property allowed to exist, it would simply be abolition in form and not in fact, and that the universal reform movement would "do more for the Slave than the anti-slavery movement."

Douglass and Remond objected to Collins' tactics of organizing an anti-slavery meeting. After discoursing at length on the limitations of Abolition, Collins would invite the audience to attend a utopian socialist meeting to be held immediately after in the same hall. They criticized the preaching of Fourierism to an audience which had come to hear about the evils of slavery, and accused Collins of using the anti-slavery platform to convert the participants to utopian socialism. Douglass made it clear that Collins had a perfect right to advocate the abolition of all property rights and the establishment of a new social system; he even had the right to advocate anti-slavery and universal reform at the same time. But he decidely had no right to serve as an agent of the Anti-Slavery Society and attack Abolitionism as useless. Douglass felt strongly about this, confiding to Maria Weston Chapman of the Massachusetts Society that if the Board of Managers sanctioned Collins' conduct he would be compelled "to write them resigning my agency in carrying out the one hundred conventions plan." But Collins resigned as general agent of the Massachusetts Society, and Douglass continued his tour.[20]

It is important again to emphasize that while Douglass was not a utopian socialist, he sympathized with Collins' desire to establish a more "equalitarian society" in which all exploitation of man by man would be abolished. But like those who correctly criticized Socialists for claiming that the struggle for Negro rights was unimportant since with the abolition of capitalism all oppression would end, Douglass condemned Collins for considering the anti-slavery movement as unimportant. It is significant that Collins resigned as an anti-slavery agent because he was convinced that nothing could be accomplished through the Abolitionist movement.

From Syracuse Douglass went to Rochester and then to Buffalo where he attended the sessions of the National Convention of Colored Men. Then, with William A. White, they pushed on to Indiana, well aware that among the inhabitants were many former southerners who had not left behind their hatred of Abolitionism. Their fears were justified. Douglass had experienced rough handling many times since his first tour as an anti-slavery agent, but these were mild compared to what he met with in Pendleton, Indiana.

Douglass and White sensed trouble as soon as they entered Pendleton on September 15. Some of the townspeople were enraged because Dr. Fussell, a prominent local physician, had invited the ex-slave to be his house guest. Only because the meeting was cancelled by rain was violence avoided the first night. The following day the meeting in the woods had barely started when a mob of rowdies, armed with pistols, clubs, stones, and eggs, broke into the gathering and began howling, screeching, and hurling brickbats. Douglass was about to get away when he was told that White had been attacked and knocked down. He quickly decided that more than "moral suasion" was needed to handle this situation. As White wrote in a report to the *Liberator:*

"Frederick Douglass who, at the time, was safe among the friends, not seeing me, thought I was knocked down, and seizing a club, rushed into the crowd. His weapon was immediately snatched from him. . . . [He] fled for his life, and ten or more of the mob followed, crying, 'kill the n——r, kill the damn n——r.' . . . The leader of the mob soon overtook him, and knocked him down and struck him once with his club, and was raising it the second time to level a blow which must have been fatal had it fallen, but I, by dint of hard running, came up in time to throw myself upon him, and stop him in his murderous purpose. . . ."

Douglass, nursed by Mrs. Fussell, was able to speak at a meeting the next day. But he never forgot the experience. Three years later he wrote to White that it still "haunted his dreams." He had gone "to bed thinking about Pendleton."[21]

After Pendleton, the rest of the trip eastward was almost routine. Everywhere they went the people wanted to hear Douglass. "All along in this State," George Bradburn wrote from Ohio, "as elsewhere, our friends complain of being made to lie to the people, in announcing Douglass for our meetings." The agents concluded their tour at Philadelphia where they joined in the celebration of the tenth anniversary of the formation of the American Anti-Slavery Society.

The Board of Managers of the Massachusetts Anti-Slavery Society hailed the Hundred Conventions as a "magnificent movement." "We doubt," they declared, "whether there has ever been in the history of the cause, so great an amount of wholesale agitation produced at so small an expense or accomplished in so short a time." Although less than $450 had been collected by the agents during their tour, the society at its annual convention in January, 1844, voted to sponsor a series of one hundred conventions within the Bay State. Douglass, White, and Pillsbury were chosen to cover the territory and in the winter months of 1844 they traveled through the central counties of Massachusetts.[22]

Once again the agents met with a favorable response. At Concord, New Hampshire, "the house was crowded with the best of our people—no clergy—and but few of the bigots who are past hearing." Douglass, wrote the reporter for the *Herald of Freedom,* "made a masterly and most impressive speech":

"It was not what you could describe as oratory or eloquence. It was sterner, darker, deeper than these. It was the volcanic outbreak of human nature, long pent up in slavery and at last bursting its imprisonment. It was the storm of insurrection; and I could not but think, as he stalked to and fro on the platform, roused up like the Numidian lion, how that terrible voice of his would ring through the pine glades of the South, in the day of her visitation, calling the insurgents to battle, and striking terror to the hearts of the dismayed and despairing mastery. He reminded me of Toussaint among the plantations of Haiti. There was a great oratory in his speech, but more of dignity and earnestness than what we call eloquence. He was not up as a speaker, performing. He was an insurgent slave, taking hold on the right of speech, and charging on his tyrants the bondage of his race. One of our editors ventured to cross his path by a rash remark. He better have run upon a lion. It was fearful, but magnificent, to see how magnanimously and lion-like the royal fellow tore him to pieces, and left his untouched fragments scattered around him.

" . . . He is a surprising lecturer. I would not praise him, or describe him; but he is a colored man, a slave, of the race who can't take care of themselves—our inferiors, and therefore to be kept in slavery—an abolitionist, and therefore to be despised. . . . He is one of the most impressive and majestic speakers I have ever heard. The close of his address Sunday was unrivalled. I have heard the leading anti-slavery speakers, as well as the pro-slavery orators, and the great advocates at the bar; and I have never seen a man leave the platform, or close a speech, with more real dignity, and eloquent majesty. . . ."[23]

Pleased though they were with Douglass' effectiveness on the platform, his associates were becoming convinced that his development had been too rapid. As early as 1841 Stephen S. Foster had warned Douglass, "People won't believe that you were ever a slave, Frederick, if you keep on in this way." Collins had added, "Better have a little of the plantation speech than not; it is not best that you seem too learned." But Douglass refused to be stereotyped and stunted, and despite repeated exhortations to "give us the facts, we will take care of the philosophy," he refused to confine himself to repeating the story of his life over and over again.

"I could not always follow the injunction," he wrote later, "for I was now reading and thinking. New views of the subject were being presented to my mind. It did not entirely satisfy me to narrate wrongs; I felt like denouncing them.... Besides I was growing and needed room."[24]

The conflict on this issue was inevitable. Many middle and upper-class white Abolitionists could not see the former Negro slave as anything but an exhibit. The white anti-slavery leaders would be the main actors; the Negroes would be the extras or only part of the stage props. Some white Abolitionists were sorry to see Douglass' rapid development as a brilliant thinker and orator. Instead of being proud that this former Negro slave had been able in such a short time to equal and even surpass many of the white spokesmen against slavery, they were worried by it and even resented it.

Yet Douglass was soon to discover that the fears of his advisers were not entirely groundless. He began to hear and read statements expressing doubt as to his ever having seen slavery.

"Many persons in the audience," wrote a Philadelphia correspondent in the *Liberator* of August 30, 1844, "seemed unable to credit the statements which he gave of himself, and could not believe that he was actually a slave. How a man, only six years out of bondage, and who had never gone to school a day in his life, could speak with such eloquence—with such precision of language and power of thought—they were utterly at a loss to devise."

Douglass was aware that if such reports continued, they would be fatal to his effectiveness as an Abolitionist agent. So he resolved to throw caution to the winds and write the story of his life. During the winter months of 1844-1845 he was busily engaged in setting down an account of his slave experiences. His *Narrative of the Life of Frederick Douglass,* a small volume of 125 pages selling for fifty cents, with introductions by Garrison and Phillips, came off the press in May, 1845. The book immediately became a fast seller, was translated into French and German, and, by January, 1848, when eleven thousand copies had been published in this country, it had gone through nine editions in England. One of a long series of autobiographies of fugitive slaves, it was by far the most effective. "Considered merely as a narrative," went a review in the *New York Tribune,* "we never read one more simple, true, coherent and warm with genuine feeling. It is an excellent piece of writing, and on that score to be prized as a specimen of the powers of the black race, which prejudice persists in disputing." The reviewer for the *Lynn Pioneer* considered that "the book, as a whole, judged as a mere work of art, would widen the fame of Bunyan or Defoe. It is the most thrilling work which the American press ever issued—*and the most important.* If it does not open the eyes of this people, they must be petrified into eternal sleep."[25]

" . . . I have many times heard the author vividly portray the evils of slavery [a woman reader wrote to Garrison]. I have often heard him recount with deep feeling the endless wrongs they are made to endure—but, oh! never before have I been brought so completely in sympathy with the slave—never before have I so fully realized the doctrine of our blessed Savior, 'Whatsoever ye do unto the least one of these, ye do it unto me.' . . . May his narrative incite us to renewed diligence in our labors for the slave! May the author become a mighty instrument to the pulling down of the strongholds of iniquity, and to the establishing of righteousness in our land!"

The *Narrative* was immediately popular in England and Ireland; newspaper notices lauded "its native eloquence." It furnished evidence that "the argument, if it can be so termed, which would uphold slavery on the ground of the slaves' natural inferiority, has no foundation as regards such a man as the writer, and therefore totally fails in its general application." One editor spoke of Douglass as "a fugitive slave, who, as but yesterday, escaped from a bondage that doomed him to ignorance and degradation, now stands up and rebukes oppression with a dignity and a fervor scarcely less glowing than that which Paul addressed to Agrippa."[26]

At the meeting of the New England Society in Boston on May 27, 1845, a resolution was adopted which "joyfully" welcomed "to our ranks the new anti-slavery lecturer, the *Narrative of the Life of Frederick Douglass,*" and commended it to all "who believe the slaves of the South to be either well treated, or happy, or ignorant of their right to freedom, or in need of preparation to make them fit for freedom." Ironically enough, when Wendell Phillips, who proposed the resolution, had first read Douglass' manuscript, he had advised the author to burn it before it went to press, fearing that since the book unmistakably divulged his identity and that of his master, he would no longer be safe in the United States. Douglass refused to heed his friend's advice, but he recognized the basis for his fears. This knowledge that his life and liberty were now in jeopardy hastened his determination to go abroad, a desire that had been growing in his mind for several months.[27] Another and probably a stronger reason for his decision to visit Europe was expressed by James N. Buffum, one of Douglass' closest friends, in a letter to Gerrit Smith on June 21, 1845:

"I write to inform you that our friend and co-labourer Frederick Douglass has concluded to visit Europe this season, to lay before the people of that country the claim of the Slave. He has come to this conclusion after a time of deliberation and consultation, with many of our wisest and best friends. He will go out as a representative from the prison-house of bondage and not as the representative of any sect or party. He will stand up before that people as one who has experienced the withering and blighting influence of Slavery upon his own Soul. His friends are confident that he will be of great service to the cause, in exciting a deeper hatred in the breasts of the English people of American Slavery, and thereby creating a warmer sympathy for our cause. When they shall see before them a man so noble and eloquent as Frederick, and learn from his own lips, that he is only seven years out of bondage; that he has now the marks of the whip upon his back, which he will carry with him until the day of his death, that he has near and dear relatives that are now pining in bondage; they will realize to a considerable extent, the horrors of the American Slave trade; the effect cannot be otherwise than good.

"In years past, the friends of the slave in this country have been cheered and encouraged by the contributions and words of sympathy which have come to them from across the waters, from the philanthropists of Europe. To express to them our deep appreciation of their benevolent labours, to encourage them to continue their friendly assistance, will be among the objects of Frederick's mission."[28]

Douglass' reluctance to leave his family which now included two more baby boys, Frederick, Junior, and Charles Remond,[29] was assuaged by the knowledge that the proceeds from the sale of the *Narrative* would go to his wife, thus substituting for his earnings on the lecture platform.[30] With a purse of $250 raised by Abolitionist friends and $350 saved from the sale of his autobiography, with letters from Phillips and Maria W. Chapman to sympathizers in England,[31] Douglass prepared to sail for Liverpool.

When Douglass left the United States he was already being hailed as the rising star among the Negro people. Wendell Phillips spoke for all the Garrisonians when he wrote to Elizabeth Pease of London: "If you ever see him, Remember that *in my opinion,* you see the most remarkable and by far the ablest colored man we have ever had here."[32] Douglass was even known to many Negroes in the South. An editor of the Philadelphia *Elevator,* a Negro paper, disclosed that when he went to Maryland, he had been visited "by at least a dozen colored persons, some of them slaves, and others freemen, who had heard that we knew Frederick at the North, and who wished to hear news of their old friend. They knew him by his assumed name as well as by his real name and related to us many interesting incidents about their former companion."[33]

"Be yourself," Phillips told Douglass as he was departing for England. "Be yourself, and you will succeed." Not even Phillips, however, dreamed that the success would reach such heights. His European visit gave Douglass an international reputation. He returned to the States a world figure, a mighty power for freedom.

A Chattel Becomes a Man

On August 16, 1845, accompanied by the Hutchinsons and James N. Buffum, Douglass sailed for Liverpool on the Cunard steamer *Cambria.* Buffum's efforts to get first-class passage for Douglass had failed for what was politely referred to as "complexional reasons," and Douglass was forced to travel steerage. Every morning during the eleven-day trip, however, he joined his colleagues on the promenade deck, mingled with the passengers, and sold copies of the *Narrative*. The captain of the steamer was disposed to be friendly to his Negro passenger and ignored the protests of southerners on board. But the night before the *Cambria* docked at Liverpool, the explosion came. Douglass, at the invitation of the captain, was lecturing on American slavery. He was constantly interrupted by catcalls, and as soon as he finished a sentence several slaveholders would yell out, "That's a lie!" When he offered to present documentary proof, they rushed at him with clenched fists. The captain knocked down one man and quieted the others by threatening to put them in irons.[1]

The cordial reception in Liverpool made it easier for Douglass to push out of his mind the bad experience on board ship. Three days after landing, Douglass and Buffum, parting company with the Hutchinsons, left for Dublin. Douglass stayed at the home of Richard D. Webb, the local agent of the *Anti-Slavery Standard,* and arranged with his host for the printing of two thousand copies of the *Narrative* for which he would not have to pay until the whole edition was sold.[2]

In Dublin, Douglass was amazed by the response to his anti-slavery work. "Our success here," he wrote to Garrison on September 16, "is even greater than I had anticipated. We have held four glorious anti-slavery meetings—two in Royal Exchange, and two in the Friends' meeting-house —all crowded to overflowing."

From the beginning of his stay in Europe, Douglass became involved in many reform movements. First he resisted this tendency, believing that he should reserve all of his efforts for the anti-slavery cause. But he soon became convinced that it was impossible to divide the struggle against oppression into separate compartments. On February 26, 1846 he explained his decision to Garrison:

" . . . though I am more closely connected and identified with one class of outraged, oppressed and enslaved people, I cannot allow myself to be insensible to the wrongs and sufferings of any part of the great family of man. I am not only an American slave, but a man, and as such, am bound to use my powers for the welfare of the whole human brotherhood."[3]

Douglass endorsed the temperance crusade sponsored by Father Theobald Mathew and spoke out for the repeal of the Act of Union which almost a half-century before had abolished the Irish Parliament. The very day of his arrival in Dublin, he spoke at a temperance gathering, and later delivered several temperance addresses in the city. In late September he spoke at a huge repeal meeting at Convention Hall where he shared honors with Daniel O'Connell, the Irish liberator. Douglass sat enthralled by O'Connell's oratory and his courageous message. O'Connell announced that he was not ashamed of being assailed for attacking American slavery and proclaimed that wherever slavery existed he was "the enemy of the system or the institution."[4]

After five happy weeks in Dublin, Douglass left for Cork. Here he was no less successful. He spoke at eleven public meetings, addressing overflow audiences on each occasion, the "suffering poor," as the *Cork Examiner* put it, "thronging to listen to exposures of the American slave system by one who has in his own person suffered under its iniquities." As in Dublin, he spoke on temperance as well as anti-slavery. He even took the temperance pledge from Father Mathew, observing that he was "the fifth of the last five of Father Mathew's 5,487,495 temperance children."[5]

Leaving Cork with the hearty good wishes of a large circle of friends, Douglass went to Belfast, then to Liverpool and Birmingham. In Birmingham he spoke to an audience of seven thousand at the annual meeting of the Birmingham Temperance Society. He then returned to Belfast on December 19 for another lecture. "I had expected a good deal from Mr. Douglass," wrote a correspondent of the *London Inquirer* from Belfast, "from what I had seen of him in public prints; but high as were my expectations, they were more than realized. He is, in truth, a wonderful man.... Who could listen to his heart-rending description of the horrors of slavery, and not heartily hate the institution." At a public breakfast in his honor, presided over by a member of Parliament, Douglass was presented with a fine edition of the Bible by the Belfast Auxiliary of the British and Foreign Anti-Slavery Society.

The four months Douglass spent in Ireland were the happiest he had ever known in his life. The complete lack of anti-Negro prejudice, the open door everywhere made him cry out for joy.

"The warm and generous cooperation extended to me by the friends of my despised race," he wrote to Garrison from Belfast on January 1, 1846, "the prompt and liberal manner with which the press has rendered me its aid—the glorious enthusiasm with which thousands have flocked to hear the cruel wrongs of my down-trodden and long enslaved countrymen portrayed—the deep sympathy of the slave, and the strong abhorrence of the slaveholder, everywhere evinced—the cordiality with which members and ministers of various religious bodies, and of various shades of religious opinion, have embraced me and lent me their aid—the kind hospitality constantly proffered to me by persons of the highest rank in society—the spirit of freedom that seems to animate all with whom I come in contact—and the entire absence of everything that looked like prejudice against me, on account of the color of my skin—contrasting so strongly with my long and bitter experience in the United States, that I look with wonder and amazement on the transition."[6]

After more than fifty lectures in Ireland, Douglass went to Scotland which he found "in a blaze of anti-slavery agitation." Here he and Buffum, who had rejoined him, became involved in the exciting battle to compel the Free Church of Scotland to return contributions made by American slaveholders. The Free Church (an organization based on the right of congregations to control the appointment of their own ministers) had sent a deputation to the United States in 1844 to form an alliance with churches in this country and to solicit funds to build Free Churches and pay Free ministers in Scotland. An outburst of indignation arose from American Abolitionists when the delegation announced its intention of visiting the southern states, but, ignoring these protests, the delegates raised £3,000 from slaveholders, entering into an alliance with southern churches. They justified their action by denouncing the Abolitionists as belonging to the tradition of "the infidels and anarchists of the French Revolution," asserting that the slaveholders were "entitled to be regarded as respectable, useful, honoured Christians, living under the power of the truth, labouring faithfully, and serving God in the Gospel of His Son." Most members of the Free Church in Scotland were not impressed either by the diatribe against the American Abolitionists or by the eulogy of the slaveholders, and a loud cry arose that the money collected in the South was tainted and should be returned. Douglass added his voice to this demand, speaking in halls decorated with posters proclaiming the slogan of the day—*"Send Back the Money."* "We shall continue to deal our blows upon them—crying out disgorge—disgorge—disgorge your horrid plunder," he wrote to Francis Jackson from Dundee, "and to this the great mass of the people here have cried Amen, Amen."[7]

Douglass toured Scotland during the spring of 1846. The most memorable part of the trip was his visit to Ayr, the birthplace of Robert Burns. An "enthusiastic admirer" of the Scottish poet, Douglass was happy to see the cottage where Burns was born and where so many of his favorite poems had been written. He cherished for a long time his meeting with Burns's sister, Mrs. Geggs. "I have ever esteemed Robert Burns," he wrote after the visit, ". . . but never could I have had the opinion of the man or his genius, which I now entertain, without my present knowledge of the country, to which he belonged—the times in which he lived, and the broad Scotch tongue in which he wrote."[8]

Douglass' happiness in Scotland was marred by an incident which was to have an important bearing on his relations with his Abolitionist friends at home. Maria Weston Chapman, leader of the Boston Female Anti-Slavery Society and editor of its gift-book, the *Liberty Bell,* had written to Richard D. Webb warning the Irish Abolitionist to keep an eye on Douglass and Buffum lest they be won over by the anti-Garrisonian wing of the English anti-slavery movement. Mrs. Chapman, it seemed, was not too concerned about Buffum who was wealthy, but was worried lest Douglass "might be bought up by the London committee." Douglass, when shown the letter, was furious at the lack of faith in his integrity and sent a sharp rebuke to Mrs. Chapman assuring her that he was still a Garrisonian, but pointing out in clear and decisive language that he would not tolerate any efforts to supervise and control his activities. "If you wish to drive me from the Anti-Slavery Society," he wrote, "put me under overseership and the work is done. Set some one to watch over me for evil and let them be so simple minded as to inform me of their office, and the last blow is struck."[9]

That Douglass was capable of thinking for himself on major issues confronting the anti-slavery movement and was prepared to challenge the Abolitionist leaders when he believed they were wrong is illustrated by two incidents which occurred about this time. When Richard D. Webb objected to the inclusion of letters of endorsement from clergymen in the English edition of the *Narrative*, the Negro shot back:

"You ought to have thought of your prejudice against priests sooner. If clergymen read my *Narrative* and approve of it, my prejudice against their office would be but a poor reason, for rejecting the benefit of such approval. The enclosed is from Mr. Nelson the Presbyterian Minister. I wish both it and that of Dr. Drew to be inserted in the second edition. To leave them out because they are ministers would be to show oneself as much and more sectarian than themselves. It would be virtually forbidding their casting out devils because they follow not us. The spirit of bigotry and sectarianism may exist, and be as deeply rooted in those who condemn sects, as those who adhere to them."[10]

While in Edinburgh, Douglass was invited by George Thompson, a leading English Abolitionist, to speak at a mammoth public meeting to be arranged in London under the auspices of the British and Foreign Anti-Slavery Society, which six years before had broken away from the Garrisonians. Well aware that his friends in America would look with disfavor upon his presence at the meeting, Douglass believed that it was his duty to "speak in any meeting where freedom of speech is allowed and where I may do any thing toward exposing the bloody system of slavery." Hence, he accepted the invitation, making it clear that his presence did not signify an endorsement of the doctrines of the organization.[11]

On his arrival in London, Douglass learned that a crowded schedule had been planned for him. "Frederick has crammed a year's sensations into the last five days," wrote George Thompson on May 23. "On Monday he poured forth at the Anti-Slavery Meeting. On Tuesday at the Peace Meeting. On Wednesday at the Complete Suffrage Meeting. On Thursday at the Temperance Meeting, and last night he had an audience of 2,500 to hear him for nearly three hours. . . ."[12] At the final meeting held at Finsbury Chapel in his honor, "with the edifice crowded to suffocation," Douglass delivered a devastating attack on American slavery. Out of his own personal experience, he presented one picture after another showing the horrors of the slave system. To the charge that American affairs should not be discussed in other countries, he replied that slavery in America was not America's problem alone, but the problem of mankind; that slavery was so monstrous a sin that no single nation by itself could achieve its removal. Since America lacked the moral stamina to remove this blight on her free institutions, he called on the people of Britain to assist in the struggle. He concluded on the following note:

> "To tear off the mask from this abominable system, to expose it to the light of heaven, aye, to the heat of the sun, that it may burn and wither it out of existence, is my object in coming to this country. I want the slaveholder surrounded, as by a wall of anti-slavery fire, so that he may see the condemnation of himself and his system glaring down in letters of light. . . . I would have condemnation blaze down upon him in every direction, till, stunned and overwhelmed with shame and confusion, he is compelled to let go the grasp he holds upon the persons of his victims, and restore them to their long-lost rights."[13]

At the conclusion of the address, Thompson arose and referred to a conversation in which Douglass spoke of how he missed his wife and children. Thompson proposed a subscription to bring Douglass' family to England. Fifty pounds were contributed while he was talking and thirty more at the end of his appeal. Thompson was certain that "an ample sum" would be raised "to bring them over and make them comfortable while they are among us."[14]

In the summer of 1846 Douglass was happy to have William Lloyd Garrison with him in England. The Abolitionist leader had been invited by the Glasgow Emancipation Society in the belief that his influence would be decisive in the campaign to compel the Free Church to return the gift to the southern clergy. On July 31 Garrison arrived at Liverpool and a few days later he and Douglass began a journey from one part of England to the other—reorganizing the enemies of slavery in Britain and denouncing the slaveholders and their apologists in America. On August 4, they attended the opening session of the World Temperance Convention held at Covent Garden Theater in London. Neither was an official delegate, but they were "politely furnished . . . with a ticket" admitting them as members of the convention.

Before the convention adjourned, Douglass had stirred up a hornet's nest with a speech attacking the official American temperance movement. He was sorry that he could not join the American delegates in lauding the progress of the cause in their country while there were three million American slaves beyond the pale of the American Temperance Society and four hundred thousand free Negroes almost as completely excluded as the slaves. He reminded the audience that on August 1, 1842, members of a temperance society in Philadelphia, composed solely of Negroes, had been assaulted by a ruthless mob, beaten and dispersed when they attempted to augment their ranks by parading through the streets. One of their churches was burned and their temperance hall destroyed. Worried by the heated emotions these remarks were arousing, the chairman whispered to Douglass that his speaking time had expired. With shouts from the audience urging him "go on! go on!" Douglass continued for a few minutes, but refrained from further reference to anything "that particularly related to the colored people of America."

The American delegates were furious. Reverend Kirk, a Boston clergyman, charged that Douglass had given a false picture of the temperance societies in the United States. Reverend Samuel Hanson Cox of Brooklyn, New York delivered a broadside against Douglass in a long, angry letter to the *New York Evangelist*. He branded him as a "colored Abolition agitator, and ultraist," charging him with "ruining almost everything [at the convention] that had preceded him." He accused him of lugging into a temperance convention an anti-slavery discussion and said he had "been well paid for the abomination." To top it all, he claimed that Douglass was trying to arouse a war spirit in England and America.

Douglass' reply to Reverend Cox was extremely effective and resulted in making friends for himself and the Abolition cause in England and in his own country. He emphasized that the motive for the attack was to ruin his influence in Britain. He pleaded guilty to the charge of being an Abolitionist, an ultraist, and expressed pride in his connection with the struggle to overthrow slavery. Furthermore, he denied the impropriety of discussing slavery in the temperance meeting and the statement that his speech had ruined all that had preceded him. He denied receiving pay for the speech he had made, but declared he had as much right to receive pay for speaking as Reverend Cox for preaching. In one of his brilliant sallies of sarcasm aimed at Dr. Cox, he said:

"And is slavery only an 'imputed evil'? Now, suppose I had lugged in anti-slavery (which I deny)—you profess to be an Abolitionist. You, therefore, ought to have been the last man in the world to have found fault with me, on that account. Your great love of liberty, and sympathy for the downtrodden slave ought to have led you to 'pardon something for the spirit of Liberty,' especially in one who had the scars of the slave-driver's whip on his back, and who, at this moment, has four sisters and one brother in slavery. But, Sir, you are not an Abolitionist, and you only assumed to be one during your recent tour in this country, that you might *sham* your way through this land, and the more effectually stab and blast the character of the real friends of emancipation. Who ever heard of a true Abolitionist speaking of slavery as an 'imputed evil,' or complaining of being 'wounded or injured' by an allusion to it—and that, too, because that allusion was in opposition to the infernal system? You took no offence when the Rev. Mr. Kirk assumed the Christian name and character for slaveholders in the World's Temperance Convention. You were not 'wounded or injured,'—it was not a 'perversion, an abuse, an iniquity against the law of reciprocal righteousness.' You have no indignation to pour out upon him. Oh, no! But when a *fugitive slave* merely alluded to slavery as obstructing the moral and social improvement of my race, you were 'wounded and injured,' and rendered indignant! This, sir, tells the whole story of your abolitionism, and stamps your pretensions to abolition as brazen hypocrisy or self-deception."[15]

Douglass' conflict with Reverend Cox revealed to a wide public on both sides of the Atlantic that in the North as well as the South there was an indifferent, if not pro-slavery, element among the clergy who did not want the evils of slavery exposed to the intelligence of the world. It also showed how deeply the pro-slavery forces feared the influence of the brilliant fugitive slave and how eagerly they sought to silence him.

Pro-slavery journals in the United States went to ridiculous lengths in their demands that the British refuse Douglass a platform, even arguing that the Negro orator was embarrassing the three million Negro people held in slavery. "The slaves," said one journal, "would be very indignant at the conduct of their representative in England could they be made acquainted with his tantrums." There was scarcely a Negro "on a South Carolina rice plantation, or in a Louisiana sugar house, but what, amid all his degradation, would scorn the acts of Frederick Douglass. The man is lowering, in the eyes of English courtesy and intelligence, the character of our slave population."[16]

To the charge that he was a menace to his native land because he was "running amuck in greedy-eared Britain against America, its people, its institutions, and even against its peace," Douglass had a ready answer. At one time, he declared, America and the American people were regarded in Europe as "the best friends and truest representatives" of the sacred cause of freedom. But the growth of slavery had created the very opposite attitude toward the United States. A person truly devoted to the interests of America and its people would seek to restore the United States to its former position as the symbol of freedom. "I am earnestly and anxiously laboring to wipe off this foul blot from the otherwise fair fame of the

American people," he wrote to Horace Greeley from Glasgow on April 15, 1846, "that they may accomplish in behalf of human freedom that which their exalted position among the nations of the earth amply fits them to do."[17]

Within a week after the Temperance Convention, Garrison formed an "Anti-Slavery League for all England," its main function being to cooperate with the American Anti-Slavery Society. At the League's first public meeting, held on August 17 at the Crown and Anchor Tavern, Henry C. Wright opened with a speech that was a "scorcher." Douglass followed, "making one of his very best efforts." "I never saw an audience more delighted," Garrison wrote to his wife. The five and a half hour meeting closed with a speech by Henry Vincent, a Chartist leader. Garrison felt encouraged by the proceedings which he described as "a real, old-fashioned, old-organized American anti-slavery meeting (such, as I am quite certain, as was never before held in *England*)."[18]

Late in August, the American Abolitionists held a meeting at Bristol. Although there was an admission charge, they spoke to an overflowing audience. The presence of the mayor of the city gave the proceedings a stiff, formal tone which took the "warmth" out of Garrison and caused Douglass to "labor under embarassment." Still the Negro made "one of his very best speeches which produced a powerful effect." From Bristol Douglass and his mentor went to Exeter and then back to London where they spent a Sunday afternoon "rolling balls on the greensward" with a Unitarian minister.[19]

Towards the end of September the visiting reformers became involved in another battle. The preceding year, a group, composed mainly of Methodists and Free Church adherents, had formed an International Evangelical Alliance. In August, 1846, at its first big meeting, the Alliance began consideration of the question of excluding slaveholders from membership. But a committee, headed by Reverend Cox, introduced a report which skillfully avoided the main question, and the Conference accepted this report with a sigh of relief.

Thus, no action was taken on slaveholder membership. But the London Abolitionists were not so easily satisfied, and, viewing the Alliance's action as an approval of slavery, called a public demonstration of protest for September 14. Garrison and Douglass were invited to share the platform with George Thompson. Hisses from Alliance sympathizers in the audience greeted Garrison when he opened the meeting, with the only effect that his speech was "less consecutive than it otherwise would have been." He was followed by Thompson who proposed a series of resolutions condemning the Alliance. Douglass brought the meeting to a close with an address which was "warmly applauded."

Following the anti-Alliance demonstration, Douglass left for northern England and Scotland. On September 25 he spoke at Sunderland in Durham County with Mayor Robert Brown in the chair. The reporter for the Durham County *Herald* was lavish with his praise. "We have rarely listened to an orator so gifted by nature," he wrote, "and never to a man who more thoroughly threw his whole heart into the work in which he is engaged." The orator journeyed to Glasgow, Paisley, Edinburgh, and Dundee as an agent of the Scottish Anti-Slavery Society, and returned to Liverpool on October 10 to meet Garrison. There by a pleasant coincidence while having breakfast one morning he happened to see a former slave associate of his in Baltimore. It was a happy reunion, and for several hours the two friends sat discussing their former life in the South and comparing notes on their experiences since their escape from bondage.[20]

Early in November Garrison sailed for America. Douglass' thoughts, too, had been turning homeward. Although England offered a permanent home for himself and his family, free from all the hardships incident to life for a Negro in America, Douglass refused to stay. There was too much to be done at home; he was anxious to get into the struggle being led by the Abolitionists against the Mexican War and to do what he could to defeat the forces who were "calling upon the free citizens .... to leave their homes families and friends to go and fight the plundering battles of Slave holding Texas." In one of his most eloquent utterances he told a London audience:

"Since I have been in this land I have had every inducement to stop here. ... I should have settled down here in a different position to what I should have been placed in the United States. But, sir, I prefer living a life of activity in the service of my brethren. I choose rather to go home; to return to America. I glory in the conflict, that I may hereafter exult in the victory. I know that victory is certain. I go, turning my back upon the ease, comfort, and respectability which I might maintain even here, ignorant as I am. Still, I will go back, for the sake of my brethren. I go to suffer with them; to toil with them; to endure insult with them; to undergo outrage with them; to lift up my voice in their behalf; to speak and write in their vindication; and struggle in their ranks for that emancipation which shall yet be achieved by the power of truth and of principle for that oppressed people."[21]

Douglass was fully aware that his former master was biding his time and awaiting his return to begin proceedings to have him restored to slavery. In July he had written to his old friend White for advice: "William do you think it would be safe for me to come home this fall? Would master Hugh stand much chance in Mass.? Think he could take me from the old Bay State? The old fellow is evidently anxious to get hold of me." Despite this concern over his safety Douglass was determined to return home and wrote his wife to expect him on November 20. Only the insistence of Garrison and Thompson that he stay abroad at least six months longer led him to alter his plans.[22]

When Douglass finally did return to America in the spring of 1847, he came home a free man. Late in 1846, his English friends, led by Ellen and Anna Richardson of Newcastle, had raised $710.96 to purchase his emancipation from Hugh Auld to whom his brother Thomas had transferred ownership. What a day in the life of Frederick Douglass when the bill of sale was handed over to him by his benefactors![23]

Douglass' joy was somewhat diminished by the storm of criticism the news of his freedom aroused among groups of Abolitionists in the United States. They charged that the purchase was a recognition of the "right to traffic in human beings." It was also "impolitic and inexpedient" because by the ransom Douglass had "lost much of that moral power which he possessed, as the representative of the three millions of his countrymen in chains, taking, as he did, his life in his hands, appearing, wherever he appeared, with all the liabilities which the law laid upon him to be returned to stripes, torture and death." Garrison, who had "gladly contributed" his "mite" to the purchase fund was deluged with indignant letters accusing him of having violated a cardinal principle of the anti-slavery creed. Justifying the negotiation, he reminded his critics that although he had always contended that the demand of the slaveholder for compensation "was an unjust one," he had never maintained that it was wrong "to ransom one held in cruel bondage." "We deny," Garrison editorialized, "that purchasing the freedom of a slave is necessarily an implied acknowledgment of the master's right to property in human beings."[24]

The heated controversy raged for more than three months in the columns of the *Liberator* and other anti-slavery journals. In a reply to Henry C. Wright who had urged him to repudiate the transaction, Douglass stressed the practical importance of the purchase, called Wright's attention to the fact that as a fugitive slave he could be seized by his master and returned to slavery the moment he set foot in the United States, and assured him that his changed status would not weaken the bonds that connected him with the slaves. "I shall be Frederick Douglass still," he concluded his masterly defense, "once a slave still. I shall neither be made to forget nor cease to feel the wrongs of my enslaved fellow-countrymen. My knowledge of slavery will be the same and my hatred of it will be the same."[25]

Douglass' last months abroad were so crammed with lecture engagements that in one month, he spoke almost every night. By March the pace was beginning to tell, and some of his addresses lacked their usual forceful delivery. An observer at Warrington noted that he appeared "to be suffering from great debility owing to the large amount of fatigue he has lately endured." Nevertheless he continued to score success after success and to convert large audiences to the cause.

Late in March Douglass prepared for his departure. In London, on March 30, his friends tendered him a public farewell attended by 1,400 persons "of great respectability." Deeply moved, the honored guest spoke regretfully of leaving the country in which he had been treated "with utmost kindness, with the utmost deference, with the utmost attention." He had known these last nineteen months "what it was for the first time in my life to enjoy freedom." The oppressed Negro people would know how England felt about slavery, and that it "would give them patience under their sorrows, and hope of a future emancipation." He would always remember the "sea of upturned faces" at the farewell meeting, for it would be "daguerreotyped upon my heart."[26]

A few days later Douglass left for Liverpool. Here he was brought back to the realities of the life that faced him in his native land. In London he had purchased a ticket for passage on the *Cambria*, but on reaching Liverpool he was informed by the Cunard agent that he could not sail unless he agreed to relinquish the berth he had ordered. These measures, he was assured, were merely precautionary. Douglass had caused a commotion on his previous passage, and the company was seeking to prevent a repetition of the disturbance.

Douglass was furious, but anxious to return home, he yielded. In a letter to the London *Times*, he laid the facts before the British public, confident that it would "pronounce a just verdict on such proceedings." His confidence was more than justified. The British press promptly condemned the agent's action in editorials carrying the headings: "A British Bow to an American Prejudice," "Pro-Slavery Persecution in England,"

"Shameful Violation of the Rights of Man," "Disgraceful Prejudice Against a Man of Color," "England Made Ashamed," "American Intolerance in the Port of Liverpool," "Disgraceful Conduct Toward Frederick Douglass, The Liberated Slave." "We call upon the whole nation," cried *Howitt's Journal,* "to resent this disgrace to the English name! ... to demand of Government to take up the matter, and to insist on the Line of Packet Company making a public apology for this surrender of the honour of the British nation." The apology came sooner than the *Journal* had expected. In a public letter to the editor of the *Times,* S. Cunard expressed his regrets and guaranteed that "nothing of the kind will *again take place in the steamships with which I am connected."* Even then the incident was not too quickly forgotten in England, and Elizabeth Pease was confident that the exclusion of Douglass "will do more ... to help the anti-slavery cause than all the lectures which F. D. has delivered on this side of the Atlantic—powerful and convincing as they have been."[27]

In his enforced privacy during the sixteen-day voyage across the Atlantic, Douglass had ample opportunity to reflect on the exciting experiences of the previous twenty months. They were happy memories. His experiences on stage-coaches, railroads, steamboats, and in taverns, hotels, and other public places had not been marred by a single instance of discrimination. He had made many warm friends and acquired a host of admirers. He had come to know many of the most distinguished men in Britain—Clarkson, Lovett, Richard Cobden, John Bright, Benjamin Disraeli, Robert Peel, Daniel O'Connell, Lord Brougham, George Thompson. He had left behind in England thousands of people who were now more than ever convinced that "a system which can doom such men as Douglass to the whip and fetter" must be destroyed. And his visit was to play an important part in increasing the sentiment in Britain toward the achievement of that goal.

He had left America a slave, he was returning a free man. He had come to England almost unknown, he was now famous. In his own country his prestige had increased. "He will be warmly welcomed by the Abolitionists," wrote Garrison upon learning that Douglass had sailed, "and, doubtless, more kindly regarded by people generally, in consequence of the generous and honorable reception given him in Great Britain." Small wonder Douglass rejoiced:

"What a contrast is my *present* with my former condition? Then a slave, now a free man; then degraded, now respected; then ignorant, despised, neglected, unknown, and unfriended, my name unheard of beyond the narrow limits of a republican slave plantation; now, my friends and benefactors, people of *both* hemispheres, to heaven the praise belongs!"[28]

Douglass returned home grown to his full stature, with a spirit fearless and daring, with a deeper hatred of slavery and discrimination, with an unyielding determination to assert his "equal right as a man and a brother,"[29] a living symbol of what millions of Negro people in the United States could contribute to civilization once their chains of bondage were broken.

Founding "The North Star"

Douglass had barely settled down after his arrival from abroad when a series of welcome-home gatherings took place. Late in April, a reception was held in the Lyceum Hall in Lynn, his home town, and numerous speeches congratulated him on the success of his "philanthropic mission." He responded with a sketch of his travels and adventures abroad, but told the audience that he had not yet "got his sea-legs off" so could not go deeply into the significance of his experiences in Europe. Ten days later, on May 3, the Negro people of Boston, assisted by their white friends, held their public welcome. They were followed by the Negro people of New York City who gathered in the Zion's Church to voice their joy at Douglass' success. On May 25 his friends in New Bedford extended their welcome, particularly praising Douglass for his decision to leave "the valuable and social inducements held out to him by the people of Great Britain, for the purpose of returning to America, to again identify himself with the suffering slave, and with those who are laboring against great obstacles to procure his liberation. . . ."[1]

At the meetings of the American Anti-Slavery Society in New York during the second week of May, Douglass was officially welcomed by his leading co-workers. On this occasion he made his first important address since his return, and startled even the most avid Garrisonians with the fervor of his remarks. He out-Garrisoned the Garrisonians as he launched into a bitter attack upon his native land in which "three millions of my brethren, some of them my own kindred, my own brothers, my own sisters, . . . are now clanking the chains of Slavery upon the plains of the South. . . ." Replying to Garrison who had referred to the Negro orator's "love and attachment" to America, Douglass declared amidst cheers and hisses:

"I cannot have any love for this country, as such, or for its Constitution. I desire to see its overthrow as speedily as possible, and its Constitution shivered in a thousand fragments, rather than this foul curse should continue to remain as now."

The remainder of the address was much calmer, as he brilliantly justified his criticism of American institutions abroad, and his role at the World's Temperance Convention. The full text of the speech, as it appeared in the *New York Tribune,* was reprinted as a pamphlet by a group of Baltimore slaveholders who pointed to it as proof of the dangers inherent in the Abolitionist movement.[2] But most readers of the *Tribune* agreed with John Greenleaf Whittier that it was "a notable refutation of the charge of the natural inferiority urged against the colored man."[3]

Once the celebrations welcoming his homecoming were over, Douglass turned his attention to the launching of an anti-slavery paper. During his last months abroad a number of his English friends had offered to supply him with an annual income sufficient to enable him to be free from worry and "to devote his whole life and energies to the Anti-Slavery Cause." Douglass had rejected the offer because it would be fatal to his effectiveness in the struggle against slavery to be separated "from mutual hardships in a common cause." Instead, he suggested that he would be happy to receive a printing press, enabling him to establish a weekly newspaper under the editorial management of Negroes. For such a paper, if run efficiently, "would be a *telling* fact against the American doctrine of natural inferiority, and the inveterate prejudice which so universally prevails in this country against the colored race." His friends eagerly seized upon the suggestion and raised a testimonial fund which rapidly exceeded two thousand dollars.[4]

On his return to the United States, Mary Howitt, one of his closest English friends, wrote Douglass asking him whether he was still interested in publishing his paper. He replied promptly:

"You speak of the printing press, and ask shall I like to have it? I answer, yes, yes! The very best instrumentalities are not too good for the cause; I should feel it quite improper to express myself thus, if the proposed present were merely an expression of personal consideration. I look upon it as an aid to a great cause, and I cannot but accept the best gifts which may be offered to it.... I hope to be able to do a good work in behalf of my race with it."[5]

The history of Negro journalism in the United States before 1847 was not one to inspire much confidence in Douglass' project. *Freedom's Journal,* the first American Negro newspaper, died a few months after its appearance in the spring of 1827. In January, 1837, the second Negro newspaper, *The Weekly Advocate,* edited by Rev. Samuel Cornish, came into being in New York City. In March of the same year, it was renamed *The Colored American* and ran until 1841, during which time it was edited successively by Cornish, Dr. James McCune Smith of New York City, a graduate of medicine of the University of Glasgow, Scotland, and Rev. Charles B. Ray. In August, 1838, David Ruggles published *The Mirror of Liberty* in New York, first a quarterly and then a monthly magazine devoted to the welfare of the free Negro. Publication ended in September, 1841.

With the 1840's came a substantial increase in the number of Negro publications. In Albany, New York, in 1842, Stephen Myers edited *The Elevator. The National Watchman,* with which William G. Allen was associated, was circulated from Troy, New York, beginning in the latter part of 1842 and lasting until 1847. *The Clarion* was published by the Rev. Henry Highland Garnet in Troy, but was short-lived. *The People's Press* was edited in New York City by Thomas Hamilton during 1843. In the same year, Martin Robinson Delany edited *The Mystery* in Pittsburgh. *The Ram's Horn,* edited in New York City by William Hodges, was published in January of 1847 and died in June of the following year.[6]

That these papers lacked stability is hardly surprising. The circulation was usually small, the subscription list confined for the most part to the city in which the journal was published. The Negro papers faced great difficulties: there were few Negro merchants and professional men who bought advertising; the Negro people were too poor to make substantial contributions to requests for funds and not many white people were interested in Negro Abolitionist journals. Thus the publications constantly needed financial assistance. Consequently, nearly all of the journals expired after a valiant battle to exist.

But this did not discourage Douglass. He did not doubt his ability to make a good editor. The literary quality of his letters from abroad had aroused considerable amazement among leading newspaper men. Horace Greeley of the *New York Tribune* wrote that in one of Douglass' letters to Garrison there were passages "which, for genuine eloquence, would do honor to any writer of the English language, however eloquent." Thurlow Weed, editor of the *Albany Evening Journal,* corroborated Greeley's judgment of the letter, commenting that it gave Douglass "rank among the most gifted and eloquent men of the age."[7]

Confident that the money to launch his project was available, Douglass broached the plan to his New England associates. He was dismayed to learn that they did not share his enthusiasm. Phillips was convinced that a newspaper would ruin him "pecuniarily" in three years.[8] Garrison argued that the paper was not needed since several journals published and edited by Negroes were already in existence; that it would fail for want of support ("The land is full of the wreck of such experiments"); that editorial work would interfere with Douglass' work as a lecturer, and that he was better fitted to speak than to write. "We have no doubt," he summarized, "that Mr. Douglass would display much editorial ability, but the experiment remains to be made. Of one thing we and his friends are certain: as a lecturer, his power over a public assembly is very high. . . . With such powers of oratory, and so few lecturers in the field where so many are needed, it seems to us as clear as the noon-day sun, that it would be no gain, but rather a loss, to the anti-slavery cause, to have him withdrawn to any considerable extent from the work of popular agitation, by assuming the cares, drudgery and perplexities of a publishing life. It is quite impracticable to combine the editor with the lecturer, without either causing the paper to be more or less neglected, or the sphere of lecturing to be seriously circumscribed."[9]

Douglass could have replied (as did some Abolitionists critical of Garrison's reasoning) that the editor of the *Liberator* seemed to be capable of combining lecturing and editorial duties. But he was unwilling to offend Garrison, who more than any other man was responsible for his success, and so he temporarily abandoned his plan. Publicly he based his decision on the four journals, which, under the exclusive editorship of Negroes, had come into existence since the entire idea of publishing a paper had taken root in his mind. His British friends assured Douglass that when he considered it advisable to launch his newspaper, the capital would be available.[10]

Resuming the lecture platform, Douglass took his place with the Abolitionists as in former days. In August he made preparations to assist Garrison "in carrying the torch of conscience into dark places of the West." The western tour grew out of an invitation extended to Garrison early in the year by the Western Anti-Slavery Society to address its annual convention at New Lynn, Ohio. When Garrison announced his acceptance, he was deluged with requests from anti-slavery societies in New York and Pennsylvania to visit them on the trip.

The tour started smoothly enough. At Norristown, where the Eastern

Pennsylvania Anti-Slavery Society was celebrating its tenth anniversary, Garrison, Sidney B. Gay, Robert Purvis and Lucretia Mott were enthusiastically received, but Douglass was "the 'lion' of the occasion." A day later a public meeting was held in honor of Garrison and Douglass by the Negro people of Philadelphia. The Negro Abolitionist held the audience "spell-bound for more than two hours."[11]

But these were deceptive signs. On a train bound for Harrisburg, Douglass was ordered out of the car by one of the passengers, a local lawyer, and dragged out of his seat when he refused to leave. The incident was but a prologue to the reception which faced the Abolitionists in the state capital. A large and attentive audience gathered in the Harrisburg courthouse, listened quietly to Garrison's speech. But when Douglass began to speak, the storm broke. Cries of "Out with the damned n——r!" began as the mob took possession. They set off firecrackers, threw cayenne pepper all over the place, and hurled stones, garbage, and rotten eggs at the speaker. The mob was still at it when Garrison arose and calmly announced that if this was a specimen of Harrisburg hospitality and "love of liberty" the visitors were quite happy to depart.

The experience did not dampen the ardor of the two men. Nor did the strenuous trip across the Alleghenies. Many times Garrison was deeply angered because Douglass was not permitted to sit at the table and, for two days and nights, "scarcely tasted a morsel of food." The greeting at Pittsburgh, where a committee of twenty white and Negro friends, "with a colored band of music," received them at the station cheered them. Douglass and Garrison, now joined by Stephen Foster who had consented to make the trip "though with much inconvenience to his domestic arrangements," held five crowded and enthusiastic meetings in two days. Garrison assured his wife that "he had seen nothing like it on this side of the Atlantic." The fact that two meetings in New Brighton had to be held in the upper room of a flour store because the churches had refused to open their doors to the Abolitionists did not diminish his enthusiasm.[12]

August 18 saw the travelers at an anti-slavery meeting at New Lyme, in northeastern Ohio, held in a huge tent with an audience of four thousand. Although many of the western Abolitionists had repudiated the Garrisonians and followed the Weld-Tappan group, Garrison's influence was still strong in the Western Reserve which, according to the Cleveland *Plain Dealer,* was "the favorite stumping ground of the fanatical disunionists of the East" where they were always "sure to gather a crowd to listen to their ravings." People came from far distant communities to see the leader of the American Anti-Slavery Society and his famous Negro companion, one Negro farmer riding three hundred miles on horseback to be present.[13]

After Benjamin S. Jones, editor of the powerful *Anti-Slavery Bugle* of Salem, Ohio, had opened the convention, a choir sang a poetical welcome to the honored guests. The verses to Douglass went:

> *And our hearts are made glad by the presence of one*
> *Who was chattelized, beaten, and sold in our land;*
> *Who is guilty of naught, save that Africa's sun*
> *Pressed his ancestor's brow with too heavy a hand.*
>
> *He can tell of the woes that have gnawed at his heart;*
> *Of the lash that has left its deep scar on his back;*
> *How the tenderest ties are torn rudely apart,*
> *And the soul and body both doomed to the rack.*[14]

The visiting Abolitionists were deeply moved by the New Lyme meetings. "Enthusiasm . . . is unequalled," wrote Garrison. "Opposition to our holy cause seems stunned." Never had he attended a convention where such fervor for the movement was displayed. They had made a "host of friends," and when the convention adjourned, they were kept "busily engaged for some time in shaking hands and bidding farewell."

Six days later, the Abolitionists were at Oberlin, having attended meetings in four towns en route. On August 27, they began a series of lectures which were well attended. Later Asa Mahan, president of Oberlin College, the great anti-slavery center, entertained Garrison and Douglass at dinner. The visitors were impressed by the courtesy displayed toward them and by the Oberlin hospitality. They welcomed the opportunity to rest in a congenial atmosphere, for the trip had proved to be more arduous than they had anticipated. They had spoken every day since entering Ohio, and, to keep the appointments arranged for them by Samuel Brooks, the agent of the Western Anti-Slavery Society, they had been compelled to travel to towns thirty to forty miles apart. Speeches delivered in tents, in drafty halls, and in the open air with rain pouring down in torrents, were detrimental to good health, and Douglass, troubled by tonsilitis, had been forced to cancel several of his scheduled addresses.

"Our friends here have so multiplied the meetings," Garrison complained on one occasion, "that not an hour is left us for rest. They are unmerciful to us, and how we are to fulfill all the engagements made, without utterly breaking down, I do not know. Douglass is not able to speak at any length without becoming very hoarse, and, in some cases, losing the ability to make himself heard."[15]

Following their Oberlin visit, the Abolitionists passed through Richfield, Medina, Massilon, and Leesburg on their way to Salem, addressing enthusiastic audiences in every town. Five thousand sympathizers welcomed them in Salem at what the *Anti-Slavery Bugle* called "the largest anti-slavery gathering ever convened in the county." A week later at Cleveland they found that the local *Plain Dealer* had prepared the city for their arrival with the announcement that the "menagerie is coming," and had slyly suggested that the visitors be given the same treatment they had received at Harrisburg. Successful meetings, however, were held, and, on the second day, Garrison told the audience that neither he nor Douglass had met with any violence since coming to Ohio. Douglass assured the gathering that he had found "nothing mean, narrow, or churlish about a true Buckeye." Discussing the two speakers, the Cleveland *True Democrat* observed:

"Mr. Garrison is a pleasant, clear, forcible, and logical speaker. He carries his point by real sledge-hammer argument. Douglass is more eloquent. He moves upon the passions of his audience and handles with a master's skill the weapons of the orator."[16]

The meetings at Cleveland were the last which Garrison and Douglass attended as friends. The pace had begun to tell on the older man, and before the Cleveland trip had ended, Garrison collapsed. He had spoken at an open-air meeting in a drizzling cold rain and had been chilled to the bone. When he returned to his rooms, feverish and exhausted, he was placed under a doctor's care. Douglass insisted on remaining with his friend but Garrison urged him to continue and carry out their scheduled engagements.

Worried and depressed, Douglass left for Buffalo. A week later he was disturbed to learn that Garrison's condition was critical. He kept reproaching himself "for leaving at all." Half-heartedly he went through his talks in Buffalo, Rochester, and Syracuse, but his mind was troubled. On October 8, 1847, Samuel J. May wrote to Garrison:

"Frederick Douglass was very much trouble[d] that he did not get any tidings from you when he reached Syracuse on the 24th. of September. He left you reluctantly, yet thinking that you would follow in a day or two; and as he did not get any word from you at Waterloo, nor at Auburn, he was almost sure he should meet you at my house. His countenance fell, and his heart failed him, when he found me likewise in sad suspense about you. Not until he arrived at West Winfield did he get any relief, and then through the *Liberator* of the 23d."[17]

May's description of Douglass' concern does not seem to have made any impression upon Garrison. Writing to his wife five weeks after Douglass' departure, the Abolitionist expressed surprise that his recent co-worker had "not written a single line to me, or to anyone else in this place, inquiring after my health, since he left me on a bed of illness."[18]

It was not Douglass' supposed indifference which was alone responsible for Garrison's annoyance. It was aggravated by Douglass' conviction that his original plan to publish an anti-slavery weekly had been correct. The hateful discrimination Douglass had encountered early on the western tour had convinced him of this. "I had not decided against the publication of a paper one month," he wrote to an English friend on November 1, "before I became satisfied that I had made a mistake and each subsequent month's experience has confirmed me in the conviction." Now more than ever he believed that the example of a journal excellently managed and edited by a Negro "would be a powerful evidence that the Negro was too much of a man to be held a chattel."[19]

Garrison was considerably vexed by Douglass' decision to go forward with his plans in spite of the objections of his colleagues. He complained to his wife that Douglass had "never opened to me his lips on the subject, nor asked my advice in any particular whatever! Such conduct grieves me to the heart. His conduct about the paper has been impulsive, inconsiderate, and inconsistent with his decision in Boston...." Douglass' insistence that he had revealed his plan to Garrison before he was taken ill in Cleveland did not help matters. Garrison had "no recollection whatever of it."[20]

Undeterred by Garrison's attitude, Douglass went forward with his project. With $2,174 forwarded by his English friends he bought "an excellent press, and nearly the necessary printing materials," and was happy to learn from expert printers that they were the best that could be obtained in the United States. Where to publish was the next problem. The site had to be removed from that of the *Liberator* and the *Anti-Slavery Standard*. Originally he had thought of publishing in Cleveland, but the following announcement in the *Ram's Horn* of November 1, 1847, revealed that he had finally decided to operate from Rochester:[21]

"PROSPECTUS FOR AN ANTI-SLAVERY PAPER TO BE ENTITLED—*THE NORTH STAR.*

"Frederick Douglass proposes to publish in Rochester, New York, a weekly anti-slavery paper with the above title. The object of *The North Star* will be to attack slavery in all its forms and aspects; advocate Universal Emancipation; exact the standard of public morality; promote the moral and intellectual improvement of the colored people; and to hasten the day of freedom to our three million enslaved fellow-countrymen.

"The paper will be printed on a double medium sheet, at $2.00 per annum, paid in advance, and $2.50 if payment be delayed over six months. . . ."[22]

Rochester offered vast potentialities for an anti-slavery publication. "Perhaps in no other communities of the north," writes a historian of the city, "was there a more intense feeling of hostility to slavery and of indignation over the wrongs inflicted upon the Negro." Most of the Abolitionists in Rochester, due to the work of Myron Holley, were not Garrisonians, but there was a tolerance and receptiveness toward anti-slavery men of all shades of opinion. Furthermore, Rochester boasted an active female Anti-Slavery Society which had been organized in 1835 and with which were associated some of the outstanding women of the country—Elizabeth Cady Stanton, Susan B. Anthony, Amy Post, Sally Holley, Sojourner Truth, and Mrs. Samuel D. Porter.[23] An anti-slavery journal would receive the support of the Female Anti-Slavery Society in building circulation and in meeting operating expenses. Douglass knew from his first visit to Rochester that the homes of many citizens would be open to him and that here he and his family could build lasting friendships.

Toward the close of 1847 Douglass moved to Rochester to prepare the first issue of his paper.

" . . . I shall enter on my duties with a full sense of my accountability to God, the slave, and to the dear friends who had aided me in the undertaking," he wrote as he prepared to depart from Lynn. "In the publication of the paper, I shall be under no party or society, but shall advocate the slave's cause in that way which in my judgment, will be best suited to the advancement of the cause."[24]

Editor and Publisher

On Friday, December 3, 1847, a new era in Negro journalism in the United States was inaugurated. The first issue of *The North Star* came off the press, its masthead proclaiming the slogan: "Right is of no Sex—Truth is of no Color—God is the Father of us all, and we are all Brethren." The role of the paper was that of a "terror to evil doers," and while it would be "mainly Anti-Slavery," its columns would be "freely opened to the candid and decorous discussion of all measures and topics of a moral and humane character, which may serve to enlighten, improve and elevate mankind. . . ." A report of the National Convention of Colored People held at Troy early in October, and a long letter by Douglass to Henry Clay commenting on the Kentuckian's speech in behalf of colonization, were the main features of the first number. The first page stated that the subscription rates were two dollars a year, *"always in advance,"* and that advertisements not exceeding ten lines would be carried three times for one dollar.

The editors were Douglass and Martin R. Delany who had just resigned the editorship of the Pittsburgh *Mystery,* a Negro paper. William C. Nell, a self-taught Negro and a devoted Garrisonian, was listed as publisher. The printing office was located at 25 Buffalo Street, in the Talman Building, opposite Reynolds Arcade. It was a simple room. Douglass' desk was in one corner; cases of type and the printing press occupied the rest of the space. Two white apprentices, William A. Atkinson and William Oliver, and Douglass' children assisted in setting the type, locking the forms, folding, wrapping and mailing the paper. Although Douglass had his own press, the paper itself was printed in the shop of the *Rochester Democrat.*[1]

On the whole, reaction to the first issue was favorable. Samuel J. May spoke of his "delight" in reading the paper, Garrison praised it, and Edmund Quincy observed in the *Liberator* that its "literary and mechanical execution would do honor to any paper new or old, anti-slavery or pro-slavery, in the country." In England, *Howitt's Journal* augmented the chorus of approval with the remark: *"The North Star* may rank with any American paper, for ability and interest; it is full of buoyancy and variety. . . ."[2]

Not all joined in welcoming the new arrival. The *New York Herald* urged the people of Rochester to throw Douglass' printing press into the lake and exile the editor to Canada. The *Albany Dispatch* was a bit more subtle. It merely warned the citizens of Rochester that the presence of a paper published by "the n——r pet of the British Abolitionists" would be a "serious detriment" to the community, and suggested that they "buy him off." Undoubtedly there were those in Rochester who approved of these suggestions, but they were a distinct minority. The Rochester *Daily Advertiser* observed that the mechanical appearance of the first issue was "exceedingly neat," that the leading article indicated "a high order of talent," and that the editor was "a man of much more than ordinary share of intellect."

More important was the welcome extended the paper and its staff by the printers' association of Rochester. In January 1848 the publishers and printers' union of the city invited Douglass and Nell to an anniversary celebration of Benjamin Franklin's birthday. When the hotel refused to allow the Negroes to enter the dining room the guests sharply protested and the manager was compelled to rescind the order. At the dinner, in response to a toast in his honor, Douglass said: "Gentlemen of the Rochester Press—promoters of knowledge, lovers of liberty, foes of ignorance, despisers of prejudice—may you continue to give the world noble examples by a free and intelligent union of *black* and *white*."[3]

In the first issue Douglass made a solemn pledge to his readers that "*The North Star* shall live." He kept his promise, but it was only by the most heroic effort. Due to the generosity of his friends abroad, Douglass started his paper debt-free, but he had to depend upon subscriptions to meet publication expenses which, in 1848, amounted to sixty dollars a week. A mailing list of seven hundred was not enough to keep the paper solvent, and, on January 12, 1848, Douglass complained to Delany who was on a subscription tour: "Subscribers come in slowly, and I am doing all I can by lectures and letters to keep our heads above the water." A week later he wrote: "The work is up hill just now, but I hope there is a good time coming." Three months later the situation had become so critical that on April 28, 1848, Douglass was compelled to mortgage his home to keep the paper alive. On May 5, 1848, *The North Star* contained an urgent appeal to its friends and readers "for immediate pecuniary aid." "We have exerted ourselves to obtain subscribers, and have succeeded to an encouraging extent; but it is impossible in our circumstances, commencing as we did with but a small number of subscribers, to obtain a sufficient number to float unencumbered from week to week." This was but the first of a series of appeals that were to accompany the existence of Douglass' paper.[4]

"Things have not turned out at all as I expected," Douglass wrote ruefully four months after launching *The North Star*. His paper had received little support from the Boston Abolitionists, partly because it had been started against their advice and partly because it did not denounce all Abolitionists who were not Garrisonians. On the other hand, the political Abolitionists had withheld their support because they regarded the weekly as too strongly tainted with Garrisonianism. In short, all groups of the Abolitionist movement felt only "a negative interest" in Douglass' paper. What was most grievous to the editor was the response of the Negro people. Douglass explained this to his own satisfaction by attributing the indifference "to the long night of ignorance which has overshadowed and subdued their spirit,"[5] but he could not hide his bitterness over the fact that in May, 1848, *The North Star* had five white subscribers to every Negro. "Tell them," he editorialized later, "that a well conducted press in the hands of colored men is essential to the progress and elevation of the colored man, and they will regard you as one merely seeking a living at public expense, 'to get along without work.' "[6]

That the paper survived the first difficult year was due mainly to Douglass' own tireless work and the assistance of a few devoted friends. Originally it had been planned that Douglass remain in Rochester and edit the paper while Delany traveled about getting subscribers. But this went by the board almost immediately. Month after month in all kinds of weather, Douglass would depart on lecture tours to raise funds, supplying his readers with a detailed account of his experiences. A typical letter from the editor went:

"The scanty editorial matter which I have sent to the paper for the past two weeks, has been written on the wing, and in the midst of pressing engagements. You will sympathize with me when I tell you that I find it necessary to go abroad in person to secure the number of subscribers requisite to the support of our paper. This ought not to be, and would not be the case if suitable agents could be obtained, who would enforce the claims of the paper upon the public, and secure subscribers and subscriptions for it. But these we have not, and in consequence find it necessary to go forth myself. I regret this only on one account, and that is, it deprives me of the time and means of making the paper what I desire and what it ought to be."[7]

During this first year, Douglass spent about six months out in the field, raising funds through lectures and subscriptions. He had mortgaged his home, was "heavily in debt," and the paper itself was over two hundred dollars in debt. But he did have the satisfaction of having completed the first volume. "It has lived through one year," he wrote joyfully on December 22, 1848, "has made its appearance regularly—has not missed a single Friday morning since the day of its first publication—those who subscribed at its commencement have not lost their money by the *'going down'* of the paper." A few weeks later Douglass' spirit soared when he learned that at an anti-slavery fair held by the Negro women of Philadelphia one hundred dollars had been raised for *The North Star*. It was not so much the money itself as the knowledge of "the esteem in which *The North Star* is held by those who feel the crushing weight of American oppression." "We believe," Douglass wrote joyfully, "it was the first fair ever held in this country by colored ladies, to sustain a press under the sole management of persons of their own complexion. We take it as an evidence that, whatever others may think of the expediency of establishing such a paper as we have tried to make the *North Star*, the oppressed themselves feel the value of it."[8]

Women had much to do with the continued existence of Douglass' weekly. Indeed, were it not for Julia Griffiths the paper on many occasions would have been forced to suspend publication. Miss Griffiths, a daughter of a close friend of Wilberforce, the British Abolitionist, had met Douglass at Newcastle-on-Tyne during his tour abroad and they had become fast friends at once. She had raised funds to help launch his paper and had furnished him with a "valuable collection of books, pamphlets, tracts and pictures." Learning, in the spring of 1848, that *The North Star* was faring poorly, she wound up her affairs in England and with her sister came to Rochester to assist in putting the journal on its feet. "She came to my relief," Douglass wrote years later, "when my paper had nearly absorbed my means, and I was heavily in debt, and when I had mortgaged my house to raise money to meet current expenses; and in a single year, by her energetic and effective management, enabled me to extend the circulation of my paper from 2,000 to 4,000 copies." In a single year, too, Miss Griffiths "paid off a debt of between seven and eight hundred dollars."[9]

An indefatigable worker, with good business sense, Julia Griffiths moved into Douglass' home soon after her arrival and devoted herself exclusively to managing his paper. She took charge of the finances of *The North Star* in the summer of 1848, and, separating Douglass' personal finances from those of the paper, enabled him to pay off the mortgage on his home by March 18, 1853. She organized numerous projects to raise funds, sponsoring fairs, mailing innumerable personal appeals for financial aid, and building a strong movement among the women Abolitionists in Rochester. Gradually the financial strain was eased. By May 1, 1851, when the paper enjoyed a circulation well over 4,000, the situation had improved so that Douglass was able to report to Gerrit Smith: "The 'North Star' sustains itself, and partly sustains my large family. It has just reached a living point. Hitherto the struggle of its life has been to live. Now it more than lives."[10]

In the summer of 1851 *The North Star* amalgamated with the *Liberty Party Paper,* a weekly journal edited and published by John Thomas in Syracuse. This paper had fewer than seven hundred subscribers and was in great financial distress. The merger resulted from a suggestion by Gerrit Smith, the financial backer of Thomas' paper. Douglass was to become the editor of the new publication, Thomas the assistant editor, and Julia Griffiths the business manager. A new printing office and a good press would result in a "good looking paper . . . free from all typographical, grammatical, orthographical, and rhetorical errors and blunders." Smith advanced two hundred dollars for the purchase of the press and type and promised to provide a monthly donation toward the paper's upkeep.

After considerable bickering with John Thomas over the salary of the assistant editor and the location of the paper, the merger became an accomplished fact. "God grant that the fruit of our union may prove a blessing to the slave, and to suffering man everywhere and of every grade," Douglass wrote to Smith on June 18, 1851. Twelve days later, the first issue of the new weekly, now named *Frederick Douglass' Paper,* appeared. Its motto, proposed by Smith, was "All Rights For All."[11]

Essentially the weekly was a continuation of *The North Star*. However, one notes the absence of the usual "F.D." at the bottom of Douglass' articles. For three years these initials had adorned every issue of *The North Star* as proof to doubters that "an uneducated fugitive slave could write the English language with such propriety and correctness. . . ." But now Douglass was assuming "in full the right and dignity of an *Editor*—a Mr. Editor if you please."[12]

With Smith contributing to its support, the paper was able for two years to meet its expenses. But after 1853 it again ran into difficulties. "Money! Money!! Money!!!" Douglass appealed to delinquent subscribers on April 8, 1853. ". . . We greatly need your assistance, just now. The expence of publishing a paper like ours is very great—and depending, as it does, almost wholly upon its *subscription* list, it can only be sustained and its Editor left unembarrassed by *prompt payment* on the part of *subscribers.*" The situation grew worse. By June, 1855, when Douglass instituted the policy of advanced subscription payments, the journal was fifteen hundred dollars in debt, and almost double that amount was due from delinquent subscribers.[13]

That the debt was not even greater was due again to the tireless efforts of Julia Griffiths. "In referring to those who have assisted us in keeping up the paper during the year," Douglass wrote later in 1854, "and for the past three years, we are indebted to none more than to that ever active and zealous friend of the slave, Miss Julia Griffiths." A year before this emphatic tribute was delivered, Miss Griffiths had launched a plan to raise one thousand dollars, in ten-dollar gifts, toward a sustaining fund for the paper. By January, 1854, she had collected four hundred and twenty dollars. Among the forty-two donors were Smith, Sumner, Chase, Greeley, Seward, William Jay, Henry Ward Beecher, Arthur and Lewis Tappan, Horace Mann, Cassius M. Clay, as well as several prominent Negroes. William Johnson, one of the Negro contributors, also published an appeal to his people urging them to support the drive for funds:

" . . . If there is any one thing more than another, that we need in a public way as a fixture, it is that of a newspaper, conducted and published by a colored man, through which our views and sentiments may be known as a people; and since God has raised up as a man in the person of Frederick Douglass, who has demonstrated to the world that he has the ability to vindicate the rights of man, with equal force, either on the platform as an orator, or as an editor of a newspaper, it becomes the duty of every colored man and woman to sustain Frederick Douglass and his paper."[14]

With the assistance of the Rochester Ladies' Anti-Slavery Society, of which she was secretary, Miss Griffiths in 1853 published a gift-book, *Autographs for Freedom,* to aid Douglass' paper. Several hundred gift-books had been issued in this country before the Civil War, and the anti-slavery cause alone had produced five before *Autographs for Freedom* made its appearance. The new feature of Miss Griffiths' volume was the autograph which followed the author's essays, letters, and speeches. Like the other anti-slavery gift-books, it was designed to be sold at Abolitionist fairs and bazaars, though Douglass also offered the volume to subscribers as a means of extending the circulation of his journal.[15]

Commenting on the English edition of *Autographs for Freedom,* the

British Banner observed: "The book is deeply interesting, and as presenting the aggregate of liberal sentiments from cultivated and enlightened minds, possesses a peculiar value." Among the "cultivated and enlightened" contributors were Negro leaders such as J. McCune Smith, George B. Vashon, William G. Allen, Charles L. Reason, James M. Whitfield, William Wells Brown, J. M. Langston and Douglass himself; public figures such as William H. Seward, Horace Greeley, Gerrit Smith, Horace Mann, and Joshua R. Giddings; preachers and philosophers such as Theodore Parker, Ralph Waldo Emerson, and Henry Ward Beecher; and women reformers such as Harriet Beecher Stowe, Antoinette Brown, Caroline M. Kirkland, Catherine M. Sedgwick, and Jane Swisshelm. Most of the contributions were brief—frequently a page in length—and few were outstanding for their literary merit. But the volumes did contain some previously unpublished work by prominent writers, and some of the contributions by the Negro authors rank high in the literature of the anti-slavery movement.[16] The 1853 issue featured a little-known work of fiction by Frederick Douglass entitled *The Heroic Slave*, a short story about Madison Washington, who led the famous uprising in 1841 on the *Creole*, a ship engaged in the domestic slave trade.

The proceeds from the two issues of *Autographs for Freedom* did not solve Douglass' multiplying financial problems. With her usual ingenuity, Miss Griffiths hit upon the plan of returning to England to raise funds. Armed with letters vouching for the merit of Douglass' journal, she arrived in her native land during the spring of 1857. Lewis Tappan's letter praised Douglass "as a man deserving entire confidence. . . . His paper is well conducted." Charles Sumner's testimonial was brief: "I have a high opinion of Frederick Douglass and his efforts. His paper is doing a very good work." Speaking for the Negro people, James McCune Smith wrote:

> "The friends of slavery, driven from argument to argument, finally point to the Blacks, and exclaim in triumph. 'See them! Are they benefiting by freedom?' So long as we can point to Frederick Douglass, and his paper, we have a triumphant reply to that question; they both stand full in clear living light, and prove more than a volume of statistics of our relative freedom from vice, crime, and poverty."[17]

Miss Griffiths was well received by the British Abolition societies. Douglass was still remembered by the English public and his paper had quite a few subscribers. In 1855 *The Anti-Slavery Reporter*, organ of the

British and Foreign Anti-Slavery Society, had urged English reformers to subscribe to Douglass' weekly.

"It is the only newspaper in America," the *Reporter* pointed out, "owned by a coloured man, who has been himself a fugitive slave; and its own intrinsic merit, as well as the interest of the Abolition cause generally, require that, above every other anti-slavery journal, it should be sustained."[18]

How much Miss Griffiths raised for the paper is difficult to determine. We do know she organized at least fourteen Ladies' Associations which pledged to aid the journal with annual donations from between five and twenty pounds. The number of English subscribers was also increased, but this did not help financially, since the added cost of postage absorbed any gain from foreign subscriptions. To meet this problem, Douglass in June, 1858, issued an edition of *Douglass' Monthly,* for circulation in the British Isles only. By excluding advertisements and items of purely local interest he was able to decrease the size of the journal so that it could be mailed overseas profitably.[19]

Meanwhile, the struggle to keep the weekly afloat in the United States continued. With debts steadily mounting it became more and more difficult to issue the paper and in 1859 the weekly came out in a reduced size. Yet even this emergency measure was of little avail. During the first six months of 1860 the paper was "running behind its income at the rate of $25 to $30 per week," and by July the receipts had fallen "nearly to nothing" while the weekly expenses were forty-five and fifty dollars. There was no alternative but to suspend its publication. With a heavy heart Douglass announced his decision to Smith on July 2, 1860:

"You may well believe that after nearly thirteen years of effort to put the paper on a permanent basis and make it an established anti-slavery instrumentality, that I am now very sorry to give up the struggle. There is no escape and I submit. I shall hereafter only publish my monthly paper."[20]

For three years longer Douglass continued to issue the *Monthly.* Although the magazine did not exert the influence of a weekly paper, Douglass made it a powerful weapon in the battle against slavery during the most critical years of the Civil War.

Despite the trying circumstances under which he was compelled to publish his journal, his busy life as a lecturer and participant in the anti-slavery movement, Douglass' paper was so interesting and instructive that it won praise from readers at home and abroad. Only when one recalls that Douglass had never had a day's schooling when he launched his paper, had had "no regular or sound rules of grammar," and had done little reading, does the magnitude of this accomplishment become clear. He owed much to Julia Griffiths who taught him the rules of grammar and spelling, and used her blue-pencil mercilessly to perfect his writing.[21] But essentially the paper was the product of Douglass' own thinking and planning. After June 29, 1848, when the joint editorship with Martin R. Delany was dissolved, the journal was under Douglass' exclusive control. It was due primarily to his own unusual powers that he was able to supply to the anti-slavery movement the only paper other than the *Liberator* and the *Anti-Slavery Standard* which survived over a number of years.

In format and typography Douglass' paper was not very different from the other anti-slavery weeklies. Like the *Liberator*, the *Anti-Slavery Standard*, the *Anti-Slavery Bugle*, and the *Pennsylvania Freeman*, it consisted of four pages of seven columns each. The first page usually featured the full text of anti-slavery speeches in Congress or at Abolitionist conventions. Foreign reports also rated a front-page position as did reports of local, statewide, and national anti-slavery meetings. The second page was filled with editorial matter which sometimes poured over onto the next page. When Douglas was ill or too busy with lectures to write his usual editorials the page was taken over by John Thomas, Julia Griffiths, James McCune Smith, William J. Watkins, and others.[22] The third and fourth pages were generally devoted to clips from other sources, a procedure common among all ante-bellum journals, poetry, instalments of novels running serially, book reviews or "literary notices" as they were elegantly called, announcements of anti-slavery tracts, advertisements of all kinds of pills, "all sorts of horse medicines" and ointments, and the letters of the paper's regular contributors.[23]

The poems bearing such titles as "The Fugitive Wife, "The Time to Die," "Wrong Not the Laboring Poor," and "Where the Spirit of the Lord is, there is Liberty," made up for their deficiencies in literary style by their spirited devotion to the cause. Since Douglass also printed many of Whittier's anti-slavery poems, his readers did not lack for good verse.

An outstanding feature was the letters from the paper's contributors, all of whom were Negroes. J. McCune Smith's weekly letter from New York signed "Communipaw," and William J. Wilson's report from Brooklyn under the pseudonym of "Ethiope" would do credit to any paper for their literary qualities and brilliant reportage. Samuel Ringgold Ward's letters from Canada, Amos Gerry Beman's from New Haven, Loguen's from Syracuse, George T. Downing's and H. O. Wagoner's from Chicago were written in a vigorous prose style and were replete with important information on developments in their communities. To ignore these articles is to overlook a significant source of information on life among the free Negroes of the United States and Canada during the ante-bellum period.

However, it was Douglass' writings which carried the paper. He brought to his newspaper writing a remarkable feeling for words, a gift for vivid phrases, a sensitiveness to language forms and a wonderful sense of humor. But he was aware of his limitations—"To those whose lives have been mainly spent in the classic shades of long-established institutions of learning (as ours have not)"[24]—and he continually sought to overcome them. He avidly read the books, pamphlets, and tracts donated by his friends, and his pursuit of knowledge was unending. "I am this summer endeavouring to make myself a little more familiar with history," he wrote to Gerrit Smith after a lecture tour. "My ignorance of the past has long been a trouble with me."[25] The results of such studies could be seen in the columns of his paper. Keen and mature observations on national and international issues written in a virile and sonorous style featured each number. Soon contemporary journals were concluding that as an editor, Douglass was even more effective than as a speaker, and this despite the fact that he was widely recognized as one of the outstanding orators of his day. A century later, Douglass' editorials retain the same vigor and freshness, the same mature and penetrating analysis that evoked such enthusiastic approval from his readers and journalistic colleagues.

Douglass set high standards for himself and his contributors. Typographical and grammatical errors angered him and he insisted on careful writing. He was determined to prove that a paper edited by a former slave compared favorably with the best-edited weeklies of the period; and he succeeded so admirably that Negroes felt a sense of pride in the paper. White reformers pointed to it constantly as a perfect refutation of the charge of inferiority of the Negro people and an answer to the question whether fugitive slaves who came North "do or do not necessarily become thieves or paupers." *The Rising Sun,* a contemporary Negro journal, voiced the sentiments of the vast majority of the free Negro population of the North when it declared: "Frederick Douglass' ability as an editor and publisher has done more for the freedom and elevation of his race than all his platform appearances."[26]

Douglass looked upon his decision to establish a paper as one of the most important acts of his life. His editorial experiences contributed immeasurably to his own development and "intellectual expansion." The very necessity to speak out week after week on every important issue of the day compelled him to analyze events carefully and to reach conclusions based upon his own thinking. He had to study for himself, make his own decisions, and shoulder all responsibilities. As he stated in his autobiography, his work as editor caused him to read and to think and to express himself in clear and concise language. It ended his period of apprenticeship under Garrison and Phillips and made him self-reliant. These were the busiest years in his life and it was of this period that he spoke when he said: "If at any time I have said or written that which is worth remembering or repeating, I must have said such things between the years 1848-1860."[27]

No less important was the fact that as newspaper editor Douglass was brought into closer contact with the Negro people and their problems. From the day that he made his first Abolitionist speech in Nantucket until the time that he founded *The North Star* he had moved almost exclusively among white Abolitionists and only occasionally had he discussed issues confronting the Negro people other than the abolition of slavery. Now he began to build a closer relationship with other Negro leaders and with the Negro people themselves, to examine the whole range of Negro problems, and to pry into every facet of discrimination. Barely eight months after the paper had started, James McCune Smith commented:

"You will be surprised to hear me say," he wrote to Gerrit Smith, "that only since his Editorial career has he seen to become a colored man! I have read his paper very carefully and find phase after phase develop itself as regularly as in one newly born among us. The Church question, the school question, separate institutions, are questions that he enters upon and argues about as our weary but active young men thought about and argued about years ago, when we had Literary Societies...."[28]

Douglass' paper was a symbol, to the Negro people, of what could be done in the way of self-improvement and achievement, to the white people, of the wealth of talent and ability that would be contributed to the national culture if the Negro were free. Every achievement of the Negro people was reported in the journal, and talented Negroes were encouraged to use their abilities to "vindicate us at the bar of public opinion from the oft-repeated assertion that genius may not flourish under a sable brow." In August, 1850, Douglass wrote proudly:

"It is not the least among the good offices of the *North Star* that it searches out and brings to the light of day those of our despised people whose manly characters serve to reflect credit upon themselves and all with whom they are identified."[29]

Throughout its career Douglass' paper carried suggestions for the betterment of the position of the Negro people, materially and otherwise. The editor minced no words in criticizing free Negroes who were indifferent to the anti-slavery cause, voted for slaveholders, and belonged to pro-slavery churches. "Every one of us should be ashamed to consider himself free while his brother is a slave," Douglass declared. To leave the struggle against slavery to the white people was to concede that the Negroes did not wish to be free, as well as to rob freedom of its value. "For our part," he proclaimed, "we despise a freedom and equality obtained for us by others, and for which we have been unwilling to labor." He called upon Negro leaders who had left the United States for a life free of prejudice in Europe to return home, join the anti-slavery crusade, and "work faithfully in the cause of our elevation—our emancipation from every species of servitude." He knew from experience that it was "very *pleasant* to be where one can inhale a pure atmosphere," but he reminded Negroes abroad that the battle to break the chains of the slaves must receive the first consideration.[30]

In editorials Douglass continually stressed that the free Negro and the slave were chained together and must rise and fall together. He deplored the indifference to education of some free Negroes as tending to keep the slaves in chains by perpetuating slanders against the Negro people. "To strengthen prejudice against the *free*," he argued, "is to rivet the fetter more firmly on the slave population. Only show that the free colored man is low, worthless, and degraded, and a warrant for enslaving him is readily acknowledged." The free Negro must not resign himself to a position of inferiority in American society. Both for his own sake and for the sake of his brother in chains, he must allow no feeling of fright or disillusionment to stand in the way of his self-improvement. The strongest argument for emancipation was a Negro proving by endeavor and achievement that he was as good as the white man. The white man and the Negro were equals, and the white man was superior only when he outstripped the Negro in improving himself; the Negro was inferior only when he proved himself incapable of accomplishing what his white brother had accomplished. It must no longer be white lawyer and Negro wood-sawyer, white editor and Negro street-cleaner, white intelligent and

Negro ignorant, "but we must take our stand side by side with our fellow countrymen, in all the trades, arts, professions, and callings of the day."[81]

Douglass' severest editorials were reserved for Negroes who accepted discrimination instead of fighting for their equal rights. When Miss Elizabeth Greenfield, "the Black Swan," sang at concerts at which the Negro people were excluded, Douglass lashed out at her for betraying her people.[32] When Samuel Ringgold Ward lectured in the Second Presbyterian Church in Philadelphia despite that fact that the notice for the meeting announced that "the lower Saloon will be appropriated exclusively to our white fellow citizens," Douglass issued a special supplement to *The North Star* denouncing his friend's "shameful concession to the spirit of slavery and prejudice...." He wrote bitterly:

"What use will the revilers and slanderers of our people make of this concession? Why this, and none else than this: that we are sensible of our own inferiority; that we are conscious of our own unfitness for the society of white people; that it is quite proper we should be separated from them in the house of prayer; that the two varieties of the same family ought not to be allowed to occupy an equal footing; that the lower and commodious part of the church —the house of *worship—should be reserved* for white people *exclusively,* and that colored people should be separated and sent up stairs—colonized."

He closed the supplement on a prophetic note:

"The colored people of this city and country have had enough of this playing fast and loose, and the time has come, unless I mistake the signs of the times, when they will demand of those who stand forth as their advocates, an inflexible adhesion to the principle of equal and impartial freedom."[33]

It was Douglass' firm conviction that a Negro leader should take issue with every case encountered of prejudice against color. The readers of his paper knew that the editor applied this principle, for they regularly came upon lengthy accounts describing Douglass' battles against segregation. The following report in *Frederick Douglass' Paper* of an encounter between the editor and a hotel clerk in Cleveland is typical:

"At the ringing of the morning bell for breakfast, I made my way to the table, supposing myself included in the call; but I was scarcely seated, when there stepped up to me a young man, apparently much agitated, saying: 'Sir, you must leave this table.' 'And why,' said I, 'must I leave this table?'

" 'I want no controversy with you. You must leave this table.'

"I replied, that I had regularly enrolled myself as a boarder in that house; I expected to pay the same charges imposed upon others; and I came to the table in obedience to the call of the bell; and if I left the table I must know the reason. 'We will serve you in your room. It is against our rules.' 'You should have informed me of *your rules* earlier. Where are your rules? Let me see them.' 'I don't want any altercation with you. You must leave this table.' 'But have I not deported myself as a gentleman? What have I done? Is there any gentleman who objects to my being seated here?' (There was silence round the table.) 'Come, sir, come, sir, you must leave this table at once.' 'Well, sir, I cannot leave it unless you will give me a better reason than you have done for my removal.' 'Well, I'll give you a reason if you'll leave the table and go to another room.' 'That, sir, I will not do. You have invidiously selected me out of all this company, to be dragged from this table, and have thereby reflected upon me as a man and a gentleman; and the reason for this treatment shall be as public as the insult you have offered.'

"At these remarks, my carrot-headed assailant left me, *as he said,* to get help to remove me from the table. Meanwhile I called upon one of the servants (who appeared to wait upon me with alacrity) to help me to a cup of coffee, and assisting myself to some of the good things before me, I quietly and thankfully partook of my morning meal without further annoyance."[84]

The frequent appearance of such reports in Douglass' paper gave courage to large sections of the Negro population in the North and made them more determined to combat segregation wherever they met it.

Douglass' vigorous denunciation of colonization is an outstanding example of the contribution he made as an editor to clarifying problems confronting the Negro people. For some time after 1835, colonization agitation was unable to get much of a hearing in the North, as it came to be considered, to paraphrase Cornish and Garrison, merely an effort to strengthen the props of slave institutions. In the late 1840's, however, Henry Clay and the various compromise groups around him renewed the colonization program in the hope that it might lessen the tensions growing in the country over the slavery question. When Douglass founded *The North Star,* colonization agitation was again in full swing. Immediately he dedicated the journal to the battle against the colonizationists.

After reading a speech by Clay on the colonization question, Douglass set out to answer him in a long discussion printed in *The North Star* for January 28, 1848. Clay's attempt to revive the Colonization Society, he claimed, was a most dangerous threat to every Negro in America, for it might easily unsettle his plans for self-improvement "by teaching him to feel that this is not his home," dishearten and subdue his enterprise by causing him to feel that all effort at self-elevation was in vain, "that neither knowledge, temperance, patience, faith, nor virtue, can avail him anything in this land." In one paragraph, he demolished Clay's speech:

"It is an insult, an insolent and tyrannical assumption on the part of Mr. Clay, or anyone else, to tell us, or any part of the Colored people of this country, that he wishes us to go anywhere. We are at home here; and our staying here is evidence that we wish to stay here; and to tell us that he wishes us to go is an insult, which, if offered to Mr. Clay instead of the despised blacks, would subject the perpetrator of the insult to the indignation of the community. Our right to stay here is as good as that of Mr. Clay, or any manstealer in this land; and God helping us, we will maintain this right before all the world."

With the publication in *The North Star* of Douglass' answer to Henry Clay, the most effective opponent of the colonization movement made his appearance on the scene. In editorial after editorial Douglass hammered away at the theme that colonization was the "twin sister of slavery"; that the United States was the native land of the Negro; that "he, of any one has a right to the soil of this continent" having for more than two hundred years "toiled over the soil of America, under a burning sun and a driver's lash—ploughing, planting, reaping, that white men might loll in ease," and having "fought and bled for this country"; that "his attachment to the place of his birth is stronger than iron," and that those who advised the Negro to emigrate were "his worst and most deadly enemies."[35]

Douglass also advanced the concept of Negro nationhood as an argument against colonization. Individuals could and might emigrate, he conceded, but nations never. And the Negro people in the United States, he maintained, "are becoming a nation in a nation which disowns them, and for weal or for woe this nation is united."[36]

The capstone of Douglass' argument and his most useful contribution to the discussion of colonization was his claim that Negroes and whites could live and work together as equals; that prejudice against color was not invincible; that it was already giving way "and must give way"; that it was an inevitable by-product of slavery and would be overcome as soon as the Negro people were given the same opportunities as their white brothers. The free Negroes, he declared, were making rapid advances in this direction, and were being retarded by the colonizationists who strengthened prejudice against the Negro people by declaring that it was inevitable and God-ordained because of "the natural inferiority of the colored race." It was the duty of the Negro people to defeat the vicious campaign which sought to prove that they were a blight upon American civilization, to "help free their brethren, rather than leave them in chains, to go and civilize Africa." We are Americans, cried Douglass, and we want to live in America on equal terms with all other Americans. "Brethren," he appealed, "stay where you are, so long as you can stay. Stay here and worthily discharge the duties of honest men, and of good citizens."[37]

Douglass' paper also combated the doctrines of white chauvinism which provided the slaveowners with ideological weapons "proving" the "inherent supremacy" of white people, and therefore their right to be masters, and the "inherent inferiority" of Negro people, and therefore their duty to be slaves. Especially did Douglass lash out against the so-called ethnologists, anthropologists, sociologists, and historians who offered alleged proof of the "natural inferiority" of the Negro and the necessity of his filling the God-ordained role of slave to the white man. He pointed out that the ideology of "white supremacy" was as necessary to the system of chattel slavery as the slave trader, the lash, and the bloodhound, and demonstrated that the fostering of a belief in the innate inferiority of the Negro people was part of slavocracy's complex system of control. Douglass called on every Abolitionist to develop the sharpest struggle to expose the propaganda from colleges, pulpits, politicians, and press which constantly drummed out the concept of the inferiority of an entire people.[38]

Douglass himself contributed considerably to the exposure of these pseudo-scientific theories. On August 4, 1854, his paper carried the entire text of his speech at Western Reserve College. Entitled *The Claims of the Negro Ethnologically Considered,* Douglass' address demolished the theories of a number of ethnologists and anthropologists who had prostituted their science in the interests of slavery by proclaiming that the Negro was not a man. After expressing his gratitude that he who had never had a day's schooling in his life had been called to speak in the halls of a university, Douglass demonstrated that the Negro was a man and that he had a common origin with all other men. This he proved by arguments in which, as the *Ohio Observer* remarked, "he exhibited considerable knowledge and research."[39]

So wide was the interest aroused by the publication of this Address in *Frederick Douglass' Paper* that it became necessary to reprint it as a pamphlet. Distributed throughout the North and West and even in Europe, it became a powerful weapon to combat the presumed "subhumanity of Negroes" dictum of the pro-slavery ethnologists and anthropologists.

"It is one of the marvels of the age," commented the *National Era* when the Address first appeared in Douglass' paper, "that a fugitive from slavery, reared to manhood under all the weight of its depressing influences, should be the author of this able and learned Address. This fact alone is the best refutation of the atheistical fanatics, who would exclude the Negro from the pale of manhood."[40]

Douglass' paper was both a powerful tribune in the anti-slavery movement and the outstanding organ of leadership for the free Negro people of the North. It clarified basic issues confronting the Negro people; it gave them courage to carry on against innumerable obstacles, and it coordinated the struggle against slavery and for full equality. The following resolution, introduced by Dr. James McCune Smith and unanimously adopted in 1854 by the New York Literary and Productive Union, composed of Negroes, voiced the sentiments of the Negro people in the United States:

"Resolved, That we recognize in *Frederick Douglass' Paper*, the organ of the enslaved and down-trodden throughout this land—an instrument, which proves beyond gainsaying, the practicability, the safety, and the glory of Emancipation, and of *Self-Emancipation*."[41]

In the next volume we shall see how Frederick Douglass used this "organ of the enslaved and down-trodden throughout this land" in developing political parties devoted to the cause of Abolition and in changing a pro-slavery United States into an anti-slavery one.

WRITINGS AND SPEECHES OF
FREDERICK DOUGLASS

Early Years, 1841-1849

I do not go back to America to sit still, remain quiet, and enjoy ease and comfort.... I glory in the conflict, that I may hereafter exult in the victory. I know that victory is certain. I go, turning my back upon the ease, comfort, and respectability which I might maintain even here ... Still, I will go back, for the sake of my brethren. I go to suffer with them; to toil with them; to endure insult with them; to undergo outrage with them; to lift up my voice in their behalf; to speak and write in their vindication; and struggle in their ranks for the emancipation which shall yet be achieved....

FAREWELL SPEECH TO THE BRITISH PEOPLE, MARCH, 1847

PART ONE: *From 1841 to the Founding of* The North Star

THE CHURCH AND PREJUDICE, speech delivered at the Plymouth Church Anti-Slavery Society, December, 1841

At the South I was a member of the Methodist Church. When I came north, I thought one Sunday I would attend communion, at one of the churches of my denomination, in the town I was staying. The white people gathered round the altar, the blacks clustered by the door. After the good minister had served out the bread and wine to one portion of those near him, he said, "These may withdraw, and others come forward"; thus he proceeded till all the white members had been served. Then he drew a long breath, and looking out towards the door, exclaimed, "Come up, colored friends, come up! for you know *God is no respecter of persons!*" I haven't been there to see the sacraments taken since.

At New Bedford, where I live, there was a great revival of religion not long ago—many were converted and "received" as they said, "into the kingdom of heaven." But it seems, the kingdom of heaven is like a net; at least so it was according to the practice of these pious Christians; and when the net was drawn ashore, they had to set down and cull out the fish. Well, it happened now that some of the fish had rather black scales; so these were sorted out and packed by themselves. But among those who experienced religion at this time was a colored girl; she was baptised in the same water as the rest; so she thought she might sit at the Lord's table and partake of the same sacramental elements with the others. The deacon handed round the cup, and when he came to the black girl, he could not pass her, for there was the minister looking right at him, and as he was a kind of abolitionist, the deacon was rather afraid of giving him offence; so he handed the girl the cup, and she tasted. Now it so happened that next to her sat a young lady who had been converted at the same time, baptised in the same water, and put her trust in the same blessed Saviour; yet when the cup, containing the precious blood which had been shed for all, came to her, she rose in disdain, and walked out of the church. Such was the religion *she* had experienced!

Another young lady fell into a trance. When she awoke, she declared she had been to heaven. Her friends were all anxious to know what and whom she had seen there; so she told the whole story. But there was one good old lady whose curiosity went beyond that of all the others—and she inquired of the girl that had the vision, if she saw any black folks in heaven? After some hesitation, the reply was, *"Oh! I didn't go into the kitchen!"*

Thus you see, my hearers, this prejudice goes even into the church of God. And there are those who carry it so far that it is disagreeable to them even to think of going to heaven, if colored people are going there too. And whence comes it? The grand cause is slavery; but there are others less prominent; one of them is the way in which children in this part of the country are instructed to regard the blacks.

"Yes!" exclaimed an old gentleman, interrupting him—"when they behave wrong, they are told, 'black man come catch you.'"

Yet people in general will say they like colored men as well as any other, *but in their proper place!* They assign us that place; they don't let us do it for ourselves, nor will they allow us a voice in the decision. They will not allow that we have a head to think, and a heart to feel, and a soul to aspire. They treat us not as men, but as dogs—they cry "Stu-boy!" and expect us to run and do their bidding. That's the way we are liked. You degrade us, and then ask why we are degraded—you shut our mouths, and then ask why we don't speak—you close your colleges and seminaries against us, and then ask why we don't know more.

But all this prejudice sinks into insignificance in *my* mind, when compared with the enormous iniquity of the system which is its cause—the system that sold my four sisters and my brothers into bondage—and which calls in its priests to defend it even from the Bible! The slaveholding ministers preach up the divine right of the slaveholders to property in their fellow-men. The southern preachers say to the poor slave, "Oh! if you wish to be happy in time, happy in eternity, you must be obedient to your masters; their interest is yours. God made one portion of men to do the working, and another to do the thinking; how good God is! Now, you have no trouble or anxiety; but ah! you can't imagine how perplexing it is to your masters and mistresses to have so much thinking to do in your behalf! You cannot appreciate your blessings; you know not how happy a thing it is for you, that you were born of that portion of the human family which has the working, instead of the thinking to do! Oh! how grateful and obedient you ought to be to your masters! How beautiful are the arrangements of Providence! Look at your hard, horny hands—see how nicely they are adapted to the labor you have to perform! Look at our delicate fingers, so exactly fitted for our station, and see how manifest it is that God designed us to be His thinkers, and you the workers—Oh! the wisdom of God!"—I used to attend a Methodist church, in which my master was a class-leader; he would talk most sanctimoniously about the dear Redeemer, who was sent "to preach deliverance to the captives, and set at liberty them that are bruised"—he could pray at morning, pray at noon, and pray at night; yet he could lash up my poor cousin by his two thumbs, and inflict stripes and blows upon his bare back, till the blood streamed to the ground! all the time quoting scripture, for his authority, and appealing to that passage of the Holy Bible which says, "He that knoweth his master's will, and doeth it not, shall be beaten with many stripes!" Such was the amount of this good Methodist's piety.

National Anti-Slavery Standard, December 23, 1841

TO WILLIAM LLOYD GARRISON

Lynn, November 8th, 1842

Dear Friend Garrison:

The date of this letter finds me quite unwell. I have for a week past been laboring, in company with bro[ther] Charles Remond, in New Bedford, with special reference to the case of our outraged brother, George Latimer,[1] and speaking almost day and night, in public and in private; and for the reward of our labor, I have the best evidence that a great good has been done. It is said by many residents, that New Bedford has never been so favorably aroused to her anti-slavery responsibility as at present. Our meetings were characterized by that deep and solemn feeling which the importance of the cause, when properly set forth, is always calculated to awaken. On Sunday, we held three meetings in the new town hall, at the usual meeting hours, morning, afternoon, and evening. In the morning, we had quite a large meeting, at the opening of which, I occupied about an hour, on the question as to whether a man is better than a sheep. Mr. Dean then made a few remarks, and after him, Mr. Clapp of Nantucket arose and gave his testimony to the truth, as it is in anti-slavery. The meeting then adjourned, to meet again in the afternoon. I said that we held our meetings at the regular meeting hours. Truth requires me to make our afternoon meeting an exception to this remark. For long before the drawling, lazy church bells commenced sounding their deathly notes, mighty crowds were making their way to the town hall. ... After a short space, allotted to secret or public prayer, bro[ther] J. B. Sanderson arose and requested the attention of the audience to the reading of a few passages of scripture, selected by yourself in the editorial of last week. They did give their attention, and as he read the solemn and soul-stirring denunciations of Jehovah, by the mouth of his prophets and apostles, against oppressors, the deep stillness that pervaded that magnificent hall was a brilliant demonstration that the audience felt that what was read was but the reiteration of words which had fallen from the great Judge of the universe. After reading, he proceeded to make some remarks on the general question of human rights. These, too, seemed to sink deep into the hearts of the gathered multitude. Not a word was lost; it was good seed, sown in good ground, by a careful hand; it must, it will bring forth fruit.

After him, rose bro[ther] Remond, who addressed the meeting in his usual happy and deeply affecting style. When he had concluded his remarks, the meeting adjourned to meet again at an early hour in the evening. ...

The meeting met according to adjournment, at an early hour. The splendid hall was brilliantly lighted, and crowded with an earnest, listening audience, and notwithstanding the efforts of our friends before named to have them seated, a large number had to stand during the meeting, which lasted about three hours; where the standing part of the audience were, at the commencement of the meeting, there they were at the conclusion of it; no moving about with them; any place was good enough, so they could but hear. From the eminence which I occupied, I could see the entire audience; and from its appearance, I should conclude that prejudice against color was not there, at any rate, it was not to be seen by me; we were all on a level, every one took a seat just where they chose; there were neither men's side, nor women's side; white pew, nor black pew; but all seats were free, and all sides free. When the meeting was fully gathered, I had something to say, and was followed by bro[thers] Sanderson and Remond. When they had concluded their remarks, I again took the stand, and called the attention of the meeting to the case of bro[ther] George Latimer, which proved the finishing stroke of my present public speaking. On taking my seat, I was seized with a violent pain in my breast, which continued till morning, and with occasional raising of blood; this past off in about two hours, after which, weakness of breast, a cough, and shortness of breath ensued, so that now such is the state of my lungs, that I am unfit for public speaking, for the present. My condition goes harder with me, much harder than it would at ordinary times. These are certainly extraordinary times; times that demand the efforts of the humblest of our most humble advocates of our perishing and dying fellow-countrymen. Those that can but whisper freedom, should be doing even that, though they can only be heard from one side of their short fire place to the other. It is a struggle of life and death with us just now. No sword that can be used, be it never so rusty, should lay idle in its scabbard. Slavery, our enemy, has landed in our very midst, and commenced its bloody work. Just look at it; here is George Latimer a man—a brother—a husband—a father, stamped with the likeness of the eternal God, and redeemed by the blood of Jesus Christ, out-lawed, hunted down like a wild beast, and ferociously dragged through the streets of Boston, and incarcerated within the walls of Leverett-st. jail. And all this is done in Boston—liberty-loving, slavery-hating Boston—intellectual, moral, and religious Boston. And why was this—what crime had George Latimer committed? He had committed the crime of availing himself of his natural rights, in defence of which the founders of this very Boston enveloped her in midnight darkness, with the smoke proceeding from their thundering artillery. What a horrible state of things is here presented. Boston has become the hunting-ground of merciless men-hunters, and man-stealers. Henceforth we need not portray to the imagination of northern people, the flying slave making his way through thick and dark woods of the South, with white fanged blood-hounds yelping on his blood-stained track; but refer to the streets of Boston, made dark and dense by crowds of professed Christians. Take a look at James B. Gray's new pack, turned loose on the track of poor Latimer. I see the blood-thirsty animals, smelling at every corner, part with each other, and meet again; they seem to be consulting as to the best mode of coming upon their victim. Now they look sad, discouraged;—tired, they drag along, as if they were ashamed of their business, and about to give up the chase; but presently they get a sight of their prey, their eyes brighten, they become more courageous, they approach their victim unlike the common hound. They come upon him softly, wagging their tails, pretending friendship, and do not pounce upon him, until they have secured him beyond possible escape. Such is the character of James B. Gray's new pack of two-legged blood-hounds that hunted down George Latimer, and dragged him away to the Leverett-street slave prison but a few days since. We need not point to the sugar fields of Louisiana, or to the rice swamps of Alabama, for the bloody deeds of this soul-crushing system, but to the city of the pilgrims. In future, we need not uncap the bloody cells of the horrible slave prisons of Norfolk, Richmond, Mobile, and New-Orleans, and depict the wretched and forlorn condition of their miserable inmates, whose groans rend the air, pierce heaven, and disturb the Almighty; listen no longer at the snappings of the bloody slavedrivers' lash. Withdraw your attention, for a moment, from the agonizing cries coming from hearts bursting with the keenest anguish at the South, gaze no longer upon the base, cold-blooded, heartless slave-dealer of the South, who lays his iron clutch upon the hearts of husband and wife, and, with one mighty effort, tears the bleeding ligaments apart which before constituted the twain one flesh. I say, turn your attention from all this cruelty abroad, look now at home—follow me to your courts of justice—mark him who sits upon the bench. He may, or he may not—God grant he may not—tear George Latimer from a beloved wife and tender infant. But let us take a walk to the prison in which George Latimer is confined, inquire for the turn-key; let him open the large iron-barred door that leads you to the inner prison. You need go no further. Hark! Listen! hear the groans and cries of George Latimer, mingling with which may be heard the cry—my wife, my child—and all is still again.

A moment of reflection ensues—I am to be taken back to Norfolk—must be torn from a wife and tender babe, with the threat from Mr. Gray that I am to be murdered, though not in the ordinary way—not to have my head severed from my shoulders, not to be hanged—not to have my heart pierced through with a dagger—not to have my brains blown out. No, no, all these are too good for me. No: I am to be killed by inches. I know not how; perhaps by cat-hauling until my back is torn all to pieces, my flesh is to be cut with the rugged lash, and I faint; warm brine must now be poured into my bleeding wounds, and through this process I must pass, until death shall end my sufferings. Good God! save me from a fate so horrible. Hark! hear him roll in his chains; "I can die, I had rather, than go back. O, my wife! O, my child!" You have heard enough. What man, what Christian can look upon this bloody state of things without his soul swelling big with indignation on the guilty perpetrators of it, and without resolving to cast in his influence with those who are collecting the elements which are to come down in ten-fold thunder, and dash this state of things into atoms?

Men, husbands and fathers of Massachusetts—put yourselves in the place of George Latimer; feel his pain and anxiety of mind; give vent to the groans that are breaking through his fever-parched lips, from a heart emersed in the deepest agony and suffering; rattle his chains; let his prospects be yours, for the space of a few moments. Remember George Latimer in bonds as bound with him; keep in view the golden rule—"All things whatsoever ye would that men should do unto you, do ye even so to them." "In as much as ye did it unto the least of these my brethren ye have done it unto me."

Now make up your minds to what your duty is to George Latimer, and when you have made your minds up, prepare to do it and take the consequences, and I have no fears of George Latimer going back. I can sympathize with George Latimer, having myself been cast into a miserable jail, on suspicion of my intending to do what he is said to have done, viz., appropriating my own body to my use.

My heart is full, and had I my voice, I should be doing all that I am capable of, for Latimer's redemption. I can do but little in any department; but if one department is more the place for me than another, that one is before the people.

I can't write to much advantage, having never had a day's schooling in my life, nor have I ever ventured to give publicity to any of my scribbling before; nor would I now, but for my peculiar circumstances.

Your grateful friend,
Frederick Douglass

The Liberator, November 18, 1842

TO MARIA (WESTON) CHAPMAN

Cambridge, Indiana, Sept. 10th, 1843

My Dear Friend:

Your favor of August 19th informing of a meeting recently held by the Board of Managers of the Massachusetts Anti-Slavery Society, and of the subject of conversation there had, came to hand Sept. 8th at Oakland. After a careful reading, I am led to conclude from the entire tone of your very kind letter, that you labor under much misapprehension concerning the whole affair of which you write, and believing this, I think a simple statement of the facts in the case may set the matter right, and render my position fully and fairly understood by yourself and the Board you represent. I intended to have given such a statement immediately after the occurrence took place at Syracuse which gave rise to the rumors of which you speak, and was only induced not to do so by the hope that some disinterested person who had taken no part in the affair would. I now regret that I did not carry out my intention, since the matter has taken the turn it has. I am, however, glad that I noted down at the time and have now in my possession the whole facts in the case, as they transpired, and will now state them as briefly as I can.

On the 30th and 31st of July, and the 1st of August, we held an Anti-slavery Convention at Syracuse. I attended and carried it on the first two days alone, Mr. Collins having remained behind at Utica after the holding of our Anti-slavery Convention, for the purpose of holding [an] antiproperty meeting, and Mr. Bradburn had gone, to visit Gerrit Smith at Peterboro. Mr. Collins was in town during the last day of our Convention, but took little part in the Convention, being unwell. Mr. Bradburn had arrived, but had gone on to Skaneatles so I was left to carry on this meeting alone, as I had been in part in Utica, during the Convention there. On the evening of the first of August, Mr. Remond arrived. We had given up the Convention for the purpose of giving our friends opportunity to attend a collation that was given by the ladies at the anti-slavery fair. At the collation Mr. Remond was called upon to speak, he complied in a short but happy speech, after this notice was given by the President of the collation that there would be a property convention held the next day in the same house in which we had just held our anti-slavery meeting the three previous days. Very soon after this notice was given, another was given by the same individual, that

Mr. Remond and myself would hold our anti-slavery meeting in the afternoon of the same day—and in the same house where the property had just been announced to be held. I know not by whose authority this conflicting notice was given, but supposed that some one of the many who wished to hear Mr. Remond had consulted the friends of the property convention and that they had decided to give up their meeting in the afternoon to give Mr. Remond an opportunity to be heard by a large number who were most anxious to hear him. Here I left the matter—until the next day just before the hour for adjourning the morning session of the community meeting. Seeing something that indicated a non-intention on the part of our property friends to give their meeting, I arose and inquired if it was understood that there would be an anti-sl[avery] meeting there in the afternoon. At this point Mr. Collins arose, and said that there would be a property meeting in the afternoon and went on to make a speech respecting the bigotry and narrowmindedness of abolitionists, he was disappointed in them, he had found them to be as sectarian as others, here they could hold a Convention three days with regard to chattel slavery, but could have no heart in the cause of universal reform, etc. etc. To this speech Mr. Remond made a short reply in which he charged Mr. Collins with weakening the anti-slavery cause, a mere stepping stone to his own favorite theory of the right of property,[2] and expressed the belief that the Board of Managers could not sanction him as their general agent. Mr. Collins again arose, and made a long speech as he said in defence of himself in which he brought forward a number of documents some of them very complimentary of himself, and purporting to have emanated from the Board and about his sentiments making Mr. Collins' half of more value to the anti-slavery than some men's whole, etc., etc. After the reading of these he went on with his speech maintaining with great warmth and earnestness the four following propositions. I give them in his own words with the exception of their classification.

1st. The anti-slavery cause is a mere dabbling with affects.

2d. If they abolish slavery, it will only be in form, it will remain in fact.

3d. To recognize property in soil is worse than to enslave man.

4th. This universal reform movement will do more for the Slave than the anti-slavery movement.

When Mr. C. sat down I asked to be heard, for I felt that the anti-slavery cause had been wantonly assailed and by one to whom I had looked up as its warmest protector and as the meeting was professedly a free meeting, where anybody might speak whenever and whatever they pleased, I felt I was violating no rule directly nor indirectly by insisting on my right there to defend the cause which had been there assailed. As it was now far beyond the hour of adjournment and the meeting seemed inclined to adjourn, I gave way for adjournment with the understanding that I should speak in the afternoon. I went home and wrote out the remarks I intended to make. At the opening of the afternoon meeting I took the floor and after a few preliminary remarks setting the question at issue fairly before the meeting. It was not that Mr. Collins had not a right to be a property man, nor was it that he had not the right to devote one half of his time to the one, and the other half to the anti-slavery cause. No. This was the question whether it was just or honorable for Mr. Collins to labor in the one for the destruction of the other. I then read from my notes the positions of Mr. Collins and went on to reply to them when I was interrupted as being out of order. The meeting, however, insisted on my being heard, and I went on about 20 minutes, and closed my remarks by saying that if the Board of Managers did sanction the course of Mr. Collins, though I did not believe they did, I should feel it my duty to write them resigning my agency in carrying out the one hundred convention plan.[3] These, dear friend, are the facts in the case, that has given rise to the rumors you have heard.

I do not think you would have felt yourself called upon, did you know me as many others do, to have said anything to me, of the Board entitling them to my gratitude and respect. I trust I have as far as one can have, a just sense of their claims to my gratitude and respect.

With great respect,
F. Douglass

P.S. I have received a few lines from my wife asking for means to carry on household affairs. I have none to send her. Will you please see that she is provided with $25 or $30.

Excuse my writing in great haste.
F. Douglass

Anti-Slavery Collection, Boston Public Library

THE FOLLY OF OUR OPPONENTS

In a note enclosing this article, Mr. Douglass says:—"It was intended for a place in The Liberty Bell, *but my literary advantages have been so limited, that I am ill prepared to decide what is, and what is not, appropriate for such a collection. I looked exceedingly strange in my own eyes, as I sat writing. The thought of writing for a book!—and only six years since a fugitive from a Southern cornfield—caused a singular jingle in my mind."*

Dr. Dewey, in his somewhat notorious defence of American Morals, published soon after his return to this country from Europe, where he had witnessed those morals subjected to a most rigid examination, treats of the conduct of the American people with regard to prejudice and Slavery; and, in extenuation of their conduct, speaks of the existence of an *"impassable barrier"* between the white and colored people of this country, and proceeds to draw a most odious picture of the character of his colored fellow-countrymen. Mean and wicked as is this position, the Doctor assumes it; and in so doing, becomes the favorite representative of a large class of his divine order, as well as of his white fellow citizens, who, like himself, being stung to very shame by the exposures abroad of their naked inhumanity at home, strive, with fig-leaf sophistry, to cover their guilt from the penetrating eye and scorching rebukes of the Christian world.

Fortunately for the cause of truth and human brotherhood, it has reached a period, when such mean-spirited efforts tend more to advance than retard its progress. Ingenious as are the arguments of its foes, they but defeat the object they are intended to promote. Their authors, in seeking thus to cover their sins, succeed only in lighting the lamp of investigation by which their guilt is more completely exposed. It is the decree of the Supreme Ruler of the universe, that he will confound the wisdom of the crafty, and bring to naught the counsels of the ungodly; and how faithfully is his decree executed upon those who bring their worldly wisdom to cover up the guilt of the American people! Their iniquity has grown too large for its robe. When one part is covered, another, equally odious and revolting, is made to appear. The efforts of priests and politicians to stretch the garment, to suit the dimensions of this giant sin, has resulted in tearing it asunder, and leaving the monster revealed as perhaps it never was before.

When they tell the world that the Negro is ignorant, and naturally and intellectually incapacitated to appreciate and enjoy freedom, they also publish their own condemnation, by bringing to light those infamous Laws by which the Slave is compelled to live in the grossest ignorance. When they tell the world that the Slave is immoral, vicious and degraded, they but invite attention to their own depravity: for the world sees the Slave stripped, *by his accusers,* of every safeguard to virtue, even of that purest and most sacred institution of marriage. When they represent the Slave as being destitute of religious principle—as in the preceding cases—they profit nothing by the plea. In addition to their moral condemnation they brand themselves with bold and daring impiety, in making it an offence punishable with fine and imprisonment, and even death, to teach a Slave to read the will of God. When they pretend that they hold the Slave out of actual regard to the Slave's welfare, and not because of any profit which accrues to themselves, as owners, they are covered with confusion by the single fact that Virginia alone has realized, in one short year, eighteen millions of dollars from the sale of human flesh. When they attempt to shield themselves by the grossly absurd and wicked pretence that the Slave is contented and happy, and, therefore, "better off" in Slavery than he could be possessed of freedom, their shield is broken by that long and bloody list of advertisements for runaway Slaves who have left their happy homes, and sought for freedom, even at the hazard of losing their lives in the attempt to gain it. When it is most foolishly asserted by Henry Clay, and those he represents, that the freedom of the colored is incompatible with the liberty of the white people of this country, the wicked intent of its author, and the barefaced absurdity of the proposition, are equally manifest. And when John C. Calhoun and Senator Walker attempt to prove that freedom is fraught with deafness, insanity and blindness to the people of color, their whole refuge of lies is swept away by the palpable inaccuracy of the last United States Census. And when, to cap the climax, Dr. Dewey tells the people of England that the white and colored people in this country are separated by an "impassable barrier," the hundreds of thousands of mulattoes, quadroons, &c. in this country, silently but unequivocally brand him with the guilt of having uttered a most egregious falsehood.

Bad, however, as are the apologies which the American people make in defence of themselves and their "peculiar institution," I am always glad to see them. I prize them very highly, as indications of a living sense of shame, which renders them susceptible of outward influences, and which shall one day bring them to repentance. Men seldom sink so deep in sin as to rid themselves of all disposition to apologize for their iniquity;—when they do, it is quite idle to labor for their reformation. Fortunately for our brethren under the accursed yoke, the American people have not yet reached that depth; and whilst there is a sense of shame left, there is strong ground for hope. The year eighteen hundred and forty-four has produced an abundant harvest of anti-slavery discussion. Slavery and prejudice cannot endure discussion, even though such discussion be had in its favor. The light necessary to reason by, is at once too painful to the eyes of these twin-monsters of darkness to be endured. Their motto is, "Put out the light!" Thanks to Heaven, "the morning light is breaking"; our cause is onward; the efforts of our enemies, not less than the efforts of our friends, are contributing to increase the strength of that sentiment at home, as well as abroad, which is very soon to dash down the bloody altar of Slavery, and "proclaim liberty through all the land, unto all the inhabitants thereof."

Lynn, Massachusetts, U. S.
The Liberty Bell, 1845, pp. 166-172

TO WILLIAM LLOYD GARRISON

Dublin, Sept. 1, 1845

Dear Friend Garrison:

Thanks to a kind Providence, I am now safe in old Ireland, in the beautiful city of Dublin, surrounded by the kind family, and seated at the table of our mutual friend, James H. Webb, brother of the well-known Richard D. Webb.... I know it will gladden your heart to hear, that from the moment we first lost sight of the American shore, till we landed at Liverpool, our gallant steam-ship was the theatre of an almost constant discussion of the subject of slavery—commencing cool, but growing hotter every moment as it advanced. It was a great time for anti-slavery, and a hard time for slavery;—the one delighting in the sunshine of free discussion, and the other horror-stricken at its God-like approach. The discussion was general. If suppressed in the saloon, it broke out in the steerage; and if it ceased in the steerage, it was renewed in the saloon; and if suppressed in both, it broke out with redoubled energy, high upon the saloon deck, in the open, refreshing, free ocean air. I was happy.

Every thing went on nobly. The truth was being told, and having its legitimate effect upon the hearts of those who heard it. At last, the evening previous to our arrival at Liverpool, the slaveholders, convinced that reason, morality, common honesty, humanity, and Christianity, were all against them, and that argument was no longer any means of defence, or at least but a poor means, abandoned their post in debate, and resorted to their old and natural mode of defending their morality by brute force.

Yes, they actually got up a *mob*—a real American, republican, democratic, Christian mob,—and that, too, on the deck of a British steamer, and in sight of the beautiful high lands of Dungarvan! I declare, it is enough to make a slave ashamed of the country that enslaved him, to think of it. Without the slightest pretensions to patriotism, as the phrase goes, the conduct of the mobocratic Americans on board the Cambria almost made me ashamed to say I *had run away* from such a country. It was decidedly the most daring and disgraceful, as well as wicked exhibition of depravity, I ever witnessed, North or South; and the actors in it showed themselves to be as hard in heart, as venomous in spirit, and as bloody in design, as the infuriated men who bathed their hands in the warm blood of the noble Lovejoy.[4]

The facts connected with, and the circumstances leading to, this most disgraceful transaction, I will now give, with some minuteness, though I may border, at times, a little on the ludicrous.

In the first place, our passengers were made up of nearly all sorts of people, from different countries, of the most opposite modes of thinking on all subjects. We had nearly all sorts of parties in morals, religion, and politics, as well as trades, callings, and professions. The doctor and the lawyer, the soldier and the sailor, were there. The scheming Connecticut wooden clock-maker, the large, surly, New-York lion-tamer, the solemn Roman Catholic bishop, and the Orthodox Quaker were there. A minister of the Free Church of Scotland, and a minister of the Church of England—the established Christian and the wandering Jew, the Whig and the Democrat, the white and the black—were there. There was the dark-visaged Spaniard, and the light-visaged Englishman—the man from Montreal, and the man from Mexico. There were slaveholders from Cuba, and slaveholders from Georgia. We had anti-slavery singing and pro-slavery grumbling; and at the same time that Governor Hammond's Letters were being read,[5] my Narrative was being circulated.

In the midst of the debate going on, there sprang up quite a desire, on the part of a number on board, to have me lecture to them on slavery. I was first requested to do so by one of the passengers, who had become quite interested. I, of course, declined, well knowing that that was a privilege which the captain alone had a right to give, and intimated as much to the friend who invited me. I told him I should not feel at liberty to lecture, unless the captain should personally invite me to speak. Things went on as usual till between five and six o'clock in the afternoon of Wednesday, when I received an invitation from the captain to deliver an address upon the saloon deck. I signified my willingness to do so, and he at once ordered the bell to be rung and the meeting cried. This was the signal for a general excitement. Some swore I should not speak, and others that I should. Bloody threats were being made against me, if I attempted it. At the hour appointed, I went upon the saloon deck, where I was expected to speak. There was much noise going on among the passengers, evidently intended to make it impossible for me to proceed. At length, our Hutchinson friends broke forth in one of their unrivalled songs, which, like the angel of old, closed the lions' mouths, so that, for a time, silence prevailed. The captain, taking advantage of this silence, now introduced me, and expressed the hope that the audience would hear me with attention. I then commenced speaking; and, after expressing my gratitude to a kind Providence that had brought us safely across the sea, I proceeded to portray the condition of my brethren in bonds. I had not uttered five words, when a Mr. Hazzard, from Connecticut, called out, in a loud voice, "That's a lie!" I went on, taking no notice of him, though he was murmuring nearly all the while, backed up by a man from New-Jersey. I continued till I said something which seemed to cut to the quick, when out bawled Hazzard, "That's a lie!" and appeared anxious to strike me. I then said to the audience that I would explain to them the reason of Hazzard's conduct. The colored man, in our country, was treated as a being without rights. "That's a lie!" said Hazzard. I then told the audience that as almost every thing I said was pronounced lies, I would endeavor to substantiate them by reading a few extracts from slave laws. The slavocrats, finding they were now to be fully exposed, rushed up about me, with hands clenched, and swore I should not speak. They were ashamed to have American laws read before an English audience. Silence was restored by the interference of the captain, who took a noble stand in regard to my speaking. He said he had tried to please all of his passengers—and a part of them had expressed to him a desire to hear me lecture to them, and in obedience to their wishes he had invited me to speak; and those who did not wish to hear, might go to some other part of the ship. He then turned, and requested me to proceed. I again commenced, but was again interrupted—more violently than before. One slaveholder from Cuba shook his fist in my face, and said, "O, I wish I had you in Cuba!" "Ah!" said another, "I wish I had him in Savannah! We would use him up!" Said another, "I will be one of a number to throw him overboard!"

We were now fully divided into two distinct parties—those in favor of my speaking, and those against me. A noble-spirited Irish gentleman assured the man who proposed to throw me overboard, that two could play at that game, and that, in the end, he might be thrown overboard himself. The clamor went on, waxing hotter and hotter, till it was quite impossible for me to proceed. I was stopped, but the cause went on. Anti-slavery was uppermost, and the mob was never of more service to the cause against which it was directed. The clamor went on long after I ceased speaking, and was only silenced by the captain, who told the mobocrats if they did not cease their clamor, he would have them put in irons; and he actually sent for the irons, and doubtless would have made use of them, had not the rioters become orderly.

Such is but a faint outline of an AMERICAN MOB ON BOARD OF A BRITISH STEAM PACKET.

Yours, to the end of the race,
Frederick Douglass

The Liberator, September 26, 1845

TO WILLIAM LLOYD GARRISON

Dublin, Sept. 16, 1845

My dear friend Garrison:

You will see that James [Buffum] and myself are still in old Ireland....

Our hearts were all made glad by the arrival of the ever welcome Liberator and Standard, yesterday—although they bore the sad intelligence of the fate of Cassius M. Clay's press.[6] I can now remember no occurrence of mobocratic violence against the anti-slavery cause which sent such a chill over my hopes, for the moment, as the one in question. I regarded the establishment of his press in Lexington, Kentucky, as one of the most hopeful and soul-cheering signs of the times,—a star shining in darkness, beaming hope to the almost despairing bondman, and bidding him to suffer on, as the day of his deliverance is certain. But, alas! the mob has triumphed, and the star apparently gone out.

The enemy came upon Cassius at an unfortunate hour. Availing themselves of his sickness, they have succeeded against him. Yet the cause shall not suffer; the star, whose feeble light had become painful, shall yet become a sun, whose brilliant rays shall scorch, blister and burn, till slavery shall be utterly consumed. I was almost sorry to be from home, when the voice of the feeblest might be of value in concentrating public indignation against so horrible an outrage upon the freedom of the press.

We shall, however, make the most of it in this land:—the damning deed shall ring throughout these kingdoms. The base, cruel, cowardly and infernal character of that organized band of plunderers, shall be as fully revealed as I am capable of doing it. What a brilliant illustration of republican love of freedom! How the monarchs and aristocrats of the old world will tremble at the rapid march of republican freedom! How they will hide their eyes for very shame, when they think of their own tyranny, in comparison with the free and noble institutions of America,—where freedom of the press means freedom to advocate slavery, and where liberty regulated by law means slavery protected by an armed band of bloody assassins! But, thank Heaven! "Oppression shall not always reign."

Our success here is even greater than I had anticipated. We have held four glorious anti-slavery meetings—two in the Royal Exchange, and two in the Friends' meeting-house—all crowded to overflowing. Only think of our holding a meeting in the *meeting-house* of the Society of Friends! When at home, they would almost bolt us out of their yards. "Circumstances alter cases." If the Lynn Friends' meeting-house could be, by some process, placed on this side of the Atlantic, its spacious walls would probably at once welcome an anti-slavery meeting; but, as things now stand, it must be closed to humanity—lest Friends get into the mixture!

I am to lecture to-morrow evening at the Music Hall. It will hold three thousand persons, and is let for about fifty dollars a night. But its generous proprietor, Mr. Classon, has kindly agreed to let me have it free of charge.

I have attended several temperance meetings, and given several temperance addresses. Friend Haughton, Buffum and myself spoke to-day on temperance, in the very prison in which O'Connell was put. I went out last Sunday to Bootertown, and saw Father Mathew administer the pledge to about one thousand. "The cause is rolling on."

One of the most pleasing features of my visit, thus far, has been a total absence of all manifestations of prejudice against me, on account of my color. The change of circumstances, in this, is particularly striking. I go on stage coaches, omnibuses, steamboats, into the first cabins, and in the first public houses, without seeing the slightest manifestation of that hateful and vulgar feeling against me. I find myself not treated as a *color,* but as a *man*—not as a thing, but as a child of the common Father of us all.

In great haste,
Ever yours,
Frederick Douglass

The Liberator, October 10, 1845

TO WILLIAM LLOYD GARRISON

Dublin, (Great Brunswick Street,) September 29th, 1845

My dear friend Garrison:

I promised on leaving America, to keep you informed of my proceedings whilst I remained abroad. I sometimes fear I shall be compelled to break my promise, if by keeping it is meant writing letters to you fit for publication. You know one of my objects in coming here was to get a little repose, that I might return home refreshed and strengthened, ready and able to join you vigorously in the prosecution of our holy cause. But, really, if the labor of the last two weeks be a fair sample of what awaits me, I have certainly sought repose in the wrong place. I have work enough here, on the spot, to occupy every inch of my time, and every particle of my strength, were I to stay in this city a whole six months. The cause of temperance alone would afford work enough to occupy every inch of my time. I have invitation after invitation to address temperance meetings, which I am compelled to decline. How different here, from my treatment at home! In this country, I am welcomed to the temperance platform, side by side with white speakers, and am received as kindly and warmly as though my skin were white.

I have but just returned from a great Repeal meeting, held at Conciliation Hall. It was a very large meeting—much larger than usual, I was told, on account of the presence of Mr. O'Connell, who has just returned from his residence at Derrynane, where he has been spending the summer, recruiting for an energetic agitation of repeal during the present autumn. ... The meeting had been in progress for some time before I got in. When I entered, one after another was announcing the Repeal rent for the week. The audience appeared to be in deep sympathy with the Repeal movement, and the announcement of every considerable contribution was followed by a hearty round of applause, and sometimes a vote of thanks was taken for the donors. At the close of this business, Mr. O'Connell rose and delivered a speech of about an hour and a quarter long. It was a great speech, skilfully delivered, powerful in its logic, majestic in its rhetoric, biting in its sarcasm, melting in its pathos, and burning in its rebukes. Upon the subject of slavery in general, and American slavery in particular, Mr. O'Connell grew warm and energetic, defending his course on this subject. He said, with an earnestness which I shall never forget, "I have been assailed for attacking the American institution, as it is called,—Negro slavery. I am not ashamed of that attack. I do not shrink from it. I am the advocate of civil and religious liberty, all over the globe, and wherever tyranny exists, I am the foe of the tyrant; wherever oppression shows itself, I am the foe of the oppressor; wherever slavery rears its head, I am the enemy of the system, or the institution, call it by what name you will. I am the friend of liberty in every clime, class and color. My sympathy with distress is not confined within the narrow bounds of my own green island. No—it extends itself to every corner of the earth. My heart walks abroad, and wherever the miserable are to be succored, or the slave to be set free, there my spirit is at home, and I delight to dwell."

Mr. O'Connell was in his happiest mood while delivering this speech. The fire of freedom was burning in his mighty heart. He had but to open his mouth, to put us in possession of "thoughts that breathe, and words that burn." I have heard many speakers within the last four years—speakers of the first order; but I confess, I have never heard one, by whom I was more completely captivated than by Mr. O'Connell. I used to wonder how such monster meetings as those of Repeal could be held peaceably. It is now no matter of astonishment at all. It seems to me that the voice of O'Connell is enough to calm the most violent passion, even though it were already manifesting itself in a mob. There is a sweet persuasiveness in it, beyond any voice I ever heard. His power over an audience is perfect.

When he had taken his seat, a number withdrew from the Hall, and, taking advantage of the space left vacant thereby, I got quite near the platform, for no higher object than that of obtaining a favorable view of the Liberator. But almost as soon as I did so, friend Buffum had by some means (I know not what) obtained an introduction to Mr. John O'Connell, and nothing would do but I must be introduced also—an honor for which I was quite unprepared, and one from which I naturally shrunk. But Buffum; in real Yankee style, had resolved (to use a Yankee term) to "put me through" at all hazards. On being introduced to Mr. O'Connell, an opportunity was afforded me to speak; and although I scarce knew what to say, I managed to say something, which was quite well received.

The Hutchinson family have been here a week or more, and have attended two of my lectures on slavery; and here, as at home, did much by their soul-stirring songs to render the meetings interesting.

My Narrative is just published, and I have sold one hundred copies in this city. Our work goes on nobly. James and myself leave here for Wexford on Monday next. We shall probably hold two meetings there, and from thence go to Waterford, and then to Cork, where we shall spend a week or ten days. I have also engagements in Belfast, which will detain me in Ireland all of one month longer.

Much love to my anti-slavery friends.

Every one with you, through good and evil report,
The Liberator, October 24, 1845   Frederick Douglass

TO R. D. WEBB

Limerick, 10th Nov., 1845

Dear Friend:

Your letter does not inform me when the great meeting is to take place in Birmingham. I cannot therefore say whether I could attend it or not. You may however inform Mr. Cadbury that my arrangements are such as to deprive me of the pleasure of attending. I now think my best plan will be to proceed immediately to Scotland from this (joining Buffum in Dublin). As to accompanying Friend Wright—I think it unwise to do so. I by no means agree with him as to the importance of discussing in this country the disunion question, and I think our difference in this matter would prevent that harmony necessary to success. Besides, Friend Wright has created against himself prejudices which I as an abolitionist do not feel myself called upon to withstand. My mission to this land is purely an anti-slavery one, and although there are other good causes which need to be advocated, I think that my duty calls me strictly to the question of Slavery. I am qualified for this, if I am for any thing, and it would be idle for me to attempt becoming any thing else at least under present circumstances. Friend Wright is identified with doctrines for which I do not wish to seem responsible. He is truly reformer in general; I only claim to be a man of one idea. I should nevertheless be delighted to see him and talk the matter over with him.

Please remember [me] to Mrs. Webb.

Truly yours,
F. Douglass

P.S. Please write me what you think of the above conclusions.

Yours truly,
F. D.

Anti-Slavery Collection, Boston Public Library

TO THURLOW WEED

Great Brunswick Street, Dublin
December 1st, 1845

Dear Sir:

Allow me to thank you for your noble and timely defence of my conduct on board the British steamship Cambria, during her passage, 27th Aug., from Boston, U. S. to Liverpool, England; and also to thank you for the friendly manner with which you regard and treat every movement tending to improve and elevate my long enslaved and deeply injured race.

In attempting to speak on board the Cambria, I acted in accordance with a sense of duty, and with no desire to wound or injure the feelings of any one on board. My object was to enlighten such of our passengers as wished to be enlightened, and to remove the objections to emancipation and false impressions concerning slavery, which I had heard urged during our passage.

Nor should I have done this, but that our popular and gentlemanly commander, as well as a most respectable number of our passengers, gave me a pressing invitation to do so. It is clear that slavery in our country can only be abolished by creating a public opinion favorable to its abolition, and this can only be done by enlightening the public mind—by exposing the character of slavery and enforcing the great principles of Justice and Humanity against it. To do this with what ability I may possess, is plainly my duty. To shrink from doing so, on any fitting occasion, from a mere fear of giving offence to those implicated in the wickedness, would be to betray the sacred trust committed to me, and to act the part of a coward.

The question to be answered is: Had the passengers, through the Captain, a right to ask me to give them my views of slavery? To ask the question is to answer it. They had as much right to ask me my views on that subject, as those on any other subject. To deny that they had such right, would be to deny that they had the right to exchange views at all. If they had the right to ask, I had the right to answer, and to answer so as to be understood by those who wished to hear. But then, it will be said, the subject of slavery is not open to discussion. Who say so? The very men who are continually speaking and writing in its favor. But who has a right to say what subject shall or shall not be discussed on board of a British steamer? Certainly not the slaveholders of South Carolina, nor their slaveholding abettors in New-York or elsewhere. If any one has such a right, the ship's commander has. Now, all I did on the occasion in question, was in perfect agreement with the wishes of the Captain and a large number of our most respectable passengers.

The English papers have had much to say respecting the affair, and of course have in all cases taken a view favorable to myself. I say of course, not because I regard English journalists more disposed to pursue an honorable course in general than those of America; but because they are all committed against Negro slavery within their own dominions and elsewhere; and in this, whatever may be said of them in other respects, they hold a decided advantage over those of America.

The whole conduct of the Americans who took part in the mob on board the Cambria, was in keeping with the base and cowardly spirit that animated the mob in Lexington, Kentucky, which murderously undertook to extinguish the light of Cassius M. Clay's noble paper, because his denunciations of slavery were offensive to their slaveholding ears. Not being able to defend their "peculiar institution" with words, they meanly—and I may add foolishly—resort to blows, vainly thinking thus to cover up their infamy. When will they learn that all such attempts only defeat the end which they are intended to promote, as it only calls attention to an institution which can pass without condemnation, only as it passes without observation. The selfishness of the slaveholder and the horrible practices of slavery must ever excite in the true heart the deepest indignation and most absolute disgust.

"To be hated, it needs but to be seen."

Again accept my thanks, and believe me to be most gratefully,
Yours,
Frederick Douglass

The Liberator, January 16, 1845

TO WILLIAM LLOYD GARRISON

Victoria Hotel, Belfast,
January 1, 1846

My Dear Friend Garrison:

I am now about to take leave of the Emerald Isle, for Glasgow, Scotland. I have been here a little more than four months. Up to this time, I have given no direct expression of the views, feelings and opinions which I have formed, respecting the character and condition of the people in this land. I have refrained thus purposely. I wish to speak advisedly, and in order to do this, I have waited till I trust experience has brought my opinions to an intelligent maturity. I have been thus careful, not because I think what I may say will have much effect in shaping the opinions of the world, but because whatever of influence I may possess, whether little or much, I wish it to go in the right direction, and according to truth. I hardly need say that, in speaking of Ireland, I shall be influenced by prejudices in favor of America. I think my circumstances all forbid that. I have no end to serve, no creed to uphold, no government to defend; and as to nation, I belong to none. I have no protection at home, or resting-place abroad. The land of my birth welcomes me to her shores only as a slave, and spurns with contempt the idea of treating me differently. So that I am an outcast from the society of my childhood, and an outlaw in the land of my birth. "I am a stranger with thee, and a sojourner as all my fathers were." That men should be patriotic is to me perfectly natural; and as a philosophical fact, I am able to give it an *intellectual* recognition. But no further can I go. If ever I had any patriotism, or any capacity for the feeling, it was whipt out of me long since by the lash of the American soul-drivers.

In thinking of America, I sometimes find myself admiring her bright blue sky—her grand old woods—her fertile fields—her beautiful rivers—her mighty lakes, and star-crowned mountains. But my rapture is soon checked, my joy is soon turned to mourning. When I remember that all is cursed with the infernal spirit of slaveholding, robbery and wrong,—when I remember that with the waters of her noblest rivers, the tears of my brethren are borne to the ocean, disregarded and forgotten, and that her most fertile fields drink daily of the warm blood of my outraged sisters, I am filled with unutterable loathing, and led to reproach myself that any thing could fall from my lips in praise of such a land. America will not allow her children to love her. She seems bent on compelling those who would be her warmest friends, to be her worst enemies. May God give her repentance before it is too late, is the ardent prayer of my heart. I will continue to pray, labor and wait, believing that she cannot always be insensible to the dictates of justice, or deaf to the voice of humanity.

My opportunities for learning the character and condition of the people of this land have been very great. I have travelled almost from the hill of "Howth" to the Giant's Causeway, and from the Giant's Causeway to Cape Clear. During these travels, I have met with much in the character and condition of the people to approve, and much to condemn—much that has thrilled me with pleasure—and very much that has filled me with pain. I will not, in this letter, attempt to give any description of those scenes which have given me pain. This I will do hereafter. I have enough, and more than your subscribers will be disposed to read at one time, of the bright side of the picture. I can truly say, I have spent some of the happiest moments of my life since landing in this country. I seem to have undergone a transformation. I live a new life. The warm and generous co-operation extended to me by the friends of my despised race—the prompt and liberal manner with which the press has rendered me its aid—the glorious enthusiasm with which thousands have flocked to hear the cruel wrongs of my down-trodden and long-enslaved fellow-countrymen portrayed—the deep sympathy for the slave, and the strong abhorrence of the slaveholder, everywhere evinced—the cordiality with which members and ministers of various religious bodies, and of various shades of religious opinion, have embraced me, and lent me their aid—the kind hospitality constantly proffered to me by persons of the highest rank in society—the spirit of freedom that seems to animate all with whom I come in contact—and the entire absence of every thing that looked like prejudice against me, on account of the color of my skin—contrasted so strongly with my long and bitter experience in the United States, that I look with wonder and amazement on the transition. In the Southern part of the United States, I was a slave, thought of and spoken of as property. In the language of the LAW, *"held, taken, reputed and adjudged to be a chattel in the hands of my owners and possessors, and their executors, administrators, and assigns, to all intents, constructions, and purposes whatsoever."*—Brev. Digest, 224. In the Northern States, a fugitive slave, liable to be hunted at any moment like a felon, and to be hurled into the terrible jaws of slavery—doomed by an inveterate prejudice against color to insult and outrage on every hand, (Massachusetts out of the question)—denied the privileges and courtesies common to others in the use of the most humble means of conveyance—shut out from the cabins on steamboats—refused admission to respectable hotels—caricatured, scorned, scoffed, mocked and maltreated with impunity by any one, (no matter how black his heart,) so he has a white skin. But now behold the change! Eleven days and a half gone, and I have crossed three thousand miles of the perilous deep. Instead of a democratic government, I am under a monarchical government. Instead of the bright blue sky of America, I am covered with the soft grey fog of the Emerald Isle. I breathe, and lo! the chattel becomes a man. I gaze around in vain for one who will question my equal humanity, claim me as his slave, or offer me an insult. I employ a cab—I am seated beside white people—I reach the hotel—I enter the same door—I am shown into the same parlor—I dine at the same table—and no one is offended. No delicate nose grows deformed in my presence. I find no difficulty here in obtaining admission into any place of worship, instruction or amusement, on equal terms with people as white as any I ever saw in the United States. I meet nothing to remind me of my complexion. I find myself regarded and treated at every turn with the kindness and deference paid to white people. When I go to church, I am met by no upturned nose and scornful lip to tell me, *"We don't allow n——rs in here"!*

I remember, about two years ago, there was in Boston, near the southwest corner of Boston Common, a menagerie. I had long desired to see such a collection as I understood were being exhibited there. Never having had an opportunity while a slave, I resolved to seize this, my first, since my escape. I went, and as I approached the entrance to gain admission, I was met and told by the door-keeper, in a harsh and contemptuous tone, *"We don't allow n——rs in here."* I also remember attending a revival meeting in the Rev. Henry Jackson's meeting-house, at New-Bedford, and going up the broad aisle to find a seat. I was met by a good deacon, who told me, in a pious tone, *"We don't allow n——rs in here"!* Soon after my arrival in New-Bedford from the South, I had a strong desire to attend the Lyceum, but was told, *"They don't allow n——rs in here"!* While passing from New York to Boston on the steamer Massachusetts, on the night of 9th Dec. 1843, when chilled almost through with the cold, I went into the cabin to get a little warm. I was soon touched upon the shoulder, and told, *"We don't allow n——rs in here"!* On arriving in Boston from an anti-slavery tour, hungry and tired, I went into an eating-house near my friend Mr. Campbell's, to get some refreshments. I was met by a lad in a white apron, *"We don't allow n——rs in here"!* A week or two before leaving the United States, I had a meeting appointed at Weymouth, the home of that glorious band of true abolitionists, the Weston family, and others. On attempting to take a seat in the Omnibus to that place, I was told by the driver, (and I never shall forget his fiendish hate,) *"I don't allow n——rs in here"!* Thank heaven for the respite I now enjoy! I had been in Dublin but a few days, when a gentleman of great respectability kindly offered to conduct me through all the public buildings of that beautiful city; and a little afterwards, I found myself dining with the Lord Mayor of Dublin. What a pity there was not some American democratic Christian at the door of his splendid mansion, to bark out at my approach, *"They don't allow n——rs in here"!* The truth is, the people here know nothing of the republican

Negro hate prevalent in our glorious land. They measure and esteem men according to their moral and intellectual worth, and not according to the color of their skin. Whatever may be said of the aristocracies here, there is none based on the color of a man's skin. This species of aristocracy belongs pre-eminently to "the land of the free, and the home of the brave." I have never found it abroad, in any but Americans. It sticks to them wherever they go. They find it almost as hard to get rid of it as to get rid of their skins.

The second day after my arrival at Liverpool, in company with my friend Buffum, and several other friends, I went to Eaton Hall, the residence of the Marquis of Westminster, one of the most splendid buildings in England. On approaching the door, I found several of our American passengers, who came out with us in the Cambria, waiting at the door for admission, as but one party was allowed in the house at a time. We all had to wait till the company within came out. And of all the faces, expressive of chagrin, those of the Americans were pre-eminent. They looked as sour as vinegar, and bitter as gall, when they found I was to be admitted on equal terms with themselves. When the door was opened, I walked in, on an equal footing with my white fellow-citizens, and from all I could see, I had as much attention paid me by the servants that showed us through the house, as any with a paler skin. As I walked through the building, the statuary did not fall down, the pictures did not leap from their places, the doors did not refuse to open, and the servants did not say, *"We don't allow n——rs in here"!*

A happy new year to you, and all the friends of freedom.

Excuse this imperfect scrawl, and believe me to be ever and always yours,

Frederick Douglass

The Liberator, January 30, 1846

TO WILLIAM LLOYD GARRISON

Perth, (Scotland), 27th Jan. 1846

Dear Friend:

For the sake of our righteous cause, I was delighted to see, by an extract copied into the Liberator of 12th Dec. 1845, from the Delaware Republican, that Mr. A. C. C. Thompson, No. 101, Market-street, Wilmington, has undertaken to invalidate my testimony against the slaveholders, whose names I have made prominent in the narrative of my experience while in slavery.

Slaveholders and slave-traders never betray greater indiscretion, than when they venture to defend themselves, or their system of plunder, in any other community than a slaveholding one. Slavery has its own standards of morality, humanity, justice, and Christianity. Tried by that standard, it is a system of the greatest kindness to the slave—sanctioned by the purest morality—in perfect agreement with justice—and, of course, not inconsistent with Christianity. But, tried by any other, it is doomed to condemnation. The naked relation of master and slave is one of those monsters of darkness, to whom the light of truth is death! The wise ones among the slaveholders know this, and they studiously avoid doing anything, which, in their judgment, tends to elicit truth. They seem fully to understand, that their safety is in their silence. They may have learned this Wisdom from Junius, who counselled his opponent, Sir William Draper, when defending Lord Granby, never to attract attention to a character, which would only pass without condemnation, when it passed without observation.

I am now almost too far away to answer this attempted refutation by Mr. Thompson. I fear his article will be forgotten, before you get my reply. I, however, think the whole thing worth reviving, as it is seldom we have so good a case for dissection. In any country but the United States, I might hope to get a hearing through the columns of the paper in which I was attacked. But this would be inconsistent with American usage and magnanimity. It would be folly to expect such a hearing. They might possibly advertise me as a runaway slave, and share the reward of my apprehension; but on no other condition would they allow my reply a place in their columns.

In this, however, I may judge the "Republican" harshly. It may be that, having admitted Mr. Thompson's article, the editor will think it but fair—Negro though I am—to allow my reply an insertion.

In replying to Mr. Thompson, I shall proceed as I usually do in preaching the slaveholders' sermon,—dividing the subject under two general heads, as follows:—

1st. The statement of Mr. Thompson, in confirmation of the truth of my narrative.

2ndly. His denials of its truthfulness.

Under the first, I beg Mr. Thompson to accept my thanks for his full, free and unsolicited testimony, in regard to my identity. There now need be no doubt on that point, however much there might have been before. Your testimony, Mr. Thompson, has settled the question forever. I give you the fullest credit for the deed, saying nothing of the motive. But for you, sir, the pro-slavery people in the North might have persisted, with some show of reason, in representing me as being an imposter—a free Negro who had never been south of Mason & Dixon's line—one whom the abolitionists, acting on the jesuitical principle, that the end justifies the means, had educated and sent forth to attract attention to their faltering cause. I am greatly indebted to you, sir, for silencing those truly prejudicial insinuations. I wish I could make you understand the amount of service you have done me. You have completely tripped up the heels of your pro-slavery friends, and laid them flat at my feet. You have done a piece of anti-slavery work, which no anti-slavery man could do. Our cautious and truth-loving people in New England would never have believed this testimony, in proof of my identity, had it been borne by an abolitionist. Not that they really think an abolitionist capable of bearing false witness intentionally; but such persons are thought fanatical, and to look at every thing through a distorted medium. They will believe you—they will believe a slaveholder. They have, some how or other, imbibed (and I confess strangely enough) the idea that persons such as yourself are dispassionate, impartial and disinterested, and therefore capable of giving a fair representation of things connected with slavery. Now, under these circumstances, your testimony is of the utmost importance. It will serve to give effect to my exposures of slavery, both at home and abroad. I hope I shall not administer to your vanity when I tell you that you seem to have been raised up for this purpose! I came to this land with the highest testimonials from some of the most intelligent and distinguished abolitionists in the United States; yet some here have entertained and expressed doubt as to whether I have ever been a slave. You may easily imagine the perplexing and embarrassing nature of my situation, and how anxious I must have been to be relieved from it. You, sir, have relieved me. I now stand before both the American and British public, endorsed by you as being just what I have ever represented myself to be—to wit, an *American slave.*

You say, "I knew this recreant slave by the name of Frederick Bailey" (instead of Douglass). Yes, that was my name; and leaving out the term recreant, which savors a little of bitterness, your testimony is direct and perfect—just what I have long wanted. But you are not yet satisfied. You seem determined to bear the most ample testimony in my favor. You say you knew me when I lived with Mr. Covey.—"And with most of the persons" mentioned in my narrative, "you are intimately acquainted." This is excellent. Then Mr. Edward Covey is not a creature of my imagination, but really did, and may yet exist.

You thus brush away the miserable insinuation of my northern pro-slavery enemies, that I have used fictitious not real names. You say—"Col. Lloyd was a wealthy planter. Mr. Gore was once an overseer for Col. Lloyd, but is now living near St. Michael's, is respected, and [you] believe he is a member of the Methodist Episcopal Church. Mr. Thomas Auld is an honorable and worthy member of the Methodist Episcopal Church. Mr. Covey, too, is a member of the Methodist Church, and all that can be said of him is, that he is a good Christian," &c., &c. Do allow me, once more, to thank you for this triumphant vindication of the truth of my statements; and to show you how highly I value your testimony, I will inform you that I am now publishing a second edition of my narrative in this country, having already disposed of the first. I will insert your article with my reply as an appendix to the edition now in progress. If you find any fault with my frequent thanks, you may find some excuse for me in the fact, that I have serious fears that you will be but poorly thanked by those whose characters you have felt it your duty to defend. I am almost certain they will regard you as running before you were sent, and as having spoken when you should have been silent. Under these trying circumstances, it is evidently the duty of those interested in your welfare to extend to you such words of consolation as may ease, if not remove, the pain of your sad disappointment. But enough of this.

Now, then, to the second part—or your denials. You are confident I did not write the book; and the reason of your confidence is, that when you knew me, I was an unlearned and rather an ordinary Negro. Well, I have to admit I was rather an ordinary Negro when you knew me, and I do not claim to be a very extraordinary one now. But you knew me under very unfavorable circumstances. It was when I lived with Mr. Covey, the Negro-breaker, *and member of the Methodist Church.* I had just been living with master Thomas Auld, where I had been reduced by hunger. Master Thomas did not allow me enough to eat. Well, when I lived with Mr. Covey, I was driven so hard, and whipt so often, that my soul was crushed and my spirits broken. I was a mere wreck. The degradation to which I was then subjected, as I now look back to it, seems more like a dream than a horrible reality. I can scarcely realize how I ever passed through it, without quite losing all my moral and intellectual energies. I can easily understand that you sincerely doubt if I wrote the narrative; for if any one had told me, seven years ago, I should ever be able to write such a one, I should have doubted as strongly as you now do. You must not judge me now by what I then was—a change of circumstances has made a surprising change in me. Frederick Douglass, the *freeman*, is a very different person from Frederick Bailey, (my former name), the *slave*. I feel myself almost a new man—freedom has given me new life. I fancy you would scarcely know me. I think I have altered very much in my general appearance, and know I have in my manners. You remember when I used to meet you on the road to St. Michaels, or near Mr. Covey's lane gate, I hardly dared to lift my head, and look up at you. If I should meet you now, amid the free hills of old Scotland, where the ancient "black Douglass" once met his foes, I presume I might summon sufficient fortitude to look you full in the face; and were you to attempt to make a slave of me, it is possible you might find me almost as disagreeable a subject, as was the Douglass to whom I have just referred. Of one thing, I am certain—you would see *a great change* in me!

I trust I have now explained away your reason for thinking I did not write the narrative in question.

You next deny the existence of such cruelty in Maryland as I reveal in my narrative; and ask, with truly marvellous simplicity, "could it be possible that charitable, feeling men could murder human beings with as little remorse as the narrative of this infamous libeller would make us believe; and that the laws of Maryland, which operate alike upon black and white, bond and free, could permit such foul murders to pass unnoticed?" "No," you say, "it is impossible." I am not to determine what charitable, feeling men can do; but, to show what Maryland slaveholders actually do, their charitable feeling is to be determined by their deeds, and not their deeds by their charitable feelings. The cowskin makes as deep a gash in my flesh, when wielded by a professed saint, as it does when wielded by an open sinner. The deadly musket does as fatal execution when its trigger is pulled by Austin Gore, the Christian, as when the same is done by Beal Bondly, the infidel. The best way to ascertain what those charitable, feeling men can do, will be to point you to the laws made by them, and which you say operate alike upon the white and the black, the bond and the free. By consulting the statute laws of Maryland, you will find the following: — "Any slave for rambling in the night, or riding horses in the day time without leave, or running away, may be punished by whipping, cropping, branding in the cheek, or otherwise—not rendering him unfit for labor."—p. 337.

Then another:—"Any slave convicted of petty treason, murder, or wilful burning of dwelling-houses, may be sentenced to have the right hand cut off, to be hanged in the usual way—his head severed from his body—the body divided into four quarters, and the head and quarters set up in the most public place where such act was committed."—page 190.

Now, Mr. Thompson, when you consider with what ease a slave may be convicted of any one or all of these crimes, how bloody and atrocious do these laws appear! Yet, sir, they are but the breath of those pious and charitable feeling men, whom you would defend. I am sure I have recorded in my narrative, nothing so revolting cruel, murderous, and infernal, as may be found in your own statute book.

You say that the laws of Maryland operate alike upon the white and black, the bond and free. If you mean by this, that the parties named are all equally protected by law, you perpetrate a falsehood as big as that told by President Polk in his inaugural address. It is a notorious fact, even on this side the Atlantic, that a black man cannot testify against a white in any court in Maryland, or any other slave State. If you do not know this, you are more than ordinarily ignorant, and are to be pitied rather than censured. I will not say "that the detection of this falsehood proves all you have said to be false"—for I wish to avail myself of your testimony, in regard to my identity,—but I will say, you have made yourself very liable to suspicion.

I will close these remarks by saying, your positive opposition to slavery is fully explained, and will be well understood by anti-slavery men, when you say the evil of the system does not fall upon the slave, but the slaveholder. This is like saying that the evil of being burnt is not felt by the person burnt, but by him who kindles up the fire about him.

Frederick Douglass.

The Liberator, February 27, 1846

TO FRANCIS JACKSON

Royal Hotel Dundee, Scotland, 29th Jan. 1846

My dear friend Jackson:

I have been promising myself the pleasure of sending you a line from this side the sea, but have been compelled to deny myself in consequence of immediate and pressing engagements here. If you demand an apology for the liberty I am now about to take, I beg you to do what I feel confident you are seldom inclined to do—namely, look over the many acts of kindness you have performed toward myself and the people with whom I am identified. These acts justify me in thinking you will not object to having a line from me. From the first day I stepped out of obscurity on the anti-slavery platform at Nantucket to the day I stepped on the deck of the Cambria for these shores you stood by me to encourage, strengthen, and defend me from the assaults of my foes, and the foes of my race. I will not trouble you with any eulogy, for I know such would be disagreeable to your ears, but you must allow me to tell you that your acts are not forgotten. When I was a stranger, rough, unpolished, just from the bellows-handle in Richmond's brass foundry in New Bedford, when I was scarce able to write two sentences of the English language correctly, you took me into your drawing room, welcomed me to your table, put me in your best bed, and treated me in every way as an equal brother at a time when to do so was to expose yourself to the hot displeasure of nearly all your neighbours. These things I still remember, and it affords me great pleasure to speak of them. Pardon me for reminding you of these things now.

I am now as you will perceive by the date of this letter in Scotland, almost every hill, river, mountain and lake of which has been made classic by the heroic deeds of her noble sons. Scarcely a stream but has been poured into song, or a hill that is not associated with some fierce and bloody conflict between liberty and slavery. I had a view the other day of what are called the Grampion mountains that divide eastern Scotland from the west. I was told that here the ancient crowned heads used to meet, contend and struggle in deadly conflict for supremacy, causing those grand old hills to run blood-warming cold steel in the others heart. My soul sickens at the thought, yet I see in myself all those elements of character which were I to yield to their promptings might lead me to deeds as bloody as those at which my soul now sickens and from which I now turn with disgust and shame. Thank God liberty is no longer to be contended for and gained by instruments of death. A higher, a nobler, a mightier than carnal weapon is placed into our hands—one which hurls defiance at all the improvements of carnal warfare. It is the righteous appeal to the understanding and the heart—with this we can withstand the most fiery of all the darts of perdition itself. I see that America is boasting of her naval, and military power—let her boast—she may build her walls and her forts making them proof against ball and bomb. But while there is a single voice in her midst to charge home upon her the duty of emancipation, neither her army nor her navy can protect her from the gnawing of a guilty conscience.

I am travelling in company with my good friend James N. Buffum. Our meetings here have been of the most soul cheering character. The present position of the free Church in Scotland makes it important to expend as much labor here as possible. You know they sent delegates to the United States to raise money to build their churches and to pay their ministers. They succeeded in getting about four thousand pounds sterling. Well, our efforts are directed to making them disgorge their ill-gotten gain—return it to the Slaveholders. Our rallying cry is "No union with Slaveholders and send back the blood-stained money." Under these rallying cries, old Scotland boils like a pot. I half think if the free Church had for a moment supposed that her conduct would have been arraigned before the Scottish people by thorough Garrisonians as H. C. Wright, James N. Buffum and myself, she would never have taken the money. She thought to get the gold and nobody see her. It was a sad mistake. It would indeed be a grand anti-slavery triumph if we could get her to send back the money. It would break upon the confounded Slaveholders and their [allies] like a clap from the sky. We shall continue to deal our blows upon them—crying out disgorge—disgorge—disgorge your horrid plunder and to this cry the great mass of the people have cried Amen, Amen.

I have disposed of nearly all the first Edition of my Narrative and am publishing a second which will be out about the sixteenth of February. I realize enough from it to meet my expenses. I shall probably remain in Scotland till the middle of March. I shall then proceed to England, as I have not yet delivered a single lecture on Slavery in that country. It is quite an advantage to be a n——r here. I find I am hardly black enough for British taste, but by keeping my hair as woolly as possible I make out to pass for at least for half a Negro at any rate. My

good friend Buffum finds the tables turned upon him here completely—
the people lavish nearly all their attention on the Negro. I can easily
understand that such a state of things would greatly embarrass a person
with less sense than he, but he stems the current thus far nobly. I have
received letters from America expressing fears that I may be spoiled by
the attention which I am receiving—well 'tis possible—but if I thought
it probable, the next steamer should bring me home to encounter again
the kicks and cuffs of pro-slavery. Indeed I shall rejoice in the day that
shall see me again by your side battling the enemy, and I should rejoice
in it though I were to be subjected to all the regulations of color-phobia
with which we used [to] encounter. I glory in the fight as well as in the
victory. Make my love to all your family.

Gratefully yours,
Frederick Douglass

Anti-Slavery Collection, Boston Public Library

TO RICHARD D. WEBB

Dundee, February 10, 1846

Dear Friend:

We held a very good meeting here last night, crowded to overflowing
with a people whose influence cannot but be felt by the free Church. Our
faithful dealing with the Church has at length had the effect to compel
them to a defense of their conduct. They have until a few days since
affected to despise our efforts, deeming this the best mode of silencing
and defeating our exposures. They now see we are not to be put down
by such cunning. Their newspaper, the Dundee *Warden,* has attempted
to ward off our blows by attacking us personally, denouncing us as
strangers, unknown to respectable people in this country, but unfortunately for this purpose they say in the next place we are in the pay of
the establishment, sent for and hired by them. Thus they give us a good
reputation by associating us with persons against whose moral characters
they dare not utter a single word. The agitation goes nobly on. All
this region is in a ferment. The very boys in the street are singing out
"Send back that money."[7] I am informed this morning by the Dundee
Courier that the St. Peter's session have unanimously recommended the
sending back the money. I meet many free Church people who are

anxious to have the money sent back. I am certain that the people are right on this point. If the money is not sent back it will be the fault of their leaders. We shall continue with unabated zeal to sound the alarm—the people shall be informed. James and myself leave here at one o'clock today for Arbroth where we hold a meeting this evening. There the people are wide awake. This battling is rather unfavorable to the sale of my book, but the cause first, everything else afterwards. My kind regards to Mrs. W. and all inquiring friends.

Yours truly,
Frederick Douglass

Anti-Slavery Collection, Boston Public Library

TO WILLIAM LLOYD GARRISON

Montrose, [Scotland], February 26, 1846

My dear Friend Garrison:

In my letter to you from Belfast, I intimated my intention to say something more about Ireland; and although I feel like fulfilling my promise, the *Liberator* comes to me so laden with foreign correspondence, that I feel some hesitancy about increasing it. I shall, however, send you this, and if it is worth a place in your columns, I need not tell you to publish it. It is the glory of the *Liberator,* that in it the oppressed of every class, color and clime, may have their wrongs fully set forth, and their rights boldly vindicated. Your brave assertion of its character in your last defense of free discussion, has inspired me with a fresh love for the *Liberator.* Though established for the overthrow of the accursed slave system, it is not insensible to other evils that afflict and blast the happiness of mankind. So also, though I am more closely connected and identified with one class of outraged, oppressed and enslaved people, I cannot allow myself to be insensible to the wrongs and sufferings of any part of the great family of man. I am not only an American slave, but a man, and as such, am bound to use my powers for the welfare of the whole human brotherhood. I am not going through this land with my eyes shut, ears stopped, or heart steeled. I am seeking to see, hear and feel, all that may be seen, heard and felt; and neither the attentions I am receiving here, nor the connections I hold to my brethren in bonds, shall prevent my disclosing the results of my observation. I believe that the sooner the wrongs of the whole human family are made known, the sooner those wrongs will be reached. I had heard much of the misery and wretchedness of the Irish people, previous to leaving the United States, and was prepared to witness much on my arrival in Ireland. But I must confess, my experience has convinced me that the half has not been told. I supposed that much that I heard from the American press on this subject was mere exaggeration, resorted to for the base purpose of impeaching the characters of British philanthropists, and throwing a mantle over the dark and infernal character of American slavery and slaveholders. My opinion has undergone no change in regard to the latter part of my supposition, for I believe a large class of writers in America, as well as in this land, are influenced by no higher motive than that of covering up our national sins, to please popular taste, and satisfy popular prejudice; and thus many have harped upon the wrongs of Irishmen, while in truth they care no more about Irishmen, or the wrongs of Irishmen, than they care about the whipped, gagged, and thumb-screwed slave. They would as willingly sell on the auction-block an Irishman, if it were popular to do so, as an African. For heart, such men have adamant—for consciences, they have public opinion. They are a stench in the nostrils of upright men, and a curse to the country in which they live. The limits of a single letter are insufficient to allow any thing like a faithful description of those painful exhibitions of human misery, which meet the eye of a stranger almost at every step. I spent nearly six weeks in Dublin, and the scenes I there witnessed were such as to make me "blush, and hang my head to think myself a man." I speak truly when I say, I dreaded to go out of the house. The streets were almost literally alive with beggars, displaying the greatest wretchedness—some of them mere stumps of men, without feet, without legs, without hands, without arms—and others still more horribly deformed, with crooked limbs, down upon their hands and knees, their feet lapped around each other, and laid upon their backs, pressing their way through the muddy streets and merciless crowd, casting sad looks to the right and left, in the hope of catching the eye of a passing stranger—the citizens generally having set their faces against giving to beggars. I have had more than a dozen around me at one time, men, women and children, all telling a tale of woe which would move any but a heart of iron. Women, barefooted and bareheaded, and only covered by rags which seemed to be held together by the very dirt and filth with which they were covered—many of these had infants in their arms, whose emaciated forms, sunken eyes and pallid cheeks, told too plainly that they had nursed till they had nursed in vain. In such a group you may hear all forms of appeal, entreaty, and expostulation. A half a dozen voices have broken upon my ear at once: "Will your honor please to give me a penny to buy some bread?" "May the Lord bless you, give the poor old woman a little sixpence." "For the love of God, leave us a few pennies—we will divide them amongst us." "Oh! my poor child, it must starve, for God's sake give me a penny. More power to you! I know your honor will leave the poor creature something. Ah, do! ah, do! and I will pray for you as long as I live." For a time I gave way to my feelings, but reason reminded me that such a course must only add another to the already long list of beggars, and I was often compelled to pass, as if I heeded not and felt not. I fear it had a hardening effect upon my heart, as I found it much easier to pass without giving to the last beggar, than the first. The spectacle that affected me most, and made the most vivid impression on my mind, of the extreme poverty and wretchedness of the poor of Dublin, was the frequency with which I met little children in the street at a late hour of the night, covered with filthy rags, and seated upon cold stone steps, or in corners, leaning against brick walls, fast asleep, with none to look upon them, none to care for them. If they have parents, they have become vicious, and have abandoned them. Poor creatures! they are left without help, to find their way through a frowning world—a world that seems to regard them as intruders, and to be punished as such. God help the poor! An infidel might ask, in view of these facts, with confusing effect—Where is your religion that takes care for the poor—for the widow and fatherless—where are its votaries—what are they doing? The answer to this would be, if properly given, wasting their energies in useless debate on hollow creeds and points of doctrine, which, when settled, neither make one hair white nor black. In conversation with some who were such rigid adherents to their faith that they would scarce be seen in company with those who differed from them in any point of their creed, I have heard them quote the text in palliation of their neglect, "The poor shall not cease out of the land"! During my stay in Dublin, I took occasion to visit the huts of the poor in its vicinity—and of all places to witness human misery, ignorance, degradation, filth and wretchedness, an Irish hut is pre-eminent. It seems to be constructed to promote the very reverse of every thing like domestic comfort. If I were to describe one, it would appear about as follows: Four mud walls about six feet high, occupying a space of ground about ten feet square, covered or thatched with straw—a mud chimney at one end, reaching about a foot above the roof—without apartments or divisions of any kind—without floor, without windows, and sometimes without a chimney—a piece of pine board laid on the top of a box or an old chest—a pile of straw covered with dirty garments, which it would puzzle any one to determine the original part of any one of them—a picture representing the crucifixion of Christ, pasted on the most conspicuous place on the wall—a few broken dishes stuck up in a corner—an iron pot, or the half of an iron pot, in one corner of the chimney—a little peat in the fireplace, aggravating one occasionally with a glimpse of fire, but sending out very little heat—a man and his wife and five children, and a pig. In front of the door-way, and within a step of it, is a hole three or four feet deep, and ten or twelve feet in circumference; into this hole all the filth and dirt of the hut are put, for careful preservation. This is frequently covered with a green scum, which at times stands in bubbles, as decomposition goes on. Here you have an Irish hut or cabin, such as millions of the people of Ireland live in. And some live in worse than these. Men and women, married and single, old and young, lie down together, in much the same degradation as the American slaves. I see much here to remind me of my former condition, and I confess I should be ashamed to lift up my voice against American slavery, but that I know the cause of humanity is one the world over. He who really and truly feels for the American slave, cannot steel his heart to the woes of others; and he who thinks himself an abolitionist, yet cannot enter into the wrongs of others, has yet to find a true foundation for his anti-slavery faith. But, to the subject.

The immediate, and it may be the main cause of the extreme poverty and beggary in Ireland, is intemperance. This may be seen in the fact that most beggars drink whiskey. The third day after landing in Dublin, I met a man in one of the most public streets, with a white cloth on the upper part of his face. He was feeling his way with a cane in one hand, and the other hand was extended, soliciting aid. His feeble step and singular appearance led me to inquire into his history. I was informed that he had been a very intemperate man, and that on one occasion he was drunk, and lying in the street. While in this state of insensibility, a hog with its fangs tore off his nose, and a part of his face! I looked under the cloth, and saw the horrible spectacle of a living man with the face of a skeleton. Drunkenness is still rife in Ireland. The temperance cause has done much—is doing much—but there is much more to do, and, as yet, comparatively few to do it. A great part of the

Roman Catholic clergy do nothing about it, while the Protestants may be said to hate the cause. I have been frequently advised to have nothing to do with it, as it would only injure the anti-slavery cause. It was most consoling to me to find that those persons who were most interested in the anti-slavery cause in the United States, were the same that distinguished themselves as the truest and warmest advocates of temperance and every other righteous reform at home. It was a pleasure to walk through the crowd with gentlemen such as the Webbs, Allens and Haughtons, and find them recognized by the multitude as the friends of the poor. My sheet is full.

Always yours,
Frederick Douglass

The Liberator, March 27, 1846

TO MARIA (WESTON) CHAPMAN

Kilmarnarck, Scotland, 29th March, 1846

My Dear Madam:

I take up my pen to thank you for the *Liberty Bell* and the kind note which you were pleased to send me by the Cambria. I have not yet found time to read the *Liberty Bell* but hope to do so soon. My time is greatly taken up with immediate engagements growing necessarily out of my present contact with friends here. I find that in order to make my visit of service to our sacred cause at home, I must as far as possible concentrate my strength upon those circles in whose midst I find myself placed. I am trying to preach and practise a genuine anti-slavery life, turning neither to the right or left, and I think not without success. I think you may safely calculate on seeing some proof of this at your next Bazaar. At the suggestion of R. D. Webb I have inserted an appeal in behalf of the Bazaar in my Narrative, so that wherever the Narrative goes there also goes an appeal in behalf of the old organized Antislavery Bazaar. One of the first objects in my lectures has been to make that Bazaar prominent by increasing its means. I have done so from no sordid motive, but because I believe it to be a powerful instrument in affording means to carry on our important anti-slavery machinery. I say this the more freely because though I consider myself as forming a humble part of that machinery, I have never received any pecuniary aid directly from it. I have never absolutely needed any such aid from it. I have ever managed to get on, and keep in the field with very little means, lived in a small house, paid a small rent, indulged in no luxuries, glad to get the common necessaries of life and have followed on with a glad heart and willing mind in the thin but brave ranks of our noble pioneer William Lloyd Garrison. Just before leaving the United States for this country, my warm and excellent friend J. N. Buffum, aware of my poverty, stepped forward with his characteristic liberality and kindly offered to collect a sufficient sum to pay my passage to this land. He tried and succeeded in getting 60 dollars, just two dollars short of my expenses in the steerage. I brought with me three hundred and fifty dollars, money which I had saved from the sale of my Narrative. And thus far I have had [no] reason to complain, having already disposed of 2000 copies. I have mentioned these facts and made these remarks because I have felt somewhat grieved to see by a letter from you to Mr. R. G. Webb of Dublin that you betray a want of confidence in me as a man, and an abolitionist, utterly inconsistent with all the facts in the history of my connection with the anti-slavery enterprise. In that letter you were pointing out to Mr. Webb the necessity of his keeping a watch on myself and friend Mr. Buffum, but as Mr. Buffum *was rich and I poor* while there was little danger but Mr. Buffum would stand firm, I might be bought up by the London committee.[8] Now, dear Madam, you do me great injustice by such comparison. They are direct insinuations and when whispered in the ear of a stranger to whom I look up as a friend, they are very embarrassing. Up to the time of hearing Mr. Webb read that letter, I supposed I shared your confidence in common with that of other members of the committee at Boston. I am disappointed. I can assure you, Dear Madam, that you have mistaken me altogether if you suppose that the love of money or the hate of poverty will drive me from the ranks of the old Antislavery Society. But had I no more confidence in them than you seem to have in me, I would not take a second breath before leaving them. I have withstood the allurements of New Organization Liberty party, and no organization at home.[9] Why should I not withstand the London committee? You have trusted me or seemed to do so at home. Why distrust me or seem to do so abroad? Of one thing I am certain, and that is I never gave you any just cause to distrust me, and if I am to be watched over for evil rather than for good by my professed friends, I can say with propriety, save me from my friends, and I will take care of my enemies. Had you, kind friend, previous to my leaving America, given me face to face that advice and friendly counsel which your long experience and superior wisdom has richly enabled you to do, or written to me a kind letter, as did my friend Mr. Phillips, warning me against the London committee, my feelings toward you as to him would be those of ardent gratitude. If you wish to drive me from the Antislavery Society, put me under overseership and the work is done. Set some one to watch over me for evil and let them be so simple minded as to inform me of their office, and the last blow is struck.

I have said what I now have because I wish you to know just how I feel toward you. I wish to be candid with my friends. It would have been quite easy to have passed the matter over had you not sent me the *Liberty Bell* and made it my duty to write to you. When I parted from you at the anti-slavery office on the morning of the 16 August 1845, I felt on leaving that you expected a faithful discharge of my duties abroad. I went forth feeling myself armed with the confidence reposed in me by yourself and the Board generally, resolved to do my duty. And although not sustained as I supposed myself to be, I can thus far challenge the strictest scrutiny into all my movements. I have neither compromised myself nor the character of my friends. But enough.

The cause goes nobly on. Our efforts—that is the efforts of friends Wright and Buffum and my own have been mainly directed toward exposing the conduct of the free Church of Scotland in holding fellowship with Slaveholders, and taking Slave money to build free Churches. The anti-slavery committee at Glasgow have succeeded in getting George Thompson to join us in an effort to get the free Church to send back the money.

Very respectfully yours,
Frederick Douglass

Anti-Slavery Collection, Boston Public Library

TO HORACE GREELEY

Glasgow (Scotland), April 15, 1846

My Dear Sir:

I never wrote nor attempted to write a letter for any other than a strictly anti-slavery press; but being greatly encouraged by your magnanimity, as shown in copying my letter written from Belfast, Ireland, to the *Liberator* at Boston, I venture to send you a few lines, direct from my pen.

I know not how to thank you for the deep and lively interest you have been pleased to take in the cause of my long neglected race, or in what language to express the gratification I feel in witnessing your unwillingness to lend your aid to "break a bruised reed," by adding your weight to the already insupportable burden to crush, the feeble though virtuous efforts of one who is laboring for the emancipation of a people, who, for two long centuries, have endured, with the utmost patience, a bondage, one hour of which, in the graphic language of the immortal Jefferson, is worse than ages of that which your fathers rose in rebellion to oppose.[10]

It is such indications on the part of the press—which, happily, are multiplying throughout all the land—that kindle up within me an ardent hope that the curse of slavery will not much longer be permitted to make its iron foot-prints in the lacerated hearts of my sable brethren, or to spread its foul mantle of moral blight, mildew and infamy, over the otherwise noble character of the American people.

I am very sorry to see that some of your immediate neighbors are very much displeased with you, for this act of kindness to myself, and the cause of which I am an humble advocate; and that an attempt has been made, on the part of some of them, by misrepresenting my sayings, motives and objects in this country, to stir up against me the already too bitter antipathy of the American people. I am called, by way of reproach, a runaway slave. As if it were a crime—an unpardonable crime—for a man to take his inalienable rights! If I had not run away, but settled down in the degrading arms of slavery, and made no effort to gain my freedom, it is quite probable that the learned gentlemen, who now brand me with being a miserable runaway slave, would have adduced the fact in proof of the Negro's adaptation to slavery, and his utter unfitness for freedom! *"There's no pleasing some people."* But why should Mr. James Brooks feel so much annoyed by the attention shown me in this country, and so anxious to excite against me the hatred and jealousy of the American people? I can very readily understand why a slaveholder—a trader in slaves—one who has all his property in human flesh, blinded by ignorance as to his own best interest, and under the dominion of violent passions engendered by the possession of discretionary and irresponsible power over the bodies and souls of his victims—

accustomed to the inhuman sight of men and women sold at auction in company with horses, sheep and swine, and in every way treated more like brutes than human beings—should repine at my success, and, in his blindness, seek to throw every discouragement and obstacle in the way of the slave's emancipation. But why a New-York editor, born and reared in the State of Maine, far removed from the contaminated and pestilential atmosphere of slavery, should pursue such a course, is not so apparent. I will not, however, stop here to ascertain the cause, but deal with fact; and I cannot better do this than by giving your readers a simple and undisguised statement of the motives and objects of my visit to this country. I feel it but just to myself to do so, since I have been denounced by the New-York Express as a "glibtongued scoundrel," and gravely charged, in its own elegant and dignified language, with "running a muck in greedy-eared Britain against America, its people, its institutions, and even against its peace."

Of the low and vulgar epithets, coupled with the false and somewhat malicious charges, very little need be said. I am used to them. Their force is lost upon me, in the frequency of their application. I was reared where they were in the most common use. They form a large and very important portion of the vocabulary of characters known in the South as plantation "Negro drivers." A slaveholding gentleman would scorn to use them. He leaves them to find their way into the world of sound, through the polluted lips of his hired "Negro driver"—a being for whom the haughty slaveholder feels incomparably more contempt than he feels toward his slave. And for the best of all reasons—he knows the slave to be degraded, because he cannot help himself; but a white "Negro driver" is degraded, because of original, ingrained meanness. If I agree with the slaveholders in nothing else, I can say I agree with them in all their burning contempt for a "Negro driver," whether born North or South. Such epithets will have no prejudicial effect against me on the mind of the class of American people, whose good opinion I sincerely desire to cultivate and deserve. And it is to these I would address this brief word of explanation.

The object, then, of my visit to this country is simply to give such an exposition of the degrading influence of slavery upon the master and his abettors as well as upon the slave—to excite such an intelligent interest on the subject of American slavery—as may react upon that country, and tend to shame her out of her adhesion to a system which all must confess to be at variance with justice, repugnant to Christianity, and at war with her own free institutions. "The head and front of my offending hath this extent, no more." I am one of those who think the best friend of a nation is he who most faithfully rebukes her for her sins—and he her worst enemy, who, under the specious and popular garb of patriotism, seeks to excuse, palliate, and defend them. America has much more to fear from such than all the rebukes of the abolitionists at home or abroad.

I am nevertheless aware, that the wisdom of exposing the sins of one nation in the ear of another, has been seriously questioned by good and clear-sighted people, both on this and on your side of the Atlantic. And the thought is not without its weight upon my own mind. I am satisfied that there are many evils which can be best removed by confining our efforts to the immediate locality where such evils exist. This, however, is by no means the case with the system of slavery. It is such a giant sin—such a monstrous aggregation of iniquity, so hardening to the human heart, so destructive to the moral sense, and so well calculated to beget a character in every one around it favorable to its own continuance, that I feel not only at liberty, but abundantly justified in appealing to the whole world to aid in its removal. Slavery exists in the United States because it is reputable, and it is reputable in the United States because it is not *dis*reputable out of the United States as it ought to be, and it is not so disreputable out of the United States as it ought to be because its character is not so well known as it ought to be. Believing this most firmly, and being a lover of Freedom, a hater of Slavery, one who has felt the bloody whip and worn the galling chain—sincerely and earnestly longing for the deliverance of my sable brethren from their awful bondage, I am bound to expose its character, whenever and wherever an opportunity is afforded me. I would attract to it the attention of the world. I would fix upon it the piercing eye of insulted Liberty. I would arraign it at the bar of Eternal Justice, and summon the Universe to witness against it. I would concentrate against it the moral and religious sentiment of Christian people of every "class, color and clime." I would have the guilty slaveholder see his condemnation written on every human face, and hear it proclaimed in every human voice, till, overwhelmed with shame and confusion, he resolved to cease his wicked course, undo the heavy burden, and let the oppressed go free.

The people in this country who take the deepest interest in the removal of Slavery from America, and the spread of Liberty throughout the world, are the same who oppose the bloody spirit of war, and are earnestly laboring to spread the blessings of peace all over the globe. I have ever found the abolitionists of this country the warmest friends of America and American institutions. I have frequently seen in their houses, and sometimes occupying the most conspicuous places in their parlors, the American Declaration of Independence.

An aged anti-slavery gentleman in Dublin, with whom I had the honor several times to dine during my stay in that city, has the Declaration of Independence and a number of the portraits of the distinguished founders of the American Republic. He bought them many years ago, in token of his admiration of the men and their principles. But, said he, after speaking of the sentiments of the Declaration—looking up as it hung in a costly frame—I am often tempted to turn its face to the wall, it is such a palpable contradiction of the spirit and practices of the American people at this time. This instrument was once the watchword of Freedom in this land, and the American people were regarded as the best friends and truest representatives of that sacred cause. But they are not so regarded now. They have allowed the crowned heads of Europe to outstrip them. While Great Britain has emancipated all her slaves, and is laboring to extend the blessings of Liberty wherever her power is felt, it seems, in the language of John Quincy Adams, that the preservation, propagation and perpetuation of slavery is the vital and animating spirit of the American Government. Even Haiti, the black Republic, is not to be spared; the spirit of Freedom, which a sanguinary and ambitious despot could not crush or extinguish, is to be exterminated by the free American Republic, because that spirit is dangerous to slavery. While the people of this country see such facts and indications, as well as the great fact that three millions of people are held in the most abject bondage, deprived of all their God-given rights—denied by law and public opinion to learn to read the sacred Scriptures, by a people professing the largest liberty and devotion to the religion of Jesus Christ—while they see this monstrous anomaly, they must look elsewhere for a paragon of civil and religious freedom. Sir, I am earnestly and anxiously laboring to wipe off this foul blot from the otherwise fair fame of the American people, that they may accomplish in behalf of human freedom that which their exalted position among the nations of the earth amply fits them to do. Would they but arise in their moral majesty and might—repent and purify themselves from this foul crime—break the galling fetters, and restore the long lost rights to the sable bondmen in their midst—they would encircle her name with a wreath of imperishable glory. Her light would indeed break forth as the morning—its brilliant beams would flash across the Atlantic, and illuminate the Eastern world.

I am, dear sir, very gratefully yours,
Frederick Douglass

The Liberator, June 26, 1846

TO WILLIAM LLOYD GARRISON

Glasgow, April 16, 1846

My dear friend:

I have given up the field of public letter-writing to my friend Buffum, who will tell you how we are getting on; but I cannot refrain from sending you a line, as a mere private correspondent. My health is good, my spirit is bright, and I am enjoying myself as well as one can be expected, when separated from home by three thousand miles of deep blue ocean. I long to be at home—"home, sweet, sweet home! Be it ever so humble, there is no place like home." Nor is it merely to enjoy the pleasure of family and friends, that I wish to be at home: it is to be in the field, at work, preaching to the best of my ability salvation from slavery, to a nation fast hastening to destruction. I know it will be hard to endure the kicks and cuffs of the pro-slavery multitude, to which I shall be subjected; but then, I glory in the battle, as well as in the victory.

I have been frequently counselled to leave America altogether, and make Britain my home. But this I cannot do, unless it shall be absolutely necessary for my personal freedom. I doubt not that my old master is in a state of mind quite favorable to an attempt at re-capture. Not that he wishes to make money by selling me, or by holding me himself, but to feed his revenge. I know he feels keenly my exposures, and nothing would afford him more pleasure than to have me in his power. He has suffered severe goadings, or he would not have broken the silence of seven years, to exculpate himself from the charges I have brought against him, by telling a positive lie. He says he can put his hand upon the Bible, and, with a clear conscience, swear he never struck me, or told any one else to do so! The same conscientious man could put his hand into my pocket, and rob me of my hard earnings; and, with a clear conscience, swear he had a right not only to my earnings, but to my body, soul and spirit! We may, in this case, reverse the old adage—"He that will lie, will steal"—and make it, "He that will steal, will lie"—especially when, by lying, he may hope to throw a veil over his stealing. This positive denial, on his part, rather staggered me at the first. I had no idea the gentleman would tell a right down untruth. He has certainly forgotten when a lamp was lost from the carriage, without my knowledge, that he came to the stable with the cart-whip, and with its heavy lash beat me over the head and shoulders, to make me tell how it was lost, until his brother Edward, who was at St. Michael's, on a visit at the time, came forward, and besought him to desist; and that he beat me until he wearied himself. My memory, in such matters, is better than his. One would think, from his readiness to swear that he never struck me, that he held it to be wrong to do so. He does not deny that he used to tie up "a cousin of mine, and lash her, and in justification of his bloody conduct quote, 'He that knoweth his master's will, and doeth it not, shall be beaten with many stripes.'" He finds fault with me for not mentioning his promising to set me free at 25. I did not tell many things which I might have told. Had I told of that promise, I should have also told that he had never set one of his slaves free; and I had no reason to believe he would treat me with any more justice and humanity, than any other one of his slaves. But enough.

Scotland is in a blaze of anti-slavery agitation—The Free Church and Slavery are the all-engrossing topics. It is the same old question of Christian union with slaveholders—old with us, but new with most people here. The discussion is followed by the same result as in America, when it was first mooted in the New-England Convention. There is such a sameness in the arguments, pro and con, that if you could be landed on this side of the Atlantic, without your knowledge, you would scarcely distinguish between our meetings here, and our meetings at home. The Free Church is in a terrible stew. Its leaders thought to get the slaveholders' money and bring it home, and escape censure. They had no idea that they would be followed and exposed. Its members are leaving it, like rats escaping from a sinking ship. There is a strong determination to have the slave money sent back, and the union broken up. In this feeling all religious denominations participate. Let slavery be hemmed in on every side by the moral and religious sentiments of mankind, and its death is certain.

I am always yours,
Frederick Douglass

The Liberator, May 15, 1846

TO ANONYMOUS

[Ayr, Scotland], April 23, 1846

... I am now in the town of Ayr. It is famous for being the birthplace of Robert Burns, the poet, by whose brilliant genius every stream, hill, glen and valley in the neighborhood have been made classic.

I have felt more interest in visiting this place than any other in Scotland, for as you are aware, (painfully perhaps) I am an enthusiastic admirer of Robt. Burns. Immediately on our arrival, Friend Buffum and myself were joined by Rev. Mr. Renwick, the minister in whose meeting house we are to lecture during our stay, and proceeded forthwith to see Burns's Monument. It is about three miles from town, and situated on the South bank of the river "Doon," and within hearing of its gentle steps as it winds its way over its pebbled path to the Ocean. The place of the Monument is well chosen, being in full view of all the places mentioned and referred to in the Poet's famous poem called "Tam O'Shanter," as well as several others of his most popular poems. From the Monument (which I have not time to describe,) may be seen the cottage where Burns was born—the old and new bridge across the Doon—"Kirk Alloway," called by Burns the "Haunted Kirk." The banks of "Doon" rising majestically from the sea toward the sky, and the Clyde stretching off to the highlands of Arran, whose dim outline is scarcely discernible through the fog by which it is almost constantly overhung, makes the spot admirably and beautifully adapted to the Monument of Scotland's noble bard. In the Monument there is a finely executed marble bust of Burns—the finest thing of the kind I ever saw. I never before, looking upon it, realized the power of man to make the marble speak. The expression is so fine, and the face is so lit up, as to cause one to forget the form in gazing upon the spirit.

In another room, there are two statues carved out of free stone—the one of Souter Johnny and the other of Tam O'Shanter, two characters named in his most famous poem. These were also finely executed and shared my attention, but I was drawn to Burns. In a glass case near his bust there was a Bible, given by Burns to his "sweet Highland Mary"—there is also in the same case a lock of hair of her he so dearly loved, and who by death was snatched from his bosom, and up to his bust glowing with expression, I received a vivid impression, and shared with him the deep melancholy portrayed in the following lines:

Ye Banks and braes of bonnie Doon,
  How can ye bloom sae fresh and fair;
How can ye chant, ye little birds,
  And I sae wary, fu' o'care?
Thou'l break my heart, thou warbling bird
  That wantons through the flowering thorn;
Thou 'minds me of departed joys,
  Departed never to return!

'Oft hae I rov'd by bonnie Doon
  To see the rose and woodbine twine,
And ilka bird sang o' its luve,
  And fondly sae did I o' mine;
Wi' lightsome heart I pri'd a rose
  Fu' sweet upon its thorny tree,
And my fause lover stole my rose
  But ah! he left the thorn wi' me.

On our way to the Monument we enjoyed a pleasure and a privilege I shall never forget. It was that of seeing and conversing with Mrs. Beggs, an own sister of Robert Burns, and also seeing and talking with the Poet's two nieces, daughters of Mrs. Beggs. They live by the road side in a small thatched cottage, humble but comfortable. When Mr. Renwick made them acquainted with the fact that we were from America they received us warmly. One of the nieces said her uncle was more highly esteemed in America than in Scotland.—Mrs. Beggs is the youngest sister of Robert Burns, and though now approaching 80, she does not look to be more than sixty. She enjoys good health, is a spirited looking woman, and bids fair to live yet many days. The two daughters are truly fine looking women. Coal black hair, full, high foreheads, and jet black eyes, sparkling with the poetic fire which illumined the breast of their brilliant uncle. Their deportment was warm and free, yet dignified and lady-like. They did every thing to make our call agreeable, and they were not ignorant as to the means of putting us fully at ease. Two letters in their uncle's own handwriting was early put into our hands. An original portrait, said to be excellent, was discoursed upon; I thought it much like those we usually see in his works.

We sat fifteen or twenty minutes. It might have been longer, as happy moments pass rapidly. Took leave—bade farewell. I saw in them so much of what I love in every body else, I felt as if leaving old and dear friends. I have ever esteemed Robert Burns a true soul but never could I have had the opinion of the man or his genius, which I now entertain, without my present knowledge of the country, to which he belonged—the times in which he lived, and the broad Scotch tongue in which he wrote. Burns lived in the midst of a bigoted and besotted clergy—a pious, but corrupt generation—a proud, ambitious, and contemptuous aristocracy, who, esteemed a little more than a man, and looked upon the plowman, such as was the noble Burns, as being little better than a brute. He became disgusted with the pious frauds, indignant at the bigotry, filled with contempt for the hollow pretensions set up by the shallow-brained aristocracy. He broke loose from the moorings which society had thrown around him. Spurning all restraint, he sought a path for his feet, and, like all bold pioneers, he made crooked paths. We may lament it, we may weep over it, but in the language of another, we shall lament and weep with him. The elements of character which urged him on are in us all, and influencing our conduct every day of our lives. We may pity him, but we can't despise him. We may condemn his faults, but only as we condemn our own. His very weakness was an index of his strength. Full of faults of a grievous nature, yet far more faultless than many who have come down to us in the page of history as saints. He was a brilliant genius, and like all of his class, did much good and much evil. Let us take the good and leave the evil—let us adopt his virtues but avoid his vices—let us pursue his wisdom but shun his folly; and as death has separated his noble spirit from the corrupt and contemptible lust with which it was encumbered, so let us separate his good from his evil deeds—thus may we make him a blessing rather than a curse to the world.

Read his "Tam O' Shanter," "Cotter's Saturday Night," "Man was made to Mourn," "To my Mary in Heaven." Indeed, dear A. read his poems, and as I know you are no admirer of Burns, read it to gratify your friend Frederick. So much for Burns.

Frederick Douglass

New York Tribune, July 9, 1846

AN APPEAL TO THE BRITISH PEOPLE, reception speech at Finsbury Chapel, Moorfields, England, May 12, 1846

I feel exceedingly glad of the opportunity now afforded me of presenting the claims of my brethren in bonds in the United States to so many in London and from various parts of Britain who have assembled here on the present occasion. I have nothing to commend me to your consideration in the way of learning, nothing in the way of education, to entitle me to your attention; and you are aware that slavery is a very bad school for rearing teachers of morality and religion. Twenty-one years of my life have been spent in slavery—personal slavery—surrounded by degrading influences, such as can exist nowhere beyond the pale of slavery; and it will not be strange, if under such circumstances, I should betray, in what I have to say to you, a deficiency of that refinement which is seldom or ever found, except among persons that have experienced superior advantages to those which I have enjoyed. But I will take it for granted that you know something about the degrading influences of slavery, and that you will not expect great things from me this evening, but simply such facts as I may be able to advance immediately in connection with my own experience of slavery.

Now, what is this system of slavery? This is the subject of my lecture this evening—what is the character of this institution? I am about to answer this inquiry, what is American slavery? I do this the more readily, since I have found persons in this country who have identified the term slavery with which I think it is not, and in some instances, I have feared, in so doing, have rather (unwittingly, I know) detracted much from the horror with which the term slavery is contemplated. It is common in this country to distinguish every bad thing by the name of slavery. Intemperance is slavery; to be deprived of the right to vote is slavery, says one; to have to work hard is slavery, says another; and I do not know but that if we should let them go on, they would say that to eat when we are hungry, to walk when we desire to have exercise, or to minister to our necessities, or have necessities at all, is slavery.

I do not wish for a moment to detract from the horror with which the evil of intemperance is contemplated—not at all; nor do I wish to throw the slightest obstruction in the way of any political freedom that any class of persons in this country may desire to obtain. But I am here to say that I think the term slavery is sometimes abused by identifying it with that which it is not. Slavery in the United States is the granting of that power by which one man exercises and enforces a right of property in the body and soul of another. The condition of a slave is simply that of the brute beast. He is a piece of property—a marketable commodity, in the language of the law, to be bought or sold at the will and caprice of the master who claims him to be his property; he is spoken of, thought of, and treated as property. His own good, his conscience, his intellect, his affections, are all set aside by the master. The will and the wishes of the master are the law of the slave. He is as much a piece of property as a horse. If he is fed, he is fed because he is property. If he is clothed, it is with a view to the increase of his value as property. Whatever of comfort is necessary to him for his body or soul that is inconsistent with his being property is carefully wrested from him, not only by public opinion, but by the law of the country. He is carefully deprived of everything that tends in the slightest degree to detract from his value as property. He is deprived of education. God has given him an intellect; the slaveholder declares it shall not be cultivated. If his moral perception leads him in a course contrary to his value as property, the slaveholder declares he shall not exercise it. The marriage institution cannot exist among slaves, and one-sixth of the population of democratic America is denied its privileges by the law of the land. What is to be thought of a nation boasting of its liberty, boasting of its humanity, boasting of its Christianity, boasting of its love of justice and purity, and yet having within its own borders three millions of persons denied by law the right of marriage?—what must be the condition of that people?

I need not lift up the veil by giving you any experience of my own. Every one that can put two ideas together must see the most fearful results from such a state of things as I have just mentioned. If any of these three millions find for themselves companions, and prove themselves honest, upright, virtuous persons to each other, yet in these cases—few as I am bound to confess they are—the virtuous live in constant apprehension of being torn asunder by the merciless men-stealers that claim them as their property. This is American slavery; no marriage—no education—the light of the gospel shut out from the dark mind of the bondman—and he forbidden by the law to learn to read. If a mother shall teach her children to read, the law in Louisiana proclaims that she may be hanged by the neck. If the father attempt to give his son a knowledge of letters, he may be punished by the whip in one instance, and in another be killed, at the discretion of the court. Three millions of people shut out from the light of knowledge! It is easy for you to conceive the evil that must result from such a state of things.

I now come to the physical evils of slavery. I do not wish to dwell at length upon these, but it seems right to speak of them, not so much to influence your minds on this question, as to let the slaveholders of America know that the curtain which conceals their crimes is being lifted abroad; that we are opening the dark cell, and leading the people into the horrible recesses of what they are pleased to call their domestic institution. We want them to know that a knowledge of their whippings, their scourgings, their brandings, their chainings, is not confined to their plantations, but that some Negro of theirs has broken loose from his chains—has burst through the dark incrustation of slavery, and is now exposing their deeds of deep damnation to the gaze of the Christian people of England.

The slaveholders resort to all kinds of cruelty. If I were disposed, I have matter enough to interest you on this question for five or six evenings, but I will not dwell at length upon these cruelties. Suffice it to say, that all the peculiar modes of torture that were resorted to in the West India islands are resorted to, I believe, even more frequently in the United States of America. Starvation, the bloody whip, the chain, the gag, the thumb-screw, cathauling, the cat-o'-nine-tails, the dungeon, the blood-hound, are all in requisition to keep the slave in his condition as a slave in the United States. If any one has a doubt upon this point, I would ask him to read the chapter on slavery in [Charles] Dickens's Notes on America. If any man has a doubt upon it, I have here the "testimony of a thousand witnesses,"[11] which I can give at any length, all going to prove the truth of my statement. The blood-hound is regularly trained in the United States, and advertisements are to be found in the southern papers of the Union, from persons advertising themselves as blood-hound trainers, and offering to hunt down slaves at fifteen dollars a piece, recommending their hounds as the fleetest in the neighborhood, never known to fail. Advertisements are from time to time inserted, stating that slaves have escaped with iron collars about their necks, with bands of iron about their feet, marked with the lash, branded with red-hot irons, the initials of their master's name burned into their flesh; and their masters advertise the fact of their being thus branded with their own signature, thereby proving to the world that, however damning it may appear to non-slaveholders, such practices are not regarded discreditable among the slaveholders themselves. Why, I believe if a man should brand his horse in this country—burn the initials of his name into any of his cattle, and publish the ferocious deed here—that the united execrations of Christians in Britain would descend upon him. Yet, in the United States, human beings are thus branded. As Whittier says—

> ... *Our countrymen in chains,*
> *The whip on woman's shrinking flesh,*
> *Our soil yet reddening with the stains*
> *Caught from her scourgings warm and fresh.*

The slave-dealer boldly publishes his infamous acts to the world. Of all things that have been said of slavery to which exception has been taken by slaveholders, this, the charge of cruelty, stands foremost, and yet there is no charge capable of clearer demonstration than that of the most barbarous inhumanity on the part of the slaveholders toward their slaves. And all this is necessary; it is necessary to resort to these cruelties, in order to make the slave a slave, and to keep him a slave. Why, my experience all goes to prove the truth of what you will call a marvelous proposition, that the better you treat a slave, the more you destroy his value as a slave, and enhance the probability of his eluding the grasp of the slaveholder; the more kindly you treat him, the more wretched you make him, while you keep him in the condition of a slave. My experience, I say, confirms the truth of this proposition. When I was treated exceedingly ill; when my back was being scourged daily; when I was whipped within an inch of my life—life was all I cared for. "Spare my life," was my continual prayer. When I was looking for the blow about to be inflicted upon my head, I was not thinking of my liberty; it was my life. But, as soon as the blow was not to be feared, then came the longing for liberty. If a slave has a bad master, his ambition is to get a better; when he gets a better, he aspires to have the best; and when he gets the best, he aspires to be his own master. But the slave must be brutalized to keep him as a slave. The slaveholder feels this necessity. I admit this necessity. If it be right to hold slaves at all, it is right to hold them in the only way in which they can be held; and this can be done only by shutting out the light of education from their minds, and brutalizing their persons.

The whip, the chain, the gag, the thumb-screw, the blood-hound, the stocks, and all the other bloody paraphernalia of the slave system are indispensably necessary to the relation of master and slave. The slave must be subjected to these, or he ceases to be a slave. Let him know that the whip is burned; that the fetters have been turned to some useful and profitable employment; that the chain is no longer for his limbs; that the blood-hound is no longer to be put upon his track; that his master's authority over him is no longer to be enforced by taking his life—and immediately he walks out from the house of bondage and asserts his freedom as a man. The slaveholder finds it necessary to have these implements to keep the slave in bondage; finds it necessary to be able to say, "Unless you do so and so; unless you do as I bid you—I will take away your life!"

Some of the most awful scenes of cruelty are constantly taking place in the middle states of the Union. We have in those states what are called the slave-breeding states. Allow me to speak plainly. Although it is harrowing to your feeling, it is necessary that the facts of the case should be stated. We have in the United States slave-breeding states. The very state from which the minister from our court to yours comes is one of these states—Maryland, where men, women, and children are reared for the market, just as horses, sheep, and swine are raised for the market. Slave-rearing is there looked upon as a legitimate trade; the law sanctions it, public opinion upholds it, the church does not condemn it. It goes on in all its bloody horrors, sustained by the auctioneer's block. If you would see the cruelties of this system, hear the following narrative. Not long since the following scene occurred. A slave-woman and a slave-man had united themselves as man and wife in the absence of any law to protect them as man and wife. They had lived together by the permission, not by right, of their master, and they had reared a family. The master found it expedient, and for his interest, to sell them. He did not ask them their wishes in regard to the matter at all; they were not consulted. The man and woman were brought to the auctioneer's block, under the sound of the hammer. The cry was raised, "Here goes; who bids cash?" Think of it—a man and wife to be sold! The woman was placed on the auctioneer's block; her limbs, as is customary, were brutally exposed to the purchasers, who examined her with all the freedom with which they would examine a horse. There stood the husband, powerless; no right to his wife; the master's right preeminent. She was sold. He was next brought to the auctioneer's block. His eyes followed his wife in the distance; and he looked beseechingly, imploringly, to the man that had bought his wife to buy him also. But he was at length bid off to another person. He was about to be separated forever from her whom he loved. No word of his, no work of his, could save him from this separation. He asked permission of his new master to go and take the hand of his wife at parting. It was denied him. In the agony of his soul he rushed from the man who had just bought him, that he might take a farewell of his wife; but his way was obstructed, he was struck over the head with a loaded whip, and was held for a moment; but his agony was too great. When he was let go, he fell a corpse at the feet of his master. His heart was broken. Such scenes are the every-day fruits of American slavery.

Some two years since, the Hon. Seth M. Gates, an anti-slavery gentleman of the state of New York, a representative in the congress of the United States, told me he saw with his own eyes the following circumstance. In the national District of Columbia, over which the star-spangled emblem is constantly waving, where orators are ever holding forth on the subject of American liberty, American democracy, American republicanism, there are two slave prisons. When going across a bridge, leading to one of these prisons, he saw a young woman run out, barefooted and bare-headed, and with very little clothing on. She was running with all speed to the bridge he was approaching. His eye was fixed upon her, and he stopped to see what was the matter. He had not paused long before he saw three men run out after her. He now knew what the nature of the case was: a slave escaping from her chains—a young woman, a sister—escaping from the bondage in which she had been held. She made her way to the bridge, but had not reached it, ere from the Virginia side there came two slaveholders. As soon as they saw them, her pursuers called out, "Stop her!" True to their Virginian instincts, they came to the rescue of their brother kidnappers across the bridge. The poor girl now saw that there was no chance for her. It was a trying time. She knew if she went back, she must be a slave forever—she must be dragged down to the scenes of pollution which the slaveholders continually provide for most of the poor, sinking, wretched young women whom they call their property. She formed her resolution; and just as those who were about to take her were going to put hands upon her, to drag her back, she leaped over the balustrades of the bridge, and down she went to rise no more. She chose death, rather than to go back into the hands of those Christian slaveholders from whom she had escaped.

Can it be possible that such things as these exist in the United States? Are not these the exceptions? Are any such scenes as this general? Are not such deeds condemned by the law and denounced by public opinion?

Let me read you a few of the laws of the slaveholding states of America. I think no better exposure of slavery can be made than is made by the laws of the states in which slavery exists. I prefer reading the laws to making my statement in confirmation of what I have said myself; for the slaveholders cannot object to this testimony, since it is the calm, the cool, the deliberate enactment of their wisest heads, of their most clear-sighted, their own constituted representatives. "If more than seven slaves together are found in any road without a white person, twenty lashes a piece; for visiting a plantation without a written pass, ten lashes; for letting loose a boat from where it is made fast, thirty-nine lashes for the first offense; and for the second shall have cut off from his head one ear; for keeping or carrying a club, thirty-nine lashes; for having any article for sale, without a ticket from his master, ten lashes; for traveling in any other than the most usual and accustomed road, when going alone to any place, forty lashes; for traveling in the night without a pass, forty lashes."

I am afraid you do not understand the awful character of these lashes. You must bring it before your mind. A human being in a perfect state of nudity, tied hand and foot to a stake, and a strong man standing behind with a heavy whip, knotted at the end, each blow cutting into the flesh, and leaving the warm blood dripping to the feet; and for these trifles. For being found in another person's Negro-quarters, forty lashes; for hunting with dogs in the woods, thirty lashes; for being on horseback without the written permission of his master, twenty-five lashes; for riding or going abroad in the night, or riding horses in the day time, without leave, a slave may be whipped, cropped, or branded in the cheek with the letter R, or otherwise punished, such punishment not extending to life, or so as to render him unfit for labor. The laws referred to may be found by consulting Brevard's Digest; Haywood's Manual; Virginia Revised Code; Prince's Digest; Missouri Laws; Mississippi Revised Code. A man, for going to visit his brethren, without the permission of his master—and in many instances he may not have that permission; his master, from caprice or other reasons, may not be willing to allow it—may be caught on his way, dragged to a post, the branding-iron heated, and the name of his master or the letter R branded into his cheek or on his forehead.

They treat slaves thus, on the principle that they must punish for light offenses in order to prevent the commission of larger ones. I wish you to mark that in the single state of Virginia there are seventy-one crimes for which a colored man may be executed; while there are only three of these crimes which, when committed by a white man, will subject him to that punishment. There are many of these crimes which if the white man did not commit he would be regarded as a scoundrel and a coward. In the state of Maryland there is a law to this effect: that if a slave shall strike his master, he may be hanged, his head severed from his body, his body quartered, and his head and quarters set up in the most prominent places in the neighborhood. If a colored woman, in the defense of her own virtue, in defense of her own person, should shield herself from the brutal attacks of her tyrannical master, or make the slightest resistance, she may be killed on the spot. No law whatever will bring the guilty man to justice for the crime.

But you will ask me, can these things be possible in a land professing Christianity? Yes, they are so; and this is not the worst. No, a darker feature is yet to be presented than the mere existence of these facts. I have to inform you that the religion of the southern states, at this time, is the great supporter, the great sanctioner of the bloody atrocities to which I have referred. While America is printing tracts and Bibles; sending missionaries abroad to convert the heathen; expending her money in various ways for the promotion of the Gospel in foreign lands—the slave not only lies forgotten, uncared for, but is trampled under foot by the very churches of the land. What have we in America? Why, we have slavery made part of the religion of the land. Yes, the pulpit there stands up as the great defender of this cursed institution, as it is called. Ministers of religion come forward and torture the hallowed pages of inspired wisdom to sanction the bloody deed. They stand forth as the foremost, the strongest defenders of this "institution."

As a proof of this, I need not do more than state the general fact, that slavery has existed under the droppings of the sanctuary of the south for the last two hundred years, and there has not been any war between the religion and the slavery of the south. Whips, chains, gags, and thumbscrews have all lain under the droppings of the sanctuary, and instead of rusting from off the limbs of the bondman, those droppings have served to preserve them in all their strength. Instead of preaching the Gospel against this tyranny, rebuke, and wrong, ministers of religion have sought, by all and every means, to throw in the background whatever in the Bible could be construed into opposition to slavery, and to bring forward that which they could torture into its support.

This I conceive to be the darkest feature of slavery, and the most difficult to attack, because it is identified with religion, and exposes those who denounce it to the charge of infidelity. Yes, those with whom I have been laboring, namely, the old organization anti-slavery society of America, have been again and again stigmatized as infidels, and for what reason? Why, solely in consequence of the faithfulness of their attacks upon the slaveholding religion of the southern states, and the northern religion that sympathizes with it. I have found it difficult to speak on this matter without persons coming forward and saying, "Douglass, are you not afraid of injuring the cause of Christ? You do not desire to do so, we know; but are you not undermining religion?" This has been said to me again and again, even since I came to this country, but I cannot be induced to leave off these exposures. I love the religion of our blessed Savior. I love that religion that comes from above, in the "wisdom of God, which is first pure, then peaceable, gentle, and easy to be entreated, full of mercy and good fruits, without partiality and without hypocrisy." I love that religion that sends its votaries to bind up the wounds of him that has fallen among thieves. I love that religion that makes it the duty of its disciples to visit the fatherless and the widow in their affliction. I love that religion that is based upon the glorious principle, of love to God and love to man; which makes its followers do unto others as they themselves would be done by. If you demand liberty to yourself, it says, grant it to your neighbors. If you claim a right to think for yourself, it says, allow your neighbors the same right. If you claim to act for yourself, it says, allow your neighbors the same right. It is because I love this religion that I hate the slaveholding, the woman-whipping, the mind-darkening, the soul-destroying religion that exists in the southern states of America. It is because I regard the one as good, and pure, and holy, that I cannot but regard the other as bad, corrupt, and wicked. Loving the one I must hate the other; holding to the one I must reject the other.

I may be asked why I am so anxious to bring this subject before the British public—why I do not confine my efforts to the United States? My answer is, first, that slavery is the common enemy of mankind, and all mankind should be made acquainted with its abominable character. My next answer is, that the slave is a man, and, as such, is entitled to your sympathy as a brother. All the feelings, all the susceptibilities, all the capacities, which you have he has. He is a part of the human family. He has been the prey—the common prey—of christendom for the last three hundred years, and it is but right, it is but just, it is but proper, that his wrongs should be known throughout the world.

I have another reason for bringing this matter before the British public, and it is this: slavery is a system of wrong, so blinding to all around, so hardening to the heart, so corrupting to the morals, so deleterious to religion, so sapping to all the principles of justice in its immediate vicinity, that the community surrounding it lacks the moral stamina necessary to its removal. It is a system of such gigantic evil, so strong, so overwhelming in its power, that no one nation is equal to its removal. It requires the humanity of Christianity, the morality of the world to remove it. Hence, I call upon the people of Britain to look at this matter, and to exert the influence I am about to show they possess, for the removal of slavery from America. I can appeal to them, as strongly by their regard for the slaveholder as for the slave, to labor in this cause. I am here, because you have an influence on America that no other nation can have. You have been drawn together by the power of steam to a marvelous extent; the distance between London and Boston is now reduced to some twelve or fourteen days, so that the denunciations against slavery, uttered in London this week, may be heard in a fortnight in the streets of Boston, and reverberating amidst the hills of Massachusetts. There is nothing said here against slavery that will not be recorded in the United States.

I am here, also, because the slaveholders do not want me to be here; they would rather that I were not here. I have adopted a maxim laid down by Napoleon, never to occupy ground which the enemy would like me to occupy. The slaveholders would much rather have me, if I will denounce slavery, denounce it in the northern states, where their friends and supporters are, who will stand by and mob me for denouncing it. They feel something as the man felt, when he uttered his prayer, in which he made out a most horrible case for himself, and one of his neighbors touched him and said, "My friend, I always had the opinion of you that you have now expressed for yourself—that you are a very great sinner." Coming from himself, it was all very well, but coming from a stranger it was rather cutting.

The slaveholders felt that when slavery was denounced among themselves, it was not so bad; but let one of the slaves get loose, let him summon the people of Britain, and make known to them the conduct of the slaveholders toward their slaves, and it cuts them to the quick, and produces a sensation such as would be produced by nothing else. The power I exert now is something like the power that is exerted by the man at the end of the lever; my influence now is just in proportion to the distance that I am from the United States. My exposure of slavery abroad will tell more upon the hearts and consciences of slaveholders than if I was attacking them in America; for almost every paper that I now receive from the United States, comes teeming with statements about this fugitive Negro, calling him a "glib-tongued scoundrel," and saying that he is running out against the institutions and people of America.

I deny the charge that I am saying a word against the institutions of America, or the people, as such. What I have to say is against slavery and slaveholders. I feel at liberty to speak on this subject. I have on my back the marks of the lash; I have four sisters and one brother now under the galling chain. I feel it my duty to cry aloud and spare not. I am not averse to having the good opinion of my fellow-creatures. I am not averse to being kindly regarded by all men; but I am bound, even at the hazard of making a large class of religionists in this country hate me, oppose me, and malign me as they have done—I am bound by the prayers, and tears, and entreaties of three millions of kneeling bondsmen, to have no compromise with men who are in any shape or form connected with the slaveholders of America.

I expose slavery in this country, because to expose it is to kill it. Slavery is one of those monsters of darkness to whom the light of truth is death. Expose slavery, and it dies. Light is to slavery what the heat of the sun is to the root of a tree; it must die under it. All the slaveholder asks of me is silence. He does not ask me to go abroad and preach in favor of slavery; he does not ask any one to do that. He would not say that slavery is a good thing, but the best under the circumstances. The slaveholders want total darkness on the subject. They want the hatchway shut down, that the monster may crawl in his den of darkness, crushing human hopes, and happiness, destroying the bondman at will, and having no one to reprove or rebuke him. Slavery shrinks from the light; it hateth the light, neither cometh to the light, lest its deed should be reproved. To tear off the mask from this abominable system, to expose it to the light of heaven, aye, to the heat of the sun, that it may burn and wither it out of existence, is my object in coming to this country. I want the slaveholder surrounded, as by a wall of anti-slavery fire, so that he may see the condemnation of himself and his system glaring down in letters of light. I want him to feel that he has no sympathy in England, Scotland, or Ireland; that he has none in Canada, none in Mexico, none among the poor wild Indians; that the voice of the civilized, aye, and savage world, is against him. I would have condemnation blaze down upon him in every direction, till, stunned and overwhelmed with shame and confusion, he is compelled to let go the grasp he holds upon the persons of his victims, and restore them to their long-lost rights.

Report of a public meeting held at Finsbury Chapel, Moorfields, to receive Frederick Douglass, the American slave, on Friday, May 12, 1846. London, 1846

TO WILLIAM LLOYD GARRISON

London, May 23, 1846

Dear Friend:

I take up my pen to give you a hasty sketch of five days' visit to this great city. I arrived here from Edinburgh, on the 18th instant, and proceeded immediately to 5 Whitehead's Grove, the house of your early and devoted friend, George Thompson, from whom I had received a most cordial letter, inviting me to make his house my home, during my stay in London. The main object of my visit was to attend the annual meeting of the British and Foreign Anti-Slavery Society—to do which, I had received a pressing invitation from the Committee of that Society. The meeting was held on the day of my arrival in Freemason's Hall, great Queen street. The chair was taken by Sir Edward North Buxton, Bart.

Having heard much of the meetings of this Society, I was surprised and disappointed by the fewness of those assembled. There were not more present, on this occasion, than what we usually have at our business meetings of the American Anti-Slavery Society. The thinness of the meeting was accounted for by the secretary, Mr. Scoble, on the ground that there were several very important philanthropic meetings in progress at the same hour—meetings in which the friends of emancipation were deeply interested, and to which many had gone, who otherwise would have been present at the anti-slavery meeting.

I will not trouble you with any minute account of this meeting, as you will find a pretty accurate sketch of its proceedings in a London paper, which I have already mailed for you. There was one pleasing feature, to which I will refer, and that was, the readiness with which the meeting responded to the sentiment of "non-christian fellowship with slaveholders," and the zeal, spirit and unanimity with which it joined in our uncompromising demand upon the Free Church of Scotland, to

"SEND BACK THE MONEY." This was the more gratifying, in view of the manner in which this subject has been treated by some of the local auxiliary societies, which have stood aloof from the subject, and refused in any way to co-operate with us, because, as they allege, we are of the "Garrison party" in America. This ground has been distinctly taken by the Edinburgh Anti-Slavery Committee. Instead of seconding our efforts, (whether intentionally, or otherwise,) they have played into the hands of the enemy, and have been quoted over and over again, by the Free Church press, against us. In assuming this position towards us, and the cause in which we are immediately engaged, they cannot but feel sensibly rebuked by the present example of the Parent Society; for that Society not only invited Mr. Thompson and myself to speak, but to speak on this very subject; and no parts of our speeches were more warmly received, or more enthusiastically cheered, than our several animadversions on the conduct of the Free Church of Scotland,—which Church now stands before this country and the world as the most prominent defender of the Christianity of man-stealers.

At the close of the meeting, Mr. Joseph Sturge came forward, and said that, in consequence of the fewness of the number who had had an opportunity of hearing me, he would do what he could to get me a meeting at the end of the week, when he was certain that a much larger meeting than the present could be obtained, if I would consent to address it. I agreed, and the meeting was held last night in Finsbury Chapel, one of the largest chapels in London. I shall also send you a newspaper report of this meeting. Meanwhile, I must say, it was one of the most effective and satisfactory meetings which I have attended since landing on these shores. You will observe, that the resolutions adopted by the meeting assert a broader and nobler platform, than that upon which our Broad-street friends have for some time past acted. They have, as you are aware, taken sides with the New Organization and Liberty party, while they have decried and disparaged the efforts of yourself, and those who are earnestly laboring with you. The fact is, they have known very little of our efforts since 1840. Mr. Scoble, the Secretary, informs me that he has been left to gather information of our movements as best he could—that, while he has never, in a single instance, omitted to send you his Annual Report, he has in no instance received ours; so that he has been compelled to silence respecting us, for the want of information necessary to an intelligent opinion of our movement. I assured him that I thought our Reports had been sent, but that they had been miscarried, or that some accident had befallen them, as I could conceive of no reason for withholding them, or neglecting to send them; especially as I knew it to be a first principle with our Society, in the fullest manner to exchange opinions with every class of abolitionists, whether they be for or against the views held by us. But to the meeting.

In adopting the resolution, moved by Dr. Campbell, a new and better way is marked out. It asserts, as it should do, the duty and prerogative of British abolitionists to be, that of co-operating with, and encouraging, fellow-laborers in the United States of every anti-slavery creed. Let this resolution be universally adopted, and scrupulously adhered to, and there will be a happy termination to the bitter jarrings which have, during the last six years, marred and defaced the beauty and excellence of our noble work. Of course, this resolution does not pledge the British and Foreign Anti-Slavery Society to the principle contained in it, as it was only adopted at a public meeting; still, I believe the ground taken is one, upon which nine-tenths of all the abolitionists in this country are anxious to stand. They are, as they ought to be, unwilling to be understood as being unfriendly to any class or creed of anti-slavery men in the United States.

This has been a week of great activity with me. I have attended a meeting every day since I came into the city. On Monday, as I have before observed, I attended the anniversary of the British and Foreign Anti-Slavery Society. On Tuesday, I received an invitation, and spoke at a large and excellent meeting of the Peace Society. On Wednesday, I was invited to speak at a meeting of the *complete* Suffrage Association, called thus in contradistinction from the Chartist party, and differing from that party, in that it repudiates the use of physical force as a means of attaining its object. I am persuaded that, after the complete triumph of the Anti-Corn Law movement, the next great reform will be that of complete suffrage.[12] The agitation which this must occasion will be louder, deeper and stronger than that attending the Anti-Corn Law movement. It comprehends dearer interests than those involved in the repeal of the Corn Laws. It is quite easy to see, that, in the triumph of complete suffrage in this country, aristocratic rule must end—class legislation must cease—the law of primogeniture and entail, the game laws, &c. will be utterly swept from the statute book. When people and not property shall govern, people will cease to be subordinate to property.

In the triumph of this movement may be read the destruction of the time-hallowed alliance of Church and State. The opposition to the gross injustice of compelling a man to support a form of worship, in which he not only feels no interest, but which he really hates, is great and increasing. The brilliant success of the Anti-Corn Law League has convinced the people of their power. The demand for the separation of Church and State, which is now but whispered, must sooner or later be heard in tones of thunder. The battle will be hot, but the right must triumph. God grant that they may make a better use of their political freedom, than the working people of the United States have hitherto done!—For, instead of taking sides with the oppressed, they have acted the unnatural and execrable part of the vilest oppressors. They stand forth in the front ranks of tyranny, and, with words of freedom on their deceitful lips, have given victory to a party,[13] the chief pride, boast and glory of which is that of having blasted one of the fairest portions of our common earth with slavery. It is but just to the friends of political freedom here to say, that they regard the hypocritical pretenders to democratic freedom in America with absolute contempt, and ineffable disgust. The time was, when America was known abroad as the land of the free, but that time is past. No intelligent and honest man, whose love of liberty does not depend on the color of a man's skin, ever thinks of America in connection with freedom, but with abhorrence. Slavery gives character to the American people. It dictates their laws, gives tone to their literature, and shapes their religion. It stands up in their midst, the only sovereign power in the land. The friends of freedom here look upon America as one of the greatest obstacles in the way of political freedom, as she is now the great fact, illustrating the alleged truth, that the tyrant many are even more tyrannical than the tyrant few.

On Thursday, I accepted an invitation to attend and speak at the anniversary meeting of the National Temperance Society, held in the far-famed Exeter Hall. It was a splendid meeting. A resolution was adopted, proposing a World's Convention to be held in London, some time during the month of August. It was supported by Mr. Joseph Sturge and myself. I mention this, simply to call attention to a noble testimony borne by Mr. Sturge against slaveholders—a testimony which must have the best effect, just now. Mr. Sturge is a thorough temperance man, and gives largely in support of the cause. While speaking of the proposed Convention, and of the possibility of slaveholders being admitted into it as members, he declared that, if slaveholders were admitted, he would not sit in the Convention, or aid it in any way whatever. He had contemplated giving the Society £50; but he must find some other benevolent object upon which to bestow that sum, if slaveholders were admitted into the Convention. Subsequently, Mr. Alexander, a friend of temperance, and a member of the Society of Friends, has taken the same ground. These sentiments were loudly applauded by the meeting. The feeling of *"No Union with Slaveholders"* is becoming more and more general in London, and throughout this country. American slaveholders must prepare, not only to be excluded from the communion of British Christians, but peremptorily driven from the platform of every philanthropic association. Let them be hemmed in on every side. Let them be placed beyond the pale of respectability, and, standing out separated, alone in their infamy, let the storm gather over them, and its hottest bolts descend. Our justification is ample:—*the slaveholder is a man-stealer*.

I ought to have said, while speaking of the anti-slavery meeting at Finsbury Chapel, that Dr. Campbell suggested that, in as much as it would be of some importance to the anti-slavery cause to have me remain in this country longer than I could be induced to remain, absent from my family, measures be at once taken, by which a sufficient amount could be realized to enable me to bring my family to this country. This suggestion being seconded by my friend Mr. Thompson, in a very few minutes between £80 and £90 were contributed for the purpose. This result was entirely unexpected to me. I had not even mentioned my desire for any such thing to the meeting. I had said, however, to Mr. Thompson, and also to Mr. Sturge, that I could not remain absent from my family more than one year, and that I must go home in August, unless I should decide to bring my family to this country; and this may have led to the suggestion by Dr. Campbell.

I have just received a letter from Mr. Sturge, the chairman of the meeting at which the money was raised, saying he will cause to be forwarded to any person whom I may mention as my friend in the United States, five hundred dollars, to be appropriated to the removal of my family to this country. So I rest in the hope of soon being joined by my family in a land where they will not be constantly harassed by apprehension, that some foul imp of a slaveholder may lay his infernal clutch upon me, and tear me from their midst. Master Hugh [Auld] must bear the loss of my service *one* year longer, and it may be, I shall remain absent *two* years. Please send him a paper, containing this announcement, and exhort him to patience. It may serve to ease, if not cure, his anxious mind. He must feel my absence keenly, and must suffer greatly; for of all pain, I believe that of suspense is the most severe. By the way, one of the charges I have preferred against master Thomas Auld, and one which he seems the most angry about, respects his meanness; and the fact illustrative of this trait brought forward in my Narrative, is that he once owned a young woman, a cousin of mine, whose right hand had been so burnt as to make it useless to her through life—and finding this young woman of little or no value to him, he very *generously* gave her to his sister Sarah. Seized, I suppose, with a similar fit of benevolence, he has transferred his legal right of property in my body and soul, to his less fortunate brother Hugh. And master Hugh (for so I suppose I must call him,) seems to be very proud of the gift, and means to play the part of a hungry blood-hound in catching me. Possess your soul in patience, *dear* master Hugh, and regale yourself on the golden dreams afforded by the prospect—"First catch your rabbit," &c. &c.

But I am wandering. My visit to this city has been exceedingly gratifying, on account of the freedom I have enjoyed in visiting such places of instruction and amusement as those from which I have been carefully excluded by the inveterate prejudice against color in the United States. Botanic and Zoological gardens, Museums and Panoramas, Halls of Statuary and Galleries of Paintings, are as free to the black as the white man in London. There is no distinction on account of color. The white man gains nothing by being white, and the black man loses nothing by being black. "A man's a man for a' that." I went on Tuesday morning, in company with Mr. and Mrs. Thompson, to see Cremore Garden, a place of recreation and amusement—a most beautiful and picturesque spot, delightfully situated on the bank of the Thames, at the west end of the city. I was admitted without a whisper of objection on the part of the proprietor or spectators. Every one looked as though they thought I had as much right there as themselves, and not the slightest dislike was manifested toward me on account of my Negro origin, unless a gentleman from Boston, who was in the Garden while I was there, be an exception—and I will not say that he was. He had just brought to the Garden a panorama of Boston, rolled up in a long case, which was so heavy as to require eight men to carry it. Soon after its arrival, the proprietor told me what it was. I then said I knew Boston, and should be glad to see a panorama of it, but was informed it would not be presented for exhibition for two or three weeks, as the place was not quite ready for it. My American friend, whom I took to be the artist, on learning that I knew Boston, at once made toward me, without the slightest ceremony or circumlocution ordinarily resorted to by gentlemen when approaching a stranger, and bolting up to me, he asked, in much the same tone which a white man employs when addressing a slave by the way-side—*"Well, boy, who do you belong to?"*—"Do you know Boston?" "Yes, Sir." "Well, if you know Boston, you know it is the handsomest city in the world!" This left me without a doubt as to the Yankee origin of my friend, and I felt quite at home in his presence. He eloquently descanted on the beauties of Boston, quoting various authorities as proof of his position, that Boston is the most beautiful city in the world. I replied, that Boston is a very handsome city, but I thought not the handsomest in the world—and proceeded to speak of Edinburgh. But a very few moments convinced me, that my patriotic friend had no ear for the praise of any other city than Boston; so we separated. We, however, met again in the course of half an hour, when his tone was quite altered, and his manner quite changed. We had a very pleasant interview. He asked if my name was Douglass, and being answered in the affirmative, expressed pleasure at seeing me, and said he had frequently heard of me since he came to this country.

There is one remarkable peculiarity in all the Americans with whom I have had the pleasure to meet on this side of the Atlantic, and that is, their adaptability to circumstances! Persons, who would feel themselves disgraced by being seen conversing with me in Boston, find no difficulty in being seated at the same table with me in London!

On Wednesday, I went to see the "assembled wisdom" of this great nation—Parliament. Through the kindness of my friend George Thompson, I gained admission to the Speaker's Gallery, which is quite a privilege. Here I found myself beside the Rev. Mr. Kirk, of Boston, who seemed in no way shocked at being seated on the same bench with a Negro, but rather pleased with having met me. I was fortunate in the choice of the time of going, for I could not have selected three hours when I could have heard a greater number of distinguished members. A bill was before the House, for restricting the hours of factory labor. Sir James Graham, Sir John Hobhouse, Lord George Bentinck, son of the Duke of Portland, Mr. Gisbourne, Mr. Wakely, Mr. Farrend, Mr. John Bright, Mr. Crawford, Mr. Brotherton, Sir Robert Peel, Lord John Russell, and several other members, addressed the House on the subject. When the vote was to be taken, the galleries were cleared, so that the spectator is not allowed to see who votes for or against a measure. I was much pleased with the respectful manner with which members spoke of each other. Never having enjoyed the privilege of witnessing the legislative proceedings of our great nation, I cannot say in what respect they differ, or in what respect the one is to be preferred to the other. All I know is, if I should presume to go into Washington as I have into London, and enter Congress as I have done the House of Parliament, the ardent defenders of democratic liberty would at once put me into prison, on suspicion of having been "created contrary to the Declaration of American Independence." On failing to prove a negative, I should be sold into slavery, to pay my jail fees! 'Hail, Columbia, happy land!' Under these circumstances, my republican friends must not think strange, when I say I would rather be in London than Washington. Liberty in Hyde Park is better than democracy in a slave prison—monarchical freedom is better than republican slavery—things are better than names. I prefer the substance to the shadow.

Since I came to this city, I have had the honor to be made a member of the Free Trade Club, composed in part of some of the most distinguished and influential gentlemen in the kingdom. But I must not speak of this, lest I should rouse the ire of the *New York Express,* or provoke the fiery indignation of Bennett's [New York] *Herald.*

I have enjoyed a fine opportunity of becoming acquainted with Mr. George Thompson. I have been with him in private and in public—at home and abroad—when in the heat of intense excitement, and when mantled with the most tranquil repose—and in all circumstances, I have found him equal to the highest estimate I had formed of the man. He is the first great orator of whom I had formed a very high opinion, on the first hearing of whom I did not feel a degree of disappointment. He is far above any opinion I had formed of him. I have found him to be, emphatically, the man of every meeting which I have attended since I came to London. The announcement of his name is attended with demonstrations of applause, such as are seldom called forth by the mention of any other name.

Mr. Thompson is now deeply engaged in exposing the corrupt and despotic rule of the East India Company, and his labors in that department are equal to all his time and strength. Yet, such is his devotion to the cause of the American slave, that he is resolved to devote one or two weeks more to the agitation now going on in Scotland, against Christian fellowship with slaveholders, to induce the Free Church to send back the blood-stained money. As usual, you see him battling for the right.

But I must close this already too lengthy letter, or I would say more of this friend of God and man. Long may he live to plead the cause of our common humanity—to open his mouth for the dumb—to demand liberty for the heart-broken captive, unconditional emancipation for the whip-scarred slave, succor for the afflicted, mercy for the suffering, and justice for the oppressed!

Yours to the end,
Frederick Douglass

The Liberator, June 26, 1846

THE FREE CHURCH AND SLAVERY, speech at Glasgow, Scotland, May 29, 1846

The abolitionists of the United States have been laboring during the last fifteen years, to establish the conviction throughout the country that slavery is a sin, and ought to be treated as such by all professing Christians. This conviction they have written about, they have spoken about, they have published about—they have used all the ordinary facilities for forwarding this view of the question of slavery. Previous to that operation, slavery was not regarded as a sin. It was spoken of as an evil—in some cases it was spoken of as a wrong—in some cases it was spoken of as an excellent institution—and it was nowhere, or scarcely anywhere, counted as a sin, or treated as a sin, except by the Society of Friends, and by the Reformed Presbyterians, two small bodies of Christians in the United States. The abolitionists, for advocating or attempting to show that slaveholding is a sin, have been called incendiaries and madmen, and they have been treated as such—only much worse, in many instances; for they have been mobbed, beaten, pelted, and defamed in every possible way, because they disclaimed the idea that slavery is not a sin—a sin against God, a violation of the rights of man, a sin demanding immediate repentance on the part of the slaveholders, and demanding the immediate emancipation of the trampled and down-crushed slave. [Cheers.] They had made considerable progress in establishing this view of the case in the United States. They had succeeded in establishing, to a considerable extent, in the northern part of the United States, a deep conviction that to hold human beings in the condition of slavery is a sin, and ought to be treated as such, and that the slaveholder ought to be treated as a sinner. [Hear! and applause.] They had called upon the religious organizations of the land to treat slaveholding as sin. They had recommended that the slaveholder should receive the same treatment from the church that is meted out to the ordinary thief. They had demanded his exclusion from the churches, and some of the largest denominations in the country had separated at Mason and Dixon's line, dividing the free states from the slave states, solely on account of slaveholding, as those who hold anti-slavery views felt that they could not stand in fellowship with men who trade in the bodies and souls of their fellowmen. [Applause.] Indeed, the anti-slavery sentiment not to sit in communion with these men, and to warn the slaveholder not to come near nor partake of the emblems of Christ's body and blood, lest they eat and drink damnation to themselves, is become very prevalent in the free States. They demand of the slaveholder, first, to put away this evil—first, to wash his hands in innocency—first, to abandon his grasp on the throat of the slave; and until he was ready to do that, they can have nothing to do with him. All was going on gloriously—triumphantly; the moral and religious sentiment of the country was becoming concentrated against slavery, slaveholders and the abettors of slaveholders, when, at this period, the Free Church of Scotland sent a deputation to the United States, with a doctrine diametrically opposed to the abolitionists, taking up the ground that, instead of no fellowship they should fellowship the slaveholders. According to them, the slaveholding system is a sin, but not the slaveholder a sinner. They taught the doctrine that it was right for Christians to unite in Christian fellowship with slaveholders, and their influence has been highly detrimental to the anti-slavery cause in the United States. [Hear! hear!] All their reasonings and arguments, instead of being quoted on behalf of the abolition cause, are quoted on behalf of slavery. [Disapprobation.] The newspapers which came from the United States came laden with eulogies of Drs. Candish and Cunningham, and of the Free Church in general. While the slaveholders have long disconnected themselves with the Secession Church in this country, I do not say that the Secession Church has formally repudiated all alliance with them; but by the faithfulness of their remonstrances, by their denunciations of slavery, from time to time, and by their opinions and arguments being known of all men, the slaveholders have disconnected themselves with them. [Hear! hear! and applause.]

Now, we want to have the matter of the Free Church thoroughly sifted here to-night. We want to call attention to the deputation particularly which admitted the principle of holding fellowship with slaveholders —to fellowship slaveholders as the type and representatives of Jesus Christ on earth, and not only that, but to take their money to build churches, and pay their ministers. The Free Church sent a deputation to America. That deputation was met by the abolitionists of New York, and remonstrated with, and begged not to stain their cause by striking hands with man-stealers, and not to take the polluted gains of slavery to pay their ministers; but, by no means, to take the side of the oppressors. The deputation had an excellent opportunity of aiming an effectual blow at slavery; but they turned a deaf ear, and refused to listen to the friends of freedom. They turned a deaf ear to the groans of the oppressed slave—they neglected the entreaties of his friends—and they went into the slave States, not for the purpose of imparting knowledge to the slave, but to strike hands with the slaveholders, in order to get money to build Free Churches and pay Free Church ministers in Scotland. [Cries of "Shame!" and applause.] Now, I am here to charge that deputation with having gone into a country, where they saw three millions of human beings deprived of every right, stripped of every privilege, ranked with four-footed beasts and creeping things, with no power over their own bodies and souls, deprived of the privilege of learning to read the name of the God who made them, compelled to live in the grossest ignorance, herded together in a state of concubinage—without marriage, without God, and without hope; they went into the midst of such a people—into the midst of those who held such a people—and never uttered a word of sympathy on behalf of the oppressed, or raised their voices against their oppressors!

We have been told, that that deputation went to the United States for the purpose of making the Christians of the United States acquainted with the position of the Free Church of Scotland; or, rather, to explain the nature of the struggles of the Free Church in behalf of religious freedom, and to preach the gospel. Now, I am here to say, that that deputation did not preach the gospel to the slave—that gospel which came from above—that gospel which is peaceable and pure, and easy to be entreated. Had they preached that God was the God of the poor slave, as well as of his rich master—had they raised their voices on behalf of that gospel—they would have been hung upon the first lamp-post. The slaveholders hate the gospel of the Lord Jesus Christ. There is nothing they hate so much. A man may go there, and preach certain doctrines connected with the gospel of Christ; but if ever he apply the principle of the love of God to man—to the slave as well as to the slaveholder—it will immediately appear how such a doctrine would be relished. But this is not all. Not only did the Free Church deputation not preach the gospel, or say a word on behalf of the slave, but they took care to preach such doctrines as would be palatable—as would be agreeably received—and as would bring them the slaveholders' money. [Cries of "Shame!" and applause.] They said, "We have only one object to accomplish"; and they justified themselves for not meddling with the sins with which they came into contact in America on the ground that they had one particular object to employ their attention. Was it to obey the voice of God? Was it to proclaim the terrors of the law against all iniquity? No. It was to get money to build Free Churches, and to pay Free Ministers. That was the object to be accomplished, and in following this course they acted more like thieves than like Christian ministers. [Applause.] I verily believe, that, had I been at the South, and had I been a slave, as I have been a slave—and I am a slave still by the laws of the United States—had I been there, and that deputation had come into my neighborhood, and my master had sold me on the auction block, and given the produce of my body and soul to them, they would have pocketed it, and brought it to Scotland to build their churches, and pay their ministers. [Cries of "No," "Yes, yes," and applause.] Why not? I am no better than the blackest slave in the Southern plantations. These men knew who were the persons they were going amongst. It may be said they were not bound to inquire as to where money comes from, when it is put into the treasury of the Lord. But in this case, there was no need for inquiry. They knew they were going to a class of people who were robbers—known stealers of men—for what is a thief? what is a robber? but he who appropriates to himself what belongs to another. The slaveholders do this continually. They publish their willingness to do so. They defend their right to do so, and the deputation knew they did this. They knew that the hat upon the head of the slaveholder, the coat upon his back, and the cash in his pocket, were the result of the unpaid toil of the fettered and bound slave; and yet, in view of this fact, they went amongst them. They went with a lighted candle in their hands. They were told what would be the consequence, but they went—purity gave way to temptation, and we see the result. The result is evil to Scotland, and evil to America, but more to the former than to the latter; for I think the Free Church has committed more sin in attempting to defend certain principles connected with this question than in accepting the money. They have had to upset all the first principles of Christianity in its defense. They have had to adopt the arguments of the Infidels, of the Socialists, and others, by which to defend themselves, and have brought a foul blot upon Christianity. [Cheers, and slight sounds of disapprobation.]

Now, what are their arguments? Why is Dr. Chalmers speaking as he does of the slaveholders and slavery, and trying to make it appear that there is a distinction without a difference? This eminent Free Church leader says, "A distinction ought to be made between the character of a system and the character of persons whom circumstances have connected therewith. Nor would it be just," continues the Doctor, "to visit upon the person all the recoil and indignation which we feel toward the system itself." Here he lays down a principle by which to justify the present policy of the Free Church. This is the rock of their present position. They say, "Distinction ought to be made; for while slavery may be very bad, a sin and a crime, a violation of the law of God, and an outrage on the rights of man; yet, the slaveholder may be a good and excellent Christian, and that in him we may embrace a type and standing representative of Christ." While they would denounce theft, they would spare the thief; while they would denounce gambling, they would spare the gambler; while they would denounce the dice, they would spare the sharper; for a distinction should be made between the character of a system and the character of the men whom circumstances have connected therewith. [Cheers and laughter.] Dr. Chalmers and his Master are at odds. Christ says, "By their fruits shall they be known." Oh, no! says Dr. Chalmers, a distinction should be made between the fruits and character of a system! Oh, the artful dodger! [Great laughter.] Well may the thief be glad, the robber sing, and the adulterer clap his hands for joy. The character of adultery and the character of the adulterer—the character of slavery and the character of the slaveholder—are not the same. We may blame the system, therefore, but not the persons whom circumstances have connected therewith.

I would like to see the slaveholder made so by circumstances, and I should like to trace out the turn of circumstances which compelled him to be a slaveholder. I know what they say about this matter. They say the law compels a slaveholder to keep his slaves, but I utterly deny that any such law exists in the United States. There is no law to compel a man to keep his slaves, or to prevent them from being emancipated. There are three or four states where the master is not allowed to emancipate his slaves on the soil, but he can remove them to a free State, or, at all events, to Canada, where the British lion prowls upon three sides of us, and there they could be free. [Cheers.] The slaveholder who wishes to emancipate his slaves has but to say, "There is the north star—that is the road to Canada—I will never claim you"—and there will be but little doubt of their finding their way to freedom. There was not a single slaveholder in America but who, if he chose, could emancipate his slaves instantly; so all the argument on this basis falls to the ground, as the fact did not exist on which it is built. [Cheers.]

Slavery—I hold it to be an indisputable proposition—exists in the United States because it is respectable. The slaveholder is a respectable man in America. All the important offices in the Government and the Church are filled by slaveholders. Slaveholders are Doctors of Divinity; and men are sold to build churches, women to support missionaries, and children to send Bibles to the heathen. Revivals in religion and revivals in the slave trade go on at the same time. Now, what we want to do is to make slavery disrespectable. Whatever tends to make it respectable, tends to elevate the slaveholder; and whatever, therefore, proclaims the respectability of the slaveholders, or of slaveholding, tends to perpetuate the existence of this vile system. Now, I hold one of the most direct, one of the most powerful means of making him a respectable man, is to say that he is a Christian: for I hold that of all other men, a Christian is most entitled to my affection and regard. Well, the Free Church is now proclaiming that these men—all blood-smeared as they are, with their stripes, gags and thumb-screws, and all the bloody paraphernalia of slaveholding, and who are depriving the slave of the right to learn to read the word of God—that these men are Christians, and ought to be in fellowship as such. [Cries of "No," and "Yes."] Does any one deny that the Free Church does this?

MR. PINKERTON—You are libelling the Free Church.

MR. DOUGLASS—What! is this disputed? Will they not fellowship those who will not teach their slaves to read? I have to say, in answer, that there is not a slaveholder in the American Union who teaches his slaves to read, and I have to inform that individual, and the Free Church, and Scotland generally, that there are several States where it is punishable with death for the second offense to teach a slave his letters. [Great applause.] And further, said Mr. Douglass, I have to tell him there is yet to be the first petition to the legislature demanding a repeal of that law. If the Free Church are to fellowship the slaveholders at all, they must fellowship them in their blood and their sins, just as they find them; and if they will not fellowship them, except they teach their slaves to read, then they will not fellowship them at all. It was necessary to keep the slave in ignorance. If he were not kept in ignorance, where there are so many facilities for escape, he would not long remain a slave, and every means is resorted to to keep him ignorant. The sentiment is general that slaves should know nothing, but to do what is told them by their masters. But a short time ago there was a Sabbath school established in Richmond, Virginia, in which the slaves, it was supposed, were being educated. The story reached the north, and was some cause of gratification; but three weeks afterwards we found in the Richmond papers an article, inquiring into the character of that school, and demanding to know why a Sabbath school had been established in Virginia. Well, they gave an account of themselves, and what was it? In that Sabbath school nothing was taught but what would tend to make the slave a better servant than before it was established; and, in the second place, that there had not been, and there never would be, any book whatever. So they have schools there without books, and learn to read without letters. You will find Sabbath schools, therefore, in many parts of the country, but you will find these such as I have described. [Applause.]

Free Church Alliance, with manstealers. Send back the money, Great anti-slavery meeting in the city hall, Glasgow..., Glasgow, 1846

TO THE EDITOR OF THE *PROTESTANT JOURNAL*

Victoria Hotel, Belfast, July 23, 1846

Mr. Editor:

My attention has just been called to an attack upon myself in your paper of the 18th July, which seems deserving a word of reply. This attack is contained in an article from an American newspaper, the *Boston Traveller*. Were I in the United States, I should deem a reply to an assault coming through that journal entirely uncalled for. I should regard its bitterest abuse as compliment rather than a condemnation. I know the paper, and am fully justified in declaring it to be notorious for its slaveholding malignity, and reckless disregard of truth in everything affecting the question of slavery in the United States. In the article before me I am pretty strongly accused of allowing the chairman of a meeting recently held in Finsbury Chapel, London, to state of me that which I knew to be false. The statement referred to is in the following words: "Our friend Douglass has been obliged to escape from America, leaving his wife and four children there, for fear of being seized by his late owner, who is vowing vengeance. He is, therefore, an exile from that country, because there is not an inch upon which he can with safety set his feet." The writer of the assault upon me says this statement "was not corrected by Douglass." I admit it was not, and for the best of all reasons—it was essentially true, and needed no correction. The writer professes to have lived in the same village with me for several years, and that the above is the first intimation he has ever seen or heard that I had any occasion to seek concealment or expatriation to avoid being again reduced to bondage. All I have to say to this is, that the writer's ignorance is through no fault of mine. I have repeatedly given as one of the reasons for leaving the United States, a fear, that in consequence of publishing a narrative of my experience in slavery, and exposing the conduct of my owner, he might, to gratify his revengeful disposition, attempt to reduce me to slavery. My object was to be out of the way during the excitement and exasperation which I had good reason to apprehend would follow the publication of my narrative. The wisdom of this course has been fully confirmed by what has transpired since I left the United States. My former owner, Mr. Thomas Auld, has transferred his legal right to my body to his brother Hugh, who has publicly declared that, cost what it may, as sure as I set my feet upon American soil, so sure I shall again be reduced to slavery. The laws of the land, and the Constitution of the United States, give him full power to arrest me anywhere in that country. There is not a State in the whole American Union, from Texas to Maine, in which I am not overshadowed with this terrible liability; and this my assailant very well knows, if he be not totally ignorant of the Constitution of the country. I think he has two purposes to serve in making the attack, and both are equally mean; one was to place me in an unfavorable light before the British public, in making me out a deceiver, and the other was to cover up the disgraceful fact, that in the United States, the land of boasted liberty and light, there is not a single inch of ground upon which a runaway slave may stand in safety. The writer speaks of my allegations against the American Board. He does not say what they are, but he says they have been nailed to the counter here (meaning in the United States). I have never made a charge against that body which I am not prepared to prove. I have charged them with neglecting to give the Bible to the slave, and of taking the price of human blood, with which to send the gospel to the heathen. They admit it, and justify themselves by the conduct of the Free Church of Scotland. The writer says—"But our American readers will be amused at the course which things are taking, in reference to this high priest of anti-ministry, anti-churchism, and anti-Sabbathism." If the writer means by this, that I have unmasked the slaveholding and woman-whipping churches and clergy of America, I plead guilty to the charge. The writer exclaims, with apparent ecstasy, "He is lost to his country forever; for one of the speakers said that they would support him handsomely during life in England." Not quite so fast, young man. No inducement could be offered strong enough to make me quit my hold upon America, as my home. Whether a slave or a freeman, America is my home, and there I mean to spend and be spent in the cause of my outraged fellow-countrymen.

Yours, &c.,
Frederick Douglass

The Liberator, August 28, 1846

TO WILLIAM A. WHITE

Edinburgh, Scotland, 30th July 1846

My Dear William:

I dreamed last night that you would not be angry at receiving a letter from your friend Frederick Douglass. It may be all a dream, yet for once I feel like acting under the direction of a dream. I have thought of you a thousand times since I left the U. S. and have as often promised myself the pleasure of writing to you—but somehow or other, I have managed to postpone it until now I am prompted by a dream. That you may the more readily excuse me for presuming to dream of you I will mention that I went to bed thinking about Pendleton Indianna [sic]. You may remember such a place, and also certain events which transpired in that region in the summer of 1843. All dreams aside I shall never forget those days and I may add those nights. I shall never forget how like two very brothers we were ready to dare, do, and even die for each other. Tragic awfully so—yet I laugh always when I think how comic I must have looked when running before the mob, darkening the air with the mud from my feet. How I looked running you can best describe but how you looked bleeding—I shall always remember. You had left home and a life of ease and even luxury that you might do something toward breaking the fetters of the Slave and elevating the despised black man. And this too against the wishes of your father and many of your friends. When I thought I did indeed wish to bleed in your stead. Such a noble blood—so warm so generous—was too holy to be poured out by the rough hand of that infernal mob. Dear William, from that hour you have been loved by Frederick Douglass.

I hold you in grateful and affectionate remembrance, and though I have not written to you before, I assure you it has not been for want of the disposition. Among those who stand forth prominently in behalf of the Antislavery cause, I looked to none upon whom I can rely in the trial hour more than yourself. I am with you in spirit, and shall welcome the day which shall again find me by your side in this good cause. I write thus freely to you because I know you to be above the miserable and contemptible prejudices, too common even among those who claim to regard the Negro as a brother. I could say many things to you about my journeys here, but I prefer to write from within rather than from without—but enough.

What is to become of Old Massachusetts? I have nearly lost all confidence in her honesty, fidelity and love of liberty. Her doom is sealed, her glory has departed. You have labored nobly, and faithfully for her salvation, but there was not enough of moral life within her borders to save her from destruction. The American government is now in the piratical grasp of Texas, and possessing all the money and patronage. Our Massachusetts politicians will follow her in her atrocious robbery of Mexico, like sharks in the bloody wake of a slave ship. Money and office is the order of the day with them, and for these they seem willing to go to perdition, and if need be drag every one else after them. Who would have believed twelve months ago, that the Whig governor of Massachusetts would be seen calling upon the free citizens of that State to leave their homes, families and friends to go and fight the plundering battles of Slave holding Texas? As low as my opinion of the Honesty sincerity and uprightness of that governor was, I should have repelled such a prediction as altogether unjust, and a malicious attempt to injure the character of Governor Briggs. He ought [to be] hurled from his place as quick as possible.

I am more than ever convinced that New England can only be saved by a dissolution of the American Union. Three years from this time will see the seat of the American government removed from Washington into the South west for the accommodation of Slave holding Texas, and as many more states of which the U. S. shall find it convenient to rob Mexico. I need not dwell upon this subject. I know you must feel the degradation of your state keenly. I will not however despair. There is yet a glorious phalanx of noble men in New England whose mighty souls if once kindled by the holy fire of freedom will consume every thing of the hay, wood and stubble of pro slavery by which they are surrounded. Go forth then, go forth, and scatter your eloquence like sparks from the smitten steel. It will have its influence.

> *Freedom's battle once begun*
> *Bequeathed from bleeding sire to son*
> *Though baffled oft, is ever won.*

You will perceive that I am now in Edinburgh. It is the capital of Scotland, and is justly regarded as one of the most beautiful cities in Europe. I never saw one with which for beauty elegance and grandeur to compare it. I have no time even had I the ability to describe it. You must come and see it if you ever visit this country. You will be delighted with it I am sure. The Monument to Sir Walter Scott, on Princes Street is just one conglomeration of architectural beauties. The Calton Hill, Salisbury Craggs and Arthur Seat give the city advantages over any city I have ever visited in this or in your country. I enjoy every thing here which may be enjoyed by those of a paler hue—no distinction here. I have found myself in the society of the Combes, the Crowe's and the Chamber's, the first people of this city and no one seemed alarmed by my presence.

I shall leave here for London on Saturday, first of August. I hope to meet Mr. Garrison there. I long to see a face which I have seen in America. I indulged a hope of seeing you over here this summer. I suppose there is no prospect of your being over now, it is so late in the season. Do tell me is it true that you are married. I think I heard you were. If you are I am glad of it. If you are not I hope you will be soon. I want to see more William A. Whites in the world as well as to see those happy who are already here.

William, do you think it would be safe for me to come home this fall? Would master Hugh stand much chance in Mass? Think he could take me from the old Bay State? The old fellow is evidently anxious to get Hold of me. Staying in this country will not be apt to increase his love for me. I am playing the mischief with the character of Slave holders in this land. The[y] will find the atmosphere very hot here for them. The Rev. Thomas Smyth D.D. of Charleston South Carolina has been kept out of every pulpit here. I think I have been partly the means of it. He is terrible mad with me for it. Pardon this poorly written scrawl. I have not time to correct the spelling or composition. It comes quick from pen as it comes warm from my heart.

Sincerely yours,
Frederick Douglass

Frederick Douglass Mss., *Douglass Memorial Home, Anacostia, D. C.*

TO MARIA (WESTON) CHAPMAN

London, August 18, 1846

My Dear Mrs. Chapman:

Yours by the kindness of Mr. Garrison has reached me. In reply I beg to state that I never for the moment doubted the purity of intention which led you to write as you did respecting me to your friend, Mr. Webb of Dublin. I have not therefore suffered myself to think of you as any other than my friend and well-wisher. Still I did feel and do now feel that it would have been far more friendly and more in keeping with all the ideas I had formed of your character, had you chosen to have given your counsel directly to me and free from what I must yet regard as uncalled for and invidious comparison of myself and Mr. Buffum. But in conveying this thought I had not the most distant expectation of its disturbing our friendship. And if anything escaped my pen which seemed to look that way, I hesitate not to confess my sorrow for it. Continue, I beseech you, to regard me as your friend, for so I am and so I wish to be and so I mean to be, and I am moreover resolved that no trifling occurrence shall be allowed to disturb the confidence which I repose in your devotion and fidelity to the cause. Still, my friend, you must be assured that I shall always speak frankly to you of any act or word of yours which I deem unjust or unkind to me. I felt that you had not done justice in the manner of introducing Mr. Webb. I have thought so and said so, and so I have done with it, and hope never to have occasion to refer to it at any future time. I hope so far from causing any alienation it may serve, to make us better friends than before, since we shall know each other better than before.

In reply to so much of your letter as relates to my having attended the recent meeting of the British and Foreign Anti-slavery in London I must say I have no confession to make or pardon to ask for my conduct in the matter. I went there with the counsel and advice of good friends who are as anxious for the emancipation of the slaves as any with whom I think I have ever met. I went for reasons which seemed good. I was not carried there by what you call money temptations. No such was offered and I may say (though you may think it an evidence of my self sufficiency) no such temptations would have been availing. When I received the invitation I, without reflection or consultation with any one, declined it. This I did from mere prejudice. My friend George Thompson was in London at the time. I was in Edinburgh. He at once wrote urging me for many reasons, most of which sprang out of our Free Church agitation, to come to London and avail myself of the opportunity afforded by that meeting of striking an important blow in behalf of "Sending back the money!" I believe Mr. Thompson now regrets having advised me to go. I do not know that he does, but I think he does since reading the article to which you refer in the *Standard*. I must, however, say that I do not regret having gone thither or having spoken when I was there. I do not believe that even the Broad Street committee, admitting them to be all you say of them, I do not think them too bad to be preached to. I will speak in any meeting where freedom of speech is allowed and where I may do any thing toward exposing the bloody system of slavery. I did not go into that meeting as a new organizationist. I distinctly told the meeting just what the Broad Street Committee knew before they invited me, that I was an old organizationist and had I been fully reported, you would have seen that I was not there in disguise or at the sacrifice of principle or friends at home. I did not indorse what under bigotry was done six years ago or what may be done by same body six years hence. I attended that meeting for a specific purpose and in doing so compromised no more than did Mr. Garrison, Leavitt, etc., who last autumn attended meetings and acted on committees together in order to prevent the annexation of Texas. I might argue the question if I had time but I have not. I have said this much that you may know just where I am in the matter and think this much due to you, since you have taken so much pains to write me respecting it. I shall not say anything about the matter in any letter I may write for the public eye as I think enough has.

I recently got a little circle to work for the Bazaar in Boston, consisting of [a] few influential young ladies in Carlisle, England. They will send a box this autumn. Mr. J. D. Carr of the same place will send you a valuable contribution to the refreshments consisting of a large box of fancy biscuits. I am sorry I can't say more, the lad is waiting to take this to the office.

Yours,
F. Douglass

Anti-Slavery Collection, Boston Public Library

TO THE LYNN ANTI-SLAVERY SEWING CIRCLE

London, August 18, 1846

My Dear Friends:

Owing to some cause at present unknown to me, but which you may understand and be able to explain, your kind letter of 16th June, did not reach me until the 3d of August. I mention this to account for what might otherwise be deemed culpable neglect. Now, what shall I say? for such are my circumstances that I can do little more than apologize for writing you a poor letter. Weighed down, oppressed, and almost overcome by constant effort—by engagements, public and private, growing out of immediate contact with deeply interested friends here—I find it very difficult to gain a moment of calm repose, during which to commune with dear friends on your side the Atlantic: you will readily understand this, when you remember that the fact of my being a fugitive slave is new here. My peculiar position, without any personal attractions, subjects me to many calls and questions from which other lecturers would be comparatively free. Thus engaged, and thus interested, you will readily see that what I write must be very imperfect. But, my dear friends, perfect or imperfect, with or without time, I have resolved to send you a line, responsive in spirit, if not in point of composition, to your warm and sympathetic letter. I thank you for it. I assure you that I speak nothing more than the truth when I say I felt gratified, cheered, and honoured, by that token of friendly interest, esteem, and affection. I felt proud in finding myself approvingly remembered by so many sterling friends, in and out of your choice circle, who placed their names under that friendly epistle. Next to the approbation of heaven and one's own conscience, stands that of clear-sighted and sincere friends; and while it is quite easy to conceive of contentment with the former, it is difficult to conceive of happiness without the latter. A strong man may be able to stand without the proper sympathy; but I know of none so strong but who could be made stronger by it.

But I must not write you an essay on the excellence of human sympathy, but speak to you of the great cause which binds our hearts sympathetically together, the deliverance from thraldom of three millions of our long-neglected and deeply-abused race. I wish I could say something to cheer and strengthen you in this cause. I wish I were able to penetrate the future, and assure you of a speedy triumph of our cause; but this is not for me. I can only say, work on; your cause is good; work on; duty is yours—consequences the Almighty's.

I confess I feel sad, and sick at heart, by the present posture of political affairs in the United States. The spirit of slavery reigns triumphant throughout all the land. Every step in the onward march of political events is marked with blood—innocent blood; shed, too, in the cause of slavery. The war with Mexico rages;[14] the green earth is drenched with warm blood, oozing out from human hearts; the air is darkened with smoke; the heavens are shaken by the terrible roar of the cannon; the groans and cries of the wounded and dying disturb the ear of God. Yet how few in that land care one farthing for it, or will move one inch to arrest and remove the cause of this horrible state of things? I am sad; I am sick; the whole land is cursed, if not given over to destruction. Massachusetts, the brightest of every other state, is now but the tool of Texas.

Texas may be said to give laws to the whole Union. She leads the way in plunder and murder; and Massachusetts, with all New England, follow in the crusade like hungry sharks in the bloody wake of a Brazilian slaveship. What a spectacle for men and angels!—Gov. Briggs issuing his order to send the sons of those who fell in the cause of freedom on Bunker Hill, to fight the battle of Slavery in Mexico! Gov. Briggs, the teetotaller! Gov. Briggs, the Baptist! issuing his order to raise troops in Massachusetts, to establish with fire and sword the man-blasting and soul-damning system of slavery! Who would have thought it? And yet it was to be expected. The deed was done long ago. The foundation of this frowning monument of infamy was laid when the States were first declared the *United States*. This is but another link around your necks of the galling chain which your fathers placed about the heels of my race. It is the legitimate fruit of compromise—of attempting a union of freedom with slavery. All was lost in that sad moment. The American Anti-Slavery Society has the right on this question. Her ground is the true one. I believe that the salvation of the country depends, under God, upon the effort of that society. The Union must be dissolved, or New England is lost and swallowed up by the slave-power of the country. Work on, dear friends, work on! walk by faith, and not by sight. Come good, or come evil—prosperity or adversity—work on! See that all which can be done by patriotic and humane women for the salvation of millions groaning in chains, is done; and whoever else may approve, you shall have the approbation of a good conscience, and the tear of grateful hearts, for your reward.

You speak of your remaining together, though unorganized. I am of course glad to hear of your prosperity, though I cannot say as much of your being *unorganized*. While it is not for me to direct you, who have laboured so long and so well in this cause, how you shall help me and my race, generally, yet you must allow me to say, that my conviction of the utility and importance of organization is strengthened by every day's experience. I find that friend H. Clapp has seen the utter absurdity of carrying forward a moral enterprise without an organization. He has changed his views, or he should not have acted as a delegate, and held the office of secretary, in the temperance World's Convention, held here last week. This he did where free speech was not tolerated, and where men spoke—only by and with the consent of the chairman. Nor was this objected to by Mr. Clapp. Is organization a curse in New England, and a blessing in Old England? Consistency thou art a jewel.

One word more. You remind me of the poor, in this country. I thank you for it. We have poverty here, but no slavery; we have crime here, but no slavery; we have suffering here, but no slavery, and in all this, England has a decided advantage over America. Still, my dear friends, I am by no means unmindful of the poor; and you may rely upon me as one who will never desert the cause of the poor, no matter whether black or white.

May kind heaven smile upon your righteous efforts, and strengthen your hearts for every duty, is the sincere wish of your grateful and devoted friend.

Frederick Douglass

National Anti-Slavery Standard, October 15, 1846

TO SAMUEL HANSON COX, D.D.

Salisbury Road, Edinburgh, October 30, 1846

Sir:

I have two objects in addressing you at this time. The first is, to deny certain charges, and to reply to certain injurious statements, recently made by yourself, respecting my conduct at a meeting of the "World's Temperance Convention," held in Covent Garden Theatre, London, in the month of August last. My second object will be to review so much of your course as relates to the anti-slavery question, during your recent tour through Great Britain and a part of Ireland. There are times when it would evince a ridiculous sensibility to the good or evil opinions of men, and when it would be a wasteful expenditure of thought, time and strength, for one in my circumstances to reply to attacks made by those who hate me, more bitterly than the cause of which I am an humble advocate. While it is all quite true, it is equally true, that there are times when it is quite proper to make such replies; and especially so, when to defend one's self is to defend great and vital principles, the vindication of which is essential to the triumph of righteousness throughout the world.

Sir, I deem it neither arrogant nor presumptuous to assume to represent three millions of my brethren, who are, while I am penning these words, in chains and slavery on the American soil, the boasted land of liberty and light. I have been one with them in their sorrow and suffering —one with them in their ignorance and degradation—one with them under a burning sun and the slavedriver's bloody lash—and am at this moment freed from those horrible inflictions only because the laws of England are commensurate with freedom, and do not permit the American man-stealer, whose Christianity you endorse, to lay his foul clutch upon me, while upon British soil. Being thus so completely identified with the slaves, I may assume that an attack upon me is an attack upon them—and especially so, when the attack is obviously made, as in the present instance, with a view to injure me in the advocacy of their cause. I am resolved that their cause shall not suffer through any misrepresentations of my conduct, which evil-minded men, in high or low places, may resort to, while I have the ability to set myself right before the public. As much as I hate American slavery, and as much as I abominate the infernal spirit which in that land seems to pervade both Church and State, there are bright spots there which I love, and a large and greatly increasing population, whose good opinion I highly value, and which I am determined never to forfeit, while it can be maintained consistently with truth and justice.

Sir, in replying to you, and in singling out the conduct of one of your age, reputation and learning, for public animadversion, I should, in most cases, deem an apology necessary—I should approach such an one with great delicacy and guardedness of language. But, in this instance, I feel entirely relieved from all such necessity. The obligations of courtesy, which I should be otherwise forward to discharge to persons of your age and standing, I am absolved from by your obviously bitter and malignant attack. I come, therefore, without any further hesitancy to the subject.

In a letter from London to the *New-York Evangelist,* describing the great meeting at Covent Garden Theatre, you say:

"They all advocated the same cause, showed a glorious unity of thought and feeling, and the effect was constantly raised—the moral scene was superb and glorious—when Frederick Douglass, the colored abolition agitator and ultraist, came to the platform, and so spoke *a la mode,* as to ruin the influence, almost, of all that preceded! He lugged in anti-slavery or abolition, no doubt prompted to it by some of the politic ones, who can use him to do what they would not themselves adventure to do in person. He is supposed to have been well paid for the abomination.

"What a perversion, an abuse, an iniquity against the law of reciprocal righteousness, to call thousands together to get them, some certain ones, to seem conspicuous and devoted for one sole and grand object, and then, all at once, with obliquity, open an avalanche on them for some imputed evil or monstrosity, for which, whatever be the wound or injury inflicted, they were both too fatigued and too hurried with surprise, and too straitened for time to be properly prepared. I say it is a trick of meanness! It is abominable!

"On this occasion Mr. Douglass allowed himself to denounce America and all its temperance societies together, and a grinding community of the enemies of his people; said evil, with no alloy of good, concerning the whole of us; was perfectly indiscriminate in his severities, talked of the American delegates, and to them, as if he had been our schoolmaster, and we his docile and devoted pupils; and launched his revengeful missiles at our country, without one palliative, and as if not a Christian or a true anti-slavery man lived in the whole of the United States. The fact is, the man has been petted, and flattered, and used, and paid by certain abolitionists not unknown to us, of the *ne plus ultra* stamp, till he forgets himself; and though he may gratify his own impulses and those of old Adam in others, yet sure I am that all this is just the way to ruin his influence, to defeat his object, and to do mischief, not good, to the very cause he professes to love. With the single exception of one cold-hearted parricide, whose character I abhor, and whom I will not name, and who has, I fear, no feeling of true patriotism or piety within him, all the delegates from our country were together wounded and indignant. No wonder at it! I write freely. It was not done in a corner. It was inspired, I believe, from beneath, and not from above. It was adapted to re-kindle, on both sides of the Atlantic, the flames of national exasperation and war. And this is the game which Mr. Frederick Douglass and his silly patrons are playing in England and in Scotland, and wherever they can find 'some mischief still for idle hands to do'! I came here his sympathizing friend—I am so no more, as I more know him.

"My own opinion is increasingly that this abominable spirit must be exorcised out of England and America, before any substantial good can be effected for the cause of the slave. It is adapted only to make bad worse, and to inflame the passions of indignant millions to an incurable resentment. None but an ignoramus or a mad man could think that this way was that of the inspired apostles of the Son of God. It may gratify the feelings of a self-deceived and malignant few, but it will do no good in any direction—least of all to the poor slave! It is short-sighted, impulsive, partisan, reckless, and tending only to sanguinary ends. None of this, with men of sense and principle.

"We all wanted to reply, but it was too late; the whole theatre seemed taken with the spirit of the Ephesian uproar; they were furious and boisterous in the extreme; and Mr. Kirk could hardly obtain a moment, though many were desirous in his behalf, to say a few words, as he did, very calm and properly, that the cause of Temperance was not at all responsible for slavery, and had no connexion with it. There were some sly agencies behind the scenes —we know!"

Now, the motive for representing, in this connexion, "the effect constantly raised," the "moral scene sublime and glorious," is very apparent. It is obviously not so much to do justice to the scene, as to magnify my assumed offence. You have drawn an exceedingly beautiful picture, that you might represent me as marring and defacing its beauty, in the hope thereby to kindle against me the fury of its admirers.

"Frederick Douglass, the colored abolitionist and ultraist, came to the platform." Well, sir, what if I did come to the platform? How did I come to it? Did I come with, or without, the consent of the meeting? Had your love of truth equalled your desire to cover me with odium, you would have said that, after loud and repeated calls from the audience, and a very pressing invitation from the chairman, "Frederick Douglass came to the platform." But, sir, this would not have served your purpose— that being to make me out an intruder, one without the wedding garment, fit to be cast out among the unbidden and unprepared. This might do very well in America, where for a Negro to stand upon a temperance platform, on terms of perfect equality with white persons, it would be regarded as an insolent assumption, not to be borne with; but, sir, it is scarcely necessary to say, that it will not serve your purpose in England. It is now pretty well known throughout the world, that color is no crime in England, and it is becoming almost equally known, that color is treated as a crime in America. *"Frederick Douglass, the colored abolition agitator and ultraist, came to the platform!"* Shocking! How could democratic Americans sit calmly by, and behold such a flagrant violation of one of the most cherished American customs—this most unnatural amalgamation! Was it not an aggravating and intolerable insult, to allow a Negro to stand upon a platform, on terms of perfect equality with pure white American *gentlemen!* Monarchical England should be taught better manners; she should know that democratic America has the sole prerogative of deciding what shall be the social and civil position of the colored race. But, sarcasm aside, Sir, you claim to be a Christian, a philanthropist, and an abolitionist. Were you truly entitled to any one of these names, you would have been delighted at seeing one of Africa's despised children cordially received, and warmly welcomed to a world's temperance platform, and in every way treated as a man and a brother. But the truth probably is, that you felt both yourself and your country severely rebuked by my presence there; and, besides this, it was undoubtedly painful to you to be placed on the same platform, on a level with a Negro, a fugitive slave. I do not assert this positively—it may not be quite true. But if it be true, I sincerely pity your littleness of soul.

You sneeringly call me an *"abolition agitator and ultraist."* Sir, I regard this as a compliment, though you intend it as a condemnation. My only fear is, that I am unworthy of those epithets. To be an abolition agitator is simply to be one who dares to think for himself—who goes beyond the mass of mankind in promoting the cause of righteousness—who honestly and earnestly speaks out his soul's conviction, regardless of the smiles or frowns of men—leaving the pure flame of truth to burn up whatever hay, wood and stubble it may find in its way. To be such an one is the deepest and sincerest wish of my heart. It is a part of my daily prayer to God, that He will raise up and send forth more to unmask a pro-slavery church, and to rebuke a man-stealing ministry—to rock the land with agitation, and give America no peace till she repent, and be thoroughly purged of this monstrous iniquity. While Heaven lends me health and strength, and intellectual ability, I shall devote myself to this agitation; and I believe that, by so acting, I shall secure the smiles of an approving God, and the grateful approbation of my down-trodden and long abused fellow-countrymen. With these on my side, of course I ought not to be disturbed by your displeasure; nor am I disturbed. I speak now in vindication of my cause, caring very little for your good or ill opinion.

You say I spoke "so as to ruin the influence of all that had preceded"! My speech, then, must have been very powerful; for I had been preceded by yourself, and some ten or twelve others, all powerful advocates of the Temperance cause, some of them the most so of any I ever heard. But I half fear my speech was not so powerful as you seem to imagine. It is barely possible that you have fallen into a mistake, quite common to persons of your turn of mind,—that of confounding your own pride with the cause which you may happen to plead. I think you will upon reflection confess, that I have now hit upon a happy solution of the difficulty. As I look back to that occasion, I remember certain facts, which seem to confirm me in this view of the case. You had eulogized in no measured or qualified terms, America and American Temperance Societies; and in this, your co-delegates were not a whit behind you. Is it not possible that the applause, following each brilliant climax of your fulsome panegyric, made you feel the moral effect raised, and the scene superb and glorious? I am not unaware of the effect of such demonstrations: it is very intoxicating, very inflating. Now, Sir, I should be very sorry, and would make any amends within my power, if I supposed I had really committed, the *"abomination"* of which you accuse me. The Temperance cause is dear to me. I love it for myself, and for the black man, as well as for the white man. I have labored, both in England and America, to promote the cause, and am ready still to labor; and I should grieve to think of any act of mine, which would inflict the slightest injury upon the cause. But I am satisfied that no such injury was inflicted. No, Sir, it was not the poor bloated drunkard, who was *"ruined"* by my speech, but your own bloated pride, as I shall presently show—as I mean to take up your letter in the order in which it is written, and reply to each part of it.

You say I lugged in anti-slavery, or abolition. Of course, you meant by this to produce the impression, that I introduced the subject illegitimately. If such were your intention, it is an impression utterly at variance with the truth. I said nothing, on the occasion referred to, which in fairness can be construed into an outrage upon propriety, or something foreign to the temperance platform—and especially a "world's Temperance platform." The meeting at Covent Garden was not a *white* temperance meeting, such as are held in the United States, but a "world's temperance meeting," embracing the black as well as the white part of the creation—practically carrying out the scriptural declaration, that "God has made of one blood, all nations of men, to dwell on all the face of the earth." It was a meeting for promoting temperance throughout the world. All nations had a right to be represented there; and each speaker had a right to make known to that body, the peculiar difficulties which lay in the way of the temperance reformation, in his own particular locality. In that Convention, and upon that platform, I was the recognized representative of the colored population of the United States; and to their cause I was bound to be faithful. It would have been quite easy for me to have made a speech upon the general question of temperance, carefully excluding all reference to my enslaved, neglected and persecuted brethren in America, and thereby secured your applause;—but to have pursued such a course, would have been, selling my birthright for a mess of pottage,—would have been to play the part of Judas, a part which even you profess to loathe and detest. Sir, let me explain the motive which animated me, in speaking as I did at Covent Garden Theatre. As I stood upon that platform, and surveyed the deep depression of the colored people of America, and the treatment uniformly adopted, by white temperance societies, towards them—the impediments and absolute barriers thrown in the way of their moral and social improvement, by American slavery, and by an inveterate prejudice against them, on account of their color—and beheld them in rags and wretchedness, in fetters and chains, left to be devoured by intemperance and kindred vices—and slavery like a very demon, standing directly in the way of their reformation, as with a drawn sword, ready to smite down any who might approach for their deliverance—and found myself in a position where I could rebuke this evil spirit, where my words would be borne to the shores of America, upon the enthusiastic shouts of congregated thousands—I deemed it my duty to embrace the opportunity. In the language of John Knox, "I was in the place where I was demanded of conscience to speak the truth—and the truth I *did* speak—impugn it who so list." But, in so doing, I spoke perfectly in order, and in such a manner as no one, having a sincere interest in the cause of Temperance, could take offence at—as I shall show by reporting, in another part of this letter my speech as delivered on that occasion.

"He was, no doubt, prompted to do it by some of the politic ones, who can use him to do what they themselves would not adventure to do in person." The right or wrong of obeying the promptings of another depends upon the character of the thing to be done. If the thing be right, I should do it, no matter by whom prompted; if wrong, I should refrain from it, no matter by whom commanded. In the present instance, I was prompted by no one—I acted entirely upon my own responsibility. If, therefore, blame is to fall anywhere, it should fall upon me.

"He is supposed to have been well paid for the abomination." This, Sir, is a cowardly way of stating your own conjecture. I should be pleased to have you tell me, what harm there is in being well paid! Is not the laborer worthy of his hire? Do you preach without pay? Were you not paid by those who sent you to represent them in the World's Temperance Convention? There is not the slightest doubt that you were paid—and *well paid*. The only difference between us, in the matter of pay, is simply this—you were paid, and I was not. I can with a clear conscience affirm that, so far from having been well paid, as you supposed, I never received a single farthing for my attendance—or for any word which I uttered on the occasion referred to—while you were in all probability well supported, "well paid," for all you did during your attendance. My visit to London was at my own cost. I mention this, not because I blame you for taking pay, or because I regard as specially meritorious my attending the meeting without pay; for I should probably have taken pay as readily as you did, had it been offered; but it was not offered, and therefore I got none.

You stigmatize my speech as an "abomination"; but you take good care to suppress every word of the speech itself. There can be but one motive for this, and that motive obviously is, because there was nothing in the speech which, standing alone, would inspire others with the bitter malignity against me, which unhappily rankles in your own bosom.

Now, Sir, to show the public how much reliance ought to be placed on your statements, and what estimate they should form of your love of truth and Christian candor, I will give the substance of my speech at Covent Garden Theatre, and the circumstances attending and growing out of its delivery. As "the thing was not done in a corner," I can with safety appeal to the FIVE THOUSAND that heard the speech, for the substantial correctness of my report of it. It was as follows:—

Mr. Chairman—Ladies and Gentlemen—I am not a delegate to this Convention. Those who would have been most likely to elect me as a delegate, could not, because they are to-night held in the most abject slavery in the United States. Sir, I regret that I cannot fully unite with the American delegates, in their patriotic eulogies of America, and American Temperance Societies. I cannot do so, for this good reason—there are, at this moment, three millions of the American population, by slavery and prejudice, placed entirely beyond the pale of American Temperance Societies. The three million slaves are completely excluded by slavery—and four hundred thousand free colored people are almost as completely excluded by an inveterate prejudice against them, on account of their color. [Cries of shame! shame!]

I do not say these things to wound the feelings of the American delegates. I simply mention them in their presence, and before this audience, that, seeing how you regard this hatred and neglect of the colored people, they may be induced, on their return home, to enlarge the field of their Temperance operations, and embrace within the scope of their influence, my long neglected race—[great cheering and some confusion on the platform]. Sir, to give you some idea of the difficulties and obstacles in the way of the Temperance reformation of the colored population in the United States, allow me to state a few facts. About the year 1840, a few intelligent, sober and benevolent colored gentlemen in Philadelphia, being acquainted with the appalling ravages of intemperance among a numerous class of colored people in that city, and finding themselves neglected and excluded from white societies, organized societies among themselves—appointed committees—sent out agents—built temperance halls, and were earnestly and successfully rescuing many from the fangs of intemperance.

The cause went nobly on till the 1st of August, 1842, the day when England gave liberty to eight hundred thousand souls in the West Indies. The colored Temperance Societies selected this day to march in procession through the city, in the hope that such a demonstration would have the effect of bringing others into their ranks. They formed their procession, unfurled their teetotal banners, and proceeded to the accomplishment of their purpose. It was a delightful sight. But, Sir, they had not proceeded down two streets, before they were brutally assailed by a ruthless mob—their banner was torn down, and trampled in the dust—their ranks broken up, their persons beaten, and pelted with stones and brickbats. One of their churches was burned to the ground, and their best temperance hall was utterly demolished.[15] [Shame! shame! shame!

from the audience—great confusion and cries of "sit down" from the American delegates on the platform.]

In the midst of this commotion, the chairman tapped me on the shoulder, and whispering, informed me that the fifteen minutes allotted to each speaker had expired; whereupon the vast audience simultaneously shouted, "Don't interrupt!—don't dictate! go on! go on! Douglass! Douglass!!" This continued several minutes; after which, I proceeded as follows:—

"Kind friends, I beg to assure you that the chairman has not, in the slightest degree, sought to alter any sentiment which I am anxious to express on the present occasion. He was simply reminding me, that the time allotted for me to speak had expired. I do not wish to occupy one moment more than is allotted to other speakers. Thanking you for your kind indulgence, I will take my seat."

Proceeding to do so, again there were loud cries of "go on! go on!" with which I complied, for a few moments, but without saying any thing more that particularly related to the colored people of America.

When I sat down, the Rev. Mr. Kirk, of Boston, rose, and said—"Frederick Douglass has unintentionally misrepresented the Temperance Societies of America. I am afraid that his remarks have produced the impression on the public mind, that the Temperance Societies support slavery—['No! no! no! no!!' shouted the audience.] If that be not the impression produced, I have nothing more to say."

Now, Dr. Cox, this is a fair unvarnished story of what took place at Covent Garden Theatre, on the 7th of August, 1846. For the truth of it, I appeal to all the Temperance papers in the land, and the "Journal of the American Union," published at New-York, Oct. 1, 1846. With this statement, I might safely submit the whole question to both the American and British public; but I wish not merely to correct your misrepresentations, and expose your falsehoods, but to show that you are animated by a fierce, bitter and untruthful spirit toward the whole anti-slavery movement.

And for this purpose, I shall now proceed to copy and comment upon extracts from your letter to the *New-York Evangelist*. In that letter, you exclaim, respecting the foregoing speech, delivered by me, every word of which you take pains to omit: "What a perversion, an abuse, an iniquity against the law of reciprocal righteousness, to call thousands together, and get them, some certain ones, to seem conspicuous and devoted for one sole and grand object, and then, all at once, with obliquity, open an avalanche on them for some imputed evil or monstrosity, for which, whatever be the wound or the injury inflicted, they were both too fatigued and too hurried with surprise, and too straitened for time, to be properly prepared. I say it is a trick of meanness! It is abominable!"

As to the "perversion," "abuse," "iniquity against the law of reciprocal righteousness," "obliquity," "a trick of meanness," "abominable,"—not one word is necessary to show their inappropriateness, as applied to myself, and the speech in question, or to make more glaringly apparent the green and poisonous venom with which your mouth, if not your heart, is filled. You represent me as opening "an avalanche upon you for some *imputed* evil or monstrosity." And is slavery only an *imputed evil?* Now, suppose I had lugged in Anti-Slavery, (which I deny,)—you profess to be an abolitionist. You, therefore, ought to have been the last man in the world to have found fault with me on that account. Your great love of liberty, and sympathy for the downtrodden slave, ought to have led you to "pardon something to the spirit of Liberty," especially in one who had the scars of the slave-drivers' whip on his back, and who, at this moment, has four sisters and a brother in slavery. But, Sir, you are not an abolitionist, and you only assumed to be one during your recent tour in this country, that you might sham your way through this land, and the more effectually stab and blast the character of the real friends of emancipation. Who ever heard of a true abolitionist speaking of slavery as an "imputed evil," or complaining of being "wounded and injured" by an allusion to it—and that, too, because that allusion was in opposition to the infernal system? You took no offence when the Rev. Mr. Kirk assumed the Christian name and character for the slaveholders in the World's Temperance Convention. You were not "wounded or injured,"— it was not a "perversion, an abuse, an iniquity against the law of reciprocal righteousness." You have no indignation to pour out upon him. Oh, no! But when a *fugitive slave* merely alluded to slavery as obstructing the moral and social improvement of my race, you were "wounded and injured," and rendered indignant! This, sir, tells the whole story of your abolitionism, and stamps your pretensions to abolition as brazen hypocrisy or self-deception.

You were "too fatigued, too hurried by surprise, too straitened for time." Why, Sir, you were in "an unhappy predicament." What would you have done, had you not been "too fatigued, too hurried by surprise, too straitened for time," and unprepared? Would you have denied a single statement in my address? I am persuaded you would not; and had you dared to do so, I could at once have given evidence in support of my statements, that would have put you to silence or to shame. My statements were in perfect accordance with historical facts—facts of so recent date that they are fresh in the memory of every intelligent American. You knew I spoke truly of the strength of American prejudice against the colored people. No man knows the truth on this subject better than yourself. I am, therefore, filled with amazement that you should seem to deny instead of confirming my statements.

Much more might be said on this point; but having already extended this letter to a much greater length than I had intended, I shall simply conclude by a reference to your remark respecting your professed sympathy and friendship for me previous to the meeting at Covent Garden. If your friendship and sympathy be of so mutable a character as must be inferred from your sudden abandonment of them I may expect that yet another change will return to me the lost treasure. At all events, I do not deem it of sufficient value to purchase it at so high a price as that of the abandonment of the cause of my colored brethren, which appears to be the condition you impose upon its continuance.

Very faithfully,
Frederick Douglass

The Liberator, November 27, 1846

TO HENRY C. WRIGHT

22, St. Ann's Square, Manchester, December 22, 1846

Dear Friend:

Your letter of the 12th December reached me at this place, yesterday. Please accept my heartfelt thanks for it. I am sorry that you deemed it necessary to assure me, that it would be the last letter of advice you would ever write me. It looked as if you were about to cast me off for ever! I do not, however, think you meant to convey any such meaning; and if you did, I am sure you will see cause to change your mind, and to receive me again into the fold of those, whom it should ever be your pleasure to advise and instruct.

The subject of your letter is one of deep importance, and upon which, I have thought and felt much; and, being the party of all others most deeply concerned, it is natural to suppose I have an opinion, and ought to be able to give it on all fitting occasions. I deem this a fitting occasion, and shall act accordingly.

You have given me your opinion: I am glad you have done so. You have given it to me direct, in your own emphatic way. You never speak insipidly, smoothly, or mincingly; you have strictly adhered to your custom, in the letter before me. I now take great pleasure in giving you my opinion, as plainly and unreservedly as you have given yours, and I trust with equal good feeling and purity of motive. I take it, that nearly all that can be said against my position is contained in your letter; for if any man in the wide world would be likely to find valid objections to such a transaction as the one under consideration, I regard you as that man. I must, however, tell you, that I have read your letter over, and over again, and have sought in vain to find anything like what I can regard a valid reason *against the purchase of my body, or against my receiving the manumission papers, if they are ever presented to me.*

Let me, in the first place, state the facts and circumstances of the transaction which you so strongly condemn. It is your right to do so, and God forbid that I should ever cherish the slightest desire to restrain you in the exercise of that right. I say to you at once, and in all the fulness of sincerity, speak out; speak freely; keep nothing back; let me know your whole mind. "Hew to the line, though the chips fly in my face." Tell me, and tell me plainly, when you think I am deviating from the strict line of duty and principle; and when I become unwilling to hear, I shall have attained a character which I now despise, and from which I would hope to be preserved. But to the facts.

I am in England, my family are in the United States. My sphere of usefulness is in the United States; my public and domestic duties are there; and there it seems my duty to go. But I am *legally* the property of Thomas Auld, and if I go to the United States, (no matter to what part, for there is no City of Refuge there, no spot sacred to freedom there,) Thomas Auld, *aided by the American Government,* can seize, bind and fetter, and drag me from my family, feed his cruel revenge upon me, and doom me to unending slavery. In view of this simple statement of facts, a few friends, desirous of seeing me released from the terrible liability, and to relieve my wife and children from the painful trepidation, consequent upon the liability, and to place me on an equal footing of safety with all other anti-slavery lecturers in the United States, and to enhance my usefulness by enlarging the field of my labors in the United States, have nobly and generously paid Hugh Auld, the agent of Thomas Auld, £150—in consideration of which, Hugh Auld (acting as his agent) and the Government of the United States agree, that I shall be free from all further liability.

These, dear friend, are the facts of the whole transaction. The principle here acted on by my friends, and that upon which I shall act in receiving the manumission papers, I deem quite defensible.

First, *as to those who acted as my friends, and their actions.* The actuating motive was, to secure me from a liability full of horrible forebodings to myself and family. With this object, I will do you the justice to say, I believe you fully unite, although some parts of your letters would seem to justify a different belief.

Then, as to the measure adopted to secure this result. Does it violate a fundamental principle, or does it not? This is the question, and to my mind the only question of importance, involved in the discussion. I believe that, on our part, no just or holy principle has been violated.

Before entering upon the argument in support of this view, I will take the liberty (and I know you will pardon it) to say, I think you should have pointed out some principle violated in the transaction, before you proceeded to exhort me to repentance. You have given me any amount of indignation against "Auld" and the United States, in all which I cordially unite, and felt refreshed by reading; but it has no bearing whatever upon the conduct of myself, or friends, in the matter under consideration. It does not prove that I have done wrong, nor does it demonstrate what is right, or the proper course to be pursued. Now that the matter has reached its present point, before entering upon the argument, let me say one other word; it is this—I do not think you have acted quite consistently with your character for promptness, in delaying your advice till the transaction was completed. You knew of the movement at its conception, and have known it through its progress, and have never, to my knowledge, uttered one syllable against it, in conversation or letter, till now that the deed is done. I regret this, not because I think your earlier advice would have altered the result, but because it would have left me more free than I can now be, since the thing is done. Of course, you will not think hard of my alluding to this circumstance. Now, then, to the main question.

The principle which you appear to regard as violated by the transaction in question, may be stated as follows:—*Every man has a natural and inalienable right to himself.* The inference from this is, *"that man cannot hold property in man"*—and as man cannot hold property in man, neither can Hugh Auld nor the United States have any right of property in me—and having no right of property in me, they have no right to sell me—and, having no right to sell me, no one has a right to buy me. I think I have now stated the principle, and the inference from the principle, distinctly and fairly. Now, the question upon which the whole controversy turns is, simply, this: does the transaction, which you condemn, really violate this principle? I own that, to a superficial observer, it would seem to do so. But I think I am prepared to show, that, so far from being a violation of that principle, it is truly a noble vindication of it. Before going further, let me state here, briefly, what sort of a purchase would have been a violation of this principle, which, in common with yourself, I reverence, and am anxious to preserve inviolate.

1st. It would have been a violation of that principle, had those who purchased me done so, *to make me a slave, instead of a free-man.* And,

2ndly. It would have been a violation of that principle, had those who purchased me done so with a view to compensate the slaveholder, for what he and they regarded as his rightful property.

In neither of these ways was my purchase effected. My liberation was, in their estimation, of more value than £150; the happiness and repose of my family were, in their judgment, more than paltry gold. The £150 was paid to the remorseless plunderer, not because he had any just claim to it, but to induce him to give up his legal claim to something which they deemed of more value than money. It was not to compensate the slaveholder, but to release me from his power; not to establish my *natural right* to freedom, but to release me from all legal liabilities to slavery. And all this, you and I, and the slaveholders, and all who know anything of the transaction, very well understand. The very letter to Hugh Auld, proposing terms of purchase, informed him that those who gave, *denied his right to it.* The error of those, who condemn this transaction, consists in their confounding the crime of buying men *into slavery,* with the meritorious act of buying men out of slavery, and the purchase of legal freedom with abstract right and natural freedom. They say, "If you BUY, you recognize the right to sell. If you receive, you recognize the right of the giver to give." And this has a show of truth, as well as of logic. But a few plain cases will show its entire fallacy.

There is now, in this country, a heavy duty on corn. The government of this country has imposed it; and though I regard it a most unjust and wicked imposition, no man of common sense will charge me with endorsing or recognizing the right of this government to impose this duty, simply because, to prevent myself and family from starving, I buy and eat this corn.

Take another case:—I have had dealings with a man. I have owed him one hundred dollars, and have paid it; I have lost the receipt. He comes upon me the second time for the money. I know, and he knows, he has no right to it; but he is a villain, and has me in his power. The law is with him, and against me. I must pay or be dragged to jail. I choose to pay the bill a second time. To say I sanctioned his right to rob me, because I preferred to pay rather than go to jail, is to utter an absurdity, to which no sane man would give heed. And yet the principle of action, in each of these cases, is the same. The man might indeed say, the claim is unjust—and declare, I will rot in jail, before I will pay it. But this would not, certainly, be demanded by any principle of truth, justice, or humanity; and however much we might be disposed to respect his daring, but little deference could be paid to his wisdom. The fact is, we act upon this principle every day of our lives, and we have an undoubted right to do so. When I came to this country from the United States, I came in the *second* cabin. And why? Not because my natural right to come in the *first* cabin was not as good as that of any other man, but because a wicked and cruel prejudice decided, that the second cabin was the place for me. By coming over in the second, did I sanction or justify this wicked proscription? Not at all. It was the best I could do. I acted from necessity.

One other case, and I have done with this view of the subject. I think you will agree with me, that the case I am now about to put is pertinent, though you may not readily pardon me for making yourself the agent of my illustration. The case respects the passport system on the continent of Europe. That system you utterly condemn. You look upon it as an unjust and wicked interference, a bold and infamous violation of the *natural* and *sacred* right of locomotion. You hold, (and so do I,) that the image of our common God ought to be a passport all over the habitable world. But bloody and tyrannical governments have ordained otherwise; they usurp authority over you, and decide for you, on what conditions you shall travel. They say, you shall have a passport, or you shall be put in prison. Now, the question is, have they a right to prescribe any such terms? and do you, by complying with these terms, sanction their interference? I think you will answer, no; submission to injustice, and sanction of injustice, are different things; and he is a poor reasoner who confounds the two, and makes them one and the same thing. Now, then, for the parallel, and the application of the passport system to my own case.

I wish to go to the United States. I have a natural right to go there, and be free. My natural right is as good as that of Hugh Auld, or James K. Polk; but that plundering government says, I shall not return to the United States in safety—it says, I must allow Hugh Auld to rob me, or my friends, of £150, or be hurled into the infernal jaws of slavery. I must have a "bit of paper, signed and sealed," or my liberty must be taken from me, and I must be torn from my family and friends. The government of Austria said to you, "Dare to come upon my soil, without a passport, declaring you to be an American citizen, (which you say you are not,) you shall at once be arrested, and thrown into prison." What said you to that Government? Did you say that the threat was a villainous one, and an infamous invasion of your right of locomotion? Did you say, "I will come upon your soil; I will go where I please! I dare and defy your government!" Did you say, "I will spurn your passports; I would not stain my hand, and degrade myself, by touching your miserable parchment. You have no right to give it, and I have no right to take it. I trample your laws, and will put your constitutions under my feet! I will not recognize them!" Was this your course? No! dear friend, it was not. Your practice was wiser than your theory. You took the passport, submitted to be examined while travelling, and availed yourself of all the advantages of your "passport"—or, in other words, escaped all the evils which you ought to have done, without it, and would have done, but for the tyrannical usurpation in Europe.

I will not dwell longer upon this view of the subject; and I dismiss it, feeling quite satisfied of the entire correctness of the reasoning, and the principle attempted to be maintained. As to the expediency of the measures, different opinions may well prevail; but in regard to the principle, I feel it difficult to conceive of two opinions. I am free to say, that, had I possessed one hundred and fifty pounds, I would have seen Hugh Auld *kicking,* before I would have given it to him. I would have waited till the emergency came, and only given up the money when nothing else would do. But my friends thought it best to provide against the contingency; they acted on their own responsibility, and I am not disturbed about the result. But, having acted on a true principle, I *do not feel free to disavow their proceedings.*

In conclusion, let me say, I anticipate no such change in my position as you predict. I shall be Frederick Douglass still, and once a slave still. I shall neither be made to forget nor cease to feel the wrongs of my enslaved fellow-countrymen. My knowledge of slavery will be the same, and my hatred of it will be the same. By the way, I have never made my own person and suffering the theme of public discourse, but have always based my appeal upon the wrongs of the three millions now in chains; and these shall still be the burthen of my speeches. You intimate that I may reject the papers, and allow them to remain in the hands of those friends who have effected the purchase, and thus avail myself of the security afforded by them, without sharing any part of the responsibility of the transaction. My objection to this is one of honor. I do not think it would be very honorable on my part, to remain silent during the whole transaction, and giving it more than my silent approval; and then, when the thing is completed, and I am safe, attempt to play the *hero*, by throwing off all responsibility in the matter. It might be said, and said with great propriety, "Mr. Douglass, your indignation is very good, and has but one fault, and that is, *it comes too late!*" It would be a show of bravery when the danger is over. From every view I have been able to take of the subject, I am persuaded to receive the papers, if presented,—not, however, as a proof of my right to be free, for *that is self-evident,* but as a proof that my friends have been legally robbed of £150, in order to secure that which is the birth-right of every man. And I will hold up those papers before the world, in proof of the plundering character of the American government. It shall be the brand of infamy, stamping the nation, in whose name the deed was done, as a great aggregation of hypocrites, thieves and liars,—and their condemnation is just. They declare that all men are created equal, and have a natural and inalienable right to liberty, while they rob me of £150, as a condition of my enjoying this natural and inalienable right. It will be their condemnation, in their own hand-writing, and may be held up to the world as a means of humbling that haughty republic into repentance.

I agree with you, that the contest which I have to wage is against the government of the United States. But the representative of that government is the slaveholder, *Thomas Auld.* He is commander-in-chief of the army and navy. The whole civil and naval force of the nation are at his disposal. He may command all these to his assistance, and bring them all to bear upon me, until I am made entirely subject to his will, or submit to be robbed myself, or allow my friends to be robbed, of seven hundred and fifty dollars. And rather than be subject to his will, I have submitted to be robbed, or allowed my friends to be robbed, of the seven hundred and fifty dollars.

Sincerely yours,
Frederick Douglass

The Liberator, January 29, 1847

FAREWELL SPEECH TO THE BRITISH PEOPLE, at London Tavern, London, England, March 30, 1847

Mr. Chairman, Ladies and Gentlemen:

I never appear before an audience like that which I now behold, without feeling my incompetency to do justice to the cause which I am here to advocate, or to meet the expectations which are generally created for me, by the friends who usually precede me in speaking. Certainly, if the eulogiums bestowed upon me this evening were correct, I should be able to chain the attention of this audience for hours by my eloquence. But, sir, I claim none of these qualities. While I feel grateful for the generosity of my friends in bestowing them upon me, I am conscious of possessing very little just right to them; for I am but a plain, blunt man —a poor slave, or, rather, one who has been a slave. [Cheers.] Never had I a day's schooling in my life; all that I have of education I have stolen. [Laughter.] I am desirous, therefore, at once to relieve you from any anticipation of a great speech, which, from what you have heard from our esteemed friend, the chairman, and the gentlemen who preceded me, you might have been led to expect. That I am deeply, earnestly, and devotedly engaged in advocating the cause of my oppressed brethren, is most true; and in that character, as their representative, I hail your kind expression of feeling towards me this evening, and receive it with the profoundest gratitude. I will make use of these demonstrations of your warm approbation hereafter; I will take them home in my memory; they shall be written upon my heart; and I will employ them in that land of boasted liberty and light, but, at the same time, of abject slavery, to which I am going, for the purpose of overthrowing that accursed system of bondage, and restoring the Negroes, throughout its wide domain, to their lost liberty and rights. Sir, the time for argument upon this question is over, so far as the right of the slave to himself is concerned; and hence I feel less freedom in speaking here this evening, than I should have done under other circumstances. Place me in the midst of a pro-slavery mob in the United States, where my rights as a man are cloven down—let me be in an assembly of ministers or politicians who call in question my claim to freedom—and then, indeed, I can stand up and open my mouth; then assert boldly and strongly the rights of my manhood. [Cheers.] But where all is admitted—where almost every man is waiting for the end of a sentence that he may respond to it with a cheer —listening for the last words of the most radical resolution that he may hold up his hand in favour of it—why, then, under such circumstances, I certainly have very little to do. You have done all for me. Still, sir, I may manage, out of the scraps of the cloth which you have left, to make a coat of many colours, not such an one as Joseph was clothed in, yet still bearing some resemblance to it. I do not, however, promise to make you a very connected speech. I have listened to the patriotic, or rather respectful, language applied to America and Americans this evening. I confess, that although I am going back to that country, though I have many dear friends there, though I expect to end my days upon its soil, I am, nevertheless, not here to make any profession whatever of respect for that country, of attachment to its politicians, or love for its churches or national institutions. The fact is, the whole system, the entire network of American society, is one great falsehood, from beginning to end. I might say, that the present generation of Americans have become dishonest men from the circumstances by which they are surrounded. Seventy years ago, they went to the battle-field in defence of liberty. Sixty years ago, they framed a constitution, over the very gateway of which they inscribed, "To secure the blessings of liberty to ourselves and posterity." In their celebrated Declaration of Independence, they made the loudest and clearest assertions of the rights of man; and yet at that very time the identical men who drew up that Declaration of Independence, and framed the American democratic constitution, were trafficking in the blood and souls of their fellow men. [Hear, hear.] From the period of the first adoption of the constitution of the United States downward, everything good and great in the heart of the American people—everything patriotic within their breasts—has been summoned to defend this great lie before the world. They have been driven from their very patriotism, to defend this great falsehood. How have they done it? Why, by wrapping it up in honeyed words. [Hear.] By disguising it, and calling it "our peculiar institution;" "our social system;" "our patriarchal institution;" "our domestic institution;" and so forth. They have spoken of it in every possible way, except the right way. In no less than three clauses of their constitution may be found a spirit of the most deadly hostility to the liberty of the black man in that country, and yet clothed in such language as no Englishman, to whom its meaning was unknown, could take offence at. For instance, the President of the United States is required, at all times and under any circumstances, to call out the army and navy to suppress "domestic insurrection." Of course, all Englishmen, upon a superficial reading of that clause of the constitution, would very readily assent to the justice of the proposition involved in it; they would agree at once in its perfect propriety. "The army and navy! what are they good for if not to suppress insurrections, and preserve the peace, tranquillity, and harmony of the state?" But what does this language really mean, sir? What is its signification, as shadowed forth practically, in that constitution? What is the idea it conveys to the mind of the American? Why, that every man who casts a ball into the American ballot-box—every man who pledges himself to raise his hand in support of the American constitution—every individual who swears to support this instrument—at the same time swears that the slaves of that country shall either remain slaves or die. [Hear, hear.] This clause of the constitution, in fact, converts every white American into an enemy to the black man in that land of professed liberty. Every bayonet, sword, musket, and cannon has its deadly aim at the bosom of the Negro: 3,000,000 of the coloured race are lying there under the heels of 17,000,000 of their white fellow creatures.

There they stand, with all their education, with all their religion, with all their moral influence, with all their means of co-operation—there they stand, sworn before God and the universe, that the slave shall continue a slave or die. [Hear, hear, and cries of "Shame."] Then, take another clause of the American constitution. "No person held to service or labour, in any state within the limits thereof, escaping into another, shall in consequence of any law or regulation therein, be released from such service or labour, but shall be delivered up to be claimed by the party to whom such service or labour may be due." Upon the face of this clause there is nothing of injustice or inhumanity in it. It appears perfectly in accordance with justice, and in every respect humane. It is, indeed, just what it should be, according to your English notion of things and the general use of words. But what does it mean in the United States? I will tell you what it signifies there—that if any slave, in the darkness of midnight, looks down upon himself, feeling his limbs and thinking himself a man, and entitled to the rights of a man, shall steal away from his hovel or quarter, snap the chain that bound his leg, break the fetter that linked him to slavery, and seek refuge from the free institutions of a democracy, within the boundary of a monarchy, that that slave, in all his windings by night and by day, in his way from the land of slavery to the abode of freedom, shall be liable to be hunted down like a felon, and dragged back to the hopeless bondage from which he was endeavouring to escape. So that this clause of the constitution is one of the most effective safeguards of that slave system of which we have met here this evening to express our detestation. This clause of the American constitution makes the whole land one vast hunting-ground for men: it gives to the slaveholder the right at any moment to set his well-trained bloodhounds upon the track of the poor fugitive; hunt him down like a wild beast, and hurl him back to the jaws of slavery, from which he had, for a brief space of time, escaped. This clause of the constitution consecrates every rood of earth in that land over which the star-spangled banner waves as slave-hunting ground. Sir, there is no valley so deep, no mountain so high, no plain so expansive, no spot so sacred, throughout the length and breadth of America, as to enable a man, not having a skin coloured like your own, to enjoy the free and unrestrained right to his own hands. If he attempt to assert such a right he may be hunted down in a moment. Sir, in the Mosaic economy, to which reference has been made this evening by a preceding speaker, we have a command given, as it were, amid the thunders and lightnings from Sinai, "Thou shalt *not* deliver unto his master the servant that is escaped unto thee: he shall dwell with thee in the place that liketh him best: thou shalt not oppress him!" America, religious America, has run into the very face of Jehovah, and said, "Thou *shalt* deliver him unto his master." [Hear, hear.] "Thou shalt deliver unto the tyrant, who usurps authority over his fellow man, the trembling bondman that escapes into your midst." Sir, this clause of the American constitution is one of the most deadly enactments against the natural rights of man: above and beyond all its other provisions, it serves to keep up that system of fraud, wrong, and inhumanity which is now crushing 3,000,000 of human beings identified with me in their complexion, and formerly in their chains. How is it? Why, the slaveholders of the South would be wholly unable to hold their slaves were it not for the existence of the protection afforded by this constitution; but for this the slaves would run away. No, no; they do not love their masters so well as the tyrants sometimes flatter themselves; they do frequently run away. You have an instance of their disposition to run away before you. [Loud cheers.]

Why, sir, the Northern States claim to be exempt from all responsibility in the matter of the slaveholding of America, because they do not actually hold slaves themselves upon their own soil. But this is a mere subterfuge. What is the actual position of those Northern States? If they are not actual slaveholders, they stand around the slave system and support it. They say to the slaveholder, "We have a sentiment against—we have a feeling opposed to—we have an abhorrence of—slavery. We would not hold slaves ourselves, and we are most sincerely opposed to slavery; but, still, if your Negroes run away from you to us, we will return them to you. And, while you can make the slaves believe that we will so return them, why, of course, they will not run away into our states: and, then, if they should attempt to gain their freedom by force, why, we will bring down upon them the whole civil, military, and naval power of the nation and crush them again into subjection. While we make them believe that we will do this, we give them the most complete evidence that we will, by our votes in congress and in the senate, by our religious assemblies, our synods, presbyteries and conferences, by our individual votes, by our deadly hate and deep prejudice against the coloured man, even when he is free, we will, by all these evidences, give you the means of convincing the slave, that, if he does attempt to gain his freedom, we will kill him. But still, notwithstanding all this, let it be clearly understood that we hate slavery." [Laughter and cheers.] This is the guilty position even of those who do not themselves hold slaves in America. And, under such circumstances, I really cannot be very patriotic when speaking of their national institutions and boasted constitution, and, therefore, I hope you will not expect any very eloquent outbursts of eulogy or praise of America from me upon the present occasion. [Loud cheers.] No, my friends; I am going back, determined to be honest with America. I am going to the United States in a few days, but I go there to do, as I have done here, to unmask her pretensions to republicanism, and expose her hypocritical professions of Christianity; to denounce her high claims to civilisation, and proclaim in her ears the wrongs of those who cry day and night to Heaven, "How long! how long! O Lord God of Sabaoth!" [Loud cheers.] I go to that land, not to foster her national pride, or utter fulsome words about her greatness. She is great in territory; great in numerical strength; great in intellectual sagacity; great in her enterprise and industry. She may boast of her broad lakes and mighty rivers; but, sir, while I remember, that with her broadest lakes and finest rivers, the tears and blood of my brethren are mingled and forgotten, I cannot speak well of her; I cannot be loud in her praise, or pour forth warm eulogiums upon her name or institutions. [Cheers.] No; she is unworthy of the name of great or free. She stands upon the quivering heartstrings of 3,000,000 of people. She punishes the black man for crimes, for which she allows the white man to escape. She declares in her statutebook, that the black man shall be seventy times more liable to the punishment of death than the white man. In the state of Virginia, there are seventy-one crimes for which a black man may be punished with death, only one of which crimes will bring upon the white man a like punishment. [Hear, hear.] She will not allow her black population to meet together and worship God according to the dictates of their own consciences. If they assemble together more than seven in number for the purpose of worshipping God, or improving their minds in any way, shape, or form, each one of them may legally be taken and whipped with thirty-nine lashes upon his bare back. If any one of them shall be found riding a horse, by day or by night, he may be taken and whipped forty lashes on his naked back, have his ears cropped, and his cheek branded with a red-hot iron. In all the slave states south, they make it a crime punishable with severe fines, and imprisonment in many cases, to teach or instruct a slave to read the pages of Inspired Wisdom. In the state of Mississippi, a man is liable to a heavy fine for teaching a slave to read. In the state of Alabama, for the third offence, it is death to teach a slave to read. In the state of Louisiana, for the second offence, it is death to teach a slave to read. In the state of South Carolina, for the third offence of teaching a slave to read, it is death by the law. To aid a slave in escaping from a brutal owner, no matter how inhuman the treatment he may have received at the hands of his tyrannical master, it is death by the law. For a woman, in defence of her own person and dignity, against the brutal and infernal designs of a determined master, to raise her hand in protection of her chastity, may legally subject her to be put to death upon the spot. [Loud cries of "Shame, shame."] Sir, I cannot speak of such a nation as this with any degree of complacency, [cheers], and more especially when that very nation is loud and long in its boasts of holy liberty and light; when, upon the wings of the press, she is hurling her denunciations at the despotisms of Europe, when she is embracing every opportunity to scorn and scoff at the English government, and taunt and denounce her people as a community of slaves, bowing under a haughty monarchy; when she has stamped upon her coin, from the cent to the dollar, from the dollar to the eagle, the sacred name of liberty; when upon every hill may be seen erected, a pole, bearing the cap of liberty, under which waves the star-spangled banner; when, upon every 4th of July, we hear declarations like this: "O God! we thank Thee that we live in a land of religious and civil liberty!" when from every platform, upon that day, we hear orators rise and say:—

> *Ours is a glorious land;*
>   *Her broad-arms stretch from shore to shore,*
> *The broad Pacific chafes her strand,*
>   *She hears the dark Atlantic roar;*
> *Enamelled on her ample breast,*
>   *A many a goodly prospect stands.*
> *Ours is the land of the free and the home of the brave.*

I say, when professions like these are put forth vauntingly before the world, and I remember the scenes I have witnessed in, and the facts I know, respecting that country, why, then, let others do as they will, I have no word of patriotic applause for America or her institutions. [Enthusiastic and protracted cheering.] America presents to the world an anomaly, such as no other nation ever did or can present before mankind. The people of the United States are the boldest in their pretensions to freedom, and the loudest in their profession of love of liberty; yet no nation upon the face of the globe can exhibit a statute-book so full of all that is cruel, malicious, and infernal, as the American code of laws. Every page is red with the blood of the American slave. O'Connell once said, speaking of Ireland—no matter for my illustration, how truly or falsely—that "her history may be traced, like the track of a wounded man through a crowd." If this description can be given of Ireland, how much more true is it when applied to the sons and daughters of Africa, in the United States? Their history is nothing but blood! blood!—blood in the morning, blood at noon, blood at night! They have had blood to drink; they have had their own blood shed. At this moment we may exclaim

> *What, ho! our countrymen in chains!*
>   *The whip on woman's shrinking flesh!*
> *Our soil still redd'ning with the stains*
>   *Caught from her scourging, warm and fresh!*

> *What! mothers from their children riven!*
> *What! God's own image bought and sold!*
> *Americans to market driven,*
> *And barter'd, as the brutes, for gold!*

And this, too, sir, in the midst of a people professing, not merely republicanism, not merely democratical institutions, but civilisation; nay, more—Christianity, in its highest, purest, and broadest sense [hear, hear]; claiming to be the heaven-appointed nation, in connexion with the British, to civilise, christianise, and evangelise the world. For this purpose, sir, we have our Tract, Bible, and Missionary Societies; our Sabbath-school and Education Societies; we have in array all these manifestations of religious life, and yet, in the midst of them all—amid the eloquence of the orators who swagger at all these meetings—may be heard the clanking of the fetter, the rattling of the chain, and the crack of the slave-driver's whip. The very man who ascends the platform, and is greeted with rounds of applause when he comes forward to speak on the subject of extending the victories of the cross of Christ, "from the rivers to the ends of the earth," has actually come to that missionary meeting with money red with the blood of the slave; with gold dripping with gore from the plantations. The very man who stands up there— Dr. Plummer, for instance, Dr. Marsh, Dr. Anderson, Dr. Cooper, or some other such doctor—comes to the missionary meeting for the purpose of promoting Christianity, Evangelical Christianity, with the price of blood in his possession. He stands up and preaches with it in his pocket, and gives it to aid the holy cause of sending missionaries to heathen lands. This is the spectacle we witness annually at New York and Philadelphia; and sometimes they have the temerity to come as far as Boston with their blood-stained money. We are a nation of inconsistencies; completely made up of inconsistencies. Mr. John C. Calhoun, the great Southern statesman of the United States, is regarded in that country as a real democrat, "dyed in the wool," "a right out-and-out democrat," "a back-bone democrat." By these and similar phrases they speak of him; and yet, sir, that very man stands upon the floor of the senate, and actually boasts that he is a robber! that he is an owner of slaves in the Southern states. He positively makes his boast of this disgraceful fact, and assigns it as a reason why he should be listened to as a man of consequence—a person of great importance. All his pretensions are founded upon the fact of his being a slaveowner. The audacity of these men is actually astounding; I scarcely know what to say in America, when I hear men deliberately get up and assert a right to property in my limbs—my very body and soul; that they have a right to *me!* that *I* am in their hands, "a chattel personal to all intents, purposes, and constructions whatsoever;" "a thing" to be bought and sold!—to be sure, having moral perceptions; certainly possessing intellect, and a sense of my own rights, and endowed with resolution to assert them whenever an opportunity occurred; and yet, notwithstanding, a slave! a marketable commodity! I do not know what to think of these men; I hardly know how to answer them when they speak in this manner. And, yet, this self-same John C. Calhoun, while he vehemently declaims for liberty, and asserts that any attempt to abridge the rights of the people should be met with the sternest resistance on all hands, deliberately stands forth at the head of the democracy of that country and talks of his right to property in me; and not only in my body, but in the bodies and souls of hundreds and thousands of others in the United States. As with this honorable gentleman, so is it with the doctors of divinity in America; for, after all, slavery finds no defenders there so formidable as them. They are more skilful, adroit, and persevering, and will descend even to greater meannesses, than any other class of opponents with whom the abolitionists have to contend in that country. The church in America is, beyond all question, the chief refuge of slavery. When we attack it in the state, it runs into the street, to the mob; when we attack it in the mob, it flies to the church; and, sir, it is a melancholy fact, that it finds a better, safer, and more secure protection from the shafts of abolitionism within the sacred enclosure of the Christian temple than from any other quarter whatever. [Hear, hear.] Slavery finds no champions so bold, brave, and uncompromising as the ministers of religion. These men come forth, clad in all the sanctity of the pastoral office, and enforce slavery with the Bible in their hands, and under the awful name of the Everlasting God. We there find them preaching sermon after sermon in support of the system of slavery as an institution consistent with the Gospel of Jesus Christ. We have commentary after commentary attempting to wrest the sacred pages of the Bible into a justification of the iniquitous system. And, sir, this may explain to you what might otherwise appear unaccountable in regard to the conduct and proceedings of American abolitionists. I am very desirous of saying a word or two on this point, upon which there has been much misrepresentation. I say, the fact that slavery takes refuge in the churches of the United States will explain to you another fact, which is, that the opponents of slavery in America are almost universally branded there—and, I am sorry to say, to some extent in this country also—as infidels. [Loud cries of "Shame, shame."] Why is this?

Simply because slavery is sheltered by the church. The warfare in favour of emancipation in America is a very different thing from the warfare which you had to wage on behalf of freedom in the West India Islands. On that occasion, thank God! religion was in its right position, and slavery in its proper place—in fierce antagonism to each other. Religion and slavery were then the enemies of each other. Slavery hated Religion with the utmost intensity; it pursued the missionary with the greatest malignity, burning down his chapel, mobbing his house, jeopardising his life, and rendering his property utterly insecure. There was an antipathy deep and lasting between slavery and the exponents of Christianity in the West India Islands. All honour to the names of Knibb and Burchell! [Loud cheers.] Those men were indeed found faithful to Him who commanded them to "Preach deliverance to the captive, and the opening of the prison to them that were bound." [Loud cheers.] But, sir, the natural consequence of such faithfulness was, that these men were hated with the most deadly hate by the slaveowners, who with their abettors, used every effort to crush that living voice of truth coming from the bosom of the Christian church, which was endeavouring to dash down the bloody altars of slavery, and scatter its guilty profits to the winds. Slavery was opposed by the church in the West Indies: not so in America; there, religion and slavery are linked and interlinked with each other—woven and interwoven together. In the United States we have slaveholders as class-leaders, ministers of the Gospel, elders, deacons, doctors of divinity, professors of theology, and even bishops. We have the slaveholder in all parts of the church. Wherever he is, he is an active, energetic, vigilant man. Slavery never sleeps or slumbers. The slaveholder who goes to his bed for the purpose of taking rest does not pass his night in tranquillity and peace; but, knowing his danger, he takes his pistol, bowie-knife, and dirk with him. He is uneasy; he is aware that he lies upon bleeding heartstrings, that he sleeps upon the wretchedness of men, that he rests himself upon the quivering flesh of his fellow creatures around him; he is conscious that there is intellect burning—a spark of divinity enkindled—within the bosoms of the men he oppresses, who are watching for, and will seize upon, the first opportunity to burst their bonds asunder, and mete out justice to the wretch who has doomed them to slavery. [Loud cheers.] The slaveowner, therefore, is compelled to be watchful; he cannot sleep; there is a morbid sensitiveness in his breast upon this subject: everything that looks like opposition to slavery is promptly met by him and put down. Whatever, either in the church or the state, may appear to have a tendency to undermine, sap, or destroy the foundation of slavery is instantly grappled with; and, by their religion, their energy, their perseverance, their unity of feeling, and identity of interest, the slaveholder and the church have ever had the power to command a majority to put down any efforts for the emancipation of the coloured race, and to sustain slavery in all its horrors. Thus has slavery been protected and sheltered by the church. Slavery has not only framed our civil and criminal code, it has not only nominated our presidents, judges, and diplomatic agents, but it has also given to us the most popular commentators on the Bible in America. [Hear, hear.] It has given to us our religion, shaped our morality, and fashioned it favourable to its own existence. Thus is it that slavery is ensconced at this moment; and, when the abolitionist sees slavery thus woven and interwoven with the very texture—with the whole network—of our social and religious organizations, why he resolves, at whatever hazard of reputation, ease, comfort, luxury, or even of life itself, to pursue, and, if possible, destroy it. [Loud cheers.] Sir, to illustrate our principle of action, I might say that we adopt the motto of Pat, upon entering a Tipperary row. Said he, "Wherever you see a head, hit it!" [Loud cheers and laughter.] Sir, the abolitionists have resolved, that wherever slavery manifests itself in the United States, they will hit it. [Renewed cheering.] They will deal out their heaviest blows upon it. Hence, having followed it from the state to the street, from the mob to the church, from the church to the pulpit, they are now hunting it down there. But slavery in the present day affects to be very pious; it is uncommonly devotional, all at once. It feels disposed to pray the very moment you touch it. The hideous fiend kneels down and pretends to engage in devotional exercises; and when we come to attack it, it howls piously—"Off! you are an infidel"; and straightway the press in America, and some portion of the press in this land also, take up the false cry. [Hear, hear.] Forthwith a clamour is got up here, not against the slaveholder, but against the man who is virtuously labouring for the overthrow of that which his assailants profess to hate—slavery. [Loud cheers.] A fierce outcry is raised, not in favour of the slave, but against him and against his best and only friends. Sir, when the history of the emancipation movement shall have been fairly written, it will be found that the abolitionists of the nineteenth century were the only men who dared to defend the Bible from the blasphemous charge of sanctioning and sanctifying Negro slavery. [Loud cheers.] It will be found that they were the only men who dared to stand up and demand, that the churches calling themselves by the name of Christ, should entirely, and for ever, purify themselves from all contact, connection, and fellowship with men who gain their fortunes by the blood of souls. It will be found that they were the men who "cried aloud and spared not;" who "lifted their voices like trumpets," against the giant iniquity by which they were surrounded. It will then be seen that they were the men who planted themselves on the immutable, eternal, and all-comprehensive principle of the sacred New Testament—"All things whatsoever ye would that men should do unto you, do ye even so unto them"—that, acting on this principle, and feeling that if the fetters were on their own limbs, the chain upon their own persons, the lash falling quick and hard upon their own quivering bodies, they would desire their fellow men about them to be faithful to their cause; and, therefore, carrying out this principle, they have dared to risk their lives, fortunes, nay, their all, for the purpose of rescuing from the tyrannous grasp of the slaveholder these 3,000,000 of trampled-down children of men. [Loud cheers.]

Sir, the foremost, strongest, and mightiest among those who have completely identified themselves with the Negroes in the United States, I will now name here; and I do so because his name has been most unjustly coupled with odium in this country. [Hear, hear.] I will name, if only as an expression of gratitude on my part, my beloved, esteemed, and almost venerated friend, William Lloyd Garrison. [Loud and prolonged cheering.] Sir, I have now been in this country for nineteen months; I have gone through its length and breadth; I have had sympathy here and sympathy there; co-operation here, and co-operation there; in fact, I have scarcely met a man who has withheld fellowship from me as an abolitionist, standing unconnected with William Lloyd Garrison. [Hear.] Had I stood disconnected from that great and good man, then numerous and influential parties would have held out to me the right hand of fellowship, sanctioned my proceedings in England, backed me up with money and praise, and have given me a great reputation, so far as they were capable; and they were men of influence. And why, sir, is William Lloyd Garrison hated and despised by certain parties in this country? What has he done to deserve such treatment at their hands? He has done that which all great reformers and pioneers in the cause of freedom or religion have ever been called upon to do—made himself unpopular for life in the maintenance of great principles. He has thrown himself, as it were, over the ditch as a bridge; his own body, his personal reputation, his individual property, his wide and giant-hearted intellect, all were sacrificed to form a bridge that others might pass over and enjoy a rich reward from the labours that he had bestowed, and the seed which he had sown. He has made himself disreputable. How? By his uncompromising hostility to slavery, by his bold, scathing denunciation of tyranny; his unwavering, inflexible adherence to principle; and by his frank, open, determined spirit of opposition to everything like cant and hypocrisy. [Loud cheers.] Such is the position in which he stands among the American people. And the same feeling exists in this country to a great extent. Because William Lloyd Garrison has upon both sides of the Atlantic fearlessly unmasked hypocrisy, and branded impiety in language in which impiety deserves to be be characterized, he has thereby brought down upon himself the fierce execrations of a religious party in this land. But, sir, I do not like, upon the present occasion, even to allude to this subject; for the party who have acted in this manner is small and insignificant; so impotent for good, so well known for its recklessness of statement, so proverbial for harshness of spirit, that I will not dwell any longer on their conduct. I feel that I ought not to trespass upon your patience any further. [Loud cheers and cries of "Go on, go on."] Well, then, as you are so indulgent to me, I will refer to another matter. It would not be right and proper, from any consideration of regard and esteem which I feel for those who have honoured me by assembling here this evening to bid me farewell—especially to some who have honoured me and the cause I am identified with, honoured themselves and our common humanity, by being present to-night upon this platform—I say it would not be proper in me, out of deference to any such persons, on this occasion, to fail to advert to what I deem one of the greatest sins of omission ever committed by British Christians in this country. I allude to the recent meeting of the Ecumenical Evangelical Alliance. [Hear.] Sir, I must be permitted to say a word or two upon this matter. [Hear.] From my very love to British Christians—out of esteem for the very motives of those excellent men who composed the British part of that great convention—from all these considerations, I am bound to state here my firm belief, that they suffered themselves to be sadly hoodwinked upon this point. [Hear, hear.] They were misled and cajoled into a position on this question, which no subsequent action can completely obliterate or entirely atone for. They had it in their power to have given slavery a blow which would have sent it reeling to its grave, as if smitten by a voice or an arm from Heaven. They had moral power; they had more—they had religious power. They were in a position which no other body ever occupied, and in which no other association will ever stand, while slavery exists in the United States. [Hear.] They were raised up on a pinnacle of great eminence: they were "a city set on a hill." They were a body to whom the whole evangelical world was looking, during that memorable month of August. Pressed down deep among evangelical Christians, under the feet of some there, were 3,000,000 of slaves looking to the Evangelical Alliance, with uplifted hands, with imploring tones—or, rather, I should say in the absence of tones, for the slave is dead; he has no voice in such assemblies; he can send no delegates to Bible and Missionary Societies, Temperance Conventions, or Evangelican Alliances; he is not permitted to send representatives there to tell his wrongs. He has his pressing evils and deeply aggravated wrongs, to which he is constantly subject; but he is not allowed to depute any voice to plead his cause. Still, in the silence of annihilation—of mental and moral annihilation—in the very eloquence of extinction, he cried to the Evangelical Alliance to utter a word on behalf of his freedom. They "passed him by on the other side." [Loud cheers.] Sir, I am sorry for this, deeply sorry; sorry on their own account, for I know they are not satisfied with their position. I am sorry that they should, from a timidity on their part—a fear of offending those who were called "The American brethren"—have given themselves the pain and trouble to repent on this question. But still, I hope they will repent; and I believe that many of them have already repented [hear, hear]; I believe that those who were hoodwinked on that occasion, when they shall be brought to see that they were miserably deceived—misled by the jack o' lanterns from America, [laughter]—that they will add another element to their former opposition to slavery, and that is, the pain and sense of injustice done to themselves on the part of the American delegates. From the very feeling of having been betrayed into a wrong position, they will feel bound to deal a sharp, powerful, and pungent rebuke to those guilty men who dared to lead them astray. Sir, after all, I do not wonder at the manner in which the British delegates were deluded; when I reflect upon the subtlety of the Americans, their apparently open, free, frank, candid, and unsophisticated disposition—how they stood up and declared to the

British brethren that they were honest, and looked so honestly, and smiled so blandly at the same time. No; I do not wonder at their success, when I think how old and skilful they are in the practice of misrepresentation —in the art of lying. [Hear.] Coarse as the expression I have here applied to them may be, Mr. Chairman, it is, nevertheless, true; the thing exists. If I am branded for coarseness on the present occasion, I must excuse myself by telling you I have a coarse thing and a foul business to lay before you. As with the president, so with these deputations from America; there is not a single inaugural speech, not an annual message, but teems with lies like this—that "in this land every man enjoys the protection of the law, the protection of his property, the protection of his person, the protection of his liberty." They iterate and reiterate these statements over and over again. Thus, these Americans, as I said before, are skilled in the art of falsehood. I do not wonder at their success, when I recollect that they brought religion to aid them in their fraud; for they not only told their falsehood with the blandness, oratory, and smiling looks of the politicians in their own country, but they combined with those seductive qualities a loud profession of piety; and in this way they have succeeded well in misleading the judgments of some of the most intrepid, bright, and illustrious of slavery's foes in the ranks of the ministers of religion of England. [Hear.] Among the arguments used at the meeting of the Evangelical Alliance, the following stood pre-eminent: "You, British ministers, should not interfere with slavery, or pass resolutions to exclude slaveholders from your fellowship, because," it was cooly said, "the slaveholders are placed in *difficult circumstances*." It was stated that the slaveholders could not get rid of their slaves if they wished; that they were anxiously desirous of emancipating their slaves, but that the laws of the states in which they lived were such as to compel them to hold them whether they would or not. It was alleged that their peculiar circumstances make it a matter of Christian duty in them to hold their slaves.

Sir, I know the stubborn and dogged manner in which these statements were made; and I am conscious how well calculated they were to excite sympathy for the slaveholders: but I am here to tell you, that there was not one word of truth in any of these plausible assertions. There was, indeed, a slight shadow of light; a glimmering might be detected by an argus eye, but not certainly by the eye of man. There was a faint semblance of truth in it; a slight shadow; but, after all, it was only a semblance. [Hear.] What are the facts of the case? Just these: that in three or four of the Southern states, when a man emancipates his slaves, he is obliged to give a bond that such slaves shall not become chargeable to the state as paupers. That is all the "impediment;" that is the whole of the "difficulty" as regards the law. But the fact is, that the free Negroes never become paupers. I do not know that I ever saw a black pauper. The free Negroes in Philadelphia, 25,000 in number, not only support their own poor, by their own benevolent societies, but actually pay 500 dollars per annum for the support of the white paupers in the state. [Loud cheers.] No, sir, the statement is false; we do not have black paupers in America; we leave pauperism to be fostered and taken care of by white people; not that I intend any disrespect to my audience in making this statement. [Hear.] I can assure you I am in nowise prejudiced against colour. [Laughter.] But the idea of a black pauper in the United States is most absurd. But, after all, what does the objection amount to? What if really they have to give a bond to the State that the slaves whom they emancipate should not become chargeable to the state? Why, sir, one would think this would be a very little matter of consideration to a just and Christian man; considering that all the wealth that this conscientious slave-holder possesses, he has wrung from the unrequited toil of the slave. It is not much, when it is recollected that he kept the poor Negro in ignorance, and worked him twenty-eight or thirty years of his life, and that he has had the fruit of his labour during the best part of his days. But yet, it is gravely stated, that the slave-owner looks on it as a great hardship, that if he emancipates his slave he is bound not to suffer him to become chargeable to the state. Why, the money which the slave should have earned in his youthful days, to support him in the season of age, has been wrung from him by his Christian master. But the slaveholder of America had no occasion ever to have had such a difficulty as this to contend with before he gets rid of his slave. I may mention a fact, which is not generally known here, that this law was adopted in the slave states —for what purpose? I will tell you why: because it was previously the custom of a large class of slaveholders to hold their slaves in bondage from infancy to old age, so long as they could toil and struggle and were worth a penny a day to their masters. While they could do this, they were kept; but, as soon as they became old and decrepit—the moment they were unable to toil—their masters, from very benevolence and humanity of course, gave them their freedom. [Hear, hear.] The inhabitants of the states, to prevent this burden upon their community, made the masters liable for their support under such circumstances. Dr. Cox did not tell you that in his famous speech in the Evangelical Alliance.

[Hear, hear.] I mean Dr. Cox of America. (Mr. Douglass here turned to Dr. Cox of Hackney, which caused much laughter.) I do rejoice that there is another Dr. Cox in the world, of a very different character from the one in America, to redeem the name of Cox from the infamy that must necessarily settle down upon the head of that Cox, who, with wiles and subtlety, led the Evangelical Alliance astray upon this question. [Cheers.] I am glad—I am delighted—I am grateful—profoundly grateful, in review of all the facts, that my friend—the slave's friend—Dr. Cox of Hackney, has been pleased to give us his presence to-night. [Renewed cheers.] But now, really if the slaveholder is watching for an opportunity to get rid of his slaves, what has he to do? Why, just nothing at all—he has only to *cease to do*. He has to undo what he has already done; nothing more. He has only to tell the slave, "I have no longer any claim upon you as a slave." That is all that is necessary; and then the work is done. The Negro, simple in his understanding as he was represented this evening—somewhat unjustly, by the by [referring to some remarks made in a former part of the evening by the vocalist, Mr. Henry Russell]— would take care of the rest of the matter. He would have no difficulty in finding some way to gain his freedom, if his master only gave him permission so to do. The truth is, that the whole of America is cursed with slavery. There is upon our Northern and Western borders a land uncursed by slavery—a territory ruled over by the British power. There—

> *The lion at a virgin's feet*
> *Crouches, and lays his mighty paw*
> *Upon her lap—an emblem meet*
> *Of England's queen and England's law.* [Cheers.]

From the slave plantations of America the slave could run, under the guidance of the North-star, to that same land, and in the mane of the British lion he might find himself secure from the talons and beak of the American eagle. The American slave-holder has only to say to his slave, "To-morrow, I shall no longer hold you in bondage," and the slave forthwith goes, and is permitted—not merely "permitted"—oh! no, he is *welcomed* and received with open arms, by the British authorities; he is welcomed, not as a slave, but as a man; not as a bondman, but as a freeman; not as a captive, but as a brother. [Cheers.] He is received with kindness, and regarded and treated with respect as a man. The Americans have only to say to their slaves, "Go and be free;" and they go and are free. No power within the states, or out of the states, attempts to disturb the master in the exercise of his right of transferring his Negro from one country to the other. "Oh! but then," Dr. Cox would say, "brethren, although all this which Douglass states may be very true, yet you must know that there are some very poor masters, who are so situated in regard to pecuniary matters"—for the doctor is a very indirect speaker—"so situated, in regard to pecuniary concerns, that they would not be able to remove their slaves. I know a brother in the South—a dear brother" (Mr. Douglass here imitated the tone and style of Dr. Cox, in a manner which caused great laughter) "to whom I spoke on this subject; and I told him what a great sin I thought it was for him to hold slaves; but he said to me, 'Brother, I feel it as much as you do, [loud laughter], but what can I do? Here are my slaves; take them; you may have them; you may take them out of the state if your please.' Said he, "I could not; and I left them. [Renewed laughter.] Now what would you do?" said the doctor to the brethren at Manchester and Liverpool—"what would you do, if placed in such difficult circumstances?" The fact is, there is no truth in the existence of these difficulties at all. Sir, let me tell you what has stood as a standing article in our anti-slavery journals for the last ten years. When this plea was first put forth in America, and those intrepid champions of the slave, Gerrit Smith, Arthur Tappan, and other noble-minded abolitionists heard of it, what did they do? They inserted their cards in all the most respectable papers in America, and stated that there were 10,000 dollars ready at the service of any poor slaveholders who might not have the means of removing the Negroes they were desirous of emancipating. [Cheers.] Now, sir, the slaveholders must have seen this advertisement, for whatever difficulties they have to encounter, they find none in seeing money. [Hear, and laughter.] But, sir, was there ever a demand for a single red copper of the whole of those 10,000 dollars? Never; never. Now what does this fact prove? Why that there were no slaveholders who stood in need of such assistance; not one who wanted it for the purpose for which it might have been easily obtained, to meet the "difficult circumstances" stated by Dr. Cox. How Dr. Cox could, knowing that fact, as he must have done—for he is not so blind that he cannot see a dollar—I say how he could set up this false and contemptible plea before the world, and attempt to mislead the public mind of England upon the subject—I will not use a harsh expression, but I will say—that I cannot see how he could reconcile its concealment with honesty at any rate. That is the strongest word I will use in regard to this portion of his conduct. [Hear, hear.] He certainly knew better; at least, I think he must have known better; he ought to have done so; for it is astonishing how quickly he sees things generally. Another brother, the Reverend Doctor Marsh, also went into this subject, and told the brethren of the difficult circumstances in which the slaveholders were placed, especially the "Christian slaveholders;" for, mark this, they never apologise for infidel slaveholders! [Hear.] You never heard one of the whole deputation apologise for that brutal man—the uneducated slavedriver. No; it is the refined, polite, highly civilised, genteel, Christian part of the slaveholders, for whom they stand up and plead. Yes; they apologise for what they call "Christian slaveholders"—*white blackbirds!* [Loud cheers and laughter.]

Dr. Marsh stated, that if any persons in the United States were to emancipate their slaves, they would instantly be put into the penitentiary. [Laughter, and cries of "Oh, oh."] I have sometimes been astonished at the credulity of their English auditory; but I do not wonder at it, for John Bull is pretty honest himself, and he thinks other people are so also. But, yet, I must say that I am surprised when I find sagacious, intelligent men really carried away by such assertions as these. Why, sir, if this statement were true, another tinge, deeper and darker than any previously exhibited, would have appeared in the character of the American people. What! men are not only *permitted* to enslave, not only allowed by the government to rob and plunder, but actually *compelled* by the first government upon earth to live by plunder! Why, these men, by such statements, stamp their country with an infamy deeper than I can cast upon it by anything I could say; that is, admitting their statements were true. But, sir, America, deeply fallen and lost as she is to moral principle, has not embodied in the form of law any such compulsion of slavery as that which these reverend gentlemen attempt to make out. No, sir; the slaveholder can free his slaves. Why, he has the same right to emancipate as he has to whip his Negro. He whips him; he has a right to do what he pleases with his own; he may give his slave away. I was given away [hear]; I was given away by my father, or the man who was called my father, to his own brother. My master was a methodist class-leader. [Hear.] When he found that I had made my escape, and was a good distance out of his reach, he felt a little spark of benevolence kindled up in his heart; and he cast his eyes upon a poor brother of his—a poor, wretched, out-at-elbows, hat-crown-knocked-in brother [laughter]—a reckless brother, who had not been so fortunate as to possess such a number of slaves as he had done. Well, looking over the pages of some British newspaper, he saw his son Frederick a fugitive slave in a foreign country, in a state of exile; and he determined now, for once in his life, that he would be a little generous to this brother out at the elbows, and he therefore said to him, "Brother, I have got a Negro; that is, I have not got him, but the English have [cheers]. When a slave, his name was Frederick—Fred. Bailey. We called him Fred" (for the Negroes never have but one name); "but he fancied that he was something better than a slave, and so he gave himself two names. Well, that same Fred. is now actually changed into Frederick Douglass, and is going through the length and breadth of Great Britain, telling the wrongs of the slaves. Now, as you are very poor, and certainly will not be made poorer by the gift I am about to bestow upon you, I transfer to you all legal right to property in the body and soul of the said Frederick Douglass." [Laughter.] Thus was I transferred by my father to my uncle. Well, really, after all, I feel a little sympathy for my uncle, Hugh Auld. I did not wish to be altogether a losing game for Hugh, although, certainly, I had no desire myself to pay him any money; but if any one else felt disposed to pay him money, of course they might do so. But at any rate I confess I had less reluctance at seeing £150 paid to poor Hugh Auld than I should have had to see the same amount of money paid to his brother, Thomas Auld, for I really think poor Hugh needed it, while Thomas did not. Hugh is a poor scamp. I hope he may read or hear of what I am now saying. I have no doubt he will, for I intend to send him a paper containing a report of this meeting.

By-the-by, though, I want to tell the audience one thing which I forgot, and that is, that I have as much right to sell Hugh Auld as Hugh Auld had to sell me. If any of you are disposed to make a purchase of him, just say the word. [Laughter.] However, whatever Hugh and Thomas Auld may have done, I will not traffic in human flesh at all; so let Hugh Auld pass, for I will not sell him. [Cheers.] As to the kind friends who have made the purchase of my freedom, I am deeply grateful to them. I would never have solicited them to have done so, or have asked them for money for such a purpose. I never could have suggested to them the propriety of such an act. It was done from the prompting or suggestion of their own hearts, entirely independent of myself. While I entertain the deepest gratitude to them for what they have done, I do not feel like shouldering the responsibility of the act. I do, however, believe that there has been no right or noble principle sacrificed in the transaction. Had I thought otherwise, I would have been willingly "a stranger and a foreigner, as all my fathers were," through my life, in a strange land, supported by those dear friends whom I love in this country. I would have contented myself to have lived here rather than have had my freedom purchased at the violation or expense of principle. But, as I said before, I do not believe that any good principle has been violated. If there is anything to which exception may be taken, it is in the expediency, and not the principle, involved in the transaction. I wish to say one word more respecting another body who have been alluded to this evening. You see that I keep harping on the church and its ministers, and I do so for the best of all reasons, that however low the ministry in a country may be (they may take this admission and make what they can of it: I know they will interpret it in their own favour, as it may be so interpreted)—that however corrupt the stream of politics and religion, nevertheless the fountain of the purity, as well as of the corruption, of the community may be found in the pulpit. (Hear.) It is in the pulpit and the press—in the publications especially of the religious press—that we are to look for our right moral sentiment. [Hear, hear.] I assert this as my deliberate opinion, I know, against the views of many of those with whom I co-operate. I do believe, however dark and corrupt they may be in any country, the ministers of religion are always higher—of necessity higher—than the community about them. I mean, of course, as a whole. There are exceptions. They cannot be enunciating those great abstract principles of right without their exerting, to some extent, a healthy influence upon their own conduct, although their own conduct is often in violation of those great principles. I go, therefore, to the churches, and I ask the churches of England for their sympathy and support in this contest. Sir, the growing contact and communication between this country and the United States, renders it a matter of the utmost importance that the subject of slavery in America should be kept before the British public. [Hear.] The reciprocity of religious deputations—the interchange of national addresses—the friendly addresses on peace and upon the subject of temperance—the ecclesiastical connections of the two countries—their vastly increasing commercial intercourse resulting from the recent relaxation of the restrictive laws upon the commerce of this country—the influx of British literature into the United States as well as of American literature into this country—the constant tourists—the frequent visits to America by literary and philanthropic men—the improvement in the facility for the transportation of letters through the post-office, in steam navigation, as well as other means of locomotion—the extraordinary power and rapidity with which intelligence is transmitted from one country to another—all conspire to make it a matter of the utmost importance that Great Britain should maintain a healthy moral sentiment on the subject of slavery. Why, sir, does slavery exist in the United States? Because it is reputable: that is the reason. Why is it thus reputable in America? Because it is not so disreputable out of America as it ought to be. Why, then, is it not so disreputable out of the United States as it should be? Because its real character has not been so fully known as it ought to have been. Hence, sir, the necessity of an Anti-slavery League [Hear, hear, and cheers]—of men leaguing themselves together for the purpose of enlightening, raising, and fixing the public attention upon this foulest of all blots upon our common humanity. Let us, then, agitate this question. [Hear.] But, sir, I am met by the objection, that to do so in this country, is to excite, irritate, and disturb the slaveholder. Sir, this is just what I want. I wish the slaveholder to be irritated. I want him jealous: I desire to see him alarmed and disturbed. Sir, by thus alarming him, you have the means of blistering his conscience, and it can have no life in it unless it is blistered. Sir, I want every Englishman to point to the star-spangled banner and say—

> *United States! Your banner wears*
> *Two emblems, one of fame:*
> *Alas! the other that it bears*
> *Reminds us of your shame,*
> *The white man's liberty in types*
> *Stands blazoned on your stars;*
> *But what's the meaning of your stripes?*
> *They mean your Negroes' scars.*

"Oh!" it is said, "but by so doing you would stir up war between the two countries." Said a learned gentleman to me, "You will only excite angry feelings, and bring on war, which is a far greater evil than slavery." Sir, you need not be afraid of war with America while they have slavery in the United States. We have 3,000,000 of peace makers there. Yes, 3,000,000, sir—3,000,000 who have never signed the pledge of the noble Burritt,[16] but who are, nevertheless, as strong and as invincible peace-men as even our friend Elihu Burritt himself. Sir, the American slaveholders can appreciate these peace-makers: 3,000,000 of them stand there on the shores of America, and when our statesmen get warm, why these 3,000,000 keep cool. [Laughter]. When our legislators' tempers are excited, these peacemakers say, "Keep your tempers down, brethren!" The Congress talks about going to war, but these peace-makers suggest, "But what will you do at home?" When these slaveholders declaim about shouldering their muskets, buckling on their knapsacks, girding on their swords, and going to beat back and scourge the foreign invaders, they are told by these friendly monitors, "Remember, your wives and children are at home! Reflect that we are at home! We are on the plantations. You had better stay at home and look after us. True, we eat the bread of freemen; we take up the room of freemen; we consume the same commodities as freemen: but still we have no interest in the state, no attachment for the country: we are slaves! You cannot fight a battle in your own land, but, at the first tap of a foreign drum—the very moment the British standard shall be erected upon your soil, at the first trumpet-call to freedom—millions of slaves are ready to rise and to strike for their own liberty." [Loud cheers.] The slaveholders know this; they understand it well enough. No, no; you need not fear about war between Great Britain and America.[17] When Mr. Polk tells you that he will have the whole of Oregon, he only means to brag a little. When this boasting president tells you that he will have all that territory or go to war, he intends to retract his words the first favourable opportunity. When Mr. Webster says, fiercely, If you do not give back Madison Washington—the noble Madison Washington, who broke his fetters on the deck of the Creole,[18] achieved liberty for himself and one hundred and thirty-five others, and took refuge within your dominions—when this proud statesman tells you, that if you do not send this noble Negro back to chains and slavery, he will go to war with you, do not be alarmed; he does not mean any such thing. Leave him alone; he will find some way—some diplomatic stratagem almost inscrutable to the eyes of common men—by which to take back every syllable he has said. [Hear, hear.] You need not fear that you will have any war with America while slavery lasts, and while you as a people maintain your opposition to the accursed system. When you cease to feel any hostility to slavery, the slave-holders will then have no fear that the slaves will desert them for you, or will hate and fight against them in favour of you. So that, if only as a means of preserving peace, it were wise policy to advocate in England the cause of the emancipation of the American slaves. But, sir, England not only has power to do great good in this matter, but it is her duty to do so to the utmost of her ability. But I fear I am speaking too long. [Loud cheers, and cries of "No, no"; "Go on, go on."] Oh, my friends, you are very kind, but you are not very wise in saying so, allow me to tell you, with all due deference.

I must conclude, and that right early; for I have to speak again to-morrow night almost 200 miles from this place; and it becomes necessary, therefore, that I should bring my address to a close, if only from motives of self-preservation, which the Americans say is the first law of slavery. But before I sit down, let me say a few words at parting to my London friends, as well as those from the country, for I have reason to believe that there are friends présent from all parts of the United Kingdom. I look around this audience, and I see those who greeted me when I first landed on your soil. I look before me here, and I see representatives from Scotland, where I have been warmly received and kindly treated. Manchester is represented on this occasion, as well as a number of other towns. Let me say one word to all these dear friends at parting; for this is probably the last time I shall ever have an opportunity of speaking to a British audience, at all events in London. I have now been in this country nineteen months, and I have travelled through the length and breadth of it. I came here a slave. I landed upon your shores a degraded being, lying under the load of odium heaped upon my race by the American press, pulpit, and people. I have gone through the wide extent of this country, and have steadily increased—you will pardon me for saying so, for I am loath to speak of myself—steadily increased the attention of the British public to this question. Wherever I have gone, I have been treated with the utmost kindness, with the greatest deference, the most assiduous attention; and I have every reason to love England. Sir, liberty in England is better than slavery in America. Liberty under a monarchy is better than despotism under a democracy. [Cheers.] Freedom under a monarchical government is better than slavery in support of the American capitol. Sir, I have known what it was for the first time in my life to enjoy freedom in this country. I say that I have here, within the last nineteen months, for the first time in my life, known what it was to enjoy liberty. I remember, just before leaving Boston for this country, that I was even refused permission to ride in an omnibus. Yes, on account of the colour of my skin, I was kicked from a public conveyance just a few days before I left that "cradle of liberty." Only three months before leaving that "home of freedom," I was driven from the lower floor of a church, because I tried to enter as other men, forgetting my complexion, remembering only that I was a man, thinking, moreover, that I had an interest in the gospel there proclaimed; for these reasons I went into the church, but was driven out on account of my colour. Not long before I left the shores of America I went on board several steamboats, but in every instance I was driven out of the cabin, and all the respectable parts of the ship, onto the forward deck, among horses and cattle, not being allowed to take my place with human beings as a man and a brother. Sir, I was not permitted even to go into a menagerie or to a theatre, if I wished to have gone there. The doors of every museum, lyceum and athenæum were closed against me if I wanted to go into them. There was the gallery, if I desired to go. I was not granted any of these common and ordinary privileges of free men. All were shut against me. I was mobbed in Boston, driven forth like a malefactor, dragged about, insulted, and outraged in all directions. Every white man—no matter how black his heart—could insult me with impunity. I came to this land—how greatly changed! Sir, the moment I stepped on the soil of England —the instant I landed on the quay at Liverpool—I beheld people as white as any I ever saw in the United States; as noble in their exterior, and surrounded by as much to commend them to admiration, as any to be found in the wide extent of America. But, instead of meeting the curled lip of scorn, and seeing the fire of hatred kindled in the eyes of Englishmen, all was blandness and kindness. I looked around in vain for expressions of insult. Yes, I looked around with wonder! for I hardly believed my own eyes. I searched scrutinizingly to find if I could perceive in the countenance of an Englishman any disapprobation of me on account of my complexion. No; there was not one look of scorn or enmity. [Loud cheers.] I have travelled in all parts of the country: in England, Ireland, Scotland, and Wales. I have journeyed upon highways, byways, railways, and steamboats. I have myself gone, I might say, with almost electric speed; but at all events my trunk has been overtaken by electric speed. In none of these various conveyances, or in any class of society, have I found any curled lip of scorn, or an expression that I could torture into a word of disrespect of me on account of my complexion; not one. Sir, I came to this city accustomed to be excluded from athenæums, literary institutions, scientific institutions, popular meetings, from the colosseum—if there were any such in the United States—and every place of public amusement or instruction. Being in London, I of course felt desirous of seizing upon every opportunity of testing the custom at all such places here, by going and presenting myself for admission as a man. From none of them was I ever ejected. I passed through them all; your colosseums, museums, galleries of painting, even into your House of Commons; and, still more, a nobleman—I do not know what to call his office, for I am not acquainted with anything of the kind in America, but I believe his name was the Marquis of Lansdowne—permitted me to go into the House of Lords, and hear what I never heard before, but what I had long wished to hear, but which I could never have heard anywhere else, the eloquence of Lord Brougham. In none of these places did I receive one word of opposition against my entrance. Sir, as my friend Buffum, who used to travel with me, would say, "I mean to tell these facts, when I go back to America." [Cheers.] I will even let them know, that wherever else I may be a stranger, that in England I am at home. [Renewed cheering.] That whatever estimate they may form of my character as a human being, England has no doubt with reference to my humanity and equality. That, however much the Americans despise and affect to scorn the Negroes, that Englishmen—the most intelligent, the noblest and best of Englishmen—do not hesitate to give the right hand of fellowship, of manly fellowship, to a Negro such as I am. I will tell them this, and endeavour to impress upon their minds these facts, and shame them into a sense of decency on this subject. Why, sir, the Americans do not know that I am a man. They talk of me as a box of goods; they speak of me in connexion with sheep, horses, and cattle. But here, how different! Why, sir, the very dogs of old England know that I am a man! [Cheers.] I was in Beckenham for a few days, and while at a meeting there, a dog actually came up to the platform, put his paws on the front of it, and gave me a smile of recognition as a man. [Laughter.] The Americans would do well to learn wisdom upon this subject from the very dogs of Old England; for these animals, by instinct, know that I am a man; but the Americans somehow or other do not seem to have attained to the same degree of knowledge. But I go back to the United States not as I landed here—I came a slave; I go back a free man. I came here a thing—I go back a human being. I came here despised and maligned—I go back with reputation and celebrity; for I am sure that if the Americans were to believe one tithe of all that has been said in this country respecting me, they would certainly admit me to be a little better than they had hitherto supposed I was. I return, but as a human being in better circumstances than when I came. Still I go back to toil. I do not go to America to sit still, remain quiet, and enjoy ease and comfort. Since I have been in this land I have had every inducement to stop here. The kindness of my friends in the north has been unbounded. They have offered me house, land, and every inducement to bring my family over to this country. They have even gone so far as to pay money, and give freely and liberally, that my wife and children might be brought to this land. I should have settled down here in a different position to what I should have been placed in the United States. But, sir, I prefer living a life of activity in the service of my brethren. I choose rather to go home; to return to America. I glory in the conflict, that I may hereafter exult in the victory. I know that victory is certain. [Cheers.] I go, turning my back upon the ease, comfort, and respectability which I might maintain even here, ignorant as I am. Still, I will go back, for the sake of my brethren. I go to suffer with them; to toil with them; to endure insult with them; to undergo outrage with them; to lift up my voice in their behalf; to speak and write in their vindication; and struggle in their ranks for that emancipation which shall yet be achieved by the power of truth and of principle for that oppressed people. [Cheers.] But, though I go back thus to encounter scorn and contumely, I return gladly. I go joyfully and speedily. I leave this country for the United States on the 4th of April, which is near at hand. I feel not only satisfied, but highly gratified, with my visit to this country. I will tell my colored brethren how Englishmen feel for their miseries. It will be grateful to their hearts to know that while they are toiling on in chains and degradation, there are in England hearts leaping with indignation at the wrongs inflicted upon them. I will endeavour to have daguerreotyped on my heart this sea of upturned faces, and portray the scene to my brethren when I reach America; I will describe to them the kind looks, the sympathetic desires, the determined hostility to everything like slavery sitting heavily or beautifully on the brow of every auditory I have addressed since I came to England. Yes, I will tell these facts to the Negroes, to encourage their hearts and strengthen them in their sufferings and toils; and I am sure that in this I shall have your sympathy as well as their blessing. Pardon me, my friends, for the disconnected manner in which I have addressed you; but I have spoken out of the fulness of my heart; the words that came up went out, and though not uttered altogether so delicately, refinedly, and systematically as they might have been, still, take them as they are—the free upgushings of a heart overborne with grateful emotions at the remembrance of the kindness I have received in this country from the day I landed until the present moment.

With these remarks I beg to bid all my dear friends, present and at a distance—those who are here and those who have departed—farewell!

Farewell Speech of Mr. Frederick Douglass Previously to Embarking on Board The Cambria *Upon His Return to America, Delivered at the Valedictory Soiree Given to Him at the London Tavern on March 30, 1847,* London, 1847

TO THE EDITOR OF THE LONDON *TIMES*

Brown's Temperance Hotel, Liverpool, April 3, 1847

Sir:

I take up my pen to lay before you a few facts respecting an unjust proscription to which I find myself subjected on board the steam-ship Cambria, to sail from this port at 10 o'clock to-morrow morning for Boston, United States.

On the 4th of March last, in company with Mr. George Moxhay, of the Hall of Commerce, London, I called upon Mr. Ford, the London agent of the Cunard line of steamers, for the purpose of securing a passage on board the steam-ship Cambria to Boston, United States. On inquiring the amount of the passage I was told 40*l*. 19*s*.; I inquired further, if a second class passage could be obtained. He answered no, there was but one fare, all distinctions having been abolished. I then gave to him 40*l*. 19*s*. and received from him in return a ticket entitling me to berth No. 72 on board the steam-ship Cambria, at the same time asking him if my colour would prove any barrier to my enjoying all the rights and privileges enjoyed by other passengers. He said "No." I then left the office, supposing all well, and thought nothing more of the matter until this morning, when in company with a few friends, agreeably to public notice, I went on board the Cambria with my luggage, and on inquiring for my berth, found, to my surprise and mortification, that it had been given to another passenger, and was told that the agent in London had acted without authority in selling me the ticket. I expressed my surprise and disappointment to the captain, and inquired what I had better do in the matter. He suggested my accompanying him to the office of the agent in Water-street, Liverpool, for the purpose of ascertaining what could be done. On stating the fact of my having purchased the ticket of the London agent, Mr. M'Iver (the Liverpool agent) answered that the London agent, in selling me the ticket, had acted without authority, and that I should not go on board the ship unless I agreed to take my meals alone, not to mix with the saloon company, and to give up the berth for which I had paid. Being without legal remedy, and anxious to return to the United States, I have felt it due to my own rights as a man, as well as to the honour and dignity of the British public, to lay these facts before them, sincerely believing that the British public will pronounce a just verdict on such proceedings.[10] I have travelled in this country 19 months, and have always enjoyed equal rights and privileges with other passengers, and it was not until I turned my face towards America that I met anything like proscription on account of my colour.

Yours respectfully,
Frederick Douglass

London *Times,* April 6, 1847

THE RIGHT TO CRITICIZE AMERICAN INSTITUTIONS, speech before the American Anti-Slavery Society, May 11, 1847

I am very glad to be here. I am very glad to be present at this Anniversary, glad again to mingle my voice with those with whom I have stood identified, with those with whom I have laboured, for the last seven years, for the purpose of undoing the burdens of my brethren, and hastening the day of their emancipation.

I do not doubt but that a large portion of this audience will be disappointed, both by the *manner* and the *matter* of what I shall this day set forth. The extraordinary and unmerited eulogies, which have been showered upon me, here and elsewhere, have done much to create expectations which, I am well aware, I can never hope to gratify. I am here, a simple man, knowing what I have experienced in Slavery, knowing it to be a bad system, and desiring, by all Christian means, to seek its overthrow. I am not here to please you with an eloquent speech, with a refined and logical address, but to speak to you the sober truths of a heart overborne with gratitude to God that we have in this land, cursed as it is with Slavery, so noble a band to second my efforts and the efforts of others, in the noble work of undoing the yoke of bondage, with which the majority of the States of this Union are now unfortunately cursed.

Since the last time I had the pleasure of mingling my voice with the voices of my friends on this platform, many interesting and even trying events have occurred to me. I have experienced, within the last eighteen or twenty months, many incidents, all of which it would be interesting to communicate to you, but many of these I shall be compelled to pass over at this time, and confine my remarks to giving a general outline of the manner and spirit with which I have been hailed abroad, and welcomed at the different places which I have visited during my absence of twenty months.

You are aware, doubtless, that my object in going from this country, was to get beyond the reach of the clutch of the man who claimed to own me as his property. I had written a book, giving a history of that portion of my life spent in the gall and bitterness and degradation of Slavery, and in which, I also identified my oppressors as the perpetrators of some of the most atrocious crimes. This had deeply incensed them against me, and stirred up within them the purpose of revenge, and, my whereabouts being known, I believed it necessary for me, if I would preserve my liberty, to leave the shores of America, and take up my abode in some other land, at least until the clamor had subsided. I went to England, monarchical England, to get rid of Democratic Slavery; and I must confess that at the very threshold I was satisfied that I had gone to the right place. Say what you will of England—of the degradation—of the poverty—and there is much of it there,—say what you will of the oppression and suffering going on in England at this time, there is Liberty there, not only for the white man, but for the black man also. The instant that I stepped upon the shore, and looked into the faces of the crowd around me, I saw in every man a recognition of my manhood, and an absence, a perfect absence, of everything like that disgusting hate with which we are pursued in this country. [Cheers.] I looked around in vain to see in any man's face a token of the slightest aversion to me on account of my complexion. Even the cabmen demeaned themselves to me as they did to other men, and the very dogs and pigs of old England treated me as a man! I cannot, however, my friends, dwell upon this anti-prejudice, or rather the many illustrations of the absence of prejudice against colour in England, but will proceed, at once, to defend the right and duty of invoking English aid and English sympathy for the overthrow of American Slavery, for the education of coloured Americans, and to forward, in every way, the interests of humanity; inasmuch as the right of appealing to England for aid in overthrowing Slavery in this country has been called in question, in public meetings and by the press, in this city.

I cannot agree with my friend Mr. Garrison, in relation to my love and attachment to this land. I have no love for America, as such; I have no patriotism. I have no country. What country have I? The institutions of this country do not know me, do not recognize me as a man. I am not thought of, spoken of, in any direction, out of the anti-slavery ranks, as a man. I am not thought of, or spoken of, except as a piece of property belonging to some *Christian* slaveholder, and all the religious and political institutions of this country, alike pronounce me a slave and a chattel. Now, in such a country as this, I cannot have patriotism. The only thing that links me to this land is my family, and the painful consciousness that here there are three millions of my fellow-creatures, groaning beneath the iron rod of the worst despotism that could be devised, even in Pandemonium; that here are men and brethren, who are identified with me by their complexion, identified with me by their hatred of Slavery, identified with me by their love and aspirations for liberty, identified with me by the stripes upon their backs, their inhuman wrongs and cruel sufferings. This, and this only, attaches me to this land, and brings me here to plead with you, and with this country at large, for the disenthralment of my oppressed countrymen, and to overthrow this system of Slavery which is crushing them to the earth. How can I love a country that dooms three millions of my brethren, some of them my own kindred, my own brothers, my own sisters, who are now clanking the chains of Slavery upon the plains of the South, whose warm blood is now making fat the soil of Maryland and of Alabama, and over whose crushed spirits rolls the dark shadow of oppression, shutting out and extinguishing forever, the cheering rays of that bright sun of Liberty lighted in the souls of all God's children by the Omnipotent hand of Deity itself? How can I, I say, love a country thus cursed, thus bedewed with the blood of my brethren? A country, the Church of which, and the Government of which, and the Constitution of which, is in favour of supporting and perpetuating this monstrous system of injustice and blood? I have not, I cannot have, any love for this country, as such, or for its Constitution. I desire to see its overthrow as speedily as possible, and its Constitution shivered in a thousand fragments, rather than this foul curse should continue to remain as now. [Hisses and Cheers.]

In all this, my friends, let me make myself understood. I do not hate

America as against England, or against any other country, or land. I love humanity all over the globe. I am anxious to see righteousness prevail in all directions. I am anxious to see Slavery overthrown here; but, I never appealed to Englishmen in a manner calculated to awaken feelings of hatred or disgust, or to influence their prejudices towards America as a nation, or in a manner provocative of national jealousy or ill-will; but I always appealed to their conscience—to the higher and nobler feelings of the people of that country, to enlist them in this cause. I always appealed to their manhood, that which preceded their being Englishmen, (to quote an expression of my friend Phillips,) I appealed to them as men, and I had a right to do so. They are men, and the slave is a man, and we have a right to call upon all men to assist in breaking his bonds, let them be born when, and live where they may.

But it is asked, "What good will this do?" or "What good has it done?" "Have you not irritated, have you not annoyed your American friends, and the American people rather, than done them good?" I admit that we have irritated them. They deserve to be irritated. I am anxious to irritate the American people on this question. As it is in physics, so in morals, there are cases which demand irritation, and counter irritation. The conscience of the American public needs this irritation. And I would *blister it all over, from centre to circumference,* until it gives signs of a purer and a better life than it is now manifesting to the world.

But why expose the sins of one nation in the eyes of another? Why attempt to bring one people under the odium of another people? There is much force in this question. I admit that there are sins in almost every country which can be best removed by means confined exclusively to their immediate locality. But such evils and such sins pre-suppose the existence of a moral power in this immediate locality sufficient to accomplish the work of renovation. But where, pray, can we go to find moral power in this nation, sufficient to overthrow Slavery? To what institution, to what party shall we apply for aid? I say, we admit that there are evils which can be best removed by influences confined to their immediate locality. But in regard to American Slavery, it is not so. It is such a giant crime, so darkening to the soul, so blinding in its moral influence, so well calculated to blast and corrupt all the humane principles of our nature, so well adapted to infuse its own accursed spirit into all around it, that the people among whom it exists have not the moral power to abolish it. Shall we go to the Church for this influence? We have heard its character described. Shall we go to politicians or political parties? Have they the moral power necessary to accomplish this mighty task? They have not. What are they doing at this moment? Voting supplies for Slavery—voting supplies for the extension, the stability, the perpetuation of Slavery in this land. What is the Press doing? The same. The pulpit? Almost the same. I do not flatter myself that there is moral power in the land sufficient to overthrow Slavery, and I welcome the aid of England. And that aid will come. The growing intercourse between England and this country, by means of steam-navigation, the relaxation of the protective system in various countries in Europe, gives us an opportunity to bring in the aid, the moral and Christian aid of those living on the other side of the Atlantic. We welcome it, in the language of the resolution. We entreat our British friends to continue to send in their remonstrances across the deep, against Slavery in this land. And these remonstrances will have a powerful effect here. Sir, the Americans may tell of their ability, and I have no doubt they have it, to keep back the invader's hosts, to repulse the strongest force that its enemies may send against this country. It may boast, and it may *rightly* boast, of its capacity to build its ramparts so high that no foe can hope to scale them, to render them so impregnable as to defy the assault of the world. But, Sir, there is one thing it cannot resist, come from what quarter it may. It cannot resist TRUTH. You cannot build your forts so strong, nor your ramparts so high, nor arm yourself so powerfully, as to be able to withstand the overwhelming MORAL SENTIMENT against Slavery now flowing into this land. For example; prejudice against color is continually becoming weaker in this land (and more and more consider this) sentiment as unworthy a lodgment in the breast of an enlightened community. And the American abroad dare not now, even in a public conveyance, to lift his voice in defence of this disgusting prejudice.

I do not mean to say that there are no practices abroad which deserve to receive an influence favourable to their extermination, from America. I am most glad to know that Democratic freedom—not the bastard democracy, which, while loud in its protestations of regard for liberty and equality, builds up Slavery, and, in the name of Freedom, fights the battles of Despotism—is making great strides in Europe. We see abroad, in England especially, happy indications of the progress of American principles. A little while ago England was cursed by a Corn monopoly—by that giant monopoly, which snatched from the mouths of the famishing poor the bread which you sent them from this land. The community, the *people* of England, demanded its destruction, and they have triumphed!

We have aided them, and they aid us, and the mission of the two nations, henceforth, is *to serve each other*.

Sir, it is said that, when abroad, I misrepresented my country on this question. I am not aware of any misrepresentation. I stated facts, and facts only. A gentleman of your own city, Rev. Dr. Cox, has taken particular pains to stigmatize me as having introduced the subject of Slavery illegitimately into the World's Temperance Convention. But what was the fact? I went to that Convention, not as a delegate. I went into it by the invitation of the Committee of the Convention. I suppose most of you know the circumstances, but I wish to say one word in relation to the spirit and the principle which animated me at the meeting. I went into it at the invitation of the Committee, and spoke not only at their urgent request, but by public announcement. I stood on the platform on the evening referred to, and heard some eight or ten Americans address the seven thousand people assembled in that vast Hall. I heard them speak of the temperance movement in this land. I heard them eulogize the temperance societies in the highest terms, calling on England to follow their example; (and England may follow them with advantage to herself;) but I heard no reference made to the 3,000,000 of people in this country who are denied the privileges, not only of temperance, but of all other societies. I heard not a word of the American slaves, who, if seven of them were found together at a temperance meeting, or any other place, would be scourged and beaten by their cruel tyrants. Yes, nine-and-thirty lashes is the penalty required to be inflicted by the law if any of the slaves get together in a number exceeding seven, for any purpose however peaceable or laudable. And while these American gentlemen were extending their hands to me, and saying, "How do you do, Mr. Douglass? I am most happy to meet you here," &c. &c. I knew that, in America, they would not have touched me with a pair of tongs. I felt, therefore, that that was the place and the time to call to remembrance the 3,000,000 of slaves, whom I aspired to represent on that occasion. I did so, not maliciously, but with a desire, only, to subserve the best interests of my race. I besought the American delegates, who had at first responded to my speech with shouts of applause, when they should arrive at home to extend the borders of their temperance societies so as to include the 500,000 coloured people in the Northern States of the Union. I also called to mind the facts in relation to the mob that occurred in the city of Philadelphia, in the year 1842. I stated these facts to show to the British public how difficult it is for a coloured man in this country to do anything to elevate himself or his race from the state of degradation in which they are plunged; how difficult it is for him to be virtuous or temperate, or anything but a menial, an outcast. You all remember the circumstances of the mob to which I have alluded. A number of intelligent, philanthropic, manly coloured men, desirous of snatching their coloured brethren from the fangs of intemperance, formed themselves into a procession, and walked through the streets of Philadelphia with appropriate banners and badges and mottoes. I stated the fact that that procession was not allowed to proceed far, in the city of Philadelphia—the American city of Brotherly Love, the city of all others loudest in its boasts of freedom and liberty—before these noble-minded men were assaulted by the citizens, their banners torn in shreds and themselves trampled in the dust, and inhumanly beaten, and all their bright and fond hopes and anticipations, in behalf of their friends and their race, blasted by the wanton cruelty of their white fellow-citizens. And all this was done for no other reason than that they had presumed to walk through the street with temperance banners and badges, like human beings.

The statement of this fact caused the whole Convention to break forth in one general expression of intense disgust at such atrocious and inhuman conduct. This disturbed the composure of some of our American representatives, who, in serious alarm, caught hold of the skirts of my coat, and attempted to make me desist from my exposition of the situation of the coloured race in this country. There was one Doctor of Divinity there, the ugliest man that I ever saw in my life, who almost tore the skirts of my coat off, so vehement was he in his *friendly* attempts to induce me to yield the floor. But fortunately the audience came to my rescue, and demanded that I should go on, and I did go on, and, I trust, discharged my duty to my brethren in bonds and the cause of human liberty, in a manner not altogether unworthy the occasion.

I have been accused of *dragging* the question of Slavery into the Convention. I had a right to do so: It was the *World's* convention—not the Convention of any sect, or number of sects—not the Convention of any particular nation—not a man's or a woman's Convention, not a black man's nor a white man's Convention, but the *World's* Convention, the Convention of ALL, *black* as well as *white, bond* as well as *free*. And I stood there, as I thought, a representative of the 3,000,000 of men whom I had left in rags and wretchedness, to be devoured by the accursed institution which stands by them, as with a drawn sword, ever ready to fall upon their devoted and defenceless heads. I felt, as I said to Dr. Cox, that it was demanded of me by conscience, to speak out boldly in behalf of those whom I had left behind. [Cheers.] And, Sir, (I think I may say this, without subjecting myself to the charge of egotism,) I deem it very fortunate for the friends of the slave, that Mr. Garrison and myself were there just at that time. Sir, the churches in this country have long repined at the position of the churches in England on the subject of Slavery. They have sought many opportunities to do away the prejudices of the English churches against American Slavery. Why, Sir, at this time there were not far from seventy ministers of the Gospel from Christian America, in England, pouring their leprous pro-slavery distilment into the ears of the people of that country, and by their prayers, their conversation, and their public speeches, seeking to darken the British mind on the subject of Slavery, and to create in the English public the same cruel and heartless apathy that prevails in this country in relation to the slave, his wrongs and his rights. I knew them by their continuous slandering of my race; and at this time, and under these circumstances, I deemed it a happy interposition of God, in behalf of my oppressed and misrepresented and slandered people, that one of their number should burst up through the dark incrustation of malice, and hate, and degradation, which had been thrown over them, and stand before the British public to open to them the secrets of the prison-house of bondage in America. [Cheers.] Sir, the slave sends no delegates to the Evangelical Alliance. [Cheers.] The slave sends no delegates to the World's Temperance Convention. Why? Because chains are upon his arms and fetters fast bind his limbs. He must be driven out to be sold at auction by some *Christian* slaveholder, and the money for which his soul is bartered must be appropriated to spread the Gospel among the heathen.

Sir, I feel that it is good to be here. There is always work to be done. Slavery is everywhere. Slavery goes everywhere. Slavery was in the Evangelical Alliance, looking saintly in the person of the Rev. Dr. Smythe; it was in the World's Temperance Convention, in the person of the Rev. Mr. Kirk. Dr. Marsh went about saying, in so many words, that the unfortunate slaveholders in America were so peculiarly situated, so environed by uncontrollable circumstances, that they could not liberate their slaves; that if they were to emancipate them they would be, in many instances, cast into prison. Sir, it did me good to go around on the heels of this gentleman. I was glad to follow him around for the sake of my country, for the country is not, after all, so bad as the Rev. Dr. Marsh represented it to be.

My fellow-countrymen, what think ye he said of you, on the other side of the Atlantic? He said you were not only pro-slavery, but that you actually aided the slaveholder in holding his slaves securely in his grasp; that, in fact, you compelled him to be a slaveholder. This I deny. You are not so bad as that. You do not compel the slaveholder to be a slaveholder.

And Rev. Dr. Cox, too, talked a great deal over there; and among other things he said, "that many slaveholders—dear Christian men!—were sincerely anxious to get rid of their slaves"; and to show how difficult it is for them to get rid of their human chattels, he put the following case: A man living in a State, the laws of which compel all persons emancipating their slaves to remove them beyond its limits, wishes to liberate his slaves, but he is too poor to transport them beyond the confines of the State in which he resides; therefore he cannot emancipate them—he is necessarily a slaveholder. But, Sir, there was one fact, which I happened, fortunately, to have on hand just at that time, which completely neutralized this very affecting statement of the Doctor's. It so happens that Messrs. Gerrit Smith and Arthur Tappan have advertised for the especial benefit of this afflicted class of slaveholders that they have set apart the sum of $10,000 to be appropriated in aiding them to remove their emancipated slaves beyond the jurisdiction of the State, and that the money would be forthcoming on application being made for it; but *no such application was ever made!* This shows that, however truthful the statements of these gentlemen may be concerning the things of the world to come, they are lamentably reckless in their statements concerning things appertaining to this world. I do not mean to say that they would designedly tell that which is false, but they did make the statements I have ascribed to them.

And Dr. Cox and others charge me with having stirred up warlike feelings while abroad. This charge, also, I deny. The whole of my arguments and the whole of my appeals, while I was abroad, were in favour of anything else than war. I embraced every opportunity to propagate the principles of peace while I was in Great Britain. I confess, honestly, that were I not a peace-man, were I a believer in fighting at all, I should have gone through England, saying to Englishmen, as Englishmen, there are 3,000,000 of men across the Atlantic who are whipped, scourged, robbed of themselves, denied every privilege, denied the right to read the Word of the God who made them, trampled under foot, denied all the rights of human-beings; go to their rescue; shoulder your muskets, buckle on your knapsacks, and in the invincible cause of Human Rights and Universal Liberty, go forth, and the laurels which you shall win will be as fadeless and as imperishable as the eternal aspirations of the human soul after that freedom which every being made after God's image instinctively feels is his birth-right. This would have been my course had I been a war man. That such was not my course, I appeal to my whole career while abroad to determine.

> *Weapons of war we have cast from the battle;*
>   TRUTH *is our armour, our watch-word is* LOVE;
> *Hushed be the sword, and the musketry's rattle,*
>   *All our equipments are drawn from above.*
>   *Praise then the God of Truth,*
>   *Hoary age and ruddy youth,*
>   *Long may our rally be*
>   *Love, Light and Liberty,*
>   *Ever our banner the banner of Peace*

National Anti-Slavery Standard, May 20, 1847

TO THOMAS VAN RENSSELAER

Lynn, Massachusetts, May 18, '47

My dear Sir:

I am at home again; and, in compliance with your earnest request, avail myself of this, my first opportunity, to send you an article for your gallant little sheet. I have to thank you for the file you sent me on board the *"Hendrick Hudson."* I have given each number a hasty perusal, and have quite satisfied myself that you are on the right ground—of the right spirit—and that you possess the energy of head and of heart to make your paper a powerful instrument in defending, improving, and elevating our brethren in the (so called) free states, as well as hastening the downfall of the fierce and blood-thirsty *evangelical* tyrants in the slave States. Blow away on your "Ram's Horn"![20] Its wild, rough, uncultivated notes may grate harshly on the ear of refined and cultivated *chimers;* but sure I am that its voice will be pleasurable to the slave, and terrible to the slaveholder. Let us have a full, clear, shrill, unmistakable sound. "No compromise—no concealment"—no lagging for those who tarry—no *"slurs"* for popular favor—no lowering your tone for the sake of harmony. The harmony of this country is discord with the ALMIGHTY. To be in harmony with God is to be in open discord and conflict with the powers of Church and State in this country. Both are drunk on the warm blood of our brethren. "Blow on—blow on," and may the God of the oppressed give effect to your blowing.

Through the kindness of a friend, I have before me the *New York Sun* of 13th May. It contains a weak, puerile, and characteristic attack upon me, on account of my speech in the Tabernacle, before the American Anti-Slavery Society on the 11th instant. The article in question affords me a text from which I could preach you a long sermon; but I will neither trespass on your space, nor weary the patience of your readers, by treating the article in that way. I do not call attention to it, because I am anxious to defend myself from its malevolent contents, but to congratulate you upon the favorable change in the public mind which it indicates, and to enjoy a little (I trust innocent) sport at the expense of the editor.

We have been laughed at and ridiculed so much, that I am glad, once in a while, to be able to turn the tables on our white brethren. The editor informs his readers, that his object in writing the article is, to protest against "the unmitigated abuse heaped upon our country by the colored man Douglass." Now, who will doubt the patriotism of a man who will venture so much on behalf of his country? The *Sun* is truly a patriot. "The colored *man* Douglass." Well done! Not "n——r" Douglass —not *black*, but *colored*—not *monkey*, but *man*—the *colored* MAN *Douglass*. This, dear sir, is a decided improvement on the old mode of speaking of us. In the brilliant light of the *Sun*, I am no longer a *monkey*, but a MAN —and, henceforth, I may claim to be treated as a man by the *Sun*. In order to prepare the patient for the pill, and prove his title to be regarded an unmixed American, he gilds the most bloody and detestable tyranny all over with the most holy and beautiful sentiments of liberty. Hear him—"*Freedom of speech in this country should receive the greatest* LATITUDE." This sounds well; but is it not a strange text, from which to preach a sermon in favor of putting down freedom of speech by *mob violence?* "If men do not speak freely of our institutions, how are we to discover their errors or reform their abuses, should any exist?" A pertinent question, truly, and worthy of the thought and study of the profound and philosophical editor of the *Sun*. But now see a nobler illustration of the story of the "cow and the milk pail"—blowing hot and blowing cold, and blowing neither hot nor cold. The editor says—

"*There is, however, a limit to this very freedom of speech. We cannot be permitted to go into a gentleman's house, accept his hospitality, yet* ABUSE *his fare, and we have no right to abuse a country under whose government, we are safely residing and securely protected.*"

Here we have it, all reasoned out as plain as logic can make it—the limit of freedom of speech accurately defined. But allow me to throw a little light upon the *Sun's* logic—if I can do so without entirely spoiling his *simile*. Poor thing, it would be a pity to hurt that. Does it not strike you as being first rate? To my mind, it is the best thing in the whole piece, and lacks only one thing—(but this probably makes no difference with the *Sun*—it may be its chief merit,) and that is, *likeness*—it lacks likeness. A gentleman's house and the government of this country are wholly dissimilar. Let me suggest to him—without meaning any disrespect to you, that a cook shop (a thing which I am surprised he should ever forget) bears a far greater resemblance to the government of this country, than that of a gentleman's house and hospitality. Let cook shop represent Country—"Bill of Fare"—"Bill of Rights;" and the "Chief Cook"—Commander-in-chief.—(I fancy I hear the editor say, this looks better.) Enters editor of the *Sun* with a keen appetite. He reads the bill of fare. It contains the names of many palatable dishes. He asks the cook for soup, he gets "dish water." For salmon, he gets a serpent; for beef, he gets bullfrogs; for ducks, he gets dogs; for salt, he gets sand; for pepper, he gets powder; and for vinegar, he gets gall; in fact, he gets for you the very opposite of everything for which you ask, and which from the bill of fare, and loudmouthed professions, you had a right to expect. This is just the treatment which the colored people receive in this country at the hand of this government. Its Bill of Rights is to practise towards us a bill of wrongs. Its self-evident truths are self-evident lies. Its majestic liberty, malignant tyranny. The foundation of this government—the great Constitution itself—is nothing more than a compromise with manstealers, and a cunningly devised complication of falsehoods, calculated to deceive foreign Nations into a belief that this is a free country; at the same time that it pledges the whole Civil, Naval and Military power of the Nation to keep three millions of people in the most abject slavery. He says I abuse a country under whose government I am safely residing, and securely protected. I am neither safely residing, nor securely protected in this country. I am living under a government which authorized Hugh Auld to rob me of seven hundred and fifty dollars, and told me if I do not submit, if I resisted this robber, I should be put to death. This is the protection given to me, and every other colored man from the South, and no one knows this better than the Editor of the New York *Sun*. And this piece of robbery, the *Sun* calls the *rights* of the Master, and says that the English people recognized those rights by giving me money with which to purchase my freedom. The *Sun* complains that I defend the right of invoking England for the overthrow of American Slavery. Why not receive aid from England to overthrow American Slavery, as well as for Americans to send bread to England to feed the hungry? Answer me that! What would the *Sun* have said, if the British press had denounced this country for sending a ship-load of grain into Ireland, and denied the right of American people to sympathize, and succor the afflicted and famine-stricken millions of that unhappy land?[21] What would it have said? Why, it and the whole American Press would have poured forth one flood of unmixed censure and scathing rebuke. England would have been denounced; the British public would have been branded as murderers. And if England had forbidden Captain Forbes to land his cargo, it might have been regarded just cause for war. And yet the interference in the one case is as justifiable as in the other. My Dear Sir, I have already extended this letter to a much greater length than I at first intended, and will now stop by wishing you every success in your noble enterprise.

Ever yours in our righteous cause,
Frederick Douglass

The Liberator, June 4, 1847

TO WILLIAM LLOYD GARRISON

Lynn, June 7th, 1847

My dear Friend:

A severe illness of two weeks' duration, from which I have now but partially recovered, has prevented me from replying to, and explaining certain representations and charges, which have recently found their way into the public press, seriously affecting my moral character.

Many reasons might be urged in favor of treating this mean and scandalous fabrication with silent contempt. The character which I have maintained for six years, open to the most searching investigation—the disguising nature of the imputations, and obvious motive for making them—and the well-known impurity and filthiness of the quarter from which they emanated—might afford some justification for pursuing a course of absolute silence; leaving the public to form what judgment they pleased of the truth or falsity, the justice or injustice of the attack upon me.

There is, however, something so direct, so impudent, and so apparently consistent in this malicious assault, that I feel that duty to the cause with which I am connected, to myself, and to the noble band of friends who have ever thrown around me the broad shield of their protection, requires at my hand a full, free and open explanation of the ground of the assault; and as complete a vindication of myself as the real facts in the case will permit me to make.

My first impulse, on being informed of this bold attempt to destroy my influence, and ruin me forever, was in favor of bringing the slanderers before some legal tribunal of the country. But upon reflection, I felt that such a course would be unwise, perplexing, and fruitless. This was not, however, because I lacked confidence in the law or its administrators, but from a knowledge of the loathsome creatures who stand forth as my accusers. The unscrupulous wretches who could string together such a list of lies, are not to be expected to have any very sacred regard for an oath. As a lawyer once said—"When a case originates in Pandemonium, we are to expect none but demons for witnesses." If, however, it shall be found necessary to bring the matter before a legal tribunal, I shall not hesitate to adopt the necessary means to bring both the perpetrators and the circulators of this foul slander, where they may have an opportunity of making good their charges, if they can. Meanwhile, I will take up their articles, all filthy as they are, and examine every material sentence in them.

The first notice of my passage from Albany to New-York, I found in a paper called *"The Switch,"* and purporting to be published in Albany. But on inquiry where it was printed, by whom edited and published, I found that those whereabouts are prudently kept unknown. The editor is unknown, and it is the policy of the managers to keep unknown, that they may lie and slander with impunity. In any other country making pretension to civilization, such a nuisance would be speedily ferreted out, and abated. But, alas for the freest nation on the globe! liberty is too often made to license all conceivable brutality, and to give impunity to the vilest slanderers. The article in the *"Switch"* begins as follows:

N——RS AND NASTINESS.
"The offence is rank—it smells to Heaven."

"A depraved portion of the people, and of the press, have for some time past been gratifying their morbid tastes in lionizing a disgusting, impertinent Negro, who styles himself Frederick Douglass. The feelings of the decent portion of the community have, times without number, been outraged by having this 'soot head' thrust into their midst. It is a needless task for us to recapitulate the instances of this 'wool head's' sauciness."

Comment on this is only necessary to fix attention upon the *animus* of the writer. It is a fit introduction to what follows. Mark! "depraved portion of the people and press"—"disgusting and impertinent Negro"—"soot head"—"wool head's sauciness," &c. These hail from the lowest of the American mould. Those who kindly regard me in this country are the purest and best in the world; they are in truth, the salt of the earth, the lights of the world; and therein is a motive for assaulting me.

My "impertinence and sauciness" have ever consisted in presuming to be, and behaving as a man—in paying no more deference to a white man, than to a black man of equal moral and intellectual worth—in bowing to no skin-deep superiority, but rendering honor only where honor is due. I am said to be 'disgusting.' How, when, where, and to whom? Not as a coach-driver, dressed in tinselled livery, driving some delicate white ladies through Albany, or Broadway, New York. Not as a footman, on some gilded carriage. Not as a waiter in some fashionable hotel. Not as a servant, a barber, a cook, or a steward. No! I am never disgusting to the most refined white Americans, in any of these capacities! Even a white lady—a *white American lady*—might be seen near me, in these capacities, without exciting vulgar abuse and filthy insinuations. But when does white complacency, in this matter, cease, and ineffable disgust commence, in the bosoms of our alabaster Fellow countrymen? Just when the colored man's inequality is dropped, and his equality is assumed. The Negro then becomes horribly disgusting! I am not insensible to this feeling of disgust. There are constant occasions for calling it forth. I was never more disgusted in my life than when in Albany, low, filthy, tobacco-chewing, slobbering white blackguards presumed to insult me on account of the color of my skin. This, I think, is something at which we may properly be disgusted.

One word more about disgust. There is a strange diversity in its manifestation, indicating how completely a pure taste may be perverted. Some animals, for instance—and man among the number—display the strangest perversity of taste. The buzzard and the condor are utterly disgusted with sound meat, and prefer to flesh their talons in carrion.

These birds go around, like the editor of the *Switch* dealing largely in the most disgusting and putrid flesh! A dog afflicted with hydrophobia, is utterly disgusted with the sight and scent of pure cold water; and a white man afflicted with colorphobia will invariably manifest signs of disgust at the sight of a respectable colored man. "Colorphobia" and buzzards—mad dogs and condors—"think of these things!"

I will now pass to the next extract. Speaking of me, he says—

"Last week he was here, and was gallanted to the Assembly Chamber by a female of this city, who so far forgot what was due to the community and to the delicacy of her sex, as to introduce this offensive creature into the Ladies' Gallery, where she left him. Mr. Stoutenburgh, the gentlemanly and attentive officer having charge of that department, on discovering him, immediately told him that a place was especially designated for colored persons, and pointed it out to him, but Sambo refused to go, on which Mr. S. was compelled to eject him forcibly. The lady soon after returned, and asked Mr. S. where her "friend and companion" had gone, on which Mr. S. informed her that he had turned him out, and directed him to the place appropriated to such as he. The female subsequently found her "friend and companion," and they left the Capital "cheek by jowl."

It is perfectly true, that I was in Albany at the time here mentioned; and quite true, that I was accompanied to the Assembly Chamber by a lady—*a white lady,* (very criminal!)—and, naturally enough, she took me to that part of the House to which, as a lady, she felt herself entitled to go. It is not true, that when Mr. Stoutenburgh discovered me, he told me that a place was especially designated for colored persons. He did point me to the gentleman's gallery, and there was no hesitancy, on my part, in going to it; and nothing imperious in his manner in pointing it out to me. Not an unfriendly word passed between us. The whole story of my being 'forcibly ejected' is a deliberate lie, to serve a purpose. I went into the gentlemen's gallery, and enjoyed a sight of the assembled wisdom of the great state of New-York, as I have frequently enjoyed a similar sight of the assembled wisdom of Great Britain. After having been permitted freely to enter Parliament—both Lords and Commons—and witness their deliberations, in company with white persons, it was not to be expected that I should be afraid to enter an Assembly Chamber, where that living embodiment of *Subterranean* filth and fury, Mike Walsh, is recognized as an *honorable* member.

Having now glanced at the lighter shades, I come at once to the darker and more important aspects of the subject. The *Switch* says—

"Shortly after this, these 'friends and companions' went to New-York in company. On the morning of their arrival, Captain Cruttenden observed that a Negro came down from the state rooms with a white woman, and was indignant on learning that the pair had occupied state rooms which communicated with each other by a door, and cautioned his assistant against permitting the like occurrence. On a return trip of the Hendrick Hudson, a few days afterwards, the same oddly matched companions were again on board, and the woman sent the chambermaid to the captain's office for two state rooms, the keys of which the chambermaid delivered to her. The female, on inspection, told the chambermaid that the rooms were not what she wanted—that they must have a door leading into each other. The person in charge of the office, without hesitation, changed their location, and gave the same rooms which these friends and companions had occupied the night before. Capt. Cruttenden discovered it in the morning, and on their coming down told the n——r never to *darken* the saloon of any boat commanded by him again, and ordered him ashore. The fellow's wool bristled somewhat, and his companion colored slightly, and they departed in company."

I will now state the circumstances of this transaction, in my own way, and shall admit all that I know to be true, and deny all that I know to be false in the above statement. On Monday, May 10th, I was in company with my wife, at Albany, where I went to see my daughter, whom I had not seen for nearly two years. Having been announced to speak the next morning at the anniversary meeting of the American Anti-Slavery Society in New-York, and suffering under severe cold and hoarseness, and well knowing the brutal manner in which colored persons are uniformly treated in steamers on the Hudson river—compelled sometimes to stroll the decks nearly all night, before they can get a place to lie down, and that place frequently unfit for a dog's accommodation—and being unwilling to risk my health to any such chances, I availed myself of the kindness of my friend alluded to, who secured for me a state room on board of the Hendrick Hudson; and also secured the adjoining one for herself. On going into mine, in the evening, I found, as above stated, that the two rooms communicated with each other by a door. But a thought of its propriety or impropriety never crossed my mind; and, at that time, I did not know but that every state room on board communicated in a similar manner. Myself and friend conversed together during the evening, when she went to her state room, and I remained in mine. I neither saw nor heard my friend till next morning, when we landed at New-York. I then went to her state-room door to assist her with her baggage; and after walking about a full half hour in the presence of the Captain, while the crowd was pressing on shore, we left the steamer together, without the slightest sign of disapprobation that I could see from any quarter. On my return from New-York, my friend secured similar state rooms, and we occupied them, without the least interruption from the Captain, or any officer, servant or passenger on board. When we left the steamer in the morning, the Captain did utter some filthy remarks, calling me a 'n——r,' &c., and telling me never to take a state room on board his steamer again. I made no reply, but went off about my business, well knowing that my color was the cause of his brutality, and that, had I been a white man, I might have occupied the state rooms a dozen times over, without calling forth any foul imputations from himself, or any one else. As to what is alleged to have been said by my friend to the chambermaid, it may or may not be true; and, true or false, it is a small matter. We needed neither bolts, bars, nor locks, to keep us in the path of virtue and rectitude. The *Switch* closes its article as follows, which shows that, vile and profligate as it is, it is a shade less atrocious than the *Subterranean*.

"We wish it distinctly understood, that we cast no imputations on the character of the white woman, who thus gads about the country with a Negro, but she certainly manifests a depravity of taste, that should induce her friends to look sharply after her—and as for this thunder-cloud, he should be kicked into his *proper place, and kept there*.

"We shall resume this subject next week."

Having disposed of the *Switch*, I come to that loathsome dabbler in *Subterranean* pollution, Mike Walsh. The depravity of the man is marvellous. My work with him will be necessarily short; for his statement is made up from the *Switch*, and improved upon to suit his own impure fancy.

My answer to it is, that, aside from the simple fact that myself and friend occupied adjoining and communicating state rooms—and the fact that the Captain was indignant that I, a *colored* person, should do so—this whole story, from beginning to end, in gross and scope, in letter and spirit, in principle and inference, is a foul, deliberate, unmixed, and malicious fabrication. The whole narration, in all its details, particulars and specifications—so far as they relate to my conduct—is a series of the most daringly wicked falsehoods; and none, but one over whom the sway of the devil is complete, could have invented and penned them.

Ever yours in the cause of purity and liberty,
Frederick Douglass

The Liberator, June 11, 1847

TO THE *BOSTON DAILY WHIG*

Lynn, Mass. 27th. June, 1847

Mr. Editor:

Sir, In the "Boston Whig" of Saturday, 26th inst, I find the following:

"The Liberator states that Frederick Douglass has given up the project of purchasing a paper in this country, and explains as a reason of the subscription being obtained in England for that purpose, the impression prevailing that no paper of the kind was published by a colored man. The Liberator enumerates four papers of the kind. It might properly be asked, how come the English people to get such an impression?"

I now beg to give you the information indirectly asked for in the last sentence of the above paragraph.

A few months previously to my leaving England for the United States, I was informed that it was the intention of my friends to make me a present of a sum of money, which would yield an annual income sufficient for my support. The object of my friends was to place me in circumstances which would enable me to devote myself unreservedly to the cause of my outraged and enslaved fellow-countrymen. Fully appreciating the motives of my benevolent friends, the proposition, nevertheless, struck me unfavorably, and I objected at once to the adoption of any measures for carrying out their kind intentions. My objections were as follows: 1st. It would make me so independent of my friends in the United States, as to disturb the sympathy which has resulted from mutual hardships in a common cause, and which is so necessary to successful cooperation. 2nd. It would be prejudicial to my influence at home, to be entirely supported abroad. 3d. It would place me in a more superannuated position, than I, being a young man, felt willing to assume. And 4thly, because of the great and increasing demands upon British sympathy and philanthropy, resulting from the awful famine with which a sister island was then and is still smitten.

I however informed my friends, (and this will answer your query), what was then the fact; that there was not a single printing press in the United States, under the control and management of colored persons; and that several attempts had been made to establish such a press, and that they had severally failed; and that I believed that the time had arrived when such a press could be established, and be a powerful means of changing the moral sentiment of the nation on the subject of slavery; and if tolerably well conducted, would be a *telling* fact against the American doctrine of natural inferiority, and the inveterate prejudice which so universally prevails in this country against the colored race. This being my opinion, I suggested that a printing press would be a useful and an acceptable testimonial, and one which would have this advantage over the former one; it would be a gift to my race, as well as a testimony of their confidence in me as their advocate. The idea pleased my friends, and the impression which it made upon their minds, they produced upon others. This, sir, is an explanation of the whole case, as my friends abroad will bear me witness.

Since my return home, three "Newspapers" under the management of colored persons have sprung into existence, and believing that this will be sufficient to accomplish the good which I sought, I have with some reluctance given up my intention of publishing a paper for the present.

I am, Sir, with sincere respect, faithfully yours,

Frederick Douglass

The Liberator, July 9, 1847

BIBLES FOR THE SLAVES

The above is the watch-word of a recent but quite numerous class of persons, whose ostensible object seems to be to give Bibles to the American Slaves. They propose to induce the public to give, of their abundance, a large sum of money, to be placed in the hands of the American Bible Society, to be employed in purchasing Bibles and distributing them among the Slaves.

In this apparently benevolent and Christian movement they desire to unite all persons friendly to the long imbruted and long neglected Slave. The religious press has already spoken out in its favor. So full of promise and popularity is this movement that many of the leaders in

Church and State are pressing into it. Churches, which have all along slumbered unmoved over the cruel wrongs and bitter woes of the Slave,—which have been as deaf as Death to every appeal of the fettered bondman for liberty,—are at last startled from their heartless stupor by this new cry of Bibles for the Slaves. Ministers of Religion, and learned Doctors of Divinity, who would not lift a finger to give the Slave to himself, are now engaged in the *professed* work of giving to the Slave the Bible. Into this enterprize have been drawn some who have been known as advocates for emancipation. One Anti-Slavery Editor has abandoned his position at the head of a widely circulating journal, and has gone forth to lecture and solicit donations in its behalf. Even the American Bible Society, which a few years ago peremptorily refused to entertain the offensive subject, and refused the offer of ten thousand dollars, has at last relented, if not repented, and now condescends to *receive money* for this object. To be sure we have had no public assurance of this from that society. It is, however, generously inferred by the friends of the movement, that they will *consent to receive money* for this purpose. Now what does all this mean? Are the men engaged in this movement sane? and if so, can they be honest? Do they seriously believe that the American Slave can receive the Bible? Do they believe that the American Bible Society cares one straw about giving Bibles to the Slaves? Do they suppose that Slaveholders, in open violation of their wicked laws, will allow their Slaves to have the Bible? How do they mean to get the Bible among the Slaves? It cannot go itself,—it must be carried. And who among them all has either the faith or the folly to undertake the distribution of Bibles among the Slaves?

Then, again, of what value is the Bible to one who may not read its contents? Do they intend to send teachers into the Slave States, with the Bibles, to teach the Slaves to read them? Do they believe that on giving the Bible, the unlettered Slave will all at once—by some miraculous transformation—become a man of letters, and be able to read the sacred Scriptures? Will they first obtain the Slaveholder's consent, or will they proceed without it? And if the former, by what means will they seek it? And if the latter, what success do they expect?

Upon these points, and many others, the public ought to be enlightened before they are called upon to give money and influence to such an enterprize. As a mere indication of the growing influence of Anti-Slavery sentiment this movement may be regarded by Abolitionists with some complacency; but as a means of abolishing the Slave system of America, it seems to me a sham, a delusion, and a snare, and cannot be too soon exposed before all the people. It is but another illustration of the folly of putting new cloth into an old garment, and new wine into old bottles. The Bible is peculiarly the companion of liberty. It belongs to a new order of things—Slavery is of the old—and will only be made worse by an attempt to mend it with the Bible. The Bible is only useful to those who can read and practise its contents. It was given to Freemen, and any attempt to give it to the Slave must result only in hollow mockery.

Give Bibles to the poor Slaves! It sounds well. It looks well. It wears a religious aspect. *It is a Protestant rebuke to the Pope,* and seems in harmony with the purely evangelical character of the great American people. It may also forestall some movement in England to give Bibles to our Slaves,—*and this is very desirable!* Now admitting (however difficult it may be to do so) the entire honesty of all engaged in this movement,—the immediate and only effect of their efforts must be to turn off attention from the main and only momentous question connected with the Slave, and absorb energies and money in giving to him the Bible that ought to be used in giving him to *himself.* The Slave is property. He cannot hold property. He cannot own a Bible. To give him a Bible is but to give his master a Bible. The Slave is a thing,—and it is the all commanding duty of the American people to make him a man. To demand this in the name of humanity, and of God, is the solemn duty of every living soul. To demand less than this, or anything else than this, is to deceive the fettered bondman, and to soothe the conscience of the Slaveholder on the very point where he should be most stung with remorse and shame.

Away with all tampering with such a question! Away with all trifling with the man in fetters! Give a hungry man a stone, and tell what beautiful houses are made of it,—give ice to a freezing man, and tell him of its good properties in hot weather,—throw a drowning man a dollar, as a mark of your good will,—but do not mock the bondman in his misery, by giving him a Bible when he cannot read it.

The Liberty Bell, June, 1847

TO WILLIAM LLOYD GARRISON

Lynn, July 18, 1847

My dear Friend:

I have observed in the *Liberator,* of the past two weeks, with considerable surprise and much regret, that the conclusion to which I have come, with respect to publishing, *at present,* an anti-slavery newspaper, has very unwisely and unnecessarily been made the occasion of attack upon yourself, and of most unkind, uncharitable and unjust imputations on the motives of leading friends of the cause in Boston. The parties engaged in this work of mischief imagine me hemmed in on every side—overpowered—and my will completely subjected to the Boston Board—and direct their efforts for my deliverance from thraldom, without stopping to inquire as to the correctness of their conjectures. This is absolutely grievous; and I feel it due to yourself and friends, and all concerned, to say at once, distinctly and publicly, that, in this matter, I have acted independently, and wholly on my own responsibility.

Yours sincerely,
Frederick Douglass

The Liberator, July 23, 1847

TO SIDNEY HOWARD GAY

[August, 1847]

My dear Gay:

I regret that my first letter for the *Standard* should be such an one as I am now about to write, and that I have to record facts which may create anxiety among the Anti-Slavery friends in the East, on account of the safety of friend Garrison, and myself. We were last night confronted by a most brutal and disgraceful mob—the first fruits of our Western tour, a sort of foretaste of what may await us further West. To the everlasting shame and infamy of the people of Harrisburg, I record the fact that they are at this moment under the domination of mob law; that the freedom of speech and the right of peaceably assembling is cloven down; and that the officers appointed to preserve order and to protect the rights and privileges of the people, have basely, by their indifference, consented to this sacrifice to the Moloch of Slavery. Let this infernal act of devotion to tyranny be published and republished at home and abroad, in the New and in the Old World, that all may learn the true character of American freedom, and our republican love of law and order. But to the facts.

A meeting was convened in the court house of this town last night, to hear addresses on Slavery by Mr. Garrison and myself. At the time appointed Mr. Garrison was present, and commenced the meeting by a calm statement of facts respecting the character of Slavery and the slave power, showing in how many ways it was a matter deeply affecting the rights and interests of the Northern people. He spoke with little or no interruption for the space of an hour, and then introduced me to the audience. I spoke only for a few moments when through the windows was poured a volley of unmerchantable eggs, scattering the contents on the desk in which I stood, and upon the wall behind me, and filling the room with the most disgusting and stifling stench. The audience appeared alarmed, but disposed to stay, though greatly at the expense of their olfactory nerves. I, thinking I could stand it as well as my audience, proceeded with my speech, but in a very few moments we were interrupted and startled by the explosion of a pack of crackers, which kept up a noise for about a minute similar to the discharge of pistols, and being on the ladies' side, created much excitement and alarm. When this subsided, I again proceeded, but was at once interrupted again by another volley of addled eggs, which again scented the house with Slavery's choice incense. Cayenne pepper and Scotch snuff were freely used, and produced their natural results among the audience. I proceeded again and was again interrupted by another grand influx of rotten eggs. One struck friend Garrison on the back, sprinkling its *essence* all over his honoured head. At this point a general tumult ensued, the people in the house became much disturbed and alarmed, and there was a press toward the doorway, which was completely wedged with people. The mob was now howling with fiendish rage. I could occasionally hear amid the tumult, fierce and bloody cries, *"throw out the n——r,* THROW OUT THE N——R." Here friend Garrison rose, with that calm and tranquil dignity, altogether peculiar to himself, and said—(speaking for himself and me.) Our mission to Harrisburg is ended. If there be not sufficient love of liberty, and self respect in this place, to protect the right of assembling, and the freedom of speech, he would not degrade himself by attempting to speak under such circumstances and he would therefore recall the appointment for Sunday night, and go where he could be heard. The wise ones knew the meaning of his speech. They saw that the character of the town was about to be consigned to deserved infamy and one of their number, a thin, delicate looking man rose, much excited. It was Mr. Petrigen, a private Secretary of the Governor of the State. He said that he for one, wished to hear Messrs. Garrison and Douglass speak, but he must defend the character of the people of Harrisburg from the charge of mobocracy, brought against them by Mr. Garrison. Nobody was to blame, as nobody could prevent the mob. It consisted of blackguards; the people of Harrisburg had nothing to do with it, nor could they prevent it, and he hoped that that gentleman (alluding to Mr. Garrison) would not go away and slander the people by making them responsible for the mob. He would repeat it, the people had nothing to do with it, and they could not prevent it. Now all this was saying to the mob—go on, mob on, there is no power anywhere to prevent you. This infamous incitement to the mob, was nobly rebuked by a gentleman of great respectability of the name of Rawen. He said, he rose to defend Harrisburg from the charge of incapacity to quell a mob, and protect the right of speech. They could do it, and if they did not do so, it was because they did not choose to do so. He asked Mr. Petrigen where was the police? If they had not the power to disperse a few blackguards and boys? Mr. Garrison again rose and said, his remarks were entirely hypothetical, and if a meeting could be conducted with order and propriety he was quite willing to remain and hold another meeting agreeable to public notice. In the midst of this discussion there was thrown in another volley of rotten eggs, and cries of "throw out the n——r, throw out the n——r," was repeated about the doors and windows of the house. It was now impossible to proceed with the meeting, and there being no attempt on the part of anybody to disperse the mob, Mr. Garrison announced the close of the meeting. The audience however remained for some time. Very few seemed willing to venture out; the doorway continued crowded and for a long time it was difficult to pass out at all. The stones now began to fly, a pile of which had been brought near the door; causing much trepidation for my safety. At this time a white lady kindly offered to walk with me and protect me, from the mob, I felt it best to decline her very disinterested offer, as I had good reason to believe that such an arrangement would exasperate the mob, and only enhance my danger. I finally took the arm of a coloured gentleman, Mr. Wolk, and several coloured friends filling up the rear, we walked out. As soon as I reached the steps I was discovered by the cowardly mob, who from their holes of darkness uttered infernal yells crying out "there he goes, there he goes," and at the same time throwing stones, and brick-bats at me—one went humming by my head and another striking me on the back, but without doing me serious injury. "Give it to him, give it to him," they cried, "let the d—d n——r have it." Two friends behind me received heavy blows, one of them was quite stunned and bruised, but they stood around me and received the blows intended for me. I very soon succeeded in disengaging myself from the crowd and by turning a corner I succeeded in very soon eluding my pursuers, and thus saved myself. All credit is due to a few coloured friends who seemed willing and glad to be ramparts for me and to receive all the blows intended for me. Mr. Garrison was not discovered by the mob. My coming out first drew off the mob from the door before he came out. I am happy to find he received no blows except the eggs, the stench of which was bad enough. Comment here, is unnecessary, the atrocious character of the proceedings is sufficiently palpable, and Harrisburg one day will be ashamed of it.

Friend Garrison and myself leave here to-morrow morning for Pittsburg, where we hope to meet with a more cordial welcome. In great haste, very sincerely yours,

Frederick Douglass

National Anti-Slavery Standard, August 19, 1847

TO SIDNEY HOWARD GAY

Austinburgh, [Ohio], August 20, 1847

My dear Friend:

I can send you but the barest outline of our Western tour thus far. Friend Garrison and myself, are moving from place to place, with such rapidity, and the places of meeting are at such "magnificent distances" from each other, that we have little or no time left us to report progress. To make our tour useful, we are compelled to devote ourselves unreservedly to the work of enlisting by private, as well as public effort, the hearts of those with whom we are brought in contact. Our private society is sought for with as much honesty and avidity, as are our public addresses. Mr. Garrison is the honoured centre of every circle into whose midst we are brought. His conversational powers are inexhaustible; he seems as fresh at midnight as at midday. Our friends eagerly flock around to hear his words of strength and cheer, while our enemies as eagerly draw around to catch him in his words. The former go away delighted with the man, while the latter skulk away, disappointed and chagrined, that they have found so little at which to be offended. Mr. Garrison's visit must do much to disabuse the public mind in this region, and to produce a mighty reaction in favour of radical Eastern Abolitionism. The Liberty party, and pro-slavery papers, have overshot themselves in regard to him.—They have so maligned, and slandered him, and have so distorted, perverted, and misrepresented his views, that they have created the most intense curiosity among the people to see and hear him, and having associated his person with the representations of his mind, that his bare presence, without the utterance of a word, is all sufficient to create an impression most favourable to him, and at once to dispel the dread, and gloomy apprehensions created concerning him. When he opens his mouth, and pours forth his truthful voice, the dark and foul spirit of slander falls before him, like Dagon before the ark.—People come expecting to see a fierce, proud, ambitious, and bitter looking man, a gloomy spirit, altogether dissatisfied with himself, and all the world around him; a stranger to peace, a man of war, if not of blood; completely wrapped up within the narrow limits of a single idea, perfectly above everything interesting to other men, an infidel, atheist, and madman, rejoicing over the triumphs of evil, and inflexibly bent upon the destruction of everything good. Such is the man which the pious, and pro-slavery papers of our land have taught the honest "Buckeyes" to look for in the person of William Lloyd Garrison, and in seeing him, they readily perceive how great has been the deception practiced upon them, and very naturally many of them are filled with indignation, and loathing, for their mean and dastardly deceivers. Thus the cause goes gloriously on, and thus is the wisdom of the crafty confounded, and the counsels of the ungodly brought to naught. Good is thus brought out of evil, and the wrath of man made to praise God.

On Wednesday, and Thursday, 11th and 12th August, we held five very interesting meetings in Pittsburg. The day meetings were held in the open air, and were very well attended. The evening meetings were held in Temperance Hall, a large room, but by no means sufficient to hold the numbers that pressed to hear.—The door-ways, and windows, and yard of the Hall, were crowded, while many were compelled to leave, without gaining admission to these. Hundreds remained on the outside of the building from an early hour till eleven o'clock at night. What a commentary on the religion of Pittsburg it is, that every church in the place was closed against us. All were too holy in which to plead the cause of our own common humanity. The great Christian cause of the age, like early Christianity itself, is too much despised by the world, to be admitted into the house of God. When saving men in our land, shall have become as popular as killing men now is in Mexico, we shall not only have churches open to our use, but, perhaps, be voted into religious societies as honorary members. In that day, the philanthropic Garrison may possibly be regarded as religious as the pious man-butcher, Zachary Taylor.

On Friday morning, 13th, we took the steamboat Beaver, from Pittsburg to New Brighton—the home of our kind friend, Milo A. Townsend, and our Anti-Slavery poetess, Grace Greenwood. A number of our friends accompanied us from Pittsburg to that place, a goodly number of whom were coloured persons. It is usual to dine on this boat between Pittsburg and Beaver, but on this occasion, strange to tell, no dinner was furnished, for the very American reason, that a goodly number of persons on board were coloured, and it was deemed probable that some of them might presume to dine, and would thus give offence to the white skinned aristocracy. So like the American delegates to the Evangelical Alliance, we concluded to preserve the peace by "going without our dinners."

We held two meetings at New Brighton, afternoon and evening, and here, too, the churches were closed against us, and we were compelled to take an upper room in a flour store. Thus making good the proposition, that humanity is received more cordially in the street than in the church. Our meetings at New Brighton were the last we held in Pennsylvania.

On Saturday, 14th instant, we took a boat on the Beaver and Warren Canal for Youngstown, Ohio, where Messrs. Foster and Walker were advertised to hold a meeting on the 14th, and 15th. On this boat, we received very kind and polite attention, and were allowed to take our meals with the other passengers. The trip from New Brighton to Youngstown, is exceedingly pleasant at this season of the year. The scenery on parts of the Beaver, is quite equal in beauty, if not in grandeur, to the Hudson. The hills on either side are lofty, precipitous, and covered with tall and finely proportioned trees. Verdant fields occasionally intersect the lofty and cragged hills, and form a beautiful variety of scene; now gratifying the eye, and at once leading it on to the discovery of new, and still more interesting points of beauty.

We reached Youngstown on Sunday morning, 15th instant, and were hospitably received by Mr. Andrews, the gentlemanly proprietor of the Youngstown Hotel. This gentleman kindly entertained us free of charge. The meetings in this place, like those held elsewhere on our Western tour, were held in the open air. Seats were arranged, and a platform erected in a beautiful grove, near the village. A good deacon of one of the churches whose doors were shut against us in this place, threatened us with prosecution, if we dared to arrange any seats on the ground during the Sabbath day. The threat, however, had no other effect than to summon a number of friends to the grove early in the morning, to arrange as many seats as might be necessary to accommodate the multitude. The meeting was large and spirited. The churches were all nearly vacated, and a large portion of their congregations came to worship in God's great temple, and to show their love for the All Good by doing good to His children.

Yours, sincerely,
Frederick Douglass

National Anti-Slavery Standard, September 2, 1847

TO SIDNEY HOWARD GAY

Austinburg, September, 1847.

The infernal system of Slavery is receiving a powerful shock in the West. The enthusiasm of our friends is unequalled. I am informed, on all sides, that the meetings now being held, are such as were never held before. The whole Western Reserve is now in a healthy state of Anti-Slavery agitation. The theme is on every lip, and is spreading far and wide. We are having a real Anti-Slavery revival. The most astonishing crowds flock to hear, and, I trust, to believe. Opposition to our holy cause seems stunned. Scarce a head is seen above the multitude to oppose the triumphant success of our glorious enterprise. The power of Church and State are shaken. The pro-slavery priesthood look woeful as they behold their glory departing. The people are fired with a noble indignation against a slaveholding Church, and filled with unutterable loathing of a slave-trading religion. The real character of our Government is being exposed. The flimsy arguments with which our Liberty party friends have attempted to make out a case of Anti-Slavery for the Constitution are blown into fragments.—The present administration is justly regarded as a combination of land-pirates and free-booters. Our *gallant* army in Mexico is looked upon as a band of legalized murderers and plunderers. Our psalm-singing, praying, pro-slavery priesthood are stamped with hypocrisy; and all their pretensions to a love for God, while they hate and neglect their fellow-man, is branded as impudent blasphemy. The fire is lighted,—let it rise—let it spread. Let the winds of an approving Heaven fan it, and guided by the hand that stays the thunder-bolt, and directs the storm, its holy flames shall burn up, and utterly consume the last vestige of tyranny in our land. The West is decidedly the best Anti-Slavery field in the country.—The people are more disposed to hear—less confined and narrowed in their views, and less circumscribed in their action by sectarian trammels, than are the people of the East. I seriously believe, had we the means to follow up the agitation already commenced in this State for six months, twelve months would not pass, ere every black law which now disgraces the statute-books of Ohio[22] would be repealed, and the free coloured people stand on as good a footing as that enjoyed by the coloured people of Massachusetts. The field here is truly ripe for the harvest, and my spirit is only cast down when I remember how few there are to labour in this part of our vineyard. With money and right-minded men we could place Ohio in advance of Massachusetts in twelve months. The people of this vast State are now ready to hear, believe, and act, but how can they hear without a preacher? We have now five lecturing agents in this field, besides Messrs. Foster, Garrison and myself; we are all labouring ardently, but we are few when you consider the vastness of the field and the readiness to hear on the subject.

I meant ere this to have sent you a hasty sketch of the character and proceedings of the Anniversary Meeting of the Western Anti-Slavery Society, but have been so hurried and driven by appointments, and so completely occupied with immediate and indispensable duties, as to make attention to this impossible. I have attended many Anti-Slavery meetings in the East, and in the West, but this exceeded, by far, any which I ever attended. It will long be remembered as one of the most interesting gatherings ever summoned at the bugle call of liberty. The presence of friends Garrison and Foster did much to give a zest and glory to the occasion, but added to these we had our cause pleaded by the magic eloquence of Music. The charms of liberty were set forth in song by the "Cowles family" of Austinburg, and greatly was the cause enhanced by their efforts. I shall never forget the impression made upon the audience by the first song. Four thousand persons stood charmed, and overcome by the melting melody of our friends; there was scarcely a dry eye among the vast audience, and all hearts seemed melted into one. The meeting was held three days, and was full of interest to the last. The first day was rather unpropitious, the weather being uncomfortably cold and cloudy, but the second and third were fine, clear, bright, warm, and beautiful. The heavens above and the earth below smiled naturally and lovingly upon our philanthropic gathering, and added their beauty and splendour to the scene, making the whole "superb and glorious." The meeting was held in what is extensively known in this region as the great "Oberlin Tent." Some idea of its greatness may be learned by the fact that it will hold five thousand persons. This portable "Farneuil Hall" was spread out in an open field near the main road through Lyme, and for three days was the scene of more human life than has been witnessed in these regions since the days of "hard Cider and Coonskins." Besides the thousands who crowded to hear on the subject of Slavery, there were hundreds who came from curiosity to see the crowd, and many for purposes of gain. Those who came for gain had their booths, and tents, and covered wagons, pitched all around us. There was a constant auctioneering going on without, while our meetings were going on within. In this respect our meeting resembled more the great political gatherings of the day than our usual Anti-Slavery meetings, except that our meeting was more orderly than they. It was pleasant to see our cause *look* popular for once. Too much praise cannot be bestowed upon the Anti-Slavery friends in New Lyme. Their industry, and hospitality were abundant and soul-cheering. You will be pleased to know that the women of the place took an active and intelligent interest in the meeting, and in the cause. When in the West four years ago, the lack of interest on the part of the women was, (you will remember,) the most painful part of our experience. I have observed that where an interest is taken in this subject there is more intellectual life and vigour among women, and much more happiness. Anti-Slavery is doing much here for the elevation and improvement of woman. The political Anti-Slavery meetings, are generally regarded as meetings with which women have nothing to do, and they can do little or nothing toward quickening their energies or expanding their intellects. On this occasion the *women* held Anti-Slavery fairs, and though little was realized, it was not for want of persevering effort. There was one mistake on their part which caused a failure, but it was a mistake on the side of liberty. They admitted all persons free of charge; and curiosity being on tiptoe, the room was so crowded with spectators that no room was left for buyers. Not one half of the useful and beautiful articles brought together were sold. They intend holding another in a few days at Ravenna, where I presume they will profit by their experience at New Lyme. The leading lady of this Bazaar movement, is well entitled to be called the Mrs. Chapman of the West. I think she will eventually be quite as successful. She is young in the cause but thoroughly devoted to it. She became deeply interested in the movement by the noble efforts of that faithful, eloquent, and intrepid advocate of the fettered bondman, Abby Kelley Foster. To this friend of God and man, the praise belongs of giving the West, and to the cause, another Maria Weston Chapman.

Since the anniversary, we have held large meetings at Painsville, Munson, Twinsbury, Oberlin, Richfield, and Medina. All the meetings have been well attended, but those of Munson and Richfield may be called monster meetings, numbering from three to six thousand. At all of these meetings, aside from the Anti-Slavery speeches, and the good resulting from them, a great deal of practical work has been done. No opportunity is missed to get in our publications, a great many useful books are sold, and subscribers to our papers obtained. We have done but little yet for the *Standard* or *Liberator,* as our efforts have been mainly directed to the support of the *Bugle.* We go to Massillon to-morrow.

F[rederick]
D[ouglass]

National Anti-Slavery Standard, September 9, 1847

TO SIDNEY HOWARD GAY

Cleveland, (O.) September 17, 1847

My dear Friend:

Mr. Garrison and myself are still pursuing our Western course, and steadily persevering (though much worn with our labours) in the fulfilment of our appointments, which are only like angels' visits in that they are "far between." Our industrious and devoted friend, the general agent, in making our appointments thus far, has studied more the wants of the cause than the weakness of our frames. We have an appointment for every day, and some of these are thirty and forty miles apart. I know that these distances will appear quite paltry to our Eastern friends, in the land of railroads and steamboats. But as the Rev. Bishop Meade says, in his celebrated sermon, on reconciling slaves to *evangelical floggings,* "if you consider it right you must needs think otherwise of it." We are carried by horses, fed with corn instead of fire—bone instead of iron. And you know, as said a certain rather windy orator, when a locomotive passed the house in which he was holding forth, and completely drowned his voice, *"wind* must yield to the superiority of *steam.*" We have any number of railroads, but they are quite similar to those you passed over four years ago, during the ever memorable "One Hundred Conventions." The mention of these conventions will be sufficient to initiate you into some of the hardships of our journey.

The enthusiasm of our friends, out here, is glorious.—They cannot wait for our arrival into their towns, but come twenty, thirty, and even forty miles, with their own teams, to meet us. They generally commence their kind communications to us by giving us some idea of the great importance of their locality, and of the importance of being promptly on the ground, and occupying every available moment in the propagation of our principles and measures; and when we are about to leave we are sympathetically informed, sometimes by the same persons, that we are fast wearing ourselves out, and that we ought to stay a day or two longer, omitting some appointment ahead, and thus secure time for necessary rest. These speeches, though somewhat inconsistent, are the natural outpourings of kind hearts. Thus far, we have resisted this sort of eloquence, and fulfilled all our appointments. Since the meetings at Medina and Richfield, of both which I believe you have been informed, we have held four meetings at Massillon and four at Leesburgh. Our meetings in these places were not so large as those held in other parts of this State, yet they would appear large in any part of New-York or New England.

This State is very justly called the giant of the West. Everything connected with it is on the most gigantic scale. She is a giant in population, in energy, and in improvement. She possesses, too, those moral elements of greatness which might easily make her the pioneer State, in resisting, successfully, the aggressions of Slavery on the North, and leading the way to the redemption of millions in the South. Her contiguity to a slave State gives her many advantages over States more removed from Slavery. Ohio may, if she will, abolish Slavery in Kentucky, and Western Virginia. At present her hands are tied,—the fetters of Slavery are on her giant limbs,—she is corrupted by Slavery. The moral pestilence that walketh in darkness along her southern border, has spread blight and mildew over her legislation. Her statute-book is polluted,—she is disgraced by her villainous black laws. Let her repeal those infernal laws—blot them forever from her statute-book, and thus cease to afford impunity to every white ruffian who may desire to insult, or plunder, who may desire to rob, or commit other outrages on her coloured population, and her power to do good would become apparent, and her moral greatness would be equal to her numerical and political strength. Till this is done, she is not in a position to exert much moral influence on the South. Before she can ask freedom for the coloured man of Kentucky, she must do justice to the black man of Ohio.

You are aware that what are called the black laws of this State, disallow and prohibit the testimony of coloured persons against white persons in courts of law. By this diabolical arrangement, law, as a means of protecting the property and persons of the weak, becomes meaningless, since it gives a "Thug" commission to any and every white villain, and permits them to insult, cheat, and plunder coloured persons with the utmost impunity. A score of facts might be mentioned of cases where persons having the fortune to have a white skin, have, in the presence of coloured persons, taken away their property without remuneration, and the guilty persons could not be brought to condign punishment, because their victims were black.

These shameful laws are not the natural expression of the moral sentiment of Ohio, but the servile work of pandering politicians, who, to conciliate the favour of slaveholders, and win their way into political power, have enacted these infernal laws. Let the people of Ohio demand their instant repeal, and the complete enfranchisement of her coloured people, and their gallant State would speedily become the paragon of all the free States, securing the gratitude and love of her coloured citizens, and wiping out a most foul imputation from the character of her white citizens. She might then well boast that *justice* within her borders, like its author in Heaven, is without respect to persons. I may mention that our friends here have it in contemplation to get up an agitation this winter, against those laws, which it is hoped will end in their repeal. Should they succeed, a staggering blow will be given to Slavery in Kentucky. The slaveholders will begin to feel that the North is fast combining against them, and must soon make their calling a bye-word and a hissing throughout all the land. Should Ohio take the step, Indiana may follow; this done and Kentucky is forsaken. The work must be done soon, or the moral effect will be lost; for the time is coming, when it will be but small work to repeal such laws, even in the slave States. The power to do good, if not soon embraced, must soon be taken from the North.

Since the above was written, we have held meetings at Salem, New Lisbon, Ravenna, Warren, and Cleveland. Our meeting at Salem was a great one—in some respects the greatest of the series. It was held two days, commencing Saturday morning, and continuing till late Sunday afternoon, deepening in interest to the last. In addition to the lofty appeals and powerful eloquence of Messrs. Garrison and Foster, we had with us, James and Lucretia Mott. I have never seen Mrs. Mott under more favourable circumstances. It was admirable to see her rise up in all her elegance and dignity of womanhood—her earnest but tranquil countenance, overshadowed and animated with the inspiration of sincere benevolence—at once arresting attention, dispelling prejudice, and commanding the entire respect of the assembled thousands. A slight pause, and all eyes are fixed, and all ears turned—a deep stillness pervades the audience, and her silvery voice, without effort or vehemence, is distinctly heard, even far beyond the vast multitude. Her truthful words came down upon the audience like great drops of summer rain upon parched ground. Mrs. Mott attended the meetings at Warren, Ravenna, and New Lisbon, and greatly added to the interest of the meetings in all these places. She parted with us at Ravenna, and pursued her course toward Indiana, where she is intending to hold religious meetings. Our meetings in this place have been well attended, and exceedingly spirited, and nothing occurred (as we somewhat feared from intimations thrown out in the *Plaindealer*) to mar the harmony and beauty of the occasion.

We shall leave here this morning for Buffalo, N. Y. where our next meeting is to be held. But one hasty word before we leave, with respect to western hospitality. Our tour thus far has been made very agreeable and happy by the noble generosity, and the kind and affable deportment of all with whom we have come in contact. There is nothing mean, narrow, or churlish about a true Buckeye—find him where or how you will, rich or poor, in a miserable log cabin, or a magnificent mansion, he is the same open, free, and truly generous man. Agreeing with or differing from you, of the same religious faith and politics, or differing from you in both, it makes no difference. Once make him feel you are an honest man and you are welcomed with all the fullness of genuine hospitality, to his heart and his home.

I ask not for his lineage
I ask not for his birth
If the stream be pure what matters it,
The source from which it burst.

Since we have been in this State, we have been as warmly welcomed and as cordially received at the homes of Liberty party men, as by Old Organizationists; and so may I say of Whigs, and sometimes Democrats. And in no case was there unfaithfulness or shunning to declare the whole truth, with reference to each and all these parties.

F[rederick]
D[ouglass]

National Anti-Slavery Standard, September 23, 1847.

AMERICAN SLAVERY, speech delivered at Market Hall, New York City, October 22, 1847

I like radical measures, whether adopted by Abolitionists or slaveholders. I do not know but I like them better when adopted by the latter. Hence I look with pleasure upon the movements of Mr. Calhoun and his party. I rejoice at any movement in the slave States with reference to this system of Slavery. Any movement there will attract attention to the system—a system, as Junius once said to Lord Granby, "which can only pass without condemnation as it passes without observation." I am anxious to have it seen of all men: hence I am delighted to see any effort to prop up the system on the part of the slaveholders. It serves to bring up the subject before the people; and hasten the day of deliverance. It is meant otherwise. I am sorry that it is so. Yet the wrath of man may be made to praise God. He will confound the wisdom of the crafty, and bring to naught the counsels of the ungodly. The slaveholders are now marshalling their hosts for the propagation and extension of the institution—Abolitionists, on the other hand, are marshalling their forces not only against its propagation and extension, but against its very existence. Two large classes of the community, hitherto unassociated with the Abolitionists, have come up so far towards the right as to become opposed to the farther extension of the crime. I am glad to hear it. I like to gaze upon these two contending armies, for I believe it will hasten the dissolution of the present unholy Union, which has been justly stigmatized as "a covenant with death, an agreement with hell." I welcome the bolt, either from the North or the South, which shall shatter this Union; for under this Union lie the prostrate forms of three millions with whom I am identified. In consideration of their wrongs, of their sufferings, of their groans, I welcome the bolt, either from the celestial or from the infernal regions, which shall sever this Union in twain. Slaveholders are promoting it—Abolitionists are doing so. Let it come, and when it does, our land will rise up from an incubus; her brightness shall reflect against the sky, and shall become the beacon light of liberty in the Western world. She shall then, indeed, become "the land of the free and the home of the brave."

For sixteen years, Wm. Lloyd Garrison and a noble army of the friends of emancipation have been labouring in season and out of season, amid smiles and frowns, sunshine and clouds, striving to establish the conviction through this land, that to hold and traffic in human flesh is a sin against God. They have been somewhat successful; but they have been in no wise so successful as they might have been, had the men and women at the North rallied around them as they had a right to hope from their profession. They have had to contend not only with skilful politicians, with a deeply prejudiced and pro-slavery community, but with eminent Divines, Doctors of Divinity, and Bishops. Instead of encouraging them as friends, they have acted as enemies. For many days did Garrison go the rounds of the city of Boston to ask of the ministers the poor privilege of entering their chapels and lifting up his voice for the dumb. But their doors were bolted, their gates barred, and their pulpits hermetically sealed. It was not till an infidel hall was thrown open, that the voice of dumb millions could be heard in Boston.

I take it that all who have heard at all on this subject, are well convinced that the stronghold of Slavery is in the pulpit. Say what we may of politicians and political parties, the power that holds the keys of the dungeon in which the bondman is confined, is the pulpit. It is that power which is dropping, dropping, constantly dropping on the ear of this people, creating and moulding the moral sentiment of the land. This they have sufficiently under their control that they can change it from the spirit of hatred to that of love to mankind. That they do it not, is evident from the results of their teaching. The men who wield the blood-clotted cow-skin come from our Sabbath Schools in the Southern States. Who act as slave-drivers? The men who go forth from our own congregations here. Why, if the Gospel were truly preached among us, a man would as soon think of going into downright piracy as to offer himself as a slave-driver.

In Farmington, two sons of members of the Society of Friends are coolly proposing to go the South and engage in the honourable office of slave-driving for a thousand dollars a year. People at the North talk coolly of uncles, cousins, and brothers who are slaveholders, and of their coming to visit them. If the Gospel were truly preached here, you would as soon talk of having an uncle or brother a brothel keeper as a slaveholder; for I hold that every slaveholder, no matter how pure he may be, is a keeper of a house of ill-fame. Every kitchen is a brothel, from that of Dr. Fuller's to that of James K. Polk's (Applause). I presume I am addressing a virtuous audience—I presume I speak to virtuous females—and I ask you to consider this one feature of Slavery. Think of a million of females absolutely delivered up into the hands of tyrants, to do what they will with them—to dispose of their persons in any way they see fit. And so entirely are they at the disposal of their masters, that if they raise their hands against them, they may be put to death for daring to resist their infernal aggression.

We have been trying to make this thing appear sinful. We have not been able to do so yet. It is not admitted, and I hardly know how to argue against it. I confess that the time for argument seems almost gone by. What do the people want? Affirmation upon affirmation,—denunciation upon denunciation,—rebuke upon rebuke?

We have men in this land now advocating evangelical flogging. I hold in my hand a sermon recently published by Rev. Bishop Meade, of Virginia. Before I read that part in favour of evangelical flogging, let me read a few extracts from another part, relating to the duties of the slave. The sermon, by the way, was published with a view of its being read by *Christian* masters to their slaves. White black birds! (Laughter.)

(*Mr. Douglass here assumed a most grotesque look, and with a canting tone of voice, read as follows.*)

"Having thus shown you the chief duties you owe to your great Master in Heaven, I now come to lay before you the duties you owe to your masters and mistresses on earth. And for this you have one general rule that you ought always to carry in your minds, and that is, *to do all services for them, as if you did it for God himself*. Poor creatures! you little consider when you are idle, and neglectful of your master's business; when you steal, waste, and hurt any of their substance; when you are saucy and impudent; when you are telling them lies and deceiving them; or when you prove stubborn and sullen, and will not do the work you are set about, without stripes and vexation; you do not consider, I say, that what faults you are guilty of towards your masters and mistresses, are faults done against God himself, who hath set your masters and mistresses over you in his own stead, and expects that you will do for them just as you would do for him. And pray, do not think that I want to deceive you, when I tell you that your *masters and mistresses are God's overseers;* and that if you are faulty towards them, God himself will punish you severely for it."

This is some of the Southern religion. Do you not think you would "grow in grace and in the knowledge of the truth." (Applause.)

I come now to evangelical flogging. There is nothing said about flogging—that word is not used. It is called correction; and that word as it is understood at the North, is some sort of medicine. (Laughter.) Slavery has always sought to hide itself under different names. The mass of the people call it "our peculiar institution." There is no harm in that. Others call it (they are the more pious sort), "our Patriarchal institution." (Laughter.) Politicians have called it "our social system"; and people in social life have called it "our domestic institution." Abbot Lawrence has recently discovered a new name for it—he calls it "unenlightened labour." (Laughter.) The Methodists in their last General Conference, have invented a new name—"the impediment." (Laughter.) To give you some idea of evangelical flogging, under the name of correction, there are laws of this description,—"any white man killing a slave shall be punished as though he shall have killed a white person, unless such a slave die under *moderate* correction." It commences with a plain proposition.

"Now when correction is given you, you either deserve it, or you do not deserve it." (Laughter.)

That is very plain, almost as safe as that of a certain orator:—"Ladies and Gentlemen, it is my opinion, my deliberate opinion, after a long consideration of the whole matter, that as a general thing, all other things being equal, there are fewer persons to be found in towns sparsely populated, than in larger towns more thickly settled." (Laughter.)

The Bishop goes on to say—

"Whether you really deserve it or not," (one would think that would make a difference), "it is your duty, and Almighty God requires that you bear it patiently. You may perhaps think that this is a hard doctrine," (and it admits of little doubt), "but if you consider it right you must needs think otherwise of it." (It is clear as mud. I suppose he is now going to reason them into the propriety of being flogged evangelically.) "Suppose you deserve correction; you cannot but see that it is just and right you should meet with it. Suppose you do not, or at least so much or so severe; you perhaps have escaped a great many more, and are at last paid for all. Suppose you are quite innocent; is it not possible you may have done some other bad thing which was never discovered, and Almighty God would not let you escape without punishment one time or another? Ought you not in such cases to give glory to Him?" (Glory!) (Much laughter.)

I am glad you have got to the point that you can laugh at the religion of such fellows as this Doctor. There is nothing that will facilitate our cause more than getting the people to laugh at that religion which brings its influence to support traffic in human flesh. It has deceived us so long that it has overawed us.

For a long time when I was a slave, I was led to think from hearing such passages as "servants obey, &c." that if I dared to escape, the wrath of God would follow me. All are willing to acknowledge my right to be free; but after this acknowledgement, the good man goes to the Bible and says "after all I see some difficulty about this thing. You know, after the deluge, there was Shem, Ham, and Japhet; and you know that Ham was black and had a curse put upon him; and I know not but it would be an attempt to thwart the purposes of Jehovah, if these men were set at liberty." It is this kind of religion I wish to have you laugh at—it breaks the charm there is about it. If I could have the men at this meeting who hold such sentiments and could hold up the mirror to let them see themselves as others see them, we should soon make head against this pro-slavery religion.

I dwell mostly upon the religious aspect, because I believe it is the religious people who are to be relied on in this Anti-Slavery movement. Do not misunderstand my railing—do not class me with those who despise religion—do not identify me with the infidel. I love the religion of Christianity—which cometh from above—which is pure, peaceable, gentle, easy to be entreated, full of good fruits, and without hypocrisy. I love that religion which sends its votaries to bind up the wounds of those who have fallen among thieves. By all the love I bear to such a Christianity as this, I hate that of the Priest and Levite, that with long-faced Phariseeism goes up to Jerusalem and worships, and leaves the bruised and wounded to die. I despise that religion that can carry Bibles to the heathen on the other side of the globe and withhold them from [the] heathen on this side—which can talk about human rights yonder and traffic in human flesh here. I love that which makes its votaries do to others as they would that others should do to them. I hope to see a revival of it—thank God it is revived. I see revivals of it in the absence of the other sort of revivals. I believe it to be confessed now, that there has not been a sensible man converted after the old sort of way, in the last five years. Le Roy Sunderland, the mesmerizer, has explained all this away, so that Knapp and others who have converted men after that sort have failed.

There is another religion. It is that which takes off fetters instead of binding them on—that breaks every yoke—that lifts up the bowed down. The Anti-Slavery platform is based on this kind of religion. It spreads its table to the lame, the halt, and the blind. It goes down after a long neglected race. It passes, link by link till it finds the lowest link in humanity's chain—humanity's most degraded form in the most abject condition. It reaches down its arm and tells them to stand up. This is Anti-Slavery—this is Christianity. It is reviving gloriously among the various denominations. It is threatening to supercede those old forms of religion having all of the love of God and none of man in it. (Applause.)

I now leave this aspect of the subject and proceed to inquire into that which probably must be the inquiry of every honest mind present. I trust I do not misjudge the character of my audience when I say they are anxious to know in what way they're contributing to uphold Slavery.

The question may be answered in various ways. I leave the outworks of political parties and social arrangements, and come at once to the Constitution, to which I believe all present are devotedly attached—I will not say all, for I believe I know some, who, however they may be disposed to admire some of the beautiful truths set forth in that instrument, recognize its pro-slavery features, and are ready to form a republic in which there shall be neither tyrant nor slave. The Constitution I hold to be radically and essentially slave-holding, in that it gives the physical and numerical power of the nation to keep the slave in his chains, by promising that that power shall in any emergency be brought to bear upon the slave, to crush him in obedience to his master. The language of the Constitution is you shall be a slave or die. We know it is such, and knowing it we are not disposed to have part nor lot with that Constitution. For my part I had rather that my right hand should wither by my side than cast a ballot under the Constitution of the United States.

Then, again, in the clause concerning fugitives—in this you are implicated. Your whole country is one vast hunting ground from Texas to Maine.

Ours is a glorious land; and from across the Atlantic we welcome those who are stricken by the storms of despotism. Yet the damning facts remain, there is not a rood of earth under the stars and the eagle of your flag, where a man of my complexion can stand free. There is no mountain so high, no plain so extensive, no spot so sacred, that it can secure to me the right of liberty. Wherever waves the star-spangled banner there the bondman may be arrested and hurried back to the jaws of Slavery. This is your "land of the free," your "home of the brave." From Lexington, from Ticonderoga, from Bunker Hill, where rises that grand shaft with its capstone in the clouds, asks, in the name of the first blood that spurted in behalf of freedom, to protect the slave from the infernal clutches of his master. That petition would be denied, and he bid go back to the tyrant.

I never knew what freedom was till I got beyond the limits of the American eagle. When I first rested my head on a British Island I felt that the eagle might scream, but from its talons and beak I was free, at least for a time. No slave-holder can clutch me on British soil. There I could gaze the tyrant in the face and with the indignation of a tyrant in my look, wither him before me. But republican, Christian America will aid the tyrant in catching his victim.

I know this kind of talk is not agreeable to what are called patriots. Indeed, some have called me a traitor. That profanely religious Journal "The Olive Branch," edited by the Rev. Mr. Norris, recommended that I be hung as a traitor. Two things are necessary to make a traitor. One is, he shall have a country. (Laughter and applause.) I believe if I had a country, I should be a patriot. I think I have all the feelings necessary—all the moral material, to say nothing about the intellectual. I do not know that I ever felt the emotion, but sometimes thought I had a glimpse of it. When I have been delighted with the little brook that passes by the cottage in which I was born,—with the woods and the fertile fields, I felt a sort of glow which I suspect resembles a little what they call patriotism. I can look with some admiration on your wide lakes, your fertile fields, your enterprise, your industry, your many lovely institutions. I can read with pleasure your Constitution to establish justice, and secure the blessings of liberty to posterity. Those are precious sayings to my mind. But when I remember that the blood of four sisters and one brother, is making fat the soil of Maryland and Virginia,—when I remember that an aged grandmother who has reared twelve children for the Southern market, and these one after another as they arrived at the most interesting age, were torn from her bosom,—when I remember that when she became too much racked for toil, she was turned out by a professed Christian master to grope her way in the darkness of old age, literally to die with none to help her, and the institutions of this country sanctioning and sanctifying this crime, I have no words of eulogy, I have no patriotism. How can I love a country where the blood of my own blood, the flesh of my own flesh, is now toiling under the lash?—America's soil reddened by the stain from woman's shrinking flesh.

No, I make no pretension to patriotism. So long as my voice can be heard on this or the other side of the Atlantic, I will hold up America to the lightning scorn of moral indignation. In doing this, I shall feel myself discharging the duty of a true patriot; for he is a lover of his country who rebukes and does not excuse its sins. It is righteousness that exalteth a nation while sin is a reproach to any people.

But to the idea of what you at the North have to do with Slavery. You furnish the bulwark of protection, and promise to put the slaves in bondage. As the American Anti-Slavery Society says, "if you will go on branding, scourging, sundering family ties, trampling in the dust your down trodden victims, you must do it at your own peril." But if you say, "we of the North will render you no assistance: if you still continue to trample on the slave, you must take the consequences," I tell you the matter will soon be settled.

I have been taunted frequently with the want of valour: so has my race, because we have not risen upon our masters. It is adding insult to injury to say this. You belong to 17,000,000, with arms, with means of locomotion, with telegraphs. We are kept in ignorance three millions to seventeen. You taunt us with not being able to rescue ourselves from your clutch. Shame on you! Stand aside—give us fair play—leave us with the tyrants, and then if we do not take care of ourselves, you may taunt us. I do not mean by this to advocate war and bloodshed.

I am not a man of war. The time was when I was. I was then a slave: I had dreams, horrid dreams of freedom through a sea of blood. But when I heard of the Anti-Slavery movement, light broke in upon my dark mind. Bloody visions fled away, and I saw the star of liberty peering above the horizon. Hope then took the place of desperation, and I was led to repose in the arms of Slavery. I said, I would suffer rather than do any act of violence—rather than that the glorious day of liberty might be postponed.

Since the light of God's truth beamed upon my mind, I have become a friend of that religion which teaches us to pray for our enemies—which, instead of shooting balls into their hearts, loves them. I would not hurt a hair of a slaveholder's head. I will tell you what else I would not do. I would not stand around the slave with my bayonet pointed at his breast, in order to keep him in the power of the slaveholder.

I am aware that there are many who think the slaves are very well off, and that they are very well treated, as if it were possible that such a thing could be. A man happy in chains! Even the eagle loves liberty.

> *Go, let a cage, with grates of gold,*
> *And pearly roof, the eagle hold;*
> *Let dainty viands be his fare,*
> *And give the captive tenderest care;*
> *But say, in luxury's limits pent,*
> *Find you the king of birds content?*
> *No, oft he'll sound the startling shriek,*
> *And dash the grates with angry beak.*
> *Precarious freedom's far more dear,*
> *Than all the prison's pampring cheer!*
> *He longs to see his eyrie's seat,*
> *Some cliff on ocean's lonely shore,*
> *Whose old bare top the tempests beat,*
> *And round whose base the billows roar,*
> *When tossed by gales, they yawn like graves,—*
> *He longs for joy to skim those waves;*
> *Or rise through tempest-shrouded air,*
> *And thick and dark, with wild winds swelling,*
> *To brave the lightning's lurid glare,*
> *And talk with thunders in their dwelling.*

As with the eagle, so with man. No amount of attention or finery, no dainty dishes can be a substitute for liberty. Slaveholders know this, and knowing it, they exclaim,—"The South are surrounded by a dangerous population, degraded, stupid savages, and if they could but entertain the idea that immediate, unconditional death would not be their portion, they would rise at once and enact the St. Domingo tragedy. But they are held in subordination by the consciousness that the whole nation would rise and crush them." Thus they live in constant dread from day to day.

Friends, Slavery must be abolished, and that can only be done by enforcing the great principles of justice. Vainly you talk about voting it down. When you have cast your millions of ballots, you have not reached the evil. It has fastened its root deep into the heart of the nation, and nothing but God's truth and love can cleanse the land. We must change the moral sentiment. Hence we ask you to support the Anti-Slavery Society. It is not an organization to build up political parties, or churches, nor to pull them down, but to stamp the image of Anti-Slavery truth upon the community. Here we may all do something.

> *In the world's broad field of battle,*
> *In the bivouac of life,*
> *Be not like dumb driven cattle—*
> *Be a hero in the strife.*

National Anti-Slavery Standard, October 28, 1847

TO J. D. CARR

Lynn, 1st Nov. 1847

My dear friend:

Your kind letter of the 1st October, enclosing a bill on London, value £445 17s. 6d. the amount collected by my friends in Great Britain, as a testimonial of their esteem, came safely and promptly to hand.

It has frequently been my lot, during my short, though varied and singular life, to respond in language of gratitude to kind friends, through whose great generosity I have been made the recipient of distinguished and valuable favours; but, in all truthfulness, never in circumstances when I could do so more sincerely and cordially than in the present instance. I accept your noble gift with emotions of gratitude, which I have no language to describe. Please accept my thanks for it, and extend the same to the generous friends of whom it was collected.

The bill sold here for two thousand, one hundred, and seventy-five dollars; a much larger sum than I had expected.

I have now to inform you that this sum is, after all, to be, and a part of it is already appropriated to the very purpose originally intended, both by myself and the donors—the establishment of a press to elevate and improve the condition of the nominally-free coloured people in the United States. . . . I had not decided against the publication of a paper one month, before I became satisfied that I had made a mistake, and each subsequent month's experience has confirmed me in the conviction. . . .

The *National Watchman,* published at Troy, by William Allen, a coloured young man, has been given up. The *Ram's Horn,* published in New York, will probably be united with my paper. The *Mystery,* published at Pittsburgh, is not issued regularly for want of means.

I have already bought an excellent and elegant press, and nearly all the necessary printing materials. The cost, in all, between nine and ten hundred dollars. My press has been examined by practical printers, and all unite in declaring it one of the best they have ever seen. My printing materials, types, &c. though not so good as what might have been secured in England, are nevertheless good, and the best that can be obtained in this country. The regular publication of the paper will begin with the commencement of the year.

As to its permanence and usefulness, I can only promise to labour for both to the very best of my ability. I am solemnly impressed with the importance of the enterprise; and I shall enter on my duties with a full sense of my accountability to God, to the slave, and to the dear friends who have aided me in the undertaking. In the publication of the paper, I shall be under no party or society, but shall advocate the slave's cause in that way which in my judgment, will be the best suited to the advancement of the cause. . . .

Frederick Douglass

"The British Friend" reprinted in *National Anti-Slavery Standard,* January 27, 1848

PART TWO: *From the Founding of* The North Star *to the Compromise of 1850*

OUR PAPER AND ITS PROSPECTS

We are now about to assume the management of the editorial department of a newspaper, devoted to the cause of Liberty, Humanity and Progress. The position is one which, with the purest motives, we have long desired to occupy. It has long been our anxious wish to see, in this slave-holding, slave-trading, and Negro-hating land, a printing-press and paper, permanently established, under the complete control and direction of the immediate victims of slavery and oppression.

Animated by this intense desire, we have pursued our object, till on the threshold of obtaining it. Our press and printing materials are bought, and paid for. Our office secured, and is well situated, in the centre of business, in this enterprising city. Our office Agent, an industrious and amiable young man, thoroughly devoted to the interests of humanity, has already entered upon his duties. Printers well recommended have offered their services, and are ready to work as soon as we are prepared for the regular publication of our paper. Kind friends are rallying round us, with words and deeds of encouragement. Subscribers are steadily, if not rapidly coming in, and some of the best minds in the country are generously offering to lend us the powerful aid of their pens. The sincere wish of our heart, so long and so devoutly cherished seems now upon the eve of complete realization.

It is scarcely necessary for us to say that our desire to occupy our present position at the head of an Anti-Slavery Journal, has resulted from no unworthy distrust or ungrateful want of appreciation of the zeal, integrity, or ability of the noble band of white laborers, in this department of our cause; but, from a sincere and settled conviction that such a Journal, if conducted with only moderate skill and ability, would do a most important and indispensable work, which it would be wholly impossible for our white friends to do for us.

It is neither a reflection on the fidelity, nor a disparagement of the ability of our friends and fellow-laborers, to assert what "common sense affirms and only folly denies," that the man who has *suffered the wrong* is the man to *demand redress*,— that the man STRUCK is the man to CRY OUT—and that he who has *endured the cruel pangs of Slavery* is the man to *advocate Liberty*. It is evident we must be our own representatives and advocates, not exclusively, but peculiarly—not distinct from, but in connection with our white friends. In the grand struggle for liberty and equality now waging, it is meet, right and essential that there should arise in our ranks authors and editors, as well as orators, for it is in these capacities that the most permanent good can be rendered to our cause.

Hitherto the immediate victims of slavery and prejudice, owing to various causes, have had little share in this department of effort: they have frequently undertaken, and almost as frequently failed. This latter fact has often been urged by our friends against our engaging in the present enterprise; but, so far from convincing us of the impolicy of our course, it serves to confirm us in the necessity, if not the wisdom of our undertaking. That others have failed, is a reason for OUR earnestly endeavoring to succeed. Our race must be vindicated from the embarrassing imputations resulting from former non-success. We believe that what *ought* to be done, *can* be done. We say this, in no self-confident or boastful spirit, but with a full sense of our weakness and unworthiness, relying upon the Most High for wisdom and strength to support us in our righteous undertaking. We are not wholly unaware of the duties, hardships and responsibilities of our position. We have easily imagined some, and friends have not hesitated to inform us of others. Many doubtless are yet to be revealed by that infallible teacher, experience. A view of them solemnize, but do not appal us. We have counted the cost. Our mind is made up, and we are resolved to go forward.

In aspiring to our present position, the aid of circumstances has been so strikingly apparent as to almost stamp our humble aspirations with the solemn sanctions of a Divine Providence. Nine years ago, as most of our readers are aware, we were held as a slave, shrouded in the midnight ignorance of that infernal system—sunken in the depths of servility and degradation—registered with four footed beasts and creeping things—regarded as property—compelled to toil without wages—with a heart swollen with bitter anguish—and a spirit crushed and broken. By a singular combination of circumstances we finally succeeded in escaping from the grasp of the man who claimed us as his property, and succeeded in safely reaching New Bedford, Mass. In this town we worked three years as a daily laborer on the wharves. Six years ago we became a Lecturer on Slavery. Under the apprehension of being re-taken into bondage, two years ago we embarked for England. During our stay in that country, kind friends, anxious for our safety, ransomed us from slavery, by the payment of a large sum. The same friends, as unexpectedly as generously, placed in our hands the necessary means of purchasing a printing press and printing materials. Finding ourself now in a favorable position for aiming an important blow at slavery and prejudice, we feel urged on in our enterprise by a sense of duty to God and man, firmly believing that our effort will be crowned with entire success.

The North Star, December 3, 1847

TO OUR OPPRESSED COUNTRYMEN

We solemnly dedicate the *North Star* to the cause of our long oppressed and plundered fellow countrymen. May God bless the offering to your good! It shall fearlessly assert your rights, faithfully proclaim your wrongs, and earnestly demand for you instant and even-handed justice. Giving no quarter to slavery at the South, it will hold no truce with oppressors at the North. While it shall boldly advocate emancipation for our enslaved brethren, it will omit no opportunity to gain for the nominally free, complete enfranchisement. Every effort to injure or degrade you or your cause—originating wheresoever, or with whomsoever—shall find in it a constant, unswerving and inflexible foe.

We shall energetically assail the ramparts of Slavery and Prejudice, be they composed of church or state, and seek the destruction of every refuge of lies, under which tyranny may aim to conceal and protect itself.

Among the multitude of plans proposed and opinions held, with reference to our cause and condition, we shall try to have a mind of our own, harmonizing with all as far as we can, and differing from any and all where we must, but always discriminating between men and measures. We shall cordially approve every measure and effort calculated to advance your sacred cause, and strenuously oppose any which in our opinion may tend to retard its progress. In regard to our position, on questions that have unhappily divided the friends of freedom in this country, we shall stand in our paper where we have ever stood on the platform. Our views written shall accord with our views spoken, earnestly seeking peace with all men, when it can be secured without injuring the integrity of our movement, and never shrinking from conflict or division when summoned to vindicate truth and justice.

While our paper shall be mainly Anti-Slavery, its columns shall be freely opened to the candid and decorous discussion of all measures and topics of a moral and humane character, which may serve to enlighten, improve, and elevate mankind. Temperance, Peace, Capital Punishment, Education,—all subjects claiming the attention of the public mind may be freely and fully discussed here.

While advocating your rights, the *North Star* will strive to throw light on your duties: while it will not fail to make known your virtues, it will not shun to discover your faults. To be faithful to our foes it must be faithful to ourselves, in all things.

Remember that we are one, that our cause is one, and that we must help each other, if we would succeed. We have drunk to the dregs the bitter cup of slavery; we have worn the heavy yoke; we have sighed beneath our bonds, and writhed beneath the bloody lash;—cruel mementoes of our oneness are indelibly marked in our living flesh. We are one with you under the ban of prejudice and proscription—one with you under the slander of inferiority—one with you in social and political disfranchisement. What you suffer, we suffer; what you endure, we endure. We are indissolubly united, and must fall or flourish together.

We feel deeply the solemn responsibility which we have now assumed. We have seriously considered the importance of the enterprise, and have now entered upon it with full purpose of heart. We have nothing to offer in the way of literary ability to induce you to encourage us in our laudable undertaking. You will not expect or require this at our hands. The most that you can reasonably expect, or that we can safely promise, is, a paper of which you need not be ashamed. Twenty-one years of severe bondage at the South, and nine years of active life at the North, while it has afforded us the best possible opportunity for storing our mind with much practical and important information, has left us little time for literary pursuits or attainments. We have yet to receive the advantage of the first day's schooling. In point of education, birth and rank, we are one with yourselves, and of yourselves. What we are, we are not only without help, but against trying opposition. Your knowledge of our history for the last seven years makes it unnecessary for us to say more on this point. What we have been in your cause, we shall continue to be; and not being too old to learn, we may improve in many ways. Patience and Perseverance shall be our motto.

We shall be the advocates of learning, from the very want of it, and shall most readily yield the deference due to men of education among us; but shall always bear in mind to accord most merit to those who have labored hardest, and overcome most, in the praiseworthy pursuit of knowledge, remembering "that the whole need not a physician, but they that are sick," and that "the strong ought to bear the infirmities of the weak."

Brethren, the first number of the paper is before you. It is dedicated to your cause. Through the kindness of our friends in England, we are in possession of an excellent printing press, types, and all other materials necessary for printing a paper. Shall this gift be blest to our good, or shall it result in our injury? It is for you to say. With your aid, co-operation and assistance, our enterprise will be entirely successful. We pledge ourselves that no effort on our part shall be wanting, and that no subscriber shall lose his subscription—"The *North Star* Shall Live."

The North Star, December 3, 1847

TO HENRY CLAY

Sir:

I have just received and read your Speech, delivered at the Mass Meeting in Lexington, Kentucky, 13th November 1847, and after a careful and candid perusal of it, I am impressed with the desire to say a few words to you on one or two subjects which form a considerable part of that speech. You will, I am sure, pardon the liberty I take in thus publicly addressing you, when you are acquainted with the fact, that I am one of those "unfortunate victims" whose case you seem to commiserate, and have experienced the cruel wrongs of Slavery in my own person. It is with no ill will, or bitterness of spirit that I address you. My position under this government, even in the State of N. Y., is that of a disfranchised man. I can have, therefore, no political ends to serve, nor party antipathy to gratify. My "intents" are not wicked but truly charitable. I approach you simply in the character of one of the unhappy millions enduring the evils of Slavery, in this otherwise highly favored and glorious land.

In the extraordinary speech before me, after dwelling at length upon the evils, disgrace, and dangers of the present unjust, mean, and iniquitous war waged by the United States upon Mexico, you disavow for yourself and the meeting, "in the most positive manner," any wish to acquire any foreign territory whatever for the purpose of introducing slavery into it. As one of the oppressed, I give you the full expression of sincere gratitude for this declaration, and the pledge which it implies, and earnestly hope that you may be able to keep your vow unsullied by compromises, (which, pardon me,) have too often marred and defaced the beauty and consistency of your humane declarations and pledges on former occasions. It is not, however, any part of my present intention to reproach you invidiously or severely for the past. Unfortunately for the race, you do not stand alone in respect to deviations from a strict line of rectitude. Poor, erring and depraved humanity, has surrounded you with a throng of guilty associates, it would not, therefore, be magnanimous in me to reproach you for the past, above all others.

Forgetting the things that are behind, I simply propose to speak to you of what you are at this time—of the errors and evils of your present, as I think, wicked position, and to point out to you the path of repentance, which if pursued, must lead you to the possession of peace and happiness, and make you a blessing to your country and the world.

In the speech under consideration, you say,

"My opinions on the subject of slavery are well known; they have the merit, if it be one, of consistency, uniformity and long duration."

The first sentence is probably true. Your opinions on slavery may be well known, but that they have the merit of consistency or of uniformity, I cannot so readily admit. If the speech before me be a fair declaration of your present opinions, I think I can convince you that even this speech abounds with inconsistencies such as materially to affect the consolation you seem to draw from this source. Indeed if you are uniform at all, you are only so in your inconsistencies.

You confess that

"Slavery is a great evil, and a wrong to its victims, and you would rejoice if not a single slave breathed the air within the limits of our country."

These are noble sentiments, and would seem to flow from a heart overborne with a sense of the flagrant injustice and enormous cruelty of slavery, and of one earnestly and anxiously longing for a remedy. Standing alone, it would seem that the author had long been in search of some means to redress the wrongs of the *"unfortunate victims"* of whom he speaks—that his righteous soul was deeply grieved, every hour, on account of the foul blot inflicted by this curse on his country's character.

But what are the facts? You are yourself a Slaveholder at this moment, and your words on this point had scarcely reached the outer circle of the vast multitude by which you were surrounded, before you poured forth one of the most helpless, illogical, and cowardly apologies for this same wrong, and *"great evil"* which I ever remember to have read. Is this consistency, and uniformity? if so, the oppressed may well pray the Most High that you may be soon delivered from it.

Speaking of "the unfortunate victims" of this "great evil," and "wrong," you hold this most singular and cowardly excuse for perpetuating the wrongs of my "unfortunate" race.

"But here they are to be dealt with as well as we can, with a due consideration of all circumstances affecting the security and happiness of both races."

What do you mean by the security, safety and happiness of both races? do you mean that the happiness of the slave is augmented by his being a slave, and if so, why call him an "unfortunate victim." Can it be that this is mere cant, by which to seduce the North into your support, on the ground of your sympathy for the slave. I cannot believe you capable of such infatuation. I do not wish to believe that you are capable of either the low cunning, or the vanity which your language on this subject would seem to imply, but will set it down to an uncontrollable conviction of the innate wickedness of slavery, which forces itself out, and defies even your vast powers of concealment.

But further, you assert,

"Every State has the supreme, uncontrolled and exclusive power to decide for itself whether slavery shall cease or continue within its limits, without any exterior intervention from any quarter."

Here I understand you to assert the most profligate and infernal doctrine, that any State in this Union has a right to plunder, scourge and enslave any part of the human family within its borders, just so long as it deems it for its interest so to do, and that no one or body of persons beyond the limits of said state has a right to interfere by word or deed against it. Is it possible that you hold this monstrous and blood-chilling doctrine? If so, what confidence can any enlightened lover of liberty place in your pretended opposition to Slavery. I know your answer to all this, but it only plunges you into lower depths of infamy than the horrible doctrines avowed above. You go on to say:

"In States where the *Slaves outnumber the whites,* as is the case in several [which I believe are only two out of fifteen] the blacks could not be emancipated without *becoming the governing power in these states.*"

This miserable bug-bear is quite a confession of the mental and physical equality of the races. You pretend that you are a Republican. You loudly boast of your Democratic principles: why then do you object to the application of your principles in this case. Is the democratic principle good in one case, and bad in another? Would it be worse for a black majority to govern a white minority than it now is for the latter to govern the former? But you conjure up an array of frightful objections in answer to this.

"*Collisions and conflicts between the two races would be inevitable,* and after shocking scenes of *rapine and carnage, the extinction or expulsion of the blacks would certainly take place.*"

How do you know that any such results would be inevitable? Where, on the page of history, do you find anything to warrant even such a conjecture? You will probably point me to the Revolution in St. Domingo,[1] the old and thread-bare falsehood under which democratic tyrants have sought a refuge for the last forty years. But the facts in that direction are all against you. It has been clearly proven that that revolution was not the result of emancipation, but of a cruel attempt to re-enslave an already emancipated people. I am not aware that you have a single fact to support your truly terrible assertion, while on the other hand I have many all going to show what is equally taught by the voice of reason and of God, "that it is always safe to do right." The promise of God is, "that thy light shall break forth as the morning, and thy health shall spring forth speedily, and thy righteousness shall go before thee, the glory of the Lord shall be thy reward: then shalt thou call and the Lord shall answer; thou shalt cry and he will say, Here I am."

The history of the world is in conformity with the words of inspired wisdom. Look, for instance, at the history of Emancipation in the British West Indies. There the blacks were, and still are, an overwhelming majority. Have there been any *"shocking scenes of rapine and carnage, extinction or expulsion."* You know there have not. Why then do you make use of this unfounded and irrational conjecture to frighten your fellow-countrymen from the righteous performance of a simple act of justice to millions now groaning in almost hopeless bondage.

I now give your argument in support of the morality of your position.

"It may be argued that, in admitting the injustice of slavery, I grant the necessity of an instantaneous separation of that injustice. Unfortunately, however, it is not always safe, practicable or possible in the great movements of States or public affairs of nations, to remedy or repair the infliction of previous injustice. In the inception of it, we may oppose and denounce it by our most strenuous exertions, but, after its consummation, there is often no other alternative left us but to deplore its perpetration, and to acquiesce as the only alternative, in its existence, as a less evil than the frightful consequences which might ensue from the vain endeavor to repair it. Slavery is one of these unfortunate instances."

The cases which you put in support of the foregoing propositions, are only wanting in one thing, and that is analogy. The plundering of the Indians of their territory, is a crime to which no honest man can look with any degree of satisfaction. It was a wrong to the Indians then living, and how muchsoever we might seek to repair that wrong, the victims are far beyond any benefit of it; but with reference to the slave, the wrong to be repaired is a present one, the slave holder is the every day robber of the slave, of his birthright to liberty, property, and the pursuit of happiness —his right to be free is unquestionable—the wrong to enslave him is self evident—the duty to emancipate him is imperative. Are you aware to what your argument on this point leads? do you not plainly see that the greatest crimes that ever cursed our common earth, may take shelter under your reasoning, and may claim perpetuity on the ground of their antiquity?

Sir, I must pass over your allusions to that almost defunct and infernal scheme which you term "unmixed benevolence" for expelling not the slave but the *free colored people* from these United States, as well as your charge against the Abolitionists.

"It is a philanthropic and consoling reflection that the moral and physical condition of the African in the United States in a state of slavery is far better than it would have been had their ancestors not been brought from their native land."

I can scarce repress the flame of rising indignation, as I read this cold blooded and cruel sentence; there is so much of Satan dressed in the livery of Heaven, as well as taking consolation from crime, that I scarcely know how to reply to it. Let me ask you what has been the cause of the present unsettled condition of Africa? Why has she not reached forth her hand unto God? Why have not her fields been made Missionary grounds, as well as the Feejee Islands? Because of this very desolating traffic from which you seem to draw consolation. For three hundred years Christian nations, among whom we are foremost, have looked to Africa only as a place for the gratification of their lust and love of power, and every means have been adopted to stay the onward march of civilization in that unhappy land.

Your declaration on this point, places your consolation with that of the wolf in devouring the lamb. You next perpetrate what I conceive to be the most revolting blasphemy. You say:

"*And if it should be the decree of the Great Ruler of the Universe, that their descendants shall be made instruments in his hands in the establishment of civilization and the Christian religion throughout Africa—our regrets on account of the original wrong will be greatly mitigated.*"

Here, Sir, you would charge home upon God the responsibility of your own crimes, and would seek a solace from the pangs of a guilty conscience by sacrilegiously assuming that in robbing Africa of her children, you acted in obedience to the great purposes, and were but fulfilling the decrees of the Most High God; but as if fearing that this refuge of lies might fail, you strive to shuffle off the responsibility of this "great evil" on Great Britain. May I not ask if you were fulfilling the great purposes of God in the share you took in this traffic, and can draw consolation from that alleged fact, is it honest to make England a sinner above yourselves, and deny her all the mitigating circumstances which you apply to yourselves?

You say that "*Great Britain inflicted the evil upon you.*" If this be true, it is equally true that she inflicted the same evil upon herself; but she has had the justice and the magnanimity to repent and bring forth fruits meet for repentance. You copied her bad example, why not avail yourself of her good one also?

Now, Sir, I have done with your Speech, though much more might be said upon it. I have a few words to say to you personally.

I wish to remind you that you are not only in the "*autumn*," but in the very winter of life. Seventy-one years have passed over your stately brow. You must soon leave this world, and appear before God, to render up an account of your stewardship. For fifty years of your life you have been a slaveholder. You have robbed the laborer who has reaped down your fields, of his rightful reward. You are at this moment the robber of nearly fifty human beings, of their liberty, compelling them to live in ignorance. Let me ask if you think that God will hold you guiltless in the great day of account, if you die with the blood of these fifty slaves clinging to your garments. I know that you have made a profession of religion, and have been baptized, and am aware that you are in good and regular standing in the church, but I have the authority of God for saying that you will stand rejected at his bar, unless you "put away the evil of your doings from before his eyes—cease to do evil, and learn to do well—seek judgment, relieve the oppressed—and plead for the widow." You must "break every yoke, and let the oppressed go free," or take your place in the ranks of "evil doers," and expect to "reap the reward of corruption."

At this late day in your life, I think it would be unkind for me to charge you with any ambitious desires to become the President of the United States. I may be mistaken in this, but it seems that you cannot indulge either the wish or expectation. Bear with me, then, while I give you a few words of further counsel, as a private individual, and excuse the plainness of one who has felt the wrongs of Slavery, and fathomed the depths of its iniquity.

Emancipate your own slaves. Leave them not to be held or sold by others. Leave them free as the Father of his country left his,[2] and let your name go down to posterity, as his came down to us, a slaveholder, to be sure, but a repentant one. Make the noble resolve, that so far as you are personally concerned, "America shall be Free."

In asking you to do this, I ask nothing which in any degree conflicts with your argument against general emancipation. The dangers which you conjecture of the latter cannot be apprehended of the former. Your own slaves are too few in number to make them formidable or dangerous. In this matter you are without excuse. I leave you to your conscience, and your God,

And subscribe myself,
Faithfully, yours,
Frederick Douglass

The North Star, December 3, 1847

COLORED NEWSPAPERS

They are sometimes objected to, on the ground that they serve to keep up an odious and wicked distinction between white and colored persons, and are a barrier to that very equality which we are wont to advocate. We have, sometimes, heard persons regret the very mention of color, on this account, and to counsel its abandonment. We confess to no such feelings; we are in no wise sensitive on this point. Facts are facts; white is not black, and black is not white. There is neither good sense, nor common honesty, in trying to forget this distinction. So far from the truth is the notion that colored newspapers are serving to keep up that cruel distinction, the want of them is the main cause of its continuance. The distinction which degrades us, is not that which exists between a *white* man and a black man. They are equal men: the one is white, and the other is black; but both are men, and equal men. The white man is only superior to the black man, when he outstrips him in the race of improvement; and the black man is only inferior, when he proves himself incapable of doing just what is done by his white brother. In order to remove this odious distinction, we must do just what white men do. It must be no longer white lawyer, and black woodsawyer,—white editor, and black street cleaner: it must be no longer white, intelligent, and black, ignorant; but we must take our stand side by side with our white fellow countrymen, in all the trades, arts, professions and callings of the day.

It is one of the most cheering signs of the times, that colored persons are becoming farmers, mechanics, lecturers, doctors, lawyers, merchants, teachers, professors and editors. The more we have of them, the better; and the sooner will the distinction of which we complain be removed. Man's greatness consists in his ability to do, and the proper application of his powers to things needful to be done, and not in the color of his skin.

The North Star, January 8, 1848

THE WAR WITH MEXICO

From aught that appears in the present position and movements of the executive and cabinet—the proceedings of either branch of the national Congress,—the several State Legislatures, North and South—the spirit of the public press—the conduct of leading men, and the general views and feelings of the people of the United States at large, slight hope can rationally be predicated of a very speedy termination of the present disgraceful, cruel, and iniquitous war with our sister republic. Mexico seems a doomed victim to Anglo Saxon cupidity and love of dominion. The determination of our slaveholding President to prosecute the war, and the probability of his success in wringing from the people men and money to carry it on, is made evident, rather than doubtful, by the puny opposition arrayed against him. No politician of any considerable distinction or eminence, seems willing to hazard his popularity with his party, or stem the fierce current of executive influence, by an open and unqualified disapprobation of the war. None seem willing to take their stand for peace at all risks; and all seem willing that the war should be carried on, in some form or other. If any oppose the President's demands, it is not because they hate the war, but for want of information as to the aims and objects of the war. The boldest declaration on this point is that of Hon. John P. Hale, which is to the effect that he will not vote a single dollar to the President for carrying on the war, until he shall be fully informed of the purposes and objects of the war. Mr. Hale knows, as well as the President can inform him, for what the war is waged; and yet he accompanies his declaration with that prudent proviso. This shows how deep seated and strongly bulwarked is the evil against which we contend. The boldest dare not fully grapple with it.

Meanwhile, "the plot thickens"; the evil spreads. Large demands are made on the national treasury, (to wit: the poor man's pockets.) Eloquent and patriotic speeches are made in the Senate, House of Representatives and State Assemblies: Whig as well as Democratic governors stand stoutly up for the war: experienced and hoary-headed statesmen tax their declining strength and ingenuity in devising ways and means for advancing the infernal work: recruiting sergeants and corporals perambulate the land in search of victims for the sword and food for powder. Wherever there is a sink of iniquity, or a den of pollution, these buzzards may be found in search of their filthy prey. They dive into the rum shop, and gambling house, and other sinks too infamous to name, with swine-like avidity, in pursuit of degraded men to vindicate the insulted honor of our Christian country. Military chieftains and heroes multiply, and towering high above the level of common men, are glorified, if not deified, by the people. The whole nation seems to "wonder after these [bloody] beasts." Grasping ambition, tyrannic usurpation, atrocious aggression, cruel and haughty pride, spread, and pervade the land. The curse is upon us. The plague is abroad. No part of the country can claim entire exemption from its evils. They may be seen as well in the State of New York, as in South Carolina; on the Penobscot, as on the Sabine. The people appear to be completely in the hands of office seekers, demagogues, and political gamblers. Within the bewildering meshes of their political nets, they are worried, confused, and confounded, so that a general outcry is heard—"Vigorous prosecution of the war!"—"Mexico must be humbled!"—"Conquer a peace!"—"Indemnity!"—"War forced upon us!"—"National honor!"—"The whole of Mexico!"—"Our destiny!"—"This continent!"—"Anglo Saxon blood!"—"More territory!"—"Free institutions!"—"Our country!" till it seems indeed "that justice has fled to brutish beasts, and men have lost their reason." The taste of human blood and the smell of powder seem to have extinguished the senses, seared the conscience, and subverted the reason of the people to a degree that may well induce the gloomy apprehension that our nation has fully entered on her downward career, and yielded herself up to the revolting idea of battle and blood. "Fire and sword," are now the choice of our young republic. The loss of thousands of her own men, and the slaughter of tens of thousands of the sons and daughters of Mexico, have rather given edge than dullness to our appetite for fiery conflict and plunder. The civilization of the age, the voice of the world, the sacredness of human life, the tremendous expense, the dangers, hardships, and the deep disgrace which must forever attach to our inhuman course, seem to oppose no availing check to the mad spirit of proud ambition, blood, and carnage, let loose in the land.

We have no preference for parties, regarding this slaveholding crusade. The one is as bad as the other. The friends of peace have nothing to hope from either. The Democrats claim the credit of commencing, and the Whigs monopolize the glory of voting supplies and carrying on the war; branding the war as dishonorably commenced, yet boldly persisting in pressing it on. If we have any preference of two such parties, that preference inclines to the one whose practice, though wicked, most accords with its professions. We know where to find the so called Democrats. They are the accustomed panderers to slaveholders: nothing is either too mean, too dirty, or infamous for them, when commanded by the merciless man stealers of our country. No one expects any thing honorable or decent from that party, touching human rights. They annexed Texas under the plea of extending the area of freedom. They elected James K. Polk, the slaveholder, as the friend of freedom; and they have backed him up in his Presidential falsehoods. They have used their utmost endeavors to crush the right of speech, abridge the right of petition, and to perpetuate the enslavement of the colored people of this country. But we do not intend to go into any examination of parties just now. That we shall have frequent opportunities of doing hereafter. We wish merely to give our readers a general portrait of the present aspect of our country in regard to the Mexican war, its designs, and its results, as they have thus far transpired.

Of the settled determination to prosecute the war, there can be no doubt: Polk has avowed it; his organs have published it; his supporters have rallied round him; all their actions bend in that direction; and every effort is made to establish their purpose firmly in the hearts of the people, and to harden their hearts for the conflict. All danger must be defied; all suffering despised; all honor eschewed; all mercy dried up; and all the better promptings of the human soul blunted, silenced and repudiated, while all the furies of hell are invoked to guide our hired assassins,—our man-killing machines,—now in and out of Mexico, to the infernal consummation. Qualities of head and heart, principles and maxims, counsels and warnings, which once commanded respect, and secured a nation's reverence, must all now be scouted; sense of decency must be utterly drowned: age nor sex must exercise any humanizing effect upon our gallant soldiers, or restrain their satanic designs. The groans of slaughtered men, the screams of violated women, and the cries of orphan children, must bring no throb of pity from our national heart, but must rather serve as music to inspire our gallant troops to deeds of atrocious cruelty, lust, and blood. The work is thus laid out, commenced, and is to be continued. Where it will end is known only to the Great Ruler of the Universe; but where the responsibility rests, and upon whom retribution will fall, is sure and certain.

In watching the effects of the war spirit, prominent among them, will be seen, not only the subversion of the great principles of Christian morality, but the most horrid blasphemy.

While traveling from Rochester to Victor, a few days ago, we listened to a conversation between two persons of apparent gentility and intelligence, on the subject of the United States' war against Mexico. A wide difference of opinion appeared between them; the one contending for the rightfulness of the war, and the other against it. The main argument in favor of the war was the meanness and wickedness of the Mexican people; and, to cap the climax, he gave it as his solemn conviction, that the hand of the Lord was in the work! that the cup of Mexican iniquity was full; and that God was now making use of the Anglo Saxon race as a rod to chastise them! The effect of this religious outburst was to stun his opponent into silence: he seemed speechless; the ground was too high and holy for him; he did not dare reply to it; and thus the conversation ended. When men charge their sins upon God, argument is idle; rebuke alone is needful; and the poor man, lacking the moral courage to do this, sat silent.

Here, then, we have religion coupled with our murderous designs. We are, in the hands of the great God, a rod to chastise this rebellious people! What say our evangelical clergy to this blasphemy? That clergy seem as silent as the grave; and their silence is the greatest sanction of the crime.[8] They have seen the blood of the innocent poured out like water, and are dumb; they have seen the truth trampled in the dust—right sought by pursuing the wrong—peace sought by prosecuting the war—honor sought by dishonorable means,—and have not raised a whisper against it: they float down with the multitude in the filthy current of crime, and are hand in hand with the guilty. Had the pulpit been faithful, we might have been saved from this withering curse. We sometimes fear, that now our case as a nation is hopeless. May God grant otherwise! Our nation seems resolved to rush on in her wicked career, though the road be ditched with human blood, and paved with human skulls. Well, be it so. But, humble as we are, and unavailing as our voice may be, we wish to warn our fellow countrymen, that they may follow the course which they have marked out for themselves; no barrier may be sufficient to obstruct them; they may accomplish all they desire; Mexico may fall before them; she may be conquered and subdued; her government may be annihilated—her name among the great sisterhood of nations blotted out; her separate existence annihilated; her rights and powers usurped; her people put under the iron arm of a military despotism, and reduced to a condition little better than that endured by the Saxons when vanquished by their Norman invaders; but, so sure as there is a God of justice, we shall not go unpunished; the penalty is certain; we cannot escape; a terrible retribution awaits us. We beseech our countrymen to leave off this horrid conflict, abandon their murderous plans, and forsake the way of blood. Peradventure our country may yet be saved. Let the press, the pulpit, the church, the people at large, unite at once; and let petitions flood the halls of Congress by the million, asking for the instant recall of our forces from Mexico. This may not save us, but it is our only hope.

The North Star, January 21, 1848

THE NORTH AND THE PRESIDENCY

The public mind is at present deeply engrossed, and apparently perplexed, on the question as to which of the manstealers, or "hired assassins," shall be nominated to run as candidates, in the approaching political campaign, for the Presidency of our slaveholding and slavery-propagating Republic.— Upon whom the nominations will fall, is exceedingly doubtful, if anything can be learned from newspaper speculations about the matter, for the greatest confusion prevails among them with respect to it. But one thing is certain: Slavery, the old President-making power, is still on the throne; and it is equally certain that, as on all former and similar occasions, it will so shape and control the decisions of each political party, as to leave liberty with nothing to hope from either.— The old game of '40 and '44, will be played off again, and the friends of freedom will be again dogged with the doctrine of choosing between two evils, as if moral evils could be separated. The people of the North are just now, if we may judge from their noisy tumult and clamor, sporting joyfully in the delusion of imagining themselves parties to a decision of the question of who shall be nominated. Infatuated and deluded men, how long will you be deceived? Your voice in this matter is without weight; your boasted power is a shadow; you have surrendered up your proper influence in the choice of rulers in your unholy union with slaveholders; you have joined hands with the wicked manstealer, to rob and plunder your equal brother; and though you may share with him, to the full, the vile profligacy and infamy of his crime, so far from being equal to him in power, you are but his mean, servile and cringing vassal. You are caught in the snare which you set for others, and are under the same yoke, in part, that you imposed on the neck of the oppressed and despised black man.

It is in strict accordance with all philosophical, as well as all experimental knowledge, that those who unite with tyrants to oppress the weak and helpless, will sooner or later find the ground-work of their own rights and liberties giving way. "The price of liberty is eternal vigilance." It can only be maintained by a sacred regard for the rights of all men. The people of the North have sought to attain and secure their rights, by a most flagrant infringement of the rights, liberties and happiness of others. They have consented to stand side by side with the tyrant, with their heels on the hearts of fettered millions, leaving them to perish under the weight of what they call "our glorious Union," and in so doing, have given the Southern slaveholder the most effective power to control and govern the North. You may flutter and flounder as you may about "Wilmot Provisos,"[4] "No extension of slavery," and a "Northern President"—you are under the yoke, you are in the traces, and will continue to be so until you end your union with slaveholders, and utterly abandon your slaveholding Constitution. You must break, or continue to hug your chains.

The grand over-ruling interest and all-pervading element in this boasted Republic, is slavery. It reigns without a rival. Representing, as it does, more than twelve hundred million dollars, it is able to bring to its aid the overwhelming influence of both political parties. To this interest, the Whig as well as the Democratic party *belong*. Yes, they belong to it. They have mutually sworn to remain true to slavery, whether within or without its present limits. "Our country however bounded," is but another phrase for slavery however bounded; and to this sentiment each political party assents.—Each party is the property of the slaveholder, and you *belong* to these parties. You think yourselves free; but the truth is, you *belong* to these parties as much as we ever belonged to the Methodist manthief, Thomas Auld.—It is theirs to command, and yours to obey. You must vote for the murderer, or the manstealer, or such other criminal as your Southern masters shall decide as being best suited to maintain Southern institutions. Flatter not yourselves with the delusion that you have any voice in nominating the persons who shall receive your support, or that you possess spirit and independence enough to oppose a slaveholder whom you deem unfit for the office, for you have neither the one nor the other; you will do as your masters bid you. It was so in 1844, and in all previous elections, and we have no reason to apprehend a different result in the approaching campaign. The plundering slaveocracy stand firmly united.—Their voice is as that of one man. To them the slave interest is dearer than Unions or Constitutions, and they are resolved to stand by it at all hazards. They avow themselves ready to be Whigs or Democrats, or neither Whigs nor Democrats, in obedience to the stern behests of slavery. The Legislature of South Carolina has adopted the following resolution, which we take to be a pretty fair exponent of the views of the South on this subject:

"Resolved, that this State is willing to bury all *minor differences of opinion,* and make common cause with the other Southern States in the most energetic possible manner, to maintain our common rights.

"Resolved, That the State of South Carolina will regard the passage of any act by the General Government upon the subject of slavery, in violation of the rights of the South, as annulling the Federal Compact, and upon the passage of such an act, will consider herself at liberty to form a new, separate and distinct Government."

The following are from the Alabama Democratic Convention, and are equally bold and decided, and we hesitate not to say, that the spirit which framed these resolutions will decide the question as to who shall be the candidate in the approaching election:

"Resolved, That this Convention pledges itself to the country, and its members pledge themselves to each other, *under no political necessity whatever,* to support for the office of President and Vice President of the United States, any person *who shall not openly and avowedly be opposed to either of the forms of excluding slavery from the territory of the United States,* mentioned in the resolutions, as being alike in violation of the Constitution, and of the just and equal rights of the citizens of the slaveholding States.

"Resolved, That these resolutions be considered as instructions to our Delegates to the Baltimore Convention, to guide them in their votes in that body; and that they vote for no man for President or Vice President, *who will not unequivocally avow themselves to be opposed to either of the forms of restricting slavery which are described in these resolutions."*

In perfect consistency with the foregoing resolutions, Congress has, within the last few days, voted down the only principle upon which the North has made the slightest show of independence. The only foundation of the North is gone, and while the South stands firm, bold and united, in favor of the complete preservation and extension of slavery, and the permanent supremacy of the slave power, the North lies disjointed, scattered, and confused, with no great and commanding interest or principle to maintain or defend.—They stand like so many Russian soldiers, respectfully awaiting the command of their superiors. A threat of dissolving the Union makes them shiver in their shoes with terror. The bleeding wounds of outraged freedom plead, but plead in vain. Liberty, insulted liberty, the most precious boon, for which the fathers poured out their warm blood on the icy earth, pleads for assistance, but has no power to move them to manliness, and is coldly, disdainfully and sacrilegiously called by them an abstraction. They are your practical men, and prove their right to the name by adroitly allowing every favorable opportunity for making an issue with, and aiming a blow at, the slave power, to pass unimproved. The Wilmot Proviso was an issue, and one of much consequence; and we have no doubt that many at the North supposed that now would come a noble struggle on the part of Northern freemen against Southern slaveholders; nor can we doubt that many, in both the Whig and the Democratic party, meant to stand by the principles of that Proviso at all hazards; but they little understood the base metal of which they were made.—Large numbers, in both the Whig and Democratic party, at the very first word of their Southern masters, meanly deserted their principles, the Whigs dropping entirely the offensive word "No more *slave* territory," and adopting the soulless one of "No more territory;" and the Democrats, repudiating the idea of making the Wilmot Proviso a test in the coming Presidential contest, thus yielding up to their masters everything which they have ever demanded. What respect can the South have for such servile dough-faces?—They have but to shake the rod, and they are down upon their knees at once, suing for pardon. We hate, with a perfect hatred, the supercilious arrogance of Southern slaveholders; but we cherish a most burning contempt for their miserable allies at the North. We feel disgust, mingled with deeper hate, for the mean subserviency of the North.

We are glad to believe that there are yet a few in each political party who would be pleased to have the coming contest waged on the principle of the Wilmot Proviso, but they are the youthful, and not the influential of the parties. They are the weak against the strong. Could John Van Buren rally a few as noble as himself, a stand might possibly be made by at least New York and New England for freedom. He, however, is unsupported, and we wait to see him crushed, though we will ever yet hope for the triumph of his movement.

The North Star, March 17, 1848

PEACE! PEACE! PEACE!

The shout is on every lip, and emblazoned on every paper. The joyful news is told in every quarter with enthusiastic delight. We are such an exception to the great mass of our fellow-countrymen, in respect to everything else, and have been so accustomed to hear them rejoice over the most barbarous outrages committed upon an unoffending people, that we find it difficult to unite with them in their general exultation at this time; and for this reason, we believe that by *peace* they mean *plunder*. In our judgment, those who have all along been loudly in favor of a vigorous prosecution of the war, and heralding its bloody triumph with apparent rapture, and glorifying the atrocious deeds of barbarous heroism on the part of wicked men engaged in it, have no sincere love of peace, and are not now rejoicing over *peace,* but *plunder.* They have succeeded in robbing Mexico of her territory, and are rejoicing over their success under the hypocritical pretence of a regard for peace. Had they not succeeded in robbing Mexico of the most important and most valuable part of her territory, many of those now loudest in their professions of favor for peace, would be loudest and wildest for war—war to the knife. Our soul is sick of such hypocricy. We presume the churches of Rochester will return thanks to God for peace they did nothing to bring about, and boast of it as a triumph of Christianity! That an end is put to the wholesale murder in Mexico, is truly just cause for rejoicing; but we are not the people to rejoice, we ought rather blush and hang our heads for shame, and in the spirit of profound humility, crave pardon for our crimes at the hands of a God whose mercy endureth forever.

The North Star, March 17, 1848

EDITORIAL CORRESPONDENCE

March 29th and 30th.—In Bath, the capital of Steuben County, New York. It is a growing town, situated on the Conhocton, a quick-moving stream, uniting with the Tioga a short distance above its confluence with the Susquehanna. The scenery surrounding Bath, like that of many other parts of this country, is picturesque and beautiful. Lofty hills surround it on all sides, and rival in beauty the far-famed Dunkeld.

The steep hill-sides are richly covered from base to top with tall and finely proportioned firs, towering up one above another, at times wholly concealing the cragged rocks, out of the midst of which they rise. It is worth a journey to Bath to enjoy the scenery. Much more can be said of the natural beauty of the place than of the actual goodness of the people. It so happens that Bath was settled, to a considerable extent, by slaveholders. It is easy to see here the fruits of slavery: the old roots of bitterness are still visible. There is here the same supercilious air to be seen on the part of whites towards colored persons, and the same display of degrading servility on the part of a portion of the latter, which we have been accustomed to see in slave States. Many of the colored people here are the children of persons formerly held as slaves in this town, and some of the elder men and women have themselves been slaves, and of course wear the marks of slavery in their tempers and dispositions. We happen here at a time when our presence is much needed, and when we can be of some service to our oppressed brethren and sisters of this place, by asserting and defending their rights.

The town has just built a large and commodious brick school-house. They have done this by imposing a special tax on all taxable property, making no distinction on account of the color of the persons owning it; and now that the school-house is completed, a petition has been put in circulation, and has been numerously signed by the white inhabitants, designed to exclude colored children from the school. We are here while this proposition is before the people, and are doing our best to defeat it. The monstrous injustice and ineffable meanness of the measure is so palpable, that one would think the community which would adopt it as destitute of shame as they are of a moral sense. They tax the property of the black man equally with that of the white man, under the pretense of building a school-house for the common benefit of all, and when it is finished, the whites combine to exclude the black man's children from all participation in the benefits which the school-house was intended to confer. A more fraudulent and disgraceful transaction could not well be enacted. It is, however, due to truth, as well as the credit of Bath, to say that some of its most wealthy and most distinguished citizens are utterly opposed to this most flagitious measure, and that there is strong reason to believe that it will be defeated. It is also highly creditable to the intelligence of the colored people themselves that they stand unanimously opposed to this measure. Unlike certain advocates for exclusive organizations amongst the colored people, they see that such separation must be injurious to all, both white and black. Let them act on this principle in church and State, and American prejudice will be of short duration. The parties here wishing to exclude the colored children from the district school, are not ignorant of their cruelty and injustice, and, as usual, they throw a veil over their motives, by saying that they are willing to contribute liberally for a colored school, which shall be exclusively for colored children. This miserable show of generosity, we are glad to say, does not deceive any part of the colored people here. All see in it the spirit of colonization, a sham, a mere snare to entrap and keep colored people in their present degraded condition. They cannot, as they ought not, trust and confide in the promises and pretensions of men who can promise so fairly and act so unjustly. They have taken the black man's money to build an elegant school house, in the most eligible part of the town, professedly for the common good of all, and after it is completed, all nicely finished, it is said, this house is too nice for "n——s," and we will build them one much better suited to their condition. Infernal as this treatment is, it is but a counterpart of that which everywhere pursues the worried footsteps of our injured fellow-countrymen. We are wronged and plundered in all directions; injustice, cruelty and fraud seem to be our doom. Oh, when shall this spirit cease to pursue and dog our footsteps! When will the American people learn to treat us with common justice! Slaves to *individuals* at the South, we are but little better than slaves to *community* at the North. The community sport with our rights with as much impunity, as if we formed no part of the family of man. They tax us, deny us the right of suffrage, take our money to build schoolhouses, and spurn our children from their doors. Prejudice pursues us in every lane of life. Even our courts of law are against us. We are tried by our enemies. The judge, jury and counsellors are all under the influence of a bitter prejudice against us. In such a state, justice is but a name.

March 31st.—Still in Bath. We have held four meetings, and another is called for tomorrow evening; and considering the urgent invitations and the general interest excited, especially with reference to excluding colored children from the new district school-house, Remond, Hathaway and ourself have concluded to stay and hold another meeting. It will be an important point gained if we secure this right. Let colored children be educated and grow up side by side with white children, come up friends from unsophisticated and generous childhood together, and it will require a powerful agent to convert them into enemies, and lead them to prey upon each other's rights and liberties. Now is the time for effort. The town is in considerable commotion. The enemies of justice, liberty and equality are active, and using their utmost endeavors to blast and destroy the force of our arguments and appeals in behalf of equal rights. The old cry of amalgamation is raised here with as much fierceness as it was ten years ago in New England. The people are just about ten years behind the times on this subject.

When about leaving the Court House after the meeting this evening, we were hailed by a pro-slavery Methodist Episcopal priest by the name of Aldin, who said that the church had no more right to abolish slavery than it had to abolish whiggery, and that the Methodist Conference did right in assuming the ground that they had no right, wish, or intention to abolish slavery, it being an institution upheld by the laws of the country. We asked him why he did not speak out his views in the public congregation when called upon to do so. He answered, "Because I would not put myself on a level with a *n——r,*" upon which we walked off, feeling that the self-righteous ruffian was not a suitable person for us to expend our breath upon. We shall, however, give the public the benefit of his views, with suitable comments, to-morrow evening. He could speak and insult us in private, but could not condescend to utter a word in regard to us in public, where his sophistry could be exposed before all.

F. D.

The North Star, April 7, 1848

FRANCE

All eyes continue fixed upon France and her infant republic, the offspring of her recent revolution.[5] The voluminous news from that quarter do not satisfy, so much as strengthen curiosity. The more we know, the more we want to know, and the more need we have of knowing. Thanks to steam navigation and electric wires, we may almost hear the words uttered, and see the deeds done, as they transpire. A revolution now cannot be confined to the place or the people where it may commence, but flashes with lightning speed from heart to heart, from land to land, till it has traversed the globe, compelling all the members of our common brotherhood at once, to pass judgment upon its merits. The revolution of France, like a bolt of living thunder, has aroused the world from its stupor. All are up and inspecting the scene. Various are the views, and mingled are the emotions which it has created. The despots of Europe—the Tories of England, and the slaveholders of America, are astonished, confused, and terrified; while the humble poor, the toil-worn laborer, the oppressed and plundered, the world around, have heard with exultation the glorious peal, and are looking forward with ardent hopes to the glorious results of which this event is but the commencement.

Simultaneously with the fall and crash of royalty in France, a terrible noise rung out from the galling chains of fettered millions in our own land, a ray of hope penetrated the lowest confines of American slave prisons, imparting firmness of faith to the whip-scarred slave, and fear and trembling to the guilty slaveholder. The pent-up fires of freedom still live, and though bound down by the strata of tyranny for ages, the sovereign element will burst all fetters. *Thank God for the event!* Slavery cannot always reign.

We occasionally see in our exchanges surprise and mortification expressed that few or no demonstrations of sympathy with France, are held in the various parts of our widely extended country. We would most respectfully ask, What sympathy have freemen with tyrants? How can the latter congratulate the former? What concord has hypocritical piety with infidel honesty? How can a nation with a manstealer in the presidential chair, and manstealers filling every other department of the government—a nation too corrupt and too mean to be fairly represented by any other than a thief and a robber, sympathise with a government which has just come into existence with the glorious motto, "Liberty—Equality—Fraternity"? and has proved its sincerity by taking steps for the immediate emancipation of all its slaves, and guaranteeing the right of suffrage to all men, independent of all complexional distinction. It would be unbecoming us to extend, and France to accept our sympathy. A nation of white men addressing "colored men"—"*negroes,*" as "Citizens, friends, and brothers," ought not to expect much, and do not expect much sympathy from a nation which proscribes, insults, plunders and enslaves the black man, in its very capitol. Should we venture into Washington to-morrow, a felon's doom awaits us for no earthly crime that we have committed, than that we are the child of a white man by a colored mother. While we write this, a paper has been handed us containing a detailed account of the arrest and imprisonment in Washington of seventy-seven slaves, for an attempt to escape from the land of slavery to a land of liberty; and for helping these men to escape, three white American citizens are confined in an American dungeon.[8] In view of these facts, and the overwhelming one, that within fifteen States of this boasted republic, nearly one-half of the people are held in the most grievous and revolting bondage, and that the whole Union is solemnly sworn to keep the slave in his chains, it would be more consistent with our character for cruelty, (if not for cowardice,) to invade France with an army, with the avowed purpose of reinstating Louis Philippe, and restoring the emancipated slaves to their tyrant masters; than to sympathise with France in her struggles for a republic.

There are only two classes in this country who are in a position sincerely to sympathise with France in her present glorious struggle in behalf of liberty, and those are the Negroes and Abolitionists. We have cause to rejoice and be glad; and can do so with some show of sincerity. All others stand rebuked by her noble example. The American people do not—cannot sympathise with any great movement in behalf of freedom, while fifteen States of the Union are cursed with slavery. It is an incubus upon their spirits—a standing rebuke, a constant reproach. To be sure, when the votes of Irishmen are wanted, a slight demonstration can be made in behalf of repeal; and when the Roman Catholic influence is needed, sympathy meetings can be held for Pope Pius IX.; but all intelligent men know, that this is mere sham—the most miserable gammon. The fact is, while Europe is becoming republican, we are becoming despotic; while France is contending for freedom, we are extending slavery; while the former are struggling to free the press, we are striving, by mobs and penal enactments, to fetter it. While France is expelling tyrants, we are glorifying them, and seeking to elevate them to the highest offices. There is no sympathy that can be called national, for France, and we ought to be ashamed to affect it. We believe that Louis Philippe would be welcomed in Washington with far more demonstrations of regard than Lamartine. We love tyrants and hate freemen.

The North Star, April 28, 1848

TO JULIA GRIFFITHS

Rochester, 28th April 1848

My very Dear Friend:

Pardon my seeming neglect in not replying to your last welcome letters. Absence from home on a long antislavery tour, from which I have but just returned has prevented an earlier letter. Do accept my warmest thanks for the unfaltering interest which you continue to take in my humble welfare. The London Times comes quite regularly, always bearing the evidence of your kind and sisterly hand. The "Illustrated News" containing a portraiture of the revolution in France came safely to hand and were most gratefully received.

My dear Julia, I have a repugnance to make a Poor face and always desire to look at the bright side of the future, and seldom can bring myself to say that I have undertaken more than I have the ability to perform. It therefore greatly pains me to tell you that my present prospects of success in my honest effort at improving my free colored Brethren by publishing a newspaper, is far from encouraging. I fear I have miscalculated in regard to the amount of support which would be extended to my enterprise. There is however the consolation in my present embarrassment, the first year is in every similar case, not only attended with more expense from various causes, but it is more difficult to obtain subscribers during that time than after the paper is established. Things have not turned out at all as I expected. The colored people themselves owing to the long night of ignorance which has overshadowed and subdued their spirit. Then again my paper is too free from party dictation to receive much support from any existing antislavery party. They have all their own party organs to support and feel only a negative interest in mine. I am also somewhat behind on account of the small assistance in getting subscribers rendered me by my Dear Friend Delany. When I united with him the understanding was that I should remain in Rochester and edit the paper, while he travelled and obtained subscribers. This from various causes, he has been able to do to a very limited extent. The consequence is I have been compelled to edit, lecture, and obtain subscribers, and furnish the money with which to proceed thus far. I will however hope on—labor on—and deserve success—though I may meet with failure. I have expended more than the sum sent me from England and shall require sixty dollars a week for six months to come in order to keep my paper afloat. The average increase of subscribers amount to twenty-five dollars a week. I feel sure if I can keep the paper in existence one year I can sustain it permanently. "The North Star" must be sustained. It has already accomplished something. It has taken a respectable stand amongst at least American newspapers, and in a measure demonstrated the slaves' capacity for higher achievements. It has also impressed the colored people themselves that they are destined [for] higher attainments even in this country than [they] now enjoy. This is very little to have accomplished but [is] something.

Frederick Douglass

Frederick Douglass MSS., Douglass Memorial Home, Anacostia, D.C.

WHAT OF THE NIGHT?

A crisis in the Anti-Slavery movement of this country, is evidently at hand. The moral and religious, no less than the political firmaments, North and South, at home and abroad, are studded with brilliant and most significant indications, pointing directly to a settlement of this all-commanding subject. Slavery is doomed to destruction; and of this slaveholders are rapidly becoming aware. Opposed or encouraged, the grand movement for its overthrow has, under God, attained a point of progress when its devoted advocates may press its claims in the full assurance that success will soon crown their righteous endeavors. We have labored long and hard. The prospect has at times been gloomy, if not hopeless. At present, we feel hopeful. In our humble judgment, there is no power within reach of the slaveholder, with all their arts, cunning and depravity, which can uphold a system at once so dark, foul and bloody as that of American slavery. The power which they have derived from the unconstitutional and perfidious annexation of Texas to the United States; the vast territories which they may acquire by our atrocious war with distracted and enfeebled Mexico; the sacrilegious support which they receive from a corrupt church and degenerate priesthood; the character and position they secure by a slaveholding President, are all transient, temporary and unavailing. They are powerful, but must give way to a mightier power.—Like huge trees in the bed of a mighty river, they only await the rising tide which, without effort, shall bear them away to the vortex of destruction. The Spirit of Liberty is sweeping in majesty over the whole

European continent, encountering and shattering dynastis, overcoming and subverting monarchies, causing thrones to crumble, courts to dissolve, and royalty and despotism to vanish like shadows before the morning sun. This spirit cannot be bound by geographical boundaries or national restrictions. It hath neither flesh nor bones; there is no way to chain it; swords and guns, armies and ramparts, are as impotent to stay it as they would be if directed against the Asiatic cholera. We cannot but be affected. These stupendous overturnings throughout the world, proclaim in the ear of American slaveholders, with all the terrible energy of an earthquake, the downfall of slavery. They have heard the royal sound—witness their reluctance on the floor of Congress to pass resolutions congratulating the French on the downfall of royalty and the triumph of republicanism; witness the course of that prince of tyrants, John C. Calhoun; witness the mean and heartless response given by the misnamed Democrats of the country. These friends of the hell-born system of slavery are painfully aware that the cause of liberty and equality are one the world over; and that its triumph in any portion of the globe foreshadows and hastens the downfall of tyranny throughout the world.

Not among the least important and significant signs of the times, are the recent debates and occurrences in Washington. A combination of events has within a few days transpired there, which may well be regarded as a Providential interference in behalf of the enslaved and plundered of our land. The bold attempt of more than seventy slaves to escape their chains—their unfortunate and mortifying recapture—the wild clamor for the blood of the men who are willing to aid them in their escape—the mobocratic demonstrations against the Era office—the violent and assassin speeches made in both branches of Congress—their utter failure to intimidate the noble-hearted Giddings, Palfrey, and Hale—the sovereign and increasing contempt with which these gentlemen treat the bullying speeches of these bowie-knife legislators, are not only signs, but facts, fixing attention on slavery, and demonstrating a progress in public opinion, directly pointing to the speedy overthrow of slavery, or a dissolution of our unhallowed Union. Should the latter come, the former must come; slavery is doomed in either case. God speed the day! Never could there have been a better place, or more fitting opportunity for such facts, than at the place and time which they transpired. Slaves escaping from the Capital of the "model Republic"! What an idea!—running *from* the Temple of Liberty to be free! Then, too, our slaveholding Belshazzars were in the midst of feasting and rejoicing over the downfall of Louis Philippe, and the establishment of a republic in France! They were all pleasure and joyous delight; "but pleasures are like poppies spread." Their joy was soon turned into moaning, their laughter into fury.

The hand-writing on the wall to these joyous congratulationists, was the fact, that more than seventy thousand dollars' worth of their human cattle had made a peaceful attempt to gain their liberty by flight. At once these thoughts of glorious liberty abroad gave way to the more urgent demands of slavery at home. These "worthless" Negroes are valuable. *These miserable creatures,* which we would gladly get rid of, must be brought back. And lo and behold! these very men who had been rejoicing over French liberty, are now armed kidnappers, and even on the Sabbath day have gone forth on the delectable business of man-hunting. Well, they have succeeded in overtaking and throttling their victims; they have brought them back before the musket's mouth, and doubtless most of them have been scourged for their temerity, and sold into Louisiana and Texas, where they will be worked to death in seven years; but as sure as there is a God, this will not be the last of it. Slavery in the District of Columbia will receive a shock from this simple event, which no earthly power can prevent or cure. The broad eye of the nation will be opened upon slavery in the District as it has never before; the North and West will feel keenly the damning disgrace of their Capital being a slave mart, and a deeper hatred of slavery will be engendered in the popular mind throughout the Union.

The North Star, May 5, 1848

NORTHERN WHIGS AND DEMOCRATS

At the imminent peril of incurring the displeasure and reproaches of our white fellow-countrymen, and being denounced as *"saucy"* and *"impudent,"* we shall now venture a few remarks on these two contending parties. We are fully aware that it is thought by many very improper for a "Negro" to entertain any opinion derogatory to the conduct or character of white men; and know full well that we have our being in what is called a "pure white Republic"—a Republic in which a white skin is considered above the criticism or scrutiny of a black man. To such persons, we doubt not that most of all we have to say on this or other subjects, has the appearance of downright bad manners. For such unfortunates, we are not entirely without compassion. They are the victims of a deplorable habit, which has to them become confounded with their very natures. Accustomed as they are to esteem the colored man as something less than a man, it is not surprising that when he, entirely forgetful of their estimate of his character, and only mindful of his own humanity, duty and dignity as a child of a common Creator, assumes the port and bearing of a man, that they should regard him as the impersonation of insolence. We are frequently reminded by such persons, that we should remember our station in life, our identity with a degraded and dependent people, and that we should be conciliatory and humble; all of which is very good, but comes from the wrong preacher. Those who preach humility to the black man, should not feed and countenance in the white men what they so readily condemn in us.

By such persons, (and they are numerous,) our presence and deportment in this city must be regarded as a painful and grievous infliction, a trying evil, only to be borne with in consideration that a greater evil might spring up in our stead. Now, we confess it is not the most agreeable thing in the world to live where one is looked upon as having nothing in common with the community by whom he may be surrounded; and such, though not our fault, is nevertheless our situation in this community. We are not, however, without consolation. The high satisfaction which results from a sense of being in the right, outweighs by far the temporary complacency which may result from being with the multitude, and we rejoice at being able to stand alone as an outcast from a pro-slavery community.

In speaking on this subject we are not merely fulfilling a duty which we owe to the slave, and to our colored fellow-countrymen, but one which we owe to our common country and our God. At such a time as the present, when the great body of the press have madly become the floodgates of political profligacy, it is the duty of even the humblest to summon from the depths of his nature the most exalted sentiments of truth and justice, and to send them forth to battle, that peradventure he may be to some extent instrumental in staying the putrid flood let loose upon the land. Neither our dark complexion nor isolated condition releases us from the high duty of rebuking corruption wherever, and whenever, and with whomsoever it may show itself. We may not be silent to gratify either the pride or the prejudice of our white fellow countrymen. We desire our white contemporaries to remember this just sentiment, when instead of answering our statements respecting them, they seek to evade their force by denouncing us "impudent," "presumptive," and out of our place. But enough.

Northern Whigs and Democrats, we may be perhaps charged with having committed a misnomer in applying these terms to any class of persons in this country; and we confess that a very ingenious case could be made out against us; for, properly speaking, there is no such thing amongst us, as a Northern Whig or Democrat. They both *belong* to the South, and are the property of the slave interest. In proof of this, as respects the Democrats, very little need be said; they have gloried in the deep shame of being the natural allies of the South. Their leaders have gone beyond all others in bowing the knee and prostrating themselves before the slave power. At the suggestion of their Southern masters, they have spurned from them, as unworthy of consideration, all self-respect and the dearest rights and interests of the working classes of the North. Have the slaveholders desired to gag to silence the voice of free speech within the halls of Congress, Northern Democracy supplied the vile tool to its accomplishment. Have they demanded new territory, over which to extend the heaven-daring curse of human bondage, Northern Democrats have supplied it. Have they demanded new and stronger safe-guards for their property in human flesh, Northern Democrats have supplied those safe-guards.

The black laws of Ohio, Indiana, Illinois, are standing proofs of the subserviency of Northern Democrats to the slave power, for these laws have been enacted at the special request of the slaveholders of Kentucky and Tennessee. The Democrats have not bowed the knee to the slave power merely in respect to the enactment of laws to uphold slavery, but have shamelessly deserted and doomed to political destruction some of the brightest ornaments that ever adorned their party.—When Thomas Morris, the noble Democratic Senator of Ohio, dared to stand up for freedom in the United States Senate, and confront the blasphemous assertion of Henry Clay, "that what the law makes property, is property," he was at once marked out for political decapitation. His murderers were of his own household; and though they found no fault in him, he was, like Innocence of old, betrayed and murdered. For manifesting a slight hesitancy about carrying out the mad wishes of Southern slaveholders in annexing Texas to the Union, Martin Van Buren, the favorite son of the Empire State, was in the same way betrayed, deserted and deposed; and from his own professed friends he received the blow which leveled him in political death—(albeit not beyond resurrection). John P. Hale, a distinguished member of the Democratic party, refused to stain his soul by voting for annexation of Texas, well knowing the measure to be fraught with deplorable and innumerable evils, and was peremptorily and immediately expelled from the party.

From the moment when it became known that Silas Wright was opposed to the extension of slavery, he was hunted and persecuted by the leaders in the Democratic party, till the day of his death. The fact is, no deed of dishonor has been regarded too base or treacherous for Northern Democrats to do at the bidding of slavery. They claim the diabolical merit of having lived a life of consistent devotion to the infernal system of slavery.—To be charged with a dislike of slavery, has been regarded by them as the most serious charge that could be preferred against them, and they have repelled it with all the energy in their power. They would rather be suspected of any crime denounced in the decalogue, than to be guilty of the slightest sympathy with three millions of enslaved and suffering bondmen.

Loyalty to the South seems to be their first duty; and should this require disloyalty to God, but little reluctance to compliance is manifested. If a lie be needed to conceal some infernal design, or to mislead the simple as to the effect of some wicked scheme, Northern Democrats and presses tell it with alacrity.—When the South moved for the annexation of Texas, for the well-known and unconcealed purpose of increasing the profits of the internal slavetrade, strengthening the slave power, and extending the curse of human bondage, with these facts before them, the Northern Democratic presses and platform declared the measure to be one to extend the area of freedom. While waging a fierce and bloody war with Mexico, by our own motion, the Democratic press and politicians persisted in saying that the war was forced upon us by the act of Mexico. There is, it seems to us, no end to the political turpitude of this vile combination, under the specious name of Democracy. Its modern history, at least, is but a series of the basest betrayals of human rights. It has professed a deep and unchangeable regard for the interests of the working man, and as an evidence of its sincerity, it has nominated a man for the Presidency[7] who was the flatterer of Louis Philippe and the calumniator of the working men in France; and who is also at this moment in favor of extending the awful curse of slavery over territory now free, while the inevitable and well-known effect of the measure must be to completely exclude the free laborer from all participation in the benefits of that territory, unless he goes there in the dishonorable and cruel capacity of a slave-driver. Now, the sooner this vile body is changed or destroyed, the better. We are glad to know that the working men at the North begin to understand its true character, and are looking to other and wiser means for protecting their rights.

But we must leave the Democrats, and turn to the Whigs. Their case is, if possible, worse than that of the Democrats. We need not go into their past history; their present position is ample proof of their unprincipled character. It is possible that we do wrong in denominating their party "the Whig party." It ought the rather be called the "Taylor party;" for as Taylor is not, and does not intend to be a Whig, the party who supports him, and whom he represents, cannot be Whig. Nothing could more satisfactorily prove the utter want of principle in that party, than the readiness with which its press and its speakers have whirled into the ranks of the "bloodhound candidate." But a few weeks ago, it was truly refreshing to read the Northern Whig journals. Their columns flamed with the most burning detestation of slavery and slavery extension. A remarkable instance of this, is furnished in our neighbor, the "Democrat." Its moral sense, humanity and religion, were all arrayed against any measure looking immediately or remotely to the extension of slavery. But oh! how changed is its tone now! The glorious uprising on the part of the independents, against the slave power, slave rule, slavery extension, and slave territory, though in perfect harmony with the views, feelings and professed principles of that paper, meets nothing but discouragement from that quarter. The paper that boasted itself freedom's friend, is now freedom's foe. If anything could deepen our sense of the servility, meanness, falsehood and corruption of the Whig party North, it is the cowardly and contemptible manner in which politicians and presses at the North have allowed themselves to be whipped into the support of this same "bloodhound," Gen. Taylor. It would seem that the Whig party is the grave of all independence, self-respect and decency. In the face of all facts, they are at this moment attempting to make out a peace character for a war candidate, a slavery limitationist of a slavery propagandist, a friend of freedom of a vile slaveholder, and an honest man of a notorious robber. There is no language fitly expressive of such villany, or the man that will stoop to it. We confess to some loathing of a sheep-stealing dog; there is something in his gait and carriage which at once proclaims his guilt; but upon such an animal we can look with ineffable complacency, compared with the loathing we feel when looking upon a traitor to freedom. The command to love our enemies can scarcely include such a person; and yet we would not harm him, but would leave him to God and his conscience.

The North Star, July 7, 1848

WHAT ARE THE COLORED PEOPLE DOING FOR THEMSELVES?

The present is a time when every colored man in the land should bring this important question home to his own heart. It is not enough to know that white men and women are nobly devoting themselves to our cause; we should know what is being done among ourselves. That our white friends have done, and are still doing, a great and good work for us, is a fact which ought to excite in us sentiments of the profoundest gratitude; but it must never be forgotten that when they have exerted all their energies, devised every scheme, and done all they can do in asserting our rights, proclaiming our wrongs, and rebuking our foes, their labor is lost—yea, worse than lost, unless we are found in the faithful discharge of our anti-slavery duties. If there be one evil spirit among us, for the casting out of which we pray more earnestly than another, it is that lazy, mean and cowardly spirit, that robs us of all manly self-reliance, and teaches us to depend upon others for the accomplishment of that which we should achieve with our own hands. Our white friends can and are rapidly removing the barriers to our improvement, which themselves have set up; but the main work must be commenced, carried on, and concluded by ourselves. While in no circumstances should we undervalue or fail to appreciate the self-sacrificing efforts of our friends, it should never be lost sight of, that our destiny, for good or for evil, for time and for eternity, is, by an all-wise God, committed to us; and that all the helps or hindrances with which we may meet on earth, can never release us from this high and heaven-imposed responsibility. It is evident that we can be improved and elevated only just so fast and far as we shall improve and elevate ourselves. We must rise or fall, succeed or fail, by our own merits. If we are careless and unconcerned about our own rights and interests, it is not within the power of all the earth combined to raise us from our present degraded condition.

> *Hereditary bondmen, know ye not*
> *Who would be free, themselves must strike the blow?*

We say the present is a time when every colored man should ask himself the question, What am I doing to elevate and improve my condition, and that of my brethren at large? While the oppressed of the old world are making efforts, by holding public meetings, putting forth addresses, passing resolutions, and in various other ways making their wishes known to the world, and the working men of our own country are pressing their cause upon popular attention, it is a shame that we, who are enduring wrongs far more grievous than any other portion of the great family of man, are comparatively idle and indifferent about our welfare. We confess, with the deepest mortification, that out of the five hundred thousand free colored people in this country, not more than two thousand can be supposed to take any special interest in measures for our own elevation; and probably not more than fifteen hundred take, read and pay for an anti-slavery paper. We say this in sorrow, not in anger. It cannot be said that we are too poor to patronize our own press to any greater extent than we now do; for in popular demonstrations of odd-fellowship, free-masonry and the like, we expend annually from ten to twelve thousand dollars. If we put forth a call for a National Convention, for the purpose of considering our wrongs, and asserting our rights, and adopting measures for our mutual elevation and the emancipation of our enslaved fellow-countrymen, we shall bring together about *fifty;* but if we call a grand celebration of odd-fellowship, or free-masonry, we shall assemble, as was the case a few days ago in New York, from *four to five thousand*—the expense of which alone would be from seventeen to twenty thousand dollars, a sum sufficient to maintain four or five efficient presses, devoted to our elevation and improvement. We should not say this of odd-fellowship and free-masonry, but that it is swallowing up the best energies of many of our best men, contenting them with the glittering follies of artificial display, and indisposing them to seek for solid and important realities. The enemies of our people see this tendency in us, and encourage it. The same persons who would puff such demonstrations in the newspapers, would mob us if we met to adopt measures for obtaining our just rights. They see our weak points, and avail themselves of them to crush us. We are imitating the inferior qualities and examples of white men, and neglecting superior ones. We do not pretend that all the members of odd-fellow societies and masonic lodges are indifferent to their rights and the means of obtaining them; for we know the fact to be otherwise. Some of the best and brightest among us are numbered with those societies; and it is on this account that we make these remarks. We desire to see these noble men expending their time, talents and strength for higher and nobler objects than any that can be attained by the weak and glittering follies of odd-fellowship and freemasonry.

We speak plainly on this point, for we feel deeply. We have dedicated ourself, heart and soul, without reserve, to the elevation and improvement of our race, and have resolved to sink or swim with them. Our inmost soul is fired with a sense of the various forms of injustice to which we are daily subjected, and we must and will speak out against anything, within ourselves or our guilty oppressors, which may tend to prolong this reign of injustice. To be faithful to our oppressors, we must be faithful to ourselves; and shame on any colored man who would have us do otherwise. For this very purpose the *North Star* was established—that it might be as faithful to ourselves as to our oppressors. In this respect, we intend that it shall be different from most of its predecessors, and if it cannot be sustained in its high position, its death will be welcomed by us. But to return.

It is a doctrine held by many good men, in Europe as well as in America, that every oppressed people will gain their rights just as soon as they prove themselves worthy of them; and although we may justly object to the extent to which this doctrine is carried, especially in reference to ourselves as a people, it must still be evident to all that there is a great truth in it.

One of the first things necessary to prove the colored man worthy of equal freedom, is an earnest and persevering effort on his part to gain it. We deserve no earthly or heavenly blessing, for which we are unwilling to labor. For our part, we despise a freedom and equality obtained for us by others, and for which we have been unwilling to labor. A man who will not labor to gain his rights, is a man who would not, if he had them, prize and defend them. What is the use of standing a man on his feet, if, when we let him go, his head is again brought to the pavement? Look out of ourselves as we will—beg and pray to our white friends for assistance as much as we will—and that assistance may come, and come at the needed time; but unless we, the colored people of America, shall set about the work of our own regeneration and improvement, we are doomed to drag on in our present miserable and degraded condition for ages. Would that we could speak to every colored man, woman and child in the land, and, with the help of Heaven, we would thunder into their ears their duties and responsibilities, until a spirit should be roused among them, never to be lulled till the last chain is broken.—But here we are mortified to think that we are now speaking to tens where we ought to speak to thousands. Unfortunately, those who have the ear of our people on Sundays, have little sympathy with the anti-slavery cause, or the cause of progress in any of its phases. They are too frequently disposed to follow the beaten paths of their fathers.—The most they aim at, is to get to heaven when they die. They reason thus: Our fathers got along pretty well through the world without learning and without meddling with abolitionism, and we can do the same.—We have in our minds three pulpits among the colored people in the North, which have the power to produce a revolution in the condition of the colored people in this country in three years.

First among these, we may mention the great Bethel Church in Philadelphia. That church is the largest colored church in this Union, and from two to three thousand persons worship there every Sabbath. It has its branches in nearly all parts of the North and West, and a few in the South. It is surrounded by numerous little congregations in Philadelphia. Its ministers and bishops travel in all directions, and vast numbers of colored people belong to its branches all over the country. The Bethel pulpit in Philadelphia may be said to give tone to the entire denomination—"as goes large Bethel, so go the small Bethels throughout the Union." Here is concentrated the talent of the church, and here is the central and ruling power.—Now, if that pulpit would but speak the right word—the word for progress—the word for mental culture—encourage reading, and would occasionally take up contributions to aid those who are laboring for their elevation, as the white churches do to aid the colonization society to send us out of the country—there is no telling the good that would result from such labors. An entire change might soon take place in that denomination; loftier views of truth and duty would be presented; a nobler destiny would be opened up to them, and a deeper happiness would at once be enjoyed through all the ramifications of that church.

Similarly situated is the "Zion Church" in New York. That church exerts a controlling influence over the next largest colored denomination in this country. It, too, is a unit—has its branches in all directions in the North rather than in the South. Its ministers are zealous men, and some of them powerful preachers. There is no estimating the good these men might do, if they would only encourage their congregations to take an interest in the subject of reform.

The next church in importance, is St. Phillip's, in New York. This church is more important on account of the talent and respectability which it comprises, than for its numbers. Now, could the influence of these churches be enlisted in exciting our people to a constant and persevering effort at self-elevation, a joyful change would soon come over us.

What we, the colored people, want, is *character,* and this nobody can give us. It is a thing we must get for ourselves. We must labor for it. It is gained by toil—hard toil. Neither the sympathy nor the generosity of our friends can give it to us. It is attainable—yes, thank God, it is attainable. "There is gold in the earth, but we must dig it"—so with character. It is attainable; but we must attain it, and attain it each for himself. I cannot for you, and you cannot for me.—What matters it to the mass of colored people of this country that they are able to point to their Peningtons, Garnets, Remonds, Wards, Purvises, Smiths, Whippers, Sandersons, and a respectable list of other men of character, which we might name, while our general ignorance makes these men exceptions to our race? Their talents can do little to give us character in the eyes of the world. We must get character for ourselves, as a people. A change in our political condition would do very little for us without this. Character is the important thing, and without it we must continue to be marked for degradation and stamped with the brand of inferiority. With character, we shall be powerful. Nothing can harm us long when we get character.—There are certain great elements of character in us which may be hated, but never despised. Industry, sobriety, honesty, combined with intelligence and a due self-respect, find them where you will, among black or white, must be *looked up to*—can never be *looked down upon.* In their presence, prejudice is abashed, confused and mortified. Encountering this solid mass of living character, our vile oppressors are ground to atoms. In its presence, the sneers of a caricaturing press, the taunts of natural inferiority, the mischievous assertions of Clay, and fine-spun sophisms of Calhoun, are innoxious, powerless and unavailing. In answer to these men and the sneers of the multitude, there is nothing in the wide world half so effective as the presentation of a character precisely the opposite of all their representations. We have it in our power to convert the weapons intended for our injury into positive blessings. That we may sustain temporary injury from gross and general misrepresentation, is most true; but the injury is but temporary, and must disappear at the approach of light, like mist from the vale. The offensive traits of character imputed to us, can only be injurious while they are true of us. For a man to say that sweet is bitter—that right is wrong—that light is darkness—is not to injure the truth, but to stamp himself a liar; and the like is true when they impute to us that of which we are not guilty. We have the power of making our enemies slanderers, and this we must do by showing ourselves worthy and respectable men.

We are not insensible to the various obstacles that throng the colored man's pathway to respectability. Embarrassments and perplexities, unknown to other men, are common to us. Though born on American soil, we have fewer privileges than aliens. The school-house, the work-shop, counting-house, attorney's office, and various professions, are opened to them, but closed to us. This, and much more, is true. A general and withering prejudice—a malignant and active hate, pursues us even in the best parts of this country. But a few days ago, one of our best and most talented men—and he a *lame man,* having lost an important limb—was furiously hurled from a car on the Niagara & Buffalo Railroad, by a band of white ruffians, who claim impunity for their atrocious outrage on the plea that New York law does not protect the rights of colored against a company of white men, and the sequel has proved them right; for the case, it appears, was brought before the grand jury, but that jury found no bill. We cannot at this time dwell on this aspect of the subject.

The fact that we are limited and circumscribed, ought rather to incite us to a more vigorous and persevering use of the elevating means within our reach, than to dishearten us. The means of education, though not so free and open to us as to white persons, are nevertheless at our command to such an extent as to make education possible; and these, thank God, are increasing. Let us educate our children, even though it should us subject to a coarser and scantier diet, and disrobe us of our few fine garments. "For the want of knowledge we are killed all the day." Get wisdom—get understanding, is a peculiarly valuable exhortation to us, and the compliance with it is our only hope in this land.—It is idle, a hollow mockery, for us to pray to God to break the oppressor's power, while we neglect the means of knowledge which will give us the ability to break this power.—God will help us when we help ourselves. Our oppressors have divested us of many valuable blessings and facilities for improvement and elevation; but, thank heaven, they have not yet been able to take from us the privilege of being honest, industrious, sober and intelligent. We may read and understand—we may speak and write—we may expose our wrongs—we may appeal to the sense of justice yet alive in the public mind, and by an honest, upright life, we may at last wring from a reluctant public the all-important confession, that we are men, worthy men, good citizens, good Christians, and ought to be treated as such.

The North Star, July 14, 1848

THE RIGHTS OF WOMEN

One of the most interesting events of the past week, was the holding of what is technically styled a Woman's Rights Convention at Seneca Falls.[8] The speaking, addresses, and resolutions of this extraordinary meeting was almost wholly conducted by women; and although they evidently felt themselves in a novel position, it is but simple justice to say that their whole proceedings were characterized by marked ability and dignity. No one present, we think, however much he might be disposed to differ from the views advanced by the leading speakers on that occasion, will fail to give them credit for brilliant talents and excellent dispositions. In this meeting, as in other deliberative assemblies, there were frequent differences of opinion and animated discussion; but in no case was there the slightest absence of good feeling and decorum. Several interesting documents setting forth the rights as well as the grievances of women were read. Among these was a Declaration of Sentiments, to be regarded as the basis of a grand movement for attaining the civil, social, political, and religious rights of women. We should not do justice to our own convictions, or to the excellent persons connected with this infant movement, if we did not in this connection offer a few remarks on the general subject which the Convention met to consider and the objects they seek to attain. In doing so, we are not insensible that the bare mention of this truly important subject in any other than terms of contemptuous ridicule and scornful disfavor, is likely to excite against us the fury of bigotry and the folly of prejudice. A discussion of the rights of animals would be regarded with far more complacency by many of what are called the *wise* and the *good* of our land, than would a discussion of the rights of women. It is, in their estimation, to be guilty of evil thoughts, to think that woman is entitled to equal rights with man. Many who have at last made the discovery that the Negroes have some rights as well as other members of the human family, have yet to be convinced that women are entitled to any. Eight years ago a number of persons of this description actually abandoned the anti-slavery cause, lest by giving their influence in that direction they might possibly be giving countenance to the dangerous heresy that woman, in respect to rights, stands on an equal footing with man. In the judgment of such persons the American slave system, with all its concomitant horrors, is less to be deplored than this *wicked* idea. It is perhaps needless to say, that we cherish little sympathy for such sentiments or respect for such prejudices. Standing as we do upon the watch-tower of human freedom, we cannot be deterred from an expression of our approbation of any movement, however humble, to improve and elevate the character of any members of the human family. While it is impossible for us to go into this subject at length, and dispose of the various objections which are often urged against such a doctrine as that of female equality, we are free to say that in respect to political rights, we hold woman to be justly entitled to all we claim for man. We go farther, and express our conviction that all political rights which it is expedient for man to exercise, it is equally so for woman. All that distinguishes man as an intelligent and accountable being, is equally true of woman, and if that government only is just which governs by the free consent of the governed, there can be no reason in the world for denying to woman the exercise of the elective franchise, or a hand in making and administering the laws of the land. Our doctrine is that "right is of no sex." We therefore bid the women engaged in this movement our humble Godspeed.

The North Star, July 28, 1848

THE REVOLUTION OF 1848, speech at West India Emancipation celebration, Rochester, New York, August 1, 1848

Mr. President and Friends:

We have met to commemorate no deed of sectional pride, or partial patriotism; to erect no monument to naval or military heroism; to applaud the character or commend the courage of no blood-stained warrior; to gloat over no fallen or vanquished foe; to revive no ancient or obsolete antipathy; to quicken and perpetuate the memory of no fierce and bloody struggle; to take from the ashes of oblivion no slumbering embers of fiery discord.

We attract your attention to no horrid strife; to no scenes of blood and carnage, where foul and unnatural murder carried its true designation, because regimentally attired. We brighten not the memories of brave men slain in the hostile array and the deadly encounter. The celebration of such men, and such deeds, may safely be left to others. We [can] thank Heaven, that [to us] is committed a more grateful and congenial task.

The day we have met to commemorate, is marked by no deeds of violence, associated with no scenes of slaughter, and excites no malignant feelings. Peace, joy and liberty shed a halo of unfading and untarnished glory around this annual festival. On this occasion, no lonely widow is reminded of a slaughtered husband; no helpless orphans are reminded of slaughtered fathers; no aged parents are reminded of slaughtered sons; no lovely sisters meet here to mourn over the memory of slaughtered brothers. Our gladness revives no sorrow; our joyous acclamation awakens no responsive mourning. The day, the deed, the event, which we have met to celebrate, is the Tenth Anniversary of West India Emancipation—a day, a deed, an event, all glorious in the annals of Philanthropy, and as pure as the stars of heaven! On this day, ten years ago, eight hundred thousand slaves became freemen. To congratulate our disenthralled brethren of the West Indies on their peaceful emancipation; to express our unfeigned gratitude to Almighty God, their merciful deliverer; to bless the memory of the noble men through whose free and faithful labors the grand result was finally brought about; to hold up their pure and generous examples to be admired and copied; and to make this day, to some extent, subservient to the sacred cause of human freedom in our own land, and throughout the world, is the grand object of our present assembling.

I rejoice to see before me white as well as colored persons; for though this is our day peculiarly, it is not so exclusively. The great fact we this day recognize—the great truth to which we have met to do honor, belongs to the whole human family. From this meeting, therefore, no member of the human family is excluded. We have this day a free platform, to which, without respect to class, color, or condition, all are invited. Let no man here feel that he is a mere spectator—that he has no share in the proceedings of this day, because his face is of a paler hue than mine. The occasion is not one of color, but of universal man—from the purest black to the clearest white, welcome, welcome! In the name of liberty and justice, I extend to each and to all, of every complexion, form and feature, a heartfelt welcome to a full participation in the joys of this anniversary....

We live in times which have no parallel in the history of the world. The grand commotion is universal and all-pervading. Kingdoms, realms, empires, and republics, roll to and fro like ships upon a stormy sea. The long pent up energies of human rights and sympathies, are at last let loose upon the world. The grand conflict of the angel Liberty with the monster Slavery, has at last come. The globe shakes with the contest.—I thank God that I am permitted, with you, to live in these days, and to participate humbly in this struggle. We are, Mr. President, parties to what is going on around us. We are more than spectators of the scenes that pass before us. Our interests, sympathies and destiny compel us to be parties to what is passing around us. Whether the immediate struggle be baptized by the Eastern or Western wave of the waters between us, the water is one, and the cause one, and we are parties to it. Steam, skill, and lightning, have brought the ends of the earth together. Old prejudices are vanishing. The magic power of human sympathy is rapidly healing national divisions, and bringing mankind into the harmonious bonds of a common brotherhood. In some sense, we realize the sublime declaration of the Prophet of Patmos, "And there shall be no more sea." The oceans that divided us, have become bridges to connect us, and the wide "world has become a whispering gallery." The morning star of freedom is seen from every quarter of the globe.

> *From spirit to spirit—from nation to nation,*
> *From city to hamlet, thy dawning is cast;*
> *And tyrants and slaves are like shadows of night,**

Standing in the far West, we may now hear the earnest debate of the Western world.— The means of intelligence is so perfect, as well as rapid, that we seem to be mingling with the thrilling scenes of the Eastern hemisphere.

In the month of February of the present year, we may date the commencement of the great movements now progressing throughout Europe. In France, at that time, we saw a king to all appearance firmly seated on his costly throne, guarded by two hundred thousand bayonets. In the pride of his heart, he armed himself for the destruction of liberty.

*Last line of poem missing.—*Ed.*

A few short hours ended the struggle. A shout went up to heaven from countless thousands, echoing back to earth, "Liberty—Equality—Fraternity." The troops heard the glorious sound, and fraternized with the people in the court yard of the Tuilleries.—Instantly the King was but a man. All that was kingly fled. The throne whereon he sat was demolished; his splendid palace sacked; his royal carriage was burnt with fire; and he who had arrayed himself against freedom, found himself, like the great Egyptian tyrant, completely overwhelmed. Out of the ruins of this grand rupture, there came up a Republican Provisional Government, and snatching the revolutionary motto of "Liberty—Equality—Fraternity," from the fiery thousands who had just rolled back the tide of tyranny, they commenced to construct a State in accordance with that noble motto. Among the first of its acts, while hard pressed from without and perplexed within, beset on every hand—to the everlasting honor of that Government, it decreed the complete, unconditional emancipation of every slave throughout the French colonies. This act of justice and consistency went into effect on the 23d of last June. Thus were three hundred thousand souls admitted to the joys of freedom.—That provisional government is now no more. The brave and brilliant men who formed it, have ceased to play a conspicuous part in the political affairs of the nation. For the present, some of the brightest lights are obscured. Over the glory of the great-hearted Lamartine, the dark shadow of suspicion is cast.—The most of the members of that government are now distrusted, suspected, and slighted.—But while there remains on the earth one man of sable hue, there will be one witness who will ever remember with unceasing gratitude this noble act of that provisional government.

Sir, this act of justice to our race, on the part of the French people, has had a widespread effect upon the question of human freedom in our own land. Seldom, indeed, has the slave power of the nation received what they regarded such bad news. It placed our slaveholding Republic in a dilemma which all the world could see. We desired to rejoice with her in her republicanism, but it was impossible to do so without seeming to rejoice over abolitionism. Here inconsistency, hypocrisy, covered even the brass face of our slaveholding Republic with confusion. Even that staunch Democrat and Christian, John C. Calhoun, found himself embarrassed as to how to vote on a resolution congratulating the French people on the triumph of Republicanism over Royalty.

But to return to Europe. France is not alone the scene of commotion. Her excitable and inflammable disposition makes her an appropriate medium for lighting more substantial fires. Austria has dispensed with Metternich, while all the German States are demanding freedom; and even iron-hearted Russia is alarmed and perplexed by what is going on around her. The French metropolis is in direct communication with all the great cities of Europe, and the influence of her example is everywhere powerful. The Revolution of the 24th February has stirred the dormant energies of the oppressed classes all over the continent. Revolutions, outbreaks, and provisional governments, followed that event in almost fearful succession. A general insecurity broods over the crowned heads of Europe. Ireland, too, the land of O'Connell, among the most powerful that ever advocated the cause of human freedom—Ireland, ever chafing under oppressive rule, famine-stricken, ragged and wretched, but warm-hearted, generous and unconquerable Ireland, caught up the inspiring peal as it swept across the bosom of St. George's Channel, and again renewed her oath, to be free or die. Her cause is already sanctified by the martyrdom of Mitchell, and millions stand ready to be sacrificed in the same manner. England, too—calm, dignified, brave old England—is not unmoved by what is going on through the sisterhood of European nations. Her toiling sons, from the buzz and din of the factory and workshop, to her endless coal mines deep down below the surface of the earth, have heard the joyful sound of "Liberty—Equality—Fraternity" and are lifting their heads and hearts in hope of better days.

These facts though unfortunately associated with great and crying evils—evils which you and I, and all of us must deeply deplore, are nevertheless interesting to the lovers of freedom and progress. They show that all sense of manhood and moral life, has not departed from the oppressed and plundered masses. They prove, that there yet remains an energy, when supported with the will that can roll back the combined and encroaching powers of tyranny and injustice. To teach this lesson, the movements abroad are important. Even in the recent fierce strife in Paris,[9] which has subjected the infant republic to a horrid baptism of blood, may be scanned a ray of goodness. The great mass of the *Blouses* behind the barricade of the Faubourgs, evidently felt themselves fighting in the righteous cause of equal rights. Wrong in head, but right in heart; brave men in a bad cause, possessing a noble zeal but not according to knowledge. Let us deplore their folly, but honor their courage; respect their aims, but eschew their means. Tyrants of the old world, and slaveholders of our own, will point in proud complacency to this awful outbreak, and say "Aha! aha! aha! *we told you so*—we told you so: this is but the result of undertaking to counteract the purposes of the Most High, who has ordained and annointed Kings and Slaveholders to rule over the people. So much for attempting to make that equal, which God made unequal!" These sentiments in other words, have already been expressed by at least one of the classes to which I have referred. To such, I say rejoice while you may, for your time is short. The day of freedom and order, is at hand. The beautiful infant may stagger and fall, but it will rise, walk and become a man. There may, and doubtless will be, many failures, mistakes and blunders attending the transition from slavery to liberty. But what then? shall the transition never be made? Who is so base, as to harbor the thought? In demolishing the old frame-work of the Bastille of civil tyranny, and erecting on its ruins the beautiful temple of freedom, some lives may indeed be lost; but who so craven, when beholding the noble structure—its grand proportions, its magnificent domes, its splendid towers and its elegant turrets, all pointing upward to heaven, as to say, That glorious temple ought never to have been built.

I look, Mr. President and friends, with the profoundest interest on all these movements, both in and out of France. Their influence upon our destiny here, is greater than may at first be perceived. Mainly, however, my confidence is reposing upon what is passing in England—brave and strong old England.—Among the first to do us wrong, and the first to do us justice. England the heart of the civilized world. The nation that gave us the deed—the glorious deed, which we, on this day humbly celebrate.

In these days of great movements, she is neither silent nor slumbering. It is true, the world is not startled by her thunder, or dazzled by her splendor. Her stillness, however, is of deeper signification, than the noise of many nations.—Like her own fuel, she has less blaze—but more heat. Her passage to freedom is not through rivers of blood; she has discovered a more excellent way. What is bloody revolution in France, is peaceful reformation in England. The friends and enemies of freedom, meet not at the barricades thrown up in the streets of London; but on the broad platform of Exeter Hall. Their weapons are not pointed bayonets, but arguments. Friends of freedom rely not upon brute force but moral power. Their courage is not that of the tiger, but that of the Christian. Their ramparts are, right and reason, and can never be stormed! Their Hotel de Ville, is the House of Commons. Their fraternity, is the unanimous sympathy of the oppressed and hungry millions, whose war cry is not "Bread or death," but bread! bread! bread!—Give this day our daily bread! That cry cannot, must not be disregarded. The last mails, brought us accounts of a stirring debate in the House of Commons, on the extension of suffrage. The opponents of the measure appeared like pigmies in the hands of giants. Friends of freedom in the House, are strong men. Among them is a man, whose name when I mention it, will call forth from this vast audience, a round of grateful applause. I allude to one, who, when he was but yet a youth, full eighteen years ago, dedicated himself to the cause of the West Indian bondman, and pleaded that cause with an eloquence the most pathetic, thrilling, and powerful ever before known to British ears—and who, when he had stirred the British heart to the core, until justice to the West India bondman rung through the British Empire—and the freedom which we celebrate, was gloriously triumphant; with life in hand, he left his native shores, to plead the cause of the bondman—and went through our land taking his lot with the despised abolitionists, and nominally free colored man; amid floods of abuse and fiery trials, he hazarded his precious life in our cause, at last was finally induced to leave our shores by the strong persuasion of his friends lest the enemies of liberty should kill him, as they had sworn to do, and returned to his own country, and is now an honorable member of the British Parliament. That man, is George Thompson. In grateful remembrance of whose labors, I now propose three cheers....

I now turn from the contemplation of men and movements in Europe, to our own great country. Great we are, in many and very important respects. As a nation, we are great in numbers and geographical extent—great in wealth—great in internal resources—great in the proclamations of great truths—great in our professions of republicanism and religion—great in our inconsistencies—great in our hypocrisy—and great in our atrocious wickedness. While our boast is loud and long of justice, freedom, and humanity, the slavewhip rings to the mockery; while we are sympathising with the progress of freedom abroad, we are extending the foul curse of slavery at home; while we are rejoicing at the progress of freedom in France, Italy, Germany, and the whole European continent, we are propagating slavery in Oregon, New Mexico, California, and all our blood-bought possessions in the South and South-west.—While we are engaged in congratulating the people of the East on casting down tyrants, we are electing tyrants and men-stealers to rule over us. Truly we are a great nation! At this moment, three million slaves clank their galling fetters and drag their heavy chains on American soil. Three million from whom all rights are robbed. Three millions, a population equal to that of all Scotland, who in this land of liberty and light, are denied the right to learn to read the name of God.—They toil under a broiling sun and a driver's lash; they are sold like cattle in the market—and are shut out from human regards—thought of and spoken of as property—sanctioned as property by cruel laws, and sanctified as such by the Church and Clergy of the country.—While I am addressing you, four of my own dear sisters and one brother are enduring the frightful horrors of American slavery. In what part of the Union, they may be, I do not know; two of them, Sarah and Catharine, were sold from Maryland before I escaped from there. I am cut off from all communication with—I cannot hear from them, nor can they hear from me—we are sundered forever.

My case, is the case of thousands; and the case of my sisters, is the case of Millions. I have no doubt, that there are hundreds here to-day, that have parents, children, sisters and brothers, who are now in slavery. Oh! how deep is the damnation of America—under what a load of crime does she stagger from day to day! What a hell of wickedness is there coiled up in her bosom, and what awful judgment awaits her impenitence! My friends, words cannot express my feelings. My soul is sick of this picture of an awful reality.—The wails of bondmen are on my ear, and their heavy sorrows weigh down my heart.

I turn from these horrors—from these God-defying, man imbruting crimes, to those who in my judgment are responsible for them. And I trace them to the door of every American citizen. Slavery exists in this land because of the moral, constitutional, political and religious support which it receives from the people of this country, especially the people of the North. As I stand before many to whom this subject may be new, I may be allowed here to explain. The people of this country are held together by a Constitution. That Constitution contains certain compromises in favor of slavery, and which bind the citizens to uphold slavery. The language of every American citizen to the slave, so far as he can comprehend that language is, "You shall be a slave or die." The history and character of the American people confirms the slave in this belief. To march to the attainment of his liberty, is to march directly upon the bristling bayonets of the whole military power of the nation. About eighteen years ago, a man of noble courage, rose among his brethren in Virginia. "We have long been subjected to slavery. The hour for our deliverance has come. Let us rise and strike for liberty. In the name of a God of justice let us stay our oppressors."[10] What was the result? He fell amid showers of American bullets, fired by *United States* troops. The fact that the Constitution guarantees to the slaveholder the naval and military support of the nation; the fact that he may under that Constitution, recapture his flying bondman in any State or territory within or belonging to this Union; and the fact that slavery alone enjoys a representation in Congress, makes every man who in good faith swears to support that Constitution and to execute its provisions, responsible for all the outrages committed on the millions of our brethren now in bonds. I therefore this day, before this large audience, charge home upon the voters of this city, county and state, the awful responsibility of enslaving and imbruting my brothers and sisters in the Southern States of this Union. Carry it home with you from this great gathering in Washington Square, that you, my white fellow-countrymen, are the enslavers of men, women, and children, in the Southern States; that what are called the compromises of your glorious Constitution, are but bloody links in the chain of slavery; and that they make you parties to that chain. But for these compromises—but for your readiness to stand by them, "in the fullness of their letter and the completeness of their letter," the slave might instantly assert and maintain his rights. The contest now would be wonderfully unequal. Seventeen millions of armed, disciplined, and intelligent people, against three millions of unarmed and uninformed. Sir, we are often taunted with the inquiry from Northern white men—"Why do your people submit to slavery? and does not that submission prove them an inferior race? Why have they not shown a desire for freedom?" Such language is as disgraceful to the insolent men who use it, as it is tantalising and insulting to us.

It is mean and cowardly for any white man to use such language toward us. My language to all such, is, Give us fair play and if we do not gain our freedom, it will be time to taunt us thus.

Before taking my seat, I will call your attention to some charges and misrepresentations of the American press, respecting the result of the great measure which we this day commemorate. We continually find statements and sentiments like this, in the whirlpool of American newspapers—"The British Colonies are ruined," "The emancipated Negroes are lazy and won't work," "Emancipation has been a failure." Now, I wish to reply to these sentiments and statements—and to say something about laziness in general, as applied to the race to which I belong. By the way, I think I may claim a superior industry for the colored man over the white man, on the showing of the white men themselves. We are just now appropriating to ourselves, vast regions of country in the Southwest.—What is the language of white men, as to the best population to develop the great resources of those vast countries? Why, in good plain English this: that white industry is unequal to it, and that none but the sinewy arm of the sable race is capable of doing so. Now, for these lazy drones to be taunting us with laziness, is a little too bad. I will answer the statements respecting the ruined condition of the West India Islands, by a declaration recently made on this very subject by Lord John Russell, present Prime Minister of England, a man remarkable for coolness and accuracy of speech. In regard to the measure of emancipation, he says, and I read from the London Times of the 17th of June, 1848:—

"The main purpose of the act of 1834 was as I have stated, to give freedom to 800,000 persons, to place those then living in a condition of slavery in a state of independence, prosperity, and happiness. That object, I think, every one admits has been accomplished. [Cheers.] I believe a class of laborers more happy, more in possession of all the advantages and enjoyments of life than the Negro population of the West Indies, does not exist. [Cheers.]—That great object has been accomplished by the act of 1834."

"It appears by evidence that the Negroes of the West India colonies since the abolition of slavery had been in the best condition. They had the best food, and were in all respects better clothed and provided for than any peasantry in the world. There was a resolution passed by a committee in 1842 declaring that the measure of emancipation had completely succeeded so far as the welfare of the Negroes was concerned. I believe the noble lord the member for Lynn, moved a similar resolution on a subsequent occasion. We have it in evidence that the Negroes were able to indulge in the luxury of dress, which they carried to an almost ridiculous excess. Some were known to have dress worth 50*l.*"

Now, sir, I call upon the press of Rochester and of this country at large, to let these facts be known, that a long abused and injured race may at last have justice done them.

I must thank you now my friends, for your kind and patient attention: asking your pardon for having trespassed so long upon your hearing, I will take my seat.

The North Star, August 4, 1848

AN ADDRESS TO THE COLORED PEOPLE OF THE UNITED STATES

Fellow Countrymen:

Under a solemn sense of duty, inspired by our relation to you as fellow sufferers under the multiplied and grievous wrongs to which we as a people are universally subjected,—we, a portion of your brethren, assembled in National Convention, at Cleveland, Ohio, take the liberty to address you on the subject of our mutual improvement and social elevation.

The condition of our variety of the human family, has long been cheerless, if not hopeless, in this country. The doctrine perseveringly proclaimed in high places in church and state, that it is impossible for colored men to rise from ignorance and debasement, to intelligence and respectability in this country, has made a deep impression upon the public mind generally, and is not without its effect upon us. Under this gloomy doctrine, many of us have sunk under the pall of despondency, and are making no effort to relieve ourselves, and have no heart to assist others. It is from this despond that we would deliver you. It is from this slumber we would rouse you. The present, is a period of activity and hope. The heavens above us are bright, and much of the darkness that overshadowed us has passed away. We can deal in the language of brilliant encouragement, and speak of success with certainty. That our condition has been gradually improving, is evident to all, and that we shall yet stand on a common platform with our fellow countrymen, in respect to political and social rights, is certain. The spirit of the age—the voice of inspiration—the deep longings of the human soul—the conflict of right with wrong—the upward tendency of the oppressed throughout the world, abound with evidence complete and ample, of the final triumph of right over wrong, of freedom over slavery, and equality over caste. To doubt this, is to forget the past, and blind our eyes to the present, as well as to deny and oppose the great law of progress, written out by the hand of God on the human soul.

Great changes for the better have taken place and are still taking place. The last ten years have witnessed a mighty change in the estimate in which we as a people are regarded, both in this and other lands. England has given liberty to nearly one million, and France has emancipated three hundred thousand of our brethren, and our own country shakes with the agitation of our rights. Ten or twelve years ago, an educated colored man was regarded as a curiosity, and the thought of a colored man as an author, editor, lawyer or doctor, had scarce been conceived. Such, thank Heaven, is no longer the case. There are now those among us, whom we are not ashamed to regard as gentlemen and scholars, and who are acknowledged to be such, by many of the most learned and respectable in our land. Mountains of prejudice have been removed, and truth and light are dispelling the error and darkness of ages. The time was, when we trembled in the presence of a white man, and dared not assert, or even ask for our rights, but would be guided, directed, and governed, in any way we were demanded, without ever stopping to enquire whether we were right or wrong. We were not only slaves, but our ignorance made us willing slaves. Many of us uttered complaints against the faithful abolitionists, for the broad assertion of our rights; thought they went too far, and were only making our condition worse. This sentiment has nearly ceased to reign in the dark abodes of our hearts; we begin to see our wrongs as clearly, and comprehend our rights as fully, and as well as our white countrymen. This is a sign of progress; and evidence which cannot be gainsayed. It would be easy to present in this connection, a glowing comparison of our past with our present condition, showing that while the former was dark and dreary, the present is full of light and hope. It would be easy to draw a picture of our present achievements, and erect upon it a glorious future.

But, fellow countrymen, it is not so much our purpose to cheer you by the progress we have already made, as it is to stimulate you to still higher attainments. We have done much, but there is much more to be done.—While we have undoubtedly great cause to thank God, and take courage for the hopeful changes which have taken place in our condition, we are not without cause to mourn over the sad condition which we yet occupy. We are yet the most oppressed people in the world. In the Southern states of this Union, we are held as slaves. All over that wide region our paths are marked with blood. Our backs are yet scarred by the lash, and our souls are yet dark under the pall of slavery.—Our sisters are sold for purposes of pollution, and our brethren are sold in the market, with beasts of burden. Shut up in the prison-house of bondage—denied all rights, and deprived of all privileges, we are blotted from the page of human existence, and placed beyond the limits of human regard. Death, moral death, has palsied our souls in that quarter, and we are a murdered people.

In the Northern states, we are not slaves to individuals, not personal slaves, yet in many respects we are the slaves of the community. We are, however, far enough removed from the actual condition of the slave, to make us largely responsible for their continued enslavement, or their speedy deliverance from chains. For in the proportion which we shall rise in the scale of human improvement, in that proportion do we augment the probabilities of a speedy emancipation of our enslaved fellow-countrymen. It is more than a mere figure of speech to say, that we are as a people, chained together. We are one people—one in general complexion, one in a common degradation, one in popular estimation. As one rises, all must rise, and as one falls all must fall. Having now, our feet on the rock of freedom, we must drag our brethren from the slimy depths of slavery, ignorance, and ruin. Every one of us should be ashamed to consider himself free, while his brother is a slave.—The wrongs of our brethren, should be our constant theme. There should be no time too precious, no calling too holy, no place too sacred, to make room for this cause. We should not only feel it to be the cause of humanity, but the cause of christianity, and fit work for men and angels. We ask you to devote yourselves to this cause, as one of the first, and most successful means of self improvement. In the careful study of it, you will learn your own rights, and comprehend your own responsibilities, and, scan through the vista of coming time, your high, and God-appointed destiny. Many of the brightest and best of our number, have become such by their devotion to this cause, and the society of white abolitionists. The latter have been willing to make themselves of no reputation for our sake, and in return, let us show ourselves worthy of their zeal and devotion. Attend anti-slavery meetings, show that you are interested in the subject, that you hate slavery, and love those who are laboring for its overthrow.— Act with white Abolition societies wherever you can, and where you cannot, get up societies among yourselves, but without exclusiveness. It will be a long time before we gain all our rights; and although it may seem to conflict with our views of human brotherhood, we shall undoubtedly for many years be compelled to have institutions of a complexional character, in order to attain this very idea of human brotherhood. We would, however, advise our brethren to occupy memberships and stations among white persons, and in white institutions, just so fast as our rights are secured to us.

Never refuse to act with a white society or institution because it is white, or a black one, because it is black. But act with all men without distinction of color. By so acting, we shall find many opportunities for removing prejudices and establishing the rights of all men. We say avail yourselves of *white* institutions, not because they are white, but because they afford a more convenient means of improvement. But we pass from these suggestions, to others which may be deemed more important. In the Convention that now addresses you, there has been much said on the subject of labor, and especially those departments of it, with which we as a class have been long identified. You will see by the resolutions there adopted on that subject, that the Convention regarded those employments though right in themselves, as being nevertheless, degrading to us as a class, and therefore, counsel you to abandon them as speedily as possible, and to seek what are called the more respectable employments. While the Convention do not inculcate the doctrine that any kind of needful toil is in itself dishonorable, or that colored persons are to be exempt from what are called menial employments, they do mean to say that such employments have been so long and universally filled by colored men, as to become a badge of degradation, in that it has established the conviction that colored men are only fit for such employments. We therefore, advise you by all means, to cease from such employments, as far as practicable, by pressing into others. Try to get your sons into mechanical trades; press them into the blacksmith's shop, the machine shop, the joiner's shop, the wheelwright's shop, the cooper's shop, and the tailor's shop.

Every blow of the sledge hammer, wielded by a sable arm, is a powerful blow in support of our cause. Every colored mechanic, is by virtue of circumstances, an elevator of his race. Every house built by black men, is a strong tower against the allied hosts of prejudice. It is impossible for us to attach too much importance to this aspect of the subject. Trades are important. Wherever a man may be thrown by misfortune, if he has in his hands a useful trade, he is useful to his fellow man, and will be esteemed accordingly; and of all men in the world who need trades we are the most needy.

Understand this, that independence is an essential condition of respectability. To be dependent, is to be degraded. Men may indeed pity us, but they cannot respect us. We do not mean that we can become entirely independent of all men; that would be absurd and impossible, in the social state. But we mean that we must become equally independent with other members of the community. That other members of the community shall be as dependent upon us, as we upon them.—That such is not now the case, is too plain to need an argument. The houses we live in are built by white men—the clothes we wear are made by white tailors—the hats on our heads are made by white hatters, and the shoes on our feet are made by white shoe-makers, and the food that we eat, is raised and cultivated by white men. Now it is impossible that we should ever be respected as a people, while we are so universally and completely dependent upon white men for the necessaries of life. We must make white persons as dependent upon us, as we are upon them. This cannot be done while we are found only in two or three kinds of employments, and those employments have their foundation chiefly, if not entirely, in the pride and indolence of the white people. Sterner necessities, will bring higher respect.

The fact is, we must not merely make the white man dependent upon us to shave him but to feed him; not merely dependent upon us to black his boots, but to make them. A man is only in a small degree dependent on us when he only needs his boots blacked, or his carpet bag carried; as a little less pride, and a little more industry on his part, may enable him to dispense with our services entirely. As wise men it becomes us to look forward to a state of things, which appears inevitable. The time will come, when those menial employments will afford less means of living than they now do. What shall a large class of our fellow countrymen do, when white men find it economical to black their own boots, and shave themselves. What will they do when white men learn to wait on themselves? We warn you brethren, to seek other and more enduring vocations

Let us entreat you to turn your attention to agriculture. Go to farming. Be tillers of the soil. On this point we could say much, but the time and space will not permit. Our cities are overrun with menial laborers, while the country is eloquently pleading for the hand of industry to till her soil, and reap the reward of honest labor. We beg and intreat you, to save your money—live economically—dispense with finery, and the gaities which have rendered us proverbial, and save your money. Not for the senseless purpose of being better off than your neighbor, but that you may be able to educate your children, and render your share to the common stock of prosperity and happiness around you. It is plain that the equality which we aim to accomplish, can only be achieved by us, when we can do for others, just what others can do for us. We should therefore, press into all the trades, professions and callings, into which honorable white men press.

We would in this connection, direct your attention to the means by which we have been oppressed and degraded. Chief among those means, we may mention the press. This engine has brought to the aid of prejudice, a thousand stings. Wit, ridicule, false philosophy, and an impure theology, with a flood of low black-guardism, come through this channel into the public mind; constantly feeding and keeping alive against us, the bitterest hate. The pulpit too, has been arrayed against us. Men with sanctimonious face, have talked of our being descendants of Ham—that we are under a curse, and to try to improve our condition, is virtually to counteract the purposes of God!

It is easy to see that the means which have been used to destroy us, must be used to save us. The press must be used in our behalf: aye! we must use it ourselves; we must take and read newspapers; we must read books, improve our minds, and put to silence and to shame, our opposers.

Dear Brethren, we have extended these remarks beyond the length which we had allotted to ourselves, and must now close, though we have but hinted at the subject. Trusting that our words may fall like good seed upon good ground; and hoping that we may all be found in the path of improvement and progress,

We are your friends and servants,
(Signed by the Committee, in behalf of the Convention)

Frederick Douglass,
H. Bibb,
W. L. Day,
D. H. Jenkins,
A. H. Francis.

The North Star, September 29, 1848

TO THOMAS AULD

September 3d, 1848

Sir:

The long and intimate, though by no means friendly relation which unhappily subsisted between you and myself, leads me to hope that you will easily account for the great liberty which I now take in addressing you in this open and public manner. The same fact may possibly remove any disagreeable surprise which you may experience on again finding your name coupled with mine, in any other way than in an advertisement, accurately describing my person, and offering a large sum for my arrest. In thus dragging you again before the public, I am aware that I shall subject myself to no inconsiderable amount of censure. I shall probably be charged with an unwarrantable, if not a wanton and reckless disregard of the rights and proprieties of private life. There are those North as well as South who entertain a much higher respect for rights which are merely conventional, than they do for rights which are personal and essential. Not a few there are in our country, who, while they have no scruples against robbing the laborer of the hard earned results of his *patient industry,* will be shocked by the extremely indelicate manner of bringing your name before the public. Believing this to be the case, and wishing to meet every reasonable or plausible objection to my conduct, I will frankly state the ground upon which I justify myself in this instance, as well as on former occasions when I have thought proper to mention your name in public. All will agree that a man guilty of theft, robbery, or murder, has forfeited the right to concealment and private life; that the community have a right to subject such persons to the most complete exposure. However much they may desire retirement, and aim to conceal themselves and their movements from the popular gaze, the public have a right to ferret them out, and bring their conduct before the proper tribunals of the country for investigation. Sir, you will undoubtedly make the proper application of these generally admitted principles, and will easily see the light in which you are regarded by me. I will not therefore manifest ill temper, by calling you hard names. I know you to be a man of some intelligence, and can readily determine the precise estimate which I entertain of your character. I may therefore indulge in language which may seem to others indirect and ambiguous, and yet be quite well understood by yourself.

I have selected this day on which to address you, because it is the anniversary of my emancipation; and knowing of no better way, I am led to this as the best mode of celebrating that truly important event. Just ten years ago this beautiful September morning, yon bright sun beheld me a slave—a poor, degraded chattel—trembling at the sound of your voice, lamenting that I was a man, and wishing myself a brute. The hopes which I had treasured up for weeks of a safe and successful escape from your grasp, were powerfully confronted at this last hour by dark clouds of doubt and fear, making my person shake and my bosom to heave with the heavy contest between hope and fear. I have no words to describe to you the deep agony of soul which I experienced on that never to be forgotten morning—(for I left by daylight). I was making a leap in the dark. The probabilities, so far as I could by reason determine them, were stoutly against the undertaking. The preliminaries and precautions I had adopted previously, all worked badly. I was like one going to war without weapons—ten chances of defeat to one of victory. One in whom I had confided, and one who had promised me assistance, appalled by fear at the trial hour, deserted me, thus leaving the responsibility of success or failure solely with myself. You, sir, can never know my feelings. As I look back to them, I can scarcely realize that I have passed through a scene so trying. Trying however as they were, and gloomy as was the prospect, thanks be to the Most High, who is ever the God of the oppressed, at the moment which was to determine my whole earthly career. His grace was sufficient, my mind was made up. I embraced the golden opportunity, took the morning tide at the flood, and a free man, young, active and strong, is the result.

I have often thought I should like to explain to you the grounds upon which I have justified myself in running away from you. I am almost ashamed to do so now, for by this time you may have discovered them yourself. I will, however, glance at them. When yet but a child about six years old, I imbibed the determination to run away. The very first mental effort that I now remember on my part, was an attempt to solve the mystery, Why am I a slave? and with this question my youthful mind was troubled for many days, pressing upon me more heavily at times than others. When I saw the slave-driver whip a slave woman, cut the blood out of her neck, and heard her piteous cries, I went away into the corner of the fence, wept and pondered over the mystery. I had, through some medium, I know not what, got some idea of God, the Creator of all mankind, the black and the white, and that he had made the blacks to serve the whites as slaves. How he could do this and be *good,* I could not tell. I was not satisfied with this theory, which made God responsible for slavery, for it pained me greatly, and I have wept over it long and often. At one time, your first wife, Mrs. Lucretia, heard me singing and saw me shedding tears, and asked of me the matter, but I was afraid to tell her. I was puzzled with this question, till one night, while sitting in the kitchen, I heard some of the old slaves talking of their parents having been stolen from Africa by white men, and were sold here as slaves. The whole mystery was solved at once. Very soon after this my aunt Jinny and uncle Noah ran away, and the great noise made about it by your father-in-law, made me for the first time acquainted with the fact, that there were free States as well as slave States. From that time, I resolved that I would some day run away. The morality of the act, I dispose as follows: I am myself; you are yourself; we are two distinct persons, equal persons. What you are, I am. You are a man, and so am I. God created both, and made us separate beings. I am not by nature bound to you, or you to me. Nature does not make your existence depend upon me, or mine to depend upon yours. I cannot walk upon your legs, or you upon mine. I cannot breathe for you, or you for me; I must breathe for myself, and you for yourself. We are distinct persons, and are each equally provided with faculties necessary to our individual existence. In leaving you, I took nothing but what belonged to me, and in no way lessened your means for obtaining an *honest* living. Your faculties remained yours, and mine became useful to their rightful owner. I therefore see no wrong in any part of the transaction. It is true, I went off secretly, but that was more your fault than mine. Had I let you into the secret, you would have defeated the enterprise entirely; but for this, I should have been really glad to have made you acquainted with my intentions to leave.

You may perhaps want to know how I like my present condition. I am free to say, I greatly prefer it to that which I occupied in Maryland. I am, however, by no means prejudiced against the State as such. Its geography, climate, fertility and products, are such as to make it a very desirable abode for any man; and but for the existence of slavery there, it is not impossible that I might again take up my abode in that State. It is not that I love Maryland less, but freedom more. You will be surprised to learn that people at the North labor under the strange delusion that if the slaves were emancipated at the South, they would flock to the North. So far from this being the case, in that event, you would see many old and familiar faces back again to the South. The fact is, there are few here who would not return to the South in the event of emancipation. We want to live in the land of our birth, and to lay our bones by the side of our fathers'; and nothing short of an intense love of personal freedom keeps us from the South. For the sake of this, most of us would live on a crust of bread and a cup of cold water.

Since I left you, I have had a rich experience. I have occupied stations which I never dreamed of when a slave. Three out of the ten years since I left you, I spent as a common laborer on the wharves of New Bedford, Massachusetts. It was there I earned my first free dollar. It was mine. I could spend it as I pleased. I could buy hams or herring with it, without asking any odds of any body. That was a precious dollar to me. You remember when I used to make seven or eight, or even nine dollars a week in Baltimore, you would take every cent of it from me every Saturday night, saying that I belonged to you, and my earnings also. I never liked this conduct on your part—to say the best, I thought it a little mean. I would not have served you so. But let that pass. I was a little awkward about counting money in New England fashion when I first landed in New Bedford. I like to have betrayed myself several times. I caught myself saying phip, for fourpence; and at one time a man actually charged me with being a runaway, whereupon I was silly enough to become one by running away from him, for I was greatly afraid he might adopt measures to get me again into slavery, a condition I then dreaded more than death.

I soon, however, learned to count money, as well as to make it, and got on swimmingly. I married soon after leaving you: in fact, I was engaged to be married before I left you; and instead of finding my companion a burden, she was truly a helpmeet. She went to live at service, and I to work on the wharf, and though we toiled hard the first winter, we never lived more happily. After remaining in New Bedford for three years, I met with Wm. Lloyd Garrison, a person of whom you have *possibly* heard, as he is pretty generally known among slaveholders. He put it into my head that I might make myself serviceable to the cause of the slave by devoting a portion of my time to telling my own sorrows, and those of other slaves which had come under my observation. This was the commencement of a higher state of existence than any to which I had ever aspired. I was thrown into society the most pure, enlightened and benevolent that the country affords. Among these I have never forgotten you, but have invariably made you the topic of conversation—thus giving you all the notoriety I could do. I need not tell you that the opinion formed of you in these circles, is far from being favorable. They have little respect for your honesty, and less for your religion.

But I was going on to relate to you something of my interesting experience. I had not long enjoyed the excellent society to which I have referred, before the light of its excellence exerted a beneficial influence on my mind and heart. Much of my early dislike of white persons was removed, and their manners, habits and customs, so entirely unlike what I had been used to in the kitchen-quarters on the plantations of the South, fairly charmed me, and gave me a strong disrelish for the coarse and degrading customs of my former condition. I therefore made an effort so to improve my mind and deportment, as to be somewhat fitted to the station to which

I seemed almost providentially called. The transition from degradation to respectability was indeed great, and to get from one to the other without carrying some marks of one's former condition, is truly a difficult matter. I would not have you think that I am now entirely clear of all plantation peculiarities, but my friends here, while they entertain the strongest dislike to them, regard me with that charity to which my past life somewhat entitles me, so that my condition in this respect is exceedingly pleasant. So far as my domestic affairs are concerned, I can boast of as comfortable a dwelling as your own. I have an industrious and neat companion, and four dear children—the oldest a girl of nine years, and three fine boys, the oldest eight, the next six, and the youngest four years old. The three oldest are now going regularly to school—two can read and write, and the other can spell with tolerable correctness words of two syllables: Dear fellows! they are all in comfortable beds, and are sound asleep, perfectly secure under my own roof. There are no slaveholders here to rend my heart by snatching them from my arms, or blast a mother's dearest hopes by tearing them from her bosom. These dear children are ours—not to work up into rice, sugar and tobacco, but to watch over, regard, and protect, and to rear them up in the nurture and admonition of the gospel—to train them up in the paths of wisdom and virtue, and, as far as we can to make them useful to the world and to themselves. Oh! sir, a slaveholder never appears to me so completely an agent of hell, as when I think of and look upon my dear children. It is then that my feelings rise above my control. I meant to have said more with respect to my own prosperity and happiness, but thoughts and feelings which this recital has quickened unfits me to proceed further in that direction. The grim horrors of slavery rise in all their ghastly terror before me, the wails of millions pierce my heart, and chill my blood. I remember the chain, the gag, the bloody whip, the death-like gloom overshadowing the broken spirit of the fettered bondman, the appalling liability of his being torn away from wife and children, and sold like a beast in the market. Say not that this is a picture of fancy. You well know that I wear stripes on my back inflicted by your direction; and that you, while we were brothers in the same church, caused this right hand, with which I am now penning this letter, to be closely tied to my left, and my person dragged at the pistol's mouth, fifteen miles, from the Bay side to Easton to be sold like a beast in the market, for the alleged crime of intending to escape from your possession. All this and more you remember, and know to be perfectly true, not only of yourself, but of nearly all of the slaveholders around you.

At this moment, you are probably the guilty holder of at least three of my own dear sisters, and my only brother in bondage. These you regard as your property. They are recorded on your ledger, or perhaps have been sold to human flesh mongers, with a view to filling your own ever-hungry purse. Sir, I desire to know how and where these dear sisters are. Have you sold them? or are they still in your possession? What has become of them? are they living or dead? And my dear old grand-mother, whom you turned out like an old horse, to die in the woods—is she still alive? Write and let me know all about them. If my grandmother be still alive, she is of no service to you, for by this time she must be nearly eighty years old—too old to be cared for by one to whom she has ceased to be of service, send her to me at Rochester, or bring her to Philadelphia, and it shall be the crowning happiness of my life to take care of her in her old age. Oh! she was to me a mother, and a father, so far as hard toil for my comfort could make her such. Send me my grandmother! that I may watch over and take care of her in her old age. And my sisters, let me know all about them. I would write to them, and learn all I want to know of them, without disturbing you in any way, but that, through your unrighteous conduct, they have been entirely deprived of the power to read and write. You have kept them in utter ignorance, and have therefore robbed them of the sweet enjoyments of writing or receiving letters from absent friends and relatives. Your wickedness and cruelty committed in this respect on your fellow-creatures, are greater than all the stripes you have laid upon my back, or theirs. It is an outrage upon the soul—a war upon the immortal spirit, and one for which you must give account at the bar of our common Father and Creator.

The responsibility which you have assumed in this regard is truly awful—and how you could stagger under it these many years is marvellous. Your mind must have become darkened, your heart hardened, your conscience seared and petrified, or you would have long since thrown off the accursed load and sought relief at the hands of a sin-forgiving God. How, let me ask, would you look upon me, were I some dark night in company with a band of hardened villains, to enter the precincts of your elegant dwelling and seize the person of your own lovely daughter Amanda, and carry her off from your family, friends and all the loved ones of her youth—make her my slave—compel her to work, and I take her wages—place her name on my ledger as property—disregard her personal rights—fetter the powers of her immortal soul by denying her the right and privilege of learning to read and write—feed her coarsely—clothe her scantily, and whip her on the naked back occasionally; more and still more horrible, leave her unprotected—a degraded victim to the brutal lust of fiendish overseers, who would pollute, blight, and blast her fair soul—rob her of all dignity—destroy her virtue, and annihilate all in her person the graces that adorn the character of virtuous womanhood? I ask how would you regard me, if such were my conduct? Oh! the vocabulary of the damned would not afford a word sufficiently infernal, to express your idea of my God-provoking wickedness. Yet sir, your treatment of my beloved sisters is in all essential points, precisely like the case I have now supposed. Damning as would be such a deed on my part, it would be no more so than that which you have committed against me and my sisters.

I will now bring this letter to a close, you shall hear from me again unless you let me hear from you. I intend to make use of you as a weapon with which to assail the system of slavery—as a means of concentrating public attention on the system, and deepening their horror of trafficking in the souls and bodies of men. I shall make use of you as a means of exposing the character of the American church and clergy—and as a means of bringing this guilty nation with yourself to repentance. In doing this I entertain no malice towards you personally. There is no roof under which you would be more safe than mine, and there is nothing in my house which you might need for your comfort, which I would not readily grant. Indeed, I should esteem it a privilege, to set you an example as to how mankind ought to treat each other.

I am your fellow man, but not your slave,

Frederick Douglass

The Liberator, September 22, 1848

THE BLOOD OF THE SLAVE ON THE SKIRTS OF THE NORTHERN PEOPLE

A victim of your power and oppression, humbly craves your attention to a few words, (in behalf of himself and three millions of his brethren, whom you hold in chains and slavery,) with respect to the election just completed. In doing so, I desire to be regarded as addressing you, individually and collectively. If I should seem severe, remember that the iron of slavery has pierced and rankled in my heart, and that I not only smart under the recollection of a long and cruel enslavement, but am even now passing my life in a country, and among a people, whose prejudices against myself and people subjects me to a thousand poisonous stings. If I speak harshly, my excuse is, that I speak in fetters of your own forging. Remember that oppression hath the power to make even a wise man mad.

In the selection of your national rulers just completed, you have made another broad mark on the page of your nation's history, and have given to the world and the coming generation a certain test by which to determine your present integrity as a people. That actions speak louder than words—that within the character of the representative may be seen that of the constituency—that no people are better than their laws or lawmakers—that a stream cannot rise higher than its source—that a sweet fountain cannot send forth bitter water, and that a tree is to be known by its fruits, are truisms; and in their light let us examine the character and pretensions of your boasted Republic.

As a people, you claim for yourselves a higher civilization—a purer morality—a deeper religious faith—a larger love of liberty, and a broader philanthropy, than any other nation on the globe. In a word, you claim yours to be a model Republic, and promise, by the force and excellence of your institutions, and the purity and brightness of your example, to overthrow the thrones and despotisms of the old world, and substitute your own in their stead. Your missionaries are found in the remotest parts of the globe, while our land swarms with churches and religious institutions. In words of Religion and Liberty, you are abundant and pre-eminent. You have long desired to get rid of the odium of being regarded as pro-slavery, and have even insisted that the charge of pro-slavery made against you was a slander and that those who made it were animated by wild and fanatical spirit. To make your innocence apparent, you have now had a fair opportunity. The issue for freedom or slavery has been clearly submitted to you, and you have deliberately chosen slavery.

General Taylor and General Cass were the chosen and admitted Southern and slavery candidates for the Presidency. Martin Van Buren, though far from being an abolitionist, yet in some sort represented the Anti-Slavery idea of the North, in a political form—him you have rejected, and elected a slaveholder to rule over you in his stead. When the question was whether New Mexico and California shall be Free or Slave States, you have rejected him who was solemnly pledged to maintain their freedom, and have chosen a man whom you knew to be pledged, by his position, to the maintenance of slavery. By your votes, you have said that slavery is better than freedom—that war is better than peace, and that cruelty is better than humanity. You have given your sanction to slave rule and slavery propagandism, and interposed whatever of moral character and standing you possess, to shield the reputation of slaveholders generally. You have said, that to be a man-stealer is no crime—to traffic in human flesh shall be a passport, rather than a barrier to your suffrages. To slaveholders you have said, Chain up your men and women, and before the bloody lash drive them to new fields of toil in California and New Mexico. To the slave in his chains you have said, Be content in your chains, and if you dare to gain your freedom by force, whether in New Mexico or California, in numbers indicated by our votes, our muskets shall find you out. In a word, you have again renewed your determination to support the Constitution of the United States, in its parts of freedom to the whites, and slavery to the blacks. If General Taylor's slaves run away, you have promised again to return them to bondage. While General Taylor is the well-known robber of three hundred human beings of all their hard earnings, and is coining their hard earnings into gold, you have conferred upon him an office worth twenty-five thousand dollars a year, and the highest honor within your power. By this act, you have endorsed his character and history. His murders in Mexico—his "bloodhound" cruelty in the Florida war—his awful profanity, together with the crimes attendant upon a slave plantation, such as theft, robbery, murder, and adultery, you have sanctioned as perfectly consistent with your morality, humanity, liberty, religion and civilization. You have said that the most available and suitable person in all this great nation, to preside over this model Republic, is a warrior, slaveholder, swearer, and bloodhound importer.—During the campaign just ended, your leaders have dubbed this man-stealer as an *honest man,* and many of you have shouted over the lie, as being a truth, thus destroying all moral distinctions. To talk of a veracious liar, a pious blasphemer, a righteous robber, a candid hypocrite, a sober drunkard, or a humane cannibal, would be quite as just and rational as to call an admitted man-stealer an honest man. Yet in the wildness of a wicked enthusiasm, you have given your countenance and support to this.

Now is it too much to say that you have made his crimes your own, and that the blood of the slave is on your garments? You have covered his theft with honesty, his blasphemy with piety, and, as far as in your power, you have rendered the blows intended to destroy slavery nugatory and innoxious. Before high heaven and the world, you are responsible for the blood of the slave. You may shut your eyes to the fact, sport over it, sleep over it, dance over it, and sing psalms over it, but so sure as there is a God of Justice and an unerring Providence, just so sure will the blood of the bondman be required at your hands.—An opportunity was presented to you by which you could have fixed an indelible mark of your utter detestation of slavery, and given a powerful blow to that bitter curse. This you have failed to do. When Christ and Barabbas were presented, you have cried out in your madness, Give us Barabbas the robber, in preference to Christ, the innocent. The perishing slave, with uplifted hands and bleeding hearts, implored you, in the name of the God you profess to serve, and the humanity you profess to cherish, not to add this mill-stone to the weight already crushing his heart and hopes. But he has appealed in vain. You have turned a deaf ear to his cries, hardened your hearts to his appeal, turned your back upon his sorrows, and united with the tyrant to perpetuate his enslavement. The efforts made in your presence to impress you with the awful sin of slavery, and to awaken you to a sense of your duty to the oppressed, have thus far been unavailing. You continue to fight against God, and declare that *injustice* exalteth a nation, and that sin is an *honor* to any people.

Do you really think to circumvent God?—Do you suppose that you can go on in your present career of injustice and political profligacy undisturbed? Has the law of righteous retribution been repealed from the statutes of the Almighty? Or what mean ye that ye bruise and bind my people? Will justice sleep forever? Oh, that you would lay these things to heart! Oh, that you would consider the enormity of your conduct, and seek forgiveness at the hands of a merciful Creator. Repent of this wickedness, and bring forth fruit meet for repentance, by delivering the despoiled out of the hands of the despoiler.

You may imagine that you have now silenced the annoying cry of abolition—that you have sealed the doom of the slave—that abolition is stabbed and dead; but you will find your mistake. You have stabbed, but the cause is not dead. Though down and bleeding at your feet, she shall rise again, and going before you, shall give you no rest till you break every yoke and let the oppressed go free. The Anti-Slavery Societies of the land will rise up and spring to action again, sending forth from the press and on the voice of the living speaker, words of burning truth, to alarm the guilty, to unmask the hypocrite, to expose the frauds of political parties, and rebuke the spirit of a corrupt and sin-sustaining church and clergy. Slavery will be attacked in its stronghold—the compromises of the Constitution, and the cry of disunion shall be more fearlessly proclaimed, till slavery be abolished, the Union dissolved, or the sun of this guilty nation must go down in blood.—F. D.

The North Star, November 17, 1848

A FEW WORDS TO OUR OWN PEOPLE

All people are ours, and we are theirs—members of a common family, with a common destiny. In the sight of the Most High and his immutable attributes, we stand upon a common and equal footing. With Him, there is neither Jew nor Gentile, barbarian nor Scythian. He is no respecter of persons, and hath made of one blood all nations for to dwell upon all the face of the earth. In what, then, some may ask, consists the propriety of using a caption which implies upon the face of it a denial of this doctrine? The question is a fair one, and deserves an answer.

Without admitting that the caption in question necessarily carries upon its face the alleged implication, we answer, that by the force of potent circumstances, now in existence, and which for ages have existed, the colored people of this country are compelled to occupy a distinct and peculiar condition, and that it is therefore right and proper to address them especially and specifically with respect to that condition, and the rights, duties and responsibilities which of necessity attach to that condition.

Though in the broad sight of a righteous God, we stand upon a common level of brotherhood with the rest of mankind, and are naturally and self-evidently entitled to all the rights, privileges and immunities common to every member of that family, we are nevertheless regarded and treated not only as distinct from, but as inferior to all others. In our case, vice and virtue are often treated with equal disfavor by our oppressors; and in some cases a premium is paid to vice, and virtue is placed under the ban of malignant proscription. In many of the Northern States of the Union, a low, idle, vicious white man stands higher in the social and political scale of society, than the most refined and virtuous colored man can do. In the States of Ohio, Indiana, and the whole South, the word of any white villain will be taken as evidence against us, while that of the most respectable and upright colored man would be rejected if in our own favor. Wherever we go, and in whichever direction we turn, we find that we are regarded as a doomed and distinct people, and unsuited to the society and friendship of our white fellow-countrymen. Let us approach the halls of science and learning—we are spurned; advance towards the proud temple dedicated to the worship of our Father, Almighty God, and we are proscribed—essay to travel by sea or land, lake or river, and in what part of this slavery-cursed land do we find our manhood admitted or respected?—Thus cast out from among the rest of mankind, it becomes us to look around and ascertain if there be any means within our reach with which we may improve our condition, regain our lost rights, and ascend to the elevated station in the scale of being for which we were evidently designed by a beneficent Creator. It is impossible to think our condition past improvement. We cannot, ought not, and must not settle down under the misanthropic idea, that we have attained all that is attainable for us in this country, and that our condition is a hopeless one. It would be to accuse the Allwise Ruler of the world's destinies with partiality, to imagine that while the rest of mankind are steadily and rapidly advancing in the arts and sciences, and the many blessings of civilization, we only are denied all means of bettering our condition.—It would be a bold contradiction of past experience to deny that we have the means, to a large degree, of our own elevation and improvement in our hands. The man among us who is looking out of ourselves for our improvement, is looking in the wrong direction, and is setting a lazy example, which, if extensively followed, must sink us below our present degraded condition. If the whites advance and we stand still, the distance which now separates us must become a gulf—and it may be an impassable gulf.

Already are our enemies gravely speculating upon our final extinction, and even venturing upon the probable time it will take to blot us out from the face of this nation. This argument has been adduced by a distinguished Free Soil man, as a reason for opposing the extension of slavery. Regarding our extension as a desirable end, and believing the extension of slavery to be unfavorable to this result, inasmuch as, by the inevitable laws of population, it must increase in proportion to the augmentation, and decrease according to the decrease of the means of living. Yes, we say that our enemies are gravely and boldly speculating upon the final extinction of the colored people of this country. They say that both the Indian and the African must perish beneath the car of the advancing civilization of America. To this end, we believe, the Hon. Mr. Hannegan, of Indiana, presented petitions the other day in the Senate of the United States, asking for grants of lands in New Mexico to be colonized and settled by free colored people. This we take to be another cunning scheme of our oppressors. Once get the free colored man confined in any one territory or locality—let us once be separated from the white people of this country, and we shall become the mere *game* of American trappers and other adventurers, and there is no reason to believe that our fate will be in any respect better than the noble Seminoles and other Indians who have perished by the perfidy and rapacity of the proud Anglo-Saxon race. It is certain that there can be no good accomplished by emigration, unless we go beyond the musket shot of white American adventurers. There is nothing to be gained by such emigration, but almost certain extinction. In a land like this, and in the circumstances by which we are surrounded, we have no better advice to give than this—"Stick by the ship"—stand to your post.—We can live where other men live, and must die if we place ourselves where other men have died. Nothing seems more evident to us, than that our destiny is sealed up with that of the white people of this country, and we believe that we must fall or flourish with them. We must banish all thoughts of emigration from our minds, and resolve to stay just where we are—not in towns and cities merely, but among white people, and avail ourselves of the civilization of America, in the very centre of its existence, and never think of trusting ourselves on its outer borders, where it ceases to be civilization, and becomes savage barbarism. It is said that we cannot prosper in a cold climate. There is no truth in the proposition. We can become acclimated just where any other members of the human family can be acclimated, and can live as well and long as any others. The idea that we cannot, is a miserable pretence, got up to afford a pretext for getting us out of this country. We can live on the banks of the Penobscot as on the Sabine, and do live there. Let us not, therefore, be gulled into the notion that this climate is unfavorable to our development and progress. There are other modes of improving our condition at hand. We need not look beyond the limits of the Northern States for every facility which we need for our improvement and elevation. Education, that grand lever for improvement, is to a large degree within our reach. Trades are not entirely closed against it. Public opinion has at last granted to us the right of speech. We can now speak of our wrongs boldly and fearlessly. We have had numerous concessions from high sources, that we are capable of the very highest attainments. We have three newspapers in the hands of our own people, as well as a large number of churches and societies for moral and benevolent purposes. Are we to turn our backs upon these, and wander away, to become the *game* of American sportsmen? We hope not; and feel assured that we shall not, notwithstanding all the efforts that may be made in high places to induce us to do so. Come, friends and brethren, let us unite firmly to do all that in us lies to improve our condition, where we are. Let us sustain our press, and keep our men in the field whose voices are never uplifted in our cause in vain. Let us not run from prejudice and hardships, but meet and overcome them. Let us keep pace with the wheels of American civilization, as the best means within our reach to prevent us from being crushed by it. Let us live savingly, that we may educate our children, and place them in favorable circumstances for maintaining an honorable position in society. Banish forever the withering heresy that our condition here is as good as we can make it, and as good as it ever will be. Such thoughts should never find a lodgment in our bosoms. They will do for the mean coward, and the miserable sluggard, but must never be tolerated for a moment among men and women situated as we are.

> *Let us then be up and doing,*
> *With a heart for any fate,*

in the full confidence that it is nobler to die struggling against the adverse currents, than to live floating idly and listlessly down to inevitable destruction.—F. D.

The North Star, January 19, 1849

COLONIZATION

In order to divert the hounds from the pursuit of the fox, a *"red herring"* is sometimes drawn across the trail, and the hounds mistaking it for the real scent, the game is often lost. We look upon the recent debate in the Senate of the United States, over this wrinkled old "red herring" of colonization as a *ruse* to divert the attention of the people from that foul abomination which is sought to be forced upon the free soil of California and New Mexico, and which is now struggling for existence in Kentucky, Virginia and the District of Columbia. The slaveholders are evidently at a stand to know what trick they shall try next to turn the scorching rays of anti-slavery light and truth from the bloodshot eyes of the monster slavery. The discussion of it is most painful and agonizing; and if it continues, the very life of this foul, unnatural and adulterous beast will be put in imminent peril; so the slaveholding *charmers* have conjured up their old *familiar spirits* of colonization, making the old *essence* of abomination to flounder about in its grave clothes before the eyes of Northern men, to their utter confusion and bewilderment. A drowning man will catch at a straw. Slavery is sinking in public estimation. It is going down. It wants help, and asks through Mr. Underwood, of Kentucky, how much of the public money (made by the honest toil of Northern men) will be at its service in the event of emancipation, "as some are in favor of emancipation, provided that the Negroes can be sent to Liberia, or beyond the limits of the United States."

Here we have the old colonization spirit revived, and the impudent proposition entertained by the Senate of the United States of expelling the free colored people from the United States, their native land, to Liberia.

In view of this proposition, we would respectfully suggest to the assembled wisdom of the nation, that it might be well to ascertain the number of free colored people who will be likely to need the assistance of government to help them out of this country to Liberia, or elsewhere, beyond the limits of these United States—since this course might save any embarrassment which would result from an appropriation more than commensurate to the numbers who might be disposed to leave this, our own country, for one we know not of. We are of opinion that the *free* colored people generally mean to live in America, and not in Africa; and to appropriate a large sum for our removal, would merely be a waste of the public money. We do not mean to go to Liberia. Our minds are made up to live here if we can, or die here if we must; so every attempt to remove us, will be, as it ought to be, labor lost. Here we are, and here we shall remain. While our brethren are in bondage on these shores; it is idle to think of inducing any considerable number of the free colored people to quit this for a foreign land.

For two hundred and twenty-eight years has the colored man toiled over the soil of America, under a burning sun and a driver's lash—plowing, planting, reaping, that white men might roll in ease, their hands unhardened by labor, and their brows unmoistened by the waters of genial toil; and now that the moral sense of mankind is beginning to revolt at this system of foul treachery and cruel wrong, and is demanding its overthrow, the mean and cowardly oppressor is meditating plans to expel the colored man entirely from the country. Shame upon the guilty wretches that dare propose, and all that countenance such a proposition. We live here—have lived here—have a right to live here, and mean to live here.—F. D.

The North Star, January 26, 1849

THE CONSTITUTION AND SLAVERY

Rochester, January 23, 1849

Frederick Douglass—Dear Sir:

I have called twice at the *Star* office. for the purpose of conferring with you about our discussion on American slavery. but did not find you. I am very anxious, in view of the good which I think may be done, to have the discussion immediately, and will cheerfully meet you at any time and place in this city, which you may propose, provided it shall be soon, as business will call me from the city in a few days. The resolution to be discussed, as you doubtless recollect, is the one which I presented at the Anti-Slavery Convention recently held in this city, at which time you challenged me to debate it, and I accepted the challenge.

"Resolved, That the Constitution of the United States, if strictly construed according to its reading, is anti-slavery in all of its provisions."

The word ALL was accepted from your suggestion. An immediate answer is especially requested.

Respectfully and truly yours,
C. H. Chase

My dear Sir:

I owe you an apology for not sooner publishing and replying to the above letter. On a close examination of the Constitution, I am satisfied that if strictly "construed according to its reading," it is not a pro-slavery instrument; and while I disagree with you as to the inference to be drawn from this admission, you will see that in the resolution, between us there is no question for debate.

I now hold, as I have ever done, that the original intent and meaning of the Constitution (the one given to it by the men who framed it, those who adopted, and the one given to it by the Supreme Court of the United States) makes it a pro-slavery instrument—such an one as I cannot bring myself to vote under, or swear to support.

Very respectfully,
Frederick Douglass

The North Star, February 9, 1849

THE ADDRESS OF SOUTHERN DELEGATES IN CONGRESS TO THEIR CONSTITUTENTS;[11] or, the Address of John C. Calhoun and Forty Other Thieves

That ponderous cloud of dismal terror which for a time overhung the national capital, darkening the blue sky of *"our glorious Union,"* and from which the simple people have only been allowed to see a few fierce, transient flashes, to keep up gloomy apprehension and dismay, has at last discharged its thunder and dissolved. The long-dreaded bolt has reached its maturity and fallen. Men whose hearts were failing for fear of those things which seemed to be coming upon the land, rest from their agonizing fears, look happier, and breathe freer. The apprehended fulmination from the secret conclave of slaveholders and slavetraders, charged with "accounts terrible, of dire confusion," and threatening the very existence of this Republic, turns out to be but an old speech of John C. Calhoun, newly vamped up, and dressed to suit the taste of some forty other slaveholders besides himself. The alarmed and appalled nation has at last seen the baseless character of its fears and we presume will not be so easily alarmed again. The thousand cats in the cellar are reduced to "our cat and another old black cat."

But lest we should be accused of treating this *grave* address with too much levity, we shall venture a brief review of it. The subject of the address is called "the most solemn and important ever presented to the consideration of the Southern people." The subject is summed up in the following ambiguous terms:

"We allude to the conflict between the two great sections of the Union, growing out of a difference of feeling and opinion in reference to the relation existing between the two races, the European and African, which inhabit the Southern section, and the acts of aggression and encroachment to which it has led."

Just read this statement of the subject over again, and try to understand what is meant by it. The "difference of feeling and opinion"—"relation existing" between two races—"inhabit the Southern section"—"acquisition and encroachment." Now, the meaning of all this is, the difference of feeling and opinion in the Northern States from the slaveholders in the Southern States. The people of the North, thank Heaven, are becoming more and more deeply impressed with the awful crime of slavery, and are manifesting it, by hesitating to extend its blighting influence to territory now free; and this is the point that gives "solemnity" to the subject. This is the calamity which produces apprehension and alarm. How carefully the above sentence is worded! European and African races, stands for slaveholders and slaves, which inhabit the Southern section. This very soft way of sliding over the hateful word slavery, shows the slaveholder conscious of his hateful crime, and is itself a confession of guilt. The signers of the address say:

"We have made it a joint address, because we believe that the magnitude of the subject required that it should assume the most impressive and solemn form."

Poor fellows! How much chagrin must they experience when they witness the mirthful levity produced by their impressive solemnity. A band of forty manstealers solemnly defending their right to plunder their fellow-men of all rights and liberties! An "impressive" scene, which ought to excite as much respect as the union of so many sheepstealers! If ever a body of men were deserving of scorn and contempt, this band of fleshmongers do deserve it. Their whole proceedings have amounted to less than an admirable farce.

The address gives a history of the "difference of feeling and opinion in reference to the *relation* between the two faces." Oh! the deceitfulness of sin! This difference disclosed itself in the Convention that framed the Constitution. Would that the difference had been stronger! What the address has to say on the subject of the compromise entered into on the part of the free States with the slave States, every Northern man should ponder well; and draw from it a lesson that will forever preclude him from entering into another like it.

It will be seen that the address assumes a clear recognition of slavery in the United States Constitution, by the clause relating to taxation and representation—that relating to the return of fugitive slaves, and that respecting the importation of slaves. We deem it unfortunate for these honorable menstealers, that in no instance have they been able to find a word in either of these clauses which bears the definition of slaves or slavery. The word slave in all these references, is the word of this conclave, and not of the Constitution.—The language in each of the provisions to which the address refers, though doubtless *intended* to bolster up slavery, and to respect slave property, has been so ambiguously worded as to bear a very different construction; and taken in connection with the preamble of that instrument, the very opposite of the construction given it by this wily band of slaveholders, and they have just reason to apprehend that such a construction may yet be placed upon that instrument as shall prove the downfall of slavery.

But granting that the slaveholding construction is the one by which the nation is to be bound and governed, we are glad to see the issue plainly put to Northern men. We say to the slaveholder, Insist upon your right to make Northern men your bloodhounds, to hunt down your slaves, and return them to bondage. We say, let this be insisted upon, the more strenuously the better, as it will the sooner awaken the North to a sense of their responsibility for slavery, not only in the District of Columbia, and in forts, arsenals and navy-yards, but in the States themselves; and will the sooner see their duty to labor for the removal of slavery from every part of this most unhallowed Union. In any case, nought but slaveholders have anything to fear. The moral sense of the North is becoming restless on this subject. It revolts at the idea of sanctioning slavery, and it must and will seek some mode by which to escape the responsibility of so foul, mean and cruel a system of wrong as is slavery. And it would not be strange if, pressed by the demand for the pound of flesh, they, in turn, should forbid the blood and thus thwart the guilty mansteater of the rewards of the guilty bargain. But we are for admitting that the Constitution is just what these slaveholders in this address say it is; and on conscientious grounds demand the immediate dissolution of the American Union, as required by liberty and the law of the living God. What man will say that the Union ought to exist for a single moment, if under it Northern men are content to act as the bloodhounds of the South, to hunt down, recapture and return to slavery and chains, every brother-man who may be so fortunate as to escape from bondage? Who, who would stain his soul by keeping a bargain so wicked and inhuman as that imposed by these merciless "forty thieves," in the name of the United States' Constitution?—The person that would so do, is a traitor to God and man.

These slaveholders say in their address, that there is not (in the clause which they allege relates to fugitive slaves) "an uncertain or equivocal word to be found in the whole provision." This is not true. If the provision in question refers to slaves escaping from slave States into free States, and was intended to define the right of masters to apprehend their slaves, and the duty of free States to deliver them up, the language used, is most ambiguous and inappropriate.—The words "held to service and labor," for instance, does not necessarily imply the relation of "master and slave," and is rather a description of minors and apprentices, than of slaves. Then the term *person*. Is not this term in itself equivocal? Are slaves, in law, regarded as persons; or are they regarded as property? and is there not a distinction, broad, deep and wide, between property and persons? If they are property, they cannot be regarded by the law as persons; and if they are regarded both in the light of persons and property, the term is imperfect, equivocal, and inappropriate. In this same clause, the term, "shall be delivered upon claim of the party to whom such service or labor may be due," carries upon its face the appearance of a contract, by which one party has a just claim upon the service and labor of another; whereas, the slaveholder has no just claim upon the labor or service of a slave, and the slave has never and can never make any contract with his master, and can never violate a contract, or owe his master any service or labor. It strikes us that the whole provision is uncertain, equivocal, and carries upon its face no recognition of the right of a slaveholder to recapture his slave; so that while we admit that this clause was *intended* to apply to fugitive slaves, and to enable their piratical owners to arrest them, and the free States to deliver them up to such claimants, we utterly deny that the clause in question is either clear or explicit.

Suppose a man from another country should read that clause of the American Constitution, with no other knowledge of the character of American institutions than what he derived from the reading of that instrument, will any one pretend that the clause in question would be thought to apply to slaves? We think not. Nor would he dream of such an outrage, such a savage monstrosity, on reading any other part of the Constitution.—Blot slavery from existence, and the whole frame-work of the Constitution might remain unchanged. There is, therefore, nothing in the Constitution which means slavery—only slavery—and nothing else than slavery. The fact is, the framers of that cunning instrument were ashamed of the *name,* while they had not the honesty to renounce the thing, slavery; and it is the same sense of shame today which leads the friends and defenders of this inhuman system to use the term "peculiar institution," "the *relation* subsisting between the European and African races" and the like. It is with a view to hide their great moral deformity from the eye of the world, and to shield slavery from the assaults and bolts which must ever descend upon it, when its gross form is presented to reflecting and humane men. But we pass from this to another point in the address.

It is this, the clear and positive testimony it bears to the efficiency of the anti-slavery agitation at the North in undermining and destroying slavery at the South. The old moonshine about putting back the cause of emancipation by agitation, has no countenance in this document. Mr. Calhoun and his "forty thieves" see and clearly comprehend the moral forces now operating against slavery, and is too honest towards his fellow-companions in crime to conceal the danger which besets, or to affect to despise that danger. He is proud, haughty, and bitter, but not defiant. He sees in the systematic agitation—the tracts, pictures, papers, pamphlets, and books—societies, lectures, and petitions, the most efficient means to bring about a state of things which will force the South into emancipation. We thank Mr. Calhoun for this testimony. It is given in circumstances which add materially to its intrinsic value.—It is extorted against pride and precedent, two very strong resisting forces. Heretofore, abolitionists have been spoken of as "fanatics," "madmen," altogether a most contemptible body, the only effect of whose efforts would be, to rivet the fetter more closely on the limbs of the slave. That they are not so viewed now, is evident. If mad, there is a "method in their madness," as alarming to Mr. Calhoun and his "forty thieves," as that of Hamlet to his murderous and incestuous uncle. Let abolitionists remember this testimony of Mr. Calhoun, and thank God, and take courage in view of the admitted adaptedness of our measures to the accomplishment of our grand and commanding object—the entire abolition of slavery throughout this country—as well in South Carolina as in California. We like the testimony of Mr. Calhoun better than his reasoning. He says:

"Slavery is a domestic institution. It belongs to the States, each for itself, to decide whether it shall be established or not; and, if it be established, whether it should be abolished or not. Such being the clear and unquestionable rights of the States, it follows necessarily that it would be a flagrant act of aggression on a State, destructive of its rights, and subversive of its independence, for the federal government, or one or more States, or their people, to undertake to force on it the emancipation of its slaves. But it is a sound maxim in politics, as well as law and morals, that no one has a right to do that indirectly, which he cannot do directly, and it may be added with equal truth, to aid, or abet, or countenance another in doing it."

Better call it *Domestic Robbery Institution*. To buy and sell, to brand and scourge human beings with the heavy lash—to rob them of all the just rewards of their labor—to compel them to live in ignorance of their relations to God and man—to blot out the institution of marriage—to herd men and women together like the beasts of the field—to deprive them of the means of learning to read the name of God—to destroy their dignity as human beings—to record their names on the ledger with horses, sheep and swine—to feed them on a peck of corn a-week—to work them under a burning sun in the rice-swamp, cotton-field, sugar-plantation, almost in a state of nudity—to sunder families for the convenience of purchasers—to examine men, women, and children, on the auction-block, as a jockey would examine a horse—to punish them for a word, look, or gesture—to burn their flesh with hot irons—to tear their backs with the poisonous claws of a living cat—to shoot, stab, and hunt humanity with bloodhounds,—for one class of men to have exclusive and absolute power over the bodies and souls of another class of human beings; this, the whole of this infernal catalogue, is comprehended in the soft and innocent term, "*domestic institution*." This is the established order of things in Carolina; and Mr. Calhoun and his "forty thieves" would have the same order of things in California. But now to the doctrine laid down in the above extract.—It goes the length of denying, on *moral* grounds, to any and every person out of the State where slavery exists, the right of saying, looking, or doing anything, directly or indirectly, for the overthrow of slavery.—According to this reasoning, it would be immoral for Northern men to refuse to wear slave-grown cotton, or to eat slave-grown rice and sugar, since by pursuing such a course, peradventure they might decrease the value of the slaves, and thereby indirectly affect the permanence of slavery. We are not to write, speak, or publish anything on the subject of human slavery, lest it serve to darken the fame of slavery, and lessen it in the popular estimation, and thereby indirectly destroy slavery, by exalting liberty. To do so, would necessarily be a flagrant aggression, a violation of the rights of a State, and subversive of its government. For what we have no right to do directly by legislation, we have no right to do indirectly by any other means.—This is strange logic for one of the most powerful minds and renowned statesmen that America affords. Coming from another quarter, it would demand no answer or comment; but from such a man, endorsed by such a company, read so universally, and put forth so imposingly, and solemnly, aiming as it does, at the very foundation of the anti-slavery movement, it may be proper to spend a few thoughts upon it.

How completely has slavery triumphed over the mind of this strong man! It holds full, complete and absolute control in his mind; so much so, that seeing it, he cannot and does not desire to see anything else than slavery. The right of speech, the freedom of the press, the liberty of assembling, and the right of petition, have in his judgment no rightful existence in the Constitution of the United States.

Slavery is there; he knows it to be there; it has a right to be there; and anything inconsistent with it is wrong, immoral, and has no right to be there. This is evidently the state of mind which Mr. Calhoun brings to the consideration of this subject. To reduce his reasoning to its real point and pith, it amounts to this—that where a people have no power to legislate for the overthrow of what *they think* an evil, they have no moral right to think, or speak, or do anything else which may induce those who have legislative power to exercise it for the removal of such evil. It is on this reasoning that he builds his complaint against the Northern States, as wanting in respect to the institutions and sovereignty of the Southern States; that they have not by legislative enactment silenced the voice of free speech, and suppressed the publications of the abolitionists. If Mr. Calhoun is right in his first position, he is right in his conclusion; but he is wrong in both. We have no legislative power to dethrone the Queen of England, but have we no moral right to say that England would be better under a republican form of government? We have no legislative right or power to alter or abolish the British tariff; but have we no moral right to say that it is unequal and oppressive, and that England would be better off without than with it. We have no legislative power to abolish the union between England and Ireland; yet is it not obviously our right to speak and write in favor of the repeal of the Union? Mr. Calhoun sinks the rights of the man in the duties of the citizen, and by confounding things which are separate and distinct, perpetrates a logical fallacy. Above and before all human institutions, stands the right of sympathizing with the oppressed and denouncing the oppressors of mankind.

Slavery is not only a wrong done to the slave, but an outrage upon man—not merely a curse to the South, but to the whole Union, and has no rightful existence anywhere.—Slaveholders have no rights more than any other thief or pirate. They have forfeited even the right to live, and if the slave should put every one of them to the sword to-morrow, who dare pronounce the penalty disproportioned to the crime, or say that the criminals deserved less than death at the hands of their long-abused chattels? All this talk about the rights of slaveholders and the rights of slave States, is the height of impudence. By what equity, by what morality are they justified? and upon what foundation do they rest their right of property in human flesh? Why, none other or better than may be set up by a band of robbers. We meet John C. Calhoun and the "forty thieves" associated with him, as being no better, or more entitled to respect, than a ship's company of pirates; and the time is coming when they will be so regarded generally. It shall not avail that the Constitution and laws sanction slavery. "There is a law above all earthly statutes, written on the heart," and by that law, unchangeable and eternal, no man can be or hold a slave.

We intended to have said something on the extension of slavery in connection with our remarks on this address, but have neither time nor space sufficient for the purpose. We leave this task to the "free soilers," both in the Whig and the Democratic ranks. The journals of each of these parties will attend to the address on this point, as well as to the right of Congress to break up the disgraceful and inhuman slave-marts in the District of Columbia, and abolish the whole system of wickedness, root and branch. As to the probable effect of this address, we believe that its most injurious consequences have already taken place. Its power to injure is destroyed. It was terrible in the distance, but tame on its approach. In the South, it may stir a slight fever. The slaveholders may be alarmed, enraged, and may "swear terribly" about it, but the North will despise the address, and the "grey fox" and "forty thieves" who gave it to the world. We think it an excellent means of agitating the public mind on the subject of slavery, and promoting the anti-slavery cause, and should not regret if Mr. Calhoun would favor us with another meeting, and make another address. We are quite sure that another meeting, though it would not probably be so large as the first, would be no less effective in exciting contempt for the whole slave power of the country.—F. D.

The North Star, February 9, 1849

THE CONSTITUTION AND SLAVERY

The assertion which we made five weeks ago, that "the Constitution, *if strictly construed according to its reading,*" is not a pro-slavery instrument, has excited some interest amongst our Anti-Slavery brethren. Letters have reached us from different quarters on the subject. Some of these express agreement and pleasure with our views, and others, surprise and dissatisfaction. Each class of opinion and feeling is represented in the letters which we have placed in another part of this week's paper. The one from our friend Gerrit Smith, represents the view which the Liberty party take of this subject, and that of Mr. Robert Forten is consistent with the ground occupied by a majority of the American Anti-Slavery Society.

Whether we shall be able to set ourselves right in the minds of those on the one side of this question or the other, and at the same time vindicate the correctness of our former assertion, remains to be seen. Of one thing, however, we can assure our readers, and that is, that we bring to the consideration of this subject no partisan feelings, nor the slightest wish to make ourselves consistent with the creed of either Anti-Slavery party, and that our only aim is to know what is truth and what is duty in respect to the matter in dispute, holding ourselves perfectly free to change our opinion in any direction, and at any time which may be indicated by our immediate apprehension of truth, unbiased by the smiles or frowns of any class or party of abolitionists. The only truly consistent man is he who will, for the sake of being right today, contradict what he said wrong yesterday. "Sufficient unto the day is the evil thereof." True stability consists not in being of the same opinion now as formerly, but in a fixed principle of honesty, even urging us to the adoption or rejection of that which may seem to us true or false at the ever-present now.

Before entering upon a discussion of the main question, it may be proper to remove a misapprehension into which Gerrit Smith and Robert Forten seem to have fallen, in respect to what we mean by the term, "strictly construed according to its reading," as used by us in regard to the Constitution. Upon a second reading of these words, we can readily see how easily they can be made to mean more than we intended. What we meant then, and what we would be understood to mean now, is simply this—that the Constitution of the United States, standing alone, and construed *only* in the light of its letter, without reference to the opinions of the men who framed and adopted it, or to the uniform, universal and undeviating practice of the nation under it, from the time of its adoption until now, is not a pro-slavery instrument. Of this admission we are perfectly willing to give our esteemed friend Gerrit Smith, and all who think with him on this subject, the fullest benefit; accompanied, however, with this explanation, that it was made with no view to give the public to understand that we held this construction to be the proper one of that instrument, and that it was drawn out merely because we were unwilling to go before the public on so narrow an issue, and one about which there could be so little said on either side. How a document would appear under one construction, is one thing; but whether the construction be the right one, is quite another and a very different thing. Confounding these two things, has led Gerrit Smith to think too favorably of us, and Robert Forten too unfavorably. We may agree with the Roman Catholic, that the language of Christ, with respect to the sacrament, if construed according to reading, teaches the doctrine of transubstantiation. But the admission is not final, neither are we understood by so doing, to sanction that irrational though literal doctrine. Neither Roman Catholic nor Protestant could attach any importance to such an admission. It would neither afford pleasure to the Catholic, nor pain to the Protestant. Hoping that we have now made ourselves understood on this point, we proceed to the general question.

THE CONSTITUTIONALITY OF SLAVERY

The Constitution of the United States.—What is it? Who made it? For whom and for what was it made? Is it from heaven or from men? How, and in what light are we to understand it? If it be divine, divine light must be our means of understanding it; if human, humanity, with all its vices and crimes, as well as its virtues, must help us to a proper understanding of it. All attempts to explain it in the light of heaven must fail. It is human, and must be explained in the light of those maxims and principles which human beings have laid down as guides to the understanding of all written instruments, covenants, contracts and agreements, emanating from human beings, and to which human beings are parties, both on the first and the second part. It is in such a light that we propose to examine the Constitution; and in this light we hold it to be a most cunningly-devised and wicked compact, demanding the most constant and earnest efforts of the friends of righteous freedom for its complete overthrow. It was "conceived in sin, and shapen in iniquity." But this will be called mere declamation, and assertion—mere "heat without light"—sound and fury signify nothing.—Have it so. Let us then argue the question with all the coolness and clearness of which an unlearned fugitive slave, smarting under the wrongs inflicted by this unholy Union, is capable. We cannot talk "lawyer like" about law—about its emanating from the bosom of God!—about government, and of its seat in the great heart of the Almighty!—nor can we, in connection with such an ugly matter-of-fact looking thing as the United States Constitution, bring ourselves to split hairs about the alleged legal rule of interpretation, which declares that an "act of the Legislature may be set aside when it contravenes natural justice." We have to do with facts, rather than theory. The Constitution is not an abstraction. It is a living, breathing fact, exerting a mighty power over the nation of which it is the bond of Union.

Had the Constitution dropped down from the blue overhanging sky, upon a land uncursed by slavery, and without an interpreter, although some difficulty might have occurred in applying its manifold provisions, yet so cunningly is it framed, that no one would have imagined that it recognized or sanctioned slavery. But having a terrestrial, and not a celestial origin, we find no difficulty in ascertaining its meaning in all the parts which we allege to relate to slavery. Slavery existed before the Constitution, in the very States by whom it was made and adopted.—Slaveholders took a large share in making it. It was made in view of the existence of slavery, and in a manner well calculated to aid and strengthen that heaven-daring crime.

Take, for instance, article 1st, section 2d, to wit: "Representatives and direct taxes shall be apportioned among the several States which may be included within this Union, according to their respective numbers, which shall be determined by adding to the whole number of *free* persons, including those bound to service for a term of years, and including Indians not taxed, *three-fifths of all other persons*."

A diversity of persons are here described—*persons* bound to service for a *term of years,* Indians not taxed, and three-fifths of *all other persons*. Now, we ask, in the name of common sense, can there be an honest doubt that, in States where there are slaves, that they are included in this basis of representation? To us, it is as plain as the sun in the heavens that this clause does, and was intended to mean, that the slave States should enjoy a representation of their human chattels under this Constitution. Beside, the term free, which is generally, though not always, used as the correlative of slave, "all other persons," settles the question forever that slaves are here included.

It is contended on this point by Lysander Spooner and others, that the words, "all other persons," used in this article of the Constitution, relates *only* to aliens. We deny that the words will bear any such construction. Are we to presume that the Constitution, which so carefully points out a class of persons for exclusion, such as "Indians not taxed," would be silent with respect to another class which it was meant equally to exclude? We have never studied logic, but it does seem to us that such a presumption would be very much like an absurdity. And the absurdity is all the more glaring, when it is remembered that the language used immediately after the words "excluding Indians not taxed," (having done with exclusions) it includes *"all other persons."* It is as easy to suppose that the Constitution contemplates *including* Indians, (against its express declaration to the contrary,) as it is to suppose that it should be construed to mean the exclusion of slaves from the basis of representation, against the express language, "including all other persons." Where all are included, none remain to be excluded. The reasonings of those who take the opposite view of this clause, appears very much like quibbling, to use no harsher word. One thing is certain about this clause of the Constitution. It is this—that under it, the slave system has enjoyed a large and domineering representation in Congress, which has given laws to the whole Union in regard to slavery, ever since the formation of the government.

Satisfied that the view we have given of this clause of the Constitution is the only sound interpretation of it, we throw at once all those parts and particulars of the instrument which refer to slavery, and constitute what we conceive to be the slaveholding compromises of the Constitution, before the reader, and beg that he will look with candor upon the comments which we propose to make upon them.

"Art. 5th, Sec. 8th.—Congress shall have power to suppress insurrections."

"Art. 1st, Sec. 9th.—The migration or importation of any such persons as any of the States now existing shall think proper to admit, shall not be prohibited by Congress prior to the year one thousand eight hundred and eight; but a tax or a duty may be imposed, not exceeding ten dollars for each person."

"Art. 4th, Sec. 2d.—No person held to service or labor in one State, escaping into another, shall in consequence of any law or regulation therein, be discharged from such service or labor, but shall be delivered up on claim of the party to whom such service or labor may be due."

"Art. 4th, Sec. 4th.—The United States shall guarantee to every State in this Union a Republican form of Government; and shall protect each of them against invasion; and on application of the Legislature, or of the Executive, (when the Legislature cannot be convened,) against domestic violence."*

*Clauses in Constitution, quoted as in Douglass' editorial—*Ed.*

The first article and ninth section is a full, complete and broad sanction of the slavetrade for twenty years. In this compromise of the Constitution, the parties to it pledged the national arm to protect that infernal trade for twenty years. While all other subjects of commerce were left under the control of Congress, this species of commerce alone was Constitutionally exempted. And why was this the case? Simply because South Carolina and Georgia declared, through their delegates that framed the Constitution, that they would not come into the Union if this traffic in human flesh should be prohibited. Mr. Rutledge, of South Carolina, (a distinguished member of the Convention that framed the Constitution,) said, "if the Convention thinks that North Carolina, South Carolina, and Georgia, will ever agree to the plan, *unless their right to import slaves be untouched,* the expectation is vain." Mr. Pinckney said, South Carolina could never receive the plan, *"if it prohibits the slavetrade."* In consequence of the determination of these States to stand out of the Union in case the traffic in human flesh should be prohibited, and from one general desire to establish a Union, this ninth section of the first article was adopted, as *a compromise;* and shameful as it is, it is by no means more shameful than others which preceded and succeeded it. The slaveholding South, by that unyielding tenacity and consistency with which they usually contend for their measures, triumphed, and the doughface North was brought to the disgraceful terms in question, just as they have been ever since on all questions touching the subject of slavery.

As a compensation for their base treachery to human freedom and justice, the North were permitted to impose a tax of ten dollars for each person imported, with which to swell the coffers of the national treasury, thus baptising the infant Republic with blood-stained gold.

Art. 4, Sec. 2.—This article was adopted with a view to restoring fugitive slaves to their masters—ambiguous, to be sure, but sufficiently explicit to answer the end sought to be attained. Under it, and in accordance with it, the Congress enacted the atrocious "law of '93," making it penal in a high degree to harbor or shelter the flying fugitive. The whole nation that adopted it, consented to become kidnappers, and the whole land converted into slave-hunting ground.

Art. 4, Sec. 4—Pledges the national arm to protect the slaveholder from *domestic violence,* and is the safeguard of the Southern tyrant against the vengeance of the outraged and plundered slave. Under it, the nation is bound to do the bidding of the slaveholder, to bring out the whole naval and military power of the country, to crush the refractory slaves into obedience to their cruel masters. Thus has the North, under the Constitution, not only consented to form bulwarks around the system of slavery, with all its bloody enormities, to prevent the slave from escape, but has planted its uncounted feet and tremendous weight on the heaving hearts of American bondmen, to prevent them from rising to gain their freedom. Could Pandemonium devise a Union more inhuman, unjust, and affronting to God and man, than this? Yet such is the Union consummated under the Constitution of the United States. It is truly a compact demanding immediate disannulment, and one which, with our view of its wicked requirements, we can never enter.

We might just here drop the pen and the subject, and assume the Constitution to be what we have briefly attempted to prove it to be, radically and essentially pro-slavery, in fact as well as in its tendency; and regard our position to be correct beyond the possibility of an honest doubt, and treat those who differ from us as mere cavillers, bent upon making the worse appear the better reason; or we might anticipate the objections which are supposed to be valid against that position. We are, however, disposed to do neither.—We have too much respect for the men opposed to us to do the former, and have too strong a desire to have those objections put in their most favorable light, to do the latter.—We are prepared to hear all sides, and to give the arguments of our opponents a candid consideration. Where an honest expression of views is allowed, Truth has nothing to fear.

And now if our friend Gerrit Smith desires to be heard on the other side, the columns of the *North Star* are at his service. We can assure him that he cannot have a stronger wish to turn every rightful instrumentality against slavery, than we have; and if the Constitution can be so turned, and he can satisfy us of the fact, we shall readily, gladly and zealously turn our feeble energies in that direction. The case which our friend Gerrit Smith put to us in his letter is a good one, but fails in a most important particular, and that is, *analogy*. The only likeness which we can see in the supposed case of a bargain with Brown, to that of the bargain entered into by the North and the South, is that there is gross dishonesty in both. So far, there is a striking similarity, but no further. The parties that made the Constitution, aimed to cheat and defraud the slave, who was not himself a party to the compact or agreement. It was entered into understandingly on both sides. They both designed to purchase their freedom and safety at the expense of the imbruted slave. The North were willing to become the body guards of slavery—suppressing insurrection—returning fugitive slaves to bondage—importing slaves for twenty years, and as much longer as the Congress should see fit to leave it unprohibited, and virtually to give slaveholders three votes for every five slaves they could plunder from Africa, and all this to form a Union by which to repel invasion, and otherwise promote their interest. No, friend Smith, we are not asked to act the honorable part of *"Judge Douglass"* with respect to this "contract," but to become a guilty party to it, and in reply we say—No!—F. D.

The North Star, March 16, 1849

WHAT GOOD HAS THE FREE SOIL MOVEMENT DONE?

The *North Star* in common with many other anti-slavery journals, gave to this movement at its commencement an earnest word of encouragement. It was regarded as a hopeful movement, containing within itself the elements of progress. The Grand National Convention held at Buffalo, indicated a vigorous vitality in the movement "deeper, sterner, and stronger," than what appeared upon the surface of its written proceedings. It however challenged favor more on account of what it might become, than what it was at that time. Its shortcomings at the commencement, were set down to the newly awakened state of the moral sense of those who gave "form and presence" to the movement. The comprehensive mantle of charity was thrown over the defective Free Soil platform. The circumstances in which the originators of that movement were placed, the *crisis* to be met, the early associations of its leading spirits, the necessity and desire for union, and the difficulty of securing it on high moral grounds—were pleaded in extenuation of the low standard erected by the Free Soil Party; and not without effect. Many good men felt that here was the time, the place, and the platform upon which to work decisively against the monster slavery, and they rushed into it....

In what we now propose to say of the free soil movement, we would not be understood to deny that it has done some good. Such a conclusion would be very unjust and wholly unnecessary to establish the point which seems to us true of its action and history thus far. Nor do we mean to find fault with political action, in a party form against slavery. There is no question with us that the anti-slavery movement will always be followed at a greater or lesser distance by a political party of some sort. It is inevitable. While anti-slavery views are propagated and the public mind is stirred and divided upon them, there will always be found politicians who will lean to the one or the other side. Each taking up the views of their respective movements, in the least objectionable manner, and thereby gaining political conspicuousness if not victory and the spoils of office.

But to the question, What good has the free soil movement done? Much in many ways but not every way. It has for once rallied a large number of the people of the North in apparent hostility to the whole system of American slavery; it has subjected this vile abomination to a wide-spread exposure; it has rebuked and humbled quite a number of corrupt and cringing politicians, by driving them to change their positions on this subject, and driven them from office. It has awakened the whole south to a sense of danger, and perhaps has checked the proud and arrogant pretensions of the slaveholder with respect to the extension of slavery. So far so good. It shall have all the credit to which it is entitled. There are men now connected with it of whom we never think but with grateful esteem and respect. Their voices have been uplifted boldly and powerfully in the councils of the nation in behalf of justice, freedom and humanity, and who must always be remembered with an abounding heart of gratitude by one who has endured as we have done, the horrors of slavery. But even these noble spirits cannot save the movement from cause of complaint, or make it worthy of the support of those who would labor effectually against slavery. The reasons which once seemed to weigh in its favor have ceased.

It promised much and has performed little. It appeared to be an active movement, flooding the land with tracts, pamphlets and papers of various descriptions, acting upon, and changing the moral sentiments from *Pro,* to *Anti*-Slavery. It proves to be a dull and indolent concern, gone to sleep and refusing to wake, until roused by the thunders of another political campaign. Not a single lecturer of that movement, dots the surface of this wide field of labor. It promised to be a progressive movement. It has not even been a standstill one, but has actually proved a retrograding movement, gradually disappearing, leaving nought but the dead body of hunkerism to occupy its place. Instead of approximating to the true standard of abolitionism, and thereby rendering the movement worthy of the countenance of anti-slavery men, it is actually seeking alliance with the enemies of that holy cause. The Free Soil movement has done, and is still doing much harm. It is standing in the way, blocking up the path, and cutting off supplies, from a higher and holier movement than it has ever aspired to be. Its papers have supplanted and crushed others which but for these, would have prospered and been useful to the cause they were established to advocate. It has swallowed up the Liberty party press of the land, and weakened its once powerful testimony against slavery. It has taken off from the old Anti-slavery platform many whose usefulness depended almost wholly upon the character and energy of their leaders, and begot in the public mind indefinite and intangible notions as to the means of overthrowing slavery, where before all was plain and straight-forward. Upon the whole it has left the public mind in a more difficult state to deal with than it found it. It found it agitated, divided, and the lines drawn distinctly, but has left it dull, stupid, undefined, and indifferent. Instead of making the task of the abolitionist lighter, it has increased his burdens. The work for abolitionists to do now, is to press their old issues upon the public mind with redoubled earnestness and zeal, blowing away the dust and fog of half-way measures, and doctrines. No abolitionist, who is truly such, will be gratified with, or encourage any measure or doctrine that does not contemplate slavery everywhere as marked out for destruction. It is a foul system—at war with the happiness of man and the laws of God, and there must be no compromise with it. To denounce it in California, to oppose its introduction in New Mexico, and give it constitutional and political sanction in New Orleans, is worse than inconsistent, and can only end in a revelation of folly and hypocrisy, without advancing the cause of freedom at all—F. D.

The North Star, March 25, 1849

TO GERRIT SMITH

Rochester, 30th March, 1849

My Dear Sir:

You kindly inquired if the *North Star is well supported.* I am sorry to say that it is not. I will explain the reasons. Many of my best friends, especially in the East, look upon it as an unnecessary, if not a useless instrumentality for promoting the cause of the slave, and believe I would be far more serviceable as a public speaker than I can be as an editor. I started the paper against their wishes and against their advice, they feel therefore little or no interest in its support. Besides this, the paper is not a party paper and looks with grateful friendship upon all classes of abolitionists and is not disposed to denounce as knaves those who believe that voting is a duty. The failure to do this is perhaps the most grievous omission of which the paper is guilty in the eyes especially of my Boston friends. On the other hand, the paper is not enough of a Liberty party paper, or in other words it is too strongly Garrisonian to be looked upon with much favor by Liberty party men. In a word there does not appear to be charity and magnanimity enough among the two classes of anti-slavery friends to support a paper that can see good in each party.

My friends in England gave me two thousand Dollars with which to commence, and I very foolishly laid out more than one half the money in printing materials such as press, types, cases, stands, etc., instead of contracting with some experienced printer to publish the paper for so much per week, until I could see if the paper could be sustained. This has proved to be quite a serious mistake. My money is now all gone—whereas if I had kept the two thousand dollars—and only paid it out as necessity required, I should have a much longer time allowed me in which to establish the paper than I now have. I am now about two hundred dollars in debt, and mean to leave the paper in the hands of my friend Nell while I go out and get the money with which to pay it. The paper shall be sustained if any effort of mine can sustain it, or cause it to be sustained. Whether the paper is doing good or not, perhaps is not for me to say, but I believe it is doing good. The simple fact that such a paper exists is serviceable to the cause of my despised and maligned race.

I thank you sincerely for the kind invitations you have given me to visit you at Peterboro, and hope the day is not distant when I shall have the pleasure of seeing you under your own roof. Please to remember me kindly to Mrs. Smith, who though I never saw but once, and that in a public meeting, I yet remember with so much distinctness, that I should know her again if I should meet her many years hence.

I am, dear Sir, Most truly yours,
Frederick Douglass

The dear little boy of ours of whom I spoke in the paper of today as being sick seems much better this morning. We have also a dear little girl under our roof—only one week old. Mrs. Douglass is doing very well—up nearly all day yesterday.

F. D.

Gerrit Smith Papers, Syracuse University

TO H. G. WARNER, ESQ., (Editor of the *Rochester Courier*)

Sir:

My reasons—I will not say my apology, for addressing to you this letter, will become evident, by perusing the following brief statement of facts.

About the middle of August of the present year—deeply desiring to give my daughter, a child between nine and ten years old, the advantages of a good school—and learning that "Seward Seminary" of this city was an institution of that character—I applied to its principal, Miss Tracy, for the admission of my daughter into that Seminary. The principal—after making suitable enquiries into the child's mental qualifications, and informing me of the price of tuition per term, agreed to receive the child into the school at the commencement of the September term. Here we parted. I went home, rejoicing that my child was about to enjoy advantages for improving her mind, and fitting her for a useful and honorable life. I supposed that the principal would be as good as her word—and was more disposed to his belief, when I learned that she was an abolitionist—a woman of religious principles and integrity—and would be faithful in the performance of her promises, as she had been prompt in making them. In all this I have been grievously—if not shamefully disappointed.

While absent from home, on a visit to Cleveland, with a view to advance the cause of education and freedom among my despised fellow countrymen—with whom I am in all respects identified, the September term of the "Seward Seminary" commenced, and my daughter was promptly sent to that school.—But instead of receiving her into the school according to agreement—and as in honor the principal was bound to do, she was merely thrust into a room separate from all other scholars, and in this prison-like solitary confinement received the occasional visits of a teacher appointed to instruct her. On my return home, I found her still going to school, and not knowing the character of the treatment extended to her, I asked with a light heart, as I took her to my side, well, my daughter, how do you get on at the Seminary? She answered with tears in her eyes, *"I get along pretty well, but father, Miss Tracy does not allow me to go into the room with the other scholars because I am colored."* Stung to the heart's core by this grievous statement, and suppressing my feelings as well as I could, I went immediately to the Seminary to remonstrate with the principal against the cruelty and injustice of treating my child as a criminal on account of her color—subjecting her to solitary confinement because guilty of a skin not colored like her own. In answer to all that I could say against such treatment, I was answered by the principal, that since she promised to receive the child into school, she had consulted with the trustees, (a body of persons I believe unknown to the public,) and that they were opposed to the child's admission to the school—that she thought at first of disregarding their opposition, but when she remembered how much they had done for her in sustaining the institution, she did not feel at liberty to do so; but she thought if I allowed her to remain and be taught separately for a term or more, that the prejudice might be overcome, and the child admitted into the school with the other young ladies and misses. At a loss to know what to do for the best interest of the child, I consulted with Mrs. Douglass and others, and the result of the consultation was, to take my child from the Seminary, as allowing her to remain there in such circumstances, could only serve to degrade her in her own eyes, and those of the other scholars attending the school. Before, however, carrying out my determination to withdraw the child from the Seminary, Miss Tracy, the principal, submitted the question of the child's reception to each scholar individually, and I am sorry to say, in a manner well calculated to rouse their prejudices against her. She told them if there was one objection to receiving her, she should be excluded; and said if any of them felt that she had a prejudice, and that that prejudice needed to be strengthened, that they might have time to whisper among themselves, in order to increase and strengthen that prejudice. To one young lady who voted to receive the child, she said, as if in astonishment; "did you mean to vote so? Are you *accustomed* to black persons?" The young lady stood silent; the question was so extraordinary, and withal so ambiguous, that she knew not what answer to make to it. Despite however, of the unwomanly conduct of the principal, (who, whatever may be her religious faith, has not yet learned the simplest principle of Christianity—do to others as ye would that others should do unto you)—thanks to the uncorruptible virtue of childhood and youth, in the fulness of their affectionate hearts, they welcomed my child among them, to share with them the blessings and privileges of the school; and when asked where she should sit if admitted, several young ladies shouted "By me, by me, by me." After this manifestation of sentiment on the part of the scholars, one would have supposed that all opposition on the part of the principal would have ceased; but this was not the case. The child's admission was subjected to a severer test. Each scholar was then told by the principal, that the question must be submitted to their parents, and that if one parent objected, the child would not be received into the school. The next morning my child went to school as usual, but returned with her books and other materials, saying that one person objected, and that she was therefore excluded from the Seminary.

Now, sir, these are the whole facts, with one important exception, and that fact is, that you are the person, the only person of all the parents sending young ladies and misses to that Seminary, who was hardened and mean enough to take the responsibility of excluding that child from school. I say, to you exclusively belongs the honor or infamy, of attempting to degrade an innocent child by excluding her from the benefit of attending a respectable school.

If this were a private affair, only affecting myself and family, I should possibly allow it to pass without attracting public attention to it; but such is not the case. It is a deliberate attempt to degrade and injure a large class of persons, whose rights and feelings have been the common sport of yourself, and such persons as yourself, for ages, and I think it unwise to allow you to do so with impunity.—Thank God, oppressed and plundered as we are, and have been, we are not without help. We have a press, open and free, and have ample means by which we are able to proclaim our wrongs as a people, and your own infamy, and that proclamation shall be as complete as the means in my power can make it. There is a sufficient amount of liberality in the public mind of Rochester to see that justice is done to all parties, and upon that liberality I rely. The young ladies of the school who saw the child, and had the best means of determining whether her presence in the schoolroom would be offensive or degrading to them, have decided in favor of admitting her, without a dissenting vote. Out of all the parents to whom the question of her admission was submitted, not one, except yourself, objected. You are in a minority of *one*. You may not remain so; there are perhaps others, whom you may corrupt, and make as much like yourself in the blindness of prejudice, as any ordinarily wicked person can be.

But you are still in a minority, and if I mistake not, you will be in a *despised minority*.—You have already done serious injury to Seward Seminary. Three young ladies left the school immediately after the exclusion of my daughter, and I have heard of three more, who had intended to go, but who have now declined going to that institution, because it has given its sanction to that anti-democratic, and ungodly caste. I am also glad to inform you that you have not succeeded as you hoped to do, in depriving my child of the means of a decent education, or the privilege of going to an excellent school. She had not been excluded from Seward Seminary five hours, before she was gladly welcomed into another quite as respectable, and *equally* christian to the one from which she was excluded. She now sits in a school among children as pure, and as white as you or yours, and no one is offended. Now I should like to know how much better are you than me, and how much better your children than mine? We are both worms of the dust, and our children are like us. We differ in color, it is true, (and not much in that respect,) but who is to decide which color is most pleasing to God, or most honorable among men? But I do not wish to waste words or argument on one whom I take to be as destitute of honorable feeling, as he has shown himself full of pride and prejudice.

Frederick Douglass

The North Star, March 30, 1849

COMMENTS ON GERRIT SMITH'S ADDRESS [12]

It will be remembered that Mr. Smith referred us in last week's paper to this address, for his views respecting the Constitutionality of slavery; and virtually said to us, Dispose of these, and if it shall then be necessary, you shall have more. To us, the address is quite unsatisfactory and unsound. About what a government ought to be so far as relates to a crime like slavery, there is no difference of opinion between us. That it is the duty of a government to protect the rights and liberties of its subjects, there is no question; and that that government which fails to do this is extremely guilty, there is equal agreement. What a government ought to do, is one thing; but not the thing germane to the question at issue between Mr. Smith and ourselves. That government ought to be just, merciful, holy, is granted. The question is not, however, what a government ought to be, or to do, but what the government of the United States is *authorized to be, and to do, by the Constitution of the United States.* The two questions should be kept separate, that the simplest may understand, as blending them only leads to confusion.

It is because we hold civil government to be solemnly bound to protect the weak against the strong, the oppressed against the oppressor, the few against the many, and to secure the humblest subject in the full possession of his rights of person and of property, that we utterly abhor and repudiate this government and the Constitution as a dark and damning conspiracy against all the purposes of government. Both its framers and administrators were, and have been until now, little better than a band of pirates.—We would make clean work of both the government and the Constitution, and not amend or force a new construction upon either, contradicted by the whole history of the nation; but would abolish both, and reconstruct a Constitution and a government which shall better answer the ends of justice. To think of good government in a Union with slaveholders, and under a Constitution framed by slaveholders, the practical operation of which for sixty years has been to strengthen, sustain and spread slavery, does seem to us delusive. We are not for mending old clothes with new cloth, or putting new wine into old bottles, but for starting afresh under a new and higher light than our piratical fathers saw, and form a Constitution and government which shall be so clear and explicit that no doubt can be entertained as to its minutest purposes.

That this cannot be truthfully affirmed of our present Constitution, we need not insist upon at this time. Even our friend Smith virtually admits that it would be dangerous to leave the question of the slave's redemption to be decided in the light of the Constitution. The "old tattered parchment" receives no great deference from him after all. Disdaining it altogether, he says, *"Whatever may be said of the lawfulness of slavery, government must abolish it. If it have a Constitution under which it cannot abolish slavery, then it must override the Constitution, and abolish slavery. But whether under or over the Constitution, it must abolish slavery."* We like this for its whole-souled devotion to a glorious object. It is revolutionary, and looks as much like the fanaticism of Wendell Phillips and William Lloyd Garrison, as if it had been cast in their mould. In plain terms, Mr. Smith is for the abolition of slavery, whether in accordance with, or in violation of, the Constitution; and while the declaration is worthy of his noble heart, we cannot think such of his head. The doctrine laid down in this declaration, runs through the whole address, and gives it a vigor and warmth from beginning to end. We shall therefore express a few thoughts upon it.

It will be seen that the doctrine in question makes the government superior to, and independent of, the Constitution, which is the very charter of the government, and without which the government is nothing better than a lawless mob, acting without any other or higher authority than its own convictions or impulses as to what is right or wrong. If this doctrine be sound, it is a mere farce to have a written Constitution at all; for if the government can override and violate its Constitution in one point, it may do so in all.—There is no limit, or safety, or certainty. If it can abolish slavery in violation of the Constitution, because it conflicts with the moral sentiments of the majority, the same may be done in other cases for the same reason. All the safe-guards of that instrument, providing for its own interpretation and its own amendment, are worthless and needless, if this doctrine be true, and government will merely be the voice of an ever-shifting majority, be that good or evil.

Among the causes which have convulsed and revolutionized Europe during the past year, none has been more prominent or effective than the want and rational desire of the people for Constitutional government—not an unwritten, but a written Constitution, accurately defining the powers of government. But these revolutions and Constitutions would be a mere mockery, if government has a character independent of, and powers superior to the Constitution creating it. In the light of such doctrine, Constitutions are impotent and useless, and not worth the trouble of making them, to say nothing of the blood and treasure expended in their support. We hold this doctrine to be radically unsound, (and although brought forward to promote a noble object,) its tendency immoral. We say to our friend Smith, and to all others who sympathize with his views on this subject, If you profess to hold to the Constitution, maintain its provisions. If you cannot, in accordance with your conscience, perform its requirements, or submit to its limitations, then we say, it is your plain duty to come out from it, forsake it, repudiate it, abandon it, do anything rather than seem to be in harmony with an instrument which you would set aside and destroy. Do not, for the sake of honesty and truth, solemnly swear to protect and defend an instrument which it is your firm and settled purpose to disregard and violate in any one particular. Such a course would unsettle all confidence, invert all the principles of trust and reliance which bind society together, and leave mankind to all the horrors of anarchy, and all the confusion of Babel. We hold in respect to this, as the apostle held of old in respect to another Constitution—"They that be under the law, are bound to do the things contained in the law." We repudiate the law, and the things contained in it, while friend Smith holds to the law, but makes it subject to the understanding of right. But, says Mr. Smith—

"Civil Government is to protect rights; and that it might as well, be openly repudiating its functions, and destroying its very existence, as to be giving countenance to searches after authorities for destroying rights. Laws, which interpret, define, secure rights, Government is to respect: and laws, which mistakingly, yet honestly, aim at this end, it is not to despise. But laws, which are enacted to destroy rights, it should trample under foot,—for, to say nothing worse of them, they are a gross insult upon it, inasmuch as they are a shameless attempt to turn it from good to evil, and from its just and Heaven-intended uses, to uses of a diametrically opposite character."

Here again, the argument goes to the extent of assuming, that civil government in this country has a separate existence from the Constitution, and, as if the Constitution were not the supreme law of the land, and that the government can consistently overthrow the Constitution whenever it shall think proper to do so. In answer to this statement, it is enough to say that the government of the United States is limited in its powers and action by the Constitution, and that beyond those limits it cannot go, by any pretext whatever; and that the Supreme Court, the appointed agent to decide the meaning of that instrument, has only to decide a law to be unconstitutional, and it is null and void.—It may indeed be said, that the Supreme Court of the United States has no right to legalize what is unjust and in derogation or against human freedom; but the answer is, that that is legal in this country which is Constitutional, and that the Supreme Court has no conscience above the Constitution of the United States, and certainly no power to set that instrument aside, either by declaring it to be null and void, or wrest it from its true intent and meaning, by a class of rules unknown and unsustained by a single precedent in this country.

As to what Mr. Smith says of determining the meaning of the Constitution by its letter alone, and disregarding as utterly worthless the intentions of the framers of that instrument, it may require consideration when he gives us some fixed and settled legal rules sustaining his views on this point. Such rules may exist, but we have not yet seen them; and until we do, we shall continue to understand the Constitution not only in the light of its letter, but in view of its history, the meaning attached to it by its framers, the men who adopted it, and the circumstances in which it was adopted. We have not read law very extensively, but so far as we have read, we have found many rules of interpretation favoring this mode of understanding the Constitution of the United States, and none against it, though there may be such.

It can scarcely be necessary, after what we have already said, to spend much time upon the following extraordinary declaration of Mr. Smith, respecting the Constitution, in which he declares that it "is drawn up with the intelligent and steadfast purpose of having it serve and be forever fully and gloriously identified with the cause of liberty, republicanism and equal rights, must of necessity be shut against the claims and pretensions of slavery." That it was drawn up with the purpose of serving the cause of the white man's liberty, is true; but that it was meant to serve the cause of the black man's liberty, is false. That a Constitution so drawn, must necessarily be shut against the claims of slavery, is an error. We are not deeply skilled in the science of human language, and use language in the sense in which it is generally used, rather than scientifically, and we do know that "Liberty, Republicanism, and Equal Rights," words constantly on the lips of this nation, are deemed to be no more hostile to Negro slavery, than the same words, when used by the Greeks, were supposed to be against the enslavement of the Helots. Ours is not the business of a lexicographer, but to receive the idea meant to be conveyed by the language of those who use it, and condemn or approve accordingly.

In the letter of Mr. Smith which we published last week, he assumes that the material thing for us to prove, in order to establish the wrongfulness of voting and acting under the United States Constitution, is, that the Federal Government has no right to abolish slavery under that instrument. With all deference, we must say, we see no such necessity laid upon us. We might, for argument's sake, grant all that Mr. Smith claims as to the power of the Federal Government to abolish slavery under the Constitution, and yet hold, as we certainly do hold, that it is wrong to vote and take office under the Constitution. It is not enough that a man can demonstrate that his plan will abolish slavery, to satisfy us that his plan is the right and best one to be adopted. Slavery might be abolished by the aid of a foreign arm; but shall we therefore invoke that aid? We might, to feed the hungry and clothe the naked, break into the house of Mr. Smith and steal the wherewithal to do these things, but the question of the rightfulness of such conduct would be still open. If there is one Christian principle more firmly fixed in our heart than another, it is this, that it is wrong to do evil that good may come; and if there is one heresy more to be guarded against than another, it is the doctrine that the end justifies the means. We say, therefore, that it is not incumbent upon us to show that, by a forced and latitudinarian construction of the Constitution, Congress may not abolish slavery in all the slaveholding States, in order to establish the doctrine which we lay down and justify the course which we feel bound to pursue in regard to voting under the Constitution of the

United States. It is enough for us to know that the Constitution requires of those who are parties to it to return the fugitive slave to the house of bondage, and to shoot down the slave if he rises to gain his freedom, to justify us in repudiating and forever casting from us, as a covenant with death, the American Constitution.

Of course those who regard the Constitution in the light that Mr. Smith does, are bound by their convictions of duty to pursue an opposite course; and we candidly confess that, could we see the Constitution as they do, we should not be slow in using the ballot-box against the system of slavery, or urging others to do so. But we have learned enough of the elements of moral power, to know that a man is lame, impotent, and worse than weak, when he ceases to regard the clear convictions of his understanding, to accomplish anything, no matter how desirable that thing may be. We shall therefore continue to denounce the Constitution and government of the United States as a most foul and bloody conspiracy against the rights of three millions of enslaved and imbruted men; for such is the conviction of our conscience in respect to both the Constitution and the government. Down with both, for it is not fit that either should exist!—F. D.

The North Star, March 30, 1849

"A TRIBUTE FOR THE NEGRO; being a vindication of the moral and religious capabilities, of the colored portion of mankind; with particular reference to the African race; illustrated by numerous biographical sketches—facts—anecdotes, &c., and many superior engravings. By Wilson Armistead."

A copy of this long looked for work has reached our table. It is a volume of five hundred and sixty-four pages, neatly bound, well printed and on excellent paper. The superior portraits referred to in the title page, raise expectations not to be gratified on looking into the book—for with but two exceptions—they are of the commonest sort. The book would have been better without than with them. The one of Mr. Pennington gives but a poor idea of the man, and does him plain injustice. That of the brave Cinque, falls far short of expressing the bold and majestic bearing of this heroic son of the forest, and is little better than a burlesque upon the fine picture of him, owned by our friend Purvis. That of Frederick Douglass, we shall leave to others to criticise, begging only to remark that, it has a much more kindly and amiable expression, than is generally thought to characterize the face of a fugitive slave. Never having seen the other persons, whom the additional portraits are designed to represent, we say nothing of them, but hope they are truer likenesses than either that of Pennington, Cinque, or Douglass. Before quitting the pictures, we shall venture one remark, which we have never heard expressed before, and which will, perhaps, be set down to the account of our Negro vanity; and it may be, not unjustly so, but we have presented it for what it may be worth. It is this, Negroes can never have impartial portraits, at the hands of white artists. It seems to us next to impossible for white men to take likenesses of black men, without most grossly exaggerating their distinctive features. And the reason is obvious. Artists, like all other white persons, have adopted a theory respecting the distinctive features of Negro physiognomy. We have heard many white persons say, that "Negroes look all alike," and that they could not distinguish between the old and the young. They associate with the Negro face, high cheek bones, distended nostril, depressed nose, thick lips, and retreating foreheads. This theory impressed strongly upon the mind of an artist exercises a powerful influence over his pencil, and very naturally leads him to distort and exaggerate those peculiarities, even when they scarcely exist in the original. The temptation to make the likeness of the Negro, rather than of the man, is very strong; and often leads the artist, as well as the player "to overstep the modesty of nature." There is the greatest variety of form and feature among us, and there is seldom one face to be found, which has all the features, usually attributed to the Negro; and there are those, from which these marks of African descent (while their color remains unchanged,) have disappeared entirely. "I am black, but comely," is as true now, as it was in the days of Solomon. Perhaps, we should not be more impartial than our white brothers, should we attempt to picture them. We should be as likely to get their lips too thin, noses too sharp and pinched up, their cheeks too lantern-like, their hair too lank and lifeless, and their faces altogether too cadaverous. But we must let the picture go, and console ourselves as Thos. Witson once did, when he told us he should become handsome, if public opinion was changed. For our part, we like a large nose, whether it be flat or sharp, no matter which, so the metal is there. Every one to his taste, so he does not trample on human rights.

A TRIBUTE FOR THE NEGRO

The Book under consideration, while it contains very little which has not been presented to the public before, in one shape or another, is, nevertheless, a most valuable work. In arrangement and literary ability it is by no means remarkable; it is plain, simple, truthful and is chiefly valuable as the repository of a luminous and brilliant array of testimony, in favor of our claims to be regarded as equal members of the great human family, with the rest of mankind, gathered with much industry, from the most valuable sources. The Author has evidently said less than he desired; possessing a warm heart, and a clear understanding, of the manifold wrongs, growing out of enormous views respecting the Negro character; he could, perhaps, have covered the whole ground, with arguments as good as those he has adduced, from more distinguished sources. But he has wisely and generously allowed others to speak, so that out of the mouths of many witnesses, the truth shall be established. In this we see a disinterested desire, to serve a righteous cause, rather than to gratify an ambitious taste for display. Mr. Armistead acknowledges his indebtedness to the writings of Abbe Gregoire, Bloomenbach, Pritchard, Horn, Phillip, Channing, Pringle, Shaw, Barrow, Valiant, Mungo Park Buffon, and many other distinguished men, writers, tourists and missionaries—all testifying to the manly capabilities of the Negro, and proving him to be a man and a brother.

In proof of the ancient greatness of the Negro race, the testimony of Herodotus and Volney is adduced. In addition to this sort of testimony, we have many extracts from the writings, speeches, poems and narratives of distinguished colored persons. The whole work abounds in evidence of the natural kindness of heart, gentleness, hospitality and honesty of the Negro race. Missionaries, sea-captains, and others, testify that the Negro is peculiarly susceptible of religious impressions. Facts are presented, showing that in many parts of Africa quite a high point of civilization has already been attained. Articles of apparel, manufactured by the natives, prove the skill and ingenuity of the African race.—Instances are referred to, illustrating the readiness and ease with which the colored race assimilate with the habits and customs of a higher civilization. The fact that Negroes are as eager to improve their condition and obtain education as other men, is alleged.

Color is accounted for by climate, food and habits. Various facts are adduced in favor of this position, and we think they are quite conclusive. Haiti, with her heroes, is strongly brought out; and the voice of youthful Liberia is heard in testimony of Negro capabilities.

The philanthropic author does not content himself with a mere cold and clear disquisition on the capabilities of the Negro, but launches forth upon the tempestuous waves of reform. His sympathies are kindled—his heart melts in pity for the long-imbruted and perishing bondman—his soul is fired with a sense of the atrocious and multiplied injustice and tyranny which the latter have endured at the hands of their oppressors; and while he weeps bitterly with the oppressed, he strongly rebukes the guilty oppressor. Into the teeth of the tyrant he hurls the truthful rebuke—"If the Negro is degraded, you are the guilty cause of his degradation; and, as O'Connell once said to England, 'Try justice to Ireland, before you resort to force.'" There is in these passages so much genuine sympathy for the suffering, and indignation for the monsters who gain their fortunes by the blood of souls, and, withal, such an intelligent view of the duties of this nation to the plundered slave, that the heart of the most radical abolitionist in this country would be warmed, cheered and strengthened by their perusal.

After all, however, we have perused this book with mingled emotions—deeply gratified that the work has been so ably and generously performed by Mr. Armistead, yet grieved and mortified that such a work seemed needful to be done. Here is a large volume, made up of extracts from the sayings of authors—travellers, missionaries, sea-captains, doctors, lawyers, and philosophers,—and all these to prove, what? Simply, that the present reviewer is a member of the human family, and ought to be so regarded. If our dark cheek could reveal our feelings, words would be unnecessary to the beholder. What a fact to be handed down to coming generations, that the Christian people of England and America had become so hardened by crime, and blinded by prejudice, that, in the year 1849, they needed the light of a volume of nearly six hundred pages to distinguish their brother man from the beast of the field. The antiquarian of coming ages will search out this work as one of the literary curiosities of the nineteenth century, and will produce it as evidence of the darkness of this age. What a commentary upon our enlightenment, that we must have books to prove what is palpable even to the brute creation—to wit: the Negro is a man!

Here we are plowing, planting, reaping—using all kinds of mechanical tools—building houses, bridges, ships—working in metals of brass, iron, copper, silver and gold—living in families as husbands and wives, brothers and sisters, parents and children—supporting and sustaining week and Sabbath-day schools—reading, writing, cyphering—acting as clerks, secretaries, merchants—having among us lawyers, ministers, doctors, poets, authors, editors, orators, teachers—building ships on land, and navigating them at sea—taming and domesticating animals on land, and pursuing the huge leviathans of the Pacific,—here we are walking, talking, acting, feeling, thinking, planning—in a word, engaged in all the professions and callings into which other men press, and which are open to us, with our minds grasping in the fulness of manly strength the awfully sublime idea, one Supreme God, who is the Common Father and Creator of us all; and yet, with these facts before the Christian world, it requires a book to prove that the Negro is a man and an equal brother, having equal capabilities with the rest of mankind. Shame on the hardness of heart and blindness of mind!

But let us not be discouraged or indignant; the world is making progress, though the movement be so slow at times as scarcely to be perceptible. We have now before us a work nearly two centuries old, "advocating and suing for the Negro's admission into *the church*," and called "A Persuasive to the Instructing and Baptising Negroes and Indians. By Morgan Godwyn."* On perusing this volume, we find that ground much lower is occupied by the writer, than that taken by the author of the "Tribute;" and that the material of the former for making his work, seems to have been far less than that of the latter. Let us hope that the time may come when it will not be necessary for our friends to write Tributes, or make persuasive appeals to the church and the world on our behalf; but when we shall present such incontestible evidence of our manhood, as shall seal the lips of calumny and persecution for ever.

We recommend this work especially to the Negro-haters of our own Christian land; we recommend it to our "Negro pew" churches and our Negro-hating priesthood, and ask them to look at its facts, statements, reasonings, and lay its mighty truths to heart; remembering that the work is not that of a wild enthusiast who bends facts, no matter how inconsistent and opposed to his theory, to suit his purpose; but that of a calm, disinterested Christian and scholar, with a heart alive to human woe, and whose only aim in these pages, appears to be to befriend the helpless. We would also commend the work to our own beloved but heart-broken brethren, the victims of prejudice and slavery. The book should be in all your houses, and those who can ought to purchase one and possess it. We

---

* Presented to Frederick Douglass, while at Whithaven, England, by John Gibson Esq.

need and ought to possess it. We need it, as a means of refuting with their own weapons and on their own ground, the cruel calumniators of our race, as well as to inspire us with higher aspirations and a nobler zeal and earnestness in the cause of our own elevation and improvement.

We observe that one of our exchanges, the *Ram's Horn*, alleges the complaint, that the work takes too low ground with respect to our abilities as a people. The complaint is not only unjust, but, in the person who prefers it, immodest. A work admitting the brilliant talents and genius of many of our number, and vindicating the capabilities of the whole people, is quite as much as we can ask or justly demand. As much or more injury is done by an over estimate of our abilities, as by an under estimation of them. We would be just, though we should thereby pluck wreaths of glory from the brow of our own people, and consign us to an inferior sphere in the ranks of human brotherhood. That Africa is behind Europe in the pathway of improvement it is madness, if nothing worse, to pretend to doubt; and in such circumstances Africa ought to be thankful for a simple vindication of her capabilities. For our part, as a man, a slave, and an humble advocate for emancipation, and as a child of Africa, we thank, from the very depth of our heart, Wilson Armistead, for the faithfulness of this book, and the great good which we believe will result from its publication on both sides the Atlantic.—F. D.

The North Star, April 7, 1849

COLORPHOBIA IN NEW YORK!

The fifth of May will long be remembered as the most trying day ever experienced by the unfortunate victims of colorphobia in the city of New York. The disease was never more malignant or general than on that day. The streets were literally crowded with persons of all classes afflicted with this terrible malady. Whole omnibus loads were attacked at the same moment, and their hideous and unearthly howls were truly distressing, excruciating. It will be impossible to describe, or give the reader any correct idea either of the extent of the disease or the agony it seemed to occasion. Like most epidemics, its chief havoc was among the baser sort. The suffering here was fearful and intense. If the genteel suffered from the plague, they managed to suppress and control their feelings better than what are called the "lower orders." But, even here, there could be no successful concealment. The strange plague defied all concealment, and would show itself in spite of veils, white pocket handkerchiefs, parasols, hats, bonnets and umbrellas. In the refined the presence of the plague might be seen by a distortion of the countenance, a red and furious look about the cheek, a singular turn up of the nose, and a *"lower me!"* expression of the eyes.

Among the low and vulgar the symptoms were different;—the hand clinched, head shaking, teeth grating, hysteric yells and horrid imprecation, marked the presence of the disease and the agony of the miserable creatures who were its unfortunate victims. Persons who, at a distance of thirty or forty yards, appeared the very pictures of health, were found, on a nearer approach, most horribly cut and marred.

But the effect upon the outward man was not half so strange and dreadful as that upon the mind. Here all was utter ruin. Gough's description of "delirium tremens" would not be much out of place in describing one haunted and afflicted with colorphobia. Monsters, goblins, demons, snakes, lizards and scorpions—all that was foul, strange and loathsome—seized upon their bewildered imaginations. Pointing with outstretched arm towards us, its victims would exclaim, as if startled by some terrible sight—"Look! look!" "Where?" "Ah, what?" "Why?" "Why, don't you see?" "See what?" "Why, that BLACK! black! *black!*" Then, with eyes turned up in horror, they would exclaim in the most unearthly manner, and start off in a furious gallop—running all around us, and gazing at us, as if they would read our very hearts. The whole scene was deeply afflicting and terrible.

But to the cause of this wide-spread plague, or rather the manifestation of it. We think it can all be made plain to the dullest comprehension. There had arrived in New York, a few days previous, two *English* Ladies, from London—friends of Frederick Douglass—and had taken apartments at the Franklin House, Broadway; and were not only called upon at that Hotel by Mr. Douglass, but really allowed themselves to take his arm, and to walk many times up and down Broadway, in broad-day light, when that great thoroughfare was crowded with pure American ladies and gentlemen. Such an open, glaring outrage upon *pure American* tastes had never before been perpetrated. Two ladies, elegantly attired, educated, and of the most approved manners, faultless in appearance and position, actually walking, and leaning upon the arm of a person, with a skin not colored like their own! Oh! monstrous! Was it not enough to cause the very stones to leap up with indignation from the pavement! and to "stir them up to mutiny and rage"? More and worse still, these ladies appeared wholly indifferent to, and oblivious of, all the indignation and fury going on about them; but walked, talked and acted as though nothing unusual was passing. In a word, they seemed to forget that they were in the greatest Commercial Emporium of this, the mightiest Nation in the world, and to act as though they had been in the paltry city of London!! instead of New York. What could they have been thinking about? How strange that they had not made themselves acquainted with the institutions and customs of the great Nation, upon whose sacred soil they were *allowed* to land? How singular that their friends had not warned them against such a monstrous outrage upon the established customs of this, the *"freest"* country in the world? They certainly must have been deceived. It is impossible "that nature so could err." "Charms, conjuration—mighty magic," must have bewildered and misled them. They would have been kindly received and hospitably entertained by some of the most respectable and refined families in the city of New York; but, with a strange hallucination, they preferred to identify themselves with the most despised and injured portion of all the people of America—and thus to make themselves of no reputation, and cut themselves off from all sympathy and attention of the highly favored and accomplished sons and daughters of America. Before quitting this subject, we wish to call attention to certain singular inconsistencies connected with the development of the feeling, called (erroneously) prejudice against color. The first is this. The poor creatures who seemed most disturbed by the fact that these ladies walked through the streets of New York in company with a colored man, felt in no wise shocked at seeing ladies seated in their gilded carriages, with colored persons seated near them, driving their horses and otherwise assisting such ladies. All this was perfectly right. They were in the capacity of servants. Hence New York toadyism is rather pleased than disgusted. It is not with colored servants that New York loafers are displeased; but with colored *gentlemen*. It is with the colored man as a gentleman that they feel the most intense displeasure. They cannot bear it, and they must pour out their pent-up wrath, whenever an opportunity is afforded for doing so.

In this same Franklin Hotel, in which we could not be allowed to dine on account of our color, we saw a large number of colored waiters in the nearest proximity to white gentlemen and ladies, without offence.

We, however, tire of this subject. This prejudice is so unjust, unnatural and irrational, that ridicule and indignation seem to be the only weapons with which to assail it.

Our friends informed us that when they landed, they were assured that they had reached the shores of a free country, and were congratulated upon that fact. But they had scarcely reached the hotel, when they were informed that a friend of theirs, who was not deemed unfit to be associated with in London, and who would have been kindly received at the best hotels in that city, and in Paris, would not be allowed to take dinner with them at the Franklin Hotel, in the city of New York. In this free country one is not permitted to choose and enjoy the society of his friends, without being subjected to innumerable insults and annoyances.

We shall not, however, despair on this point. A marked improvement has already taken place in the manner of treating colored travelers, and the change is going on still. Nothing, however, facilitates this more than such examples of fidelity to principle, and indifference to a corrupt and brutal public opinion, as is presented in the conduct of these two English ladies, and others. This prejudice must be removed; and the way for abolitionists and colored persons to remove it, is to act as though it did not exist, and to associate with their fellow creatures irrespective of all complexional differences. We have marked out this path for ourselves, and we mean to pursue it at all hazards.—F. D.

The North Star, May 25, 1849

THE AMERICAN COLONIZATION SOCIETY, speech in Faneuil Hall, June 8, 1849

Mr. Chairman, Ladies and Gentlemen: I never rise to speak in Faneuil Hall, without a deep sense of my want of ability to do justice to the subject upon which I undertake to speak. I can do a pretty good business, some have said, in the country school houses in Western New York and elsewhere; but when I come before the people of Boston in Faneuil Hall, I feel my exceeding weakness. I am all the more embarrassed this evening, because I have to speak to you in respect to a subject concerning which an apology seems to be demanded. I allude to the subject of the American Colonization Society—a subject which has had a large measure of anti-slavery attention, and been long since disposed of at the hands of Wm. Lloyd Garrison. The only apology that I can make for calling attention to it this evening is, that it has had a sort of "revival," of late, through the agency of a man whom I presume a large portion of this audience esteem and admire. I allude to the Honorable Henry Clay of Kentucky. [Applause.] Though not a Yankee, you see I guessed correctly. I have presumed rightly that you esteem and admire that gentleman. Now if you admire Mr. Clay, of course you would like to know all about him. You would like, of course, to hear whatever can be said of him, and said fairly, although a black man may presume to say it.

Mr. Clay has recently given to the world a letter, purporting to advocate the emancipation of the slaves of Kentucky.[18] That letter has been extensively published in New England as well as other parts of the United States; and in almost every instance where a Whig paper has spoken of the letter it has done so in terms of high approval. The plan which Mr. Clay proposes is one which seems to meet almost the universal assent of the Whig party at the North; and many religious papers have copied the article, and spoken in terms of high commendation of the humanity, of the clear-sightedness and philanthropy of Henry Clay. Now, my friends, I am going to speak to you in a manner that, unless you allow your reason and not your prejudices to prevail, will provoke from you demonstrations of disapprobation. I beg of you, then, to hear me calmly—without prejudice or opposition. You, it must be remembered, have in your hands all power in this land. I stand here not only in a minority, but identified with a class whom everybody can insult with impunity. Surely, the ambition for superiority must be great indeed in honorable men to induce them to insult a poor black man, whom the basest fellow in the street can insult with impunity. Keep this in mind, and hear what I have to say with regard to Mr. Clay's letter, and his position as a slaveholder.

The letter of Mr. Clay commences in a manner that gives promise to the reader that he shall find it a consistent, straightforward anti-slavery document. It commences by refuting, with one or two strokes of the pen, the vast cart-loads of sophistry piled up by Mr. Calhoun and others in favor of perpetual slavery. He shows clearly that Mr. Calhoun's theory of slavery, if admitted to be sound, would enslave the whites as readily as it enslaves the blacks—this would follow necessarily. Glancing at the question of the natural inferiority of the colored man, he says: "Admitting a question he does not raise—admitting that the whites of this country are superior to the blacks, the fact devolves upon the former the duty of enlightening, instructing and improving the condition of the latter." These are noble sentiments, worthy of the heart and head of a great and good man. But how does Mr. Clay propose to carry out this plan? He goes on to state that, in carrying out his proposed plan of gradual emancipation, great care should be taken that the rights and interests of the slaveholder should not be jeopardized. He proceeds to state that the utmost caution and prudence should guide the hand that strikes down slavery in Kentucky. With reference to emancipation, he affirms that it should not commence until the year 1885. The plan is that all children born of slave parents in Kentucky after the year 1860 shall be free after arriving at the age of twenty-five. He sets, therefore, the day of emancipation beyond the average length of the slave's life, for a generation of slaves in the far South dies out in seven years. But how would he have these children of slave parents free? Not free to work for themselves—not free to live on the soil that they have cultivated with their own hard hands—that they have nourished with their best blood, and toiled over and beautified and adorned—but that then they shall be let out under an agent of the State for three long years, to raise one hundred and fifty dollars with which to pay the price of their own expatriation from their family and friends. [Voices—"Shame!"]

I hear the cry of shame—yes, it is a deep and damning shame. He declares in that letter that not only shall these emancipated slaves work three years, but that he, Mr. Clay, will oppose any measure for emancipation without the expatriation of the emancipated slaves. Just look at the peculiar operation of this plan. Let us suppose that it is adopted, and that in the year 1860 it commences. All children born of slave parents are to be free in the year 1888. It is well known that all persons in the South have contracted marriages long before this period, and have become parents, some having children from one to four years of age. Henry Clay's plan is that when these persons arrive at the age of twenty-eight, these parents shall be torn away from their tender children, and hurried off to Liberia or somewhere else; and that the children taken from these parents, before they have become acquainted with the paternal relation, shall remain another twenty-eight years; and when they have remained that period, and have contracted matrimonial alliances, and become fathers and mothers, they, too, shall be taken from their children, the slaveholders having kept them at work for twenty-eight years, and hurried off to Liberia.

But a darker, baser feature than all these appears in this letter of Mr. Clay. It is this: He speaks of the loss which the slaveholders will be called on to experience by the emancipation of his slaves. But he says that even this trifling expenditure may be prevented by leaving the slaveholder the right to sell—to mortgage—to transfer his slave property any time during the twenty-five years. Only look at Henry Clay's generosity to the slaveholders of Kentucky. He has twenty-five long years during which to watch the slave markets of New Orleans, of Memphis, of Vicksburg and other Southern cities, and to watch the prices of cotton and rice and tobacco on the other side of the Atlantic, and as the prices rise there in these articles, he may expect a corresponding rise in the price of flesh in the slave markets, and then he can sell his slaves to the best advantage. Thus it is that the glorious State of Kentucky shall be made free, and yet her purse be made the heavier in consequence of it. This is not a proposition for emancipation, but a proposition to Kentucky to sell off the slaves she holds in her possession, and throw them off into the far Southern States—and then hypocritically boast of being a free State, while almost every slave born upon her soil remains a slave. And this is the plan of the good Henry Clay, whom you esteem and admire so much. [Applause and hisses.] You that like to hiss, if you had the chain on your own limbs, and were pent up in Henry Clay's own quarter, and had free access to Henry Clay's own meal-tub, I think would soon change your tune. [Laughter.]

I want to say a word about the Colonization Society, of which Henry Clay is President. He is President of nothing else. [Laughter.] That Society is an old enemy of the colored people in this country. Almost every respectable man belongs to it, either by direct membership or by affinity. I meet with colonizationists everywhere; I met with a number of them the other day, on board the steamer *Alida,* going from Albany to New York. I wish to state my experience on board of that steamer, and as it is becoming a subject of newspaper remark, it may not be out of place to give my version of the story: On Thursday last, I took my passage on board the steamer *Alida,* as I have stated, to go from Albany to New York. I happened to have, very contrary to American taste and American prejudices and customs, in my company, a couple of friends from England—persons who had not been ashamed—nor had they cause to be ashamed from any feeling that exists in that country against the colored man—of being found on equal social terms with him in the city of London. They happen now to be sojourning in this country; and as if unaware of the prejudice existing in this country, or, if aware, perfectly regardless of it, they accompanied me on the steamer, and shared, of course, my society, or permitted me to share theirs on the passage to New York. About noon, I went into the cabin, and inquired of one of the waiters if we could have dinner. The answer was, we could. They had on a sign on each side of the captain's office words to this effect: "Meals can be received in the cabin at any hour during the day, by application to the steward." I made the application, and expected, of course, that dinner would be forthcoming at the time appointed. The bell rung—and though I do not know as it was altogether wise and prudent, I took a lady on each arm—for my friends were white ladies, you must know—and moved forward to the cabin. The fact of their being white ladies will enable you more readily to understand the cause of the intensity of hate displayed towards me. I went below forgetting all about my complexion, the curl of my hair, or the flatness of my nose, only remembering I had two elbows and a stomach, and was exceedingly hungry. [Laughter.] I walked below, as I have said, and took my seat at the table, supposing that the table was the place where a man should eat.

I had been there but a few moments, before I observed a large number of American gentlemen rising up gradually—for we are gradualists in this country—and moving off to another table, on the other side. But feeling I was there on my own responsibility, and that those gentlemen could not eat dinner for me, and I must do it for myself, I preferred to sit still, unmoved by what was passing around me. I had been there but a few moments, when a white man—after the order of American white men—for I would say, for your consolation, that you are growing darker and darker every year—the steward came up to me in a very curious manner, and said, "Yer must get up from that table." [Laughter.] I demanded by what authority he ordered me from the table. "Well," said he, "yer know the rule?" "Sir," said I, "I know nothing of your rules. I know that the rule is, that the passengers can receive their meals at any hour of the day on applying to the steward." Says he, "Now, it is no use for yer to talk, yer must leave." [Laughter.] "But where is the rule?" "Well," said he, "yer cannot get dinner on any boat on this river." I told him I went up the river in the *Confidence,* and took dinner, and no remark had been made. "Well," said he, "what yer can do on the *Confidence,* yer can't do on the *Alida.* [Laughter.] Are yer a going to get up?" "No, sir," said I. "Well," says he, "I will have you up." So off he goes to the upper deck, and brings down the captain, mate, clerk, and two or three hands. I sat still during the time of his absence; but finding they were mustering pretty strong, and remembering I had but one coat, and not caring to have it torn, and feeling I had borne a sufficient testimony against their unrighteous treatment, I arose from the table, and walked to the other end of the cabin, in company with my friends. A scene then occurred which I shall never forget; not because of its impudence, but because of its malignity. A large number of American ladies and gentlemen, seated around the table on the other side of the cabin, the very moment we walked away, gave three cheers for the captain, and applauded in the most uproarious manner the steward, for having driven two ladies and one gentleman from the table, and deprived them of dinner.

Mr. Garrison: That is a fact for Europe.

Mr. Douglass: They drove us from the table, and gave three cheers for the captain for driving us away. I looked around on the audience there assembled, to see if I could detect one line of generous magnanimity on any face—any indignation manifested against the outrage that had been perpetrated upon me and my friends. But not a look, not a word, not the slightest expression of disapprobation in any part of the vessel. Now, I have traveled in England, Ireland, and Scotland—I mention this, not by way of boast, but because I want to contrast the freedom of our glorious country—and it is a glorious one, after all—with that of other countries through which I have traveled—by railroads, in highways and byways, steamboats, stagecoaches, and every imaginable kind of vehicle—I have stayed at some of the first hotels in London, Liverpool, Edinburgh, Glasgow, Dublin, and elsewhere—and I must say to you, good Americans, that I never, in any of those cities or towns, received the first mark, or heard the first word of disapprobation on account of the color of my skin. I may tell you that one of the ladies with me on the steamboat, though not a believer in the right of women to speak in public, was so excited and so indignant at the outrage perpetrated, that she went to the American captain and told him that she had heard much of the country, much of the gallantry of American gentlemen—that they would be willing to rise from their seats to allow a lady to be seated—and she was very happy in having the opportunity of witnessing a manifestation of American gallantry and American courtesy. I do think I saw one neck hang when this rebuke was administered. [Applause.]

Most of the passengers were of the baser sort, very much like some Western men—dark-complexioned, lean, lank, pinched up, about the ugliest set of men I ever saw in my life. [Laughter.] I went to the steward about two hours after they had cleared off the dinner table for those hungry, wolfish-looking people. [Laughter.] My dear friends, if you had seen them, you would have agreed with me. I then inquired of the steward if now, after this hungry multitude had been fed, we could have a cup of coffee and a biscuit. Said he—"Who are you? If you are the servant of those ladies, you shall have what you want." I thought that was kind, anyhow. "Yes," said I, "I am their most humble servant." [Great laughter.] "Well," said he, "what are you walking about on deck with them for, if you are their servant?" I told him they were very courteous to me—putting him off in that way. He then told me if I did not get out of the cabin, he would split my head open. He was rather a diminutive being, and would not have been a mouthful for anything like a Tom Hyer man. [Applause.] However, seeing his Anglo-Saxon blood was up, I thought I would move off; but tapping him on the shoulder, I told him I wanted to give him a piece of advice: "I am a passenger, you are a servant; and therefore you should always consult the wants of the passengers." [Laughter.] He finally told me he was ready to give me my dinner in the capacity of a servant, but not otherwise. This acknowledgment told the whole story of American prejudice. There were two or three slaveholders on board. One was a lady from New Orleans; rather a dark looking person—for individuals from that quarter are dark, except the blacks, and they are getting lighter. [Laughter.] This woman was perfectly horrified with my appearance, and she said to gentlemen standing by, that she was really afraid to be near me, and that I would draw a bowie knife. Indeed, she had liked to have fainted. This woman, I learned from good authority, owned three hundred slaves in Louisiana; and yet she was afraid of a black man, and expected every moment I would attempt to commit violence on her. At the time she was affecting this horror of a Negro, she was being waited on at the table by colored men. It was, "Waiter, come here!" and "Waiter, go there!" and there they were actually, cutting up the meat, standing right over it, quite near those white persons who really shouted when I was driven out.

This tells the whole story. You have no prejudice against blacks—no more than against any other color—but it is against the black man appearing as the colored gentleman. He is then a contradiction of your theory of natural inferiority in the colored race. It was not in consequence of my complexion that I was driven out of the cabin, for I could have remained there as a servant; but being there as a gentleman, having paid my own passage, and being in company with intelligent, refined persons, was what awakened the hatred, and brought down upon me the insulting manifestations I have alluded to.

It is because the American Colonization Society cherishes and fosters this feeling of hatred against the black man, that I am opposed to it. And I am especially disposed to speak out my opposition to this colonization scheme to-night, because not only of the renewed interest excited in the colonization scheme by the efforts of Henry Clay and others, but because there is a lecturer in the shape of the Rev. Mr. Miller, of New Jersey, now in England, soliciting funds for our expatriation from this country, and going about trying to organize a society, and to create an impression in favor of removing us from this country. I would ask you, my friends, if this is not mean and impudent in the extreme, for one class of Americans to ask for the removal of another class? I feel, sir, I have as much right in this country as any other man. I feel that the black man in this land has as much right to stay in this land as the white man. Consider the matter in the light of possession in this country. Our connection with this country is contemporaneous with your own. From the beginning of the existence of this people, as a people, the colored man has had a place upon the American soil. To be sure, he was not driven from his home in pursuit of a greater liberty than he enjoyed at home, like the Pilgrim fathers; but in the same year that the Pilgrims were landing in this State, slaves were landing on the James River, in Virginia. We feel on this score, then, that we have as much right here as any other class of people.

We have other claims to being regarded and treated as American citizens. Some of our number have fought and bled for this country, and we only ask to be treated as well as those who have fought against it. We are lovers of this country, and we only ask to be treated as well as the haters of it. We are not only told by Americans to go out of our native land to Africa, and there enjoy our freedom—for we must go there in order to enjoy it—but Irishmen newly landed on our soil, who know nothing of our institutions, nor of the history of our country, whose toil has not been mixed with the soil of the country as ours—have the audacity to propose our removal from this, the land of our birth. For my part, I mean, for one, to stay in this country; I have made up my mind to live among you. I had a kind offer, when I was in England, of a little house and lot, and the free use of it, on the banks of the river Eden. I could easily have stayed there, if I had sought for ease, undisturbed, unannoyed by American skin-aristocracy; for it is an aristocracy of skin [applause]—

those passengers on board the *Alida* only got their dinners that day in virtue of color; if their skins had been of my color, they would have had to fast all day. Whatever denunciations England may be entitled to on account of her treatment of Ireland and her own poor, one thing can be said of her, that no man in that country, or in any of her dominions, is treated as less than a man on account of his complexion. I could have lived there; but when I remembered this prejudice against color, as it is called, and slavery, and saw the many wrongs inflicted on my people at the North that ought to be combated and put down, I felt a disposition to lay aside ease, to turn my back on the kind offer of my friends, and to return among you—deeming it more noble to suffer along with my colored brethren, and meet these prejudices, than to live at ease, undisturbed, on the other side of the Atlantic. [Applause.] I had rather be here now, encountering this feeling, bearing my testimony against it, setting it at defiance, than to remain in England undisturbed. I have made up my mind wherever I go, I shall go as a man, and not as a slave. When I go on board of your steamboats, I shall always aim to be courteous and mild in my deportment towards all with whom I come in contact, at the same time firmly and constantly endeavoring to assert my equal right as a man and a brother.

But the Colonization Society says this prejudice can never be overcome—that it is natural—God has implanted it. Some say so; others declare that it can only be removed by removing the cause, that is, by removing us to Liberia. I know this is false, from my own experience in this country. I remember that, but a few years ago, upon the railroads from New Bedford and Salem and in all parts of Massachusetts, a most unrighteous and proscriptive rule prevailed, by which colored men and women were subjected to all manner of indignity in the use of those conveyances. Anti-slavery men, however, lifted up their testimony against this principle from year to year; and from year to year, he whose name cannot be mentioned without receiving a round of applause, Wendell Phillips [applause] went abroad, exposing this proscription in the light of justice. What is the result? Not a single railroad can be found in any part of Massachusetts, where a colored man is treated and esteemed in any other light than that of a man and a traveller. Prejudice has given way and must give way. The fact that it is giving way proves that this prejudice is not invincible. The time was when it was expected that a colored man, when he entered a church in Boston, would go into the Jim Crow pew—and I believe such is the case now, to a large extent; but then there were those who would defend the custom. But you can scarcely get a defender of this proscription in New England now.

The history of the repeal of the intermarriage law shows that the prejudice against color is not invincible. The general manner in which white persons sit with colored persons shows plainly that the prejudice against color is not invincible. When I first came here, I felt the greatest possible diffidence of sitting with whites. I used to come up from the shipyard, where I worked, with my hands hardened with toil, rough and uncomely, and my movements awkward (for I was unacquainted with the rules of politeness), I would shrink back, and would not have taken my meals with the whites had they not pressed me to do so. Our president, in his earlier intercourse with me, taught me, by example, his abhorrence of this prejudice. He has, in my presence, stated to those who visited him, that if they did not like to sit at the table with me, they could have a separate one for themselves.

The time was, when I walked through the streets of Boston, I was liable to insult if in company with a white person. To-day I have passed in company with my white friends, leaning on their arm and they on mine, and yet the first word from any quarter on account of the color of my skin I have not heard. It is all false, this talk about the invincibility of prejudice against color. If any of you have it, and no doubt some of you have, I will tell you how to get rid of it. Commence to do something to elevate and improve and enlighten the colored man, and your prejudice will begin to vanish. The more you try to make a man of the black man, the more you will begin to think him a man.

> Mr. Douglass here related an anecdote of his having once visited the town of Pittsfield, Massachusetts, for the purpose of lecturing. He was invited to the house of a friend, an anti-slavery man, who was filled with the prejudice against color. This man allowed him to walk to the place of the lecture without offering to take him into his carriage, and then left him, after the afternoon meeting to come home alone. While standing there, it began to rain, and the Hon. —— ——, a pro-slavery man, invited him into his house. The children, on seeing him enter, cried "n——r, n——r," and fled, and the whole family treated him with coldness. Determined to overcome it, he complained of a hoarseness, with which he was affected, and asked Mrs. —— if she would be kind enough to give him a glass of cold water, with a little sugar in it, to relieve his cold. Mrs. —— brought the articles, and Mr. Douglass thanked her, he said, with a swimming heart; and from that moment her coldness and formality were gone,

and he was invited, whenever he visited Pittsfield again, to make his stay at their house.

Mr. Garrison desired to make a remark with reference to the exclamation of the children on the approach of Mr. Douglass, "There's a n——r in the house," and their precipitate flight. It was the same kind of feeling that was evinced on another occasion. When Mungo Park, the celebrated English traveler, visited Africa, he found himself, at a certain period, in a village where the inhabitants had never seen a white person before. On going into one of the huts, he greeted the children, who exhibited great trepidation, and ran out with all possible expedition, crying, "The devil! the devil!" [Great laughter.]

Mr. Douglass: It is a poor rule that won't work both ways. [Laughter and applause.] Most people think their Lord is like themselves. A certain very pious man was horribly shocked by hearing an abolitionist say that the Negro was made in the image of God. The Lord is in their image, they seem to think, and the devil in the image of the black man. [Laughter.]

I desire to bear my testimony, after hearing the eulogy pronounced by Mr. Garrison, with regard to our departed brother and co-laborer, John Murray, of Scotland. About three years ago I had the pleasure of bidding that noble man farewell on the shores of Scotland; and I remember well the deep interest he took in the anti-slavery questions of this country. His last battle in behalf of the slave was with the Free Church of Scotland; and while he lived, that Church, for its alliance with slaveholders—for receiving their money into its treasury, and extending to them its fellowship in return—obtained no repose. He bore a noble testimony against it; he had borne a noble testimony against slavery before. For the last twenty-eight years, John Murray stood up in Scotland, the firm, the untiring, the devoted friend of the slave. There are two or three colored persons, at least, now in this Hall, who have shared his generous hospitality, and received his hearty "God-speed" in their endeavors to break down slavery and prejudice against color in this country, by creating a public sentiment on that side of the Atlantic that should react in favor of human liberty here. I have no more to say respecting this good man; his consistent and irreproachable character is his best eulogy.

Some one has asked me to say a word about General Worth. I only know General Worth by his acts in Mexico and elsewhere, in the service of this slaveholding and slave-trading government. I know why that question is put: it is because one of your city papers, which does not rise to the dignity of being called a paper—a sheet of the basest sort—has said that my tongue ought to be cut out by its roots, because, upon hearing of the death of that man, I made use of the remark—(it is not stated in what connection I made it, or where)—that another legalized murderer had gone to his account. I say so yet! [Loud cheering and some hisses.] I will not undertake to defend what I then said, or to show up his character or history. You know as well as I do, that Faneuil Hall has resounded with echoing applause of a denunciation of the Mexican war, as a murderous war—as a war against the free states—as a war against freedom, against the Negro, and against the interests of the workingmen of this country—and as a means of extending that great evil and damning curse, Negro slavery. [Immense applause.] Why may not the oppressed say, when an oppressor is dead, either by disease or by the hand of the foeman on the battlefield, that there is one the less of his oppressors left on earth? For my part, I would not care if, to-morrow, I should hear of the death of every man who engaged in that bloody war in Mexico, and that every man had met the fate he went there to perpetrate upon unoffending Mexicans. [Applause and hisses.]

A word more. There are three millions of slaves in this land, held by the United States Government, under the sanction of the American Constitution, with all the compromises and guaranties contained in that instrument in favor of the slave system. Among those guaranties and compromises is one by which you, the citizens of Boston, have sworn, before God, that three millions of slaves shall be slaves or die—that your swords and bayonets and arms shall, at any time at the bidding of the slaveholder, through the legal magistrate or governor of a slave State, be at his service in putting down the slaves. With eighteen millions of freemen standing upon the quivering hearts of three millions of slaves, my sympathies, of course, must be with the oppressed. I am among them, and you are treading them beneath your feet. The weight of your influence, numbers, political combinations and religious organizations, and the power of your arms, rest heavily upon them, and serve at this moment to keep them in their chains. When I consider their condition—the history of the American people—how they bared their bosoms to the storm of British artillery, in order to resist simply a three-penny tea tax, and to assert their independence of the mother country—I say, in view of these things, I should welcome the intelligence to-morrow, should it come, that the slaves had risen in the South, and that the sable arms which had been engaged in beautifying and adorning the South were engaged in spreading death and devastation there. [Marked sensation.] There is a state of war at the South at this moment. The slaveholder is waging a war of aggression on the oppressed. The slaves are now under his feet. Why, you welcomed the intelligence from France, that Louis Philippe had been barricaded in Paris—you threw up your caps in honor of the victory achieved by Republicanism over Royalty—you shouted aloud—"Long live the republic!"—and joined heartily in the watchword of "Liberty, Equality, Fraternity"—and should you not hail, with equal pleasure, the tidings from the South that the slaves had risen, and achieved for himself, against the iron-hearted slaveholder, what the republicans of France achieved against the royalists of France? [Great applause, and some hissing.]

The Liberator, June 8, 1849

THE UNION OF THE OPPRESSED FOR THE SAKE OF FREEDOM

We have placed this motto at the head of our editorial column, not as a rhetorical flourish, nor as something to catch the eye for a moment, and then to be withdrawn, but as an important and solid end to be attained. Much has been said about uniting the free colored people in a general organization for opposing slavery and improving their own condition; but as yet all efforts have been unsuccessful. We have been, and still are a divided and scattered people; and, in consequence, we have not distinguished ourselves by doing much for our elevation and improvement. It has ever been the policy of our enemies to divide us, and to create jealousies among us, and thus to render union as difficult as possible. They well understand that we are more easily managed and victimized, while disunited, than we could be if protected by a bond of union. We are now without this protection. We have no general understanding among ourselves; and the question for every colored man to answer, is, Shall we have it? Different answers will undoubtedly be returned to this question. Some will say, with our oppressors, that any general union among us is out of the question; that, as a class, we are too ignorant, and too suspicious of each other, to organize ourselves in a comprehensive manner for prosecuting any important measure, or for achieving any great purpose whatsoever. It will be contended, that we are too indifferent to our condition, and too well satisfied with our degradation, to rally in behalf of our own rights. Such will be the gloomy apprehensions of the faithless many among ourselves. Incapable of doing anything towards bettering their own condition, they are ever ready, with their doubts and fears, to discourage others.

Against all precedents—against all lukewarmness—against all doubts and fears, we believe that the oppressed colored population of this country can and will be largely and effectively united; and, single handed, we mean to bend our energies to this end, until we are convinced of its hopelessness or gratified by its success.

As a means of having something definite before our people, we take the liberty to submit the rough outlines of a constitution, or a basis of Union, which may serve the better to illustrate our subject and facilitate our object.

PREAMBLE

Whereas, the voice of reason, and the admonitions of experience, in all ages alike, impress us with the wisdom and the necessity of combination; and that union and concert of action are highly essential to the speedy success of any good cause; that as in division there is weakness, so in union there is strength; and whereas, we have long deplored the distracted and divided state of the oppressed, and the manifold evils resulting therefrom, and desiring as we do to see an union formed which shall enable us the better to grapple with the various systems of injustice and wrong by which we are environed, and to regain our plundered rights, we solemnly agree to unite in accordance with the following

CONSTITUTION

Article 1.—This Society shall be designated, "The National League."

Article 2.—The sentiments of the Society are, that slavery is a heinous sin again God—a monstrous outrage upon man—a fruitful source of pride, prejudice and oppression; and that it ought to be immediately and forever abolished; that resistance to slavery is the right and duty of every member of the human family; that, of all other men, it is especially the right and duty of the oppressed to vindicate their own rights; that, if they are indifferent to their condition, it is idle to hope that others will be interested for them; that to be worthy of human freedom, we should seek to attain it; that the best evidence of a man's fitness for social equality, is to make the best use of his civil rights; that no people ever obtained their freedom worthily that did not manifest a willingness to make sacrifices in reaching that end.

Article 3.—The object of the National League shall be, the abolition of slavery, and the elevation and improvement of the free colored people of the United States.

Article 4.—The Society will seek to attain these objects by means of lectures and the press, and all other means within their power, consistent with Christian morality.

Article 5.—The officers of this Society shall consist of a President, Vice-President, Secretary, Treasurer, and a Council of nine....

We may remark, that this constitution is merely thrown out as a means of directing attention to the subject of union. It makes no attempt at perfection; nor do we propose to insist upon its adoption, in its present form; but we present it to the consideration of our people, as a means of leading them to adopt something better.

We shall be happy to receive any communications on the subject; and as we anticipate that many may wish to make their sentiments known, we would recommend brevity to all who may write for the *North Star*. The subject is one of vital concern to us all, and should receive our most serious and earnest attention.—F. D.

The North Star, August 10, 1849

TO W. M. RATTEN

Rochester, Aug. 27, 1849

My Dear Friend:

The deep interest which you take in the cause of the perishing Slave in the Southern States, and the improvement and elevation of the nominally free colored people in the Northern States, emboldens me to appeal to you in their name and behalf for your assistance and co-operation in the work of extending the circulation of the *North Star*. Of the origin and history of that paper you are perhaps fully aware. It was established with money contributed by anti-slavery friends in Great Britain with a view to enable the despised colored man of this country to make known to the world his own wrongs, and to plead for his own rights. To this end it has, during the last eighteen months, been humbly but sincerely and faithfully devoted. Its existence and permanence as an auxiliary to the cause is of vital importance, and its claims to support are inferior to those of no other anti-slavery journal in the land. Conducted by persons belonging to the very race now doomed to endure the wrongs which it would remove—its claims to the aid and sympathy of philanthropists are strong and peculiar. To allow a paper thus circumstanced to fail of support cannot be other than disastrous to the cause of the slave. The presence of the *North Star* in this country is necessary to the proper vindication of the colored race from the charge of natural intellectual inferiority, and to assert their equal claim to be esteemed members of the common human Brotherhood.

The downfall of the paper would be hailed with a thrill of delight by those who "gain their fortunes by the blood of souls," and who of all things hate to be confronted by the objects of their own injustice and cruelty. While it lives, it cheers the hearts of the oppressed, and helps to arouse the fears of the guilty slave-holder. That the paper has been useful, we have had the best and most abundant evidence. What it has been, if it continues, it will continue to be. The question is, shall it be continued? It ought to be, and with your assistance it shall be continued.

My plan is this: to get every subscriber to the *North Star* to obtain at least one other subscriber, and to forward the same to the *North Star* office, with the subscription money, at once. At the same time you get this circular every other subscriber will receive one, and each is earnestly solicited to obtain one subscriber. Should this be done, and I hope no one will think the task a severe or heavy one—the paper will be placed upon a good basis, and the editor will have a much larger share of time to devote to it than he has hitherto found himself able to command.

Dear Friend, the case is briefly stated, and now is before you. Let me entreat you to render the cause this great service. Remember, that many hands make light work, and although your part may be small, its faithful performance is of the greatest importance. That you may feel the force of this appeal, and be moved to respond to it encouragingly is the sincere desire of your friend and fellow worker in a common cause.

Very Sincerely yours,
Frederick Douglass

Frederick Douglass Mss., University of Rochester

TO CAPT. THOMAS AULD, FORMERLY MY MASTER

No. 4 Alexander St., Rochester, September 3d, 1849

Dear Sir:

I propose to celebrate this, the 11th anniversary of my escape from your dominion, by addressing to you a friendly epistle on the subject of slavery.

I do this partly with a view to the fulfilment of a promise I made you on this day one year ago, and partly to neutralize certain charges which I then brought against you.

Ungrateful and unjust as you, perhaps, deem me, I should despise myself if I could wilfully malign the character even of a slaveholder; and if, at any time, I have appeared to you guilty of such conduct, you have greatly misapprehended me. I can say, with a clear conscience, in all that I have ever written or spoken respecting yourself, I have tried to remember that, though I am beyond your power and control, I am still accountable to our common Father and Judge, in the sight of whom I believe that I stand acquitted of all intentional misrepresentation against you. Of course, I said many hard things respecting yourself; but all has been based upon what I knew of you at the time I was a slave in your family. Of the past, therefore, I have nothing to take back; but information concerning you and your household, lately received, makes it unjust and unkind for me to continue the style of remark, in regard to your character, which I primarily adopted. I have been told by a person intimately acquainted with your affairs, and upon whose word I can rely, that you have ceased to be a slaveholder, and have emancipated all your slaves, except my poor old grandmother, who is now too old to sustain herself in freedom; and that you have taken her from the desolate hut in which she formerly lived, into your own kitchen, and are providing for her in a manner becoming a man and a Christian.

This, sir, is good news; it is all the more gratifying to me, since it deprives the pro-slavery public of the North of what they deem a powerful argument against me, and the abolitionists generally. It proves that the agitation of the subject of slavery does not hinder, if it does not help, the emancipation of slaves at the South. I have been frequently told that my course would have an unfavorable influence upon the condition of my friends and relatives in your possession; and the common argument against abolitionists may be stated as follows: Let slaveholders alone, and they will emancipate their slaves; and that agitation only retards the progress of the slave's liberation. It is alleged that the slaveholder is induced to clutch more firmly what is attempted to be wrested from him. To this argument, your case is a plain contradiction. If the effect of anti-slavery were such as is thus alleged, you would have been among the first to have experienced it; for few slaveholders in this land have had a larger share of public exposure and denunciation than yourself; and this, too, from a quarter most calculated to annoy, and to provoke resentment. All this, however, has not prevented you from nobly discharging the high duty you owed alike to God and to the slaves in your possession. I congratulate you warmly, and I rejoice most sincerely, that you have been able, against all the suggestions of self-interest, of pride, and of love of power, to perform this act of pure justice and humanity. It has greatly increased my faith in man, and in the *latent virtue* even of slaveholders. I say *latent virtue,* not because I think slaveholders are worse than all other men, but because, such are the power and influence of education and habit upon even the best constituted minds, that they paralyze and disorder, if not destroy their moral energy; and of all persons in the world, slaveholders are in the most unfavorable position for retaining their power. It would be easy for me to give you the reason of this, but you may be presumed to know it already.

Born and brought up in the presence and under the influence of a system which at once strikes at the very foundation of morals, by denying—if not the existence of God—the equal brotherhood of mankind, by degrading one part of the human family to the condition of brutes, and by reversing all right ideas of justice and of brotherly kindness, it is almost impossible that one so environed can greatly grow in virtuous rectitude.

You, however, sir, have risen superior to these unhallowed influences, and have added another striking proof to those already existing, that the heart of the slaveholder is still within the reach of the truth, and that to him the duty of letting "the oppressed go free," is not in vain.

I shall no longer regard you as an enemy to freedom, nor to myself—but shall hail you as a friend to both.—Before doing so, however, I have one reasonable request to make of you, with which you will, I hope, comply. It is thus: That you make your conversion to anti-slavery known to the world, by precept as well as example. A publication of the facts relating to the emancipation of the slaves, with the reasons that have led you to this humane act, would doubtless prove highly beneficial to the cause of freedom generally—at the same time that it would place yourself in that high estimation of the public mind to which your generous conduct justly entitles you. I think you have no right to put your candle under a bushel. Your case is different in many respects from that of most repentant slaveholders. You have been publicly and peculiarly exposed before the world for being a slaveholder; and, since you have ceased to be such, a just regard for your own standing among men, as well as a desire to promote the happiness of a deeply injured people, requires you to make known your sentiments on this important subject. It would be truly an interesting and a glorious spectacle to see *master* and *slave,* hand in hand, laboring together for the overthrow of American slavery. I am sure that such an example would tell with thrilling effect upon the public mind of this section. We have already had the example of slaves and slaveholders side by side battling for freedom; but we yet lack a master working by the side of his former slave on the anti-slavery platform. You have it in your power to supply this deficiency; and if you can bring yourself to do so, you will attain a larger degree of happiness for yourself, and will confer a greater blessing on the cause of freedom, than you have already done by the generous act of emancipating your own slaves. With the example before me, I shall not despair of yet having the pleasure of giving you the right hand of fellowship on the anti-slavery platform.

Before closing the present letter, I wish to set you right about a matter which is, perhaps, of small importance to yourself, but is of considerable consequence to me.

In your letter, written three years ago, to Mr. A. C. C. Thompson, of Wilmington, respecting the validity of my narrative, you complained that I failed to mention your intention to emancipate me at the age of 25. The reason of this failure is as follows: You will remember that your promise to emancipate me preceded my first attempt to escape; and that you then told me that you would have emancipated me, had I not made the attempt in question. If you ask me why I distrusted your promise in the first instance, I could give you many reasons; but the one that weighed most with me was the passage of a law in Maryland, throwing obstructions in the way of emancipation; and I had heard you refer to that law as an excuse for continuing your slaves in bondage; and, supposing the obstructions alluded to might prove insuperable barriers to my freedom, I resolved upon flight as the only alternative left me short of a life of slavery. I hope this explanation will be satisfactory. I do not regret what I have done, but rather rejoice in it, as well for your sake as mine. Nevertheless, I wish to be fairly understood, and have, therefore, made the explanation.

I shall here conclude this letter, by again expressing my sincere gratitude at the magnanimous deed with which your name is now associated—and by repeating the ardent hope that you will publicly identify yourself with the holy cause of freedom, to which, since I left your service, I have been most unremittingly devoting myself.

I am, Dear Sir, very respectfully yours,
Frederick Douglass

The Liberator, September 14, 1849

PHILADELPHIA

The papers give an account of another ferocious mob in this mobocratic city. Its violence was directed against the colored people in the neighborhood of Sixth and St. Thomas' street—a large number of whom are represented as having been wounded, and ten or twelve as having been killed. As usual, the excuse for this bloody outbreak is represented to be the fact that white and colored persons were living in the same families together, and associating on equal terms. One of the papers states that this is a mere pretext. But whether it be true or false it conveys an instructive lesson on the bitterness and baseness of the hatred with which colored people are regarded in Philadelphia. When, in any community, a violation of a mere custom, or a disregard of a particular taste, is esteemed an available excuse for setting aside all law, and for resorting to violence and bloodshed, it shows such custom and taste to be profoundly wedded to the affections of the people; and proves them to be most difficult of eradication.

Slavery and prejudice are, evidently, above law and order in Philadelphia—and we are not surprised that *"the society of killers"* should adduce this reason for every outbreak of which they may be guilty. When the Mayor of Philadelphia informed "the *Hutchinson family"* that "he could not protect them from the violence of a mob if they permitted colored persons to attend their concerts," he gave up the government, the peace, and the property of that disgraced city into the hands of a band of atrocious mobocrats. They took authority from the hands of the Mayor, he virtually telling them that they were to have full liberty to endanger the lives, and to destroy the property of any and all persons who should be found acting in disregard of public taste and prejudice, by associating, in any way, with colored persons—and thus, also, he marked out the people of color for destruction whenever the brutal propensities of base white men should prompt them to the work of murderous outrage.

The authority has gone from the government of Philadelphia; and the struggle will be long and fearful, before it will be regained. Since the burning of Pennsylvania Hall,[14] Philadelphia has been from time to time, the scene of a series of most foul and cruel mobs, waged against the people of color—and it is now justly regarded as one of the most disorderly and insecure cities in the Union. No man is safe—his life—his property—and all that he holds dear, are in the hands of a mob, which may come upon him at any moment—at midnight or mid-day, and deprive him of his all.

Shame upon the guilty city! Shame upon its law-makers, and law administrators!—Philadelphia will never be redeemed from the curse of mobs, until it copies the examples set by the government of New York in the late Riots in Astor Place.[15]—F. D.

The North Star, October 19, 1849

PUMPKINS

Yes! Pumpkins! we raised a nice lot of them this season in our own garden. Some of them were very large—yellow as the gold of California—and as deliciously sweet as ever pleased the taste of the most fastidious epicure, or appeased the appetite of the most hungry laborer. It does us good to look upon those pumpkins—and then to partake of them in company with our dear little ones. But it is not so much the good *quality* of the pumpkins to which we would call attention, as to the good *moral* we have extracted from them.—The ground was prepared—seed sown—and the plant cultivated by our own colored hands; and although the soil is *American*, it took no offence on account of our color—but yielded a generous return for our industry. From this we infer that the earth has no prejudice against color, and that nature is no respecter of persons. It pours its treasures as liberally into the lap of colored industry, as into that of the white husbandman. The earth is a preacher of righteousness; it inculcates justice—love—and mercy; repudiates the factitious distinctions of pride and prejudice—and owns all the sons and daughters of men (without regard to color) as its own dear children. Oh! ye Negro hating Americans! our mouth is open unto you! Come, and learn wisdom and goodness from our mother earth, and treat the colored man no longer as an outcast and a despicable being; but as the child of a common Father, who causes His sun to shine alike upon the black and the white—and the elements of nature to respond to the wants of all His creatures.—F. D.

The North Star, October 19, 1849

THE NATIONAL LEAGUE

It is astonishing and mortifying that the people of all others under the broad canopy of heaven, who ought to be the most united, present to the world the least evidence of that union. Smarting under wrongs, and denied rights which should cause all hearts to throb together, as the heart of one man, in a common effort to redress those wrongs, and to achieve those rights, we are yet a disunited, separated, and scattered people, and we present to the world no grand movement, nor comprehensive scheme for bettering our condition.

Without wishing to censure unjustly, or to compare unwarrantably, we do think, that a cause like ours, were it in the hands of any other people, would certainly rally larger numbers, excite a deeper interest, and obtain a better support than now falls to its lot. It is always grievous to be compelled to speak in disparagement of an oppressed people: if we ever do so, it is with a view of inciting them to make the needful exertions for their deliverance: and this is the only apology we deem necessary.

There is not an intelligent colored man in the land who does not know that the colored people in this country need organization; and it has been a cause of deep grief to the noble minded among us that no effort has been made for a general organization, by which the moral power of our people could be made available to our cause. Go where we will we hear a general lament that we are a disunited people; yet how few there are who have the energy and the will to remedy the evil of which all so readily complain.

On the 10th of August last, we suggested the rough outline of a Constitution, which should serve as a landmark to those of our people, who are desirous to secure an *"union of the oppressed for the sake of freedom,"* and although a few among us have readily and wholly responded to our suggestion, the overwhelming mass have remained silent as the grave on the subject. *The Impartial Citizen,* edited by a colored man, did not even notice it. *The Ram's Horn* has been dumb over it. Very few of our public men have, as yet, given to the idea the slightest encouragement. Pittsburgh, that should always be ready to speak, as she always has an opinion, has been silent. Cincinnati, containing a colored population as intelligent, active, and wealthy as any in the country, has not lisped a word, *pro* or *con,* on the subject. New York, as usual, has nothing to say.

What can be the cause of this apparent indifference? Can it be that the professions of regret with which we meet, from time to time, that there is not an union among the colored people, are false and hypocritical? Can it be that the profession is put forth merely as a cloak for indifference and indolence? We cannot believe it. The true reason of the apparent general apathy and unconcern with which the idea of a National League has been received by the people, must be found in the fact, that the subject has not been fairly brought before them. Our leading men have not taken it up, nor pressed its importance upon them. In addition to this, we have reason to believe that sectarianism is not among the least of the causes of the hesitation and coldness with which the movement has been received. Colored people, in common with white people, have their different religious creeds and sects to support—nor are we disposed to quarrel with them on that account; but when they allow their religious differences to stand in the way of proper efforts for their enfranchisement, they, at once, become suitable objects for exposure and rebuke.

There is nothing, necessarily, in a difference of religious opinions, to divide us on subjects pertaining to our civil, social, and political rights and relations; but, in the causes that separate us, there is something more difficult and bitter than mere differences of religious opinions:—it is the bigotry of sect—so narrow and near-sighted that it can see good nowhere beyond the limits of its own particular communion. It is this ignorance and intolerance that stand directly in the way of that union "so devoutly to be wished" for. There is that among us, as among other people, which leads us to reject a thing, good in itself, merely because the person, or the party bringing it forward may entertain opinions on other subjects not stamped with orthodoxy.

We have among us, our little Popes and Bishops, who claim and assume to decide for the colored people what shall be the religious opinions of those who undertake to instruct them. Such men love the uppermost seats in the synagogue, and they will have them or they will have nothing. But it is not our purpose to give an *expose* of the hindrances with which our proposed movement must contend. We see no impediments but what may be easily removed. It is impossible to keep a people asunder for any long time, who are so strongly and peculiarly identified together, when there is a vigorous effort made to unite them. We shall never despair of our people—an union shall yet be effected—our ranks cannot always be divided. The injuries which we mutually suffer—the contempt in which we are held—the wrongs which we endure, together with a sense of our own dignity as men, *must,* eventually lead us to combine. It will one day, become obvious to all, that the evils that afflict us all, require the united strength of all for their removal. At present we as a people, do not feel nor see this. We have not yet learned the philosophy of reform—nor the appreciation of moral forces. There are many among us who easily perceive the change going on in our condition and circumstances, but who have not the most remote conception of the means by which this change is effected. Of the action of mind upon mind they are wholly ignorant. Tell such persons that a well written address, emanating from a colored man, setting forth the wrongs of his people, and pleading for their rights, serves to elevate and improve the condition of the whole colored population; and the thing is so entirely above their comprehension, that it does not even rise in their estimation to the dignity of an idle tale. Tell them that a grand convention of colored persons, assembled from all quarters of the Northern States, in one of our large cities, with its proceedings characterized by intelligence, earnestness, and dignity would command a larger share of respect for our whole people than is now extended to us; and they cannot understand it. They can easily see that a man can be knocked down by brute force; that, if the slaves were able to conquer the country they might be free; but they cannot comprehend that by changing the moral sentiment of the nation, we change its institutions.

Of course in the formation of the National League, it will be idle to look to this class for co-operation. *The success of the movement will depend entirely upon the intelligent and philanthropic portion of our people.* To this class we shall look;—it is upon their moral and intellectual power that the League must rely;—since it is they alone who can exert any considerable influence upon the public mind. *To this class, therefore, we appeal. Let us hear from them.* Let no one hesitate to speak because he may think he sees insurmountable difficulties in the way of the movement. *We want discussion;—we want action:*—the former must precede the latter.

We call upon Pittsburgh, Cincinnati, New York and Boston, to hold public meetings, and to express their opinions freely on the wisdom and desirableness of such a combination as that proposed under the title of *"the National League."* Philadelphia, Chicago, Buffalo and Albany have already spoken, and will undoubtedly, stand ready to give the measure their warmest and most energetic support. A Grand Convention in which these cities with others, are largely represented by the wise and the good, would produce a thrilling effect and a lasting impression on the public mind.—F. D.

The North Star, October 26, 1849

TO ELIZABETH PEASE

Rochester, 8th Nov. '49

My dear friend:

I take up my pen to thank you for the generous donation which you have kindly sent me by the hand of our mutual friend Eliza Nicholson of Carlisle. I am the more grateful because you had already contributed the amount which you had decided to give for this year. I take it as marked kindness that you have thus thought me worthy of your encouragement and support.

The North Star has had a multitude of difficulties to struggle with—perhaps greater than any of my English friends can well understand. I commenced the paper against the advice of many of my best friends, and in this I may have acted unwisely, since they of course do not feel that interest in its success that my former and present relations to them led me to expect. Of the motives which led me to commence the paper, I need say but little. The general contempt with which my people are regarded, the low estimate entertained of the Negro's mental and moral qualities among the white people of this land, and the absence of any very striking confutation of the debasing and depressing theories universally prevailing against us, and the knowledge that the colored people feel a hesitance about speaking through columns of papers conducted by white persons, led me to establish this paper as a means of bring[ing] out their powers in such a manner as to silence hurtful misrepresentations, and to remove the cruel and unnatural prejudices which may be safely set down as the most powerful agency in holding Slavery in this country. How far the motive has been justified by the result, I may leave to others to decide. I am, however, convinced that the effort has not wholly failed. Good, lasting good, has been done by the paper, and I am resolved that it shall continue while I have anything like the necessary means for continuing it.

My own poor abilities as a writer have been heavily taxed and I have performed my part with very little credit, but then I have done the best I could and reason can ask no more. Without ever having had a day's schooling and with no regular or sound knowledge of the rules of grammar, and very little reading, I have managed to keep my paper up nearly two years with very little complaint against me either from its readers or from a sneering contemporaneous press, although the latter have uniformly treated others rudely on this score. Upon the whole I feel a degree of complacency on account of the respect and consideration thus far extended to me by the press and public generally. Especially do I feel gratified for the spirit with which the enterprise is regarded by the people for whose benefit the paper was established. Most of the papers started by colored persons had failed its establishment, and as a consequence our people were generally disheartened and hopeless, and of course they feared that the fate which had consigned all others to defeat would also make mine a failure. It is, therefore, a matter of surprise and gratification that the paper continues, and the more intelligent and respectable among us are exerting themselves hopefully to keep the paper in existence. This is particularly the case with the colored people in Philadelphia who are industriously endeavoring to put the paper on a permanent footing.

Believe me, dear friend, I shall do my utmost to honorably serve the cause of my race, and thereby merit your esteem and approbation.

My family—wife and five children—are all well. I have three boys and two girls. Two boys, Lewis and Fred'k, go to school, and my daughter, of whom you have heard, is also regularly going to school.

I am most sincerely yours,
Frederick Douglass

Anti-Slavery Collection, Boston Public Library

GOVERNMENT AND ITS SUBJECTS

It has long been regarded as the dictate of wisdom, by sagacious legislators, that a government should conciliate, as far as possible, every class of its subjects. It is always deemed unpardonable folly, and flagrant wickedness, for any government needlessly to afflict and insult a portion of its people. Governments are, either exceedingly strong, or exceedingly weak; and that government is strongest which has the fewest foes. This is peculiarly true of our own; it, of all others, should make friends with its subjects, and with every class of its subjects, for the day may come when it will need them all. It is not to be disguised that, in the matter of slave-holding, our nation stands before the world, pre-eminent in infamy; that the existence of slavery, in this country, is looked upon by other nations, as the peculiar weakness, as well as the crime, of the American people; and it is quite easy to perceive that, in the event of a conflict between this and any European power, this vulnerable point would be the first to be attacked. The colored people of this country would be counted as the natural allies of any power which should inscribe on its banners, *Liberty for the black, as well as for the white man.*

But with these truths so obvious to common sense before them, our legislators appear to take the utmost pleasure in wantonly displaying their contempt for the rights and feelings of the growing colored population of the United States. It would be impossible for a government to devise a policy better calculated to make itself the object of hatred than that adopted by our government toward its free colored people; to make us detest the land of our birth—to abhor the government under which we live—and to welcome the approach of an invading enemy as our only salvation, would seem to be the animating spirit and purpose of all the legislative enactments of the country with respect to us. With all its boasted wisdom and dignity, it does not hesitate to use every opportunity of persecuting, insulting and assailing the weakest, and most defenceless part of its subjects or citizens. It acts towards us as though the highest crime we could commit is that of patriotism; and all manner of insult, neglect and contempt, are necessary to prevent the commission of this crime on our part. Our thoughts have been turned in this direction by the contemptible meanness of our present Secretary of State, in refusing to grant to William W. Brown the usual passport granted to citizens about to travel in foreign countries. Mr. Brown remarks (in a recent letter to Mr. Garrison,) that one of his fellow passengers to Europe, was accompanied by a colored servant, and that this servant had with him a regular passport, signed by the Secretary of State, Mr. Buchanan.

This fact presents the American government in its true light. It has no objection whatever to extend its protection to colored servants, but it is resolved, on no occasion, to grant protection to colored gentlemen. A colored man who travels for the benefit of a white man, will have thrown over him the shield and panoply of the United States; but, if he travels for his own profit or pleasure, he forfeits all the immunities of an American citizen. The government in this particular, fairly reflects the lights and shades of the whole American mind; as appendages to white men we are universally esteemed; as independent and responsible men we are universally despised.

In keeping with this spirit, and in pursuance of this policy, the colored man is not permitted to carry a United States' mail bag across the street, nor hand it from a stage driver to a post-master. In the navy, no matter how great may be his talents, skill and acquirements—no matter how daring, heroic, and patriotic he may be, he is forbidden, by the government, to rise above the office of a cook, or a steward, under the flag of the United States.

The colored man, if a slave, may travel in company with his master, into any state or territory in the Union; but if he be a free man, he may not even visit the capitol of the nation (which he helps to support by his taxes), without the liability of being cast into prison, kept there for months together, and then taken out, and sold like a beast of burden, under the auctioneer's hammer, for his jail fees. Besides the gross frauds and ruinous wrongs, heaped, with scandalous profusion, on the heads of the colored people, by the government, the white population at large, (saints and sinners,) are constantly exerting their skill and ingenuity in devising schemes which serve to embitter our lot, and to destroy our happiness.

From places of instruction and amusement, open to all other nations under the sun, we are *excluded;* from the cabins of steamboats, and the tables of Hotels (which are free to English, Irish, Dutch, Scotch and also to the most rude Hoosier of the West) we are *excluded;* from the ecclesiastical convention, and the political caucus, we are generally *excluded;* from the bar and the jury-box of our country we are *excluded;* from respectable trades and employments, and from nearly all the avenues to wealth and power, we are *excluded;* from the Lyceum Hall and the common school, the sources of light and education, we are as a people *excluded.* Meanwhile societies are organized under the guise of philanthropy and religion, whose chief business it is to propagate the most malignant slanders against us, and to keep up in the public mind a violent animosity between us and our white fellow-citizens. Upon this the government smiles with approbation, and exerts its utmost powers to execute the behests of this unnatural and cruel prejudice. What is this but the most discreditable disregard of sound political wisdom, to say nothing of the dictates of justice and magnanimity? Can the colored man be expected to entertain for such a government any feelings but those of intense hatred? Or can he be expected to do other than to seize the first moment which shall promise him success to gratify his vengeance? To apprehend that he would not do so would evince the most deplorable ignorance of the elements of human nature.

We warn the American people, and the American Government to be wise in their day and generation. The time may come that those whom they now despise and hate, may be needed. Those compelled foes may, by and by be wanted as friends. America cannot always sit, as a queen, in peace and repose. Prouder and stronger governments than hers have been shattered by the bolts of the wrath of a *just God*. We beseech her to have a care how she goads the *sable oppressed* in the land. We warn her in the name of retribution, to look to her ways, for in an evil hour those hands that have been engaged in beautifying and adorning the fair fields of our country, may yet become the instruments of spreading desolation, devastation, and death throughout our borders.—F. D.

The North Star, November 9, 1849

ZION CHURCH SCHOOL

We recorded our protest last week against huddling the colored children of this city into the miserable cellar of Zion Church. The colored citizens of this city pay as freely for the support of schools as any other class, and their children are as much entitled to school privileges as are the sons of the wealthiest of this community; and there can be no reason founded in justice why they should be shut out of the fine, airy schoolhouses of the districts, and driven into the dull, damp, dark, and badly ventilated cellar of Zion Church.—It is a disgrace to the city of Rochester that such an act of flagrant injustice and cruelty can be perpetrated against any class of its citizens. The Board of Education have not only stained themselves with the sin of partiality and proscription, but have degraded themselves by duping the stupid creatures who officiate as Trustees in Zion Church. If the colored people of this city must be driven into a separate school, one would think that such a degradation would be sufficient to satisfy the Negro haters, without adding to it the cruelty of crowding them into a cellar. We hope that our brethren in this city will show themselves in earnest about this matter, and will continue to agitate the question of our children's admission into the District Schools.—We must not tamely submit to this violation of our educational rights. This is, just now, the question of questions for the colored people of this place. If we yield willingly to this encroachment, perhaps the next demand will require us to live in a certain part of the city—Our children are to go to a particular school—colored people are to attend their own meeting; and it may, by and bye, follow that we are to occupy a given place in the town. *For one, we say, most distinctly, to the Board of Education, that in no emergency,* will we send a child of ours to the miserable cellar under Zion Church.—F. D.

The North Star, November 9, 1849

THE DESTINY OF COLORED AMERICANS

It is impossible to settle, by the light of the present, and by the experience of the past, any thing, definitely and absolutely, as to the future condition of the colored people of this country; but, so far as present indications determine, it is clear that this land must continue to be the home of the colored man so long as it remains the abode of civilization and religion. For more than two hundred years we have been identified with its soil, its products, and its institutions; under the sternest and bitterest circumstances of slavery and oppression—under the lash of Slavery at the South—under the sting of prejudice and malice at the North—and under hardships the most unfavorable to existence and population, we have lived, and continue to live and increase. The persecuted red man of the forest, the original owner of the soil, has, step by step, retreated from the Atlantic lakes and rivers; escaping, as it were, before the footsteps of the white man, and gradually disappearing from the face of the country. He looks upon the steamboats, the railroads, and canals, cutting and crossing his former hunting grounds; and upon the ploughshare, throwing up the bones of his venerable ancestors, and beholds his glory departing—and his heart sickens at the desolation. He spurns the civilization—he hates the race which has despoiled him, and unable to measure arms with his superior foe, he dies.

Not so with the black man. More unlike the European in form, feature and color—called to endure greater hardships, injuries and insults than those to which the Indians have been subjected, he yet lives and prospers under every disadvantage. Long have his enemies sought to expatriate him, and to teach his children that this is not their home, but in spite of all their cunning schemes, and subtle contrivances, his footprints yet mark the soil of his birth, and he gives every indication that America will, for ever, remain the home of his posterity. We deem it a settled point that the destiny of the colored man is bound up with that of the white people of this country; be the destiny of the latter what it may.

It is idle—worse than idle, ever to think of our expatriation, or removal. The history of the colonization society must extinguish all such speculations. We are rapidly filling up the number of four millions; and all the gold of California combined, would be insufficient to defray the expenses attending our colonization. We are, as laborers, too essential to the interests of our white fellow-countrymen, to make a very grand effort to drive us from this country among probable events. While labor is needed, the laborer cannot fail to be valued; and although passion and prejudice may sometimes vociferate against us, and demand our expulsion, such efforts will only be spasmodic, and can never prevail against the sober second thought of self-interest. *We are here,* and here we are likely to be. To imagine that we shall ever be eradicated is absurd and ridiculous. We can be remodified, changed, and assimilated, but never extinguished. We repeat, therefore, that *we are here;* and that this is *our* country; and the question for the philosophers and statesmen of the land ought to be, What principles should dictate the policy of the action towards us? We shall neither die out, nor be driven out; but shall go with this people, either as a testimony against them, or as an evidence in their favor throughout their generations. We are clearly on their hands, and must remain there for ever. All this we say for the benefit of those who hate the Negro more than they love their country. In an article, under the caption of "Government and its Subjects," (published in our last week's paper,) we called attention to the unwise, as well as the unjust policy usually adopted, by our Government, towards its colored citizens. We would continue to direct attention to that policy, and in our humble way, we would remonstrate against it, as fraught with evil to the white man, as well as to his victim.

The white man's happiness cannot be purchased by the black man's misery. Virtue cannot prevail among the white people, by its destruction among the black people, who form a part of the whole community. It is evident that white and black "must fall or flourish together." In the light of this great truth, laws ought to be enacted, and institutions established— all distinctions, founded on complexion, ought to be repealed, repudiated, and for ever abolished—and every right, privilege, and immunity, now enjoyed by the white man, ought to be as freely granted to the man of color.

Where "knowledge is power," that nation is the most powerful which has the largest population of intelligent men; for a nation to cramp, and circumscribe the mental faculties of a class of its inhabitants, is as unwise as it is cruel, since it, in the same proportion, sacrifices its power and happiness. The American people, in the light of this reasoning, are, at this moment, in obedience to their pride and folly, (we say nothing of the wickedness of the act,) wasting one sixth part of the energies of the entire nation by transforming three millions of its men into beasts of burden.— What a loss to industry, skill, invention, (to say nothing of its foul and corrupting influence,) is *Slavery!* How it ties the hand, cramps the mind, darkens the understanding, and paralyses the whole man! Nothing is more evident to a man who reasons at all, than that America is acting an irrational part in continuing the slave system at the South, and in oppressing its free colored citizens at the North. Regarding the nation as an individual, the act of enslaving and oppressing thus, is as wild and senseless as it would be for Nicholas to order the amputation of the right arm of every Russian soldier before engaging in a war with France. We again repeat that Slavery is the peculiar weakness of America, as well as its peculiar crime; and the day may yet come when this visionary and oft repeated declaration will be found to contain a great truth.—F. D.

The North Star, November 16, 1849

MR. WHIPPER'S OBJECTIONS TO THE PROPOSED NATIONAL LEAGUE CONSIDERED

Necessary and unavoidable engagements abroad, must be our only apology for not sooner replying to Mr. Whipper's late letter on the "National League," published in the *North Star,* No. 48. Anything from that source, touching the interests and prospects of the oppressed and proscribed people to whom we belong, is entitled to very high respect. He is a gentleman of acknowledged ability, a profound thinker, an eloquent and forcible writer, and withal an earnest friend of liberty. From such a man we always differ reluctantly. His letter before us, displays all the qualities of head and heart which we have with pride and pleasure, ascribed to him; and while we differ widely from him in his reasonings and conclusions, upon the subject in question, we are sincerely glad that so able a pen as his, should be wielded by a *sable* hand, and that he has felt called upon to record publicly, his opinions, with respect to the projected League. Perhaps it will not be assuming too much, to account for the difference between us and our esteemed friend, on the ground that we are more practical and less theoretical than he. With abstractions, and theories, he is at home, and in these he can easily find objections to measures which we deem of immediate and practical importance. He sees a seeming (certainly not real) inconsistency between the *end,* and the means by which that *end* is proposed to be attained.—With him the necessary, but rude scaffolding must not be arranged, lest its awkward appearance should obscure the magnificent edifice proposed to be erected.

As an illustration of the truth of what we have just remarked we take the following from his letter:

"The expediency of an organized union among our people, has long engaged my attention, and I do most freely confess that it appears to me to be a subject that is fraught with difficulties and dangers, as well as promises and blessings."

Having confessed the difficulties and dangers to be apprehended from the formation of the proposed League Mr. W. gives his reasons for those apprehensions as follows:

"I believe that the motto, 'Union of the oppressed for the sake of freedom,' will be interpreted by the pro-slavery press, to mean an union of the black against the white man, and the overthrow of American Institutions. For however strange and unnatural it may appear, it is nevertheless true, that the success of any movement among ourselves is more dependent on the praise of our enemies, than the labors of our friends. For of late our denunciations have been as unerringly directed against abolitionists as slaveholders. When you shall have launched the 'League' in the pro-slavery current of this nation, you will be obliged to answer the nautical questions, viz.: 'From whence do you hail? What is your object? and to what port you are destined?' or receive a broadside.

"You well know that we have no security in the divine nature of our object, for that being interpreted in the popular tongue, means 'devil incarnate,' and vestal purity of motive—a rapacious desire to corrupt all that is 'good and holy' in the affections of the multitude. So deeply seated are the religious and political prejudices against which we have to contend, that virtue and vice change their character to suit the complexion of the actor. During the recent eventful period of nations, the press has been teeming with the fate of 'Leagues' for civil and religious reform, and the proclamation has gone forth that God is on the side of the strong.

"It will be useless to say that this is not a complexional question, for its success would depend on so stating it,—and the collision springing from its action against public sentiment, would be more likely to increase and concentrate existing prejudices, than scatter and disseminate them. It is, therefore, no less a dictate of interest than humanity, to avoid a 'complexional issue.' "

Here then are the reasons alleged against the League plainly and strongly stated. Let us examine them. The first point made is, that such a "League" will be interpreted by the pro-slavery press "to mean an union of the black against the white man, and the overthrow of American Institutions."

It may be said, in reply, that the objection is an old one, and is as true as it is old. For never since the day that Moses called upon the Egyptian Monarch to let the Israelites go free, until the day that William Lloyd Garrison startled this guilty land by a similar demand, has there been a movement against slavery and oppression, but which has had in its course, to submit to the embarrassment of *mis*-interpretation, *mis*-representation, and even slander. It is the common Baptism of all great movements. It is the forty days fasting in the wilderness to try the faith, and to test the integrity of their projectors. Let him who cannot stand *mis*-interpretation, never attempt to stem the popular current, for such an one will only attempt, to fail. But after all, we think the apprehensions of our esteemed correspondent are much greater than the occasion will justify. If the public mind were as dark now, on the subject of human rights, as it was twenty years ago, and such a movement had been proposed, the grounds urged

OBJECTIONS TO NATIONAL LEAGUE CONSIDERED 421

would wear a more rational aspect—But now, when colored men can speak, write, and publish their views to the world, with the utmost impunity in the Northern States, it seems almost worse than timidty for us to hesitate in the adoption of measures for our improvement and elevation, from the fear of *mis*-interpretation. There is now in this country a willingness, nay, a waiting, to hear what we have to say. We are, therefore, fully able to set ourselves right before the community. In the first place, we should attempt nothing but what would be right, just; and secondly, we should, of course, have the sympathy of the wise and good of every color in our righteous endeavors. But, says our friend, *"any movement among ourselves is more dependent on the praise of our enemies than the labors of our friends."* A singular notion truly. Are our movements then to be shaped to the pleasure of our enemies? Are we then to conform to their wishes to secure their praises? Shall we adopt such measures, and such measures only, as shall secure the approbation of our oppressors? No—we do not believe that friend Whipper would have us pursue any such unmanly, cringing, and contemptible policy, and yet such might easily be inferred from the idea thrown out by him. We do not know what he means when he says, "Of late our denunciations have been as unerringly directed against abolitionists as slaveholders." If this be true, we are not aware of it, and the offenders ought to be exposed. The "Nautical questions which the League will have to answer, or receive a broadside," are such as may be easily and proudly answered, since its mission will be open and above board. The *"Fate of the Leagues,"* so eloquently referred to, has no terrors to us. They relied upon the sword. "Our weapons are not carnal." The difference is great. But the grand argument against the formation of the "League" is, that it will present a *"complexional issue."* This is a danger to be avoided. But is it true of this movement? Do colored men, by associating themselves together for the purpose of obtaining equal rights with all other citizens, thereby make a "complexional issue" with their white fellow-countrymen? *So it does not seem to us.* It strikes us that the issue is tendered from the other side. "The ground has already been taken, that colored men shall not possess equal, civil, social, and political advantages with white men, leaving us no other alternative but to submit, or to resist.—Now, shall we tamely, quietly submit? shall we remain in the house all day, when others are at work, and merely sally forth in the dark unseen, lest we should seem to make a "complexional issue?" We are not to say to treacherous Pennsylvania, *restore* the *black* man's right of suffrage, for fear of making "complexional issues." We are not to ask admission for our children into common schools, to avoid "complexional issues."—We are not to go into the cabin of steamboats among *white* men, that we may avoid "complexional issues." But seriously, the objection is too palpably absurd to require the aid of ridicule to expose it, and yet it has its advocates in high quarters.

For our part we wish colored men could be induced to make any kind of an issue. We want some signs of life—some evidence of a common desire to improve our present condition and to take some position in the moral world. At present we are for the most part dead. We are seen in the world's activities only by proxy. An occasional head is seen to rise above the surface, but his legs soon give way for the want of sympathy and he falls—perhaps to rise again—perhaps not.—Now an organization such as that suggested by the "League," would at least put us in the way of doing something. It would give us a position. But says our Correspondent, "the thing is impossible—the oppressed have adopted the religious creeds of our oppressors, &c." This is true, but only true of a part of us. There are some among us who repudiate at least, most part of the religion of the land, that assumes the natural inferiority of the colored man. We must, however, stop here, simply by saying that whatever may be the difficulties, dangers and hardships attending it, we are for the formation of a colored National League—and hope to have the influence of our esteemed friend Whipper to help forward that result.—F. D.

The North Star, December 14, 1849

Reference Notes
to Biography of Frederick Douglass

FROM SLAVERY TO FREEDOM

1. *Frederick Douglass' Paper*, April 29, 1853. "It has always been a source of dissatisfaction to the writer," Douglass wrote in 1870, "that he neither knows when nor exactly where he was born." As late as 1894, a year before his death, he was still trying to fill in gaps in his early life. On March 16, 1894, he called upon Dr. Thomas Edward Sears, a grandson of his former owners, Thomas and Lucretia Auld, and discovered that he had been sent to live with Hugh Auld in Baltimore in 1825. "I know," he wrote in his diary, "that it must have been in that year that I went to live in Baltimore because the spring lambs were big enough to be sent to market, and I helped to drive a flock of them from Smiths Dock to Fells Point on the day I landed in Baltimore." (*Frederick Douglass Diary*, Mar. 17, 1894, entry, Douglass Papers, Frederick Douglass Memorial Home, Anacostia, D. C.)
2. In his first autobiography, *Narrative of the Life of Frederick Douglass*, published in Boston, 1845, Douglass stated positively: "My father was a white man. He was admitted to be such by all I ever heard speak of my parentage" (p. 2). On several occasions Douglass intimated that his master might have been his father. In May, 1850, he introduced himself to a New York audience with the remark: "The son of a slaveholder stands before you, by a colored mother." (*National Anti-Slavery Standard*, May 23, 1850.)
3. Harriet Bailey was the mother of an older son, Perry, and of four daughters, two of whom were named Sarah and Eliza. "While I am addressing you," said Douglass in 1848, "four of my own dear sisters and one brother are enduring the frightful horrors of American slavery." (*The North Star*, Aug. 4, 1848.)
4. Frederick Douglass, *My Bondage and My Freedom*, New York, 1855, pp. 56-57.
5. Douglass to Theodore Tilton [September, 1867], *The Independent*, Sept. 12, 1867.
6. *New York Herald*, Sept. 6, 1866.
7. Ethan Allen Andrews, *Slavery and the Slave Trade in the United States*, Boston, 1836, p. 42; John L. Carey, *Slavery in Maryland Briefly Considered*, Baltimore, 1845, pp. 25-27; *Narrative of the Life of Frederick Douglass*, Boston, 1845, p. 31. Hereafter cited as *Narrative*.
8. "The education of free Negroes and slaves was not forbidden by law in Maryland, but the black was indebted for what he got to the interest of individuals or of such societies as the Society of Friends." (Jeffrey R. Brackett, *The Negro in Maryland*, Baltimore, 1889, p. 196.)
9. Speech of Frederick Douglass in Belfast, *Anti-Slavery Standard*, Feb. 26, 1846; *Narrative*, pp. 38-39.
10. In January, 1856, *The Columbian Orator* was listed as one of the Abolition books found in southern schools. (See *De Bow's Review*, vol. XX, p. 69.) The copy of *The Columbian Orator* purchased by Douglass is still preserved in the Frederick Douglass Memorial Home in Anacostia.

11. *My Bondage and My Freedom*, p. 99; Douglass to Mrs. Livermore, Apr. 4, 1885, Douglass *Mss.*, Frederick Douglass Memorial Home, Anacostia, D. C.
12. *Narrative*, pp. 35-36; *Baltimore Gazette*, May 19, 1870.
13. *Narrative*, p. 73; Reception Speech at Finsbury Chapel, Moorfelds, England, May 12, 1846.
14. In *My Bondage and My Freedom*, Douglass prefaced his account of his experiences at Gardiner's shipyards with a brilliant analysis of the effects of slavery upon the southern white workers. He was confident that the "competition and its injurious consequences, will, one day, array the non-slaveholding white people of the slave states, against the slave system, and make them the most effective workers against this great evil" (pp. 309-10). For a discussion of relations between white and Negro workers in the South, see Philip S. Foner, *History of the Labor Movement in the United States*, New York, 1947, pp. 258-65.
15. In addition to these benevolent societies, both male and female, each with from thirty-five to fifty members, the free Negro population of Baltimore had ten churches. ". . . Also, among us," went a report of the free Negroes, "there are various mechanics and others, who have by industry and frugality purchased houses and lots of grounds, horses, drays, carts and carriages. . . ." ("A Reply to a Note from 'A White Citizen,'" signed by John Fortie, Nathaniel Peck, William Levington, *Niles' Register*, vol. XLIX, Oct. 3, 1835, p. 72.)
16. *My Bondage and My Freedom*, p. 330.
17. Douglass did not publicly divulge the method of his escape until March 10, 1873, when, in a speech at the Academy of Music in Philadelphia, he broke his long silence. Even in July, 1865, he was reluctant to permit the story to be made public. "Use the story of my life in any way you see fit," he wrote to Lydia M. Child. ". . . I do not think it well to make known the manner of my escape from slavery. No good end could be served by such publication and some evil might possibly come of it." (Douglass to Lydia M. Child, July 12, 1865, Douglass *Mss.*) Douglass kept the story secret for fear that the conductor who had passed him from Baltimore to Philadelphia would be responsible to Hugh Auld for the loss (from $500 to $650) he had sustained in his slave's escape. Also, he did not want to expose his friends Stanley and Rhodes and did not wish to reveal to slave owners a method employed by fugitive slaves. In his *Narrative*, Douglass sharply criticized some of the Abolitionists in the Underground Railroad for publicizing their activities. Such procedures stimulated the master "to greater watchfulness, and enhance his power to capture his slaves. We owe something to the slaves south of the line as well as to those north of it; and in aiding the latter on their way to freedom, we should be careful to do nothing which would be likely to hinder the former from escaping from slavery. I would keep the merciless slaveholder profoundly ignorant of the means of flight adopted by the slave." (*Narrative*, pp. 100-01.)
18. Quoted by Philip S. Foner, *Business and Slavery*, Chapel Hill, N. C., 1941, p. 1.
19. The New York Vigilance Committee was founded in November, 1835, by a group of white and Negro "Friends of Human Rights" to assist any colored person who might be arrested under pretense of being an escaped slave. But much of its work was to feed and clothe runaways and send them on to some points of safety outside of New York with money and letters of introduction to friends. Ruggles, who had been a traveling agent for *The Emancipator*, a New York anti-slavery newspaper, was, at the time Douglass came to him for aid, publishing *The Mirror for Liberty*, the first magazine edited by a Negro. (For a study of Ruggles, see Dorothy B. Parker, "David B. Ruggles,

An Apostle for Human Freedom," *Journal of Negro History*, vol. XXVIII, Jan., 1943, pp. 23-50.) Ruggles estimated that during the five years he was secretary of the Vigilance Committee, he aided over six hundred slaves to escape. (*The North Star*, Apr. 14, 1848.)
20. *Life and Times of Frederick Douglass*, Hartford, Conn., 1881, p. 183.
21. *Anti-Slavery Standard*, Dec. 23, 1841. Reverend Thomas James relates in his autobiography that while he was preaching in New Bedford in 1841 he heard Douglass speak and licensed him to preach. (*Wonderful Eventful Life of Thomas James, By Himself*, Rochester, 1887, p. 6.) This may actually have happened, but there is no mention of Douglass in the official list of ministers and preachers of the African Methodist Church in 1842. (See *African Methodist Episcopal Church Magazine*, vol. I, Dec., 1842, p. 89.)
22. *Narrative*, p. 117.
23. *Anti-Slavery Standard*, Aug. 26, 1841; *Liberator*, July 9, 1841.
24. Frederick Douglass, "Reminiscences," *The Cosmopolitan*, vol. VII, Aug., 1889, p. 378; *Liberator*, Aug. 20, Sept. 3, 1841.
25. *Boston Evening Transcript*, Aug. 11, 1841; *Anti-Slavery Standard*, Aug. 26, 1841.
26. *Anti-Slavery Standard*, Aug. 26, 1841. No authentic account of Douglass' speech is available. The Nantucket papers did not even mention it and none of the Abolition journals carried a verbatim report. Parker Pillsbury, who was present, recalls that in the course of his remarks, Douglass "gave a most side-splitting specimen of a slave-holding minister's sermon, 'servants obey your masters.' . . ." (*The Acts of the Anti-Slavery Apostles*, Boston, 1884, p. 326.) None of the other accounts mention this and it is doubtful whether Douglass would have used this material on this occasion.
27. In later years different Abolitionists claimed credit for having been the first to induce Douglass to become an anti-slavery lecturer. Garrison's children wrote that it was their father who had advised this step. (W. F. Garrison and F. J. Garrison, *Life of William Lloyd Garrison* [4 vols., New York, 1885-1889], vol. III, p. 292.) However, Edmund Quincy wrote in 1845, "I believe I was the first person who suggested to him becoming an Anti-Slavery speaker." (Quincy to Richard D. Webb, Dec. 13, 1845, Anti-Slavery Letters to William Lloyd Garrison and others, Boston Public Library.) Forty years later still another Abolitionist, James Buffum, insisted that he, too, was responsible for bringing Douglass into the movement as a lecturer. "Mr. Garrison and myself thought it would be a good thing if a man who had endured some of the penalties of slavery could go out and tell his story. And so he was engaged." (James N. Buffum, *Commemoration of the Fiftieth Anniversary of the American Anti-Slavery Society*, Philadelphia, 1884, p. 42.)

THE GARRISONIANS

1. See Gilbert H. Barnes, *The Anti-Slavery Impulse*, New York, 1933; Dwight L. Dumond, *Anti-Slavery Origins of the Civil War*, Ann Arbor, Michigan, 1939, pp. 99-100; Gilbert H. Barnes and Dwight L. Dumond, editors, *Letters of Theodore Dwight Weld, Angelina Grimké Weld and Sarah Grimké*, New York 1934, pp. v-xxvii. (Hereafter cited as *Weld-Grimké Letters*.) Barnes and Dumond are guilty of overemphasizing Weld's influence and underestimating Garrison's. For a summary of their views, see Dwight L. Dumond, "Race Prejudice and Abolition," *Michigan Alumni Quarterly Review*, vol. XLI, Apr., 1935, pp. 377-85.

2. Mary Stoughton Locke, *Anti-Slavery in America, 1619-1808*, Boston, 1901, pp. 15-32; Philip S. Foner, editor, *The Complete Writings of Thomas Paine*, New York, 1945, vol. II, pp. 15-18; Philip S. Foner, editor, *Basic Writings of Thomas Jefferson*, New York, 1944, pp. 14-28, Herbert Aptheker, *To Be Free*, New York, 1948, p. 43; Herbert Aptheker, *The Negro in the American Revolution*, New York, 1940, pp. 7-13.
3. The organization was known, after 1818, as the American Convention for Promoting the Abolition of Slavery and Improving the Condition of the African Race.
4. Quoted by Alice Dana Adams, The *Neglected Period of Anti-Slavery in America, 1808-31*, Boston, 1908, p. 178.
5. L. R. Mehlinger, "The Attitude of the Free Negro toward African Colonization," *Journal of Negro History*, vol. I, July, 1916, pp. 276-301.
6. See *Liberator*, June 18, 1831; *Minutes and Proceedings of the Second National Negro Convention, held in Philadelphia, June 6-11, 1831*.
7. Aptheker, *To Be Free*, p. 50.
8. Arthur M. Schlesinger, *New Viewpoints in American History*, New York, 1932, pp. 201-20; Avery Craven, *The Coming of the Civil War*, New York, 1942, pp. 128-34; Vernon L. Parrington, *Main Currents in American Thought*, New York, 1926, vol. II, pp. 339-78; Albert Bushnell Hart, *Slavery and Abolition*, New York, 1906, pp. 170-74.
9. Garrison was brought to the anti-slavery movement by Benjamin Lundy, a New Jersey Quaker who had learned to hate slavery while working at the saddler's trade in Virginia. Garrison became Lundy's assistant in Baltimore, and edited the weekly *Genius of Universal Emancipation* which Lundy had founded at Mount Pleasant, Tennessee, in 1821. When Garrison began calling the known slave-traffickers by name, his audacity was rewarded with seven weeks in a Baltimore jail.

    Garrison moved rapidly ahead of his mentor after his return to Boston. Lundy had never been won over to the radical idea of immediate emancipation and remained a staunch colonizationist. At first Garrison shared his teacher's views, but, moved by the arguments of the Negro people against the Colonization Society, he investigated for himself. Soon he became an outstanding enemy of the African Colonization Society and the champion of immediate emancipation. (See William Lloyd Garrison, *Address to the Colored People*, 1831, and *Thoughts on African Colonization*, 1832.)
10. *Liberator*, Dec. 14, 1833. The following Negroes were among the delegates to the founding convention of the American Society: James G. Barbadoes, of Massachusetts; James McCrummell, Robert Purvis, James Forten, John B. Vashon and Abraham D. Shadd of Pennsylvania; and Peter Williams of New York. The Negroes who signed the Declaration of Sentiments were: James G. Barbadoes, Robert Purvis, and James McCrummell.
11. See G. M. Stroud, *A Sketch of the Laws Relating to Slavery*, New York, 1858, pp. 33-34.
12. Quoted by Dwight L. Dumond, "Race Prejudice and Abolition," *Michigan Alumni Quarterly Review*, vol. XLI, Apr., 1935, p. 378.
13. Quoted by Henry Wilson, *History of the Rise and Fall of the Slave Power in America*, Boston and New York, 1872, vol. I, p. 257.
14. Printed in *The Liberty Bell*, 1842, pp. 64-66.

15. *Fourteenth Annual Report of the Massachusetts Anti-Slavery Society*, 1846, p. 48; Elizur Wright to James G. Birney, July 16, 1836, Dwight L. Dumond, ed., *Letters of James Gillespie Birney*, New York, 1938, vol. I, p. 334. Theodore Weld, an outstanding worker for the cause, received an annual salary of $416 from the American Anti-Slavery Society (Wright to Weld, Dec. 31, 1833, Barnes and Dumond, editors, *Weld-Grimké Letters*, vol. I, p. 122). Many agents did not even receive the meager salary allotted to them. In 1840 Henry B. Stanton's salary was two years in arrears. (Weld to Tappan, Apr. 10, 1840, *Weld-Grimké Letters*, vol. II, p. 828.) For a detailed study of Abolitionist finances, see Benjamin Quarles, "Sources of Abolitionist Income," *Mississippi Valley Historical Review*, vol. XXXII, June, 1945, pp. 63-76.

16. Weld, son of a New York State Presbyterian minister, had been influenced by Charles G. Finney in the Great Revival, and became chief assistant to the revivalist. Later he went to Oneida Institute to prepare for the ministry. In the winter of 1833-1834 he organized a great anti-slavery revival among the students of Lane Seminary at which they discussed the question of immediate emancipation. When the trustees objected to the discussion, Weld and his followers left Lane Seminary and went to Oberlin which was founded as an Abolitionist institution with Finney as its president. Twelve of the Lane rebels became agents of the American Anti-Slavery Society, and, under Weld's leadership, abolitionized Ohio. All American Society agents were trained by Weld. At the Agents' Convention in New York City, Weld met the Grimké sisters, daughters of a Charleston slaveholder, who had become Abolitionists and come north. Weld married Angelina Grimké.

    When Weld turned his talents to writing and editing, the cause gained a remarkable force whose achievements are miracles even by today's standards. Determined to publish a factual, first-hand proof that emancipation of slaves would work, James A. Thomas and Joseph A. Kimball were sent off to the West Indies to gather facts on the results of emancipation. After the enormous work of cutting and editing, Weld published their *Emancipation in the West Indies* and ran it through several editions of which one alone totaled one hundred thousand copies. When bought in quantity, the book sold for twelve cents a copy.

    Together with his wife, Angelina Grimké Weld, he wrote the greatest of all anti-slavery pamphlets, *Slavery as it is; the testimony of a thousand witnesses*. Assiduously assembling facts on the conditions of the slaves in the South from southern newspapers and from statements of fugitive slaves, Weld and his wife arranged them in a pamphlet of 224 pages which became one of the most powerful weapons in the struggle against slavery.

    In 1842, Weld went to Washington, where he took the leading part in organizing the anti-slavery Congressmen into an effective group.

17. Charlotte Morse to Elizur Wright, Oct. 28, 1845, Elizur Wright Papers, Library of Congress.

18. *National Anti-Slavery Standard*, Nov. 11, 1841; *Liberator*, Jan. 1, 1841; Quarles, *op. cit.*, pp. 75-76; Hart, *op. cit.*, pp. 170-87; *Quarterly Anti-Slavery Magazine*, vol. I, Oct., 1835, p. 104; vol. II, Apr., 1836, p. 310; vol. III, July, 1837, p. 340.

19. Barnes, *op. cit.*, pp. 121-27.

20. Quoted by Philip S. Foner, *History of the Labor Movement in the United States*, p. 267.

21. Wilson, *op. cit.*, vol. I, p. 405; Oliver Johnson, *William Lloyd Garrison*, Boston, 1881, p. 314; *Fourth Annual Report of the American Anti-Slavery Society*, Boston,

1839, p. 23; Wendell Phillips to the *Liberator*, Dec. 2, 1841, in *Liberator*, Dec. 31, 1841.
22. William Lloyd Garrison, *An Address to the Abolitionists of Massachusetts on the subject of Political Action*, pp. 7, 15.
23. *Liberator*, Dec. 15, 1837; Massachusetts Abolition Society, *The True History of the Late Division in the Anti-Slavery Societies*, Boston, 1841; Wendell Phillips Stafford, *Wendell Phillips*, New York, 1911, p. 18; Parker Pillsbury, *The Anti-Slavery Advocate*, Dec., 1844, pp. 218-19; Eliza Wigham, *The Anti-Slavery Cause in America and its Martyrs*, London, 1863, pp. 67-71.
24. Elaine Brooks, "The Massachusetts Anti-Slavery Society," *Journal of Negro History*, vol. XXX, July, 1945, pp. 311-31.
25. W. P. and F. J. Garrison, *Life of William Lloyd Garrison*, vol. II, p. 347; *Liberator*, Apr. 24, 1840; Wilson, *op. cit.*, vol. I, pp. 415-20.
26. Barnes and Dumond, editors, *Weld-Grimké Letters*, vol. II, p. 849.
27. Hart, *op. cit.*, p. 201; *Tenth Annual Report of the Massachusetts Anti-Slavery Society*, Boston, 1842, Appendix, p. 8.
28. Garrison to Henry C. Wright, Oct. 1, 1844, Garrison *Mss.*, Boston Public Library. On Mar. 21, 1856, Garrison wrote to Samuel J. May: "The dissolution of the Union must first precede the abolition of slavery." (Garrison *Mss.*, Boston Public Library.)

ANTI-SLAVERY AGENT

1. One writer branded the whole galaxy of Abolitionists as "a group of fanatics or zealots who never saw a slave in slavery." (J. B. Robinson, *Pictures of Slavery and Anti-Slavery*, Philadelphia, 1853, pp. 74-75.
2. "A South Carolinian," *An Appeal to the People of the Northern and Eastern States*, New York, 1834, pp. 14, 18; A. E. Miller, *A Refutation*, Charleston, 1822, pp. 53-54; H. Manly, *The South Vindicated*, Philadelphia, 1836, *passim*. See also Wilfred Carsel, "The Slaveholders' Indictment of Northern Wage Slavery," *Journal of Southern History*, vol. VI, Nov., 1940, pp. 514-20.
3. Anonymous, *Twofold Slavery*, Baltimore, 1838, p. 122. See also J. L. Carey, *Slavery in Maryland*, Philadelphia, 1836, p. 13.
4. G. Barnes and D. L. Dumond, editors, *Weld-Grimké Correspondence*, vol. II, p. 717.
5. John A. Collins to Garrison, Jan. 18, 1842, *Liberator*, Jan. 21, 1842. See also Vernon Loggens, *The Negro Author*, New York, 1931, pp. 131-32.
6. See *Liberator*, Sept. 17, 24, Oct. 15, 29, Nov. 12, 19, Dec. 3, 14, 1841; Jan. 14, 1842; *Herald of Freedom*, (Concord), Dec. 10, 1841.
7. Abby Kelley to *Herald of Freedom*, (Concord), Nov. 12, 1841; See also *Providence Journal*, Jan. 1, 1842; *Anti-Slavery Standard*, Dec. 23, 1841.
8. See *Liberator*, Oct. 12, 26, Dec. 3, 1841; *Anti-Slavery Standard*, Dec. 23, 1841.
9. Quoted by Parker Pillsbury, *Acts of the Anti-Slavery Apostles*, p. 31; Frederic May Holland, *Frederick Douglass*, New York, 1891, pp. 68-69.
   There is no complete copy of Douglass' famous "Slaveholders' Sermon." The text used here is from reports of the meeting at Faneuil Hall on Jan. 8, 1842, and before the Plymouth County Anti-Slavery Society in December, 1841. See *Tenth Annual Report of the Board of Managers of the Massachusetts Anti-Slavery Society*, Appendix, p. 19, and *Anti-Slavery Standard*, Dec. 23, 1841. For another version of the "Sermon," see *Anti-Slavery Standard*, Oct. 25, 1847.

REFERENCE NOTES 429

10. *Tenth Annual Report of the Board of Managers of the Massachusetts Anti-Slavery Society*, Boston, 1842, pp. 105-06.
11. Douglass was paid $170.34 by the Society for his three months' service. (*Ibid.*, p. 106.)
12. *Herald of Freedom* (Concord), June 3, 1842; A.W.P. in *Liberator*, June 17, 1842. See also *Nantucket Islander* in *Ibid.*, July 8, 1842.
13. *Liberator*, Oct. 1, 8, 15, 1841; Aug. 26, Sept. 2, 1842; *Herald of Freedom* (Concord), Aug. 19, 1842.
14. *Eleventh Annual Report of the Board of Managers of the Massachusetts Anti-Slavery Society*, Boston, 1843, pp. 45-46.
15. *Liberator*, Nov. 18, 1842.
16. *The Latimer Journal and North Star*, Nov. 26, 1842. After Latimer's purchase, the Abolitionists presented a petition to the State Legislature praying that fugitive slaves should never again be arrested by town or city officials, nor held as prisoners in the jails of Massachusetts, and that the State Constitution should be "so amended as shall forever separate the people of Massachusetts from all connection with slavery." The petition, signed by 60,000 persons headed by George Latimer himself, was presented on February 17, 1843, to the Massachusetts House of Representatives. It resulted in the passage of a law, with very few dissenting votes, making it a penal offense for any magistrate or executive officer of the state to assist in the arrest or delivery of any person claimed as a fugitive slave and prohibiting those having charge of the jails and other places of confinement to use them for his detention. (See *The Latimer Journal and North Star*, Nov. 23, 1842; *Twelfth Annual Report of the Massachusetts Anti-Slavery Society*, Boston, 1844, p. 45.)
17. *Salem Register* reprinted in *Liberator*, Dec. 9, 1842.
18. *Twelfth Annual Report of the Massachusetts Anti-Slavery Society*, Boston, 1844, pp. 34-35.
    Early in the year the Rhode Island Anti-Slavery Society employed Douglass to lecture and collect funds. He worked for three months for the Society, meanwhile continuing his lectures in Massachusetts.
19. Frederic May Holland, *op. cit.*, pp. 86-87.
20. Douglass to Maria W. Chapman, Sept. 10, 1843, *Anti-Slavery Letters to Garrison*, Boston Public Library.
    Douglass was dismayed by Mrs. Chapman's reaction to his letter. "Strange to say," he reveals in his autobiography, "my course in this matter did not meet the approval of Mrs. M. W. Chapman, an influential member of the board of managers of the Massachusetts Anti-Slavery Society, and called out a sharp reprimand from her, for insubordination to my superiors. This was a strange and distressing revelation to me, and one of which I was not soon relieved." (*Life and Times of Frederick Douglass*, p. 255.) Douglass' role in this incident foreshadowed his later controversy with the Garrisonians.
    After his resignation, Collins deserted the anti-slavery movement and devoted his entire energies to an experiment in community living in Skaneateles, New York. In 1869 he wrote to Douglass recalling their conflict in Syracuse. (John A. Collins to Douglass, Apr. 12, 1869, Douglass Papers, Frederick Douglass Memorial Home, Anacostia, D. C.)
21. William A. White to Garrison, Sept. 22, 1843, *Liberator*, Oct. 13, 1843; Douglass to William A. White, July 30, 1846, Douglass *Mss.*, Frederick Douglass Memorial Home, Anacostia, D. C.

22. George Bradburn to John A. Collins, Nov. 21, 1843, Anti-Slavery Letters to Garrison, Boston Public Library; F. M. Holland, *op. cit.*, p. 97; *Twelfth Annual Report of the Massachusetts Anti-Slavery Society*, Boston, 1844, pp. 34-35; *Liberator*, Mar. 15, 1844.

23. *Herald of Freedom* (Concord), Feb. 16, 23, 1844.

24. *Life and Times of Frederick Douglass*, p. 242.

25. *The North Star*, Jan. 8, 1848; Frederika Bremer, *The Homes of the New World*, translated by Mary Howitt, New York, 1853, pp. 583-85.

26. *Lynn Pioneer* in *Liberator*, May 30, 1845; *The North Star*, Mar. 12, 1848.

27. As early as Feb. 24, 1845, Wendell Phillips wrote to Elizabeth Pease: "Douglass who is now writing out his story thinks of relaxing by a voyage whether with the Hutchinsons or alone I don't know." (Anti-Slavery Letters to Garrison, Boston Public Library.) According to a statement made by Douglass in 1886, it was Phillips who first suggested that he go abroad. (See Douglass' speech before the Wendell Phillips Club of Boston, *Boston Journal*, Sept. 13, 1886.)

28. James N. Buffum to Gerrit Smith, June 21, 1845, Gerrit Smith Papers, Syracuse University. Buffum urged Smith to raise funds for Douglass' voyage, adding: "Frederick feels a natural delicacy in soliciting funds for this purpose."

29. Frederick, junior, was born in New Bedford early in 1842. Charles Remond was born Oct. 21, 1844, in Lynn.

30. For 1842 Douglass received $300.36 from the Massachusetts Society. For 1843 there was no listing of any payment to Douglass, but it is likely that Collins paid him out of the funds allotted to the general agent. At any rate, Douglass felt keenly the need of money during this year. "I have received a few lines from my wife," he wrote to Maria W. Chapman on Sept. 10, 1843, "asking for means to carry on household affairs. I have none to send her. Will you please see that she is provided with $25 or $30." (Anti-Slavery Letters to Garrison, Boston Public Library.)

    For 1844 Douglass received $142 from the Massachusetts Society. (See *Thirteenth Annual Report of the Massachusetts Anti-Slavery Society*, Appendix, p. 6.)

31. Wendell Phillips to R. D. Webb, July, 1845; Wendell Phillips to James Haughton, Richard Allen and R. D. Webb, Aug. 13, 1845; Maria W. Chapman to R. D. Webb, Aug. 16, 1845, Anti-Slavery Letters to Garrison, Boston Public Library; *Herald of Freedom* (Concord), July 11, 1845. Douglass insisted that only $60 had been raised to help him pay for the passage. (See Douglass to Maria W. Chapman, Mar. 29, 1846, Anti-Slavery Letters to Garrison, Boston Public Library.)

32. Wendell Phillips to Elizabeth Pease, Feb. 24, 1845, Anti-Slavery Letters to Garrison, Boston Public Library. "Language, taste, fancy—eloquence—vigor of thoughts—good sound common sense—manliness are all his," Phillips added. "His imitation is so large that they say he lays in all under contribution & grows fat on the spoils of all the other speakers he hears—but he does not want originality. He never thinks of his color & we never do. He is one of our ablest men."

33. *Philadelphia Elevator* reprinted in *The British and Foreign Anti-Slavery Reporter*, vol. VI, no. 25, Dec. 10, 1845.

A CHATTEL BECOMES A MAN

1. *British and Foreign Anti-Slavery Reporter*, vol. I, new series, Nov. 12, 1845, p. 212; John Wallace Hutchinson, *Story of the Hutchinsons*, Boston, 1896, vol. I, p. 145; Douglass to Thurlow Weed, Dec. 1, 1845, *Liberator*, Jan. 16, 1845; Douglass to Garrison, Sept. 1, 1845, *Liberator*, Sept. 26, 1845.
2. Richard D. Webb to Elizabeth Pease, Sept. 25, 1845, Anti-Slavery Letters to Garrison, Boston Public Library. Webb supplied Douglass with paper and binding for the edition "at cut prices," and estimated that when all of the volumes were sold the author would gain a profit of £180.
3. Douglass to Garrison, Sept. 16, 1845, *Liberator*, Oct. 10, 1845; Douglass to Richard D. Webb, Nov. 10, 1845, Anti-Slavery Letters to Garrison, Boston Public Library; Douglass to Garrison, Feb. 26, 1846, *Liberator*, Mar. 27, 1846.
4. James N. Buffum to Henry Clapp, Jr., Sept. 1, 1845; *Lynn Pioneer*, Sept. 25, 1845; Douglass to Garrison, Sept. 29, 1845, *Liberator*, Oct. 24, 1845; Dublin *Evening Post* reprinted in *Liberator*, Oct. 24, 1845.
5. Cork *Examiner* reprinted in *Liberator*, Nov. 28, 1845; Douglass to Garrison, Oct. 28, 1845, *Liberator*, Nov. 28, 1845.
6. Douglass to Garrison, Jan. 1, 1846, *Liberator*, Jan. 20, 1846.
7. *Free Church Alliance with Manstealers, Glasgow*, 1846, p. 11; *Letter from the Executive Committee of the American and Foreign Anti-Slavery Society to the Commissioners of the Free Church of Scotland, April 2, 1844*, Edinburgh, 1844; Douglass to Richard D. Webb, Feb. 10, 1846; Douglass to Francis Jackson, Jan. 29, 1846; Anti-Slavery Letters to Garrison, Boston Public Library.
8. Douglass to Anonymous, Apr. 23, 1846, *Albany Evening Journal* reprinted in *New York Tribune*, July 8, 1846. In reprinting the letter, the *Tribune* remarked: "The writer, be it remembered, is a 'Runaway Slave,' who, during his eight years of stolen Freedom, in defiance of all the disadvantages under which his class labors, has qualified himself to think and write thus."
9. Douglass to Richard D. Webb, Mar. 29, 1846; Douglass to Maria W. Chapman, Mar. 29, 1849, Anti-Slavery Letters to Garrison, Boston Public Library. Years later, Douglass wrote that Mrs. Chapman's suspicions "stuck in my crop. I could not get it 'down' no how." (Douglass to Richard D. Webb, Sept. 12, 1850, Anti-Slavery Letters to Garrison, Boston Public Library.)
10. Douglass to Richard D. Webb, Apr. 16[?], 1846, Anti-Slavery Letters to Garrison.
    Webb was somewhat critical of Douglass. He wrote to Maria W. Chapman as early as Aug. 30, 1845, that he found Douglass "touchy, huffish, haughty, and I think selfish," and "ever ready to sacrifice his friends to his joke." He admitted, however, that the Negro had "many of the characteristics of the man of genius," and was "a much greater and more powerful man than Remond." "As an advocate and orator—as a company man—as a remarkable example of the triumph over difficulties he is a wonder indeed," he added. "He is exceedingly pleasant and amusing when he pleases." (Anti-Slavery Letters to Garrison, Boston Public Library.)
    Douglass must have heard of this criticism, for in an undated letter to Webb he wrote: "If Mr. Garrison or Phillips have given you any reason to expect perfection in me, they did both you and me a serious wrong." (Anti-Slavery Letters to Garrison, Boston Public Library.)
11. Douglass to Maria W. Chapman, Aug. 18, 1846, Anti-Slavery Letters to Garrison, Boston Public Library.

12. George Thompson to Henry C. Wright, May 23, 1846, Anti-Slavery Letters to Garrison, Boston Public Library.
13. *Report of a public meeting held at Finsbury Chapel, Moorefields, to receive Frederick Douglass, the American slave, on Friday, May 22, 1846*, London, 1846.
14. George Thompson to Henry C. Wright, May 23, 1846, Anti-Slavery Letters to Garrison, Boston Public Library.
    Douglass told Thompson that he could not remain away from his family much longer and would be forced to return home in August unless he should decide to bring his family to England. The conversation led to the raising of a fund for this purpose. "This result was entirely unexpected to me," wrote Douglass to Garrison on May 23, 1846. (*Liberator*, June 26, 1846.)
15. W. P. Garrison and F. J. Garrison, *Life of William Lloyd Garrison*, vol. III, p. 157. (Letter dated London, Aug. 4, 1846); Douglass to Samuel Hanson Cox, D.D., Oct. 30, 1846, *Liberator*, Nov. 27, 1846.
16. *Oswego Daily Advertiser*, reprinted in *Anti-Slavery Standard*, Oct. 29, 1846.
17. Douglass to Horace Greeley, Apr. 15, 1846, *Liberator*, June 26, 1846.
18. Garrison to his wife, Aug. 18, 1846, Garrison *Mss.*, Boston Public Library.
19. Garrison to Henry Clapp, Jr., Aug. 27, 1846, Garrison *Mss.*, Boston Public Library; Garrison to Henry C. Wright, W. P. Garrison and F. J. Garrison, *op. cit.*, vol. III, p. 170.
20. Garrison to his wife, Sept. 17, 1846, W. P. Garrison and F. J. Garrison, *op. cit.*, vol. III, p. 167; *Dunham Herald*, reprinted in *Liberator*, Nov. 13, 1846; *Liberator*, Dec. 25, 1846.
21. Douglass to William A. White, July 30, 1846, Douglass *Mss.*, Frederick Douglass Memorial Home, Anacostia, D. C.; *Farewell Speech of Mr. Frederick Douglass Previously to Embarking on Board the Cambria upon his Return to America, Delivered at the Valedictory Soiree Given to Him at the London Tavern, on March 30, 1847*, London, 1847.
22. Douglass to William A. White, July 30, 1846; Douglass to Isabel Jennings, Sept. 22, 1846; Douglass *Mss.*, Frederick Douglass Memorial Home, Anacostia, D. C.; Garrison to Elizabeth Pease, April 1, 1847, Garrison *Mss.*, Boston Public Library.
23. The manumission document read: "To all whom it may concern: Be it known, that I, Hugh Auld, of the city of Baltimore, in Baltimore county, in the State of Maryland, for divers good causes and considerations, me thereunto moving, have released from slavery, liberated, manumitted, and set free, and by these presents do hereby release from slavery, liberate, manumit, and set free, *My Negro Man*, named *Frederick Bailey*, otherwise called *Douglass*, being of the age of twenty-eight years, or thereabouts, and able to work and gain a sufficient livelihood and maintainence; and him the said Negro man, named *Frederick Bailey*, otherwise called *Frederick Douglass*, I do declare to be henceforth free, manumitted and discharged from all manner of servitude to me, my executors, and administrators forever.
    "In witness whereof, I the said Hugh Auld, have hereunto set my hand and seal, the fifth of December, in the year one thousand eight hundred and forty-six.
    "*Hugh Auld.*"
    To this document was annexed the bill of sale.
    Douglass published these documents in *The North Star*, December 3, 1847. He added these words as a preface: "We give our readers the evidence of our right to be free in this democratic and Christian country—not so much however

to establish our right to ourself as to expose the cold-blooded Methodist man-stealer, who claimed us as his property, and the hypocritical nation that has sanctioned his infamous claim. We shall send him a copy of this paper."
24. Lucretia Mott to Richard D. Webb, Feb. 21, 1847, Anti-Slavery Letters to Garrison, Boston Public Library; Philadelphia Female Anti-Slavery Society in *Liberator*, Mar. 19, 1847; Increase S. Smith in *Ibid.*, Jan. 15, 1847; Garrison to Elizabeth Pease, Apr. 1, 1847, Garrison *Mss.*, Boston Public Library; *Liberator*, Mar. 19, 1847.
25. Douglass to Henry C. Wright, Dec. 22, 1846, *Liberator*, Jan 29, 1847.
26. *Liberator*, Apr. 30, 1847; *London Morning Advertiser*, reprinted in *Liberator*, Apr. 30, 1847; *Farewell Speech of Mr. Frederick Douglass . . . March 30, 1847*, London, 1847.
27. Douglass to the London *Times*, Apr. 6, 1847; Douglass to Garrison, Apr. 21, 1847, *Liberator*, Apr. 30, 1847; *Liberator*, May 14, 1847; *Howitt's Journal*, vol. I, 1847, p. 225.
28. Ralph Varian to *British and Foreign Anti-Slavery Reporter*, vol. VI, Dec. 10, 1845. See also the poems "Farewell to Frederick Douglass who sailed from England for America, April 4th, 1847, Easter Sunday," *Howitt's Journal*, vol. I, 1847, pp. 222-23; *Poem on the Embarkation at Liverpool of Mr. Frederick Douglass upon his return to America, by F. N. D.*, Manchester, July 8, 1847 (pamphlet in Schomburg Collection, New York Public Library, 135th Street Branch); Garrison to Elizabeth Pease, Apr. 1, 1847, Garrison *Mss.*, Boston Public Library; Douglass to Julia Griffiths, Oct. 13, 1847, *Howitt's Journal*, vol. II, 1848, p. 319.
29. *Liberator*, June 8, 1849.

FOUNDING *THE NORTH STAR*

1. *Lynn Pioneer and Herald of Freedom*, Apr. 25, 1847; *Anti-Slavery Standard*, May 6, 1847; *Liberator*, May 21, June 4, 1847; *Sixteenth Annual Report of the Massachusetts Anti-Slavery Society*, Boston, 1848, p. 41.
2. *Abolition Fanaticism in New York: Speech of a Runaway Slave from Baltimore at an Abolition meeting in New York Held May 11, 1847.*
   The introduction to the pamphlet went: "The following report will show to Marylanders, how a runaway slave talks, when he reaches the Abolition regions of the country. This presumptive Negro was even present at the London World's Temperance Convention last year; and in spite of all the efforts of the American Delegates to prevent it, he palmed off his Abolition bombast upon an audience of 7000 persons! Of this high-handed measure he now makes his boast in New-York, one of the hot-beds of Abolitionism. The Report is given exactly as published in The New York Tribune. The reader will make his own comments."
3. *The National Era*, June 3, 1847.
4. *Howitt's Journal*, vol. I, 1847, p. 239; Douglass to the *Boston Daily Whig* reprinted in *Liberator*, July 9, 1847; *The North Star*, Dec. 22, 1848.
5. Douglass to Mary Howitt, May 10 [1848], *Howitt's Journal*, vol. I, 1847, p. 352.
6. I. G. Penn, the *Afro-American Press and its Editors*, Springfield, Mass., pp. 25-57.
   There is also record of the *Albany Sentinel* issued by a Negro in 1832. I am indebted to Dr. Herbert Aptheker for this information.
7. *New York Tribune* and *Albany Evening Journal*, reprinted in *Liberator*, Feb. 13, 1846.

434 LIFE AND WRITINGS OF FREDERICK DOUGLASS

8. Wendell Phillips to Elizabeth Pease, Aug. 29, 1847, Anti-Slavery Letters to Garrison, Boston Public Library. Phillips suggested that the money raised for the launching of a paper should be invested "in stock yielding 7 or 8 percent—say $240 per year—which will relieve him for staying at home, more than his press would. Even at 6 per cent it would do well. He is gathering golden opinion—rolling up popularity—all wonder at his talents, so much improved by travel."
9. *Liberator,* July 23, 1847.
10. London *People's Journal,* July 24, 1847, reprinted in *Anti-Slavery Standard,* Aug. 26, 1847.

    The journals referred to were *The Mystery,* published in Pittsburgh and edited by Martin R. Delaney; *The Genius of Freedom,* published and edited in New York City by David Ruggles; *The Ram's Horn* also published in New York City and edited by Willis Hodges and Thomas Van Rensselaer.

    The Ram's Horn announced that it had offered to suspend publication if Douglass decided to publish his paper, "that there might be no strife between us. . . ." (Reprinted in *Liberator,* July 23, 1847.)

    For some months after abandoning his project, Douglass served as an assistant editor for *The Ram's Horn* and as a regular contributor for the *Anti-Slavery Standard.* The *Standard* proudly announced its accession of "a writer of no common power." (Reprinted in *Liberator,* Aug. 20, 1847.)
11. Quoted by Goldwin Smith, *William Lloyd Garrison,* New York and London, 1892, p. 150; *Liberator,* Sept. 3, 10, 1847.
12. Douglass to Sidney B. Gay, Aug. 7, 1847, *Anti-Slavery Standard,* Aug. 19, 1847; *Liberator,* July 23, Aug. 20, 1847; Frederic May Holland, *Frederick Douglass,* pp. 155-57; Garrison to his wife, Aug. 12, 13, 1847, W. P. Garrison and F. J. Garrison, *Life of William Lloyd Garrison,* vol. III, p. 193.
13. *Cleveland Plaindealer,* reprinted in *Anti-Slavery Standard,* Sept. 9, 1847; Garrison to his wife, Aug. 25, 1847, *Liberator,* Sept. 10, 1847.
14. Minute Book of the Western Anti-Slavery Society, Library of Congress, Manuscript Division.
15. Garrison to his wife, Aug. 20, 28, 1847, W. P. Garrison and F. J. Garrison, *op. cit.,* vol. III, pp. 203-04; *Liberator,* Sept. 10, 1847.
16. *Anti-Slavery Bugle,* Sept. 10, 1847; *Cleveland True-Democrat,* reprinted in *Anti-Slavery Standard,* Sept. 23, 1847.
17. Samuel J. May to Garrison, Oct. 8, 1847, Anti-Slavery Letters to Garrison, Boston Public Library.
18. Garrison to his wife, Oct. 20, 1847, Anti-Slavery Letters to Garrison, Boston Public Library.
19. Douglass to J. D. Carr, Nov. 1, 1847, *British Friend,* reprinted in *Anti-Slavery Standard,* Jan. 27, 1848; *Life and Times of Frederick Douglass,* p. 317.
20. Garrison to his wife, Oct. 20, 1847, Samuel J. May to Mary Carpenter, Mar. 4, 1848, W. P. Garrison and F. J. Garrison, *op. cit.,* vol. III, p. 209.
21. Douglass to J. D. Carr, Nov. 1, 1847, *British Friend,* reprinted in *Anti-Slavery Standard,* Jan. 27, 1848; *Anti-Slavery Bugle,* reprinted in *Anti-Slavery Standard,* Sept. 30, 1847. In his letter to his wife from Cleveland, Oct. 30, 1847, Douglass referred to his intention "for establishing a paper here, to be called 'The North Star'. . . . " (W. P. Garrison and F. J. Garrison, *op. cit.,* vol. III, p. 209.)
22. In explaining the choice of the title for his journal, Douglass wrote in its first issue: "Of all the stars in this 'brave old, overhanging sky,' *The North Star* is

our choice. To thousands now free in the British dominions it has been the *Star of Freedom*. To millions, now in our boasted land of liberty, it is the *Star of Hope*...."

A newspaper issued during the Latimer case was called the *Latimer Journal and North Star*, and a paper published in Danville, Vermont, was called *The North Star*.

It is well known, that one of the most celebrated of the songs of fugitive slaves referred to the north star:
> *I kept my eye on the bright north star,*
> *And thought of liberty.*

23. William Peck, *History of Rochester and Monroe County*, Rochester, 1892, vol. I, p. 77; Orlo J. Price, "The Significance of the Early Religious History of Rochester," *Publications of the Rochester Historical Society*, Rochester, N. Y., vol. III, 1924, pp. 180-81; Adelaide Elizabeth Dorn, "A History of the Anti-Slavery Movement in Rochester and Vicinity," unpublished M.A. Thesis, University of Buffalo, pp. 49-51.

24. Douglass to J. D. Carr, Nov. 1, 1847, *British Friend*, reprinted in *Anti-Slavery Standard*, Jan. 27, 1948.

THE EDITOR AND PUBLISHER

1. Douglass to Gerrit Smith, May 1, 1851, Gerrit Smith Papers, Syracuse University; Horace McGuire, "Two Episodes of Anti-Slavery Days," *Publications of the Rochester Historical Society*, Rochester, N. Y., vol. IV. 1925, p. 219. Douglass laid the blame for frequent errors and inaccuracies in *The North Star* on the fact that the paper was printed outside of his shop.

2. *The North Star*, Jan. 8, 1848; *Liberator*, Jan. 28, 1848; *Anti-Slavery Standard*, Jan. 27, 1848; Frederick G. Detweiler, *The Negro Press in the United States*, Chicago, 1922, p. 42; *Howitt's Journal*, vol. III, 1848, p. 288.

3. *Sunday Dispatch* reprinted in *The North Star*, Jan. 21, 1848; *Rochester Daily Advertiser*, Dec. 18, 1847; William C. Nell to Garrison, Jan. 23, 1848, *Liberator*, Feb. 11, 1848.

4. Douglass to Martin R. Delany, Jan. 12, 1848, Douglass *Mss.*, Frederick Douglass Memorial Home, Anacostia, D. C.

The mortgage deed was for $500. The deed itself is in the Douglass Papers in the Frederick Douglass Memorial Home at Anacostia, D. C.

5. Douglass to Julia Griffiths, Apr. 28, 1848, Douglass *Mss.*, Frederick Douglass Memorial Home, Anacostia, D. C.

6. *The North Star*, Apr. 27, 1849.

7. *Ibid.*, Nov. 17, 1848.

"I have been on a little lecturing tour to Geneva," Douglass wrote on Feb. 21, 1848, "and had to ride all night in order to meet my engagements here. This riding all night is killing me, and I am resolved to stop it." (Douglass to Abigail and Lydia Mott, Feb. 21, 1848, Frederick Douglass *Mss.*, Henry E. Huntington Library. See also *The North Star*, Jan. 8, 1848.)

It is of some interest in this connection to consider a remark made by one of Garrison's sons in 1891 who wrote that "selfishly considered his [Douglass'] journalistic step was advantageous in giving him a more settled life than that of an itinerant lecturer." (*The Nation*, vol. LII, May 7, 1891, p. 388.)

8. Douglass to Gerrit Smith, Mar. 1, 1849, Gerrit Smith Papers, Syracuse Uni-

versity; *The North Star*, Dec. 22, 1848, Jan. 19, 1849; *Anti-Slavery Standard*, July 12, 1849.
9. Douglass to Julia Griffiths, Oct. 13, 1847, Douglass *Mss.*, Frederick Douglass Memorial Home, Anacostia, D. C.; *Life and Times of Frederick Douglass*, p. 242; Douglass to Gerrit Smith, May 1, 1851, Gerrit Smith Papers, Syracuse University.
10. Douglass to Gerrit Smith, May 1, 1851, Gerrit Smith Papers, Syracuse University; *The North Star*, Mar. 15, Apr. 12, May 30, Oct. 31, Dec. 5, 1850. *Frederick Douglass' Paper* of Jan. 15, 1858, printed documents showing that the mortgage was paid off in 1853. (See *The Anti-Slavery Reporter*, Apr. 1, 1858, p. 96.)
11. John Thomas to Gerrit Smith, Jan. 27, Feb. 4, May 6, June 14, Dec. 30, 1850, Gerrit Smith Papers, Syracuse University; Douglass to Gerrit Smith, May 1, 28, June 4, 18, 1851, Gerrit Smith Papers, Syracuse University.

Thomas wanted to receive eight dollars a week as assistant editor while Douglass thought he could only afford to pay six dollars. Furthermore, Thomas wished the paper to be published in Syracuse while Douglass insisted on Rochester. Douglass won out on both points. (See John Thomas to Gerrit Smith, June 14, 1851; Douglass to Gerrit Smith, May 28, 29, June 4, 1851, Gerrit Smith Papers, Syracuse University.)
12. *Frederick Douglass' Paper*, June 26, 1851.

In 1852 Smith contributed $1200 to the paper. (See *Frederick Douglass' Paper*, Dec. 17, 1852.) On Jan. 14, 1853, Douglass wrote to Smith: "Paper getting along well." (Gerrit Smith Papers, Syracuse University.)
13. *Frederick Douglass' Paper*, June 26, 1851.
14. *Frederick Douglass' Paper*, Jan. 9, 1854.
15. *Frederick Douglass' Paper*, Feb. 24, 1854.
16. *British Banner*, reprinted in *Frederick Douglass' Paper*, Apr. 8, 1853; *Autographs for Freedom*, Rochester, 1854, pp. 44-60, 70-76.
17. "The Anti-Slavery Appeal to Christian Public of Glasgow and Edinburgh," *The Anti-Slavery Reporter*, Apr. 1, 1857, pp. 80-82; May 1, 1857, pp. 118-19; Sept. 1, 1857, p. 215.
18. *The Anti-Slavery Reporter*, Nov. 1, 1855, p. 263.
19. *Ibid.*, Apr. 1, 1857, pp. 80-82, May 1, 1857, pp. 119-20, May 2, 1859, p. 120; Douglass to Mrs. Maxwell, Treasurer of the Clogher Anti-Slavery Society, Oct. 10, 1857, *The Anti-Slavery Reporter*, Dec. 1, 1857, p. 279, Oct. 1, 1858, p. 238.
20. Douglass to Gerrit Smith, July 2, 1860, Gerrit Smith Papers, Syracuse University. A copy of the weekly for July 8, 1859, is in the Wisconsin State Historical Society at Madison. Very few copies of *Frederick Douglass' Paper* for the period 1856-1860 are in existence.
21. Douglass to Elizabeth Pease, Nov. 8, 1849, Anti-Slavery Letters to Garrison, Boston Public Library; Jane Marsh Parker, "Reminiscences of Frederick Douglass," *The Outlook*, vol. LI, Apr. 6, 1895, p. 552. "Think what editing a paper was to me before Miss Griffiths came," Douglass once wrote.
22. Not infrequently the subscribers would read: "We have been so much on the wing of late as to have little time to devote to our editorial duties. . . ." (*Frederick Douglass' Paper*, Sept. 10, 1852.) In the Dec. 18, 1851, issue Douglass wrote: "I have during the last month, been for the most part, too much disabled by illness to attend to the Editorial department of this paper—or to do anything towards its publication."

23. One of the books serialized was Charles Dickens' *Bleak House*. The book reviews were usually written by Julia Griffiths, but occasionally Douglass would review an important book on the editorial page.
24. *Frederick Douglass' Paper*, May 26, 1854.
25. Douglass to Gerrit Smith, Apr. 24, 1868, Gerrit Smith Papers, Syracuse University.
26. *New York Tribune*, Sept. 18, 1857; Francis Julius Lemoyne to Gerrit Smith, July 28, 1851, Gerrit Smith Papers, Syracuse University; Quoted in A. H. Payne, "The Negro in New York Prior to 1860," *The Howard Review*, vol. I, June, 1923, p. 24.
27. Lindsly M. Moore to Gerrit Smith, Nov. 10, 1852, Gerrit Smith Papers, Syracuse University; *Life and Times of Frederick Douglass*, p. 323.
28. Dr. James McCune Smith to Gerrit Smith, July 28, 1848, Gerrit Smith Papers, Syracuse University.
29. *The North Star*, Jan. 7, 1848; *Anti-Slavery Bugle*, Aug. 24, 1850.
30. *The North Star*, July 14, 21, 1848; *Frederick Douglass' Paper*, Apr. 3, 1855.
31. *Anti-Slavery Bugle*, Aug. 10, 1850; *The North Star*, Jan. 7, 1848.
32. *Frederick Douglass' Paper*, Apr. 8, 1855. "She should be called no longer the *Black Swan*, but the White Raven," wrote Douglass. (*Ibid.*, Feb. 26, 1852.)
33. *The North Star*, May 30, 1850.
34. *Frederick Douglass' Paper* reprinted in *Autographs for Freedom*, edited by Julia Griffiths, Rochester, 1853, pp. 158-60.
35. *The North Star*, Jan. 26, Mar. 23, 1849; *Frederick Douglass' Paper*, Feb. 26, 1852; *Douglass' Monthly*, Feb., 1859. *The African Repository* (vol. XXVI, Oct., 1850, pp. 289-94) contains several excerpts from Douglass' editorials dealing with colonization as well as the answer of the emigrationists.
36. Annual Report of the American and Foreign Anti-Slavery Society for 1853, New York, 1854.
37. *The North Star*, Feb. 18, 1848; *Frederick Douglass' Paper*, Jan. 22, 1852. Douglass made it quite clear that he did not oppose missionary work in Africa. In a letter to Benjamin Coates he wrote: "My heart can never be indifferent to any legitimate movement for spreading the blessings of Christianity and civilization in that country. But the effort must not be to get the Negroes out of this country but to get Christianity into that." (Douglass to Benjamin Coates, Apr. 17, 1856, William M. Coates Papers, Historical Society of Pennsylvania.)
38. *Frederick Douglass' Paper*, Jan. 12, 1855.

Reference Notes
to Writings and Speeches of Frederick Douglass

PART I

1. See pp. 52-53.
2. John Anderson Collins (1810-1899) was general agent of the Massachusetts Anti-Slavery Society in 1839, and served as its agent in Europe from July, 1840, to November, 1841. Later editor of the *Monthly Garland,* he established a co-operative community in New York state based on Fourieristic principles. He advocated that the reform movement concern itself *"not to free Negro slaves alone, but to remove the cause which makes us all slaves."* (*The Social Pioneer and Herald of Progress,* Boston, 1844, pp. 13-14.)
3. See pp. 53-56.
4. In 1837, Elijah P. Lovejoy (1802-1837), a clergyman who had edited an anti-slavery paper in St. Louis, was forced to leave that city and to carry on his work in Alton, Illinois. Here he organized the Illinois Anti-Slavery Society and edited the *Alton Observer.* Pro-slavery mobs destroyed one printing press after another, and, on November 7, 1837, the night after the third press was installed, the printing office was attacked and Lovejoy was killed while defending his property. Thereafter he was referred to as the "martyr abolitionist."
5. John L. Brown of Fairfield, South Carolina, was convicted in the fall of 1843 of aiding a slave to escape, and was sentenced to be hanged. Petitions poured in to Governor James Henry Hammond (1810-1864) demanding that he reprieve the sentence. To one of the Memorials, that from the Free Church of Glasgow, Hammond replied, defending slavery. He also sent two letters to Thomas Clarkson, elaborating his pro-slavery arguments. The Free Church and Clarkson letters were published in pamphlet form in late May and June, 1845, by the Charleston *Mercury;* were translated and circulated all over Europe. They were republished in 1853 in the *Pro-Slavery Argument,* and again in 1860 in *Cotton is King and Pro-Slavery Arguments.*
6. Cassius M. Clay (1810-1903), the son of a large slaveholder in Kentucky, was inspired by William Lloyd Garrison whom he heard at Yale College and became an Abolitionist. In June, 1845, he founded the newspaper, *True American,* in Lexington which campaigned to rid Kentucky of slavery. Two months later a committee of sixty prominent Lexingtonians visited his office while he was absent, boxed up his equipment, and dispatched it to Cincinnati. Clay continued to publish his paper from this city, and later, changing its name to the *Examiner,* he moved to Louisville.
7. See pp. 62-63.
8. The reference is to the Committee of the British and Foreign Anti-Slavery Society. The committee was founded at a general anti-slavery convention held in London, in June, 1840, and authorized to call world conventions to which friends of the cause on both sides of the Atlantic would be invited. William Allen was the first chairman of the committee.
9. At the 1840 convention of the American Anti-Slavery Society, Abby Kelley was

appointed to serve upon a committee. A group of delegates who opposed this action withdrew from the Society, and, at the call of Lewis Tappan, formed a new society, the American and Foreign Anti-Slavery Society, from which women were carefully excluded. Referred to as the New Organization to distinguish it from the American Anti-Slavery Society under Garrison's leadership, the members were called the New Organizationists.

A section of those who formed the new organization, believing in political action, organized in 1840 the Liberty Party and nominated James G. Birney for President. In 1843 the Garrisonians remarked: "The distinction which was at first attempted to be made between New Organization and Third party, is now proved to be scarcely a difference." (*Eleventh Annual Report of the Massachusetts Anti-Slavery Society*, Boston, 1843, pp. 63-64.)

The no-organization Abolitionists were men and women disgusted with both the old and new organization. Thus Gerrit Smith wrote to Theodore Weld on July 11, 1840: "Like yourself, I can go neither with the Old nor New Anti-slavery Organization *at the present*. I am sick, heart sick, of the quarrels of abolitionists between themselves. . . ." (Gilbert Barnes and Dwight W. Dumond, eds., *Letters of Theodore Dwight Weld, Angelina Grimké Weld and Sarah Grimké*, New York, 1934, vol. II, p. 849.)

10. In 1786, Thomas Jefferson wrote to M. de Meusnier: "What a stupendous, what an incomprehensible machine is man! Who can endure toil, famine, stripes, imprisonment, and death itself, in vindication of his own liberty, and, the next moment, be deaf to all those motives whose power supported him through his trial, and inflict on his fellow men a bondage, one hour of which is fraught with more misery, than ages of that which he rose in rebellion to oppose." (Philip S. Foner, ed., *Thomas Jefferson: Selections from his Writings*, New York, 1943, p. 67.)

11. The reference is to *Slavery as it is: the testimony of a thousand witnesses*, prepared by Theodore D. Weld and published in 1839 by the American Anti-Slavery Society. From fugitive slaves in the North and from Southern newspapers Weld assembled facts on conditions of slaves in the South. In 1886, Douglass wrote that "His [Weld's] 'Testimony of a Thousand Witnesses' did as much for the cause of the Slave in the early times as 'Uncle Tom's Cabin' did for it in the later years." (Douglass to Garrison, May 1, 1886, Douglass *Mss.*, Frederick Douglass Memorial Home, Anacostia, D. C.)

12. In June, 1838, the laboring classes of England under the leadership of the London Working Men's Association drew up a manifesto known as "The People's Charter" which made six political demands: universal (manhood) suffrage, annual parliaments, vote by ballot, the abolition of property qualifications for membership in the House of Commons, payment of members of Parliament, and equal electoral districts. In addition to these demands the Chartist movement came out for numerous social and economic reforms. In 1840 the National Charter Association was formed.

The Anti-Corn Law League under the leadership of Richard Cobden and John Bright led the battle for repeal of the Corn Law which fixed duties on the importation of corn according to the price of corn in England. This was a terrible hardship for the laboring classes who were impoverished by low wages and the soaring cost of living.

13. The reference is to the Democratic Party. (For an analysis of northern labor's role in the struggle over slavery, see Philip S. Foner, *History of the Labor Movement in the United States*, New York, 1947, pp. 266-96.)

14. On April 25, 1846, an encounter took place between American troops, commanded by Captain Thornton, and Mexican troops under General Arista in which several American soldiers were killed. The report of the encounter reached Washington May 9. Two days later President Polk informed Congress that war existed between Mexico and the United States. On May 13, Congress authorized the President to accept volunteers for the prosecution of the war.

15. The riot began when a group of young hoodlums attacked a parade of colored men and boys organized to celebrate the progress of the temperance cause and the emancipation of the slaves in the British West Indies. The attack on the Negroes spread rapidly. In the next few days Negroes were stoned and beaten, a hall designed for the holding of their meetings was burned, and a Presbyterian Church set on fire. The cause of the riot was said to be a banner in the parade which carried the motto "Liberty or Death" over the figure of a Negro and showed St. Domingo in flames with white people massacred by the slaves. A reporter for the Philadelphia *Public Ledger* investigated this charge and found it to be completely false. "The banner," he wrote, "contains nothing more than the figure of an *emancipated slave,* pointing with one hand to the broken chains at his feet, and with the other to the word 'Liberty' in gold letters over his head. The burning town turns out to be a representation of the *rising sun,* and a *sinking ship,* emblematic of the dawn of freedom and the wreck of tyranny." (*Public Ledger,* Aug. 4, 1842.)

16. In 1846 the League of Universal Brotherhood was founded by Elihu Burritt (1810-1879), to lead a movement against war. Its members, numbering in a few years 20,000 Americans and 20,000 Englishmen, took an iron-clad oath never to support any war for whatever purpose. During the Oregon crisis, when Burritt was also editing the *Advocate of Peace and Universal Brotherhood,* he co-operated with friends in Manchester, England, in an exchange of "Friendly Addresses" between British and American cities, merchants, ministers, and laborers.

17. The territory west of the Rocky Mountains, north of 42° and south of 54° 40′, was claimed by Spain, Great Britain, the United States, and Russia, but in 1818 by the terms of the Joint Occupation Treaty the territory was jointly occupied by Great Britain and the United States. On April 27, 1846, Congress authorized President James K. Polk to give notice of the termination of this treaty and claim the area for the United States. The situation seemed likely to lead to war, but on June 18, 1846, a compromise was agreed upon which settled the Oregon dispute by continuing the boundary east of the Rockies to the sea.

18. In October, 1841, the brig *Creole* sailed from Virginia for New Orleans, laden with over 100 slaves. During the voyage the slaves, led by Madison Washington, rose in revolt, killed one owner, overpowered the crew, and brought the vessel into the English port of Nassau. At the request of the American consul, the governor imprisoned nineteen involved in the mutiny, allowing the others to go free. Secretary of State Daniel Webster demanded the surrender of all the slaves, but the British refused. Finally, in 1853, an Anglo-American Commission awarded an indemnity of $110,330 to the United States.

19. For excerpts from editorials in the London press on the incident, see *The Liberator,* May 14, May 28, 1847. These editorials denounced the Cunard Line, carrying the headings: "A British Bow to an American Prejudice," "Shameful Violation of the Rights of Man," "Disgraceful Prejudice Against a Man of Color," "Disgraceful Conduct Toward Frederick Douglass, The Liberated Slave."

20. *The Ram's Horn*, a Negro paper, appeared in New York City on January 1, 1847, and lasted until June, 1848. Thomas Van Rensselaer and Willis Hodges were its editors, the latter raising money to put out the paper by working as a whitewasher. The paper had as many as 2,500 subscribers. Douglass assisted in editing the paper for a time.
21. Hundreds of thousands starved in Ireland during the potato famine of 1845-47. Nearly 307,000 tenants in Ireland held less than five acres each, and when their crop failed, death and migration reduced the population 20 per cent. (For detailed descriptions of American aid during the famine, see *The Voyage of the Jamestown on her Errand of Mercy*, Boston, 1847, and *Report of the General Executive Committee for the relief of Ireland of the City and County of Philadelphia, Appointed by the Town Meeting of February 17, 1847, to provide means to relieve the sufferings in Ireland*, Philadelphia, 1847.)
22. The Black Laws of Ohio greatly curtailed the rights of Negro residents to testify against white persons in court and to a proportionate share of the school fund, and required that they furnish bonds that they would not become public charges.

PART II

1. In August, 1791, after two years of the French Revolution, the slaves in San Domingo revolted. The struggle lasted for twelve years during which time the slaves defeated in turn their local white rulers and the soldiers of the French monarchy, a Spanish invasion, a British expedition of some 60,000 men, and a French expedition of similar size under Napoleon Bonaparte's brother-in-law. The defeat of Bonaparte's expedition in 1803 led to the establishment of the Negro republic of Haiti which has lasted to this day.
2. In his will George Washington provided for the manumission of all his slaves after his wife's death. He likewise provided for the support of those thus freed who were either too old or too young to support themselves. In the case of the children he provided further that they were "to be taught to read and write and to be brought up to some useful occupation." (John C. Fitzpatrick, ed., *George Washington. Writings from the Original Manuscript Sources*, Washington, 1931-1940, vol. XXXI, pp. 279-80.)
3. Douglass is not entirely correct, for the Congregationalist, Unitarian, and Quaker churches opposed the war. But as one historian has pointed out: ". . . One may search through the journals and newspaper reports of the many state conventions of the Protestant Episcopal Church held during the war without being aware of its existence." Also: "Officially the Baptists in the North were almost silent." Clayton Sumner Ellsworth, "The American Churches and the Mexican War," *American Historical Review*, vol. XLV, Jan., 1940, pp. 309, 311.)
4. Shortly after the Mexican War began, President Polk requested $2,000,000 from Congress with which to negotiate peace. On August 8, 1846, a bill to appropriate that sum was introduced in the House. David Wilmot, a Democrat from Pennsylvania, proposed the following amendment to the bill: "Provided, That, as an express and fundamental condition to the acquisition of any territory from the Republic of Mexico by the United States, by virtue of any Treaty which may be negotiated between them, and to the use of the Executive of the moneys herein appropriated, neither slavery nor involuntary servitude shall exist in any part of said territory." This amendment became known as the

Wilmot Proviso. The appropriation bill with the Wilmot Proviso passed the House, but the Senate adjourned without voting on it. It was again passed in the House on Feb. 1, 1847, but it was defeated in the Senate.

5. On Feb. 24, 1848, the working class of Paris which had driven King Louis Phillipe from the Tuileries, routed the Royalist deputies from the Chamber of the Palais Bourbon, and a Provisional Republican government was proclaimed by Alphonse Lamartine. Soon afterwards, owing to the insistence of the unemployed, the government founded the National Workshops under the direction of Louis Blanc.

6. In the spring of 1848 the schooner *Pearl*, with 77 fugitive slaves aboard, was captured at the mouth of the Potomac River and was brought back to Washington. The slaves and their white rescuers, Daniel Drayton, Capton Sayres, and Chester English, were imprisoned. The Negroes were turned over to slave-dealers to be sold in the lower South, and the white men were brought to trial. During the excitement of this event, a mob attempted to destroy the office of the *National Era* in Washington, and to force Dr. Bailey, its editor, to leave the district. Drayton and Sayres were found guilty of transporting slaves and were sentenced to life imprisonment. Exceptions were taken to the judge's rulings and a new trial was ordered, which took place in May, 1849. Once again the men were convicted and returned to the district jail, remaining there until 1852, when Charles Sumner, who had just been elected to the United States Senate, began a campaign for their release. Sumner submitted to the attorney-general an elaborate treatise on the injustice of the sentence, and President Fillmore granted the men an unconditional pardon. When it was learned that the governor of Virginia intended to arrest them at their release, Drayton and Sayres were taken by night to Baltimore, and then sent to Harrisburg and Philadelphia.

7. The reference is to Lewis Cass (1782-1866) who was the Democratic candidate for President in 1848. Cass had praised Louis Phillipe in his book, *France, its King, Court, and Government* (New York, 1840, pp. 19-21), had favored the occupation of all of Mexico, and had opposed the adoption of the Wilmot Proviso. Later he supported the Compromise of 1850 and defended the Fugitive Slave Law.

8. See Vol. II for discussion of Douglass' role in the Convention.

9. On May 15, 1848, the working class of Paris broke into the Assembly to protest the manipulations of the bourgeoisie in emasculating the socialist National Workshops program. A month later, on the morning of June 23, civil war broke out in Paris. After two days of fighting, the working class uprising was crushed with the loss of 3,000 workers' lives. Soon afterwards, the reaction set in in full force, ending on Dec. 10, 1848, with the election of Louis Napoleon as President of the Republic.

10. The reference is to Nat Turner (1800-1831) the leader of the great Negro slave insurrection in Southampton County, Virginia, in 1831.

11. At Calhoun's instigation, 69 senators and representatives from the South met for deliberation on Dec. 23, 1848, in the Senate Chamber. A Committee of Fifteen was appointed, which designated a sub-committee to draw up an address. When this sub-committee met, Calhoun submitted the draft of an "Address of the Southern Delegates in Congress to their Constituents." The Committee of Fifteen debated the address vigorously, and it was finally adopted by a majority of only one vote. The address was ultimately issued, but only

forty southern members of Congress signed it, including only two members of the Whig Party. Even several Democrats refused to sign the document.

12. Smith delivered several addresses and wrote many letters on the constitutional aspects of slavery, the most detailed of which is his speech in March, 1850, before a joint meeting of the Senate and Assembly of the State of New York. (See *Constitutional Argument vs. American Slavery*, Utica, 1844; *Letter of Gerrit Smith to S. P. Chase, on the unconstitutionality of every part of American slavery*, Albany, New York, 1847; *Speech of Gerrit Smith before a joint meeting of the Senate and Assembly of the State of New York, March 11-12, 1850*, Syracuse, New York, second edition, enlarged.)

13. In the Pindell letter written from New Orleans in January, 1849, Clay set forth in detail his plan for gradual emancipation. He proposed that all slave children born after 1855 or 1860 should be free on their twenty-fifth birthday, then should be hired out under the authority of the state for a period not exceeding three years, in order that they might earn a sum sufficient to pay the expenses of their transportation to Liberia and provide them with an outfit for six months after their arrival there. Their children were to be free from their birth, but to be apprenticed until the age of twenty-one, and were also to be sent to Liberia. The letter was addressed to Richard Pindell of Lexington, but was intended for the people of Kentucky. (For a summary of Clay's views on colonization, see Eugene P. Southall, "Henry Clay and the African Colonization Movement, *"The Quarterly Journal of the Florida Agricultural and Mechanical College,* May 15, 1932, pp. 11-16.)

14. Of all the acts of violence and lawlessness against Abolitionists during the 1830's, the burning of Pennsylvania Hall aroused the greatest indignation. Unable to use churches and halls for their meetings, the Abolitionists and other proponents of free discussion in Philadelphia erected in that city, at the cost of $40,000, Pennsylvania Hall. Dedicated on May 14, 1838, the ceremonies lasted for three days, during which time speeches on slavery, the temperance cause, and the protection of the Indian were delivered. Simultaneously a national convention of anti-slavery women was being held in Philadelphia, and the delegates came to address the audience in the hall on the evening of the third day. A huge mob gathered outside the building and with stones and riotous demonstrations sought to break up the meeting. Another mob tried to interrupt the proceedings by similar activities inside the hall. They were defied in moving speeches by Garrison, Maria W. Chapman, Angelina Grimké, and Abby Kelley.

Early on the morning of May 17 the mob again began to mill about the hall. The board of managers called upon the police and the mayor for protection, and finally towards sunset the mayor replied that he would disperse the mob if the building were placed in his hands. Then, after assuring the mob that "we never call out the military here," he retired to his office. During the night, while fifteen thousand persons looked on, the building was burned to the ground. In its report the police blamed the owners of the building and the Abolitionists because they had insisted on advancing "doctrines repulsive to the moral sense of a large majority of our community." (For the entire story in detail, see *History of Pennsylvania Hall which was Destroyed by a Mob, on the 17th of May, 1838*. Philadelphia, 1838.)

15. The reference is to the riots in New York City resulting from the rivalry between the actors Edward Forrest and William C. Macready. Both were performing in separate productions of *Macbeth* on the evening of May 7, 1849. Mac-

ready, an English actor, was attacked by a mob during his performance. A few days later, on May 10, at another performance at the Astor Place Opera House, Macready was again interrupted by a mob which proceeded to demolish the place. The police and the infantry were called in, and in the process of quelling the riot twenty-two persons were killed and thirty wounded. (See J. T. Headley, *The Great Riots of New York*, New York, 1873, pp. 111-35; *Account of the Terrific and Fatal Riots at the New York Astor Place Opera House, on the night of May 10th, 1849*, New York, 1849.)

INDEX

The specific activities of Frederick Douglass himself and the main events of his life during the period covered by this volume are included under the heading, Douglass, Frederick.

Abolition, and civil liberty, 38-39; and political action, 40-41; early history of, 28-45; in West, 259-69; militant nature of, 398-99; organization of, 33-45; role of Negroes in, 35, 46, 59; role of women in, 37-38, 43, 83, 186-87
Abolitionist bazaars, 37-38, 142, 186
Abolitionist press, 37
Adams, John Quincy, 39, 148
Allen, William G., 77, 90
American and Foreign Anti-Slavery Society, 43-44, 438-40
American Anti-Slavery Society, 33-44
American Union, Garrisonians favor dissolution of, 41, 44-45
Anthony, Aaron, 15
Anthony, Susan B., 83
Anti-Corn Law League, 167-68, 439
Auld, Hugh, 17, 21, 22
Auld, Lucretia, 16-17
Auld, Thomas, 16, 19, 336-43, 403-06
Autographs for Freedom, 89-90

Bailey, Frederick Augustus Washington; *See* Douglass, Frederick
Barbadoes, James G., 33
Beecher, Henry Ward, 89, 90
Beman, Amos, G., 92
Birney, James G., 439
Bradburn, George, 55, 57
Brisbane, Albert, 56
Brooks, James, 145
Brown, Antoinette, 90
Brown, William Wells, 90
Buffum, James N., 122, 136, 137, 143
Buffum, Robert, 65
Burns, Robert, 65, 151-53
Burritt, Elihu, 227, 440

Calhoun, John C., 39, 114, 214, 353-60, 442
Cass, Lewis, 442
Channing, William E., 32
Chapman, Maria Weston, 33, 37-38, 43, 56, 61, 65, 142-43, 443
Chartism, 70, 167, 439
Chase, Salmon P., 89
Child, Lydia M., 37, 43
Church, denounced by Garrisonians, 42, 44-45; and prejudice, 103-04; and slavery, 50-51, 104-05, 113-15, 161-62, 173-78, 218-26, 253-55, 271-74; *see also* Free Church of Scotland
Civil liberty, and Abolition, 38-39
Clarkson, Thomas, 33
Clay, Cassius M., 89, 118, 125, 438
Clay, Henry, 97-98, 114, 284-90, 388-91, 442
Coffin, William C., 26
Collins, John A., 27, 46, 47, 48, 51, 53, 55, 59, 110-12, 438
Colonization, attitude of Negroes toward, 25-26, 30-31, 84-90, 97-99; Douglass opposes, 350-52, 387-99, 416-18
Constitution of the United States, and slavery, 41, 44-45, 209-10, 274-75, 328-29, 352-67, 374-79
Cornish, Samuel, 77
Covey, Edward, 19-20, 132
Cox, Samuel Hanson, 68-69
Cuffee, William, 29

Delany, Martin R., 77, 84, 92
Dickens, Charles, 156
Dorr, Thomas Wilson, 48
Douglass, Anna Murray, aids Douglass escape 21; assists Douglass in early strug-

445

gles, 24, 340, 372; marries Douglass, 23
Douglass, Charles, 61
Douglass, Frederick (chronology), life as a slave, 15-22, 130-34, 423-24; escapes from slavery, 22, 426; early life as a freeman, 23-25; joins Abolitionist movement, 25-27, 427; early speeches, 46 ff.; praised as a speaker, 47-48, 51-52, 54-55, 58-59; and Latimer (fugitive slave) case, 54-55; and Hundred Conventions, 55-58; attacked by mobs, 53, 57, 79, 181-82, 256-59, 384-87; writes *Narrative*, 59-60; decides to visit England, 61; trip on *Cambria*, 62, 115-18, 123-25; becomes interested in temperance movement, 63; attacks Free Church of Scotland, 64-65; justifies attacking American institutions while in Europe, 67, 69-70, 146-48, 234-43; attacks American temperance movement, 67-68; denounces Mexican War, 182-83, 187-88, 291-96, 300; enjoys freedom in England, 125-29; freedom purchased by English friends, 72-73, 199-206, 432; bids farewell to England, 73, 206-33; return voyage to United States, 233-34; welcomed home from abroad, 75; abandons plans to publish paper, 78, 252-53, 256; publishes *The North Star*, 81, 278-84, 434; moves family to Rochester, 83; role as editor, 93-94, 435-37; efforts to educate himself, 93; battles discrimination, 96-97, 250-52, 384-87, 390-92; attacks colonization, 97-99, 350-52, 387-99, 416-18; attacks white chauvinism, 99-100; insists Negroes must participate in struggle against slavery, 314-20; supports woman's rights, 320-21; fights jim-crow schools, 371-74, 415-16; favors militant Abolitionism, 398-99; proposes National League, 399-401, 408-09, 419-22
Douglass, Frederick, junior, 61
Douglass, Lewis, 24
Douglass, Rosetta, 24, 371-74
Douglass' Monthly, 91
Downing, George T., 93

Education, 301-02, 415-16
Election of 1848, 296-99, 309-14, 343-47
Evangelical Alliance, 218-19

Father Mathew, 120
Ferris, Jacob, 55
Forten, James, 31
Foster, Stephen S., 27, 33, 59, 79
France, revolution in, 303-05, 321-30, 442
Frederick Douglass' Paper, difficulties in publishing, 88-91; founding of, 88
Friedland, William, 20
Free Church of Scotland, 64-65, 136, 144, 150, 174-78
Free Soil Party, 367-69

Gardner, William, 21
Garrison, William Lloyd, anti-slavery principles of, 40-44; Douglass' first impression of, 26; Douglass' friendship with, 143, 217-18, 257-59, 270, 340, 375, 388; joins Douglass in England, 67; opposes Douglass' plan to publish paper, 78; publishes *Liberator*, 32-33
Gay, Sidney B., 55, 79, 259, 262
Greeley, Horace, 56, 70, 77, 89, 90, 144
Greenfield, Elizabeth, 96
Griffiths, Julia, 87-92, 306-07
Grimké, Angelina, 443

Hall, Prince, 29
Hamilton, Thomas, 77
Holley, Myron, 83
Howitt, Mary, 76
Hundred Conventions, 55-58
Hutchinson family, 62, 117, 122, 406

Ireland, poverty in, 139-42, 246, 441

Jackson, Francis, 26, 65, 135
Jay, William, 89
Jefferson, Thomas, 28-29, 439
Johnson, Nathan, 23
Johnson, William, 89
Jones, Absalom, 29

Kelley, Abby, 43, 47, 48, 53, 443

INDEX 447

Langston, John M., 90
Latimer case, 54-55, 104-09, 429
League of Universal Brotherhood, 227, 440
Liberator, the, 25, 32-33
Liberty Party, 43, 439
Lloyd, Edward, 15
Lovejoy, Elijah P., 33, 116, 438

Mahan, Isa, 80
Mann, Horace, 89, 90
Manumission, 441
May, Samuel J., 52, 81, 84
McCrummell, James, 33
Mexican War, 182-83, 187-88, 291-96, 300, 439-41
Meyers, Stephen, 75
Moral suasion, 40
Mott, Lucretia, 33, 43, 79

Narrative of the Life of Frederick Douglass, 59-60, 136, 142-43
National League, 399-401, 408-11, 419-22
Negroes, address to, 331-36; and Abolitionist movement, 46, 59, 426; and temperance movement, 67-68, 440; as a nation, 98; churches of, 317-19; in Baltimore, 21; in New Bedford, 24-25; journalism among, 76-77, 291; must participate in struggle against slavery, 314-20; need for national organization among, 399-401, 410-12, 421-24; oppose colonization, 25-26, 30-31, 84-89, 97-99; prejudice against, 384-99, 406-07; schools for, 301-02, 415-16
Nell, William C., 84
New York Express, 145
New York Tribune, 56, 70, 77, 89, 90, 144
North Star, The, difficulties in publishing, 85-88, 306-07, 369-70, 401-02, 413-15, 435-37; first issue greeted, 84-85; founding of, 81, 278-84, 434; objectives of, 83-84

Oberlin College, 80, 265
O'Connell, Daniel, 33, 63, 121-22
Otis, James, 28

Paine, Thomas, 28
Parker, Theodore, 33
Pease, Elizabeth, 62, 411-12
Pennsylvania Hall, burning of, 443
Phillips, Wendell, 33, 38, 40, 42, 53, 61-62, 78, 375, 430
Pillsbury, Parker, 47, 48
"Pinckney gag," 39
Political action, 40-41, 296-99, 309-14, 343-47; *see also* Constitution of the U.S.; Garrison, William Lloyd; Liberty Party
Polk, James K., 134, 441
Purvis, Robert, 33, 79

Quincy, Edmund, 85

Ray, Charles B., 77
Reason, Charles L., 90
Remond, Charles Lenox, 52, 54, 55
Revolution of 1848, 303-05, 321-30, 442
Rhode Island, suffrage in, 48
Rhodes, Isaac, 22
Rochester, anti-slavery movement in, 53-54, 83
Rogers, N. P., 47
Ruggles, David B., 23, 26, 77, 424-25

Seward, William H., 89, 90
Shadd, Abraham, 33
Slavery, abolished in North, 29; character of, 154-65; defense of, 33-34, 45-46
Smith, Gerrit, 33, 37, 44, 88, 90, 91, 93, 366, 369, 374-79, 442
Smith, James McCune, 77, 90, 92, 94, 100
Stanton, Elizabeth Cady, 83
Stein, Frederick, 22
Stowe, Harriet Beecher, 90
Stuart, Charles, 34
Sumner, Charles, 89, 90, 442
Swisshelm, Jane, 90

Tappan, Arthur, 33, 89
Tappan, Lewis, 33, 89, 90
Temperance movement, 63, 67-68, 120, 189-99, 440
Thompson, George, 33, 66, 171-72

Trade unions, 39
Truth, Sojourner, 83
Turner, Nat, 19, 31, 442

Utopian socialism, 56, 111-12

Vashon, John B., 33

Walker, David, 31
Wagoner, H. O., 93
Ward, Samuel Ringgold, 92, 96
Warner, H. G., 371
Washington, George, 441
Washington, Madison, 90, 228, 440
Webb, Richard D., 65, 142

Webster, Daniel, 440
Weed, Thurlow, 78, 123
Weld, Theodore D., 33, 35-36, 44, 46, 427, 439
West India Emancipation, 35, 321-22
White chauvinism, 99-100
White, William A., 55-56, 181-82
Whittier, John Greenleaf, 33, 54, 76
Williams, Peter, 33
Wilmot Proviso, 299, 441
Women, rights of, 320-21; role of, in Abolitionist movement, 37-38, 42-43, 83, 186-87, 438-39
Wright, Elizur, 35
Wright, Frances, 39
Wright, Henry C., 44, 70, 72-73, 136, 199

www.ingramcontent.com/pod-product-compliance
Lightning Source LLC
Chambersburg PA
CBHW032029150426
43194CB00006B/201